SAS Publishing

SAS® Certification Prep Guide
Base Programming for SAS® 9

The Power to Know®

The correct bibliographic citation for this manual is as follows: SAS Institute Inc. 2006. *SAS® Certification Prep Guide: Base Programming for SAS®9*. Cary, NC: SAS Institute Inc.

SAS® Certification Prep Guide: Base Programming for SAS®9

ISBN 1-59047-922-X
ISBN 978-1-59047-922-3

1st printing, March 2006

SAS Publishing provides a complete selection of books and electronic products to help customers use SAS software to its fullest potential. For more information about our e-books, e-learning products, CDs, and hard-copy books, visit the SAS Publishing Web site at **support.sas.com/pubs** or call 1-800-727-3228.

Contents

About This Book

Purpose

The SAS Certification Prep Guide: Base Programming for SAS9 prepares you to take the SAS Base Programming for SAS9 exam. The book covers all of the objectives tested on the exam, including basic concepts, producing reports, creating and modifying SAS data sets, and reading various types of raw data.

The book includes quizzes that enable you to test your understanding of material in each chapter. In addition, the companion *SAS Certification Prep Guide: Base Programming for SAS9 CD-ROM* contains sample data and sample programs that enable you to practice your new skills in your actual SAS environment.

Audience

The SAS Certification Prep Guide: Base Programming for SAS9 is for new or experienced SAS programmers who want to prepare for the SAS Base Programming for SAS9 exam.

Programming Environments

This book assumes you are running Base SAS or SAS Enterprise Guide software in the Windows environment. You will learn how to write and manage your SAS programs in either the SAS Windowing Environment workspace or in the SAS Enterprise Guide workspace.

If you are not sure which programming workspace you are using, select **Help→About** from the SAS software main menu. If you are using SAS Enterprise Guide, the About window displays the name "Enterprise Guide." If you are using the SAS Windowing Environment, the About window displays the name "SAS for Windows."

Because the two programming workspaces differ, you will occasionally see notes in this book that provide information specific to either SAS Enterprise Guide or to the SAS Windowing Environment. These notes use the following icons to identify information that is unique to these workspaces:

    SAS Enterprise Guide

       SAS Windowing Environment

How to Use This Book and CD-ROM

The SAS Certification Prep Guide: Base Programming for SAS9 includes a companion CD-ROM, which can be found in the envelope inside the back cover of this book.

The CD-ROM contains tutorials that teach you how to operate within the SAS and SAS Enterprise Guide programming workspaces. Before using the CD-ROM, check online for any updates at **support.sas.com/certbasetutorials**.

After completing Chapter 1 in this book and before continuing to Chapter 2, go to the CD-ROM, print and go through the tutorial that matches the version of SAS you are using. For each chapter in the book, starting with Chapter 2,

1. complete the chapter text and summary in the book.

2. use the sample data and programs on the CD-ROM to practice what you learned in each chapter.

3. complete the end-of-chapter quiz in the book. You can check your answers by using the answer key in the appendix at the back of this book.

After completing the book, you can take the SAS Certification Practice Exam: Base Programming for SAS9 at **support.sas.com/selfpaced**.

Syntax Conventions for This Book

This is an example of how the general form of SAS code is shown in the book:

```
DATA output-SAS-data-set
     (DROP=variable(s) | KEEP=variable(s));
   SET SAS-data-set <options>;
   BY variable(s);
RUN;
```

For example, in the general form above,

- **DATA**, **DROP=**, **KEEP=**, **SET**, **BY**, and **RUN** are in uppercase bold because they must be spelled as shown

- *output-SAS-data-set*, *variable(s)*, *SAS-data-set*, and *options* are in italics because each represents a value that you supply

- *<options>* is enclosed in angle brackets because it is optional syntax

- **DROP=** and **KEEP=** are separated by a vertical bar (|) to indicate that they are mutually exclusive.

The general forms of SAS statements and commands that are shown in this book include only the syntax that you need to know to prepare for the certification exam. For complete syntax, see the appropriate SAS reference guide.

Additional Resources

Other resources might be helpful when learning SAS programming. You can refer to them as needed to enhance your understanding of the material covered in this book. You can access SAS online Help, documentation, and other resources from your SAS software or on the Web.

From SAS Software	
General help	SAS 9: Select **Help** → **SAS Help and Documentation**.
	SAS Enterprise Guide: Select **Help** → **Enterprise Guide Help**.
Online documentation	SAS 9: Select **Help** → **SAS Help and Documentation**.
	SAS Enterprise Guide: Access online documentation on the Web (see **On the Web** below).

On the Web	
SAS OnlineDoc	SAS OnlineDoc, Version 9: `support.sas.com/v9doc`
Customer Support Center	`support.sas.com`
Training (General)	`support.sas.com/training`
e-Learning	`support.sas.com/selfpaced`
Online documentation	`support.sas.com/documentation`
Books	`support.sas.com/pubs`
SAS sample programs	`support.sas.com/techsup/sample/sample_library.html`

SAS Certification Practice Exam: Base Programming for SAS9

The SAS Certification Practice Exam: Base Programming for SAS9 was designed to help you prepare for the SAS Base Programming for SAS9 exam. This practice exam was constructed to test the same knowledge and skills as the official certification exam. You can access this exam under the SAS Certification category at **support.sas.com/selfpaced**.

SAS Base Programming for SAS9

For information about how to register for the official SAS Base Programming for SAS9 exam, see the SAS Certified Professional Programmer Web site at **support.sas.com/certify/**.

Chapter **1**   Basic Concepts

Overview

Introduction

To program effectively using SAS, you need to understand basic concepts about **SAS programs** and the **SAS files** that they process. In particular, you need to be familiar with **SAS data sets**.

In this chapter, you'll examine a simple SAS program and see how it works. You'll see how SAS data sets are stored temporarily or permanently in **SAS libraries**. You'll also learn details about SAS data sets, which are files that contain data that is logically arranged in a form that SAS can understand.

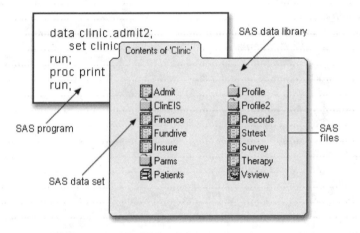

Objectives

In this chapter, you learn about

- the structure and components of SAS programs
- the steps involved in processing SAS programs
- SAS libraries and the types of SAS files that they contain
- temporary and permanent SAS libraries
- the structure and components of SAS data sets.

SAS Programs

You can use SAS programs to access, manage, analyze, or present your data. Let's begin by looking at a simple SAS program.

```
data clinic.admit2;
    set clinic.admit;
run;
proc print data=clinic.admit2;
run;
```

This program creates a new SAS data set from an existing SAS data set and then prints a listing of the new data set. A SAS data set is a data file that is formatted in a way that SAS can understand.

Let's see how this program works.

Components of SAS Programs

Our sample SAS program contains two steps: a **DATA step** and a **PROC step**.

```
data clinic.admit2;
    set clinic.admit;
run;
proc print data=clinic.admit2;
run;
```

These two types of steps, alone or combined, form most SAS programs.

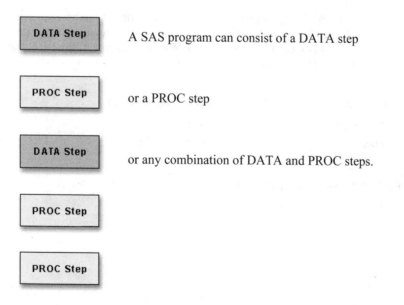

A SAS program can consist of a DATA step

or a PROC step

or any combination of DATA and PROC steps.

DATA steps typically create or modify SAS data sets. They can also be used to produce custom-designed reports. For example, you can use DATA steps to

- put your data into a SAS data set

- compute values

- check for and correct errors in your data

- produce new SAS data sets by subsetting, merging, and updating existing data sets.

PROC (procedure) steps are pre-written routines that enable you to analyze and process the data in a SAS data set and to present the data in the form of a report. PROC steps sometimes create new SAS data sets that contain the results of the procedure. PROC steps can list, sort, and summarize data. For example, you can use PROC steps to

- create a report that lists the data

- produce descriptive statistics

- create a summary report

- produce plots and charts.

Characteristics of SAS Programs

Next let's look at the individual statements in our sample program. SAS programs consist of **SAS statements**. A SAS statement has two important characteristics:

- It usually begins with a SAS **keyword**.

- It always ends with a **semicolon**.

As you've seen, a DATA step begins with a DATA statement, which begins with the keyword DATA. A PROC step begins with a PROC statement, which begins with the keyword PROC. Our sample program contains ❶a DATA statement, ❷a SET statement, ❸a RUN statement, ❹a PROC PRINT statement, and ❺another RUN statement.

Statements	Sample Program Code
❶a DATA statement	`data clinic.admit2;`
❷a SET statement	`set clinic.admit;`
❸a RUN statement	`run;`
❹a PROC PRINT statement	`proc print data=clinic.admit2;`
❺another RUN statement	`run;`

Layout for SAS Programs

SAS statements are in free format. This means that

- they can begin and end anywhere on a line

- one statement can continue over several lines

- several statements can be on a line.

Blanks or special characters separate "words" in a SAS statement.

 You can specify SAS statements in uppercase or lowercase. In most situations, text that is enclosed in quotation marks is case sensitive.

You've examined the general structure of our sample program. But what happens when you run the program?

Processing SAS Programs

When you submit a SAS program, SAS begins reading the statements and checking them for errors.

DATA and PROC statements signal the beginning of a new step. When SAS encounters a subsequent DATA, PROC, or RUN statement (for DATA steps and most procedures) or a QUIT statement (for some procedures), SAS stops reading statements and executes the previous step in the program. In our sample program, each step ends with a RUN statement.

```
data clinic.admit2;
   set clinic.admit;
run;
proc print data=clinic.admit2;
run;
```

 The beginning of a new step (DATA or PROC) implies the end of the previous step. Though the RUN statement is not always required between steps in a SAS program, using it can make the SAS program easier to read and debug, and it makes the SAS log easier to read.

Log Messages

Each time a step is executed, SAS generates a log of the processing activities and the results of the processing. The SAS log collects messages about the processing of SAS programs and about any errors that occur.

When SAS processes our sample program, you see the log messages shown below. Notice that you get separate sets of messages for each step in the program.

SAS Log

```
1     data clinic.admit2;
2         set clinic.admit;
3     run;

NOTE: The data set CLINIC.ADMIT2 has 21
      observations and 9 variables.
NOTE: The DATA statement used 1.03 seconds

4     proc print data=clinic.admit2;
5     run;

NOTE: The PROCEDURE PRINT used 0.2 seconds.
```

Results of Processing

Suppose you submit the sample program below.

```
data clinic.admit2;
    set clinic.admit;
run;
proc print data=clinic.admit2;
run;
```

When the program is processed, it

- creates the SAS data set **Clinic.Admit2** in the DATA step. The DATA step produces messages in the SAS log, but it does not create a report or other output.

- creates the following HTML report of the SAS data set **Clinic.Admit2**:

Obs	ID	Name	Sex	Age	Date	Height	Weight	ActLevel	Fee
1	2458	Murray, W	M	27	1	72	168	HIGH	85.20
2	2462	Almers, C	F	34	3	66	152	HIGH	124.80
3	2501	Bonaventure, T	F	31	17	61	123	LOW	149.75
4	2523	Johnson, R	F	43	31	63	137	MOD	149.75
5	2539	LaMance, K	M	51	4	71	158	LOW	124.80
6	2544	Jones, M	M	29	6	76	193	HIGH	124.80
7	2552	Reberson, P	F	32	9	67	151	MOD	149.75
8	2555	King, E	M	35	13	70	173	MOD	149.75
9	2563	Pitts, D	M	34	22	73	154	LOW	124.80
10	2568	Eberhardt, S	F	49	27	64	172	LOW	124.80
11	2571	Nunnelly, A	F	44	19	66	140	HIGH	149.75
12	2572	Oberon, M	F	28	17	62	118	LOW	85.20
13	2574	Peterson, V	M	30	6	69	147	MOD	149.75
14	2575	Quigley, M	F	40	8	69	163	HIGH	124.80
15	2578	Cameron, L	M	47	5	72	173	MOD	124.80
16	2579	Underwood, K	M	60	22	71	191	LOW	149.75
17	2584	Takahashi, Y	F	43	29	65	123	MOD	124.80
18	2586	Derber, B	M	25	23	75	188	HIGH	85.20
19	2588	Ivan, H	F	22	20	63	139	LOW	85.20
20	2589	Wilcox, E	F	41	16	67	141	HIGH	149.75
21	2595	Warren, C	M	54	7	71	183	MOD	149.75

Throughout this book, procedure output is shown in HTML in the style shown above unless otherwise noted. You can learn how to create HTML output in Chapter 2, **Referencing Files and Setting Options**.

You've seen the results of submitting our sample program. For other SAS programs, the results of processing might vary:

- SAS programs often invoke procedures that create output in the form of a report, as is the case with the TABULATE procedure.

```
proc tabulate data=clinic.admit;
   class sex;
   var height weight;
   table sex*(height weight),mean;
run;
```

		Mean
Sex		
F	**Height**	64.82
	Weight	141.73
M	**Height**	72.00
	Weight	172.80

- Other SAS programs perform tasks such as sorting and managing data, which have no visible results except for **messages in the log**. (All SAS programs produce log messages, but some SAS programs produce **only** log messages.)

```
proc copy in=clinic out=work;
   select admit;
run;
```

SAS Log

```
6   proc copy in=clinic out=work;
7   select admit;
8   run;

NOTE: Copying CLINIC.ADMIT to WORK.ADMIT (memtype=DATA).
NOTE: There were 21 observations read from the data set
      CLINIC.ADMIT.
NOTE: The data set WORK.ADMIT has 21 observations and 9
      variables.
NOTE: PROCEDURE COPY used (Total process time):
      real time           0.13 seconds
      cpu time            0.08 seconds
```

You can turn off log messages by using system options, which you can learn about in Chapter 2, **Referencing Files and Setting Options**.

SAS Libraries

You've learned about SAS programs and SAS data sets. Now let's look at **SAS libraries** to see how SAS data sets and other SAS files are organized and stored.

How SAS Files Are Stored

Every SAS file is stored in a **SAS library**, which is a collection of SAS files. A SAS data library is the highest level of organization for information within SAS.

SAS libraries have different implementations depending on your operating environment, but a library usually corresponds to the level of organization that your host operating system uses to access and store files. In some operating environments, a library is a physical collection of files. In others, the files are only logically related.

For example, in the Windows and UNIX environments, a library is typically a group of SAS files in the same folder or directory.

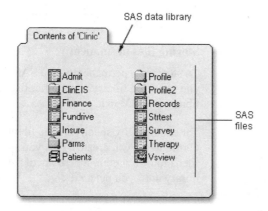

The table below summarizes the implementation of SAS libraries in various operating environments.

Environment	Library
Windows, UNIX, OpenVMS (directory based-systems)	a group of SAS files that are stored in the same directory. Other files can be stored in the directory, but only the files that have SAS file extensions are recognized as part of the SAS library. (Refer to the online documentation for more information.)
CMS	a group of SAS files that have the same file type.
z/OS	a specially formatted host data set in which only SAS files are stored.

Storing Files Temporarily or Permanently

Depending on the library name that you use when you create a file, you can store SAS files temporarily or permanently.

Storing files temporarily:

If you don't specify a library name when you create a file (or if you specify the library name **Work**), the file is stored in the temporary SAS data library. When you end the session, the temporary library and all of its files are deleted.

Temporary SAS libraries last only for the current SAS session.

Storing files permanently:

To store files permanently in a SAS data library, you specify a library name other than the default library name **Work**.

For example, by specifying the library name **Clinic** when you create a file, you specify that the file is to be stored in a permanent SAS data library until you delete it.

Permanent SAS libraries are available to you during subsequent SAS sessions.

 You can learn how to set up permanent SAS libraries in Chapter 2, **Referencing Files and Setting Options**.

Referencing SAS Files

Two-Level Names

To reference a permanent SAS data set in your SAS programs, you use a **two-level name**:

libref.filename

In the two-level name, *libref* is the name of the SAS data library that contains the file, and *filename* is the name of the file itself. A period separates the libref and filename.

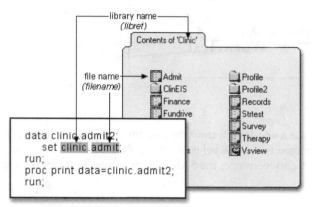

For example, in our sample program, **Clinic.Admit** is the two-level name for the SAS data set **Admit**, which is stored in the library named **Clinic**.

LIBREF.FILENAME

Clinic.Admit

Referencing Temporary SAS Files

To reference temporary SAS files, you can specify the default libref **Work**, a period, and the filename. For example, the two-level name **Work.Test** references the SAS data set named **Test** that is stored in the temporary SAS library **Work**.

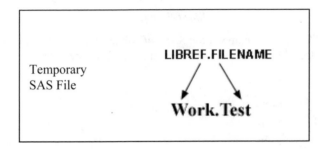

Alternatively, you can use a **one-level name** (the filename only) to reference a file in a temporary SAS library. When you specify a one-level name, the default libref **Work** is assumed. For example, the one-level name **Test** also references the SAS data set named **Test** that is stored in the temporary SAS library **Work**.

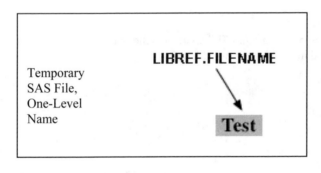

> If the USER library is assigned, SAS uses the **User** library rather than the **Work** library for one-level names. **User** is a permanent library. For more information, see the *SAS Language Reference: Concepts* documentation.

Referencing Permanent SAS Files

You can see that **Clinic.Admit** and **Clinic.Admit2** are permanent SAS data sets because the library name is **Clinic,** not **Work**.

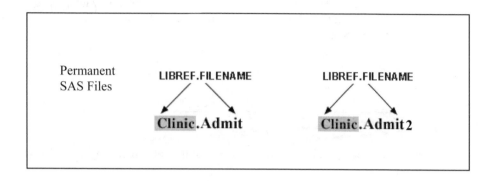

So referencing a SAS file in any library **except Work** indicates that the SAS file is stored permanently. For example, when our sample program creates **Clinic.Admit2**, it stores the new **Admit2** data set permanently in the SAS library **Clinic.**

Rules for SAS Names

SAS data set names

- can be 1 to 32 characters long

- must begin with a letter (A–Z, either uppercase or lowercase) or an underscore (_)

- can continue with any combination of numbers, letters, or underscores.

These are examples of valid data set names:

- **Payroll**

- **LABDATA1995_1997**

- **_EstimatedTaxPayments3**

SAS Data Sets

So far, you've seen the components and characteristics of SAS programs, including how they reference SAS data sets. Data sets are one type of SAS file. There are other types of SAS files (such as catalogs), but this chapter focuses on SAS data sets. For many procedures and for some DATA step statements, data must be in the form of a SAS data set to be processed. Now let's take a closer look at SAS data sets.

Overview of Data Sets

As you saw in our sample program, for many of the data processing tasks that you perform with SAS, you

- access data in the form of a SAS data set

- analyze, manage, or present the data.

Conceptually, a SAS data set is a file that consists of two parts: a **descriptor portion** and a **data portion**. Sometimes a SAS data set also points to one or more indexes, which enable SAS to locate records in the data set more efficiently. (The data sets that you see in this chapter do not contain indexes.)

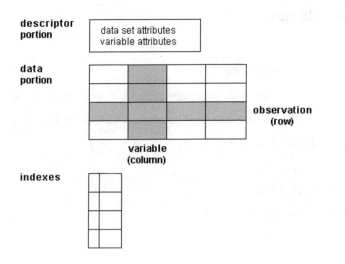

Descriptor Portion

The descriptor portion of a SAS data set contains information about the data set, including

- the name of the data set

- the date and time that the data set was created

- the number of observations

- the number of variables.

Let's look at another SAS data set. The table below lists part of the descriptor portion of the data set **Clinic.Insure**, which contains insurance information for patients who are admitted to a wellness clinic. (It's a good idea to give your data set a name that is descriptive of the contents.)

```
Data Set Name:       CLINIC.INSURE
Member Type:         DATA
Engine:              V8
Created:             10:05 Tuesday, March 30, 1999
Observations:        21
Variables:           7
Indexes:             0
Observation Length:  64
```

Data Portion

The data portion of a SAS data set is a collection of data values that are arranged in a rectangular table. In the example below, the name *Jones* is a data value, the weight *158.3* is a data value, and so on.

Data portion

Name	Sex	Age	Weight
Jones	M	48	128.6
Laverne	M	58	158.3
Jaffe	F	.	115.5
Wilson	M	28	170.1

Observations (Rows)

Rows (called **observations**) in the data set are collections of data values that usually relate to a single object. The values *Jones*, *M*, *48*, and *128.6* constitute a single observation in the data set shown below.

	Name	Sex	Age	Weight
	Jones	M	48	128.6
Observation	Laverne	M	58	158.3
	Jaffe	F	.	115.5
	Wilson	M	28	170.1

This data set has four observations, each containing information about an individual. A SAS data set can store any number of observations.

Variables (Columns)

Columns (called **variables**) in the data set are collections of values that describe a particular characteristic. The values *Jones*, *Laverne*, *Jaffe*, and *Wilson* constitute the variable Name in the data set shown below.

	Name	Sex	Age	Weight
	Jones	M	48	128.6
Variable	Laverne	M	58	158.3
	Jaffe	F	.	115.5
	Wilson	M	28	170.1

This data set contains four variables for each observation: Name, Sex, Age, and Weight. A SAS data set can store thousands of variables.

Missing Values

The rectangular arrangement of rows and columns in a SAS data set implies that every variable must exist for each observation. If a data value is unknown for a particular observation, a missing value is recorded in the SAS data set.

Missing value

Name	Sex	Age	Weight
Jones	M	48	128.6
Laverne	M	58	158.3
Jaffe	F	.	115.5
Wilson	M	28	170.1

Variable Attributes

In addition to general information about the data set, the descriptor portion contains information about the attributes of each variable in the data set. The attribute information includes the variable's name, type, length, format, informat, and label.

When you write SAS programs, it's important to understand the attributes of the variables that you use. For example, you might need to combine SAS data sets that contain same-named variables. In this case, the variables must be the same type (character or numeric).

The following is a partial listing of the attribute information in the descriptor portion of the SAS data set **Clinic.Insure**. Let's look at the **name**, **type**, and **length** variable attributes. You'll learn about the format, informat, and label attributes later in this chapter.

```
Variable Type Length Format     Informat Label

Policy   Num  8                          Policy Number

Total    Num  8      DOLLAR8.2 COMMA10. Total Balance
Name     Char 20                         Patient Name
```

Name

Each variable has a name that conforms to SAS naming conventions. Variable names follow exactly the same rules as SAS data set names. Like data set names, variable names

- can be 1 to 32 characters long
- must begin with a letter (A–Z, either uppercase or lowercase) or an underscore (_)
- can continue with any combination of numbers, letters, or underscores.

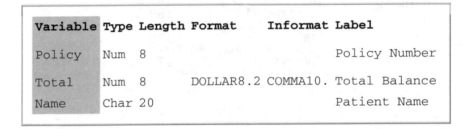

Variable	Type	Length	Format	Informat	Label
Policy	Num	8			Policy Number
Total	Num	8	DOLLAR8.2	COMMA10.	Total Balance
Name	Char	20			Patient Name

Type

A variable's type is either **character** or **numeric**.

- Character variables, such as Name (shown below), can contain **any values**.
- Numeric variables, such as Policy and Total (shown below), can contain **only numeric values** (the digits 0 through 9, +, -, ., and E for scientific notation).

Variable	Type	Length	Format	Informat	Label
Policy	Num	8			Policy Number
Total	Num	8	DOLLAR8.2	COMMA10.	Total Balance
Name	Char	20			Patient Name

A variable's type determines how missing values for a variable are displayed. In the following data set, `Name` and `Sex` are character variables, and `Age` and `Weight` are numeric variables.

- For character variables such as `Name`, a **blank** represents a missing value.

- For numeric variables such as `Age`, a **period** represents a missing value.

Name	Sex	Age	Weight
	M	48	128.6
Laverne	M	58	158.3
Jaffe	F	.	115.5
Wilson	M	28	170.1

Length

A variable's **length** (the number of bytes used to store it) is related to its type.

- Character variables can be up to **32,767 bytes** long. In the example below, `Name` has a length of 20 characters and uses 20 bytes of storage.

- All numeric variables have a default length of **8**. Numeric values (no matter how many digits they contain) are stored as floating-point numbers in 8 bytes of storage, unless you specify a different length.

```
Variable  Type  Length  Format      Informat  Label

Policy    Num   8                             Policy Number

Total     Num   8       DOLLAR8.2   COMMA10.  Total Balance
Name      Char  20                            Patient Name
```

You've seen that each SAS variable has a name, type, and length. In addition, you can define **format**, **informat**, and **label** attributes for variables. Let's look briefly at these optional attributes—you'll learn more about them in later chapters as you need to use them.

Format

Formats are variable attributes that affect the way data values are written. SAS software offers a variety of character, numeric, and date and time formats. You can also create and store your own formats. To write values out using a particular form, you select the appropriate format.

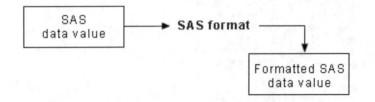

For example, to display the value *1234* as $1234.00 in a report, you can use the DOLLAR8.2 format, as shown for `Total` below.

Variable	Type	Length	Format	Informat	Label
Policy	Num	8			Policy Number
Total	Num	8	DOLLAR8.2	COMMA10.	Total Balance
Name	Char	20			Patient Name

Usually you have to specify the maximum width (*w*) of the value to be written. Depending on the particular format, you might also need to specify the number of decimal places (*d*) to be written. For example, to display the value *5678* as 5,678.00 in a report, you can use the COMMA8.2 format, which specifies a width of 8 including 2 decimal places.

You can permanently assign a format to a variable in a SAS data set, or you can temporarily specify a format in a PROC step to determine the way the data values appear in output.

Informat

Whereas **formats** write values **out** by using some particular form, **informats** read data values in certain forms **into** standard SAS values. Informats determine how data values are read into a SAS data set. You **must** use informats to read numeric values that contain letters or other special characters.

For example, the numeric value *$1,234.00* contains two special characters, a dollar sign ($) and a comma (,). You can use an informat to read the value while removing the dollar sign and comma, and then store the resulting value as a standard numeric value. For `Total` below, the COMMA10. informat is specified.

Variable	Type	Length	Format	Informat	Label
Policy	Num	8			Policy Number
Total	Num	8	DOLLAR8.2	COMMA10.	Total Balance
Name	Char	20			Patient Name

Label

A variable can have a **label**, which consists of descriptive text up to 256 characters long. By default, many reports identify variables by their names. You might want to display more descriptive information about the variable by assigning a label to the variable.

For example, you can label `Policy` as **Policy Number**, `Total` as **Total Balance**, and `Name` as **Patient Name** to display these labels in reports.

Variable	Type	Length	Format	Informat	Label
Policy	Num	8			Policy Number
Total	Num	8	DOLLAR8.2	COMMA10.	Total Balance
Name	Char	20			Patient Name

You might even want to use labels to shorten long variable names in your reports. Assigning labels to variables is discussed in Chapter 4, **Creating List Reports**.

Summary

Text Summary

Components of SAS Programs

SAS programs consist of two types of steps: DATA steps and PROC (procedure) steps. These two steps, alone or combined, form most SAS programs. A SAS program can consist of a DATA step, a PROC step, or any combination of DATA and PROC steps. **DATA steps** typically create or modify SAS data sets, but they can also be used to produce custom-designed reports. **PROC steps** are pre-written routines that enable you to analyze and process the data in a SAS data set and to present the data in the form of a report. PROC steps sometimes create new SAS data sets that contain the results of the procedure.

Characteristics of SAS Programs

SAS programs consist of **SAS statements**. A SAS statement usually begins with a SAS keyword and always ends with a semicolon. A DATA step begins with the keyword DATA. A PROC step begins with the keyword PROC. SAS statements are in free format, so they can begin and end anywhere on a line. One statement can continue over several lines, and several statements can be on a line. Blanks or special characters separate "words" in a SAS statement.

Processing SAS Programs

When you submit a SAS program, SAS reads SAS statements and checks them for errors. When it encounters a subsequent DATA, PROC, RUN, or QUIT statement, SAS executes the previous step in the program.

Each time a step is executed, SAS generates a log of the processing activities and the results of the processing. The SAS log collects messages about the processing of SAS programs and about any errors that occur.

The results of processing can vary. Some SAS programs open an interactive window or invoke procedures that create output in the form of a report. Other SAS programs perform tasks such as sorting and managing data, which have no visible results other than messages in the log.

SAS Libraries

Every SAS file is stored in a **SAS library**, which is a collection of SAS files such as SAS data sets and catalogs. In some operating environments, a SAS library is a physical collection of files. In others, the files are only logically related. In the Windows and UNIX environments, a SAS library is typically a group of SAS files in the same folder or directory.

Depending on the libref you use, you can store SAS files in temporary SAS libraries or in permanent SAS libraries.

- Temporary SAS files that are created during the session are held in a special workspace that is assigned the default libref **Work**. If you don't specify a libref when you create a file (or if you specify **Work**), then the file is stored in the temporary SAS library. When you end the session, the temporary library is deleted.

- To store a file permanently in a SAS library, you assign it a libref other than the default **Work**. For example, by assigning the libref **Clinic** to a SAS library, you specify that files within the library are to be stored until you delete them.

Referencing SAS Files

To reference a SAS file, you use a two-level name, *libref.filename*. In the two-level name, *libref* is the name for the SAS library that contains the file, and *filename* is the name of the file itself. A period separates the libref and filename.

To reference temporary SAS files, you specify the default libref **Work**, a period, and the filename. Alternatively, you can simply use a one-level name (the filename only) to reference a file in a temporary SAS library. Referencing a SAS file in any library **except Work** indicates that the SAS file is stored permanently.

SAS data set names can be 1 to 32 characters long, must begin with a letter (A–Z, either uppercase or lowercase) or an underscore (_), and can continue with any combination of numbers, letters, or underscores.

Overview of SAS Data Sets

For many of the data processing tasks that you perform with SAS, you access data in the form of a **SAS data set** and use SAS programs to analyze, manage, or present the data. Conceptually, a SAS data set is a file that consists of two parts: a descriptor portion and a data portion. Some SAS data sets also contain one or more indexes, which enable SAS to locate records in the data set more efficiently.

The **descriptor portion** of a SAS data set contains information about the data set.

The **data portion** of a SAS data set is a collection of data values that are arranged in a rectangular table. **Observations** in the data set correspond to rows or data lines in a raw data file or in an external database. An observation is the information about each object in a SAS data set. **Variables** in the data set correspond to columns in a raw data file or in an external database. A variable is the set of data values that describe a particular characteristic. If a data value is unknown for a particular observation, a missing value is recorded in the SAS data set.

Variable Attributes

In addition to general information about the data set, the descriptor portion contains attribute information for each variable in the data set. The attribute information includes the variable's name, length, and type. A variable's type determines how missing values for a variable are displayed by SAS. For character variables, a **blank** represents a missing value. For numeric variables, a **period** represents a missing value.

Points to Remember

- Before referencing SAS files, you must assign a name (libref, or library reference) to the library in which the files are stored (or specify that SAS is to assign the name automatically).

- You can store SAS files either temporarily or permanently.

- Variable names follow the same rules as SAS data set names. However, your site might choose to restrict variable names to those valid in SAS Version 6, to uppercase variable names automatically, or to remove all restrictions on variable names.

 After completing Chapter 1 and before continuing with Chapter 2 of this book, you should take one of the tutorials located on the CD that accompanies this book. These tutorials teach you how to create and manage your SAS programs by using the programming workspace provided in SAS and SAS Enterprise Guide.

Which tutorial you take will depend on the version of SAS that you are running on your machine.
- If you are running SAS9, take the **Using the Programming Workspace: SAS Windowing Environment** tutorial.
- If you are running SAS Enterprise Guide 3.0, take the **Using the Programming Workspace: SAS Enterprise Guide 3.0** tutorial.
- If you are running SAS Enterprise Guide 4.1, take the **Using the Programming Workspace: SAS Enterprise Guide 4.1** tutorial.

Now, insert the CD and print one of the following tutorials:

- Using the Programming Workspace: SAS Windowing Environment
- Using the Programming Workspace: SAS Enterprise Guide 3.0
- Using the Programming Workspace: SAS Enterprise Guide 4.1

If you do not find the release or version of SAS that you are running at your site, check the following companion Web site for updates:

support.sas.com/certbasetutorials

Ensure that you read the **Before You Begin** section on the CD for instructions on how to create the sample data and how to use the contents of the CD.

Practice

After you complete this chapter, practice what you learned by using the sample data and SAS programs for Chapter 1, **Basic Concepts**, which are located on the CD-ROM. Follow the directions for creating your sample data in the Before You Begin section.

Quiz

Select the best answer for each question. After completing the quiz, you can check your answers using the answer key in the appendix.

1. How many observations and variables does the data set below contain?

Name	Sex	Age
Picker	M	32
Fletcher		28
Romano	F	.
Choi	M	42

    a. 3 observations, 4 variables
    b. 3 observations, 3 variables
    c. 4 observations, 3 variables
    d. can't tell because some values are missing

2. How many program steps are executed when the program below is processed?

```
data user.tables;
    infile jobs;
    input date name $ job $;
run;
proc sort data=user.tables;
    by name;
run;
proc print data=user.tables;
run;
```

    a. three
    b. four
    c. five
    d. six

3. What type of variable is the variable AcctNum in the data set below?

AcctNum	Balance
3456_1	M
2451_2	
Romano	F
Choi	M

    a. numeric
    b. character
    c. can be either character or numeric
    d. can't tell from the data shown

4. What type of variable is the variable Wear in the data set below?

Brand	Wear
Acme	43
Ajax	34
Atlas	.

    a. numeric
    b. character
    c. can be either character or numeric
    d. can't tell from the data shown

5. Which of the following variable names is valid?

    a. 4BirthDate
    b. $Cost
    c. _Items_
    d. Tax-Rate

6. Which of the following files is a permanent SAS file?

    a. `Sashelp.PrdSale`
    b. `Sasuser.MySales`
    c. `Profits.Quarter1`
    d. all of the above

7. In a DATA step, how can you reference a temporary SAS data set named **Forecast**?

   a. `Forecast`
   b. `Work.Forecast`
   c. `Sales.Forecast` (after assigning the libref `Sales`)
   d. only *a* and *b* above

8. What is the default length for the numeric variable Balance?

Name	Balance
Adams	105.73
Geller	107.89
Martinez	97.45
Noble	182.50

   a. 5
   b. 6
   c. 7
   d. 8

9. How many statements does the following SAS program contain?

   ```
   proc print data=new.prodsale
                   label double;
     var state day price1 price2; where state='NC';
     label state='Name of State';
   run;
   ```

   a. three
   b. four
   c. five
   d. six

10. What is a SAS data library?

    a. a collection of SAS files, such as SAS data sets and catalogs
    b. in some operating environments, a physical collection of SAS files
    c. in some operating environments, a logically related collection of SAS files
    d. all of the above

Chapter **2** Referencing Files and Setting Options

Overview

 Have you reviewed the appropriate tutorial for your programming environment on the companion CD-ROM? If you have not, please review the appropriate tutorial before beginning this chapter.

Introduction

When you begin a SAS session, it's often convenient to set up your environment first. For example, you might want to

- define libraries that contain the SAS data sets that you intend to use
- set features of your SAS listings, such as whether the date and time appear
- specify how two-digit year values should be interpreted.

Objectives

In this chapter, you learn to

- define new libraries by using programming statements
- reference SAS files to be used during your SAS session
- set system options to determine how date values are read and to control the appearance of listing output that is created during your SAS session.

Referencing Files

SAS Libraries

In the previous chapter, you learned that SAS files are stored in **SAS libraries**. By default, SAS defines several libraries for you:

- **Sashelp** is a permanent library that contains sample data and other files that control how SAS works at your site. This is a read-only library.
- **Sasuser** is a permanent library that contains SAS files in the Profile catalog that store your personal settings. This is also a convenient place to store your own files.
- **Work** is a temporary library for files that do not need to be saved from session to session.

You can also define additional libraries. In fact, often the first step in setting up your SAS session is to define the libraries.

To define a library, you assign a **library name** (a **libref**) to it and specify a **path**, such as a directory path. You will use the libref as the first part of the file's two-level name (**libref.filename**) to reference the file within the library. You can use programming statements to assign library names.

Assigning Librefs

To define libraries, you can use a **LIBNAME statement**. You can store the LIBNAME statement with any SAS program so that the SAS data library is assigned each time the program is submitted.

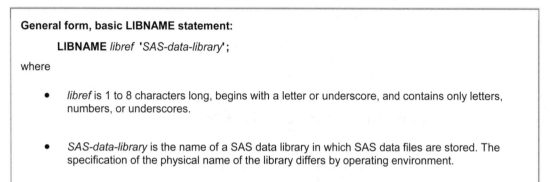

General form, basic LIBNAME statement:

       LIBNAME *libref* **'***SAS-data-library***'** ;

where

- *libref* is 1 to 8 characters long, begins with a letter or underscore, and contains only letters, numbers, or underscores.

- *SAS-data-library* is the name of a SAS data library in which SAS data files are stored. The specification of the physical name of the library differs by operating environment.

The LIBNAME statement below assigns the libref **Clinic** to the SAS data library **D:\Users\Qtr\Reports** in the Windows environment.

```
libname clinic 'd:\users\qtr\reports';
```

The table below gives examples of physical names for SAS data libraries in various operating environments.

Environment	Sample Physical Name
Windows	c:\fitness\data
UNIX	/users/april/fitness/sasdata
OpenVMS	dua0:[april.fitness]
CMS	b
z/OS (OS/390)	april.fitness.sasdata

The code examples in this book are shown in the Windows operating environment. If you are running SAS within another operating environment, then the platform-specific names and locations will look different. Otherwise, SAS programming code will be the same across operating environments.

You can use multiple LIBNAME statements to assign as many librefs as needed.

Verifying Librefs

After assigning a libref, it is a good idea to check the Log window to verify that the libref has been assigned successfully.

SAS Log

```
17     libname clinic 'd:\users\qtr\reports';

NOTE: Libref CLINIC was successfully assigned as follows:
      Engine:          V9
      Physical Name: d:\users\qtr\reports
```

How Long Librefs Remain in Effect

The LIBNAME statement is **global**, which means that the librefs remain in effect until you modify them, cancel them, or end your SAS session.

Therefore, the LIBNAME statement assigns the libref for the current SAS session only. Each time you begin a SAS session, you must assign a libref to each permanent SAS data library that contains files that you want to access in that session. (Remember that **Work** is the default libref for a temporary SAS data library.)

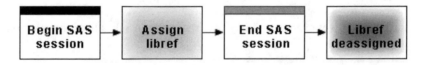

When you end your SAS session or delete a libref, SAS no longer has access to the files in the library. However, the contents of the library still exist on your operating system.

Specifying Two-Level Names

After you assign a libref, you specify the libref as the first element in the two-level name for a SAS file.

For example, in order for the PRINT procedure to read **Clinic.Admit**, you specify the two-level name of the file as follows:

```
proc print data=clinic.admit;
run;
```

Other Formats

You can use the LIBNAME statement to reference not only SAS files but also files that were created with other software products, such as database management systems.

SAS can read or write these files by using the appropriate **engine** for that file type. Depending on your operating environment and on the SAS/ACCESS products that you license, you can create libraries with various engines. Each engine enables you to read a different file format, including file formats from other software vendors.

For some file types, you need to tell SAS which engine to use. For others, SAS automatically chooses the appropriate engine.

A SAS engine is a set of internal instructions that SAS uses for writing to and reading from files in a SAS library.

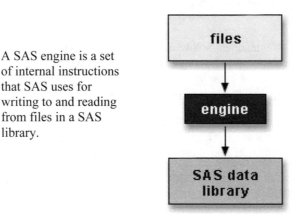

Specifying Engines

To indicate which engine to use, you specify the engine name in the LIBNAME statement, as shown below.

General form, LIBNAME statement for files in other formats:

> **LIBNAME** *libref engine* '*SAS-data-library*' ;

where

- *libref* is 1 to 8 characters long, begins with a letter or underscore, and contains only letters, numbers, or underscores.

- *engine* is the name of a library engine that is supported in your operating environment.

- *SAS-data-library* is the name of a SAS library in which SAS data files are stored. The specification of the physical name of the library differs by operating environment.

Interface Library Engines

Interface library engines support read-only access to BMDP, OSIRIS, and SPSS files. With these engines, the physical filename that is associated with a libref is an **actual filename**, not a SAS library. This is an exception to the rules for librefs.

Engine	Description
BMDP	allows read-only access to BMDP files
OSIRIS	allows read-only access to OSIRIS files
SPSS	allows read-only access to SPSS files

For example, the LIBNAME statement below specifies the libref **Rptdata** and the engine **SPSS** for the file **G:\Myspss.dat** in the Windows operating environment.

```
libname rptdata spss 'g:\myspss.dat';
```

For more information about interface library engines, see the SAS documentation for your operating environment.

SAS/ACCESS Engines

If your site licenses SAS/ACCESS software, then you can use the LIBNAME statement to access data that is stored in a DBMS file. The types of data that you can access depend on your operating environment and on which SAS/ACCESS products you have licensed.

Relational Databases	Nonrelational Files	PC Files
ORACLE	ADABAS	Excel (.xls)
SYBASE	IMS/DL-I	Lotus (.wk*n*)
Informix	CA-IDMS	DBF
DB2 for z/OS (OS/390)	SYSTEM 2000	DIF
DB2 for UNIX and PC		
Oracle Rdb		
ODBC		
CA-OpenIngres		

Viewing the Contents of SAS Libraries

The CONTENTS Procedure

You've learned how to use SAS windows to view the contents of a SAS library or of a SAS file. Alternatively, you can use the **CONTENTS procedure** to create SAS output that describes either of the following:

- the contents of a library
- the descriptor information for an individual SAS data set.

General form, basic PROC CONTENTS step:

> **PROC CONTENTS DATA=**_libref._**_ALL_ NODETAILS;**
> **RUN;**

where

- *libref* is the libref that has been assigned to the SAS library.

- **_ALL_** requests a listing of all files in the library. Use a period (.) to append _ALL_ to the libref.

- **NODETAILS (NODS)** suppresses the printing of detailed information about each file when you specify _ALL_. You can specify NODS **only** when you specify _ALL_.

Example

To view the contents of the **Mylib** library, submit the following PROC CONTENTS step:

```
proc contents data=mylib._all_ nods;
run;
```

The output from this step lists only the names, types, sizes, and modification dates for the SAS files in the **Mylib** library.

-----Directory-----	
Libref:	MYLIB
Engine:	V8
Physical Name:	C:\WINNT\Profiles\Personal\My SAS Files\V8
File Name:	C:\WINNT\Profiles\Personal\My SAS Files\V8

#	Name	Memtype	File Size	Last Modified
1	ADMIT	DATA	9216	23JUN2000:16:30:38
2	ADMITJUNE	DATA	9216	23JUN2000:16:30:38
3	COMPANY	DATA	5120	23JUN2000:16:30:38
4	CREDIT	DATA	5120	23JUN2000:16:30:38
5	CUSTDET1	DATA	33792	04MAY2000:13:45:49
6	DIABETES	DATA	9216	23JUN2000:16:30:38
7	DMDATA	CATALOG	21504	04MAY2000:13:59:19

To view the descriptor information for the **Mylib.Admit** data set, you can submit the following PROC CONTENTS step:

```
proc contents data=mylib.admit;
run;
```

The output from this step lists information for **Mylib.Admit**, including an alphabetic list of the variables in the data set.

Data Set Name	MYLIB.ADMIT	**Observations**	21
Member Type	DATA	**Variables**	9
Engine	V8	**Indexes**	0
Created	15:05 Thursday, July 17, 2003	**Observation Length**	64
Last Modified	15:05 Thursday, July 17, 2003	**Deleted Observations**	0
Protection		**Compressed**	NO
Data Set Type		**Sorted**	NO
Label			

Engine/Host Dependent Information	
Data Set Page Size	8192
Number of Data Set Pages	1
First Data Page	1
Max Obs per Page	127
Obs in First Data Page	21
Number of Data Set Repairs	0
File Name	C:\WINNT\Profiles\Personal\My SAS Files\V8\admit.sas7bdat
Release Created	8.0202M0
Host Created	XP_PRO

Alphabetic List of Variables and Attributes				
#	Variable	Type	Len	Format
8	ActLevel	Char	4	
4	Age	Num	8	
5	Date	Num	8	
9	Fee	Num	8	7.2
6	Height	Num	8	
1	ID	Char	4	
2	Name	Char	14	
3	Sex	Char	1	
7	Weight	Num	8	

The DATASETS Procedure

In addition to PROC CONTENTS, you can also use **PROC DATASETS** with the CONTENTS statement to view the contents of a SAS library or a SAS data set.

General form, PROC DATASETS step with CONTENTS statement:

PROC DATASETS;
   CONTENTS DATA=*libref.***_ALL_ NODETAILS;**
QUIT;

where

- **CONTENTS** describes the contents of one or more SAS data sets and prints the directory of the SAS data library.

- *libref* is the libref that has been assigned to the SAS data library.

- **_ALL_** requests a listing of all files in the library. Use a period (.) to append _ALL_ to the libref.

- **NODETAILS (NODS)** suppresses the printing of detailed information about each file when you specify _ALL_. You can specify NODS **only** when you specify _ALL_.

For example, the following PROC steps produce essentially the same output (with minor formatting differences):

```
proc datasets;
   contents data=sasuser._all_ nods;
quit;
proc contents data=sasuser._all_ nods;
run;
```

The major difference between the CONTENTS procedure and the CONTENTS statement in PROC DATASETS is the default for *libref* in the DATA= option. For PROC CONTENTS, the default is either **Work** or **User**. For the CONTENTS statement, the default is the libref of the procedure input library. Notice also that PROC DATASETS is an interactive procedure that requires a QUIT statement rather than a RUN statement.

In addition to the CONTENTS statement, PROC DATASETS also uses several other statements. These statements enable you to perform tasks that PROC CONTENTS does not perform. For more information about PROC DATASETS, see the SAS documentation for your operating environment.

Viewing Descriptor Information for a SAS Data Set

As with PROC CONTENTS, you can also use PROC DATASETS to display the descriptor information for a specific SAS data set.

By default, PROC CONTENTS and PROC DATASETS list variables **alphabetically**. To list variable names in the order of their **logical** position (or creation order) in the data set, you can specify the **VARNUM option** in PROC CONTENTS or in the CONTENTS statement in PROC DATASETS.

For example, either of these programs creates output that includes the list of variables shown below:

```
proc datasets;
   contents data=sasuser.admit varnum;
quit;

proc contents data=sasuser.admit varnum;
run;
```

Variables in Creation Order			
#	**Variable**	**Type**	**Len**	**Format**
1	ID	Char	4	
2	Name	Char	14	
3	Sex	Char	1	
4	Age	Num	8	
5	Date	Num	8	
6	Height	Num	8	
7	Weight	Num	8	
8	ActLevel	Char	4	
9	Fee	Num	8	7.2

Setting SAS System Options

SAS Output

Next, let's consider the appearance and format of your SAS output. You can specify **result formats** to create your output as

- an HTML document

- a listing (traditional SAS output)

- both of the above.

You can create HTML output by using programming statements on any SAS platform. In addition, in desktop operating environments, you can use windows to specify result formats. You can learn more about how to create HTML output in Chapter 10, **Producing HTML Output**.

If you create your procedure output as a SAS listing, you can also control the appearance of your output by setting system options such as

- line size (the maximum width of the log and output)

- page size (the number of lines per printed page of output)

- the display of page numbers

- the display of date and time.

 The above options do not affect the appearance of HTML output.

All SAS system options have default settings that are used unless you specify otherwise. For example, page numbers are automatically displayed (unless your site modifies this default).

```
                                          Date and time              Page numbers

                                                                          5
                               10:31  Tuesday,  March  3,  1998

                          Sex    Age    Height    Weight

                           M      27      72       168
            Page           F      34      66       152
            Size           F      31      61       123
                           F      43      63       137
                           M      51      71       158
                           M      29      76       193
                           F      32      67       151
                           M      35      70       173
                           M      34      73       154

                                          Line size
```

To modify system options, you submit an OPTIONS statement. You can place an OPTIONS statement anywhere in a SAS program to change the settings from that point onward. However, it is good programming practice to place OPTIONS statements outside of DATA or PROC steps so that your programs are easier to read and debug.

 Because the OPTIONS statement is **global**, the settings remain in effect until you modify them, or until you end your SAS session.

General form, OPTIONS statement:

  OPTIONS *options*;

where *options* specifies one or more system options to be changed. The available system options depend on your host operating system.

Example: NUMBER | NONUMBER and DATE | NODATE Options

By default, page numbers and dates appear with output. The following OPTIONS statement suppresses the printing of both page numbers and the date and time in listing output.

```
options nonumber nodate;
```

In the following example, page numbers and the current date are not displayed in the PROC PRINT output. Page numbers are not displayed in the PROC FREQ output, either, but the date does appear at the top of the page that contains the PROC FREQ report.

```
options nonumber nodate;
proc print data=clinic.admit;
   var id sex age height weight;
   where age>=30;
run;
options date;
proc freq data=clinic.diabetes;
   where fastgluc>=300;
   tables sex;
run;
```

```
                        The SAS System

    Obs      ID     Sex      Age      Height      Weight

     2      2462      F       34        66          152
     3      2501      F       31        61          123
     4      2523      F       43        63          137
     5      2539      M       51        71          158
     7      2552      F       32        67          151
     8      2555      M       35        70          173
     9      2563      M       34        73          154
    10      2568      F       49        64          172
    11      2571      F       44        66          140
    13      2574      M       30        69          147
    14      2575      F       40        69          163
    15      2578      M       47        72          173
    16      2579      M       60        71          191
    17      2584      F       43        65          123
    20      2589      F       41        67          141
    21      2595      M       54        71          183
```

```
                        The SAS System
              15:19 Thursday, September 23, 1999

                                      Cumulative     Cumulative
   Sex     Frequency      Percent     Frequency      Percent
   --------------------------------------------------------------
   F           2           25.0           2            25.0
   M           6           75.0           8           100.0
```

Example: PAGENO= Option

If you print page numbers, you can specify the beginning page number for your report by using the PAGENO= option. If you don't specify the PAGENO= option, output is numbered sequentially throughout your SAS session, starting with page 1.

In the following example, the output pages are numbered sequentially throughout the SAS session, beginning with number 3.

```
options nodate pageno=3;
proc print data=hrd.funddrv;
run;
```

```
                              The SAS System                     3
     Obs    LastName     Qtr1     Qtr2     Qtr3     Qtr4

      1     ADAMS         18       18       20       20
      2     ALEXANDER     15       18       15       10
      3     APPLE         25       25       25       25
      4     ARTHUR        10       25       20       30
      5     AVERY         15       15       15       15
      6     BAREFOOT      20       20       20       20
      7     BAUCOM        25       20       20       30
      8     BLAIR         10       10        5       10
      9     BLALOCK        5       10       10       15
     10     BOSTIC        20       25       30       25
     11     BRADLEY       12       16       14       18
```

Example: PAGESIZE= Option

The PAGESIZE= option specifies how many lines each page of output contains. In the following example, each page of the output that the PRINT procedure produces contains 15 lines (including those used by the title, date, and so on).

```
options pageno=1 pagesize=15;
proc print data=clinic.admit;
run;
```

```
                              The SAS System                    1
                      15:19 Thursday, September 23, 1999

    Obs    ID     Name              Sex     Age     Date

     1    2458    Murray, W          M       27       1
     2    2462    Almers, C          F       34       3
     3    2501    Bonaventure, T     F       31      17
     4    2523    Johnson, R         F       43      31
     5    2539    LaMance, K         M       51       4
     6    2544    Jones, M           M       29       6
     7    2552    Reberson, P        F       32       9
     8    2555    King, E            M       35      13
     9    2563    Pitts, D           M       34      22
    10    2568    Eberhardt, S       F       49      27
```

Example: LINESIZE= Option

The LINESIZE= option specifies the width of the print line for your procedure output and log. Observations that do not fit within the line size continue on a different line.

In the following example, the observations are longer than 64 characters, so the observations continue on a subsequent page.

```
options pageno=1 linesize=64;
proc print data=flights.europe;
run;
```

```
                                      The SAS System                     1
                              15:19 Thursday, September 23, 1999

  Obs   Flight    Date    Depart  Orig  Dest  Miles  Mail  Freight  Boarded

   1      821    04MAR99   9:31   LGA   LON   3442   403    209      167
   2      271    04MAR99  11:40   LGA   PAR   3856   492    308      146
   3      271    05MAR99  12:19   LGA   PAR   3857   366    498      177
   4      821    06MAR99  14:56   LGA   LON   3442   345    243      167
   5      821    07MAR99  13:17   LGA   LON   3635   248    307      215
   6      271    07MAR99   9:31   LGA   PAR   3442   353    205      155
   7      821    08MAR99  11:40   LGA   LON   3856   391    395      186
   8      271    08MAR99  12:19   LGA   PAR   3857   366    279      152
   9      821    09MAR99  14:56   LGA   LON   3442   219    368      203
  10      271    09MAR99  13:17   LGA   PAR   3635   357    282      159
```

```
                                        The SAS System                      2
                                15:19 Thursday, September 23, 1999

     Obs  Transfer  NonRev  Deplaned  Capacity  MonthDay  Revenue

      1       17       7       222       250        1      150634
      2        8       3       163       250        1      156804
      3       15       5       227       250        1      190098
      4       13       4       222       250        1      150634
      5       14       6       158       250        1      193930
      6       18       7       172       250        2      166470
      7        8       1       114       250        2      167772
      8        7       4       187       250        2      163248
      9        6       3       210       250        2      183106
     10       15       4       191       250        2      170766
```

Handling Two-Digit Year Values: Year 2000 Compliance

If you use **two-digit year values** in your data lines, external files, or programming statements, you should consider another important system option, the YEARCUTOFF= option. This option specifies which 100-year span is used to interpret two-digit year values.

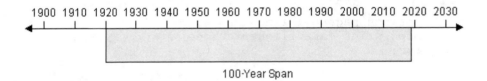

100-Year Span

All versions of SAS represent dates correctly from 1582 A.D. to 20,000 A.D. (Leap years, century, and fourth-century adjustments are made automatically. Leap seconds are ignored, and SAS does not adjust for daylight saving time.) However, you should be aware of the YEARCUTOFF= value to ensure that you are properly interpreting two-digit years in data lines.

As with other system options, you specify the YEARCUTOFF= option in the OPTIONS statement:

```
  options yearcutoff=1925;
```

How the YEARCUTOFF= Option Works

When a two-digit year value is read, SAS interprets it based on a 100-year span that starts with the YEARCUTOFF= value. The default value of YEARCUTOFF= is **1920**.

1920 ← 100 years → **2019**

Date Expression	Interpreted As
12/07/41	12/07/1941
18Dec15	18Dec2015
04/15/30	04/15/1930
15Apr95	15Apr1995

However, you can override the default and change the value of YEARCUTOFF= to the first year of another 100-year span. For example, if you specify YEARCUTOFF=1950, then the 100-year span will be from 1950 to 2049.

```
options yearcutoff=1950;
```

Using YEARCUTOFF=1950, dates are interpreted as shown below:

1950 ← 100 years → 2049

Date Expression	Interpreted As
12/07/41	**12/07/2041**
18Dec15	18Dec2015
04/15/30	**04/15/2030**
15Apr95	15Apr1995

How Four-Digit Year Values Are Handled

Remember, the value of the YEARCUTOFF= system option affects only **two-digit year values**. A date value that contains a four-digit year value will be interpreted correctly even if it does not fall within the 100-year span set by the YEARCUTOFF= system option.

 You can learn more about reading date values in Chapter 19, **Reading Date and Time Values**.

Using System Options to Specify Observations

You've seen how to use SAS system options to change the appearance of output and interpret two-digit year values. You can also use the **OBS=** and **FIRSTOBS=** system options to specify the observations to process from SAS data sets.

You can specify either or both of these options as needed. That is, you can use

- OBS= to specify the last observation to be processed

- FIRSTOBS= to specify the first observation to be processed

- FIRSTOBS= and OBS= together to specify a range of observations to be processed.

General form, FIRSTOBS= and OBS= options in an OPTIONS statement:

> **OPTIONS FIRSTOBS=**n;
>
> **OPTIONS OBS=**n;

where n is a positive integer. For FIRSTOBS=, n specifies the number of the **first** observation to process. For OBS=, n specifies the number of the **last** observation to process. By default, FIRSTOBS=1. The default value for OBS= is MAX, which is the largest signed, four-byte integer that is representable in your operating environment.

 Each of these options applies to every input data set that is used in a program or a SAS process.

Example: FIRSTOBS= and OBS= Options

The data set **Sasuser.Heart** contains 20 observations. If you specify FIRSTOBS=10, SAS reads the 10th observation of the data set first and reads through the last observation (for a total of 11 observations).

```
options firstobs=10;
proc print data=sasuser.heart;
run;
```

The PROC PRINT step produces the following output:

Obs	Patient	Sex	Survive	Shock	Arterial	Heart	Cardiac	Urinary
10	509	2	SURV	OTHER	79	84	256	90
11	742	1	DIED	HYPOVOL	100	54	135	0
12	609	2	DIED	NONSHOCK	93	101	260	90
13	318	2	DIED	OTHER	72	81	410	405
14	412	1	SURV	BACTER	61	87	296	44
15	601	1	DIED	BACTER	84	101	260	377
16	402	1	SURV	CARDIO	88	137	312	75
17	98	2	SURV	CARDIO	84	87	260	377
18	4	1	SURV	HYPOVOL	81	149	406	200
19	50	2	SURV	HYPOVOL	72	111	332	12
20	2	2	DIED	OTHER	101	114	424	97

If you specify OBS=10 instead, SAS reads through the 10th observation, in this case for a total of 10 observations. (Notice that FIRSTOBS= has been reset to the default value.)

```
options firstobs=1 obs=10;
proc print data=sasuser.heart;
run;
```

Now the PROC PRINT step produces this output:

Obs	Patient	Sex	Survive	Shock	Arterial	Heart	Cardiac	Urinary
1	203	1	SURV	NONSHOCK	88	95	66	110
2	54	1	DIED	HYPOVOL	83	183	95	0
3	664	2	SURV	CARDIO	72	111	332	12
4	210	2	DIED	BACTER	74	97	369	0
5	101	2	DIED	NEURO	80	130	291	0
6	102	2	SURV	OTHER	87	107	471	65
7	529	1	DIED	CARDIO	103	106	217	15
8	524	2	DIED	CARDIO	145	99	156	10
9	426	1	SURV	OTHER	68	77	410	75
10	509	2	SURV	OTHER	79	84	256	90

Combining FIRSTOBS= and OBS= processes observations in the middle of the data set. For example, the following program processes only observations 10 through 15, for a total of 6 observations:

```
options firstobs=10 obs=15;
proc print data=sasuser.heart;
run;
```

Here is the output:

Obs	Patient	Sex	Survive	Shock	Arterial	Heart	Cardiac	Urinary
10	509	2	SURV	OTHER	79	84	256	90
11	742	1	DIED	HYPOVOL	100	54	135	0
12	609	2	DIED	NONSHOCK	93	101	260	90
13	318	2	DIED	OTHER	72	81	410	405
14	412	1	SURV	BACTER	61	87	296	44
15	601	1	DIED	BACTER	84	101	260	377

To reset the number of the last observation to process, you can specify OBS=MAX in the OPTIONS statement.

```
options obs=max;
```

This instructs any subsequent SAS programs in the SAS session to process through the last observation in the data set being read.

Using FIRSTOBS= and OBS= for Specific Data Sets

As you saw above, using the FIRSTOBS= or OBS= system options determines the first or last observation, respectively, that is read for all steps for the duration of your current SAS session or until you change the setting. However, you might want to

- override these options for a given data set
- apply these options to a specific data set only.

To affect any single file, you can use FIRSTOBS= or OBS= as **data set options** instead of as system options. You specify the data set option in parentheses immediately following the input data set name.

A FIRSTOBS= or OBS= specification from a data set option overrides the corresponding FIRSTOBS= or OBS= system option.

Example: FIRSTOBS= and OBS as Data Set Options

As shown in the last example, this program processes only observations 10 through 15, for a total of 6 observations:

```
options firstobs=10 obs=15;
proc print data=sasuser.heart;
run;
```

You can create the same output by specifying FIRSTOBS= and OBS= as data set options. The data set options override the system options for this instance only.

```
options firstobs=10 obs=15;
proc print data=sasuser.heart(firstobs=4 obs=20);
run;
```

To specify FIRSTOBS= or OBS= for this program only, you could omit the OPTIONS statement altogether and simply use the data set options.

Viewing System Options

The OPTIONS Procedure

You can use the OPTIONS procedure to display the current setting of one or all SAS system options. The results are displayed in the log.

General form, OPTIONS procedure:

> **PROC OPTIONS** <*option(s)*>;
> **RUN;**

where *option(s)* specifies how SAS system options are displayed.

Example

To list all SAS system options, their settings, and a description, submit the following code:

```
proc options;
run;
```

The log lists the options and their settings:

Partial Log

```
1          proc options;
2          run;
SAS (r) Proprietary Software Release 9 TS2M0
Portable Options:
 APPLETLOC=C:\Program Files\SAS Institute\Shared Files\applets\9
               Location of Java applets
 ARMAGENT=         ARM Agent to use to collect ARM records
 ARMLOC=ARMLOC.LOG Identify location where ARM records are to be
               written
 ARMSUBSYS=(ARM_NONE)
               Enable/Disable ARMing of SAS subsystems
 NOASYNCHIO        Do not enable asynchronous input/output
               AUTOSAVELOC=        Identifies the location
               where program editor contents are auto saved
```

To list the value of one particular system option, use the OPTION= option in the PROC OPTIONS statement as shown below:

```
proc options option=yearcutoff;
run;
```

> If a SAS system option uses an equal sign, such as YEARCUTOFF=, you do not include the equal sign when specifying the option to OPTION=.

The log shows that the setting of the YEARCUTOFF= option is 1920.

```
3              proc options option=yearcutoff;
4              run;
   SAS (r) Proprietary Software Release 9 TS2M0
   YEARCUTOFF=1920 Cutoff year for DATE and DATETIME informats
   and functions
```

Additional System Options

When you set up your SAS session, you can set SAS system options that affect listing output, information written to the SAS log, and much more. Here are some additional system options that you are likely to use with SAS procedures:

Option	Description
FORMCHAR='*formatting-characters*'	specifies the formatting characters for your output device. Formatting characters are used to construct the outlines of tables, and dividers for various procedures, such as the FREQ and TABULATE procedures. If you do not specify formatting characters as an option in the procedure, then the default specifications given in the FORMCHAR= system option are used.
FORMDLIM='*delimiting-character*'	specifies a character that is used to delimit page breaks in SAS System output. Normally, the delimiting character is null. When the delimiting character is null, a new physical page starts whenever a page break occurs.
LABEL | NOLABEL	permits SAS procedures to temporarily replace variable names with descriptive labels. The LABEL system option must be in effect before the LABEL option of any procedure can be used. If NOLABEL is specified, then the LABEL option of a procedure is ignored. The default setting is LABEL.
OBS=*n*	specifies the observation from a data set (or the record from a raw data file) that SAS reads last. You can also use the OBS= system option to control the analysis of SAS data sets in PROC steps. *n* specifies the number of the last observation to process.
SOURCE | NOSOURCE	controls whether SAS source statements are written to the SAS log. NOSOURCE specifies not to write SAS source statements to the SAS log. The default setting is SOURCE.

You can also use programming statements to control the result format of each item of procedure output individually. For more information, see Chapter 10, **Producing HTML Output**.

Summary

Text Summary

Referencing Files in SAS Libraries

To reference a SAS file, you assign a libref (library reference) to the SAS library in which the file is stored. Then you use the libref as the first part of the two-level name (*libref.filename*) for the file.

To reference a SAS library, you can submit a **LIBNAME statement**. You can store the LIBNAME statement with any SAS program to reference the SAS library automatically when you submit the program. The LIBNAME statement assigns the libref for the current SAS session only. You must assign a libref each time you begin a SAS session in order to access SAS files that are stored in a permanent SAS library. (**Work** is the default libref for a temporary SAS library.)

You can also use the LIBNAME statement to reference data in files that were created with other software products, such as database management systems. SAS can write to or read from the files by using the appropriate **engine** for that file type. For some file types, you need to tell SAS which engine to use. For others, SAS automatically chooses the appropriate engine.

Viewing the Contents of SAS Libraries

To list the contents of a library, use the **CONTENTS procedure**. Append a period and the _ALL_ option to the libref to get a listing of all files in the library. Add the NODS option to suppress detailed information about the files. As an alternative to PROC CONTENTS, you can use **PROC DATASETS.**

Setting SAS System Options

For your listing output, you can also control the appearance of your output by setting system options such as line size, page size, the display of page numbers, and the display of the date and time. (These options do not affect the appearance of HTML output.)

All SAS system options have default settings that are used unless you specify otherwise. For example, page numbers are automatically displayed (unless your site modifies this default). To modify system options, you submit an **OPTIONS statement**. You can place an OPTIONS statement anywhere in a SAS program to change the current settings. Because the OPTIONS statement is global, the settings remain in effect until you modify them or until you end your SAS session.

If you use two-digit year values in your SAS data lines, you must be aware of the **YEARCUTOFF= option** to ensure that you are properly interpreting two-digit years in your SAS program. This option specifies which 100-year span is used to interpret two-digit year values.

Viewing SAS System Options

You can use the **OPTIONS procedure** to display the value of one or more SAS system options. The output of this procedure is included in the log.

Points to Remember

- LIBNAME and OPTIONS statements remain in effect for the current SAS session only.

- When you work with date values,

  - check the default value of the YEARCUTOFF= system option and change it if necessary

  - specify the proper informat for reading a date value or the proper format for writing a date value

  - specify the correct field width so that the entire date value is read or written.

Practice

After you complete this chapter, practice what you learned by using the sample data and SAS programs for Chapter 2, **Referencing Files and Setting Options**, which are located on the CD-ROM. Follow the directions for creating your sample data in the Before You Begin section.

Quiz

Select the best answer for each question. After completing the quiz, check your answers using the answer key in the appendix.

1. If you submit the following program, how does the output look?

    ```
    options pagesize=55 nonumber;
    proc tabulate data=clinic.admit;
       class actlevel;
       var age height weight;
       table actlevel,(age height weight)*mean;
    run;
    options linesize=80;
      proc means data=clinic.heart min max maxdec=1;
      var arterial heart cardiac urinary;
      class survive sex;
    run;
    ```

    a. The PROC MEANS output has a print line width of 80 characters, but the PROC TABULATE output has no print line width.

    b. The PROC TABULATE output has no page numbers, but the PROC MEANS output has page numbers.

    c. Each page of output from both PROC steps is 55 lines long and has no page numbers, and the PROC MEANS output has a print line width of 80 characters.

    d. The date does not appear on output from either PROC step.

2. In order for the date values 05May1955 and 04Mar2046 to be read correctly, what value must the YEARCUTOFF= option have?

    a. a value between 1947 and 1954, inclusive

    b. 1955 or higher

    c. 1946 or higher

    d. any value

3. When you specify an engine for a library, you are always specifying

    a. the file format for files that are stored in the library.

    b. the version of SAS that you are using.

    c. access to other software vendors' files.

    d. instructions for creating temporary SAS files.

4. Which statement prints a summary of all the files stored in the library named Area51?

    a. `proc contents data=area51._all_ nods;`
    b. `proc contents data=area51 _all_ nods;`
    c. `proc contents data=area51 _all_ noobs;`
    d. `proc contents data=area51 _all_.nods;`

5. The following PROC PRINT output was created immediately after PROC TABULATE output. Which SAS system options were specified when the report was created?

```
                                              1
                    10:03 Friday, March 17, 2000
                                 Act
     Obs  ID   Height  Weight  Level    Fee

      1  2458    72      168    HIGH    85.20
      2  2462    66      152    HIGH   124.80
      3  2501    61      123    LOW    149.75
      4  2523    63      137    MOD    149.75
      5  2539    71      158    LOW    124.80
      6  2544    76      193    HIGH   124.80
      7  2552    67      151    MOD    149.75
      8  2555    70      173    MOD    149.75
      9  2563    73      154    LOW    124.80
```

    a. OBS=, DATE, and NONUMBER
    b. PAGENO=1 and DATE
    c. NUMBER and DATE only
    d. none of the above

6. Which of the following programs correctly references a SAS data set named SalesAnalysis that is stored in a permanent SAS library?

    a.
    ```
    data saleslibrary.salesanalysis;
       set mydata.quarter1sales;
       if sales>100000;
    run;
    ```
    b.
    ```
    data mysales.totals;
       set sales_99.salesanalysis;
       if totalsales>50000;
    run;
    ```
    c.
    ```
    proc print data=salesanalysis.quarter1;
       var sales salesrep month;
    run;
    ```
    d.
    ```
    proc freq data=1999data.salesanalysis;
       tables quarter*sales;
    run;
    ```

7. Which time span is used to interpret two-digit year values if the YEARCUTOFF= option is set to 1950?

    a. 1950-2049
    b. 1950-2050
    c. 1949-2050
    d. 1950-2000

8. Assuming you are using SAS code and not special SAS windows, which one of the following statements is false?

    a. LIBNAME statements can be stored with a SAS program to reference the SAS library automatically when you submit the program.
    b. When you delete a libref, SAS no longer has access to the files in the library. However, the contents of the library still exist on your operating system.
    c. Librefs can last from one SAS session to another.
    d. You can access files that were created with other vendors' software by submitting a LIBNAME statement.

9. What does the following statement do?

    ```
    libname osiris spss 'c:\myfiles\sasdata\data';
    ```

    a. defines a library called Spss using the OSIRIS engine
    b. defines a library called Osiris using the SPSS engine
    c. defines two libraries called Osiris and Spss using the default engine
    d. defines the default library using the OSIRIS and SPSS engines

10. What does the following OPTIONS statement do?

    ```
    options pagesize=15 nodate;
    ```

    a. suppresses the date and limits the page size of the log
    b. suppresses the date and limits the vertical page size for text output
    c. suppresses the date and limits the vertical page size for text and HTML output
    d. suppresses the date and limits the horizontal page size for text output

Chapter 3 Editing and Debugging SAS Programs

Overview

Introduction

Now that you're familiar with the basics, you can learn how to correct errors in your programs and resolve common problems effectively.

```
┌─ Output - (Untitled) ──────────────  _□×
│ Browse output from
│ your SAS session
│     ┌─ Log - (Untitled) ──────────────  _□×
│     │
│     │            Get messages
│     │            about your SAS
│     │            session and
│     │            the programs
│     │            you submit
│     │
│     │     ┌─ Editor - Untitled1 * ──────  _□×
│     │     │
│     │     │        Enter, edit, and
│     │     │        submit SAS
│     │     │        programs
│     │     │
│     │     │
```

Objectives

In this chapter, you learn to

- enhance the readability of your SAS programs

- interpret error messages in the SAS log

- correct errors

- resolve common problems.

SAS Program Layout

Before discussing how to edit and debug programs, let's review the characteristics of SAS statements and look at enhancing the readability of your SAS programs.

Remember that SAS programs consist of SAS statements.

SAS statements...

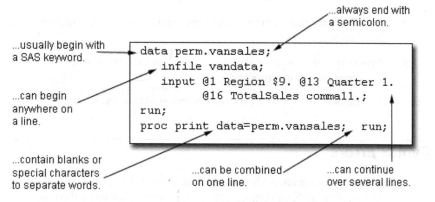

...always end with a semicolon.

...usually begin with a SAS keyword.

...can begin anywhere on a line.

...contain blanks or special characters to separate words.

...can be combined on one line.

...can continue over several lines.

```
data perm.vansales;
   infile vandata;
   input @1 Region $9. @13 Quarter 1.
         @16 TotalSales comma11.;
run;
proc print data=perm.vansales;  run;
```

Although you can write SAS statements in almost any format, a consistent layout enhances readability and helps you understand the program's purpose. It's a good idea to

- begin DATA and PROC steps in column one

- indent statements within a step

- begin RUN statements in column one

- include a RUN statement after every DATA step or PROC step.

```
data work.bankacct;
   infile records;
   input Name $ 1-10 AccountType $ 12-20
         Deposit 22-25 Withdrawal 27-30;
run;
proc print data=work.bankacct;
run;
proc means mean;
   var deposit withdrawal;
run;
```

Interpreting Error Messages

Error Types

So far, the programs that you've seen in this book have been error free, but programming errors do occur. SAS can detect several types of errors. The most common are

- **syntax errors** that occur when program statements do not conform to the rules of the SAS language

- **data errors** that occur when some data values are not appropriate for the SAS statements that are specified in a program.

This chapter focuses on identifying and correcting **syntax errors**.

Syntax Errors

When you submit a program, SAS scans each step for syntax errors, then processes the step (if no syntax errors are found). SAS then goes to the next step and repeats the process. Syntax errors, such as misspelled words, generally cause SAS to stop processing the step in which the error occurred.

You already know that information is written to the SAS log while a SAS program is executing. When a program that contains an error is submitted, messages regarding the problem also appear in the SAS log. When a syntax error is detected, the SAS log

- displays the word ERROR

- identifies the possible location of the error

- gives an explanation of the error.

Example

The program below contains a syntax error. The DATA step copies the SAS data set **Clinic.Admit** into a new data set named **Clinic.Admitfee**. The PROC step should print the values for the variables ID, Name, Actlevel, and Fee in the new data set. However, *print* is misspelled in the PROC PRINT statement.

```
data clinic.admitfee;
   set clinic.admit;
run;
proc prin data=clinic.admitfee;
   var id name actlevel fee;
run;
```

When the program is submitted, messages in the SAS log indicate that the procedure PRIN was not found and that SAS stopped processing the PRINT step due to errors. No output is produced by the PRINT procedure, because the second step fails to execute.

error notification   possible   explanation
                          location   of the error
                          of the error

```
24b6           proc prin data=clinic.admitfee;
ERROR: PROCEDURE PRIN not found.
2467             var id name actlevel fee;
2468           run;

NOTE:   The SAS System stopped processing this
        step because of errors.
NOTE:   PROCEDURE PRIN used (Total process time):
        real time              0.03 seconds
        cpu time               0.00 seconds
```

  Problems with your statements or data might not be evident when you look at results. Therefore, it's important to review the messages in the log each time you submit a SAS program.

Correcting Errors

To modify programs that contain errors, you can edit them in the Editor window. You can correct simple errors, such as the spelling error in the following program, by typing over the incorrect text, deleting text, or inserting text.

```
data clinic.admitfee;
   set clinic.admit;
run;
proc prin data=clinic.admitfee;
   var id name actlevel fee;
run;
```

In the program below, the missing **t** has been inserted into the PRINT keyword that is specified in the PROC PRINT statement.

```
data clinic.admitfee;
   set clinic.admit;
run;
proc print data=clinic.admitfee;
   var id name actlevel fee;
run;
```

Some problems are relatively easy to diagnose and correct. But sometimes you might not know right away how to correct errors. The online Help provides information about individual procedures as well as help that is specific to your operating environment. From the **Help** menu, you can also select **SAS on the Web** for links to Technical Support and Frequently Asked Questions, if you have Internet access.

Resubmitting a Revised Program

After correcting your program, you can submit it again.

 When you submit the code, SAS Enterprise Guide prompts you to choose whether or not you want to replace the previous results. If you choose not to replace the results, SAS Enterprise Guide makes a copy of the code and a new code item is added to the project.

Previously, because there was an error in the PRINT procedure, the code that contained the error did not produce output. This time, the PRINT procedure executes and produces output.

Obs	ID	Name	ActLevel	Fee
1	2458	Murray, W	HIGH	85.20
2	2462	Almers, C	HIGH	124.80
3	2501	Bonaventure, T	LOW	149.75
4	2523	Johnson, R	MOD	149.75
5	2539	LaMance, K	LOW	124.80
6	2544	Jones, M	HIGH	124.80
7	2552	Reberson, P	MOD	149.75
8	2555	King, E	MOD	149.75
9	2563	Pitts, D	LOW	124.80
10	2568	Eberhardt, S	LOW	124.80
11	2571	Nunnelly, A	HIGH	149.75
12	2572	Oberon, M	LOW	85.20
13	2574	Peterson, V	MOD	149.75
14	2575	Quigley, M	HIGH	124.80
15	2578	Cameron, L	MOD	124.80
16	2579	Underwood, K	LOW	149.75
17	2584	Takahashi, Y	MOD	124.80
18	2586	Derber, B	HIGH	85.20
19	2588	Ivan, H	LOW	85.20
20	2589	Wilcox, E	HIGH	149.75
21	2595	Warren, C	MOD	149.75

Remember to check the SAS log again to verify that your program ran correctly.

SAS Log

```
54      data clinic.admitfee;
55          set clinic.admit;
56      run;


NOTE:   The data set CLINIC.ADMITFEE has
        21 observations and 9 variables.
NOTE:   DATA statement used:
        real time            0.09  seconds
        cpu time             0.03  seconds


57      proc print data=clinic.admitfee;
58          var id name actlevel fee;
59      run;


NOTE:   PROCEDURE PRINT used;
        real time            1.78  seconds
        cpu time             0.03  seconds
```

Resolving Common Problems

In addition to correcting spelling mistakes, you might need to resolve several other types of common syntax errors. These errors include

- omitting semicolons
- leaving quotation marks unbalanced
- specifying invalid options.

Another common problem is omitting a RUN statement at the end of a program. Although this is not technically an error, it can produce unexpected results. For the sake of convenience, we'll consider it together with syntax errors.

The table below lists these problems and their symptoms.

Problem	Symptom
missing RUN statement	"PROC (or DATA) step running" at top of active window
missing semicolon	log message indicating an error in a statement that seems to be valid
unbalanced quotation marks	log message indicating that a text string enclosed in quotation marks has become too long or that a statement is ambiguous
invalid option	log message indicating that an option is invalid or not recognized

Missing RUN Statement

Each step in a SAS program is compiled and executed independently from every other step. As a step is compiled, SAS recognizes the end of the current step when it encounters

- a DATA or PROC statement, which indicates the beginning of a new step
- a RUN or QUIT statement, which indicates the end of the current step.

When the program below is submitted, the DATA step executes, but the PROC step does not. The PROC step does not execute because there is no following DATA or PROC step to indicate the beginning of a new step, nor is there a following RUN statement to indicate the end of the step.

```
data clinic.admitfee;
   set clinic.admit;
run;
proc print data=clinic.admitfee;
   var id name actlevel fee;
```

 If you submit this code using the SAS windowing environment, the PRINT procedure waits before executing because there is nothing to indicate the end of the PROC step. A "PROC PRINT running" message appears at the top of the active window.

 SAS Enterprise Guide automatically adds a RUN statement at the end of code when it is submitted to SAS. So although you need to learn to add a RUN statement to the end of your steps, you will not encounter this problem if you forget to add a RUN statement when using SAS Enterprise Guide.

Resolving the Problem

To correct the error, submit a RUN statement to complete the PROC step.

```
run;
```

Missing Semicolon

One of the most common errors is the omission of a semicolon at the end of a statement. The program below is missing a semicolon at the end of the PROC PRINT statement.

```
data clinic.admitfee;
  set clinic.admit;
run;
proc print data=clinic.admitfee
  var id name actlevel fee;
run;
```

When you omit a semicolon, SAS reads the statement that lacks the semicolon, plus the following statement, as one long statement. The SAS log then lists errors that relate to the combined statement, not the actual mistake (the missing semicolon).

SAS Log

```
1832        proc print data=clinic.admitfee
1833            var id name actlevel fee;
                ---
                22
                76
ERROR 22-322:Syntax error, expecting one of the following:
             ;, (, DATA, DOUBLE, HEADING, LABEL,
             N, NOOBS, OBS, ROUND, ROWS, SPLIT, UNIFORM, WIDTH.
ERROR 76-322:Syntax error, statement will be ignored.
1834        run;

NOTE: The SAS System stopped processing this step
      because of errors.
NOTE: PROCEDURE PRINT used:
      real time           0.35 seconds
      cpu time            0.03 seconds
```

Resolving the Problem

To correct the error, do the following:

1. Find the statement that lacks a semicolon. You can usually locate the statement that lacks the semicolon by looking at the underscored keywords in the error message and working backwards.

2. Add a semicolon in the appropriate location.

3. Resubmit the corrected program.

4. Check the SAS log again to make sure there are no other errors.

Unbalanced Quotation Marks

Some syntax errors, such as the missing quotation mark after *HIGH* in the program below, cause SAS to misinterpret the statements in your program.

```
data clinic.admitfee;
   set clinic.admit;
   where actlevel= 'HIGH;
run;
proc print data=clinic.admitfee;
   var id name actlevel fee;
run;
```

When you have unbalanced quotation marks, SAS is often unable to detect the end of the statement in which the error occurs. When the program above is submitted, SAS is unable to resolve the DATA step, and a "DATA STEP running" message appears at the top of the active window.

In addition, when unbalanced quotation marks appear in a program that contains TITLE or FOOTNOTE statements, there is sometimes a warning in the SAS log which indicates that

- a text string enclosed in quotation marks has become too long

- a statement that contains quotation marks (such as a TITLE or FOOTNOTE statement) is ambiguous due to invalid options or unquoted text.

SAS Log (PROC PRINT Running)

```
93 proc print data=clinic.admitfee;
94   var id name actlevel fee;
95   title 'Patient Billing;
96   title2 'January 1998';
WARNING: The TITLE statement is ambiguous due to
         invalid options or unquoted text.
97 run;
```

Simply adding a quotation mark and resubmitting your program usually does **not** solve the problem. SAS still considers the quotation marks to be unbalanced.

 If you do not resolve this problem when it occurs, it is likely that any subsequent programs that you submit in the current SAS session will generate errors.

Resolving the Problem

 When you submit a program with unbalanced quotation marks, you might not receive an error message. This is because SAS Enterprise Guide automatically submits an ending quotation mark for you. However, you will not get valid results.

Because there might be no visual indicator in the Project window that there is an error in your program, you should learn to detect this syntax error before you submit your program. The Code Editor window uses color coding to help you recognize errors.

In the SAS windowing environment, you must cancel the program before you recall, correct, and resubmit the code. To submit a line of SAS code that cancels the program, complete the following steps:

1. Submit an asterisk followed by a quotation mark, a semicolon, and a RUN statement.

   ```
   *'; run;
   ```

2. Delete the line that contains the asterisk followed by the quotation mark, the semicolon, and the RUN statement.
3. Insert the missing quotation mark in the appropriate place in your program.
4. Submit the corrected program.

SAS Log

```
98  *'; run;

NOTE: There were 7 observations read from the data set
      CLINIC.ADMITFEE.
NOTE: PROCEDURE PRINT used (Total process time):
            real time            31.38 seconds
            cpu time             1.21 seconds

99  proc print data=clinic.admitfee;
99     var id name actlevel fee;
100    title 'Patient Billing';
101    title2 'January 1998';
102 run;

NOTE: There were 7 observations read from the data set
      CLINIC.ADMITFEE.
NOTE: PROCEDURE PRINT used (Total process time):
      real time            0.16 seconds
      cpu time             0.15 seconds
```

Invalid Option

An **invalid option** error occurs when you specify an option that is not valid in a particular statement. In the program below, the KEYLABEL option is not valid when used with the PROC PRINT statement.

```
data clinic.admitfee;
   set clinic.admit;
run;
proc print data=clinic.admitfee keylabel;
   label actlevel='Activity Level';
run;
```

When a SAS statement that contains an invalid option is submitted, a message appears in the SAS log indicating that there is a syntax error. The message lists the options that are valid in the statement.

SAS Log

```
12    proc print data=clinic.admitfee keylabel;

                               22        200
ERROR 22-322:  Syntax error, expecting one of the following: ;,
               (,
               N, NOOBS, OBS, ROUND, ROWS, SPLIT, STYLE,
               UNIFORM,
ERROR 200-322:  The symbol is not recognized and will be ignored.
13        label actlevel='Activity Level';
14    run;

NOTE: The SAS System stopped processing this step
      because of errors.
NOTE: PROCEDURE PRINT used:
      real time              0.23 seconds
      cpu time               0.04 seconds
```

Resolving the Problem

To correct the error:

1. Remove or replace the invalid option, and check your statement syntax as needed.

2. Resubmit the corrected program.

3. Check the SAS log again to make sure there are no other errors.

Additional Features

Comments in SAS Programs

You can insert comments into a SAS program to document the purpose of the program, to explain segments of the program, or to describe the steps in a complex program or calculation. A comment statement begins and ends with a comment symbol. There are two forms of comment statements:

```
*text;
```

or

```
/*text*/
```

SAS ignores text in comments during processing.

The following program shows some of the ways comments can be used to describe a SAS program.

```
/* Read national sales data for vans */
/* from an external raw data file */
data perm.vansales;
   infile vandata;
   input @1 Region $9.
         @13 Quarter 1. /* Values are 1, 2, 3, or 4 */
         @16 TotalSales comma11.;
   /* Print the entire data set */
proc print data=perm.vansales;
run;
```

SAS System Options

SAS includes several system options that enable you to control error handling and SAS log messages. The table shown below contains brief descriptions of some of these options. You can use the OPTIONS statement to specify these options.

Option	Description
ERRORS=n	Specifies the maximum number of observations for which complete data error messages are printed.
FMTERR | NOFMTERR	Controls whether SAS generates an error message when a format of a variable cannot be found. NOFMTERR results in a warning instead of an error. FMTERR is the default.
SOURCE | NOSOURCE	Controls whether SAS writes source statements to the SAS log. SOURCE is the default.

Summary

Text Summary

SAS Program Layout

SAS programs consist of SAS statements. Although you can write SAS statements in almost any format, a consistent layout enhances readability and enables you to understand the program's purpose.

Interpreting Error Messages

When a SAS program that contains errors is submitted, error messages appear in the SAS log. SAS can detect several types of errors, including syntax and data errors. This chapter focuses on identifying and resolving common syntax errors.

Correcting Errors

To modify a program that contains syntax errors, you can correct the errors in the Editor window and then resubmit the revised program. You can delete any error-free steps from a revised program before resubmitting it.

Detecting and Resolving Common Problems

You might need to resolve several types of common problems: missing RUN statements, missing semicolons, unbalanced quotation marks, and invalid options.

Points to Remember

- It's a good idea to begin DATA steps, PROC steps, and RUN statements on the left and to indent statements within a step.
- End each step with a RUN statement.
- Review the messages in the SAS log each time you submit a SAS program.

Practice

After you complete this chapter, practice what you learned by using the sample data and SAS programs for Chapter 3, **Editing and Debugging SAS Programs**, which are located on the CD-ROM. Follow the directions for creating your sample data in the Before You Begin section.

Quiz

Select the best answer for each question. After completing the quiz, check your answers using the answer key in the appendix.

1. As you write and edit SAS programs, it's a good idea to

   a. begin DATA and PROC steps in column one.
   b. indent statements within a step.
   c. begin RUN statements in column one.
   d. all of the above.

2. What usually happens when a syntax error is detected?

   a. SAS continues processing the step.
   b. SAS continues to process the step, and the SAS log displays messages about the error.
   c. SAS stops processing the step in which the error occurred, and the SAS log displays messages about the error.
   d. SAS stops processing the step in which the error occurred, and the Output window displays messages about the error.

3. A syntax error occurs when

   a. some data values are not appropriate for the SAS statements that are specified in a program.
   b. the form of the elements in a SAS statement is correct, but the elements are not valid for that usage.
   c. program statements do not conform to the rules of the SAS language.
   d. none of the above.

4. How can you tell whether you have specified an invalid option in a SAS program?

   a. A log message indicates an error in a statement that seems to be valid.
   b. A log message indicates that an option is not valid or not recognized.
   c. The message "PROC running" or "DATA step running" appears at the top of the active window.
   d. You can't tell until you view the output from the program.

5. Which of the following programs contain a syntax error?

   a.
   ```
   proc sort data=sasuser.mysales;
      by region;
   run;
   ```
   b.
   ```
   dat sasuser.mysales;
      set mydata.sales99;
   run;
   ```
   c.
   ```
   proc print data=sasuser.mysales label;
      label region='Sales Region';
   run;
   ```
   d. none of the above.

6. What does the following log indicate about your program?

   ```
   proc print data=sasuser.cargo99
     var origin dest cargorev;
      22
      76
   ERROR 22-322: Syntax error, expecting one of the
   following:
                  ;, (, DATA, DOUBLE, HEADING, LABEL,
                  N, NOOBS, OBS, ROUND, ROWS, SPLIT, STYLE,
                  UNIFORM, WIDTH.
   ERROR 76-322: Syntax error, statement will be ignored.
   11         run;
   ```

   a. SAS identifies a syntax error at the position of the VAR statement.
   b. SAS is reading VAR as an option in the PROC PRINT statement.
   c. SAS has stopped processing the program because of errors.
   d. all of the above

Chapter **4** Creating List Reports

Overview

Introduction

To list the information in a data set, you can create a report with a PROC PRINT step. Then you can enhance the report with additional statements and options to create reports like those shown below.

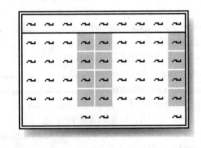

Basic Report

Column Totals

Sorting and Labels

Selected Observations and Variables

Objectives

In this chapter you learn to

- specify SAS data sets to print

- select variables and observations to print

- sort data by the values of one or more variables

- specify column totals for numeric variables

- double-space SAS listing output

- add titles and footnotes to procedure output

- assign descriptive labels to variables

- apply formats to the values of variables.

Types of Reports

Basic Report

You can easily list the contents of a SAS data set by using a simple program like the one shown below.

```
libname clinic 'your-SAS-data-library';
proc print data=clinic.admit;
run;
```

Obs	ID	Name	Sex	Age	Date	Height	Weight	ActLevel	Fee
1	2458	Murray, W	M	27	1	72	168	HIGH	85.20
2	2462	Almers, C	F	34	3	66	152	HIGH	124.80
3	2501	Bonaventure, T	F	31	17	61	123	LOW	149.75
4	2523	Johnson, R	F	43	31	63	137	MOD	149.75
5	2539	LaMance, K	M	51	4	71	158	LOW	124.80
6	2544	Jones, M	M	29	6	76	193	HIGH	124.80
7	2552	Reberson, P	F	32	9	67	151	MOD	149.75
8	2555	King, E	M	35	13	70	173	MOD	149.75
9	2563	Pitts, D	M	34	22	73	154	LOW	124.80
10	2568	Eberhardt, S	F	49	27	64	172	LOW	124.80
11	2571	Nunnelly, A	F	44	19	66	140	HIGH	149.75
12	2572	Oberon, M	F	28	17	62	118	LOW	85.20
13	2574	Peterson, V	M	30	6	69	147	MOD	149.75
14	2575	Quigley, M	F	40	8	69	163	HIGH	124.80
15	2578	Cameron, L	M	47	5	72	173	MOD	124.80
16	2579	Underwood, K	M	60	22	71	191	LOW	149.75
17	2584	Takahashi, Y	F	43	29	65	123	MOD	124.80
18	2586	Derber, B	M	25	23	75	188	HIGH	85.20
19	2588	Ivan, H	F	22	20	63	139	LOW	85.20
20	2589	Wilcox, E	F	41	16	67	141	HIGH	149.75
21	2595	Warren, C	M	54	7	71	183	MOD	149.75

Column Totals

You can produce column totals for numeric variables within your report.

```
libname clinic 'your-SAS-data-library';
proc print data=clinic.admit;
   sum fee;
run;
```

Obs	ID	Name	Sex	Age	Date	Height	Weight	ActLevel	Fee
1	2458	Murray, W	M	27	1	72	168	HIGH	85.20
2	2462	Almers, C	F	34	3	66	152	HIGH	124.80
3	2501	Bonaventure, T	F	31	17	61	123	LOW	149.75
4	2523	Johnson, R	F	43	31	63	137	MOD	149.75
5	2539	LaMance, K	M	51	4	71	158	LOW	124.80
6	2544	Jones, M	M	29	6	76	193	HIGH	124.80
7	2552	Reberson, P	F	32	9	67	151	MOD	149.75
8	2555	King, E	M	35	13	70	173	MOD	149.75
9	2563	Pitts, D	M	34	22	73	154	LOW	124.80
10	2568	Eberhardt, S	F	49	27	64	172	LOW	124.80
11	2571	Nunnelly, A	F	44	19	66	140	HIGH	149.75
12	2572	Oberon, M	F	28	17	62	118	LOW	85.20
13	2574	Peterson, V	M	30	6	69	147	MOD	149.75
14	2575	Quigley, M	F	40	8	69	163	HIGH	124.80
15	2578	Cameron, L	M	47	5	72	173	MOD	124.80
16	2579	Underwood, K	M	60	22	71	191	LOW	149.75
17	2584	Takahashi, Y	F	43	29	65	123	MOD	124.80
18	2586	Derber, B	M	25	23	75	188	HIGH	85.20
19	2588	Ivan, H	F	22	20	63	139	LOW	85.20
20	2589	Wilcox, E	F	41	16	67	141	HIGH	149.75
21	2595	Warren, C	M	54	7	71	183	MOD	149.75
									2686.95

Sorting and Labels

You can sort data by the values of one or more variables and replace variable names with descriptive labels.

```
libname clinic 'your-SAS-data-library';
proc sort data=clinic.admit out=admit;
  by age;
run;
proc print data=admit label;
  var age height weight fee;
  label fee='Admission Fee';
run;
```

Obs	Age	Height	Weight	Admission Fee
1	22	63	139	85.20
2	25	75	188	85.20
3	27	72	168	85.20
4	28	62	118	85.20
5	29	76	193	124.80
6	30	69	147	149.75
7	31	61	123	149.75
8	32	67	151	149.75
9	34	66	152	124.80
10	34	73	154	124.80
11	35	70	173	149.75
12	40	69	163	124.80
13	41	67	141	149.75
14	43	63	137	149.75
15	43	65	123	124.80
16	44	66	140	149.75
17	47	72	173	124.80
18	49	64	172	124.80
19	51	71	158	124.80
20	54	71	183	149.75
21	60	71	191	149.75

Selected Observations and Variables

You can choose the observations and variables that appear in your report. In addition, you can remove the default Obs column that displays observation numbers.

```
libname clinic 'your-SAS-data-library';
proc print data=clinic.admit noobs;
   var age height weight fee;
   where age>30;
run;
```

Age	Height	Weight	Fee
34	66	152	124.80
31	61	123	149.75
43	63	137	149.75
51	71	158	124.80
32	67	151	149.75
35	70	173	149.75
34	73	154	124.80
49	64	172	124.80
44	66	140	149.75
40	69	163	124.80
47	72	173	124.80
60	71	191	149.75
43	65	123	124.80
41	67	141	149.75
54	71	183	149.75

Creating a Basic Report

To produce a simple list report, you first reference the library in which your SAS data set is stored. If you want, you can also set SAS system options to control the appearance of your reports. Then you submit a basic PROC PRINT step.

General form, basic PROC PRINT step:

> **PROC PRINT <DATA=***SAS-data-set***>;**
> **RUN;**

where *SAS-data-set* is the name of the SAS data set to be printed.

In the program below, the PROC PRINT statement invokes the PRINT procedure and specifies the data set Therapy in the SAS data library to which the libref Patients has been assigned.

*libname 1st,
then statement*

```
libname patients 'c:\records\patients';
proc print data=patients.therapy;
run;
```

Notice the layout of the resulting report. By default,

- all observations and variables in the data set are printed

- a column for observation numbers appears on the far left

- variables appear in the order in which they occur in the data set.

Obs	Date	AerClass	WalkJogRun	Swim
1	JAN1999	56	78	14
2	FEB1999	32	109	19
3	MAR1999	35	106	22
4	APR1999	47	115	24
5	MAY1999	55	121	31
6	JUN1999	61	114	67
7	JUL1999	67	102	72
8	AUG1999	64	76	77
9	SEP1999	78	77	54
10	OCT1999	81	62	47
11	NOV1999	84	31	52
12	DEC1999	2	44	55
13	JAN2000	37	91	83
14	FEB2000	41	102	27
15	MAR2000	52	98	19
16	APR2000	61	118	22
17	MAY2000	49	88	29
18	JUN2000	24	101	54
19	JUL2000	45	91	69
20	AUG2000	63	65	53
21	SEP2000	60	49	68
22	OCT2000	78	70	41
23	NOV2000	82	44	58
24	DEC2000	93	57	47

 Be sure to specify the equal sign in the DATA= option in SAS procedures. If you omit the equal sign, your program produces an error similar to the following in the SAS log.

SAS Log

```
1   proc print data patients.therapy;
        ----------------
            73

2   run;
ERROR 73-322: Expecting an =.

NOTE: The SAS System stopped processing this step
          because of errors.
```

Selecting Observations

By default, a PROC PRINT step lists all the variables in a data set. You can select variables and control the order in which they appear by using a VAR statement in your PROC PRINT step.

General form, VAR statement:

VAR *variable(s)*;

where *variable(s)* is one or more variable names, separated by blanks.

For example, the following VAR statement specifies that only the variables Age, Height, Weight, and Fee be printed, in that order:

```
proc print data=clinic.admit;
   var age height weight fee;
run;
```

The procedure output from the PROC PRINT step with the VAR statement lists only the values for the variables Age, Height, Weight, and Fee.

Obs	Age	Height	Weight	Fee
1	27	72	168	85.20
2	34	66	152	124.80
3	31	61	123	149.75
4	43	63	137	149.75
5	51	71	158	124.80
6	29	76	193	124.80
7	32	67	151	149.75
8	35	70	173	149.75
9	34	73	154	124.80
10	49	64	172	124.80

Obs	Age	Height	Weight	Fee
11	44	66	140	149.75
12	28	62	118	85.20
13	30	69	147	149.75
14	40	69	163	124.80
15	47	72	173	124.80
16	60	71	191	149.75
17	43	65	123	124.80
18	25	75	188	85.20
19	22	63	139	85.20
20	41	67	141	149.75
21	54	71	183	149.75

In addition to selecting variables, you can control the default Obs column that PROC PRINT displays to list observation numbers. If you prefer, you can choose not to display observation numbers.

Obs	Age	Height	Weight	Fee
1	27	72	168	85.20
2	34	66	152	124.80
3	31	61	123	149.75
4	43	63	137	149.75
5	51	71	158	124.80

Removing the OBS Column

To remove the Obs column, specify the NOOBS option in the PROC PRINT statement.

```
proc print data=work.example noobs;
  var age height weight fee;
run;
```

Age	Height	Weight	Fee
27	72	168	85.20
34	66	152	124.80
31	61	123	149.75
43	63	137	149.75
51	71	158	124.80

Identifying Observations

You've learned how to remove the Obs column altogether. As another alternative, you can use one or more **variables** to replace the Obs column in the output.

To specify which variables should replace the Obs column, use the ID statement. This technique is particularly useful when observations are too long to print on one line.

General form, ID statement:

    ID *variable(s)*;

where *variable(s)* specifies one or more variables to print instead of the observation number at the beginning of each row of the report.

Example

To replace the Obs column and identify observations based on an employee's ID number and last name, you can submit the following program.

```
proc print data=sales.reps;
   id idnum lastname;
run;
```

This is HTML output from the program:

IDnum	LastName	FirstName	City	State	Sex	JobCode	Salary	Birth	Hired	HomePhone
1269	CASTON	FRANKLIN	STAMFORD	CT	M	NA1	41690.00	06MAY60	01DEC80	203/781-3335
1935	FERNANDEZ	KATRINA	BRIDGEPORT	CT		NA2	51081.00	31MAR42	19OCT69	203/675-2962
1417	NEWKIRK	WILLIAM	PATERSON	NJ	,	NA2	52270.00	30JUN52	10MAR77	201/732-6611
1839	NORRIS	DIANE	NEW YORK	NY	F	NA1	43433.00	02DEC58	06JUL81	718/384-1767
1111	RHODES	JEREMY	PRINCETON	NJ	M	NA1	40586.00	17JUL61	03NOV80	201/812-1837
1352	RIVERS	SIMON	NEW YORK	NY	M	NA2	5379.80	05DEC48	19OCT74	718/383-3345
1332	STEPHENSON	ADAM	BRIDGEPORT	CT	M	NA1	42178.00	20SEP58	07JUN79	203/675-1497
1443	WELLS	AGNES	STAMFORD	CT	F	NA1	422.74	20NOV56	01SEP79	203/781-5546

 In listing output, the IDnum and LastName columns are repeated for each observation that is printed on more than one line.

```
IDnum    LastName   FirstName    City       State    Sex    JobCode

1269    CASTON     FRANKLIN    STAMFORD    CT       M      NA1
1935    FERNANDEZ  KATRINA     BRIDGEPO    CT              NA2
1417    NEWKIRK    WILLIAM     PATERSON    NJ       ,      NA2
1839    NORRIS     DIANE       NEW YORK    NY       F      NA1
1111    RHODES     JEREMY      PRINCETO    NJ       M      NA1
1352    RIVERS     SIMON       NEW YORK    NY       M      NA2
1332    STEPHENS   ADAM        BRIDGEPO    CT       M      NA1
1443    WELLS      AGNES       STAMFORD    CT       F      NA1


IDnum    LastName    Salary     Birth     Hired      HomePhone

1269    CASTON      41690.00   06MAY60   01DEC80    203/781-3335
1935    FERNANDEZ   51081.00   31MAR42   19OCT69    203/675-2962
1417    NEWKIRK     52270.00   30JUN52   10MAR77    201/732-6611
1839    NORRIS      43433.00   02DEC58   06JUL81    718/384-1767
1111    RHODES      40586.00   17JUL61   03NOV80    201/812-1837
1352    RIVERS       5379.80   05DEC48   19OCT74    718/383-3345
1332    STEPHENS    42178.00   20SEP58   07JUN79    203/675-1497
1443    WELLS         422.74   20NOV56   01SEP79    203/781-5546
```

If a variable in the ID statement also appears in the VAR statement, the output contains two columns for that variable. In the example below, the variable IDnum appears twice.

```
proc print data=sales.reps;
   id idnum lastname;
   var idnum sex jobcode salary;
run;
```

IDnum	LastName	IDnum	Sex	JobCode	Salary
1269	CASTON	1269	M	NA1	41690.00
1935	FERNANDEZ	1935		NA2	51081.00
1417	NEWKIRK	1417	,	NA2	52270.00
1839	NORRIS	1839	F	NA1	43433.00
1111	RHODES	1111	M	NA1	40586.00
1352	RIVERS	1352	M	NA2	5379.80
1332	STEPHENSON	1332	M	NA1	42178.00
1443	WELLS	1443	F	NA1	422.74

Selecting Observations

By default, a PROC PRINT step lists all the observations in a data set. You can control which observations are printed by adding a WHERE statement to your PROC PRINT step. There can be only one WHERE statement in a step.

General form, WHERE statement:

> **WHERE** *where-expression*;

where *where-expression* specifies a condition for selecting observations. The *where-expression* can be any valid SAS expression.

For example, the following WHERE statement selects only observations for which the value of Age is greater than 30:

```
proc print data=clinic.admit;
   var age height weight fee;
   where age>30;
run;
```

Here is the procedure output from the PROC PRINT step with the WHERE statement:

Obs	Age	Height	Weight	Fee
2	34	66	152	124.80
3	31	61	123	149.75
4	43	63	137	149.75
5	51	71	158	124.80
7	32	67	151	149.75
8	35	70	173	149.75
9	34	73	154	124.80
10	49	64	172	124.80
11	44	66	140	149.75
14	40	69	163	124.80
15	47	72	173	124.80
16	60	71	191	149.75
17	43	65	123	124.80
20	41	67	141	149.75
21	54	71	183	149.75

Specifying WHERE Expressions

In the WHERE statement you can specify any variable in the SAS data set, not just the variables that are specified in the VAR statement. The WHERE statement works for both character and numeric variables. To specify a condition based on the value of a character variable, you must

- enclose the value in quotation marks
- write the value with lowercase and uppercase letters exactly as it appears in the data set.

You use the following **comparison operators** to express a condition in the WHERE statement:

Symbol	Meaning	Example
= or **eq**	equal to	`where name='Jones, C.';`
^= or **ne**	not equal to	`where temp ne 212;`
> or **gt**	greater than	`where income>20000;`
< or **lt**	less than	`where partno lt "BG05";`
>= or **ge**	greater than or equal to	`where id>='1543';`
<= or **le**	less than or equal to	`where pulse le 85;`

 You can learn more about valid SAS expressions in Chapter 5, **Creating SAS Data Sets from Raw Data**.

Using the CONTAINS Operator

The CONTAINS operator selects observations that include the specified substring. The mnemonic equivalent for the CONTAINS operator is **?**. You can use either the CONTAINS keyword or the mnemonic equivalent in your code, as shown below.

```
  where firstname CONTAINS 'Jon';
  where firstname ? 'Jon';
```

Specifying Compound WHERE Expressions

You can also use WHERE statements to select observations that meet **multiple** conditions. To link a sequence of expressions into compound expressions, you use **logical operators**, including the following:

Operator	Meaning
AND or **&**	and, both. If both expressions are true, then the compound expression is true.
OR or **|**	or, either. If either expression is true, then the compound expression is true.

Examples of WHERE Statements

- Here are some examples of WHERE statements that use logical operators:

```
where age<=55 and pulse>75;
where area='A' or region='S';
where ID>1050 and state='NC';
```

- When you test for **multiple values of the same variable**, you specify the variable name in each expression:

```
where actlevel='LOW' or actlevel='MOD';
where fee=124.80 or fee=178.20;
```

- You can use the **IN operator** as a convenient alternative:

```
where actlevel in ('LOW','MOD');
where fee in (124.80,178.20);
```

- To control the way compound expressions are evaluated, you can use **parentheses** (expressions in parentheses are evaluated first):

```
where (age<=55 and pulse>75) or area='A';
where age<=55 and (pulse>75 or area='A');
```

Sorting Data

By default, PROC PRINT lists observations in the order in which they appear in your data set. To sort your report based on values of a variable, you must use PROC SORT to sort your data before using the PRINT procedure to create reports from the data.

The SORT procedure

- rearranges the observations in a SAS data set
- creates a new SAS data set that contains the rearranged observations
- replaces the original SAS data set by default
- can sort on multiple variables
- can sort in ascending or descending order
- does not generate printed output
- treats missing values as the smallest possible values.

General form, simple PROC SORT step:

> **PROC SORT DATA=***SAS-data-set* **<OUT=***SAS-data-set***>;**
>   **BY <DESCENDING>** *BY-variable(s)*;
> **RUN;**

[handwritten margin note: → throws output into a new data set o/w overrides Original data set]

where

- the **DATA=** option specifies the data set to be read.

- the **OUT=** option specifies the output data set that contains the data in sorted order.

- *BY-variable(s)* in the required **BY** statement specifies one or more variables whose values are used to sort the data.

- the **DESCENDING** option in the BY statement sorts observations in descending order. If you have more than one variable in the BY statement, DESCENDING applies only to the variable that immediately follows it.

If you don't use the OUT= option, PROC SORT **permanently** sorts the data set that is specified in the DATA= option. If you need your data to be sorted to produce output for only one SAS session, then you should specify a temporary SAS data set as the output data set.

Example

In the following program, the PROC SORT step sorts the permanent SAS data set **Clinic.Admit** by the values of the variable `Age` within the values of the variable `Weight` and creates the temporary SAS data set **Wgtadmit**. Then the PROC PRINT step prints the **Wgtadmit** data set.

```
proc sort data=clinic.admit out=work.wgtadmit;
   by weight age;
run;
proc print data=work.wgtadmit;
   var age height weight fee;
   where age>30;
run;
```

The report displays observations in ascending order of age within weight.

Obs	Age	Height	Weight	Fee
2	31	61	123	149.75
3	43	65	123	124.80
4	43	63	137	149.75
6	44	66	140	149.75
7	41	67	141	149.75
9	32	67	151	149.75
10	34	66	152	124.80
11	34	73	154	124.80
12	51	71	158	124.80

Obs	Age	Height	Weight	Fee
13	40	69	163	124.80
15	49	64	172	124.80
16	35	70	173	149.75
17	47	72	173	124.80
18	54	71	183	149.75
20	60	71	191	149.75

Adding the DESCENDING option to the BY statement sorts observations in ascending order of age within descending order of weight. Notice that DESCENDING applies only to the variable `Weight`.

```
proc sort data=clinic.admit out=work.wgtadmit;
   by descending weight age;
run;
proc print data=work.wgtadmit;
   var age height weight fee;
   where age>30;
run;
```

Obs	Age	Height	Weight	Fee
2	60	71	191	149.75
4	54	71	183	149.75
5	35	70	173	149.75
6	47	72	173	124.80
7	49	64	172	124.80
9	40	69	163	124.80
10	51	71	158	124.80
11	34	73	154	124.80
12	34	66	152	124.80
13	32	67	151	149.75
15	41	67	141	149.75
16	44	66	140	149.75
18	43	63	137	149.75
19	31	61	123	149.75
20	43	65	123	124.80

Generating Column Totals

To produce column totals for numeric variables, you can list the variables to be summed in a **SUM statement** in your PROC PRINT step.

General form, SUM statement:

> **SUM** *variable(s)*;

where *variable(s)* is one or more variable names, separated by blanks. You do not need to name the variables in a VAR statement if you specify them in the SUM statement.

The SUM statement in the following PROC PRINT step requests column totals for the variable BalanceDue:

```
proc print data=clinic.insure;
   var name policy balancedue;
   where pctinsured < 100;
   sum balancedue;
run;
```

Column totals appear at the end of the report in the same format as the values of the variables.

Obs	Name	Policy	BalanceDue
2	Almers, C	95824	156.05
3	Bonaventure, T	87795	9.48
4	Johnson, R	39022	61.04
5	LaMance, K	63265	43.68
6	Jones, M	92478	52.42
7	Reberson, P	25530	207.41
8	King, E	18744	27.19
9	Pitts, D	60976	310.82
10	Eberhardt, S	81589	173.17
13	Peterson, V	75986	228.00
14	Quigley, M	97048	99.01
15	Cameron, L	42351	111.41
17	Takahashi, Y	54219	186.58
18	Derber, B	74653	236.11
20	Wilcox, E	94034	212.20
21	Warren, C	20347	164.44
			2279.01

Requesting Subtotals

You might also want to subtotal numeric variables. To produce subtotals, add both a **SUM statement** and a **BY statement** to your PROC PRINT step.

General form, BY statement in the PRINT procedure:

> **BY** <DESCENDING> *BY-variable-1*
> <...<DESCENDING> <*BY-variable-n*>>
> <NOTSORTED>;

where

- *BY-variable* specifies a variable that the procedure uses to form BY groups. You can specify more than one variable, separated by blanks.

- the **DESCENDING** option specifies that the data set is to be sorted in descending order by the variable that immediately follows.

- the **NOTSORTED** option specifies that the observations are not necessarily sorted in alphabetic or numeric order. If observations that have the same values for the BY variables are not contiguous, then the procedure treats each contiguous set as a separate BY group.

 If you do not use the NOTSORTED option in the BY statement, the observations in the data set must either be sorted by all the variables that you specify, or they must be indexed appropriately.

Example

The SUM statement in the following PROC PRINT step requests column totals for the variable Fee, and the BY statement produces a subtotal for each value of ActLevel.

```
proc sort data=clinic.admit out=work.activity;
   by actlevel;
run;
proc print data=work.activity;
   var age height weight fee;
   where age>30;
   sum fee;
   by actlevel;
run;
```

In the output, the BY variable name and value appear before each BY group. The BY variable name and the subtotal appear at the end of each BY group.

ActLevel=HIGH

Obs	Age	Height	Weight	Fee
2	34	66	152	124.80
4	44	66	140	149.75
5	40	69	163	124.80
7	41	67	141	149.75
ActLevel				549.10

ActLevel=LOW

Obs	Age	Height	Weight	Fee
8	31	61	123	149.75
9	51	71	158	124.80
10	34	73	154	124.80
11	49	64	172	124.80
13	60	71	191	149.75
ActLevel				673.90

ActLevel=MOD

Obs	Age	Height	Weight	Fee
15	43	63	137	149.75
16	32	67	151	149.75
17	35	70	173	149.75
19	47	72	173	124.80
20	43	65	123	124.80
21	54	71	183	149.75
ActLevel				848.60
				2071.60

Creating a Customized Layout with BY Groups and ID Variables

In the previous example, you might have noticed the redundant information for the BY variable. For example, in the partial PROC PRINT output below, the BY variable ActLevel is identified both before the BY group and for the subtotal.

ActLevel=HIGH

Obs	Age	Height	Weight	Fee
2	34	66	152	124.80
4	44	66	140	149.75
5	40	69	163	124.80
7	41	67	141	149.75
ActLevel				549.10

To show the BY variable heading only once, you can use an **ID statement** and a **BY statement** together with the SUM statement. When an ID statement specifies the same variable as the BY statement,

- the Obs column is suppressed
- the ID/BY variable is printed in the left-most column
- each ID/BY value is printed only at the start of each BY group and on the line that contains that group's subtotal.

Example

The ID, BY, and SUM statements work together to produce the output shown below. The ID variable is listed only once for each BY group and once for each sum. The BY lines are suppressed. Instead, the value of the ID variable, ActLevel, identifies each BY group.

```
proc sort data=clinic.admit out=work.activity;
   by actlevel;
run;
proc print data=work.activity;
   var age height weight fee;
   where age>30;
   sum fee;
   by actlevel;
   id actlevel;
run;
```

ActLevel	Age	Height	Weight	Fee
HIGH	34	66	152	124.80
	44	66	140	149.75
	40	69	163	124.80
	41	67	141	149.75
HIGH				**549.10**
LOW	31	61	123	149.75
	51	71	158	124.80
	34	73	154	124.80
	49	64	172	124.80
	60	71	191	149.75
LOW				**673.90**
MOD	43	63	137	149.75
	32	67	151	149.75
	35	70	173	149.75
	47	72	173	124.80
	43	65	123	124.80
	54	71	183	149.75
MOD				**848.60**
				2071.60

Requesting Subtotals on Separate Pages

As another enhancement to your PROC PRINT report, you can request that each BY group be printed on a separate page by using the **PAGEBY statement**.

General form, PAGEBY statement:

> **PAGEBY** *BY-variable*;

where *BY-variable* identifies a variable that appears in the BY statement in the PROC PRINT step. PROC PRINT begins printing a new page if the value of any of the variables in the BY statement changes.

 The variable that is specified in the PAGEBY statement must also be specified in the BY statement in the PROC PRINT step.

Example

The PAGEBY statement in the program below prints BY groups for the variable `ActLevel` separately. The BY groups appear on separate pages in the output.

```
proc sort data=clinic.admit out=work.activity;
   by actlevel;
run;
proc print data=work.activity;
   var age height weight fee;
   where age>30;
   sum fee;
   by actlevel;
   id actlevel;
   pageby actlevel;
run;
```

ActLevel	Age	Height	Weight	Fee
HIGH	34	66	152	124.80
	44	66	140	149.75
	40	69	163	124.80
	41	67	141	149.75
HIGH				**549.10**

ActLevel	Age	Height	Weight	Fee
LOW	31	61	123	149.75
	51	71	158	124.80
	34	73	154	124.80
	49	64	172	124.80
	60	71	191	149.75
LOW				**673.90**

ActLevel	Age	Height	Weight	Fee
MOD	43	63	137	149.75
	32	67	151	149.75
	35	70	173	149.75
	47	72	173	124.80
	43	65	123	124.80
	54	71	183	149.75
MOD				848.60
				2071.60

Double-Spacing Listing Output

If you are generating SAS listing output, one way to control the layout is to double-space it. To double-space, specify the **DOUBLE option** in the PROC PRINT statement.

```
proc print data=clinic.stress double;
  var resthr maxhr rechr;
  where tolerance='I';
run;
```

Double-spacing does not apply to HTML output.

SAS Output

OBS	RestHR	MaxHR	RecHR
2	68	171	133
3	78	177	139
8	70	167	122
11	65	181	141
14	74	152	113
15	75	158	108
20	78	189	138

To generate SAS listing output, you must select Text output on the Results tab of the Options window.

Specifying Titles and Footnotes

Now you've learned how to structure your PROC PRINT output. However, you might also want to make your reports easy to interpret by

- adding titles and footnotes

- replacing variable names with descriptive labels

- formatting variable values.

Although this chapter focuses on PROC PRINT, you can apply these enhancements to most SAS procedure output.

TITLE and FOOTNOTE Statements

To make your report more meaningful and self-explanatory, you can specify up to 10 titles with procedure output by using **TITLE statements** before the PROC step. Likewise, you can specify up to 10 footnotes by using **FOOTNOTE statements** before the PROC step.

 Because TITLE and FOOTNOTE statements are global statements, place them before the PRINT procedure. Titles and footnotes are assigned as soon as TITLE or FOOTNOTE statements are read; they apply to all subsequent output.

General form, TITLE and FOOTNOTE statements:

> **TITLE**<*n*> *'text'*;

> **FOOTNOTE**<*n*> *'text'*;

where

- *n* is a number from 1 to 10 that specifies the title or footnote line

- *'text'* is the actual title or footnote to be displayed.

⚠ Be sure to match quotation marks that enclose the title or footnote text.

 The maximum title or footnote length depends on your operating environment and on the value of the LINESIZE= option.

The keyword `title` is equivalent to title1. Likewise, the keyword `footnote` is equivalent to footnote1.

If you don't specify a title, the default title is **The SAS System**. No footnote is printed unless you specify one.

Examples: Titles

The two TITLE statements below, specified for lines 1 and 3, define titles for the PROC PRINT output.

```
title1 'Heart Rates for Patients with';
title3 'Increased Stress Tolerance Levels';
proc print data=clinic.stress;
   var resthr maxhr rechr;
   where tolerance='I';
run;
```

In **HTML output**, title lines appear consecutively, without extra spacing to indicate skipped title numbers.

**Heart Rates for Patients with
Increased Stress Tolerance Levels**

Obs	RestHR	MaxHR	RecHR
2	68	171	133
3	78	177	139
8	70	167	122
11	65	181	141
14	74	152	113
15	75	158	108
20	78	189	138

In **SAS listing output**, title line 2 is blank, as shown below. Titles are centered by default.

```
            Heart Rates for Patients with

        Increased Stress Tolerance Levels

     OBS      RestHR      MaxHR      RecHR

       2        68        171        133
       3        78        177        139
       8        70        167        122
      11        65        181        141
      14        74        152        113
      15        75        158        108
      20        78        189        138
```

Examples: Footnotes

The two FOOTNOTE statements below, specified for lines 1 and 3, define footnotes for the PROC PRINT output.

```
footnote1 'Data from Treadmill Tests';
footnote3 '1st Quarter Admissions';
proc print data=clinic.stress;
   var resthr maxhr rechr;
   where tolerance='I';
run;
```

Footnotes appear at the bottom of each page of procedure output. Notice that footnote lines are "pushed up" from the bottom. The FOOTNOTE statement that has the largest number appears on the bottom line.

In **HTML output**, footnote lines simply appear consecutively, without extra spacing to indicate skipped footnote numbers.

Obs	RestHR	MaxHR	RecHR
2	68	171	133
3	78	177	139
8	70	167	122
11	65	181	141
14	74	152	113
15	75	158	108
20	78	189	138
Data from Treadmill Tests			
1st Quarter Admissions			

In **SAS listing output**, footnote line 2 is blank, as shown below. Footnotes are centered by default.

```
   OBS      RestHR      MaxHR      RecHR

     2         68        171        133
     3         78        177        139
     8         70        167        122
    11         65        181        141
    14         74        152        113
    15         75        158        108
    20         78        189        138

          Data from Treadmill Tests

          1st Quarter Admissions
```

Modifying and Canceling Titles and Footnotes

TITLE and FOOTNOTE statements are **global statements**. That is, after you define a title or footnote, it remains in effect until you modify it, cancel it, or end your SAS session.

For example, the footnotes that are assigned in the PROC PRINT step below also appear in the output from the PROC TABULATE step.

```
footnote1 'Data from Treadmill Tests';
footnote3 '1st Quarter Admissions';
proc print data=clinic.stress;
   var resthr maxhr rechr;
   where tolerance='I';
run;
proc tabulate data=clinic.stress;
   where tolerance='I';
   var resthr maxhr;
   table mean*(resthr maxhr);
run;
```

Re-defining a title or footnote line cancels any higher-numbered title or footnote line, in that order. In the example below, defining a title for line 2 in the second report automatically cancels title line 3.

```
title3 'Participation in Exercise Therapy';
proc print data=clinic.therapy;
   var swim walkjogrun aerclass;
run;
title2 'Report for March';
proc print data=clinic.therapy;
run;
```

To cancel all previous titles or footnotes, specify a null TITLE or FOOTNOTE statement (a TITLE or FOOTNOTE statement with no number or text) or a TITLE1 or FOOTNOTE1 statement with no text. This will also cancel the default title **The SAS System**.

For example, in the program below, the null TITLE1 statement cancels all titles that are in effect before either PROC step executes. The null FOOTNOTE statement cancels all footnotes that are in effect after the PROC PRINT step executes. The PROC TABULATE output appears without a footnote.

```
title1;
footnote1 'Data from Treadmill Tests';
footnote3 '1st Quarter Admissions';
proc print data=clinic.stress;
   var resthr maxhr rechr;
   where tolerance='I';
run;
footnote;
proc tabulate data=clinic.stress;
   var timemin timesec;
   table max*(timemin timesec);
run;
```

Assigning Descriptive Labels

Temporarily Assigning Labels to Variables

You can also enhance your PROC PRINT report by labeling columns with more descriptive text. To label columns, you use

- the **LABEL statement** to assign a descriptive label to a variable
- the **LABEL option** in the PROC PRINT statement to specify that the labels be displayed.

General form, LABEL statement:

LABEL   *variable1*='*label1*'
  variable2='*label2*'
  ... ;
Labels can be up to 256 characters long. Enclose the label in quotation marks.

The LABEL statement applies only to the PROC step in which it appears.

Example

In the PROC PRINT step below, the variable name `WalkJogRun` is displayed with the label **Walk/Jog/Run**. Note the LABEL option in the PROC PRINT statement.

```
proc print data=clinic.therapy label;
   label walkjogrun='Walk/Jog/Run';
run;
```

Obs	Date	AerClass	Walk/Jog/Run	Swim
1	JAN1999	56	78	14
2	FEB1999	32	109	19
3	MAR1999	35	106	22
4	APR1999	47	115	24
5	MAY1999	55	121	31
6	JUN1999	61	114	67
7	JUL1999	67	102	72
8	AUG1999	64	76	77
9	SEP1999	78	77	54
10	OCT1999	81	62	47
11	NOV1999	84	31	52
12	DEC1999	2	44	55
13	JAN2000	37	91	83
14	FEB2000	41	102	27
15	MAR2000	52	98	19

Obs	Date	AerClass	Walk/Jog/Run	Swim
16	APR2000	61	118	22
17	MAY2000	49	88	29
18	JUN2000	24	101	54
19	JUL2000	45	91	69
20	AUG2000	63	65	53
21	SEP2000	60	49	68
22	OCT2000	78	70	41
23	NOV2000	82	44	58
24	DEC2000	93	57	47

Using Single or Multiple LABEL Statements

You can assign labels in separate LABEL statements ...

```
proc print data=clinic.admit label;
  var age height;
  label age='Age of Patient';
  label height='Height in Inches';
run;
```

...or you can assign any number of labels in a single LABEL statement.

```
proc print data=clinic.admit label;
  var actlevel height weight;
  label actlevel='Activity Level'
        height='Height in Inches'
        weight='Weight in Pounds';
run;
```

Formatting Data Values

Temporarily Assigning Formats to Variables

In your SAS reports, formats control how the data values are displayed. To make data values more understandable when they are displayed in your procedure output, you can use the FORMAT statement, which associates formats with variables.

Formats affect only how the data values appear in output, **not** the actual data values as they are stored in the SAS data set.

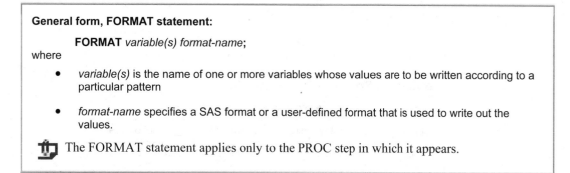

You can use a separate FORMAT statement for each variable, or you can format several variables (using either the same format or different formats) in a single FORMAT statement.

This FORMAT Statement	Associates	To display Values as
`format date mmddyy8.;`	the format **MMDDYY8.** with the variable `Date`	06/05/03
`format net comma5.0 gross comma8.2;`	the format **COMMA5.0** with the variable `Net` and the format **COMMA8.2** with the variable `Gross`	1,234 5,678.90
`format net gross dollar9.2;`	the format **DOLLAR9.2** with both variables, `Net` and `Gross`	$1,234.00 $5,678.90

For example, the FORMAT statement below writes values of the variable `Fee` using dollar signs, commas, and no decimal places:

```
proc print data=clinic.admit;
   var actlevel fee;
   where actlevel='HIGH';
   format fee dollar4.;
run;
```

Obs	ActLevel	Fee
1	HIGH	$85
2	HIGH	$125
6	HIGH	$125
11	HIGH	$150
14	HIGH	$125
18	HIGH	$85
20	HIGH	$150

Specifying SAS Formats

The table below describes some SAS formats that are commonly used in reports.

Format	Specifies These Values	Example
COMMA*w.d*	that contain commas and decimal places	`comma8.2`
DOLLAR*w.d*	that contain dollar signs, commas, and decimal places	`dollar6.2`
MMDDYY*w.*	as date values of the form 09/12/97 (MMDDYY8.) or 09/12/1997 (MMDDYY10.)	`mmddyy10.`
w.	rounded to the nearest integer in *w* spaces	`7.`
w.d	rounded to *d* decimal places in *w* spaces	`8.2`
$w.	as character values in *w* spaces	`$12.`
DATE*w.*	as date values of the form 16OCT99 (DATE7.) or 16OCT1999 (DATE9.)	`date9.`

Field Widths

All SAS formats specify the total field width (*w*) that is used for displaying the values in the output. For example, suppose the longest value for the variable `Net` is a four-digit number, such as *5400*. To specify the COMMA*w.d* format for `Net`, you specify a field width of 5 or more. You must count the comma, because it occupies a position in the output, as shown in the table below.

 When you use a SAS format, be sure to specify a field width (*w*) that is wide enough for the largest possible value. Otherwise, values might not be displayed properly.

Stored Value	5400
Desired Format	COMMA*w.d*
Displayed Value	5,400
Positions Displayed in Output	5
FORMAT statement	`format net comma5.0;`

Decimal Places

For numeric variables you can also specify the number of decimal places (*d*), if any, to be displayed in the output. Numbers are rounded to the specified number of decimal places.

Writing the whole number *2030* as 2,030.00 requires eight print positions, including two decimal places and the decimal point.

Stored Value	2030
Desired Format	COMMA*w.d*
Displayed Value	2,030.00
Positions Displayed in Output	8
FORMAT statement	`format qtr3tax comma8.2;`

Formatting *15374* with a dollar sign, commas, and two decimal places requires 10 print positions.

Stored Value	15374
Desired Format	DOLLAR*w.d*
Displayed Value	$15,374.00
Positions Displayed in Output	10
FORMAT statement	`format totsales dollar10.2;`

Examples

This table shows you how data values are displayed when different format, field width, and decimal place specifications are used.

Stored Value	Format	Displayed Value
38245.3975	COMMA12.2	38,245.40
38245.3975	12.2	38245.40
38245.3975	DOLLAR12.2	$38,245.40
38245.3975	DOLLAR9.2	$38245.40
38245.3975	DOLLAR8.2	38245.40
0	MMDDYY8.	01/01/60
0	MMDDYY10.	01/01/1960
0	DATE7.	01JAN60
0	DATE9.	01JAN1960

 If a format is too small, the following message is written to the SAS log: "NOTE: At least one W.D format was too small for the number to be printed. The decimal may be shifted by the 'BEST' format."

Using Permanently Assigned Labels and Formats

You have seen how to **temporarily** assign labels and formats to variables. When you use a LABEL or FORMAT statement within a PROC PRINT step, the label or format applies only to the output from that step.

However, in your PROC PRINT steps, you can also take advantage of **permanently** assigned labels or formats. Permanent labels and formats can be assigned in the DATA step. These labels and formats are saved with the data set, and they can later be used by procedures that reference the data set.

For example, the DATA step below creates **Flights.March** and defines a format and label for the variable `Date`. Because the LABEL and FORMAT statements are inside the DATA step, they are written to the **Flights.March** data set and are available to the subsequent PRINT procedure.

```
data flights.march;
  set flights.mar01;
  label date='Departure Date';
  format date date9.;
run;
proc print data=flights.march label;
run;
```

Partial Listing

Obs	Departure Date	Dest	Boarded
1	01MAR2000	LON	198
2	01MAR2000	PAR	207
3	01MAR2000	LON	205
4	01MAR2000	COP	138
5	01MAR2000	MUN	147

Notice that the PROC PRINT statement still requires the LABEL option in order to display the permanent labels. Many other SAS procedures display permanently assigned labels and formats without additional statements or options.

 You can learn more about permanently assigning labels and formats in Chapter 11, **Creating and Managing Variables**.

Additional Features

When you create list reports, you can use several other features to enhance your procedure output. For example, you can

- control where text strings split in labels by using the SPLIT= option.

```
proc print data=reps split='*';
   var salesrep type unitsold net commission;
   label salesrep='Sales*Representative';
run;
```

- create your own formats, which are particularly useful for formatting character values.

```
proc format;
   value $repfmt
        'TFB'='Bynum'
        'MDC'='Crowley'
        'WKK'='King';
proc print data=vcrsales;
   var salesrep type unitsold;
   format salesrep $repfmt.;
run;
```

 You can learn more about user-defined formats in Chapter 7, **Creating and Applying User-Defined Formats**.

Summary

Text Summary

Creating a Basic Report

To list the information in a SAS data set, you can use **PROC PRINT**. You use the PROC PRINT statement to invoke the PRINT procedure and to specify the data set that you are listing. Include the DATA= option to specify the data set that you are using. By default, PROC PRINT displays all observations and variables in the data set, includes a column for observation numbers on the far left, and displays variables in the order in which they occur in the data set. If you use a LABEL statement with PROC PRINT, you must specify the LABEL option or the SPLIT= option in the PROC PRINT statement.

To refine a basic report, you can

- select which variables and observations are processed
- sort the data
- generate column totals for numeric variables.

Selecting Variables

You can select variables and control the order in which they appear by using a **VAR statement** in your PROC PRINT step. To remove the Obs column, you can specify the **NOOBS option** in the PROC PRINT statement. As an alternative, you can replace the Obs column with one or more variables by using the **ID statement**.

Selecting Observations

The **WHERE statement** enables you to select observations that meet a particular condition in the SAS data set. You use **comparison operators** to express a condition in the WHERE statement. You can also use the CONTAINS operator to express a condition in the WHERE statement. To specify a condition based on the value of a character variable, you must enclose the value in quotation marks, and you must write the value with lowercase and uppercase letters exactly as it appears in the data set. You can also use WHERE statements to select a subset of observations based on multiple conditions. To link a sequence of expressions to compound expressions, you use **logical operators**. When you test for multiple values of the same variable, you specify the variable name in each expression. You can use the **IN operator** as a convenient alternative. To control how compound expressions are evaluated, you can use parentheses.

Sorting Data

To display your data in sorted order, you use **PROC SORT** to sort your data before using PROC PRINT to create reports. By default, PROC SORT sorts the data set that is specified in the DATA= option and overwrites this data set with the sorted data set. If you do not want your original data to be sorted permanently, you must create an output data set that contains the data in sorted order. The OUT= option in the PROC SORT statement specifies an output data set. If you need sorted data to produce output for only one SAS session, you should specify a temporary SAS data set as the output data set. The BY statement, which is required with PROC SORT, specifies the variable(s) whose values are used to sort the data.

Generating Column Totals

To total the values of numeric variables, use the **SUM statement** in the PROC PRINT step. You do not need to specify the variables in a VAR statement if you specify them in the SUM statement. Column totals appear at the end of the report in the same format as the values of the variables. To produce subtotals, add both the SUM statement and the **BY statement** to your PROC PRINT step. To show **BY variable headings** only once, use an ID and BY statement together with the SUM statement. As another enhancement to your report, you can request that each BY group be printed on a separate page by using the **PAGEBY statement**.

Double-Spacing Output

To double-space your SAS listing output, you can specify the **DOUBLE option** in the PROC PRINT statement.

Specifying Titles

To make your report more meaningful and self-explanatory, you can specify up to 10 titles with procedure output by using **TITLE statements** anywhere within or preceding the PROC step. After you define a title, it remains in effect until you modify it, cancel it, or end your SAS session. Re-defining a title line cancels any higher-numbered title lines. To cancel all previous titles, specify a null TITLE statement (a TITLE statement with no number or text).

Specifying Footnotes

To add footnotes to your output, you can use the **FOOTNOTE statement**. Like TITLE statements, FOOTNOTE statements are global. Footnotes appear at the bottom of each page of procedure output, and footnote lines are "pushed up" from the bottom. The FOOTNOTE statement that has the largest number appears on the bottom line. After you define a footnote, it remains in effect until you modify it, cancel it, or end your SAS session. Re-defining a footnote line cancels any higher-numbered footnote lines. To cancel all previous footnotes, specify a null FOOTNOTE statement (a FOOTNOTE statement with no number or text).

Assigning Descriptive Labels

To label the columns in your report with more descriptive text, you use the **LABEL statement**, which assigns a descriptive label to a variable. To display the labels that were assigned in a LABEL statement, you must specify the **LABEL option** in the PROC PRINT statement.

Formatting Data Values

To make data values more understandable when they are displayed in your procedure output, you can use the **FORMAT statement**, which associates formats with variables. The FORMAT statement remains in effect only for the PROC step in which it appears. Formats affect only how the data values appear in output, not the actual data values as they are stored in the SAS data set. All SAS formats specify the total field width (w) that is used for displaying the values in the output. For numeric variables you can also specify the number of decimal places (d), if any, to be displayed in the output.

Using Permanently Assigned Labels and Formats

You can take advantage of permanently assigned labels or formats without adding LABEL or FORMAT statements to your PROC step. Some SAS procedures require a LABEL option in order to display permanent labels. Many other SAS procedures display permanently assigned labels and formats within additional statements or options.

Points to Remember

- VAR, WHERE, and SUM statements remain in effect only for the PROC step in which they appear.
- If you don't use the OUT= option, PROC SORT permanently sorts the data set that is specified in the DATA= option.
- TITLE and FOOTNOTE statements remain in effect until you modify them, cancel them, or end your SAS session.
- Be sure to match the quotation marks that enclose the text in TITLE, FOOTNOTE, and LABEL statements.
- To display labels in PRINT procedure output, remember to add the LABEL option to the PROC PRINT statement.
- To permanently assign labels or formats to data set variables, place the LABEL or FORMAT statement inside the DATA step.

Practice

After you complete this chapter, practice what you learned by using the sample data and SAS programs for Chapter 4, **Creating List Reports**, which are located on the CD-ROM. Follow the directions for creating your sample data in the Before You Begin section.

Quiz

Select the best answer for each question. After completing the quiz, check your answers using the answer key in the appendix.

1. Which PROC PRINT step below creates the following output?

Date	On	Changed	Flight
04MAR99	232	18	219
05MAR99	160	4	219
06MAR99	163	14	219
07MAR99	241	9	219
08MAR99	183	11	219
09MAR99	211	18	219
10MAR99	167	7	219

   a. ```
      proc print data=flights.laguardia noobs;
         var on changed flight;
         where on>=160;
      run;
      ```

   b. ```
      proc print data=flights.laguardia;
         var date on changed flight;
         where changed>3;
      run;
      ```

   c. ```
      proc print data=flights.laguardia label;
         id date;
         var boarded transferred flight;
         label boarded='On' transferred='Changed';
         where flight='219';
      run;
      ```

   d. ```
      proc print flights.laguardia noobs;
         id date;
         var date on changed flight;
         where flight='219';
      run;
      ```

2.   Which of the following PROC PRINT steps is correct if labels are not stored with the data set?

   a.
```
proc print data=allsales.totals label;
    label region8='Region 8 Yearly Totals';
run;
```

   b.
```
proc print data=allsales.totals;
    label region8='Region 8 Yearly Totals';
run;
```

   c.
```
proc print data allsales.totals label noobs;
run;
```

   d.
```
proc print allsales.totals label;
run;
```

3.   Which of the following statements selects from a data set only those observations for which the value of the variable `Style` is *RANCH, SPLIT,* or *TWOSTORY?*

   a. `where style='RANCH' or 'SPLIT' or 'TWOSTORY';`

   b. `where style in 'RANCH' or 'SPLIT' or 'TWOSTORY';`

   c. `where style in (RANCH, SPLIT, TWOSTORY);`

   d. `where style in ('RANCH','SPLIT','TWOSTORY');`

4.   If you want to sort your data and create a temporary data set named **Calc** to store the sorted data, which of the following steps should you submit?

   a.
```
proc sort data=work.calc out=finance.dividend;
run;
```

   b.
```
proc sort dividend out=calc;
    by account;
run;
```

   c.
```
proc sort data=finance.dividend out=work.calc;
    by account;
run;
```

   d.
```
proc sort from finance.dividend to calc;
    by account;
run;
```

5. Which options are used to create the following PROC PRINT output?

```
                                    13:27 Monday, March 22, 1999
    Patient     Arterial     Heart     Cardiac     Urinary

     203          88          95          66          110

      54          83         183          95            0

     664          72         111         332           12

     210          74          97         369            0

     101          80         130         291            0
```

   a. the DATE system option and the LABEL option in PROC PRINT

   b. the DATE and NONUMBER system options and the DOUBLE and NOOBS options in PROC PRINT

   c. the DATE and NONUMBER system options and the DOUBLE option in PROC PRINT

   d. the DATE and NONUMBER system options and the NOOBS option in PROC PRINT

6. Which of the following statements can you use in a PROC PRINT step to create this output?

Month	Instructors	AerClass	WalkJogRun	Swim
01	1	37	91	83
02	2	41	102	27
03	1	52	98	19
04	1	61	118	22
05	3	49	88	29
	8	240	497	180

   a. `var month instructors;`
       `sum instructors aerclass walkjogrun swim;`

   b. `var month;`
       `sum instructors aerclass walkjogrun swim;`

   c. `var month instructors aerclass;`
       `sum instructors aerclass walkjogrun swim;`

   d. all of the above

7. What happens if you submit the following program?

```
proc sort data=clinic.diabetes;
run;
proc print data=clinic.diabetes;
   var age height weight pulse;
   where sex='F';
run;
```

   a. The PROC PRINT step runs successfully, printing observations in their sorted order.

   b. The PROC SORT step permanently sorts the input data set.

   c. The PROC SORT step generates errors and stops processing, but the PROC PRINT step runs successfully, printing observations in their original (unsorted) order.

   d. The PROC SORT step runs successfully, but the PROC PRINT step generates errors and stops processing.

8. If you submit the following program, which output does it create?

```
proc sort data=finance.loans out=work.loans;
   by months amount;
run;
proc print data=work.loans noobs;
   var months;
   sum amount payment;
   where months<360;
run;
```

   a.

Months	Amount	Payment
12	$3,500	$308.52
24	$8,700	$403.47
36	$10,000	$325.02
48	$5,000	$128.02
	$27,200	$1,165.03

   b.

Months	Amount	Payment
12	$3,500	$308.52
24	$8,700	$403.47
36	$10,000	$325.02
48	$5,000	$128.02
	27,200	1,165.03

c.

Months	Amount	Payment
12	$3,500	$308.52
48	$5,000	$128.02
24	$8,700	$403.47
36	$10,000	$325.02
	$27,200	$1,165.03

d.

Months	Amount	Payment
12	$3,500	$308.52
24	$8,700	$403.47
36	$10,000	$325.02
48	$5,000	$128.02
		$1,165.03

9. Choose the statement below that selects rows in which

- the amount is less than or equal to $5000
- the account is 101–1092, or the rate equals 0.095.

a. ```
where amount <= 5000 and
      account='101-1092' or rate = 0.095;
```

*b.* ```
where (amount le 5000 and account='101-1092')
      or rate = 0.095;
```

c. ```
where amount <= 5000 and
      (account='101-1092' or rate eq 0.095);
```

*d.* ```
where amount <= 5000 or account='101-1092'
      and rate = 0.095;
```

10. What does PROC PRINT display by default?

a. PROC PRINT does not create a default report; you must specify the rows and columns to be displayed.

b. PROC PRINT displays all observations and variables in the data set. If you want an additional column for observation numbers, you can request it.

c. PROC PRINT displays columns in the following order: a column for observation numbers, all character variables, and all numeric variables.

d. PROC PRINT displays all observations and variables in the data set, a column for observation numbers on the far left, and variables in the order in which they occur in the data set.

Chapter 5 Creating SAS Data Sets from Raw Data

Overview

Introduction

In order to create reports with SAS procedures, your data must be in the form of a SAS data set. If your data is not stored in the form of a SAS data set, then you need to create a SAS data set by entering data, by reading raw data, or by accessing external files (files that were created by other software).

This shows you how to design and write a DATA step program to create a SAS data set from **raw data** that is stored in an external file. It also shows you how to read data from a SAS data set and write observations out to a raw data file.

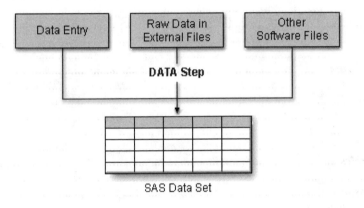

Objectives

In this chapter, you learn to

- reference a SAS library

- reference a raw data file

- name a SAS data set to be created

- specify a raw data file to be read

- read standard character and numeric values in fixed fields

- create new variables and assign values

- select observations based on conditions

- read instream data

- submit and verify a DATA step program

- read a SAS data set and write the observations out to a raw data file.

Raw Data Files

A raw data file is an external text file whose records contain data values that are organized in fields. Raw data files are non-proprietary and can be read by a variety of software programs. The sample raw data files in this book are shown with a ruler to help you identify where individual fields begin and end. The ruler is not part of the raw data file.

Raw Data File

The table below describes the record layout for a raw data file that contains readings from exercise stress tests that have been performed on patients at a health clinic. Exercise physiologists in the clinic use the test results to prescribe various exercise therapies. The file contains **fixed fields**; that is, values for each variable are in the same location in all records.

Field Name	Starting Column	Ending Column	Description of Field
ID	1	4	patient ID number
Name	6	25	patient name
RestHR	27	29	resting heart rate
MaxHR	31	33	maximum heart rate during test
RecHR	35	37	recovery heart rate after test
TimeMin	39	40	time, complete minutes
TimeSec	42	43	time, seconds
Tolerance	45	45	comparison of stress test tolerance between this test and the last test (I=increased, D=decreased, S=same, N=no previous test)

Steps to Create a SAS Data Set

Let's take a look at the steps for creating a SAS data set from a raw data file. In the first part of this chapter, you will learn the steps to create a SAS data set from a raw data file that contains fixed fields. The examples shown use a raw data file that contains data from exercise stress tests, which was introduced on the previous page.

Before reading the raw data from the file, you must first reference the SAS library in which you will store the data set. Then you can write a DATA step program to read the raw data file and create a SAS data set.

To read the raw data file, the DATA step must provide the following instructions to SAS:

- the location or name of the external text file
- a name for the new SAS data set
- a reference that identifies the external file
- a description of the data values to be read.

After using the DATA step to read the raw data, you can use a PROC PRINT step to produce a list report that displays the data values that are in the new data set.

The table below outlines the basic statements that you'll use to construct your program. Throughout this chapter, you'll see similar tables that show sample SAS statements for reading raw data in fixed fields.

To Do This	Use This SAS Statement
Reference a SAS data library	LIBNAME statement
Reference an external file	FILENAME statement
Name a SAS data set	DATA statement
Identify an external file	INFILE statement
Describe data	INPUT statement
Execute the DATA step	RUN statement
List the data	PROC PRINT statement
Execute the final program step	RUN statement

You can also use additional SAS statements to perform tasks that customize your data for your needs. For example, you might want to create new variables from the values of existing variables.

Referencing a SAS Library

Using a LIBNAME Statement

As you begin to write the program, remember that you use a LIBNAME statement to reference the permanent SAS library in which the data set will be stored.

To Do This	Use This SAS Statement	Example
Reference a SAS data library	LIBNAME statement	`libname` *`libref`* `'SAS-data-library';`

For example, the LIBNAME statement below assigns the libref **Taxes** to the SAS library **C:\Users\Acct\Qtr1\Report** in the Windows environment.

```
libname taxes 'c:\users\acct\qtr1\report';
```

You do not need to use a LIBNAME statement in all situations. For example, you do not need to use a LIBNAME statement if you are storing the data set in a temporary SAS data set or if SAS has automatically assigned the libref for the permanent library that you are using.

Referencing a Raw Data File

Using a FILENAME Statement

Before you can read your raw data, you must point to the location of the external file that contains the data. You use the FILENAME statement to point to this location.

To Do This	Use This SAS Statement	Example
Reference a SAS data library	LIBNAME statement	`libname` *`libref`* `'SAS-data-library';`
Reference an external file	FILENAME statement	`filename tests 'c:\users\tmill.dat';`

Just as you assign a libref by using a LIBNAME statement, you assign a fileref by using a FILENAME statement.

Filerefs perform the same function as librefs: they temporarily point to a storage location for data. However, librefs reference SAS data libraries, whereas filerefs reference external files.

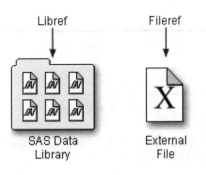

Libref   Fileref

SAS Data Library   External File

General form, FILENAME statement:

> **FILENAME** *fileref* **'***filename***';**

where

- *fileref* is a name that you associate with an external file. The name must be 1 to 8 characters long, begin with a letter or underscore, and contain only letters, numbers, or underscores.

- *filename* is the fully qualified name or location of the file.

Defining a Fully Qualified Filename

The following FILENAME statement temporarily associates the fileref **Tests** with the external file that contains the data from the exercise stress tests. The complete filename is specified as **C:\Users\Tmill.dat** in the Windows environment.

```
filename tests 'c:\users\tmill.dat';
```

Raw Data File Tests

```
1---+----10---+----20---+----30---+----40---+--
2458   Murray,  W         72    185 128 12 38 D
1215 RAINTREE CIRCLE
2462   Almers,  C         68    171 133 10 5  I
2501   Bonaventure, T     78    177 139 11 13 I
2523   Johnson, R         69    162 114 9  42 S
2539   LaMance, K         75    168 141 11 46 D
2552   Reberson, P        69    158 139 15 41 D
2555   King, E            70    167 122 13 13 I
```

Defining an Aggregate Storage Location

You can also use a FILENAME statement to associate a fileref with an aggregate storage location, such as a directory that contains multiple external files.

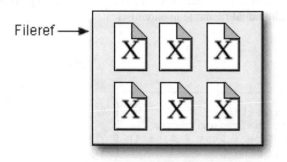

This FILENAME statement temporarily associates the fileref **Finance** with the aggregate storage directory **C:\Users\Personal\Finances**:

```
filename finance 'c:\users\personal\finances';
```

Both the LIBNAME and FILENAME statements are global. In other words, they remain in effect until you change them, cancel them, or end your SAS session.

Referencing a Fully Qualified Filename

When you associate a fileref with an individual external file, you specify the fileref in subsequent SAS statements and commands.

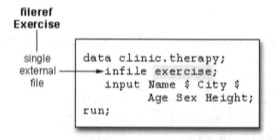

Referencing a File in an Aggregate Storage Location

To reference an external file with a fileref that points to an aggregate storage location, you specify the fileref followed by the individual filename in parentheses:

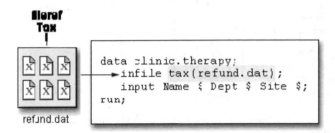

```
data clinic.therapy;
   infile tax(refund.dat);
   input Name $ Dept $ Site $;
run;
```

 In the Windows operating environment, you can omit the filename extension but you will need to add quotation marks when referencing the external file, as in

```
infile tax('refund');
```

For details about referencing external files stored in aggregate storage locations, see the SAS documentation for your operating environment.

Writing a DATA Step Program

Naming the Data Set

The DATA statement indicates the beginning of the DATA step and names the SAS data set to be created.

To Do This	Use This SAS Statement	Example
Reference a SAS data library	LIBNAME statement	`libname libref 'SAS-data-library';`
Reference an external file	FILENAME statement	`filename tests 'c:\users\tmill.dat';`
Name a SAS data set	DATA statement	`data clinic.stress;`

General form, basic DATA statement:

> **DATA** *SAS-data-set-1* <...*SAS-data-set-n*>;

where *SAS-data-set* names (in the format *libref.filename*) the data set or data sets to be created.

In the following example, the two-level name **Clinic.Admit** specifies that the file **Admit** is stored in the permanent SAS library to which the libref **Clinic** has been assigned.

Clinic.Admit

Libref   Filename

Specifying the Raw Data File

When reading raw data, use the INFILE statement to indicate which file the data is in.

To Do This	Use This SAS Statement	Example
Reference a SAS data library	LIBNAME statement	`libname libref 'SAS-data-library';`
Reference an external file	FILENAME statement	`filename tests 'c:\users\tmill.dat';`
Name a SAS data set	DATA statement	`data clinic.stress;`
Identify an external file	INFILE statement	`infile tests obs=10;`

General form, INFILE statement:

INFILE *file-specification <options>*;

where

- *file-specification* can take the form *fileref* to name a previously defined file reference or *'filename'* to point to the actual name and location of the file

- *options* describes the input file's characteristics and specifies how it is to be read with the INFILE statement.

To read the raw data file to which the fileref **Tests** has been assigned, you write the following INFILE statement:

```
infile tests;
```

 Instead of using a FILENAME statement, you can choose to identify the raw data file by specifying the entire filename and location in the INFILE statement. For example, the following statement points directly to the **C:\Irs\Personal\Refund.dat** file:

```
infile 'c:\irs\personal\refund.dat';
```

Column Input

In this chapter, you'll be working with column input, the most common input style. Column input specifies actual column locations for values. However, column input is appropriate only in certain situations. When you use column input, your data **must** be

- standard character or numeric values
- in fixed fields.

Standard and Nonstandard Numeric Data

Standard numeric data values can contain only

- numbers
- decimal points
- numbers in scientific or E-notation (*2.3E4*, for example)
- plus or minus signs.

Nonstandard numeric data includes

- values that contain special characters, such as percent signs (%), dollar signs ($), and commas (,)
- date and time values
- data in fraction, integer binary, real binary, and hexadecimal forms.

The external file that is referenced by the fileref **Staff** contains the personnel information for a technical writing department of a small computer manufacturer. The fields contain values for each employee's last name, first name, job title, and annual salary.

Notice that the values for Salary contain commas. The values for Salary are considered to be nonstandard numeric values. You cannot use column input to read these values.

Raw Data File Staff

```
1---+----10---+----20---+---
EVANS    DONNY 112 29,996.63
HELMS    LISA  105 18,567.23
HIGGINS  JOHN  111 25,309.00
LARSON   AMY   113 32,696.78
MOORE    MARY  112 28,945.89
```

Fixed-Field Data

Raw data can be organized in several different ways.

This external file contains data that is in free format, meaning data that is not arranged in columns. Notice that the values for a particular field do not begin and end in the same columns. You cannot use column input to read this file.

```
1---+----10---+----20
BARNES   NORTH 360.98
FARLSON  WEST 243.94
LAWRENCE NORTH 195.04
NELSON   EAST 169.30
STEWART  SOUTH 238.45
TAYLOR   WEST 318.87
```

This external file contains data that is arranged in columns or fixed fields. You can specify a beginning and ending column for each field. Let's look at how column input can be used to read this data.

```
1---+----10---+----20
2810 61 MOD   F
2804 38 HIGH  F
2807 42 LOW   M
2816 26 HIGH  M
2833 32 MOD   F
2823 29 HIGH  M
```

Describing the Data

The INPUT statement describes the fields of raw data to be read and placed into the SAS data set.

To Do This	Use This SAS Statement	Example
Reference a SAS data library	LIBNAME statement	`libname libref 'SAS-data-library';`
Reference an external file	FILENAME statement	`filename tests 'c:\users\tmill.dat';`
Name a SAS data set	DATA statement	`data clinic.stress;`
Identify an external file	INFILE statement	`infile tests obs=10;`
Describe data	INPUT statement	`input ID 1-4 Age 6-7 ...;`
Execute the DATA step	RUN statement	`run;`

General form, INPUT statement using column input:

> **INPUT** *variable* <$> *startcol-endcol* . . . ;

where

- *variable* is the SAS name that you assign to the field

- the dollar sign ($) identifies the variable type as character (if the variable is numeric, then nothing appears here)

- *startcol* represents the starting column for this variable

- *endcol* represents the ending column for this variable.

Look at the small data file shown below. For each field of raw data that you want to read into your SAS data set, you must specify the following information in the INPUT statement:

- a valid SAS variable name

- a type (character or numeric)

- a range (starting column and ending column).

Raw Data File Exercise

```
1---+----10---+----20
2810 61 MOD   F
2804 38 HIGH  F
2807 42 LOW   M
2816 26 HIGH  M
2833 32 MOD   F
2823 29 HIGH  M
```

The INPUT statement below assigns the character variable ID to the data in columns 1–4, the numeric variable Age to the data in columns 6–7, the character variable ActLevel to the data in columns 9–12, and the character variable Sex to the data in column 14.

```
filename exer 'c:\users\exer.dat';
data exercise;
   infile exer;
   input ID $ 1-4 Age 6-7 ActLevel $ 9-12 Sex $ 14;
run;
```

SAS Data Set Work.Exercise

Obs	ID	Age	ActLevel	Sex
1	2810	61	MOD	F
2	2804	38	HIGH	F
3	2807	42	LOW	M
4	2816	26	HIGH	M
5	2833	32	MOD	F
6	2823	29	HIGH	M

When you use column input, you can

- read any or all fields from the raw data file

- read the fields in any order

- specify only the starting column for values that occupy only one column.

```
input ActLevel $ 9-12 Sex $ 14 Age 6-7;
```

Remember, when you create a new variable, you must specify it in the exact case that you want it stored. An example is NewBalance. Thereafter, you can specify the variable in lowercase.

Specifying Variable Names

Each variable has a name that conforms to SAS naming conventions. Variable names

- must be 1 to 32 characters in length

- must begin with a letter (A–Z) or an underscore (_)

- can continue with any combination of numbers, letters, or underscores.

Let's look at an INPUT statement that uses column input to read the three data fields in the raw data file below.

Raw Data File Admit

```
1---+----10---+----20
58MOD M
29LOW F
34LOW M
41HIGHF
30MOD F
22HIGHM
```

The values for the variable that you are naming Age are located in columns 1–2. Because Age is a numeric variable, you do not specify a dollar sign ($) after the variable name.

```
input Age 1-2
```

The values for the variable ActLevel are located in columns 3–6. You specify a $ to indicate that ActLevel is a character variable.

```
input Age 1-2 ActLevel $ 3-6
```

The values for the character variable Sex are located in column 7. Notice that you specify only a single column.

```
input Age 1-2 ActLevel $ 3-6 Sex $ 7;
```

Submitting the DATA Step Program

Verifying the Data

To verify your data, it is a good idea to use the **OBS= option** in the INFILE statement. Adding OBS=*n* to the INFILE statement enables you to process only records 1 through *n*, so you can verify that the correct fields are being read before reading the entire data file.

The program below reads the first 10 records in the raw data file referenced by the fileref **Tests**. The data is stored in a permanent SAS data set named **Clinic.Stress**. Don't forget a RUN statement, which tells SAS to execute the previous SAS statements.

```
data clinic.stress;
   infile tests obs=10;
   input ID 1-4 Name $ 6-25
         RestHR 27-29 MaxHR 31-33
         RecHR 35-37 TimeMin 39-40
         TimeSec 42-43 Tolerance $ 45;
run;
```

SAS Data Set Clinic.Stress

ID	Name	RestHR	MaxHR	RecHR	TimeMin	TimeSec	Tolerance
2458	Murray, W	72	185	128	12	38	D
2462	Almers, C	68	171	133	10	5	I
2501	Bonaventure, T	78	177	139	11	13	I
2523	Johnson, R	69	162	114	9	42	S
2539	LaMance, K	75	168	141	11	46	D
2544	Jones, M	79	187	136	12	26	N
2552	Reberson, P	69	158	139	15	41	D
2555	King, E	70	167	122	13	13	I
2563	Pitts, D	71	159	116	10	22	S
2568	Eberhardt, S	72	182	122	16	49	N

Checking DATA Step Processing

After submitting the previous program, messages in the log verify that the raw data file was read correctly. The notes in the log indicate that

- 10 records were read from the raw data file
- the SAS data set **Clinic.Stress** was created with 10 observations and 8 variables.

SAS Log

```
NOTE: The infile TESTS is:
      File Name=C:\My SAS Files\tests.dat,
      RECFM=V,LRECL=256

NOTE: 10 records were read from the infile TESTS.
      The minimum record length was 80.
      The maximum record length was 80.
NOTE: The data set CLINIC.STRESS has 10 observations
      and 8 variables.
NOTE: DATA statement used  0.07 seconds
```

Listing the Data Set

The messages in the log seem to indicate that the DATA step program correctly accessed the raw data file. But it is a good idea to look at the ten observations in the new data set before reading the entire raw data file. You can submit a PROC PRINT step to view the data.

To Do This	Use This SAS Statement	Example
Reference a SAS data library	LIBNAME statement	`libname libref 'SAS-data-library';`
Reference an external file	FILENAME statement	`filename tests 'c:\users\tmill.dat';`
Name a SAS data set	DATA statement	`data clinic.stress;`
Identify an external file	INFILE statement	`infile tests obs=10;`
Describe data	INPUT statement	`input ID 1-4 Name $ 6-25 ...;`
Execute the DATA step	RUN statement	`run;`
List the data	PROC PRINT statement	`proc print data=clinic.stress;`
Execute the final program step	RUN statement	`run;`

The following PROC PRINT step lists the **Clinic.Stress** data set.

```
proc print data=clinic.stress;
run;
```

The PROC PRINT output indicates that the variables in the **Clinic.Stress** data set were read correctly for the first 10 records.

Obs	ID	Name	RestHR	MaxHR	RecHR	TimeMin	TimeSec	Tolerance
1	2458	Murray, W	72	185	128	12	38	D
2	2462	Almers, C	68	171	133	10	5	I
3	2501	Bonaventure, T	78	177	139	11	13	I
4	2523	Johnson, R	69	162	114	9	42	S
5	2539	LaMance, K	75	168	141	11	46	D
6	2544	Jones, M	79	187	136	12	26	N
7	2552	Reberson, P	69	158	139	15	41	D
8	2555	King, E	70	167	122	13	13	I
9	2563	Pitts, D	71	159	116	10	22	S
10	2568	Eberhardt, S	72	182	122	16	49	N

Raw Data File

…he log and verified your data, you can modify the DATA step to read the
…o, remove the OBS= option from the INFILE statement and re-submit the

```
                   s;
              e $ 6-25
              29 MaxHR 31-33
              7 TimeMin 39-40
              -43 Tolerance $ 45;
```

…TA step and check the log, you see a note indicating that invalid
…auie RecHR in line 14 of the raw data file, columns 35–37.

This note is followed by a column ruler and the actual data line that contains the invalid value for
RecHR.

```
NOTE: Invalid data for RecHR in line 14 35-37.
RULE:       ----+----1----+----2----+----3----+----4----+----5---
14        2575 Quigley, M          74   152 Q13 11 26 I 45
ID=2575 Name=Quigley, M RestHR=74 MaxHR=152 RecHR=. TimeMin=11
TimeSec=26 Tolerance=I _ERROR_=1
_N_=14
NOTE: 21 records were read from the infile TESTS.
      The minimum record length was 80.
      The maximum record length was 80.
NOTE: The data set CLINIC.STRESS has 21 observations
      and 8 variables.
NOTE: DATA statement used 0.13 seconds
```

The value *Q13* is a data-entry error. It was entered incorrectly for the variable RecHR.

RecHR is a numeric variable, but *Q13* is not a valid number. So RecHR is assigned a missing value,
as indicated in the log. Because RecHR is numeric, the missing value is represented with a period.

Notice, though, that the DATA step does not fail as a result of the invalid data but continues to
execute. Unlike syntax errors, invalid data errors do not cause SAS to stop processing a program.

Assuming you have a way to edit the file and can justify a correction, you can correct the invalid
value and re-run the DATA step. If you did this, the log would then show that the data set
Clinic.Stress was created with 21 observations, 8 variables, and no messages about invalid data.

```
NOTE: The infile TESTS2 is:
      File Name=C:\My SAS Files\tests2.dat,
      RECFM=V,LRECL=256

NOTE: 21 records were read from the infile TESTS2.
      The minimum record length was 80.
      The maximum record length was 80.
NOTE: The data set CLINIC.STRESS has 21 observations
      and 8 variables.
NOTE: DATA statement used 0.14 seconds
```

After correcting the raw data file, you can list the data again to verify that it is correct.

```
proc print data=clinic.stress;
run;
```

Obs	ID	Name	RestHr	MaxHR	RecHR	TimeMin	TimeSec	Tolerance
1	2458	Murray, W	72	185	128	12	38	D
2	2462	Almers, C	68	171	133	10	5	I
3	2501	Bonaventure, T	78	177	139	11	13	I
4	2523	Johnson, R	69	162	114	9	42	S
5	2539	LaMance, K	75	168	141	11	46	D
6	2544	Jones, M	79	187	136	12	26	N
7	2552	Reberson, P	69	158	139	15	41	D
8	2555	King, E	70	167	122	13	13	I
9	2563	Pitts, D	71	159	116	10	22	S
10	2568	Eberhardt, S	72	182	122	16	49	N
11	2571	Nunnelly, A	65	181	141	15	2	I
12	2572	Oberon, M	74	177	138	12	11	D
13	2574	Peterson, V	80	164	137	14	9	D
14	2575	Quigley, M	74	152	113	11	26	I
15	2578	Cameron, L	75	158	108	14	27	I

Whenever you use the DATA step to read raw data, remember the steps that you followed in this chapter, which help ensure that you don't waste resources when accessing data:

- Write the DATA step using the OBS= option in the INFILE statement.
- Submit the DATA step.
- Check the log for messages.
- View the resulting data set.
- Remove the OBS= option and re-submit the DATA step.
- Check the log again.
- View the resulting data set again.

Creating and Modifying Variables

So far in this book, you've read existing data. But sometimes existing data doesn't provide the information that you need. To modify existing values or to create new variables, you can use an **assignment statement** in any DATA step.

General form, assignment statement:

> *variable=expression*;

where

- *variable* names a new or existing variable
- *expression* is any valid SAS expression.

The assignment statement is one of the few SAS statements that doesn't begin with a keyword.

For example, here is an assignment statement that assigns the character value *Toby Witherspoon* to the variable `Name`:

```
Name='Toby Witherspoon';
```

SAS Expressions

You use SAS expressions in assignment statements and many other SAS programming statements to

- transform variables
- create new variables
- conditionally process variables
- calculate new values
- assign new values.

An expression is a sequence of operands and operators that form a set of instructions. The instructions are performed to produce a new value:

- **Operands** are variable names or constants. They can be numeric, character, or both.

- **Operators** are special-character operators, grouping parentheses, or functions. You can learn about functions in Chapter 14, **Transforming Data with SAS Functions**.

Using Operators in SAS Expressions

To perform a calculation, you use **arithmetic operators**. The table below lists arithmetic operators.

Operator	Action	Example	Priority
-	negative prefix	`negative=-x;`	I
**	exponentiation	`raise=x**y;`	I
*	multiplication	`mult=x*y;`	II
/	division	`divide=x/y;`	II
+	addition	`sum=x+y;`	III
-	subtraction	`diff=x-y;`	III

When you use more than one arithmetic operator in an expression,

- operations of priority I are performed before operations of priority II, and so on

- consecutive operations that have the same priority are performed

  o from right to left within priority I

  o from left to right within priorities II and III

- you can use parentheses to control the order of operations.

 When a value that is used with an arithmetic operator is missing, the result of the expression is **missing**. The assignment statement assigns a **missing value** to a variable if the result of the expression is missing.

You use the following **comparison operators** to express a condition.

Operator	Meaning	Example
= or **eq**	equal to	`name='Jones, C.'`
^= or **ne**	not equal to	`temp ne 212`
> or **gt**	greater than	`income>20000`
< or **lt**	less than	`partno lt "BG05"`
>= or **ge**	greater than or equal to	`id>='1543'`
<= or **le**	less than or equal to	`pulse le 85`

To link a sequence of expressions into compound expressions, you use **logical operators**, including the following.

Operator	Meaning
AND or **&**	and, both. If both expressions are true, then the compound expression is true.
OR or **|**	or, either. If either expression is true, then the compound expression is true.

More Examples of Assignment Statements

The assignment statement in the DATA step below creates a new variable, `TotalTime`, by multiplying the values of `TimeMin` by 60 and then adding the values of `TimeSec`.

```
data clinic.stress;
   infile tests;
   input ID 1-4 Name $ 6-25 RestHr 27-29 MaxHR 31-33
         RecHR 35-37 TimeMin 39-40 TimeSec 42-43
         Tolerance $ 45;
   TotalTime=(timemin*60)+timesec;
run;
```

SAS Data Set Clinic.Stress (Partial Listing)

ID	Name	RestHR	MaxHR	RecHR	TimeMin	TimeSec	Tolerance	TotalTime
2458	Murray, W	72	185	128	12	38	D	758
2462	Almers, C	68	171	133	10	5	I	605
2501	Bonaventure, T	78	177	139	11	13	I	673
2523	Johnson, R	69	162	114	9	42	S	582
2539	LaMance, K	75	168	141	11	46	D	706

The expression can also contain the variable name that is on the left side of the equal sign, as the following assignment statement shows. This statement re-defines the values of the variable `RestHR` as 10 percent higher.

```
data clinic.stress;
   infile tests;
   input ID 1-4 Name $ 6-25 RestHr 27-29 MaxHR 31-33
         RecHR 35-37 TimeMin 39-40 TimeSec 42-43
         Tolerance $ 45;
   resthr=resthr+(resthr*.10);
run;
```

When a variable name appears on both sides of the equal sign, the original value on the right side is used to evaluate the expression. The result is assigned to the variable on the left side of the equal sign.

```
data clinic.stress;
   infile tests;
   input ID 1-4 Name $ 6-25 RestHr 27-29 MaxHR 31-33
         RecHR 35-37 TimeMin 39-40 TimeSec 42-43
         Tolerance $ 45;
   resthr=resthr+(resthr*.10);
run;     ^           ^
         result   original value
```

Date Constants

You can assign date values to variables in assignment statements by using **date constants**. To represent a constant in SAS date form, specify the date as *'ddmmmyy'* or *'ddmmmyyyy'*, followed by a D.

General form, date constant:

> *'ddmmm<yy>yy'*D

> or

> *"ddmmm<yy>yy"*D

where

- *dd* is a one- or two-digit value for the day

- *mmm* is a three-letter abbreviation for the month (JAN, FEB, and so on)

- *yy* or *yyyy* is a two- or four-digit value for the year, respectively.

  Be sure to enclose the date in quotation marks.

Example

In the following program, the second assignment statement assigns a date value to the variable
`TestDate`.

```
data clinic.stress;
    infile tests;
    input ID 1-4 Name $ 6-25 RestHr 27-29 MaxHR 31-33
          RecHR 35-37 TimeMin 39-40 TimeSec 42-43
          Tolerance $ 45;
    TotalTime=(timemin*60)+timesec;
    TestDate='01jan2000'd;
run;
```

 You can also use SAS **time constants** and SAS **datetime constants** in assignment
statements.

```
Time='9:25't;
DateTime='18jan2005:9:27:05'dt;
```

Subsetting Data

As you read your data, you can subset it by processing only those observations that meet a specified
condition. To do this, you can use a **subsetting IF statement** in any DATA step.

The subsetting IF statement causes the DATA step to continue processing only those raw data
records or observations that meet the condition of the expression specified in the IF statement. The
resulting SAS data set or data sets contain a subset of the original external file or SAS data set.

General form, subsetting IF statement:

> **IF** *expression*;

where *expression* is any valid SAS expression.

- If the expression is **true**, the DATA step continues to process that record or observation.

- If the expression is **false**, no further statements are processed for that record or observation,
  and control returns to the top of the DATA step.

For example, the subsetting IF statement below selects only observations whose values for
`Tolerance` are *D*. The IF statement is positioned in the DATA step so that other statements do not
need to process unwanted observations.

```
data clinic.stress;
    infile tests;
    input ID 1-4 Name $ 6-25 RestHr 27-29 MaxHR 31-33
          RecHR 35-37 TimeMin 39-40 TimeSec 42-43
          Tolerance $ 45;
    if tolerance='D';
    TotalTime=(timemin*60)+timesec;
run;
```

Because Tolerance is a character variable, the value *D* must be enclosed in quotation marks, and it must be the same case as in the data set.

See the SAS documentation for your operating environment for a comparison of the WHERE and subsetting IF statements when they are used in the DATA step.

Reading Instream Data

Throughout this chapter, our program has contained an INFILE statement that identifies an **external file** to read.

```
data clinic.stress;
    infile tests;
    input ID 1-4 Name $ 6-25 RestHr 27-29 MaxHR 31-33
          RecHR 35-37 TimeMin 39-40 TimeSec 42-43
          Tolerance $ 45;
    if tolerance='D';
    TotalTime=(timemin*60)+timesec;
run;
```

However, you can also read **instream data lines** that you enter directly in your SAS program, rather than data that is stored in an external file. Reading instream data is extremely helpful if you want to create data and test your programming statements on a few observations that you can specify according to your needs.

To read instream data, you use

- a **DATALINES statement** as the last statement in the DATA step (except for the RUN statement) and immediately preceding the data lines

- a **null statement** (a single semicolon) to indicate the end of the input data.

```
data clinic.stress;
    input ID 1-4 Name $ 6-25 RestHr 27-29 MaxHR 31-33
          RecHR 35-37 TimeMin 39-40 TimeSec 42-43
          Tolerance $ 45;
    datalines;
    .
    .
    .
    data lines go here
    .
    .
    .
;
```

General form, DATALINES statement:

    DATALINES;

 You can use only one DATALINES statement in a DATA step. Use separate DATA steps to enter multiple sets of data.

 You can also use **CARDS;** as the last statement in a DATA step (except for the RUN statement) and immediately preceding the data lines. The CARDS statement is an alias for the DATALINES statement.

 If your data contains semicolons, use the DATALINES4 statement plus a null statement that consists of four semicolons (;;;;) to indicate the end of the input data.

Example

To read the data for the treadmill stress tests as instream data, you can submit the following program:

```
data clinic.stress;
    input ID 1-4 Name $ 6-25 RestHr 27-29 MaxHR 31-33
          RecHR 35-37 TimeMin 39-40 TimeSec 42-43
          Tolerance $ 45;
    if tolerance='D';
    TotalTime=(timemin*60)+timesec;
    datalines;
2458 Murray, W          72  185 128 12 38 D
2462 Almers, C          68  171 133 10  5 I
2501 Bonaventure, T     78  177 139 11 13 I
2523 Johnson, R         69  162 114  9 42 S
2539 LaMance, K         75  168 141 11 46 D
2544 Jones, M           79  187 136 12 26 N
2552 Reberson, P        69  158 139 15 41 D
2555 King, E            70  167 122 13 13 I
2563 Pitts, D           71  159 116 10 22 S
2568 Eberhardt, S       72  182 122 16 49 N
2571 Nunnelly, A        65  181 141 15  2 I
2572 Oberon, M          74  177 138 12 11 D
2574 Peterson, V        80  164 137 14  9 D
2575 Quigley, M         74  152 113 11 26 I
2578 Cameron, L         75  158 108 14 27 I
2579 Underwood, K       72  165 127 13 19 S
2584 Takahashi, Y       76  163 135 16  7 D
2586 Derber, B          68  176 119 17 35 N
2588 Ivan, H            70  182 126 15 41 N
2589 Wilcox, E          78  189 138 14 57 I
2595 Warren, C          77  170 136 12 10 S
;
```

> Notice that you do not need a RUN statement following the null statement (the semicolon after the data lines). The null statement functions as a step boundary when the DATALINES statement is used, so the DATA step is executed as soon as SAS encounters it. If you do place a RUN statement after the null statement, any statements between the null statement and the RUN statement are **not** executed as part of the DATA step.

Steps to Create a Raw Data File

Look at the SAS program and SAS data set created earlier in this chapter.

```
data clinic.stress;
   infile tests;
   input ID 1-4 Name $ 6-25 RestHR 27-29 MaxHR 31-33
         RecHR 35-37 TimeMin 39-40 TimeSec 42-43
         Tolerance $ 45;
   if tolerance='D';
   TotalTime=(timemin*60)+timesec;
run;
```

SAS Data Set Clinic.Stress

ID	Name	RestHR	MaxHR	RecHR	TimeMin	TimeSec	Tolerance	TotalTime
2458	Murray, W	72	185	128	12	38	D	758
2539	LaMance, K	75	168	141	11	46	D	706
2552	Reberson, P	69	158	139	15	41	D	941
2572	Oberon, M	74	177	138	12	11	D	731
2574	Peterson, V	80	164	137	14	9	D	849
2584	Takahashi, Y	76	163	135	16	7	D	967

As you can see, the data set has been modified with SAS statements. If you wanted to write the new observations to a raw data file, you could reverse the process that you've been following and write out the observations from a SAS data set as records or lines to a new raw data file.

Using the_NULL_ Keyword

Because the goal of your SAS program is to create a raw data file and not a SAS data set, it is inefficient to list a data set name in the DATA statement. Instead, use the keyword _NULL_, which enables you to use the DATA step without actually creating a SAS data set. A SET statement specifies the SAS data set that you want to read from.

```
data _null_;
   set clinic.stress;
```

The next step is to specify the output file.

Specifying the Raw Data File

You use the FILE and PUT statements to write the observations from a SAS data set to a raw data file, just as you used the INFILE and INPUT statements to create a SAS data set. These two sets of statements work almost identically.

When writing observations to a raw data file, use the FILE statement to specify the output file.

General form, FILE statement:

> **FILE** *file-specification*;

where *file-specification* can take the form *fileref* to name a previously defined file reference or '*filename*' to point to the actual name and location of the file.

For example, if you want to read the **Clinic.Stress** data set to a raw data file that is referenced by the fileref **Newdat**, you would begin your program with the following SAS statements.

```
data _null_;
   set clinic.stress;
   file newdat;
```

Instead of identifying the raw data file with a SAS fileref, you can choose to specify the entire filename and location in the FILE statement. For example, the following FILE statement points directly to the **C:\Clinic\Patients\Stress.dat** file. Note that the path specifying the filename and location must be enclosed in quotation marks.

```
data _null_;
   set clinic.stress;
   file 'c:\clinic\patients\stress.dat';
```

Describing the Data

Whereas the FILE statement specifies the output file, the PUT statement describes the lines to write to the raw data file.

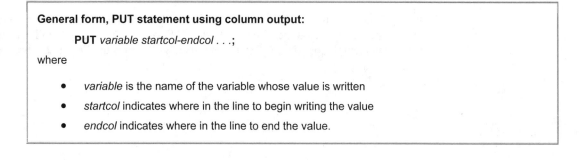

General form, PUT statement using column output:

> **PUT** *variable startcol-endcol . . .*;

where

- *variable* is the name of the variable whose value is written
- *startcol* indicates where in the line to begin writing the value
- *endcol* indicates where in the line to end the value.

In general, the PUT statement mirrors the capabilities of the INPUT statement. In this case you are working with column output. Therefore, you need to specify the variable name, starting column, and ending column for each field that you want to create. Because you are creating raw data, you don't need to follow character variable names with a dollar sign ($).

```
data _null_;
    set clinic.stress;
    file 'c:\clinic\patients\stress.dat';
    put id 1-4 name  6-25 resthr 27-29 maxhr 31-33
        rechr 35-37 timemin 39-40 timesec 42-43
        tolerance 45 totaltime 47-49;
run;
```

SAS Data Set Clinic.Stress

ID	Name	RestHR	MaxHR	RecHR	TimeMin	TimeSec	Tolerance	TotalTime
2458	Murray, W	72	185	128	12	38	D	758
2539	LaMance, K	75	168	141	11	46	D	706
2552	Reberson, P	69	158	139	15	41	D	941
2572	Oberon, M	74	177	138	12	11	D	731
2574	Peterson, V	80	164	137	14	9	D	849
2584	Takahashi, Y	76	163	135	16	7	D	967

The resulting raw data file would look like this:

Raw Data File Stress.Dat

```
1---+----10---+----20---+----30---+----40---+----50---+
2458 Murray, W      72  185 128 12 38 D 758
2539 LaMance, K     75  168 141 11 46 D 706
2552 Reberson, P    69  158 139 15 41 D 941
2572 Oberon, M      74  177 138 12 11 D 731
2574 Peterson, V    80  164 137 14 9  D 849
2584 Takahashi, Y   76  163 135 16 7  D 967
```

In later chapters you'll learn how to use INPUT and PUT statements to read and write raw data in other forms and record types.

If you do not execute a FILE statement before a PUT statement in the current iteration of the DATA step, then SAS writes the lines to the SAS log. If you specify the PRINT option in the FILE statement, before the PUT statement, then SAS writes the lines to the procedure output file.

Additional Features

In this chapter, you learned to read raw data by writing an INPUT statement that uses column input. You also learned how to write to a raw data file by using the FILE statement with column input. However, column input is appropriate only in certain situations. When you use column input, your data must be

- **standard character and numeric values**. If the raw data file contains nonstandard values, then you need to use formatted input, another style of input. To learn about formatted input, see Chapter 17, **Reading Raw Data in Fixed Fields**.

- **in fixed fields**. That is, values for a particular variable must be in the same location in all records. If your raw data file contains values that are not in fixed fields, then you need to use list input. To learn about list input, see Chapter 18, **Reading Free-Format Data**.

Other forms of the INPUT statement enable you to read

- nonstandard data values such as hexadecimal, packed decimal, SAS date values, and monetary values that contain dollar signs and commas

- free-format data (data that is not in fixed fields)

- implied decimal points

- variable-length data values

- variable-length records

- different record types.

Summary

Text Summary

Raw Data Files
A **raw data file** is an external file whose records contain data values that are organized in fields. The raw data files in this chapter contain fixed fields.

Steps to Create a SAS Data Set
You need to follow several steps to create a SAS data set using raw data.

1. Reference the raw data file to be read.

2. Name the SAS data set.

3. Identify the location of the raw data.

4. Describe the data values to be read.

Referencing a SAS Library
To begin your program, you might need to use a LIBNAME statement to reference the SAS library in which your data set will be stored.

Referencing a Raw Data File
Before you can read your raw data, you must reference the raw data file by creating a fileref. Just as you assign a libref by using a LIBNAME statement, you assign a fileref by using a FILENAME statement.

Writing a DATA Step Program
The DATA statement indicates the beginning of the DATA step and names the SAS data set(s) to be created.

Next, you specify the raw data file by using the INFILE statement. The OBS= option in the INFILE statement enables you to process a specified number of observations.

This chapter teaches column input, the most common input style. Column input specifies actual column locations for data values. The INPUT statement describes the raw data to be read and placed into the SAS data set.

Submitting the DATA Step Program
When you submit the program, you can use the OBS= option with the INFILE statement to verify that the correct data is being read before reading the entire data file.

After you submit the program, view the log to check the DATA step processing. You can then list the data set by using the PROC PRINT procedure.

After you've checked the log and verified your data, you can modify the DATA step to read the entire raw data file by removing the OBS= option from the INFILE statement.

If you are working with a raw data file that contains invalid data, the DATA step continues to execute. Unlike syntax errors, invalid data errors do not cause SAS to stop processing a program. If you have a way to edit the invalid data, it's best to correct the problem and re-run the DATA step.

Creating and Modifying Variables
To modify existing values or to create new variables, you can use an **assignment statement** in any DATA step. Within assignment statements, you can specify any **SAS expression**.

You can use **date constants** to assign dates in assignment statements. You can also use SAS time constants and SAS datetime constants in assignment statements.

Subsetting Data
To process only observations that meet a specified condition, use a **subsetting IF statement** in the DATA step.

Reading Instream Data
To read instream data lines instead of an external file, use a **DATALINES statement** or a CARDS statement and enter data directly in your SAS program. Omit the RUN statement at the end of the DATA step.

Creating a Raw Data File
When the goal of your SAS program is to create a raw data file and not a SAS data set, it is inefficient to list a data set name in the DATA statement. Instead use the keyword **_NULL_**, which allows the power of the DATA step without actually creating a SAS data set. A SET statement specifies the SAS data set that you want to read from.

You can use the **FILE** and **PUT** statements to write out the observations from a SAS data set to a raw data file the same way you used the INFILE and INPUT statements to create a SAS data set. These two sets of statements work almost identically.

Points to Remember

- LIBNAME and FILENAME statements are **global**. Librefs and filerefs remain in effect until you change them, cancel them, or end your SAS session.

- For each field of raw data that you read into your SAS data set, you must specify the following in the INPUT statement: a valid SAS **variable name**, a **type** (character or numeric), a **starting column**, and if necessary, an **ending column**.

- When you use column input, you can read **any or all fields** from the raw data file, read the fields **in any order**, and **specify only the starting column for variables whose values occupy only one column**.

- Column input is appropriate only in some situations. When you use column input, your data must be **standard character and numeric values,** and these values must be in **fixed fields**. That is, values for a particular variable must be in the same location in all records.

Practice

After you complete this chapter, practice what you learned by using the sample data and SAS programs for Chapter 5, **Creating SAS Data Sets from Raw Data**, which are located on the CD-ROM. Follow the directions for creating your sample data in the Before You Begin section.

Quiz

Select the best answer for each question. After completing the quiz, check your answers using the answer key in the appendix.

1. Which SAS statement associates the fileref **Crime** with the raw data file **C:\States\Data\Crime**?

   a. `filename crime 'c:\states\data\crime';`
   b. `filename crime c:\states\data\crime;`
   c. `fileref crime 'c:\states\data\crime';`
   d. `filename 'c:\states\data\crime' crime;`

2. Filerefs remain in effect until

   a. you change them.
   b. you cancel them.
   c. you end your SAS session.
   d. all of the above

3. Which statement identifies the name of a raw data file to be read with the fileref **Products** and specifies that the DATA step read only records 1–15?

   a. `infile products obs 15;`
   b. `infile products obs=15;`
   c. `input products obs=15;`
   d. `input products 1-15;`

4. Which of the following programs correctly writes the observations from the data set below to a raw data file?

   SAS Data Set Work.Patients

ID	Sex	Age	Height	Weight	Pulse
2304	F	16	61	102	100
1128	M	43	71	218	76
4425	F	48	66	162	80
1387	F	57	64	142	70
9012	F	39	63	157	68
6312	M	52	72	240	77
5438	F	42	62	168	83
3788	M	38	73	234	71
9125	F	56	64	159	70
3438	M	15	66	140	67

a.
```
data _null_;
   set work.patients;
   infile 'c:\clinic\patients\referrals.dat';
   input id 1-4 sex 6 age 8-9 height 11-12
        weight 14-16 pulse 18-20;
run;
```

b.
```
data referrals.dat;
   set work.patients;
   input id 1-4 sex 6 age 8-9 height 11-12
        weight 14-16 pulse 18-20;
run;
```

c.
```
data _null_;
   set work.patients;
   file c:\clinic\patients\referrals.dat;
   put id 1-4 sex 6 age 8-9 height 11-12
        weight 14-16 pulse 18-20;
    run;
```

d.
```
data _null_;
   set work.patients;
   file 'c:\clinic\patients\referrals.dat';
   put id 1-4 sex 6 age 8-9 height 11-12
        weight 14-16 pulse 18-20;
run;
```

5. Which raw data file can be read using column input?

a.
```
1---+----10---+----20---+
Henderson CA 26 ADM
Josephs SC 33 SALES
Williams MN 40 HRD
Rogan NY RECRTN
```

b.
```
1---+----10---+----20---+----30
2803 Deborah Campos  173.97
2912 Bill    Marin   205.14
3015 Helen   Stinson 194.08
3122 Nicole  Terry   187.65
```

c
```
1---+----10---+----20---+
Avery John       $601.23
Davison Sherrill $723.15
Holbrook Grace   $489.76
Jansen Mike      $638.42
```

d. all of the above

6. Which program creates the output shown below?

```
1---+----10---+----20---+----30
3427 Chen     Steve Raleigh
1436 Davis    Lee   Atlanta
2812 King     Vicky Memphis
1653 Sanchez  Jack  Atlanta
```

Obs	ID	LastName	FirstName	City
1	3427	Chen	Steve	Raleigh
2	1436	Davis	Lee	Atlanta
3	2812	King	Vicky	Memphis
4	1653	Sanchez	Jack	Atlanta

a.
```
data work.salesrep;
    infile empdata;
    input ID $ 1-4 LastName $ 6-12
        FirstName $ 14-18 City $ 20-29;
run;
proc print data=work.salesrep;
run;
```

b.
```
data work.salesrep;
    infile empdata;
    input ID $ 1-4 Name $ 6-12
        FirstName $ 14-18 City $ 20-29;
run;
proc print data=work.salesrep;
run;
```

c.
```
data work.salesrep;
    infile empdata;
    input ID $ 1-4 name1 $ 6-12
        name2 $ 14-18 City $ 20-29;
run;
proc print data=work.salesrep;
run;
```

d. all of the above

7. Which statement correctly reads the fields in the following order: StockNumber, Price, Item, Finish, Style?

Field Name	Start Column	End Column	Data Type
StockNumber	1	3	character
Finish	5	9	character
Style	11	18	character
Item	20	24	character
Price	27	32	numeric

```
1---+----10---+----20---+----30---+
310 oak    pedestal table  329.99
311 maple pedestal table  369.99
312 brass floor     lamp   79.99
313 glass table     lamp   59.99
313 oak    rocking   chair  153.99
```

a. input StockNumber $ 1-3 Finish $ 5-9 Style $ 11-18
        Item $ 20-24 Price 27-32;

b. input StockNumber $ 1-3 Price 27-32
        Item $ 20-24 Finish $ 5-9 Style $ 11-18;

c. input $ StockNumber 1-3 Price 27-32
        $ Item   20-24 $ Finish 5-9 $ Style 11-18;

d. input StockNumber $ 1-3 Price $ 27-32
        Item $ 20-24 Finish $ 5-9 Style $ 11-18;

8. Which statement correctly re-defines the values of the variable Income as 100 percent higher?

a. income=income*1.00;

b. income=income+(income*2.00);

c. income=income*2;

d. income= *2;

9. Which program correctly reads instream data?

a.
```
data finance.newloan;
     input datalines;
     if country='JAPAN';
     MonthAvg=amount/12;
  1998 US       CARS     194324.12
  1998 US       TRUCKS  142290.30
  1998 CANADA CARS       10483.44
  1998 CANADA TRUCKS    93543.64
  1998 MEXICO CARS       22500.57
  1998 MEXICO TRUCKS    10098.88
  1998 JAPAN   CARS      15066.43
  1998 JAPAN   TRUCKS   40700.34
  ;
```

b.
```
data finance.newloan;
     input Year 1-4 Country $ 6-11
           Vehicle $ 13-18 Amount 20-28;
     if country='JAPAN';
     MonthAvg=amount/12;
     datalines;
run;
```

c.
```
data finance.newloan;
     input Year 1-4 Country 6-11
           Vehicle 13-18 Amount 20-28;
     if country='JAPAN';
     MonthAvg=amount/12;
     datalines;
  1998 US       CARS     194324.12
  1998 US       TRUCKS  142290.30
  1998 CANADA CARS       10483.44
  1998 CANADA TRUCKS    93543.64
  1998 MEXICO CARS       22500.57
  1998 MEXICO TRUCKS    10098.88
  1998 JAPAN   CARS      15066.43
  1998 JAPAN   TRUCKS   40700.34
  ;
```

d.
```
data finance.newloan;
     input Year 1-4 Country $ 6-11
           Vehicle $ 13-18 Amount 20-28;
     if country='JAPAN';
     MonthAvg=amount/12;
     datalines;
  1998 US       CARS     194324.12
  1998 US       TRUCKS  142290.30
  1998 CANADA CARS       10483.44
  1998 CANADA TRUCKS    93543.64
  1998 MEXICO CARS       22500.57
  1998 MEXICO TRUCKS    10098.88
  1998 JAPAN   CARS      15066.43
  1998 JAPAN   TRUCKS   40700.34
  ;
```

10. Which SAS statement subsets the raw data shown below so that only the observations in which Sex (in the second field) has a value of *F* are processed?

```
1----+----10---+----20---+--
Alfred  M 14 69.0 112.5
Becka   F 13 65.3 98.0
Gail    F 14 64.3 90.0
Jeffrey M 13 62.5 84.0
John    M 12 59.0 99.5
Karen   F 12 56.3 77.0
Mary    F 15 66.5 112.0
Philip  M 16 72.0 150.0
Sandy   F 11 51.3 50.5
Tammy   F 14 62.8 102.5
William M 15 66.5 112.0
```

a. if sex=f;

b. if sex=F;

c. if sex='F';

d. *a* or *b*

Chapter 6 Understanding DATA Step Processing

Overview

Introduction

In Chapter 5, **Creating SAS Data Sets from Raw Data**, you learned how to read data, perform basic modifications, and create a new SAS data set.

This chapter teaches you what happens "behind the scenes" when the DATA step reads raw data. You'll examine the **program data vector**, which is a logical framework that SAS uses when creating SAS data sets.

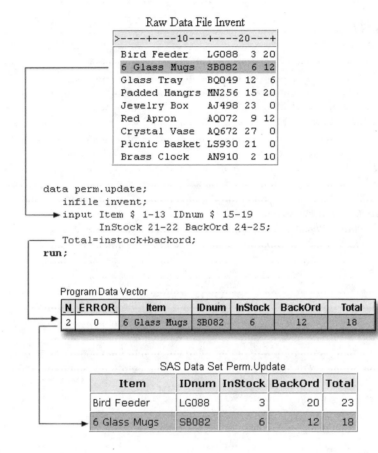

Understanding how the program operates can help you to anticipate how variables will be created and processed, to plan your modifications, and to interpret and debug program errors. It also gives you useful strategies for preventing and correcting common DATA step errors.

Objectives

In this chapter, you learn to

- identify the two phases that occur when a DATA step is processed

- interpret automatic variables

- identify the processing phase in which an error occurs

- debug SAS DATA steps

- test programs by limiting the number of observations that are created

- flag errors in the SAS log.

Writing Basic DATA Steps

In Chapter 5, **Creating SAS Data Sets from Raw Data**, you learned how to write a DATA step to create a permanent SAS data set from raw data that is stored in an external file.

Raw Data File Tests (Partial)

```
1---+----10---+----20---+----30---+----40---+-
2458 Murray, W          72     185 128 12 38 D
2462 Almers, C          68     171 133 10  5 I
2501 Bonaventure, T     78     177 139 11 13 I
2523 Johnson, R         69     162 114  9 42 S
2539 LaMance, K         75     168 141 11 46 D
2544 Jones, M           79     187 136 12 26 N
2552 Reberson, P        69     158 139 15 41 D
2555 King, E            70     167 122 13 13 I
```

```
data clinic.stress;
    infile tests obs = 8;
    input ID 1-4 Name $ 6-25 RestHR 27-29
          MaxHR 31-33 RecHR 35-37
          TimeMin 39-40 TimeSec 42-43
          Tolerance $ 45;
run;
```

You learned how to submit the DATA step and how to check the log to see whether the step ran successfully.

SAS Log

```
NOTE: The infile TESTS is:
      FILENAME=may/t1/rawdata.dat
NOTE: 8 records were read from the infile TESTS.
NOTE: The data set CLINIC.STRESS has 8
      observations and 8 variables.
NOTE: The DATA statement used 0:00:07.00 real
      0:00:07.10 cpu.
```

You also learned how to display the contents of the data set with the PRINT procedure.

```
proc print data=clinic.stress;
run;
```

Obs	ID	Name	RestHr	MaxHR	RecHR	TimeMin	TimeSec	Tolerance
1	2458	Murray, W	72	185	128	12	38	D
2	2462	Almers, C	68	171	133	10	5	I
3	2501	Bonaventure, T	78	177	139	11	13	I
4	2523	Johnson, R	69	162	114	9	42	S
5	2539	LaMance, K	75	168	141	11	46	D
6	2544	Jones, M	79	187	136	12	26	N
7	2552	Reberson, P	69	158	139	15	41	D
8	2555	King, E	70	167	122	13	13	I

How SAS Processes Programs

When you submit a DATA step, SAS processes the DATA step and then creates a new SAS data set. Let's see exactly how that happens.

A SAS DATA step is processed in two phases:

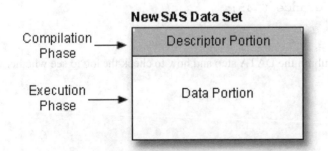

- During the **compilation phase**, each statement is scanned for syntax errors. Most syntax errors prevent further processing of the DATA step. When the compilation phase is complete, the descriptor portion of the new data set is created.

- If the DATA step compiles successfully, then the **execution phase** begins. During the execution phase, the DATA step reads and processes the input data. The DATA step executes once for each record in the input file, unless otherwise directed.

The diagram below shows the flow of DATA step processing for reading raw data. We'll examine both the compilation phase and the execution phase in this chapter.

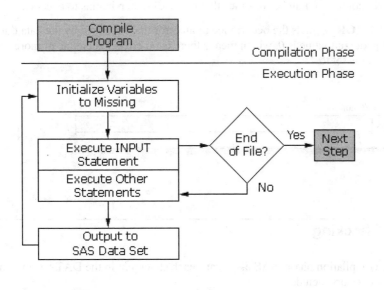

Let's start with the compilation phase.

Compilation Phase

Input Buffer

At the beginning of the compilation phase, the **input buffer** (an area of memory) is created to hold a record from the external file. The input buffer is created only when raw data is read, not when a SAS data set is read. The term **input buffer** refers to a logical concept; it is not a physical storage area.

Input Buffer

1	2	3	4	5	6	7	8	9	10	11	12	13	14	15	16	17	18	19	20	21

Program Data Vector

After the input buffer is created, the **program data vector** is created. The program data vector is the area of memory where SAS builds a data set, one observation at a time. Like the term **input buffer**, the term **program data vector** refers to a logical concept.

The program data vector contains two **automatic variables** that can be used for processing but which are not written to the data set as part of an observation.

- **_N_** counts the number of times that the DATA step begins to execute.

- **_ERROR_** signals the occurrence of an error that is caused by the data during execution. The default value is *0*, which means there is no error. When one or more errors occur, the value is set to *1*.

Program Data Vector

_N_	_ERROR_	

Syntax Checking

During the compilation phase, SAS also scans each statement in the DATA step, looking for syntax errors. Syntax errors include

- missing or misspelled keywords
- invalid variable names
- missing or invalid punctuation
- invalid options.

Data Set Variables

As the INPUT statement is compiled, a slot is added to the program data vector for each variable in the new data set. Usually, variable attributes such as length and type are determined the first time a variable is encountered.

```
data perm.update;
   infile invent;
   input Item $ 1-13 IDnum $ 15-19
         InStock 21-22 BackOrd 24-25;
   Total=instock+backord;
run;
```

Program Data Vector

N	ERROR	Item	IDnum	InStock	BackOrd	

Any variables that are created with an assignment statement in the DATA step are also added to the program data vector. For example, the assignment statement below creates the variable `Total`. As the statement is compiled, the variable is added to the program data vector. The attributes of the variable are determined by the expression in the statement. Because the expression produces a numeric value, `Total` is defined as a numeric variable and is assigned the default length of 8.

```
data perm.update;
   infile invent;
   input Item $ 1-13 IDnum $ 15-19
         InStock 21-22 BackOrd 24-25;
   Total=instock+backord;
run;
```

Program Data Vector

N	ERROR	Item	IDnum	InStock	BackOrd	Total

Descriptor Portion of the SAS Data Set

At the bottom of the DATA step (in this example, when the RUN statement is encountered), the compilation phase is complete, and the descriptor portion of the new SAS data set is created. The descriptor portion of the data set includes

- the name of the data set

- the number of observations and variables

- the names and attributes of the variables.

Data Set Descriptor

```
Data Set Name: PERM.UPDATE                 Observations:          0
Member Type:   DATA                        Variables:             5
Engine:        V9                          Indexes:               0
Created:       14:38 Thursday, June 20, 2002   Observation Length: 48
Last Modified: 14:38 Thursday, June 20, 2002   Deleted Observations: 0
Protection:                                Compressed:            NO
Data Set Type:                             Sorted:                NO
Label:


             -----Engine/Host Dependent Information-----

Data Set Page Size:          4096
Number of Data Set Pages:    1
First Data Page:             1
Max Obs per Page:            84
Obs in First Data Page:      0
Number of Data Set Repairs:  0
File Name:                   C:\WINNT\My SAS Files\V8\update.sas7bdat
Release Created:             9.0000M0
Host Created:                WIN_NT


           -----Alphabetic List of Variables and Attributes-----
           # Variable         Type      Len     Pos
           ----------------------------------------
           4 BackOrd          Num        8       8
           2 IDnum            Char       5      37
           3 InStock          Num        8       0
           1 Item             Char      13      24
           5 Total            Num        8      16
```

At this point, the data set contains the five variables that are defined in the input data set and in the assignment statement. Remember, _N_ and _ERROR_ are not written to the data set. There are no observations because the DATA step has not yet executed. During execution, each raw data record is processed and is then written to the data set as an observation.

 For additional information about assigning attributes to variables, see the SAS documentation for your operating environment.

Summary of the Compilation Phase

Let's review the compilation phase.

```
data perm.update;
   infile invent;
   input Item $ 1-13 IDnum $ 15-19
         InStock 21-22 BackOrd 24-25;
   Total=instock+backord;
run;
```

During the compilation phase, the input buffer is created to hold a record from the external file.

Input Buffer

1	2	3	4	5	6	7	8	9	10	11	12	13	14	15	16	17	18	19	20	21

The program data vector is created to hold the current observation.

Program Data Vector

N	ERROR	Item	IDnum	InStock	BackOrd	Total

The descriptor portion of the SAS data set is created.

Data Set Descriptor (Partial)

```
Data Set Name:       PERM.UPDATE
Member Type:         DATA
Engine:              V9
Created:             11:25 Friday, June 21, 2002
Observations:        0
Variables:           5
Indexes:             0
Observation Length:  30
```

Execution Phase

After the DATA step is compiled, it is ready for execution. During the execution phase, the data portion of the data set is created. The data portion contains the data values.

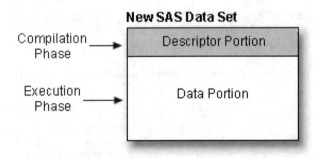

During execution, each record in the input raw data file is read, stored in the program data vector, and then written to the new data set as an observation. The DATA step executes once for each record in the input file, unless otherwise directed by additional statements.

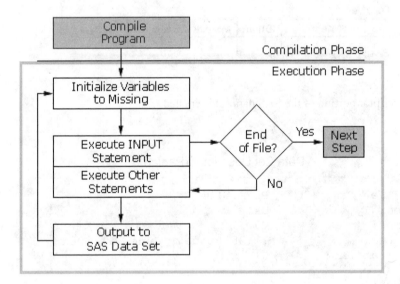

Example

The following DATA step reads values from the file **Invent** and executes nine times because there are nine records in the file.

Raw Data File Invent

```
1---+----10---+----20---+-
Bird Feeder    LG088  3 20
6 Glass Mugs   SB082  6 12
Glass Tray     BQ049 12  6
Padded Hangrs  MN256 15 20
Jewelry Box    AJ498 23  0
Red Apron      AQ072  9 12
Crystal Vase   AQ672 27  0
Picnic Basket  LS930 21  0
Brass Clock    AN910  2 10
```

```
data perm.update;
    infile invent;
    input Item $ 1-13 IDnum $ 15-19
            InStock 21-22 BackOrd 24-25;
    Total=instock+backord;
run;
```

Initializing Variables

At the beginning of the execution phase, the value of _N_ is *1*. Because there are no data errors, the value of _ERROR_ is *0*.

```
data perm.update;
    infile invent;
    input Item $ 1-13 IDnum $ 15-19
          InStock 21-22 BackOrd 24-25;
    Total=instock+backord;
run;
```

Program Data Vector

_N_	_ERROR_	Item	IDnum	InStock	BackOrd	Total
1	0			.	.	.

Initialized to Missing

The remaining variables are initialized to missing. Missing numeric values are represented by periods, and missing character values are represented by blanks.

Input Data

Next, the INFILE statement identifies the location of the raw data.

```
data perm.update;
    infile invent;
    input Item $ 1-13 IDnum $ 15-19
          InStock 21-22 BackOrd 24-25;
    Total=instock+backord;
run;
```

Input Pointer

When an INPUT statement begins to read data values from a record that is held in the input buffer, it uses an input pointer to keep track of its position (the input pointer is represented by an arrow in the examples in this book).

The input pointer starts at column 1 of the first record, unless otherwise directed. As the INPUT statement executes, the raw data in columns 1–13 is read and is assigned to Item in the program data vector.

```
data perm.update;
    infile invent;
    input Item $ 1-13 IDnum $ 15-19
          InStock 21-22 BackOrd 24-25;
    Total=instock+backord;
run;
```

Raw Data File Invent

```
↓---+----10---+----20---+-
Bird Feeder   LG088   3 20
6 Glass Mugs  SB082   6 12
Glass Tray    BQ049  12  6
Padded Hangrs MN256  15 20
Jewelry Box   AJ498  23  0
Red Apron     AQ072   9 12
Crystal Vase  AQ672  27  0
Picnic Basket LS930  21  0
Brass Clock   AN910   2 10
```

Program Data Vector

N	ERROR	Item	IDnum	InStock	BackOrd	Total
1	0	Bird Feeder		.	.	.

Notice that the input pointer now rests on column 14. With column input, the pointer moves as far as the INPUT statement instructs it, and it stops in the column immediately following the last one read.

Raw Data File Invent

```
1---+----10--↓+----20---+
Bird Feeder    LG088   3 20
6 Glass Mugs   SB082   6 12
Glass Tray     BQ049  12  6
Padded Hangrs  MN256  15 20
Jewelry Box    AJ498  23  0
Red Apron      AQ072   9 12
Crystal Vase   AQ672  27  0
Picnic Basket  LS930  21  0
Brass Clock    AN910   2 10
```

Next, the data in columns 15–19 is read and is assigned to IDnum in the program data vector, as shown below. Likewise, the INPUT statement reads the values for InStock from columns 21–22, and it reads the values for BackOrd from columns 24–25. At the end of the INPUT statement processing, the input pointer is in column 26.

```
data perm.update;
   infile invent;
   input Item $ 1-13 IDnum $ 15-19
         InStock 21-22 BackOrd 24-25;
   Total=instock+backord;
run;
```

Raw Data File Invent

```
1---+----10---+----20---+↓
Bird Feeder    LG088   3 20
6 Glass Mugs   SB082   6 12
Glass Tray     BQ049  12  6
Padded Hangrs  MN256  15 20
Jewelry Box    AJ498  23  0
Red Apron      AQ072   9 12
Crystal Vase   AQ672  27  0
Picnic Basket  LS930  21  0
Brass Clock    AN910   2 10
```

Program Data Vector

N	ERROR	Item	IDnum	InStock	BackOrd	Total
1	0	Bird Feeder	LG088	3	20	.

Next, the assignment statement executes. The values for `InStock` and `BackOrd` are added to produce the values for `Total`.

```
data perm.update;
    infile invent;
    input Item $ 1-13 IDnum $ 15-19
          InStock 21-22 BackOrd 24-25;
    Total=instock+backord;
run;
```

Program Data Vector

N	ERROR	Item	IDnum	InStock	BackOrd	Total
1	0	Bird Feeder	LG088	3	20	23

End of the DATA Step

At the end of the DATA step, several actions occur. First, the values in the program data vector are written to the output data set as the first observation.

```
data perm.update;
    infile invent;
    input Item $ 1-13 IDnum $ 15-19
          InStock 21-22 BackOrd 24-25;
    Total=instock+backord;
run;
```

SAS Data Set Perm.Update

Item	IDnum	InStock	BackOrd	Total
Bird Feeder	LG088	3	20	23

Next, the value of _N_ is set to 2 and control returns to the top of the DATA step. Finally, the variable values in the program data vector are re-set to missing. Notice that the automatic variable _ERROR_ retains its value.

```
data perm.update;
    infile invent;
    input Item $ 1-13 IDnum $ 15-19
                InStock 21-22 BackOrd 24-25;
    Total=instock+backord;
run;
```

Raw Data File Invent

```
↓---+----10---+----20---+-
Bird Feeder    LG088  3 20
6 Glass Mugs   SB082  6 12
Glass Tray     BQ049 12  6
Padded Hangrs  MN256 15 20
Jewelry Box    AJ498 23  0
Red Apron      AQ072  9 12
Crystal Vase   AQ672 27  0
Picnic Basket  LS930 21  0
Brass Clock    AN910  2 10
```

Finally, the variable values in the program data vector are re-set to missing. Notice that the automatic variables _N_ and _ERROR_ retain their values.

Program Data Vector

_N_	_ERROR_	Item	IDnum	InStock	BackOrd	Total
2	0			•	•	•

└─────────────── Set to Missing ───────────────┘

When reading variables from **raw data**, SAS sets the value of each variable in the DATA step to missing at the beginning of each cycle of execution, with these exceptions:

- variables that are named in a RETAIN statement

- variables that are created in a SUM statement

- data elements in a _TEMPORARY_ array

- any variables that are created with options in the FILE or INFILE statements

- automatic variables.

In contrast, when reading variables from a **SAS data set**, SAS sets the values to missing only before the first cycle of execution of the DATA step. Thereafter, the variables retain their values until new values become available—for example, through an assignment statement or through the next execution of a SET or MERGE statement. Variables that are created with options in the SET or MERGE statements also retain their values from one cycle of execution to the next. (You will learn about reading SAS data sets and about arrays, the SET statement, and the MERGE statement in later chapters.)

Iterations of the DATA Step

You can see that the DATA step works like a loop, repetitively executing statements to read data values and create observations one by one. Each loop (or cycle of execution) is called an **iteration**. At the beginning of the second iteration, the value of _N_ is set to *2,* and _ERROR_ is still *0*. Notice that the input pointer rests in column 1 of the second record.

```
data perm.update;
    infile invent;
    input Item $ 1-13 IDnum $ 15-19
          InStock 21-22 BackOrd 24-25;
    Total=instock+backord;
run;
```

Raw Data File Invent

```
↓---+----10---+----20---+-
Bird Feeder    LG088  3 20
6 Glass Mugs   SB082  6 12
Glass Tray     BQ049 12  6
Padded Hangrs  MN256 15 20
Jewelry Box    AJ498 23  0
Red Apron      AQ072  9 12
Crystal Vase   AQ672 27  0
Picnic Basket  LS930 21  0
Brass Clock    AN910  2 10
```

Program Data Vector

N	ERROR	Item	IDnum	InStock	BackOrd	Total
2	0			.	.	.

As the INPUT statement executes for the second time, the values from the second record are held in the input buffer and then read into the program data vector.

```
data perm.update;
    infile invent;
    input Item $ 1-13 IDnum $ 15-19
          InStock 21-22 BackOrd 24-25;
    Total=instock+backord;
run;
```

Raw Data File Invent

```
1---+----10---+----20---+↓
Bird Feeder    LG088  3 20
6 Glass Mugs   SB082  6 12
Glass Tray     BQ049 12  6
Padded Hangrs  MN256 15 20
Jewelry Box    AJ498 23  0
Red Apron      AQ072  9 12
Crystal Vase   AQ672 27  0
Picnic Basket  LS930 21  0
Brass Clock    AN910  2 10
```

Program Data Vector

N_	ERROR_	Item	IDnum	InStock	BackOrd	Total
2	0	6 Glass Mugs	SB082	6	12	

Next, the value for `Total` is calculated based on the current values for `InStock` and `BackOrd`. The RUN statement indicates the end of the DATA step.

Program Data Vector

N_	ERROR_	Item	IDnum	InStock	BackOrd	Total
2	0	6 Glass Mugs	SB082	6	12	18

$$\text{└} + \text{└} = \text{↑}$$

At the bottom of the DATA step, the values in the program data vector are written to the data set as the second observation.

SAS Data Set Perm.Update

Item	IDnum	InStock	BackOrd	Total
Bird Feeder	LG088	3	20	23
6 Glass Mugs	SB082	6	12	18

Next, the value of _N_ is set to 3, control returns to the top of the DATA step, and the values for Item, `IDnum`, `InStock`, `BackOrd`, and `Total` are re-set to missing.

Raw Data File Invent

```
↓---+----10---+----20---+-
Bird Feeder    LG088   3 20
6 Glass Mugs   SB082   6 12
Glass Tray     BQ049  12  6
Padded Hangrs  MN256  15 20
Jewelry Box    AJ498  23  0
Red Apron      AQ072   9 12
Crystal Vase   AQ672  27  0
Picnic Basket  LS930  21  0
Brass Clock    AN910   2 10
```

Program Data Vector

N	ERROR_	Item	IDnum	InStock	BackOrd	Total
3	0			•	•	•

Reset to Missing

End-of-File Marker

The execution phase continues in this manner until the end-of-file marker is reached in the raw data file. When there are no more records in the raw data file to be read, the data portion of the new data set is complete.

Raw Data File Invent

```
1---+----10---+----20---+-
Bird Feeder    LG088   3 20
6 Glass Mugs   SB082   6 12
Glass Tray     BQ049  12  6
Padded Hangrs  MN256  15 20
Jewelry Box    AJ498  23  0
Red Apron      AQ072   9 12
Crystal Vase   AQ672  27  0
Picnic Basket  LS930  21  0
Brass Clock    AN910   2 10
```

SAS Data Set Perm.Update

Item	IDnum	InStock	BackOrd	Total
Bird Feeder	LG088	3	20	23
6 Glass Mugs	SB082	6	12	18
Glass Tray	BQ049	12	6	18
Padded Hangrs	MN256	15	20	35
Jewelry Box	AJ498	23	0	23
Red Apron	AQ072	9	12	21
Crystal Vase	AQ672	27	0	27
Picnic Basket	LS930	21	0	21
Brass Clock	AN910	2	10	12

Remember, the order in which variables are defined in the DATA step determines the order in which the variables are stored in the data set. The DATA step below, which reverses the order of `Item` and `IDnum`, produces a different data set from the same raw data.

```
data perm.update;
   infile invent;
   input IDnum $ 15-19 Item $ 1-13      ← reversed
         InStock 21-22 BackOrd 24-25;
   Total=instock+backord;
run;
```

SAS Data Set Perm.Update

IDnum	Item	InStock	BackOrd	Total
LG088	Bird Feeder	3	20	23
SB082	6 Glass Mugs	6	12	18
BQ049	Glass Tray	12	6	18
MN256	Padded Hangrs	15	20	35
AJ498	Jewelry Box	23	0	23
AQ072	Red Apron	9	12	21
AQ672	Crystal Vase	27	0	27
LS930	Picnic Basket	21	0	21
AN910	Brass Clock	2	10	12

--reversed--

Summary of the Execution Phase

You've seen how the DATA step iteratively reads records in the raw data file. Now take a minute to review execution-phase processing.

During the execution phase

- variables in the program data vector are initialized to missing before each execution of the DATA step

- each statement is executed sequentially

- the INPUT statement reads the next record from the external file identified by the INFILE statement, and it writes the values into the program data vector

- other statements can then further modify the current observation

- the values in the program data vector are written to the SAS data set at the end of the DATA step

- program flow is returned to the top of the DATA step

- the DATA step is executed until the end-of-file marker is reached in the external file.

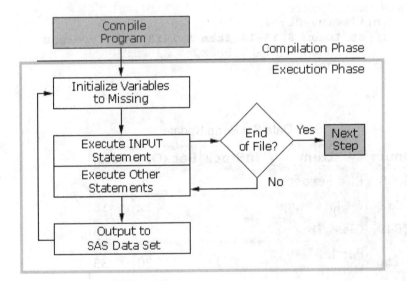

End of the Execution Phase

At the end of the execution phase, the SAS log confirms that the raw data file was read, and it displays the number of observations and variables in the data set.

SAS Log (Partial)

```
NOTE: 9 records were read from the infile INVENT.
NOTE: The data set PERM.UPDATE has 9 observations
      and 5 variables.
```

You already know how to display the data set with the PRINT procedure.

```
proc print data=perm.update;
run;
```

Obs	Item	IDnum	InStock	BackOrd	Total
1	Bird Feeder	LG088	3	20	23
2	6 Glass Mugs	SB082	6	12	18
3	Glass Tray	BQ049	12	6	18
4	Padded Hangrs	MN256	15	20	35
5	Jewelry Box	AJ498	23	0	23
6	Red Apron	AQ072	9	12	21
7	Crystal Vase	AQ672	27	0	27
8	Picnic Basket	LS930	21	0	21
9	Brass Clock	AN910	2	10	12

Debugging a DATA Step

Diagnosing Errors in the Compilation Phase

Now that you know how a DATA step is processed, you can use that knowledge to correct errors. Many errors are detected during the compilation phase, including

- misspelled keywords and data set names
- missing semicolons
- unbalanced quotation marks
- invalid options.

During the compilation phase, SAS can interpret some syntax errors (such as the keyword DATA misspelled as DAAT). If it cannot interpret the error, SAS

- prints the word ERROR followed by an error message in the log

- compiles but does **not** execute the step where the error occurred, and prints the following message to warn you:

  ```
  NOTE: The SAS System stopped processing this step because of
        errors.
  ```

Some errors are explained fully by the message that SAS prints; other error messages are not as easy to interpret. For example, because SAS statements are in free format, when you fail to end a SAS statement with a semicolon, SAS does not always detect the error at the point where it occurs.

Diagnosing Errors in the Execution Phase

As you have seen, errors can occur in the compilation phase, resulting in a DATA step that is compiled but not executed. Errors can also occur during the execution phase. When SAS detects an error in the execution phase, the following can occur, depending on the type of error:

- A note, warning, or error message is displayed in the log.

- The values that are stored in the program data vector are displayed in the log.

- The processing of the step either continues or stops.

Example

Suppose you misspelled the fileref in the INFILE statement below. This is not a syntax error, because SAS does not validate the file that you reference until the execution phase. During the compilation phase, the fileref **Invnt** is assumed to reference some external raw data file.

```
data perm.update;
    infile invnt;
    input Item $ 1-13 IDnum $ 15-19
          InStock 21-22 BackOrd 24-25;
    Total=instock+backord;
run;
```

This error is not detected until the execution phase begins. Because there is no external file that is referenced by the fileref **Invnt**, the DATA step stops processing.

SAS Log

```
07   data perm.update;
08      infile invnt;
09      input Item $ 1-13 IDnum $ 15-19
10            InStock 21-22 BackOrd 24-25;
11      Total=instock+backord;
12   run;


ERROR: No logical assign for filename INVNT.
NOTE: The SAS System stopped processing this step
      because of errors.
WARNING: The data set PERM.UPDATE may be incomplete.
         When this step was stopped there were
         0 observations and 5 variables.
```

Because **Invent** is misspelled as Invnt, the statement in the DATA step that identifies the raw data is incorrect. Note, however, that the correct number of variables was defined in the descriptor portion of the data set.

Incorrectly identifying a variable's type is another common execution-time error. As you know, the values for IDnum are character values. Suppose you forget to place the dollar sign ($) after the variable's name in your INPUT statement. This is not a compile-time error, because SAS cannot verify IDnum's type until the data values for IDnum are read.

```
data perm.update;
   infile invent;
   input Item $ 1-13 IDnum 15-19
         InStock 21-22 BackOrd 24-25;
   Total=instock+backord;
run;
```

Raw Data File Invent

```
1---+----10---+----20---+-
Bird Feeder    LG088  3 20
6 Glass Mugs   SB082  6 12
Glass Tray     BQ049 12  6
Padded Hangrs  MN256 15 20
Jewelry Box    AJ498 23  0
Red Apron      AQ072  9 12
Crystal Vase   AQ672 27  0
Picnic Basket  LS930 21  0
```

In this case, the DATA step completes the execution phase, and the observations are written to the data set. However, several notes appear in the log.

SAS Log

```
NOTE: Invalid data for IDnum in line 7 15-19.
RULE: ----+----1----+----2----+----3----+----4--
07     Crystal Vase  AQ672 27 0
Item=Crystal Vase IDnum=. InStock=27 BackOrd=0
Total=27 _ERROR_=1 _N_=7
NOTE: Invalid data for IDnum in line 8 15-19.
08     Picnic Basket LS930 21 0
Item=Picnic Basket IDnum=. InStock=21 BackOrd=0
Total=21 _ERROR_=1 _N_=8
NOTE: Invalid data for IDnum in line 9 15-19.
09     Brass Clock   AN910 2 10
Item=Brass Clock IDnum=. InStock=2 BackOrd=10
Total=12 _ERROR_=1 _N_=9

NOTE: 9 records were read from the infile INVENT.
NOTE: The data set PERM.UPDATE has 9 observations
      and 5 variables.
```

Each note identifies the location of the invalid data for each observation. In this example, the invalid data is located in columns 15–19 for all observations.

The second line in each note (excluding the Rule line) displays the raw data record. Notice that the second field displays the values for IDnum, which are obviously character values.

SAS Log

```
NOTE: Invalid data for IDnum in line 7 15-19.
RULE: ----+----1----+----2----+----3----+----4--
07     Crystal Vase  AQ672 27 0
Item=Crystal Vase IDnum=. InStock=27 BackOrd=0
Total=27 _ERROR_=1 _N_=7
NOTE: Invalid data for IDnum in line 8 15-19.
08     Picnic Basket LS930 21 0
Item=Picnic Basket IDnum=. InStock=21 BackOrd=0
Total=21 _ERROR_=1 _N_=8
NOTE: Invalid data for IDnum in line 9 15-19.
09     Brass Clock   AN910 2 10
Item=Brass Clock IDnum=. InStock=2 BackOrd=10
Total=12 _ERROR_=1 _N_=9

NOTE: 9 records were read from the infile INVENT.
NOTE: The data set PERM.UPDATE has 9 observations
      and 5 variables.
```

The third and fourth lines display the values that are stored in the program data vector. Here, the values for IDnum are missing, although the other values have been correctly assigned to their respective variables. Notice that _ERROR_ has a value of *1*, indicating that an error has occurred.

SAS Log

```
NOTE: Invalid data for IDnum in line 7 15-19.
RULE: ----+----1----+----2----+----3----+----4--
07    Crystal Vase  AQ672 27 0
Item=Crystal Vase IDnum=. InStock=27 BackOrd=0
Total=27 _ERROR_=1 _N_=7
NOTE: Invalid data for IDnum in line 8 15-19.
08    Picnic Basket LS930 21 0
Item=Picnic Basket IDnum=. InStock=21 BackOrd=0
Total=21 _ERROR_=1 _N_=8
NOTE: Invalid data for IDnum in line 9 15-19.
09    Brass Clock   AN910 2 10
Item=Brass Clock IDnum=. InStock=2 BackOrd=10
Total=12 _ERROR_=1 _N_=9

NOTE: 9 records were read from the infile INVENT.
NOTE: The data set PERM.UPDATE has 9 observations
      and 5 variables.
```

The PRINT procedure displays the data set, showing that the values for IDnum are missing. In this example, the periods indicate that IDnum is a numeric variable, although it should be defined as a character variable.

```
proc print data=perm.update;
run;
```

Obs	Item	IDnum	InStock	BackOrd	Total
1	Bird Feeder	.	3	20	23
2	6 Glass Mugs	.	6	12	18
3	Glass Tray	.	12	6	18
4	Padded Hangrs	.	15	20	35
5	Jewelry Box	.	23	0	23
6	Red Apron	.	9	12	21
7	Crystal Vase	.	27	0	27
8	Picnic Basket	.	21	0	21
9	Brass Clock	.	2	10	12

When you read raw data with the DATA step, it's important to check the SAS log to verify that your data was read correctly. Here is a typical message.

SAS Log

```
WARNING: The data set PERM.UPDATE may be incomplete.
         When this step was stopped there were
         0 observations and 5 variables.
```

When no observations are written to the data set, you should check to see whether your DATA step was completely executed. Most likely, a syntax error or another error is being detected at the beginning of the execution phase.

An **invalid data** message indicates that the program executed, but the data is not acceptable. Typically, the message indicates that a variable's type has been incorrectly identified in the INPUT statement, or that the raw data file contains some invalid data value(s).

SAS Log

```
NOTE: Invalid data for IDnum in line 7 15-19.
```

Testing Your Programs

Writing a NULL Data Set

After you write or edit a DATA step, you can compile and execute your program without creating a data set. This enables you to detect the most common errors and saves you development time. A simple way to test a DATA step is to specify the keyword **_NULL_** as the data set name in the DATA statement.

```
data _null_;
   infile invent;
   input Item $ 1-13 IDnum $ 15-19
         InStock 21-22 BackOrd 24-25;
   Total=instock+backord;
run;
```

When you submit the DATA step, no data set is created, but any compilation or execution errors are written to the log after the values of the variables are read and verified. After correcting any errors, you can replace _NULL_ with the name of the data set that you want to create.

Limiting Observations

Remember that you can use the **OBS= option** in the INFILE statement to limit the number of observations that are read or created during the execution of the DATA step.

```
data perm.update;
   infile invent obs=10;
   input Item $ 1-13 IDnum $ 15-19
         InStock 21-22 BackOrd 24-25;
   Total=instock+backord;
run;
```

When processed, this DATA step creates the **Perm.Update** data set with variables but with only 10 observations.

PUT Statement

When the source of program errors is not apparent, you can use the **PUT statement** to examine variable values and to print your own message in the log. For diagnostic purposes, you can use IF-THEN/ELSE statements to conditionally check for values. You can learn about IF-THEN/ELSE statements in detail in Chapter 11, **Creating and Managing Variables**.

```
data work.test;
   infile loan;
   input Code $ 1 Amount 3-10 Rate 12-16
       Account $ 18-25 Months 27-28;
   if code='1' then type='variable';
   else if code='2' then type='fixed';
   else put 'MY NOTE: invalid value:'
       code=;
run;
```

In this example, if CODE does not have the expected values of *1* or *2*, the PUT statement writes a message to the log:

SAS Log

```
MY NOTE: invalid value: Code=V
NOTE: The data set WORK.TEST has 9 observations
      and 6 variables.
```

General form, simple PUT statement:

> **PUT** *specification(s)*;

where each *specification* specifies what is written, how it is written, and where it is written. This can include

- a character string

- one or more data set variables

- the automatic variables _N_ and _ERROR_

- the automatic variable _ALL_

and much more. The following pages show examples of PUT specifications.

Character Strings

You can use a PUT statement to specify a character string to identify your message in the log. The character string must be enclosed in quotation marks.

```
put 'MY NOTE: The condition was met.';
```

SAS Log

```
MY NOTE: The condition was met.
NOTE: The data set WORK.TEST has 9 observations
      and 6 variables.
```

Data Set Variables

You can use a PUT statement to specify one or more data set variables to be examined for that iteration of the DATA step.

```
put 'MY NOTE: invalid value: '
     code type;
```

SAS Log

```
MY NOTE: invalid value: V FIXED
NOTE: The data set WORK.TEST has 9 observations
      and 6 variables.
```

When you specify a variable in the PUT statement, only the value of the variable is written to the log. To write both the variable name and its value in the log, add an equal sign (=) to the variable name.

```
put 'MY NOTE: invalid value: '
     code= type=;
```

SAS Log

```
MY NOTE: invalid value: Code=V type=FIXED
NOTE: The data set WORK.TEST has 9 observations
      and 6 variables.
```

Automatic Variables

You can use a PUT statement to display the values of the automatic variables _N_ and _ERROR_. In some cases, knowing the value of _N_ can help you locate an observation in the data set.

```
put 'MY NOTE: invalid value: '
    code= _n_= _error_=;
```

SAS Log

```
MY NOTE: invalid value: Code=V N=4 ERROR=0
NOTE: The data set WORK.TEST has 9 observations
      and 6 variables.
```

You can also use a PUT statement to write all variable names and variable values, including automatic variables, to the log. Use the _ALL_ specification.

```
put 'MY NOTE: invalid value: ' _all_ ;
```

SAS Log

```
MY NOTE: invalid value: Account=101-3144
         Amount=$3,500 Rate=10.50% Months=1
         Code=V type=C ERROR=0 N=4
NOTE: The data set WORK.TEST has 9 observations
      and 6 variables.
```

Conditional Processing

You can use a PUT statement with conditional processing (that is, with IF-THEN/ELSE statements) to flag program errors or data that is out of range. In the example below, the PUT statement is used to flag any missing or zero values for the variable Rate.

```
data finance.newcalc;
    infile newloans;
    input LoanID $ 1-4 Rate 5-8 Amount 9-19;
    if rate>0 then
        Interest=amount*(rate/12);
    else put 'DATA ERROR ' rate= _n_=;
run;
```

The PUT statement can accomplish a wide variety of tasks. This chapter shows a few ways to use the PUT statement to help you debug a program or examine variable values. For a complete description of the PUT statement, see the SAS documentation for your operating environment.

Summary

Text Summary

How SAS Processes Programs

A SAS DATA step is processed in two distinct phases. During the **compilation phase**, each statement is scanned for syntax errors. During the **execution phase**, the DATA step writes observations to the new data set.

Compilation Phase

At the beginning of the compilation phase, the input buffer and the **program data vector** are created. The program data vector is the area of memory where data sets are built, one observation at a time. Two automatic variables are also created: _N_ counts the number of DATA step executions, and _ERROR_ signals the occurrence of an error. DATA step statements are checked for syntax errors, such as invalid options or misspellings.

Execution Phase

During the execution phase, each record in the input file is processed, stored in the program data vector, and then written to the new data set as an observation. The DATA step executes once for each record in the input file, unless otherwise directed.

Diagnosing Errors in the Compilation Phase

Missing semicolons, misspelled keywords, and invalid options cause syntax errors in the compilation phase. Detected errors are underlined and are identified with a number and message in the log. If SAS can interpret a syntax error, then the DATA step compiles and executes; if SAS cannot interpret the error, then the DATA step compiles but doesn't execute.

Diagnosing Errors in the Execution Phase

Illegal mathematical operations or processing a character variable as numeric causes errors in the execution phase. Depending on the type of error, the log might show a warning and might include invalid data from the program data vector, and the DATA step either stops or continues.

Testing Your Programs

To detect common errors and save development time, compile and execute your program without creating observations. Specify the keyword **_NULL_** as the data set name to view compilation or execution errors without creating a data set. Or use the **OBS= option** in the INFILE statement to limit the number of observations that are read or created during the DATA step. You can also use the **PUT statement** to examine variable values and to generate your own message in the log.

Points to Remember

- Making, diagnosing, and resolving errors is part of the process of writing programs. However, checking for common errors will save you time and trouble. Ensure that

    o   each SAS statement ends with a semicolon

    o   filenames are spelled correctly

    o   keywords are spelled correctly.

- In SAS output, missing numeric values are represented by periods, and missing character values are left blank.

- The order in which variables are defined in the DATA step determines the order in which the variables are stored in the data set.

- Standard character values can include numbers, but numeric values cannot include characters.

Practice

After you complete this chapter, practice what you learned by using the sample data and SAS programs for Chapter 6, **Understanding DATA Step Processing**, which are located on the CD-ROM. Follow the directions for creating your sample data in the Before You Begin section.

Quiz

Select the best answer for each question. After completing the quiz, check your answers using the answer key in the appendix.

1. Which of the following is **not** created during the compilation phase?

    a. the data set descriptor
    b. the first observation
    c. the program data vector
    d. the _N_ and _ERROR_ automatic variables

2. During the compilation phase, SAS scans each statement in the DATA step, looking for syntax errors. Which of the following is **not** considered a syntax error?

    a. incorrect values and formats
    b. invalid options or variable names
    c. missing or invalid punctuation
    d. missing or misspelled keywords

3. Unless otherwise directed, the DATA step executes

    a. once for each compilation phase.
    b. once for each DATA step statement.
    c. once for each record in the input file.
    d. once for each variable in the input file.

4. At the beginning of the execution phase, the value of _N_ is *1*, the value of _ERROR_ is *0*, and the values of the remaining variables are set to

    a. *0*
    b. *1*
    c. undefined
    d. missing

5. Suppose you run a program that causes three DATA step errors. What is the value of the automatic variable _ERROR_ when the observation that contains the third error is processed?

    a. *0*
    b. *1*
    c. *2*
    d. *3*

6. Which of the following actions occurs at the end of the DATA step?

    a. The automatic variables _N_ and _ERROR_ are incremented by one.

    b. The DATA step stops execution.

    c. The descriptor portion of the data set is written.

    d. The values of variables created in programming statements are re-set to missing in the program data vector.

7. Look carefully at the DATA step shown below. Based on the INPUT statement, in what order will the variables be stored in the new data set?

    ```
    data perm.update;
      infile invent;
      input IDnum $ 15-19 Item $ 1-13 Instock 21-22
            BackOrd 24-25;
      Total=instock+backord;
     run;
    ```

    a. IDnum Item InStock BackOrd Total

    b. Item IDnum InStock BackOrd Total

    c. Total IDnum Item InStock BackOrd

    d. Total Item IDnum InStock BackOrd

8. If SAS cannot interpret syntax errors, then

    a. data set variables will contain missing values.

    b. the DATA step does not compile.

    c. the DATA step still compiles, but it does not execute.

    d. the DATA step still compiles and executes.

9. What is wrong with this program?

    ```
    data perm.update;
      infile invent
      input Item $ 1-13 IDnum $ 15-19 Instock 21-22
            BackOrd 24-25;
      total=instock+backord;
     run;
    ```

    a. missing semicolon on second line

    b. missing semicolon on third line

    c. incorrect order of variables

    d. incorrect variable type

10. Look carefully at this section of a SAS session log. Based on the note, what was the most likely problem with the DATA step?

```
NOTE: Invalid data for IDnum in line 7 15-19.
RULE: ----+----1----+----2----+----3----+----4
7        Bird Feeder LG088 3 20
Item=Bird Feeder IDnum=. InStock=3 BackOrd=20
Total=23 _ERROR_=1 _N_=1
```

    a. A keyword was misspelled in the DATA step.

    b. A semicolon was missing from the INFILE statement.

    c. A variable was misspelled in the INPUT statement.

    d. A dollar sign was missing in the INPUT statement.

Chapter **7** Creating and Applying User-Defined Formats

Overview

Introduction

In Chapter 4, **Creating List Reports**, you learned to associate formats with variables either temporarily or permanently.

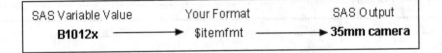

But sometimes you might want to create custom formats for displaying variable values. For example, you can format a product number so that it is displayed as descriptive text, as shown below.

SAS Variable Value	Your Format	SAS Output
B1012x	$itemfmt	35mm camera

Using the FORMAT procedure, you can define your own formats for variables. You can store your formats temporarily or permanently, and you can display a list of all your formats and descriptions of their values.

Objectives

In this chapter, you learn to

- create your own formats for displaying variable values
- permanently store the formats that you create
- associate your formats with variables.

Introduction to PROC FORMAT

Sometimes variable values are stored according to a code. For example, when the PRINT procedure displays the data set **Perm.Empinfo**, notice that the values for JobTitle are coded, and they are not easily interpreted.

Obs	FirstName	LastName	JobTitle	Salary
1	Donny	Evans	112	29996.63
2	Lisa	Helms	105	18567.23
3	John	Higgins	111	25309.00
4	Amy	Larson	113	32696.78
5	Mary	Moore	112	28945.89
6	Jason	Powell	103	35099.50
7	Judy	Riley	111	25309.00
8	Neal	Ryan	112	28180.00

You can display more descriptive values for these variables. Here is how a report that contains formatted values for the variable `JobTitle` might look. The predefined SAS formats cannot help here.

Obs	FirstName	LastName	JobTitle	Salary
1	Donny	Evans	technical writer	29996.63
2	Lisa	Helms	text processor	18567.23
3	John	Higgins	assoc. technical writer	25309.00
4	Amy	Larson	senior technical writer	32696.78
5	Mary	Moore	technical writer	28945.89
6	Jason	Powell	manager	35099.50
7	Judy	Riley	assoc. technical writer	25309.00
8	Neal	Ryan	technical writer	28180.00

However, you can use the **FORMAT** procedure to define your own formats for displaying values of variables.

Invoking PROC FORMAT

To begin a PROC FORMAT step, you use a PROC FORMAT statement.

General form, PROC FORMAT statement:

> **PROC FORMAT** *<options>*;

where *options* includes

- **LIBRARY=***libref* specifies the libref for a SAS data library that contains a permanent catalog in which user-defined formats are stored

- **FMTLIB** prints the contents of a format catalog.

Any time you use PROC FORMAT to create a format, the format is stored in a format catalog. If the SAS data library does not already contain a format catalog, SAS automatically creates one. If you do not specify the LIBRARY= option, then the formats are stored in a default format catalog named **Work.Formats**.

As the libref **Work** implies, any format that is stored in **Work.Formats** is a temporary format that exists only for the current SAS session. At the end of the current session, the catalog is erased.

Permanently Storing Your Formats

You can store your formats in a **permanent format catalog named Formats** when you specify the LIBRARY= option in the PROC FORMAT statement.

```
PROC FORMAT LIBRARY=libref;
```

But first, you need a LIBNAME statement that associates the libref with the permanent SAS data library in which the format catalog is to be stored. It is recommended, but not required, that you use the word **Library** as the libref when creating your own permanent formats.

```
libname library 'c:\sas\formats\lib';
libname library 'c:\data\setup\library';
libname library 'c:\sales\ancillary\libset';
```

When you associate a permanent format with a variable in a subsequent DATA or PROC step, you use the **Library** libref to reference the location of the format catalog.

We'll discuss the use of permanent user-defined formats later, after you learn how to create them.

Now, any format that you create in this PROC FORMAT step is stored in a permanent format catalog called **Library.Formats**.

```
libname library 'c:\sas\formats\lib';
proc format library=library;
   ... ;
run;
```

In the program above, the catalog **Library.Formats** is located in the SAS data library **C:\Sas\Formats\Lib**, which is referenced by the libref **Library**.

You can use LIB= as an abbreviation for the LIBRARY= option.

```
proc format lib=library;
```

You can specify a catalog name in the LIBRARY= option, and you can store formats in any catalog. The catalog name must conform to SAS naming conventions.

```
proc format lib=library.catalog;
```

Now that you know how to store your own formats, let's learn how to create them.

Defining a Unique Format

You can use the VALUE statement to define a format for displaying one or more values.

General form, VALUE statement:

> **VALUE** *format-name*
> *range1=*'*label1*'
> *range2=*'*label2*'
> ... ;

where

- *format-name* names the format that you are creating. The format name

    o must begin with a dollar sign ($) if the format applies to character data

    o cannot be longer than eight characters

    o cannot be the name of an existing SAS format

    o cannot end with a number

    o does not end in a period when specified in a VALUE statement.

- *range* specifies one or more variable values and a character string or an existing format

- *label* is a text string enclosed in quotation marks.

Notice that the statement begins with the keyword VALUE and ends with a semicolon after all the labels have been defined. The following VALUE statement creates the JOBFMT format to specify descriptive labels that will later be assigned to the variable `JobTitle`:

```
proc format lib=library;
    value jobfmt
            103='manager'
            105='text processor'
            111='assoc. technical writer'
            112='technical writer'
            113='senior technical writer';
run;
```

The VALUE range specifies

- a **single value**, such as *24* or *'S'*

- a **range of numeric values**, such as *0–1500*

- a **range of character values** enclosed in quotation marks, such as 'A'–'M'.

- a **list of unique values** separated by commas, such as *90,180,270* or *'B','D','F'*. These values can be character values or numeric values, but not a combination of character and numeric values (because formats themselves are either character or numeric).

When the specified values are **character values**, they must be enclosed in quotation marks and must match the case of the variable's values. The format's name must also start with a dollar sign ($). For example, the VALUE statement below defines the $GRADE format, which displays the character values as text labels.

```
proc format lib=library;
   value $grade
           'A'='Good'
           'B'-'D'='Fair'
           'F'='Poor'
           'I','U'='See Instructor';
run;
```

When the specified values are **numeric values**, they are not enclosed in quotation marks, and the format's name should not begin with a dollar sign ($). The VALUE statement that defines the format JOBFMT assigns labels to numeric values.

```
proc format lib=library;
   value jobfmt
           103='manager'
           105='text processor'
           111='assoc. technical writer'
           112='technical writer'
           113='senior technical writer';
run;
```

Specifying Value Ranges

You can specify a non-inclusive range of numeric values by using the "less than" symbol (<) to avoid any overlapping. In this example, the range of values from 0 to less than 13 is labeled as **child**. The next range begins at 13, so the label **teenager** would be assigned to the values 13 to 19.

```
proc format lib=library;
   value agefmt
           0-<13='child'
           13-<20='teenager'
           20-<65='adult'
           65-100='senior citizen';
run;
```

You can also use the keywords **LOW** and **HIGH** to specify the lower and upper limits of a variable's value range. The keyword LOW does not include missing numeric values. The keyword **OTHER** can be used to label missing values as well as any values that are not specifically addressed in a range.

```
proc format lib=library;
   value agefmt
           low-<13='child'
           13-<20='teenager'
           20-<65='adult'
           65-high='senior citizen'
           other='unknown';
run;
```

If applied to a character format, the keyword LOW includes missing character values.

When specifying a label for displaying each range, remember to

- enclose the label in quotation marks

- limit the label to 256 characters

- use double quotation marks if you want an apostrophe to appear in the label, as in this example:

  ```
  000="employee's jobtitle unknown";
  ```

Defining Multiple Formats

To define several formats, you can use multiple VALUE statements in a single PROC FORMAT step. In this example, each VALUE statement defines a different format.

```
proc format lib=library;
    value jobfmt
            103='manager'
            105='text processor'
            111='assoc. technical writer'
            112='technical writer'
            113='senior technical writer';
    value $respnse
            'Y'='Yes'
            'N'='No'
            'U'='Undecided'
            'NOP'='No opinion';
run;
```

The SAS log prints notes informing you that the formats have been created.

SAS Log (Partial Listing)

```
01   proc format lib=library;
02      value jobfmt
03              103='manager'
04              105='text processor'
05              111='assoc. technical writer'
06              112='technical writer'
07              113='senior technical writer';
     NOTE: Format JOBFMT has been written to LIBRARY.FORMATS.
```

Because you have defined the JOBFMT format for displaying the values of `JobTitle`, the format can be used with PROC PRINT for more legible output.

(Without Format)

FirstName	LastName	JobTitle	Salary
Donny	Evans	112	29996.63
Lisa	Helms	105	18567.23
John	Higgins	111	25309.00
Amy	Larson	113	32696.78
Mary	Moore	112	28945.89
Jason	Powell	103	35099.50

(With Format)

FirstName	LastName	JobTitle	Salary
Donny	Evans	technical writer	29996.63
Lisa	Helms	text processor	18567.23
John	Higgins	assoc. technical writer	25309.00
Amy	Larson	senior technical writer	32696.78
Mary	Moore	technical writer	28945.89
Jason	Powell	manager	35099.50

The next section shows how to apply your formats to variables.

Associating User-Defined Formats with Variables

Referencing Your Formats

Remember that permanent, user-defined formats are stored in a format catalog. For example, the program below stores the format JOBFMT in a catalog named **Library.Formats**, which is located in the directory **C:\Sas\Formats\Lib** in the Windows environment.

```
libname library 'c:\sas\formats\lib';
proc format lib=library;
    value jobfmt
           103='manager'
           105='text processor'
           111='assoc. technical writer'
           112='technical writer'
           113='senior technical writer';
run;
```

To use the JOBFMT format in a subsequent SAS session, you must assign the libref **Library** again.

```
libname library 'c:\sas\formats\lib';
data ... ;
```

SAS searches for the format JOBFMT in two libraries, in this order:

- the temporary library referenced by the libref **Work**
- a permanent library referenced by the libref **Library**.

SAS uses the first instance of a specified format that it finds.

> You can delete formats by using PROC CATALOG or the SAS Explorer window.

Assigning Your Formats to Variables

Just as with SAS formats, you associate a user-defined format with a variable in a **FORMAT statement**.

```
data perm.empinfo;
   infile empdata;
   input @9 FirstName $5. @1 LastName $7. +7 JobTitle 3.
         @19 Salary comma9.;
   format salary comma9.2 jobtitle jobfmt.;
run;
```

> Don't worry about @ pointer controls in programs in this chapter (as in @9
> FirstName), because they don't affect the behavior of formats. To learn more about
> using @ pointer controls in SAS programs, see Chapter 17, **Reading Raw Data in Fixed
> Fields**.

Remember, you can place the FORMAT statement in either a DATA step or a PROC step. By placing the FORMAT statement in a DATA step, you can permanently associate a format with a variable. Note that you do not have to specify a width value when using a user-defined format.

When you submit the PRINT procedure, the output for **Perm.Empinfo** now shows commas in the values for Salary, and it shows descriptive labels in place of the values for JobTitle.

```
proc print data=perm.empinfo;
run;
```

Obs	FirstName	LastName	JobTitle	Salary
1	Donny	Evans	technical writer	29,996.63
2	Lisa	Helms	text processor	18,567.23
3	John	Higgins	assoc. technical writer	25,309.00
4	Amy	Larson	senior technical writer	32,696.78
5	Mary	Moore	technical writer	28,945.89
6	Jason	Powell	manager	35,099.50
7	Judy	Riley	assoc. technical writer	25,309.00
8	Neal	Ryan	technical writer	28,180.00

When associating a format with a variable, remember to

- use the **same format name** in the FORMAT statement that you specified in the VALUE statement

- place a **period** at the end of the format name when it is used in the FORMAT statement.

```
libname library 'c:\sas\formats\lib';
proc format lib=library;
    value jobfmt
            103='manager'
            105='text processor'
            111='assoc. technical writer'
            112='technical writer'
            113='senior technical writer';
run;
libname perm 'c:\data\perm';
filename empdata 'c:\data\temp\newhires.txt';
data perm.empinfo;
    infile empdata;
    input @9 FirstName $5. @1 LastName $7. +7 JobTitle 3.
            @19 Salary comma9.;
    format salary comma9.2 jobtitle jobfmt.;
run;
```

Notice that a period is **not** required at the end of the SAS format COMMA9.2 in the FORMAT statement. The period in this format occurs between the width specification and the decimal place specification. All formats contain periods, but only user-defined formats invariably require periods at the end of the name.

If you do not format all of a variable's values, then those values that are not listed in the VALUE statement are printed as they appear in the SAS data set, as shown in the following example:

```
proc format lib=library;
    value jobfmt
            103='manager'
            105='text processor';
            112='technical writer';
run;
proc print data=perm.empinfo;
run;
```

Obs	FirstName	LastName	JobTitle	Salary
1	Donny	Evans	112	29996.63
2	Lisa	Helms	text processor	18567.23
3	John	Higgins	111	25309.00
4	Amy	Larson	113	32696.78
5	Mary	Moore	112	28945.89
6	Jason	Powell	manager	35099.50
7	Judy	Riley	111	25309.00
8	Neal	Ryan	technical writer	28180.00

Displaying a List of Your Formats

When you build a large catalog of permanent formats, it can be easy to forget the exact spelling of a specific format name or its range of values. Adding the keyword **FMTLIB** to the PROC FORMAT statement displays a list of all the formats in your catalog, along with descriptions of their values.

```
libname library 'c:\sas\formats\lib';
proc format library=library fmtlib;
run;
```

When you submit this PROC step, a description of each format in your permanent catalog is displayed as output.

SAS Output

Format Name: JobFmt Length: 23 Number of Values: 5 Min Length: 1 Max Length: 40 Default Length: 23 Fuzz: Std		
START	END	LABEL (VER. 9.00 29AUG2002:11:13:14)
103	103	manager
105	105	text processor
111	111	assoc. technical writer
112	112	technical writer
113	113	senior technical writer

In addition to the name, range, and label, the format description includes the

- length of the longest label
- number of values defined by this format
- version of SAS that this format is compatible with
- date and time of creation.

Summary

Text Summary

Invoking PROC FORMAT

The **FORMAT** procedure enables you to substitute descriptive text values for the values of variables. The **LIBRARY=** option stores the new formats in a specified format catalog. Otherwise, they are stored in a default catalog named **Work.Formats**. The keyword **FMTLIB** displays the formats and values that are currently stored in the catalog. The **VALUE** statement defines a new format for the values of a variable.

Defining a Unique Format

Formats can be specified for a single value, a range of numeric values, or a list of unique values. Unique values must be separated by commas. When character values are specified, the values must be enclosed in quotation marks, and the format name must begin with a dollar sign ($). You can specify non-inclusive numeric ranges by using the "less than" sign (<). The keywords HIGH, LOW, and OTHER can be used to label values that are not specifically addressed in a range.

Associating User-Defined Formats with Variables

To access the permanent, user-defined formats in a **format catalog**, you'll need to use a LIBNAME statement to reference the catalog library. To associate user-defined formats with variables in the FORMAT statement, use the same format names in both the FORMAT and VALUE statements, but place a period at the end of the format name when it is used in the FORMAT statement.

Points to Remember

- Formats—even permanently associated ones—do not affect the values of variables in a SAS data set. Only the appearance of the values is changed.

- A user-defined format name must begin with a dollar sign ($) when it is assigned to character variables. A user-defined format name cannot end with a number.

- Use two double quotation marks when you want an apostrophe to appear in a label.

- Place a period at the end of the format name when you use the format name in the FORMAT statement.

Practice

After you complete this chapter, practice what you learned by using the sample data and SAS programs for Chapter 7, **Creating and Applying User-Defined Formats**, which are located on the CD-ROM. Follow the directions for creating your sample data in the Before You Begin section.

Quiz

Select the best answer for each question. After completing the quiz, check your answers using the answer key in the appendix.

1. If you don't specify the LIBRARY= option, your formats are stored in **Work.Formats**, and they exist

   a. only for the current procedure.
   b. only for the current DATA step.
   c. only for the current SAS session.
   d. permanently.

2. Which of the following statements will store your formats in a permanent catalog?

   a. ```
      libname library 'c:\sas\formats\lib';
      proc format lib=library
         ...;
      ```
   b. ```
      libname library 'c:\sas\formats\lib';
      format lib=library
         ...;
      ```
   c. ```
      library='c:\sas\formats\lib';
      proc format library
         ...;
      ```
   d. ```
      library='c:\sas\formats\lib';
      proc library
         ...;
      ```

3. When creating a format with the VALUE statement, the new format's name
   o cannot end with a number
   o cannot end with a period
   o cannot be the name of a SAS format, and

   a. cannot be the name of a data set variable.
   b. must be at least two characters long.
   c. must be at least eight characters long.
   d. must begin with a dollar sign ($) if used with a character variable.

4. Which of the following FORMAT procedures is written correctly?

```
a.  proc format lib=library
        value colorfmt;
              1='Red'
              2='Green'
              3='Blue'
    run;
b.  proc format lib=library;
        value colorfmt
              1='Red'
              2='Green'
              3='Blue';
    run;
c.  proc format lib=library;
        value colorfmt;
              1='Red'
              2='Green'
              3='Blue'
    run;
d.  proc format lib=library;
        value colorfmt
              1='Red';
              2='Green';
              3='Blue';
    run;
```

5. Which of these is **false**? Ranges in the VALUE statement can specify

   a. a single value, such as *24* or *'S'*.
   b. a range of numeric values, such as *0–1500*.
   c. a range of character values, such as *'A'–'M'*.
   d. a list of numeric and character values separated by commas, such as *90,'B',180,'D',270*.

6. How many characters can be used in a label?

   a. 40
   b. 96
   c. 200
   d. 256

7. Which keyword can be used to label missing values as well as any values that are not specified in a range?

   a. LOW
   b. MISS
   c. MISSING
   d. OTHER

8. You can place the FORMAT statement in either a DATA step or a PROC step. What happens when you place the FORMAT statement in a DATA step?

   a. You temporarily associate the formats with variables.
   b. You permanently associate the formats with variables.
   c. You replace the original data with the format labels.
   d. You make the formats available to other data sets.

9. The format JOBFMT was created in a FORMAT procedure. Which FORMAT statement will apply it to the variable `JobTitle` in the program output?

   a. `format jobtitle jobfmt;`
   b. `format jobtitle jobfmt.;`
   c. `format jobtitle=jobfmt;`
   d. `format jobtitle='jobfmt';`

10. Which keyword, when added to the PROC FORMAT statement, will display all the formats in your catalog?

   a. CATALOG
   b. LISTFMT
   c. FMTCAT
   d. FMTLIB

Chapter **8** Creating Enhanced List and Summary Reports

Overview

Introduction

List and summary reports are often created from SAS data. To produce a variety of reports using a single report-writing tool, you can use **PROC REPORT**. In addition to creating list reports, PROC REPORT enables you to

- create custom reports
- request separate subtotals and grand totals
- calculate columns
- create and store report definitions.

You can use PROC REPORT in three ways:

- in a windowing mode with a prompting facility that guides you as you build a report
- in a windowing mode without the prompting facility
- in a nonwindowing mode. In this case, you submit a series of statements with the PROC REPORT statement, just as you do in other SAS procedures.

 In SAS Enterprise Guide, you work with PROC REPORT in a nonwindowing mode. You can access PROC REPORT in a windowing mode through the SAS programming interface.

This chapter shows you how to use PROC REPORT by submitting SAS statements. Although PROC REPORT enables you to create highly customized reports, we'll focus on basic statements and will add a few enhancements. By the end of the chapter, you'll create a list report and a summary report.

PROC REPORT List Report

Flight Number	Flight Origin	Flight Destination	Mail / Pounds	Freight / Pounds	Revenue
821	LGA	LON	403	209	$150,634.00
821	LGA	LON	345	243	$150,634.00
821	LGA	LON	248	307	$193,930.00
821	LGA	LON	391	395	$167,772.00
821	LGA	LON	219	368	$183,106.00
821	LGA	LON	389	479	$169,576.00
821	LGA	LON	448	282	$143,561.00
821	LGA	LON	403	209	$170,766.00
821	LGA	LON	345	243	$129,560.00
821	LGA	LON	248	307	$196,736.00
821	LGA	LON	391	395	$125,344.00

Flight Number	Flight Origin	Flight Destination	Mail / Pounds	Freight / Pounds	Revenue
821	LGA	LON	219	368	$166,543.00
821	LGA	LON	389	479	$129,745.00

PROC REPORT Summary Report

Flight Number	Flight Origin	Flight Destination	Mail / Pounds	Freight / Pounds	Total Revenue
821	LGA	LON	4,438	4,284	$2,077,907.00
271	LGA	PAR	5,050	4,421	$1,969,201.00
219	LGA	LON	2,700	2,513	$1,111,647.00

Objectives

In this chapter, you learn to

- invoke the REPORT procedure and specify a windowing or nonwindowing environment
- select columns for your report
- define the usage for columns
- specify attributes, options, and justification for columns
- specify features of column headings, including split characters, underlining, and blank lines.

Creating a Default List Report

Let's start by creating a list report. Suppose you want to create a listing of mail, freight, and passenger revenue for flights between LaGuardia Airport and London or Paris.

As with other SAS procedures, you first reference the library in which your data is stored, and then you submit a basic PROC REPORT step.

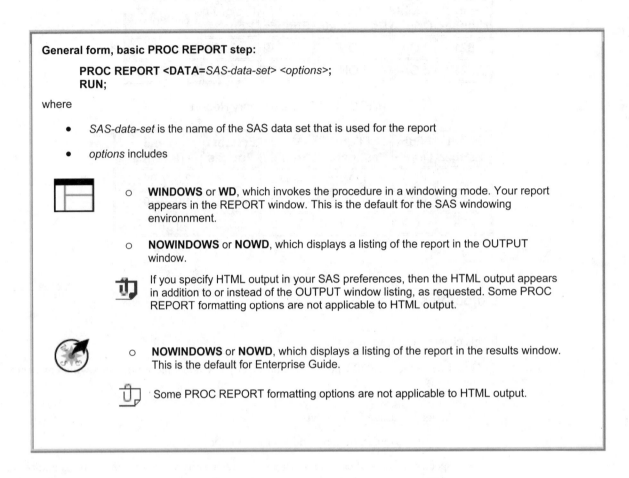

General form, basic PROC REPORT step:

> **PROC REPORT <DATA=***SAS-data-set***> <***options***>;**
> **RUN;**

where

- *SAS-data-set* is the name of the SAS data set that is used for the report

- *options* includes

   - **WINDOWS** or **WD**, which invokes the procedure in a windowing mode. Your report appears in the REPORT window. This is the default for the SAS windowing environnment.

   - **NOWINDOWS** or **NOWD**, which displays a listing of the report in the OUTPUT window.

   If you specify HTML output in your SAS preferences, then the HTML output appears in addition to or instead of the OUTPUT window listing, as requested. Some PROC REPORT formatting options are not applicable to HTML output.

   - **NOWINDOWS** or **NOWD**, which displays a listing of the report in the results window. This is the default for Enterprise Guide.

   Some PROC REPORT formatting options are not applicable to HTML output.

Example

In this program, PROC REPORT reads the **Flights.Europe** data set and creates a report in a nonwindowing mode.

```
proc report data=flights.europe nowd;
run;
```

This is HTML output from the PROC REPORT step. Notice that by default

- all observations and variables in the data set are printed

- variables appear in the order in which they occur in the data set.

Flight	Date	Depart	Orig	Dest	Miles	Mail	Freight	Boarded	Transferred	NonRevenue	Deplaned	Capacity	DayOfMonth	Revenue
821	04MAR99	9:31	LGA	LON	3442	403	209	167	17	7	222	250	1	150634
271	04MAR99	11:40	LGA	PAR	3856	492	308	146	8	3	163	250	1	156804
271	05MAR99	12:19	LGA	PAR	3857	366	498	177	15	5	227	250	1	190098
821	06MAR99	14:56	LGA	LON	3442	345	243	167	13	4	222	250	1	150634
821	07MAR99	13:17	LGA	LON	3635	248	307	215	14	6	158	250	1	193930
271	07MAR99	9:31	LGA	PAR	3442	353	205	155	18	7	172	250	2	166470
821	08MAR99	11:40	LGA	LON	3856	391	395	186	8	1	114	250	2	167772
271	08MAR99	12:19	LGA	PAR	3857	366	279	152	7	4	187	250	2	163248
821	09MAR99	14:56	LGA	LON	3442	219	368	203	6	3	210	250	2	183106
271	09MAR99	13:17	LGA	PAR	3635	357	282	159	15	4	191	250	2	170766
821	10MAR99	9:31	LGA	LON	3442	389	479	188	8	6	211	250	3	169576
271	10MAR99	11:40	LGA	PAR	3856	415	463	182	9	6	153	250	3	195468
622	03MAR99	12:19	LGA	FRA	3857	296	414	180	16	4	200	250	3	187636
821	03MAR99	14:56	LGA	LON	3442	448	282	151	17	4	172	250	3	143561
271	03MAR99	13:17	LGA	PAR	3635	352	351	147	29	7	183	250	3	123456
219	04MAR99	9:31	LGA	LON	3442	331	376	232	18	0	250	250	4	189065
387	04MAR99	11:40	LGA	CPH	3856	395	217	81	21	1	103	250	4	196540
622	04MAR99	12:19	LGA	FRA	3857	296	232	137	14	4	155	250	4	165456
821	04MAR99	14:56	LGA	LON	3442	403	209	167	9	6	182	250	4	170766
271	04MAR99	13:17	LGA	PAR	3635	492	308	146	13	4	163	250	4	125632
219	05MAR99	9:31	LGA	LON	3442	485	267	160	4	3	167	250	5	197456
387	05MAR99	11:40	LGA	CPH	3856	393	304	142	8	2	152	250	5	134561
622	05MAR99	12:19	LGA	FRA	3857	340	311	185	11	3	199	250	5	125436
271	05MAR99	13:17	LGA	PAR	3635	366	498	177	22	4	203	250	5	128972
219	06MAR99	9:31	LGA	LON	3442	388	298	163	14	6	183	250	6	162343
821	06MAR99	14:56	LGA	LON	3442	345	243	167	16	2	185	250	6	129560
219	07MAR99	9:31	LGA	LON	3442	421	356	241	9	0	250	250	7	134520
387	07MAR99	11:40	LGA	CPH	3856	546	204	131	5	6	142	250	7	135632
622	07MAR99	12:19	LGA	FRA	3857	391	423	210	22	5	237	250	7	107865
821	07MAR99	14:56	LGA	LON	3442	248	307	215	11	5	231	250	7	196736
271	07MAR99	13:17	LGA	PAR	3635	353	205	155	21	4	180	250	7	153423
219	08MAR99	9:31	LGA	LON	3442	447	299	183	11	3	197	250	8	106753
387	08MAR99	11:40	LGA	CPH	3856	415	367	150	9	3	162	250	8	128564
622	08MAR99	12:19	LGA	FRA	3857	346		176	5	6	187	250	8	178543
821	08MAR99	14:56	LGA	LON	3442	391	395	186	11	5	202	250	8	125344
271	08MAR99	13:17	LGA	PAR	3635	366	279	152	20	4	176	250	8	133345
219	09MAR99	9:31	LGA	LON	3442	356	547	211	18	6	235	250	9	122766
387	09MAR99	11:40	LGA	CPH	3856	363	297	128	14	3	145	250	9	134523
622	09MAR99	12:19	LGA	FRA	3857	317	421	173	11	5	189	250	9	100987
821	09MAR99	14:56	LGA	LON	3442	219	368	203	11	4	218	250	9	166543
271	09MAR99	13:17	LGA	PAR	3635	357	282	159	18	5	182	250	9	126543
219	10MAR99	9:31	LGA	LON	3442	272	370	167	7	7	181	250	10	198744
387	10MAR99	11:40	LGA	CPH	3856	336	377	154	18	5	177	250	10	109885
622	10MAR99	12:19	LGA	FRA	3857	272	363	129	12	6	147	250	10	134459
821	10MAR99	14:56	LGA	LON	3442	389	479	188	5	4	197	250	10	129745
271	10MAR99	13:17	LGA	PAR	3635	415	463	182	9	7	198	250	10	134976

Selecting Variables

Now let's see how you can choose the data that you want to display.

To select and order the variables that appear in your list report, you can use the COLUMN statement.

General form, COLUMN statement:

    COLUMN *variable(s)*;

where *variable(s)* is one or more variable names, separated by blanks.

Example

The following COLUMN statement specifies that only the variables Flight, Orig, Dest, Mail, Freight, and Revenue be printed, in that order.

```
proc report data=flights.europe nowd;
   column flight orig dest mail freight revenue;
run;
```

Flight	Orig	Dest	Mail	Freight	Revenue
821	LGA	LON	403	209	150634
271	LGA	PAR	492	308	156804
271	LGA	PAR	366	498	190098
821	LGA	LON	345	243	150634
821	LGA	LON	248	307	193930
271	LGA	PAR	353	205	166470
821	LGA	LON	391	395	167772
271	LGA	PAR	366	279	163248
821	LGA	LON	219	368	183106
271	LGA	PAR	357	282	170766
821	LGA	LON	389	479	169576
271	LGA	PAR	415	463	195468
622	LGA	FRA	296	414	187636
821	LGA	LON	448	282	143561
271	LGA	PAR	352	351	123456
219	LGA	LON	331	376	189065
387	LGA	CPH	395	217	196540
622	LGA	FRA	296	232	165456
821	LGA	LON	403	209	170766

Flight	Orig	Dest	Mail	Freight	Revenue
271	LGA	PAR	492	308	125632
219	LGA	LON	485	267	197456
387	LGA	CPH	393	304	134561
622	LGA	FRA	340	311	125436
271	LGA	PAR	366	498	128972
219	LGA	LON	388	298	162343
821	LGA	LON	345	243	129560
219	LGA	LON	421	356	134520
387	LGA	CPH	546	204	135632
622	LGA	FRA	391	423	107865
821	LGA	LON	248	307	196736
271	LGA	PAR	353	205	153423
219	LGA	LON	447	299	106753
387	LGA	CPH	415	367	128564
622	LGA	FRA	346	.	178543
821	LGA	LON	391	395	125344
271	LGA	PAR	366	279	133345
219	LGA	LON	356	547	122766
387	LGA	CPH	363	297	134523
622	LGA	FRA	317	421	100987
821	LGA	LON	219	368	166543
271	LGA	PAR	357	282	126543
219	LGA	LON	272	370	198744
387	LGA	CPH	336	377	109885
622	LGA	FRA	272	363	134459
821	LGA	LON	389	479	129745
271	LGA	PAR	415	463	134976

Selecting Observations

You might also want to select rows for your report based on a condition. To select observations, you can use the **WHERE statement**, just as you have learned to do with PROC PRINT.

Example

The following WHERE statement specifies that only observations that have the value *LON* or *PAR* for the variable Dest be printed.

```
proc report data=flights.europe nowd;
   column flight orig dest mail freight revenue;
   where dest in ('LON','PAR');
run;
```

Flight	Orig	Dest	Mail	Freight	Revenue
821	LGA	LON	403	209	150634
271	LGA	PAR	492	308	156804
271	LGA	PAR	366	498	190098
821	LGA	LON	345	243	150634
821	LGA	LON	248	307	193930
271	LGA	PAR	353	205	166470
821	LGA	LON	391	395	167772
271	LGA	PAR	366	279	163248
821	LGA	LON	219	368	183106
271	LGA	PAR	357	282	170766
821	LGA	LON	389	479	169576
271	LGA	PAR	415	463	195468
821	LGA	LON	448	282	143561
271	LGA	PAR	352	351	123456
219	LGA	LON	331	376	189065
821	LGA	LON	403	209	170766
271	LGA	PAR	492	308	125632
219	LGA	LON	485	267	197456
271	LGA	PAR	366	498	128972
219	LGA	LON	388	298	162343
821	LGA	LON	345	243	129560
219	LGA	LON	421	356	134520
821	LGA	LON	248	307	196736
271	LGA	PAR	353	205	153423
219	LGA	LON	447	299	106753

Flight	Orig	Dest	Mail	Freight	Revenue
821	LGA	LON	391	395	125344
271	LGA	PAR	366	279	133345
219	LGA	LON	356	547	122766
821	LGA	LON	219	368	166543
271	LGA	PAR	357	282	126543
219	LGA	LON	272	370	198744
821	LGA	LON	389	479	129745
271	LGA	PAR	415	463	134976

Defining Variables

Overview of Defining Variables

In the output that you've seen in this chapter so far, you might have noticed that PROC REPORT displays

- each data value the way it is stored in the data set
- variable names as column headings in the report
- a default width for the report columns
- left-justified character values
- right-justified numeric values
- observations in the order in which they are stored in the data set.

Partial PROC REPORT Output

Flight	Orig	Dest	Mail	Freight	Revenue
821	LGA	LON	403	209	150634
271	LGA	PAR	492	308	156804

You can enhance the report by

- defining how each variable is used in the report
- assigning formats to variables
- specifying column headings and widths
- justifying the variable values and column headings within the report columns
- changing the order of the rows in the report.

Using DEFINE Statements

To describe how to use and display variables in your report, you use one or more **DEFINE statements**. You can list DEFINE statements in any order, and you can list options (usages, attributes, and so on) in any order in a DEFINE statement.

General form, simple DEFINE statement:

> **DEFINE** *variable / <usage> <attribute(s)> <option(s)>*
> *<justification> <'column-heading'>* ;

where

- *variable* is the name of the variable that you want to define.

- *usage* specifies how to use the variable. Valid options are ACROSS, ANALYSIS, COMPUTED, DISPLAY, GROUP, and ORDER.

- *attribute(s)* specifies attributes for the variable, including FORMAT=, WIDTH=, and SPACING=.

- *option(s)* specifies formatting options, including DESCENDING, NOPRINT, NOZERO, and PAGE.

- *<justification>* specifies column justification (CENTER, LEFT, or RIGHT).

- *'column-heading'* specifies a label for the column heading.

Example

These DEFINE statements specify attributes, usages, options, justification, and column headings for the variables `Flight` and `Orig`.

```
proc report data=flights.europe nowd;
    where dest in ('LON','PAR');
    column flight orig dest mail freight revenue;
    define flight / order descending 'Flight Number'
           center width=6 spacing=5;
    define orig / 'Flight Origin' center width=6;
run;
```

In this chapter, you'll look at each of these ways of defining variables.

Defining Column Attributes

You can easily change the appearance of your PROC REPORT output by specifying attributes for variables. For example, you can select a format for data values, specify the column width, and specify the spacing between columns.

To enhance your PROC REPORT output, you'll use the following attributes.

Attribute	Action
FORMAT=*format*	Assigns a SAS format or a user-defined format to the item.
SPACING=*horizontal-positions*	Specifies how many blank characters to leave between the selected column and the column immediately to its left. The default is 2.
WIDTH=*column-width*	Specifies the width of the column. The default column width is just large enough to handle the specified format.

Assigning Formats

In previous chapters, you learned that **formats** determine how data values appear in SAS output. If you do not specify a format for a variable within the PROC REPORT step, PROC REPORT uses the format that is stored in the data set. If no format is stored in the data set, PROC REPORT uses the default format for that variable type.

To assign a format to a specific report column, use the **FORMAT= attribute** in the DEFINE statement for that column. You can specify any appropriate SAS format or user-defined format.

Example

The variable Revenue has no format assigned to it in the **Flights.Europe** data set. So in your current report, revenue values appear as shown in the example below.

Partial PROC REPORT Output, HTML

Flight	Orig	Dest	Mail	Freight	Revenue
821	LGA	LON	403	209	150634
271	LGA	PAR	492	308	156804
271	LGA	PAR	366	498	190098
821	LGA	LON	345	243	150634
821	LGA	LON	248	307	193930

But suppose you want your revenue figures to be formatted with a dollar sign, commas, and two decimal places, in a total width of 15 positions. To do this, you can assign the DOLLAR15.2 format to Revenue.

```
proc report data=flights.europe nowd;
    where dest in ('LON','PAR');
    column flight orig dest mail freight revenue;
    define revenue / format=dollar15.2;
run;
```

Here is part of the HTML output from the previous program.

Partial PROC REPORT Output, HTML

Flight	Orig	Dest	Mail	Freight	Revenue
821	LGA	LON	403	209	$150,634.00
271	LGA	PAR	492	308	$156,804.00
271	LGA	PAR	366	498	$190,098.00
821	LGA	LON	345	243	$150,634.00
821	LGA	LON	248	307	$193,930.00

Notice that the format supplies the dollar sign, comma, decimal point, and decimal places. However, because the HTML table column conforms to the width of its contents, assigning the format does not increase the column width beyond the length of the data values.

By contrast, the monospace SAS listing of the report does display the increased column width.

Partial PROC REPORT Output, SAS Listing

```
Fli   Ori   Des
ght   g     t              Mail    Freight         Revenue
821   LGA   LON            403        209     $150,634.00
271   LGA   PAR            492        308     $156,804.00
271   LGA   PAR            366        498     $190,098.00
821   LGA   LON            345        243     $150,634.00
821   LGA   LON            248        307     $193,930.00
```

You can also use FORMAT statements with PROC REPORT. However, the DEFINE statement enables you to specify more than one column attribute at a time. Also, you can use the FORMAT= attribute to define report columns (such as statistics or computed variables) that are not data set variables.

Specifying Column Widths

In the previous example of SAS listing output, you might have noticed that several headings were wrapped over two lines. (In HTML output, the longest cell value determines the column width, so wrapping doesn't occur.)

If a variable in the input data set doesn't have a format associated with it, then the default PROC REPORT column width is

- **the variable's length** for character variables
- **9** for numeric variables.

The character variables `Flight`, `Orig`, and `Dest` each have a length of 3, and no format is associated with them. So 3 is their default column width.

Partial PROC REPORT Output, SAS Listing

```
Fli  Ori  Des
ght  g    t           Mail   Freight        Revenue
821  LGA  LON          403        209   $150,634.00
271  LGA  PAR          492        308   $156,804.00
271  LGA  PAR          366        498   $190,098.00
821  LGA  LON          345        243   $150,634.00
821  LGA  LON          248        307   $193,930.00
```

To specify a width for columns in your report, use the **WIDTH= attribute** in the DEFINE statement. You can specify values from 1 to the value of the LINESIZE= system option.

The WIDTH= attribute has no effect on HTML output.

Example

To specify column widths that accommodate the column headings for `Flight`, `Orig`, and `Dest`, you can use the following DEFINE statements in your PROC REPORT step:

```
proc report data=flights.europe nowd;
   where dest in ('LON','PAR');
   column flight orig dest mail freight revenue;
   define revenue / format=dollar15.2;
   define flight / width=6;
   define orig / width=4;
   define dest / width=4;
run;
```

Now the headings appear on one line.

Partial PROC REPORT Output, SAS Listing

```
Flight  Orig  Dest       Mail   Freight        Revenue
821     LGA   LON         403        209   $150,634.00
271     LGA   PAR         492        308   $156,804.00
271     LGA   PAR         366        498   $190,098.00
821     LGA   LON         345        243   $150,634.00
821     LGA   LON         248        307   $193,930.00
```

Specifying Column Spacing

Another way to enhance your PROC REPORT output is to specify **column spacing**, which is the number of blank characters between the selected column and the column immediately to its left. The default column spacing is 2. To specify a different column spacing, use the **SPACING= attribute** in the DEFINE statement.

The SPACING= attribute has no effect on HTML output.

Example

In the following PROC REPORT output, no spacing has been specified. Orig and Dest have two blank characters preceding their columns.

Partial PROC REPORT Output, SAS Listing

```
Flight  Orig  Dest       Mail  Freight         Revenue
821     LGA   LON        403      209      $150,634.00
271     LGA   PAR        492      308      $156,804.00
271     LGA   PAR        366      498      $190,098.00
821     LGA   LON        345      243      $150,634.00
821     LGA   LON        248      307      $193,930.00
```

To specify five blank spaces before the column headings for Orig and Dest, you can use DEFINE statements as shown below in your PROC REPORT step:

```
proc report data=flights.europe nowd;
    where dest in ('LON','PAR');
    column flight orig dest mail freight revenue;
    define revenue / format=dollar15.2;
    define flight / width=6;
    define orig / width=4 spacing=5;
    define dest / width=4 spacing=5;
run;
```

Now the two columns display the extra spacing.

Partial PROC REPORT Output, SAS Listing

```
Flight     Orig     Dest      Mail  Freight         Revenue
821        LGA      LON        403      209      $150,634.00
271        LGA      PAR        492      308      $156,804.00
271        LGA      PAR        366      498      $190,098.00
821        LGA      LON        345      243      $150,634.00
821        LGA      LON        248      307      $193,930.00
```

Defining Column Headings

In addition to specifying column widths and spacing, you might want to change **column headings**. To define a column heading, enclose the heading text in quotation marks in the DEFINE statement.

Example

Suppose you want to label `Flight` as **Flight Number**, `Orig` as **Flight Origin** and `Dest` as **Flight Destination**. Add these column headings to the DEFINE statements, being sure to match quotation marks. You can also change the WIDTH= specifications to accommodate the new headings.

```
proc report data=flights.europe nowd;
    where dest in ('LON','PAR');
    column flight orig dest mail freight revenue;
    define revenue / format=dollar15.2;
    define flight / width=13 'Flight Number';
    define orig / width=13 spacing=5 'Flight Origin';
    define dest / width=18 spacing=5 'Flight Destination';
run;
```

Partial PROC REPORT Output, SAS Listing

```
Flight Number        Flight Origin        Flight Destination
821                  LGA                  LON
271                  LGA                  PAR
271                  LGA                  PAR
821                  LGA                  LON
821                  LGA                  LON
```

Here is HTML output from the same program.

Partial PROC REPORT Output, HTML

Flight Number	Flight Origin	Flight Destination	Mail	Freight	Revenue
821	LGA	LON	403	209	$150,634.00
271	LGA	PAR	492	308	$156,804.00
271	LGA	PAR	366	498	$190,098.00
821	LGA	LON	345	243	$150,634.00
821	LGA	LON	248	307	$193,930.00

Now you have the column headings that you want. But the columns are so wide that you might prefer to split the long column headings across two lines.

Splitting Column Headings across Multiple Lines

To control how words break in column headings, you can use a **split character** in the column label. When PROC REPORT encounters the split character in a column heading, it breaks the heading and continues the heading on the next line. The split character itself does not appear in the heading.

To use a split character, you can do either of the following:

- Use the **default slash** (*/*) as the split character.

- Define a split character by using the **SPLIT= option** in the PROC REPORT statement.

Example

Suppose you want to break headings so that only one word appears on a line. Using the default slash as the split character, you can submit this PROC REPORT step. Notice that the column width has been reduced.

```
proc report data=flights.europe nowd;
    where dest in ('LON','PAR');
    column flight orig dest mail freight revenue;
    define revenue / format=dollar15.2;
    define flight / width=6 'Flight/Number';
    define orig / width=6 spacing=5 'Flight/Origin';
    define dest / width=11 spacing=5 'Flight/Destination';
run;
```

Or you can submit this program, which uses the SPLIT= option and produces exactly the same output:

```
proc report data=flights.europe nowd split='*';
    where dest in ('LON','PAR');
    column flight orig dest mail freight revenue;
    define revenue / format=dollar15.2;
    define flight / width=6 'Flight*Number';
    define orig / width=6 spacing=5 'Flight*Origin';
    define dest / width=11 spacing=5 'Flight*Destination';
run;
```

Here are both types of output from both programs.

Partial PROC REPORT Output, HTML

Flight Number	Flight Origin	Flight Destination	Mail	Freight	Revenue
821	LGA	LON	403	209	$150,634.00
271	LGA	PAR	492	308	$156,804.00
271	LGA	PAR	366	498	$190,098.00
821	LGA	LON	345	243	$150,634.00
821	LGA	LON	248	307	$193,930.00

Partial PROC REPORT Output, SAS Listing

```
Flight      Flight      Flight
Number      Origin      Destination     Mail     Freight          Revenue
821         LGA         LON              403         209      $150,634.00
271         LGA         PAR              492         308      $156,804.00
271         LGA         PAR              366         498      $190,098.00
821         LGA         LON              345         243      $150,634.00
821         LGA         LON              248         307      $193,930.00
```

Specifying Column Justification

You might also want to specify **justification** for columns in your report. Remember that by default in listing output, PROC REPORT left-justifies character variables and right-justifies numeric variables. For each variable that you define, you can specify the justification option **CENTER**, **LEFT**, or **RIGHT** in the DEFINE statement.

Each option justifies both the formatted values of the report item within the column width and the column headings over the values.

Example

To center headings and values for `Flight`, `Orig`, and `Dest`, you can specify the CENTER option in your DEFINE statements as shown below:

```
proc report data=flights.europe nowd;
   where dest in ('LON','PAR');
   column flight orig dest mail freight revenue;
   define revenue / format=dollar15.2;
   define flight / width=6 'Flight/Number' center;
   define orig / width=6 spacing=5 'Flight/Origin' center;
   define dest / width=11 spacing=5 'Flight/Destination' center;
run;
```

Partial PROC REPORT Output, SAS Listing

```
Flight      Flight      Flight
Number      Origin      Destination     Mail     Freight          Revenue
821         LGA            LON            403         209      $150,634.00
271         LGA            PAR            492         308      $156,804.00
271         LGA            PAR            366         498      $190,098.00
821         LGA            LON            345         243      $150,634.00
821         LGA            LON            248         307      $193,930.00
```

Enhancing the Heading's Appearance

To complete the job of enhancing headings in your list report, you can take advantage of two useful options in the PROC REPORT statement:

- **HEADLINE**, which underlines all column headings and the spaces between them

- **HEADSKIP**, which writes a blank line beneath all column headings or after the underline if the HEADLINE option is used.

These options have no effect on HTML output.

Example

In this PROC REPORT step, the PROC REPORT statement specifies both HEADLINE and HEADSKIP.

```
proc report data=flights.europe nowd headline headskip;
    where dest in ('LON','PAR');
    column flight orig dest mail freight revenue;
    define revenue / format=dollar15.2;
    define flight / width=6 'Flight/Number' center;
    define orig / width=6 spacing=5 'Flight/Origin' center;
    define dest / width=11 spacing=5 'Flight/Destination' center;
run;
```

In the SAS listing output, the column headings are underlined and are followed by a blank line.

Partial PROC REPORT Output, SAS Listing

Flight Number	Flight Origin	Flight Destination	Mail	Freight	Revenue
821	LGA	LON	403	209	$150,634.00
271	LGA	PAR	492	308	$156,804.00
271	LGA	PAR	366	498	$190,098.00
821	LGA	LON	345	243	$150,634.00
821	LGA	LON	248	307	$193,930.00

Defining Variable Usage

So far, you've selected data for your list report and defined column attributes and headings. Next, let's look at a more complex PROC REPORT feature: **usage** for variables in your report. You've seen that you define variable usage in the DEFINE statement. Now you can see how each usage affects the layout of your report and the values that the report contains.

How PROC REPORT Uses Variables

PROC REPORT uses each variable in one of six ways (DISPLAY, ORDER, GROUP, ACROSS, ANALYSIS, or COMPUTED). By default, PROC REPORT uses

- character variables as **display** variables

- numeric variables as **analysis** variables, which are used to calculate the SUM statistic.

Because you haven't explicitly defined any variable usages, your current list report contains only display and analysis variables:

- The character variables `Flight`, `Orig`, and `Dest` are display variables. Display variables don't affect the order of rows in the report. A report that contains one or more display variables has a detail row for each observation that is read from the data set. Each detail row contains a value for each display variable.

- The numeric variables `Mail`, `Freight`, and `Revenue` are analysis variables. Analysis variables are used to calculate a statistic (in this case, the default SUM).

In the illustration below, columns for display variables are shown in white. Columns for analysis variables are shown in gray.

Illustration of Partial PROC REPORT Output

	Flight Number	Flight Origin	Flight Destination	Mail	Freight	Revenue	
character variables	821	LGA	LON	403	209	$150,634.00	numeric variables
	271	LGA	PAR	492	308	$156,804.00	
(default= DISPLAY)	271	LGA	PAR	366	498	$190,098.00	(default= ANALYSIS)
	821	LGA	LON	345	243	$150,634.00	
	821	LGA	LON	248	307	$193,930.00	

Using Order Variables

How you use a variable in a report determines, among other things, the order of the rows in your report.

An **order variable** orders the detail rows in a report according to their formatted values. For example, suppose you want to see values in your list report ordered by flight number. To use Flight as an order variable, you specify the **ORDER** usage option in the DEFINE statement, as shown below.

```
proc report data=flights.europe nowd headline headskip;
   where dest in ('LON','PAR');
   column flight orig dest mail freight revenue;
   define revenue / format=dollar15.2;
   define flight / order 'Flight/Number' width=6 center;
   define orig / width=6 spacing=5 'Flight/Origin' center;
   define dest / width=11 spacing=5 'Flight/Destination'
                 center;
run;
```

In the ordered output shown below, notice that PROC REPORT displays only the first occurrence of each value of an order variable in a set of rows that have the same value for all order variables.

Flight Number	Flight Origin	Flight Destination	Mail	Freight	Revenue
219	LGA	LON	331	376	$189,065.00
	LGA	LON	485	267	$197,456.00
	LGA	LON	388	298	$162,343.00
	LGA	LON	421	356	$134,520.00
	LGA	LON	447	299	$106,753.00
	LGA	LON	356	547	$122,766.00
	LGA	LON	272	370	$198,744.00
271	LGA	PAR	492	308	$156,804.00
	LGA	PAR	366	498	$190,098.00
	LGA	PAR	353	205	$166,470.00
	LGA	PAR	366	279	$163,248.00
	LGA	PAR	357	282	$170,766.00
	LGA	PAR	415	463	$195,468.00
	LGA	PAR	352	351	$123,456.00
	LGA	PAR	492	308	$125,632.00
	LGA	PAR	366	498	$128,972.00
	LGA	PAR	353	205	$153,423.00

Flight Number	Flight Origin	Flight Destination	Mail	Freight	Revenue
	LGA	PAR	366	279	$133,345.00
	LGA	PAR	357	282	$126,543.00
	LGA	PAR	415	463	$134,976.00
821	LGA	LON	403	209	$150,634.00
	LGA	LON	345	243	$150,634.00
	LGA	LON	248	307	$193,930.00
	LGA	LON	391	395	$167,772.00
	LGA	LON	219	368	$183,106.00
	LGA	LON	389	479	$169,576.00
	LGA	LON	448	282	$143,561.00
	LGA	LON	403	209	$170,766.00
	LGA	LON	345	243	$129,560.00
	LGA	LON	248	307	$196,736.00
	LGA	LON	391	395	$125,344.00
	LGA	LON	219	368	$166,543.00
	LGA	LON	389	479	$129,745.00

By default, the order is ascending, but you can change it with the **DESCENDING option** in the DEFINE statement:

```
proc report data=flights.europe nowd headline headskip;
    where dest in ('LON','PAR');
    column flight orig dest mail freight revenue;
    define revenue / format=dollar15.2;
    define flight / order descending 'Flight/Number' width=6
                  center;
    define orig / width=6 spacing=5 'Flight/Origin' center;
    define dest / width=11 spacing=5 'Flight/Destination'
                  center;
run;
```

Using Group Variables

Your list report is complete. But suppose you now want to create a **summary report**. That is, rather than a list of the mail, freight, and revenue for each flight, you want the total mail, freight, and revenue by flight number. Here is the summary report that you want to create.

Flight Number	Flight Origin	Flight Destination	Mail	Freight	Revenue
219	LGA	LON	2700	2513	$1,111,647.00
271	LGA	PAR	5050	4421	$1,969,201.00
821	LGA	LON	4438	4284	$2,077,907.00

To summarize your data using PROC REPORT, you can define one or more **group** variables. A group variable groups the detail rows in a report according to their formatted values. If a report contains one or more group variables, then PROC REPORT consolidates into one row all observations from the data set that have a unique combination of values for all group variables.

To define a group variable, you specify the **GROUP** usage option in the DEFINE statement.

Example

If you submit the following PROC REPORT step, with Flight defined as a group variable, you get the output shown below.

```
proc report data=flights.europe nowd headline headskip;
   where dest in ('LON','PAR');
   column flight orig dest mail freight revenue;
   define revenue / format=dollar15.2;
   define flight / group 'Flight/Number' width=6 center;
   define orig / width=6 spacing=5 'Flight/Origin' center;
   define dest / width=11 spacing=5 'Flight/Destination'
                 center;
run;
```

Flight Number	Flight Origin	Flight Destination	Mail	Freight	Revenue
219	LGA	LON	331	376	$189,065.00
	LGA	LON	485	267	$197,456.00
	LGA	LON	388	298	$162,343.00
	LGA	LON	421	356	$134,520.00
	LGA	LON	447	299	$106,753.00
	LGA	LON	356	547	$122,766.00
	LGA	LON	272	370	$198,744.00
271	LGA	PAR	492	308	$156,804.00
	LGA	PAR	366	498	$190,098.00
	LGA	PAR	353	205	$166,470.00
	LGA	PAR	366	279	$163,248.00
	LGA	PAR	357	282	$170,766.00

Flight Number	Flight Origin	Flight Destination	Mail	Freight	Revenue
	LGA	PAR	415	463	$195,468.00
	LGA	PAR	352	351	$123,456.00
	LGA	PAR	492	308	$125,632.00
	LGA	PAR	366	498	$128,972.00
	LGA	PAR	353	205	$153,423.00
	LGA	PAR	366	279	$133,345.00
	LGA	PAR	357	282	$126,543.00
	LGA	PAR	415	463	$134,976.00
821	LGA	LON	403	209	$150,634.00
	LGA	LON	345	243	$150,634.00
	LGA	LON	248	307	$193,930.00
	LGA	LON	391	395	$167,772.00
	LGA	LON	219	368	$183,106.00
	LGA	LON	389	479	$169,576.00
	LGA	LON	448	282	$143,561.00
	LGA	LON	403	209	$170,766.00
	LGA	LON	345	243	$129,560.00
	LGA	LON	248	307	$196,736.00
	LGA	LON	391	395	$125,344.00
	LGA	LON	219	368	$166,543.00
	LGA	LON	389	479	$129,745.00

But this output looks exactly like the list output in which `Flight` was an order variable. What happened?

The problem with the preceding output is that your report contains display variables. As character variables, `Orig` and `Dest` are defined as display variables by default.

All of the variables in a summary report must be defined as **group**, **analysis**, **across**, or **computed** variables. This is because PROC REPORT must be able to summarize all variables across an observation in order to collapse observations. If PROC REPORT can't create groups, it displays group variables as order variables.

Revising the Report

To group data in your report, you need to define the character variables (Flight, Orig, and Dest) as group variables, as shown below:

```
proc report data=flights.europe nowd headline headskip;
    where dest in ('LON','PAR');
    column flight orig dest mail freight revenue;
    define revenue / format=dollar15.2;
    define flight / group 'Flight/Number' width=6 center;
    define orig / group width=6 spacing=5 'Flight/Origin'
                  center;
    define dest / group width=11 spacing=5
                  'Flight/Destination' center;
run;
```

Now PROC REPORT can create groups, and your summary report displays the total mail, freight, and revenue by flight number. Remember that the default statistic for the analysis variables is SUM.

Flight Number	Flight Origin	Flight Destination	Mail	Freight	Revenue
219	LGA	LON	2700	2513	$1,111,647.00
271	LGA	PAR	5050	4421	$1,969,201.00
821	LGA	LON	4438	4284	$2,077,907.00

The following table compares the effects of using order variables and group variables.

Effect on Report	Order	Group
Rows are ordered	yes	yes
Repetitious printing of values is suppressed	yes	yes
Rows that have the same values are collapsed	no	yes
Type of report produced	list	summary

Specifying Statistics

As you saw in the previous example, the default statistic for analysis variables is SUM. However, you might want to display other statistics in your PROC REPORT output. To associate a statistic with an analysis variable, specify the statistic as an attribute in the DEFINE statement.

Here's the previous sample output, which displays the default statistic SUM for the three analysis variables:

Flight Number	Flight Origin	Flight Destination	Mail	Freight	Revenue
219	LGA	LON	2700	2513	$1,111,647.00
271	LGA	PAR	5050	4421	$1,969,201.00
821	LGA	LON	4438	4284	$2,077,907.00

By specifying **MEAN** in the DEFINE statement for Revenue, you can display the average revenue for each flight number. The optional column heading **Average Revenue** clarifies that the MEAN statistic is displayed.

```
proc report data=flights.europe nowd headline headskip;
   where dest in ('LON','PAR');
   column flight orig dest mail freight revenue;
   define revenue / mean format=dollar15.2
                  'Average/Revenue';
   define flight / group 'Flight/Number' width=6 center;
   define orig / group width=6 spacing=5 'Flight/Origin'
               center;
   define dest / group width=11 spacing=5
               'Flight/Destination' center;
run;
```

Flight Number	Flight Origin	Flight Destination	Mail	Freight	Average Revenue
219	LGA	LON	2700	2513	$158,806.71
271	LGA	PAR	5050	4421	$151,477.00
821	LGA	LON	4438	4284	$159,839.00

You can use the following statistics in PROC REPORT.

Statistic	Definition
CSS	Corrected sum of squares
USS	Uncorrected sum of squares
CV	Coefficient of variation
MAX	Maximum value
MEAN	Average
MIN	Minimum value
N	Number of observations with nonmissing values
NMISS	Number of observations with missing values
RANGE	Range

Statistic	Definition
STD	Standard deviation
STDERR	Standard error of the mean
SUM	Sum
SUMWGT	Sum of the `Weight` variable values
PCTN	Percentage of a cell or row frequency to a total frequency
PCTSUM	Percentage of a cell or row sum to a total sum
VAR	Variance
T	Student's *t* for testing the hypothesis that the population mean is 0
PRT	Probability of a greater absolute value of student's *t*

Using Across Variables

So far, we've looked at display, analysis, order, and group variables. You can also define variables as **across** variables, which are functionally similar to group variables. However, PROC REPORT displays the groups that it creates for an across variable **horizontally** rather than vertically.

Let's look at an example of across variables to clarify this usage.

Example

The following program uses **group** variables to produce the output shown. The table shows unique combinations of values of the group variables, and sums of each analysis variable for each combination.

```
proc report data=flights.europe nowd headline headskip;
   where dest in ('LON','PAR');
   column flight dest mail freight revenue;
   define revenue / format=dollar15.2;
   define flight / group 'Flight/Number' width=6 center;
   define dest / group width=11 spacing=5
                 'Flight/Destination' center;
run;
```

Flight Number	Flight Destination	Mail	Freight	Revenue
219	LON	2700	2513	$1,111,647.00
271	PAR	5050	4421	$1,969,201.00
821	LON	4438	4284	$2,077,907.00

Now let's suppose you change the group variables to **across** variables, as in this program.

```
proc report data=flights.europe nowd headline headskip;
   where dest in ('LON','PAR');
   column flight dest mail freight revenue;
   define revenue / format=dollar15.2;
   define flight / across 'Flight/Number' width=6 center;
   define dest / across width=11 spacing=5
                 'Flight/Destination' center;
run;
```

In this case, for each across variable, the table cells contain a frequency count for each unique value. For each analysis variable, the table cells represent the sum of all the variable's values.

Flight Number			Flight Destination				
219	271	821	LON	PAR	Mail	Freight	Revenue
7	13	13	20	13	12188	11218	$5,158,755.00

Using Computed Variables

The last type of variable usage is reserved for **computed** variables, which are numeric or character variables that you define for the report. They are not in the input data set, and PROC REPORT doesn't add them to the input data set. You can't change the usage of a computed variable.

In the nonwindowing environment, you add a computed variable as follows:

1. Include the computed variable in the COLUMN statement.

2. Define the variable's usage as COMPUTED in the DEFINE statement.

3. Compute the value of the variable in a compute block that is associated with the variable.

 The position of a computed variable is important. PROC REPORT assigns values to the columns in a row of a report from left to right. Consequently, you can't base the calculation of a computed variable on any variable that appears to its right in the report.

Let's see how you create a new variable for your report.

Example

Suppose you want to determine the number of empty seats for each flight. To do so, you can compute the variable `EmptySeats` by subtracting the number of passengers deplaning (`Deplaned`) from the plane's total seats (`Capacity`), assuming that the plane is full.

In the following program, you

- specify `EmptySeats` in the COLUMN statement to the right of the variables that are used in its calculation.

- define `EmptySeats` as a computed variable in a DEFINE statement.

- begin a compute block by specifying `EmptySeats` in a COMPUTE statement.

- use DATA step statements in the compute block to calculate the values of `EmptySeats`. Notice that when you refer to an analysis variable, you use a **compound name** that identifies both the original variable and the statistic that PROC REPORT now calculates from it. The compound name has the form *variable-name.statistic*.

- close the compute block with an ENDCOMP statement.

```
proc report data=flights.europe nowd;
    where dest in ('LON','PAR');
    column flight capacity deplaned emptyseats;
    define flight / width=6;
    define emptyseats / computed 'Empty Seats';
    compute emptyseats;
        emptyseats=capacity.sum-deplaned.sum;
    endcomp;
run;
```

The program creates the following output.

Partial PROC REPORT Output

Flight	Capacity	Deplaned	Empty Seats
821	250	222	28
271	250	163	87
271	250	227	23
821	250	222	28
821	250	158	92

Summary

Text Summary

Creating a Default List Report

To create a default list report, you submit a basic PROC REPORT step. You can specify options to invoke the procedure in either a windowing or nonwindowing mode. By default, all observations and variables in the data set are printed, and variables appear in the order in which they occur in the data set.

Selecting Variables

To select and order the variables that appear in your list report, you can use the **COLUMN statement**.

Selecting Observations

To select rows for your report, you can use the **WHERE statement** as you do with many other SAS procedures.

Defining Variables

You can enhance your report by defining how each variable is used in the report. To describe how to use and display variables in your report, you use one or more **DEFINE statements**.

Defining Column Attributes

To assign a format to a specific report column, use the **FORMAT= attribute** in the DEFINE statement for that column. To specify a width for columns in your report, use the **WIDTH= attribute** in the DEFINE statement. To specify a different column spacing, use the **SPACING= attribute** in the DEFINE statement. To define a column heading, enclose the heading text in quotation marks in the DEFINE statement. To control how words break in column headings, you can use a **split character** in the column label. For each variable that you define, you can specify the **justification option** CENTER, LEFT, or RIGHT in the DEFINE statement.

Enhancing the Heading's Appearance

To enhance headings in your report, you can use the **HEADLINE option**, which underlines all column headings and the spaces between them, and the **HEADSKIP option**, which writes a blank line before the data values. These options have no effect on HTML output.

Defining Variable Usage

PROC REPORT uses each variable in one of six ways (DISPLAY, ORDER, GROUP, ACROSS, ANALYSIS, or COMPUTED). By default, PROC REPORT uses character variables as display variables, and it uses numeric variables as analysis variables, which are used to calculate the SUM statistic. You can define usage for variables in the DEFINE statement.

Variable Usage in PROC REPORT	
Display variables	do not affect the order of rows in the report. A report that contains one or more display variables has a detail row for each observation in the data set. Each detail row contains a value for each display variable. By default, PROC REPORT treats all character variables as display variables.
Order variables	order the detail rows in a report according to their formatted values.
Group variables	order the detail rows in a report according to their formatted values. If a report contains one or more group variables, PROC REPORT tries to consolidate into one row all observations from the data set that have a unique combination of values for all group variables.
Across variables	are functionally similar to group variables; however, PROC REPORT displays the groups that it creates for an across variable horizontally rather than vertically.
Analysis variables	are used to calculate a statistic. By default, PROC REPORT uses numeric variables as analysis variables, which are used to calculate the SUM statistic.
Computed variables	are variables that you define for the report. They are not in the data set. You cannot change the usage of a computed variable. Computed variables can be either numeric or character variables.

Specifying Statistics

To associate a statistic with an analysis variable, specify the statistic as an attribute in the DEFINE statement.

Points to Remember

- You can use PROC REPORT in either a windowing or nonwindowing mode.
- You can use FORMAT statements with PROC REPORT, but the DEFINE statement enables you to specify more than one column attribute at a time.
- For HTML output, the FORMAT= option cannot increase cell width beyond the width of cell values. The WIDTH= and SPACING= attributes, along with the HEADSKIP and HEADLINE options, have no effect on HTML output.
- You can use the default slash as the split character, or you can specify a split character using the SPLIT= option in the PROC REPORT statement.
- By default, PROC REPORT uses character variables as display variables and numeric variables as analysis variables, which are used to calculate the SUM statistic.
- All of the variables in a summary report must be defined as group, analysis, across, or computed variables. If PROC REPORT can't create groups, it displays group variables as order variables.
- You can't change the usage of a computed variable.
- The position of a computed variable is important. You can't base the calculation of a computed variable on any variable that appears to its right in the report.

Practice

After you complete this chapter, practice what you learned by using the sample data and SAS programs for Chapter 8, **Creating Enhanced List and Summary Reports**, which are located on the CD-ROM. Follow the directions for creating your sample data in the Before You Begin section.

Quiz

Select the best answer for each question. After completing the quiz, check your answers using the answer key in the appendix.

1. If `Style` has four unique values and you submit the following program, which output do you get? (Assume that all the other variables are numeric.)

   ```
   proc report data=sasuser.houses nowd;
      column style sqfeet bedrooms price;
      define style / group;
   run;
   ```

   a.

Style	SqFeet	Bedrooms	Price
CONDO	6755	11	$397,250
RANCH	5005	9	$274,300
SPLIT	4110	8	$233,950
TWOSTORY	5835	12	$335,300

   b.

Style	SqFeet	Bedrooms	Price
CONDO	1400	2	$80,050
	1390	3	$79,350
	2105	4	$127,150
	1860	2	$110,700
RANCH	1250	2	$64,000
	1500	3	$86,650
	1535	3	$89,100
	720	1	$34,550
SPLIT	1190	1	$65,850
	1615	4	$94,450
	1305	3	$73,650
TWOSTORY	1810	4	$107,250
	1040	2	$55,850
	1240	2	$69,250
	1745	4	$102,950

c.

Style	SqFeet	Bedrooms	Price
15	21705	40	$1,240,800

d.

Style	SqFeet	Bedrooms	Price
RANCH	1250	2	$64,000
SPLIT	1190	1	$65,850
CONDO	1400	2	$80,050
TWOSTORY	1810	4	$107,250
RANCH	1500	3	$86,650
SPLIT	1615	4	$94,450
SPLIT	1305	3	$73,650
CONDO	1390	3	$79,350
TWOSTORY	1040	2	$55,850
CONDO	2105	4	$127,150
RANCH	1535	3	$89,100
TWOSTORY	1240	2	$69,250
RANCH	720	1	$34,550
TWOSTORY	1745	4	$102,950
CONDO	1860	2	$110,700

2. When you define an order variable,

    a. the detail rows are ordered according to their formatted values.

    b. you can't create summary reports.

    c. PROC REPORT displays only the first occurrence of each order variable value in a set of rows that have the same value for all order variables.

    d. all of the above

3. Which attributes or options are reflected in this PROC REPORT output?

Style	SqFeet	Price
RANCH	720	$34,550
TWOSTORY	1040	$55,850
SPLIT	1190	$65,850
TWOSTORY	1240	$69,250
RANCH	1250	$64,000
SPLIT	1305	$73,650
CONDO	1390	$79,350
CONDO	1400	$80,050
RANCH	1500	$86,650
RANCH	1535	$89,100
SPLIT	1615	$94,450
TWOSTORY	1745	$102,950
TWOSTORY	1810	$107,250
CONDO	1860	$110,700
CONDO	2105	$127,150

a. SKIPLINE and FORMAT=

b. CENTER, HEADLINE, HEADSKIP, and either WIDTH=, SPACING=, or FORMAT=

c. SPACING= only

d. CENTER, FORMAT=, and HEADLINE

4. To create a summary report that shows the average number of bedrooms and the maximum number of baths for each style of house, which DEFINE statements do you use in your PROC REPORT step?

a.
```
define style / center 'Style of/House';
   define bedrooms / mean 'Average/Bedrooms';
   define baths / max 'Maximum/Baths';
```
b.
```
define style / group;
   define bedrooms / mean 'Average/Bedrooms';
   define baths / max 'Maximum/Baths';
```
c.
```
define style / order;
   define bedrooms / mean 'Average/Bedrooms';
   define baths / max 'Maximum/Baths';
```
d.
```
define style / group;
   define bedrooms / 'Average/Bedrooms';
   define baths / 'Maximum/Baths'
```

5. Which program does **not** contain an error?

   a.
   ```
   proc report data=sasuser.houses nowd;
      column style bedrooms baths;
      define style / order;
      define bedbathratio / computed format=4.2;
      compute bedbathratio;
         bedbathratio=baths.sum/bedrooms.sum;
      endcomp;
   run;
   ```

   b.
   ```
   proc report data=sasuser.houses nowd;
      column style bedrooms baths BedBathRatio;
      define style / order;
      define bedbathratio / order format=4.2;
      compute bedbathratio;
         bedbathratio=baths.sum/bedrooms.sum;
      endcomp;
   run;
   ```

   c.
   ```
   proc report data=sasuser.houses nowd;
      column style bedrooms baths BedBathRatio;
      define style / order;
      define bedbathratio / computed format=4.2;
      compute bedbathratio;
         bedbathratio=baths.sum/bedrooms.sum;
      endcomp;
   run;
   ```

   d.
   ```
   proc report data=sasuser.houses nowd;
      column style bedrooms baths BedBathRatio;
      define style / order;
      define bedbathratio / computed format=4.2;
      compute bedbathratio;
         bedbathratio=baths/bedrooms;
      endcomp;
   run;
   ```

6. What output does this PROC REPORT step produce?

   ```
   proc report data=sasuser.houses nowd;
      column style sqfeet bedrooms price;
   run;
   ```

   a. a list report ordered by values of the first variable in the COLUMN statement

   b. a summary report ordered by values of the first variable in the COLUMN statement

   c. a list report that displays a row for each observation in the input data set and which calculates the SUM statistic for numeric variables

   d. a list report that calculates the N (frequency) statistic for character variables

7. Which of the following programs produces this output?

Style				
CONDO	RANCH	SPLIT	TWOSTORY	Average Price
4	4	3	4	$82,720

a.
```
proc report data=sasuser.houses nowd;
    column style condo range split
           twostory price;

    define price / mean 'Average Price';
run;
```

b.
```
proc report data=sasuser.houses nowd;
    column style price;
    define style / group;
    define price / mean 'Average Price';
run;
```

c.
```
proc report data=sasuser.houses nowd;
    column style price;
    define style / across;
    define price / mean 'Average Price';
run;
```

d.
```
proc report data=sasuser.houses nowd;
    column style price;
    define style / across 'CONDO' 'RANCH'
            'SPLIT' 'TWOSTORY';
    define price / mean 'Average Price';
run;
```

8. If you submit this program, where does your PROC REPORT output appear?

```
proc report data=sasuser.houses nowd;
    column style sqfeet bedrooms price;
    define style / group;
run;
```

a. in the PROC REPORT window
b. as HTML and/or SAS listing output
c. both of the above
d. neither of the above

9. How can you create output with headings that break as shown below?

```
Style of     Average    Maximum
  House      Bedrooms     Baths
  CONDO         2.75        2.5
  RANCH         2.25          3
  SPLIT     2.666666          3
TWOSTORY           3          3
```

   a. You must specify the SPLIT= option in the PROC REPORT statement and use the split character in column headings in DEFINE statements.

   b. You must use the default split character in column headings in DEFINE statements.

   c. You must specify either the WIDTH= or the SPACING= attribute in DEFINE statements.

   d. These headings split this way by default.

10. Suppose you want to create a report using both character and numeric variables. If you don't use any DEFINE statements in your PROC REPORT step,

   a. your PROC REPORT step will not execute successfully.

   b. you can produce only list reports.

   c. you can order rows by specifying options in the PROC REPORT statement.

   d. you can produce only summary reports.

Chapter 9 Producing Descriptive Statistics

Overview

Introduction

As you have seen, one of the many features of PROC REPORT is the ability to summarize large amounts of data by producing descriptive statistics. However, there are SAS procedures that are designed specifically to produce various types of descriptive statistics and to display them in meaningful reports. The type of descriptive statistics that you need and the SAS procedure that you should use depend on whether you need to summarize continuous data values or discrete data values.

If the data values that you want to describe are continuous numeric values (for example, people's ages), then you can use the MEANS procedure or the SUMMARY procedure to calculate statistics such as the mean, sum, minimum, and maximum.

Variable	N	Mean	Std Dev	Minimum	Maximum
Age	20	47	13	15	63
Height	20	67	4	61	75
Weight	20	175	36	102	240
Pulse	20	75	8	65	100
FastGluc	20	299	126	152	568
PostGluc	20	355	126	206	625

If the data values that you want to describe are discrete (for example, the color of people's eyes), then you can use the FREQ procedure to show the distribution of these values, such as percentages and counts.

Eye Color	Frequency	Percent	Cumulative Frequency	Cumulative Percent
Brown	92	58.60	92	58.60
Blue	65	41.40	157	100.00

This chapter shows you how to use the MEANS, SUMMARY, and FREQ procedures to describe your data.

Objectives

In this chapter, you learn to

- determine the *n*-count, mean, standard deviation, minimum, and maximum of numeric variables using the MEANS procedure
- control the number of decimal places used in PROC MEANS output
- specify the variables for which to produce statistics
- use the SUMMARY procedure to produce the same results as the MEANS procedure
- describe the difference between the SUMMARY and MEANS procedures

- create one-way frequency tables for categorical data using the FREQ procedure
- create two-way and *n*-way crossed frequency tables
- control the layout and complexity of crossed frequency tables.

Computing Statistics for Numeric Variables

Computing Statistics Using PROC MEANS

Descriptive statistics such as the mean, minimum, and maximum can provide useful information about numeric data. The MEANS procedure provides these and other data summarization tools, as well as helpful options for controlling your output.

The MEANS procedure can include many statements and options for specifying needed statistics. For simplicity, let's consider the procedure in its basic form.

General form, basic MEANS procedure:

> **PROC MEANS <DATA=***SAS-data-set*>
> <*statistic-keyword(s)*> <*option(s)*>;
> **RUN;**

where

- *SAS-data-set* is the name of the data set to be used

- *statistic-keyword(s)* specifies the statistics to compute

- *option(s)* controls the content, analysis, and appearance of output.

In its simplest form, PROC MEANS prints the *n*-count (number of nonmissing values), the mean, the standard deviation, and the minimum and maximum values of every numeric variable in a data set.

```
proc means data=perm.survey;
run;
```

Variable	N	Mean	Std Dev	Minimum	Maximum
Item1	4	3.7500000	1.2583057	2.0000000	5.0000000
Item2	4	3.0000000	1.6329932	1.0000000	5.0000000
Item3	4	4.2500000	0.5000000	4.0000000	5.0000000
Item4	4	3.5000000	1.2909944	2.0000000	5.0000000
Item5	4	3.0000000	1.6329932	1.0000000	5.0000000
Item6	4	3.7500000	1.2583057	2.0000000	5.0000000
Item7	4	3.0000000	1.8257419	1.0000000	5.0000000
Item8	4	2.7500000	1.5000000	1.0000000	4.0000000
Item9	4	3.0000000	1.4142136	2.0000000	5.0000000
Item10	4	3.2500000	1.2583057	2.0000000	5.0000000
Item11	4	3.0000000	1.8257419	1.0000000	5.0000000

Variable	N	Mean	Std Dev	Minimum	Maximum
Item12	4	2.7500000	0.5000000	2.0000000	3.0000000
Item13	4	2.7500000	1.5000000	1.0000000	4.0000000
Item14	4	3.0000000	1.4142136	2.0000000	5.0000000
Item15	4	3.0000000	1.6329932	1.0000000	5.0000000
Item16	4	2.5000000	1.9148542	1.0000000	5.0000000
Item17	4	3.0000000	1.1547005	2.0000000	4.0000000
Item18	4	3.2500000	1.2583057	2.0000000	5.0000000

Specifying Statistics

The default statistics that the MEANS procedure produces (*n*-count, mean, standard deviation, minimum, and maximum) are not always the ones that you need. You might prefer to limit output to the mean of the values. Or you might need to compute a different statistic, such as the median or range of the values.

To specify statistics, include statistic keywords as options in the PROC MEANS statement. When you specify a statistic in the PROC MEANS statement, default statistics are not produced. For example, to see the median and range of **Perm.Survey** numeric values, add the MEDIAN and RANGE keywords as options.

```
proc means data=perm.survey median range;
run;
```

Variable	Median	Range
Item1	4.0000000	3.0000000
Item2	3.0000000	4.0000000
Item3	4.0000000	1.0000000
Item4	3.5000000	3.0000000
Item5	3.0000000	4.0000000
Item6	4.0000000	3.0000000
Item7	3.0000000	4.0000000
Item8	3.0000000	3.0000000
Item9	2.5000000	3.0000000
Item10	3.0000000	3.0000000
Item11	3.0000000	4.0000000
Item12	3.0000000	1.0000000
Item13	3.0000000	3.0000000
Item14	2.5000000	3.0000000
Item15	3.0000000	4.0000000
Item16	2.0000000	4.0000000
Item17	3.0000000	2.0000000
Item18	3.0000000	3.0000000

The following keywords can be used with PROC MEANS to compute statistics:

Descriptive Statistics

Keyword	Description
CLM	Two-sided confidence limit for the mean
CSS	Corrected sum of squares
CV	Coefficient of variation
KURTOSIS / KURT	Kurtosis
LCLM	One-sided confidence limit below the mean
MAX	Maximum value
MEAN	Average
MIN	Minimum value
N	Number of observations with non-missing values
NMISS	Number of observations with missing values
RANGE	Range
SKEWNESS / SKEW	Skewness
STDDEV / STD	Standard deviation
STDERR / STDMEAN	Standard error of the mean
SUM	Sum
SUMWGT	Sum of the `Weight` variable values
UCLM	One-sided confidence limit above the mean
USS	Uncorrected sum of squares
VAR	Variance

Quantile Statistics

Keyword	Description
MEDIAN / P50	Median or 50th percentile
P1	1st percentile
P5	5th percentile
P10	10th percentile
Q1 / P25	Lower quartile or 25th percentile
Q3 / P75	Upper quartile or 75th percentile
P90	90th percentile
P95	95th percentile
P99	99th percentile
QRANGE	Difference between upper and lower quartiles: Q3-Q1

Hypothesis Testing

Keyword	Description
PROBT	Probability of a greater absolute value for the t value
T	Student's t for testing the hypothesis that the population mean is 0

Limiting Decimal Places

By default, PROC MEANS output uses the BEST. format to display values in the report. As the following example shows, this can result in unnecessary decimal places, making your output difficult to read.

```
proc means data=clinic.diabetes min max;
run;
```

Variable	Minimum	Maximum
Age	15.0000000	63.0000000
Height	61.0000000	75.0000000
Weight	102.0000000	240.0000000
Pulse	65.0000000	100.0000000
FastGluc	152.0000000	568.0000000
PostGluc	206.0000000	625.0000000

To limit decimal places, use the **MAXDEC=** option in the PROC MEANS statement, and set it equal to the length that you prefer.

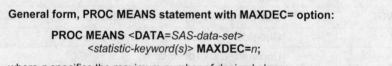

General form, PROC MEANS statement with MAXDEC= option:

> **PROC MEANS** <**DATA**=*SAS-data-set*>
> <*statistic-keyword(s)*> **MAXDEC**=*n*;

where *n* specifies the maximum number of decimal places.

```
proc means data=clinic.diabetes min max maxdec=0;
run;
```

Variable	Minimum	Maximum
Age	15	63
Height	61	75
Weight	102	240
Pulse	65	100
FastGluc	152	568
PostGluc	206	625

Specifying Variables in PROC MEANS

By default, the MEANS procedure generates statistics for every numeric variable in a data set, although you'll typically want to focus on only a few variables, particularly if the data set is large. It also makes sense to exclude certain types of variables. The values of employee identification numbers, for example, are unlikely to yield useful statistics.

To specify the variables that PROC MEANS analyzes, add a **VAR statement** and list the variable names.

> **General form, VAR statement:**
>
> **VAR** *variable(s)*;
>
> where *variable(s)* lists numeric variables for which to calculate statistics.

```
proc means data=clinic.diabetes min max maxdec=0;
   var age height weight;
run;
```

Variable	Minimum	Maximum
Age	15	63
Height	61	75
Weight	102	240

In addition to listing variables separately, you can use a numbered range of variables.

```
proc means data=perm.survey mean stderr maxdec=2;
   var item1-item5;
run;
```

Variable	Mean	Std Error
Item1	3.75	0.63
Item2	3.00	0.82
Item3	4.25	0.25
Item4	3.50	0.65
Item5	3.00	0.82

Group Processing Using the CLASS Statement

You will often want statistics for grouped observations, instead of for observations as a whole. For example, census numbers are more useful when grouped by region than when viewed as a national total. To produce separate analyses of grouped observations, add a **CLASS statement** to the MEANS procedure.

> **General form, CLASS statement:**
>
> **CLASS** *variable(s)*;
>
> where *variable(s)* specifies category variables for group processing.

PROC MEANS does not generate statistics for CLASS variables, because their values are used only to categorize data. CLASS variables can be either character or numeric, but they should contain a limited number of discrete values that represent meaningful groupings.

The output of the program shown below is categorized by values of the variables Survive and Sex. The order of the variables in the CLASS statement determines their order in the output table.

```
proc means data=clinic.heart maxdec=1;
   var arterial heart cardiac urinary;
   class survive sex;
run;
```

Survive	Sex	N Obs	Variable	N	Mean	Std Dev	Minimum	Maximum
DIED	1	4	Arterial	4	92.5	10.5	83.0	103.0
			Heart	4	111.0	53.4	54.0	183.0
			Cardiac	4	176.8	75.2	95.0	260.0
			Urinary	4	98.0	186.1	0.0	377.0
	2	6	Arterial	6	94.2	27.3	72.0	145.0
			Heart	6	103.7	16.7	81.0	130.0
			Cardiac	6	318.3	102.6	156.0	424.0
			Urinary	6	100.3	155.7	0.0	405.0
SURV	1	5	Arterial	5	77.2	12.2	61.0	88.0
			Heart	5	109.0	32.0	77.0	149.0
			Cardiac	5	298.0	139.8	66.0	410.0
			Urinary	5	100.8	60.2	44.0	200.0
	2	5	Arterial	5	78.8	6.8	72.0	87.0
			Heart	5	100.0	13.4	84.0	111.0
			Cardiac	5	330.2	87.0	256.0	471.0
			Urinary	5	111.2	152.4	12.0	377.0

Group Processing Using the BY Statement

Like the CLASS statement, the **BY statement** specifies variables to use for categorizing observations.

> **General form, BY statement:**
>
> **BY** *variable(s)*;
>
> where *variable(s)* specifies category variables for group processing.

But BY and CLASS processing differ in two key ways:

1. Unlike CLASS processing, BY processing requires that your data already be sorted or indexed in the order of the BY variables. Unless data set observations are already sorted, you will need to run the SORT procedure before using PROC MEANS with any BY group.

Be careful when sorting data sets to enable group processing. If you don't specify an output data set by using the OUT= option, then PROC SORT will overwrite your initial data set with the newly sorted observations.

2. BY group results have a layout that is different from the layout of CLASS group results. Note that the BY statement in the program below creates four small tables; a CLASS statement would produce a single large table.

```
proc sort data=clinic.heart out=work.heartsort;
   by survive sex;
run;
proc means data=work.heartsort maxdec=1;
   var arterial heart cardiac urinary;
   by survive sex;
run;
```

Survive=DIED Sex=1

Variable	N	Mean	Std Dev	Minimum	Maximum
Arterial	4	92.5	10.5	83.0	103.0
Heart	4	111.0	53.4	54.0	183.0
Cardiac	4	176.8	75.2	95.0	260.0
Urinary	4	98.0	186.1	0.0	377.0

Survive=DIED Sex=2

Variable	N	Mean	Std Dev	Minimum	Maximum
Arterial	6	94.2	27.3	72.0	145.0
Heart	6	103.7	16.7	81.0	130.0
Cardiac	6	318.3	102.6	156.0	424.0
Urinary	6	100.3	155.7	0.0	405.0

Survive=SURV Sex=1

Variable	N	Mean	Std Dev	Minimum	Maximum
Arterial	5	77.2	12.2	61.0	88.0
Heart	5	109.0	32.0	77.0	149.0
Cardiac	5	298.0	139.8	66.0	410.0
Urinary	5	100.8	60.2	44.0	200.0

Survive=SURV Sex=2

Variable	N	Mean	Std Dev	Minimum	Maximum
Arterial	5	78.8	6.8	72.0	87.0
Heart	5	100.0	13.4	84.0	111.0
Cardiac	5	330.2	87.0	256.0	471.0
Urinary	5	111.2	152.4	12.0	377.0

Because it doesn't require a sorting step, the CLASS statement is easier to use than the BY statement. However, BY-group processing can be more efficient when you are categorizing data that includes many variables.

Creating a Summarized Data Set Using PROC MEANS

You might want to create an output SAS data set that contains only the summarized variable. You can do this by using the OUTPUT statement in PROC MEANS.

General form, OUTPUT statement:

> **OUTPUT** OUT=*SAS-data-set* <*statistic-keyword=variable-name(s)*>;

where

- *SAS-data-set* specifies the name of the output data set

- *statistic-keyword=* specifies the summary statistic to be written out

- *variable-name(s)* specifies the names of the variables that will be created to contain the values of the summary statistic. These variables correspond to the analysis variables that are listed in the VAR statement.

When you use the OUTPUT statement without specifying the *statistic-keyword=* option, the summary statistics N, MEAN, STD, MIN, and MAX are produced for **all** of the numeric variables or for **all** of the variables that are listed in a VAR statement.

Specifying the *statistic-keyword=* Option

To specify which statistics to produce in the output data set, you must specify the keyword for the statistic and then list all of the variables. The variables must be listed in the **same order** as in the VAR statement. You can specify more than one statistic in the OUTPUT statement.

The following program creates a typical PROC MEANS report and also creates a summarized output data set that includes only the MEAN and MIN statistics:

```
proc means data=clinic.diabetes;
    var age height weight;
    class sex;
    output out=work.sum_gender
        mean=AvgAge AvgHeight AvgWeight
        min=MinAge MinHeight MinWeight;
run;
```

Sex	N Obs	Variable	N	Mean	Std Dev	Minimum	Maximum
F	11	Age	11	48.9090909	13.3075508	16.0000000	63.0000000
		Height	11	63.9090909	2.1191765	61.0000000	68.0000000
		Weight	11	150.4545455	18.4464828	102.0000000	168.0000000
M	9	Age	9	44.0000000	12.3895117	15.0000000	54.0000000
		Height	9	70.6666667	2.6457513	66.0000000	75.0000000
		Weight	9	204.2222222	30.2893454	140.0000000	240.0000000

To see the contents of the output data set, submit the following PROC PRINT step:

```
proc print data=work.sum_gender;
run;
```

Obs	Sex	_TYPE_	_FREQ_	AvgAge	AvgHeight	AvgWeight	MinAge	MinHeight	MinWeight
1		0	20	46.7000	66.9500	174.650	15	61	102
2	F	1	11	48.9091	63.9091	150.455	16	61	102
3	M	1	9	44.0000	70.6667	204.222	15	66	140

> You can use the NOPRINT option in the PROC MEANS statement to prevent the default report from being created. For example, the following program creates only the output data set:
>
> ```
> proc means data=clinic.diabetes noprint;
>   var age height weight;
>   class sex;
>   output out=work.sum_gender
>     mean=AvgAge AvgHeight AvgWeight;
>
>   run;
> ```

> In addition to the variables that you specify, the procedure adds the _TYPE_ and _FREQ_ variables to the output data set. When no statistic keywords are specified, PROC MEANS also adds the variable _STAT_. For more information about these variables, see the SAS documentation for the MEANS procedure.

Creating a Summarized Data Set Using PROC SUMMARY

You can also create a summarized output data set by using the SUMMARY procedure. When you use PROC SUMMARY, you use the same code to produce the output data set that you would use with PROC MEANS.

The difference between the two procedures is that PROC MEANS produces a report by default (remember that you can use the NOPRINT option to suppress the default report). By contrast, to produce a report in PROC SUMMARY, you must include a PRINT option in the PROC SUMMARY statement.

Example

The following example creates an output data set but does not create a report:

```
proc summary data=clinic.diabetes;
  var age height weight;
  class sex;
  output out=work.sum_gender
    mean=AvgAge AvgHeight AvgWeight;
run;
```

If you placed a PRINT option in the PROC SUMMARY statement above, this program would produce the same report as if you replaced the word SUMMARY with MEANS:

```
proc summary data=clinic.diabetes print;
    var age height weight;
    class sex;
    output out=work.sum_gender
        mean=AvgAge AvgHeight AvgWeight;
run;
```

Sex	N Obs	Variable	N	Mean	Std Dev	Minimum	Maximum
F	11	Age	11	48.9090909	13.3075508	16.0000000	63.0000000
		Height	11	63.9090909	2.1191765	61.0000000	68.0000000
		Weight	11	150.4545455	18.4464828	102.0000000	168.0000000
M	9	Age	9	44.0000000	12.3895117	15.0000000	54.0000000
		Height	9	70.6666667	2.6457513	66.0000000	75.0000000
		Weight	9	204.2222222	30.2893454	140.0000000	240.0000000

Producing Frequency Tables

Producing Frequency Tables Using PROC FREQ

The FREQ procedure is a descriptive procedure as well as a statistical procedure. It produces one-way and *n*-way frequency tables, and it concisely describes your data by reporting the distribution of variable values. You can use the FREQ procedure to create crosstabulation tables that summarize data for two or more categorical variables by showing the number of observations for each combination of variable values.

The FREQ procedure can include many statements and options for controlling frequency output. For simplicity, let's consider the procedure in its basic form.

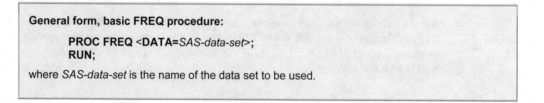

General form, basic FREQ procedure:

    PROC FREQ <DATA=*SAS-data-set***>;**
    RUN;

where *SAS-data-set* is the name of the data set to be used.

By default, PROC FREQ creates a one-way table with the **frequency**, **percent**, **cumulative frequency**, and **cumulative percent** of every value of all variables in a data set.

Variable	Frequency	Percent	Cumulative Frequency	Cumulative Percent
Value	Number of observations with the value	Frequency of the value divided by the total number of observations	Sum of the frequency counts of the value and all other values listed above it in the table	Cumulative frequency of the value divided by the total number of observations

For example, the following FREQ procedure creates a frequency table for each variable in the data set **Parts.Widgets**. All the unique values are shown for ItemName, LotSize, and Region.

```
proc freq data=parts.widgets;
run;
```

ItemName	Frequency	Percent	Cumulative Frequency	Cumulative Percent
Bolt	2930	34.52	2930	34.52
Locknut	3106	36.60	6036	71.12
Washer	2451	28.88	8487	100.00

LotSize	Frequency	Percent	Cumulative Frequency	Cumulative Percent
1	4256	50.15	4256	50.15
2	1009	11.89	5265	62.04
3	3222	37.96	8487	100.00

Region	Frequency	Percent	Cumulative Frequency	Cumulative Percent
East	2848	33.56	2848	33.56
North	1355	15.97	4203	49.53
South	1706	20.10	5909	69.63
West	2578	30.38	8487	100.00

Specifying Variables in PROC FREQ

By default, the FREQ procedure creates frequency tables for every variable in your data set. But this isn't always what you want. A variable that has continuous numeric values—such as DateTime—can result in a lengthy and meaningless table. Likewise, a variable that has a unique value for each observation—such as FullName—is unsuitable for PROC FREQ processing. Frequency distributions work best with variables whose values can be described as categorical, and whose values are best summarized by counts rather than by averages.

To specify the variables to be processed by the FREQ procedure, include a **TABLES** statement.

General form, TABLES statement:

> **TABLES** *variable(s)*;

where *variable(s)* lists the variables to include.

Example

The order in which the variables appear in the TABLES statement determines the order in which they are listed in the PROC FREQ report.

Consider the SAS data set **Finance.Loans**. The variables Rate and Months are best described as categorical values, so they are the best choices for frequency tables.

Account	Amount	Rate	Months	Payment
101-1092	$22,000	10.00%	60	$467.43
101-1731	$114,000	9.50%	360	$958.57
101-1289	$10,000	10.50%	36	$325.02
101-3144	$3,500	10.50%	12	$308.52
103-1135	$8,700	10.50%	24	$403.47
103-1994	$18,500	10.00%	60	$393.07
103-2335	$5,000	10.50%	48	$128.02
103-3864	$87,500	9.50%	360	$735.75
103-3891	$30,000	9.75%	360	$257.75

```
proc freq data=finance.loans;
   tables rate months;
run;
```

Rate	Frequency	Percent	Cumulative Frequency	Cumulative Percent
9.50%	2	22.22	2	22.22
9.75%	1	11.11	3	33.33
10.00%	2	22.22	5	55.56
10.50%	4	44.44	9	100.00

Months	Frequency	Percent	Cumulative Frequency	Cumulative Percent
12	1	11.11	1	11.11
24	1	11.11	2	22.22
36	1	11.11	3	33.33
48	1	11.11	4	44.44
60	2	22.22	6	66.67
360	3	33.33	9	100.00

In addition to listing variables separately, you can use a numbered range of variables.

```
proc freq data=perm.survey;
   tables item1-item3;
run;
```

Item1	Frequency	Percent	Cumulative Frequency	Cumulative Percent
2	1	25.00	1	25.00
4	2	50.00	3	75.00
5	1	25.00	4	100.00

Item2	Frequency	Percent	Cumulative Frequency	Cumulative Percent
1	1	25.00	1	25.00
3	2	50.00	3	75.00
5	1	25.00	4	100.00

Item3	Frequency	Percent	Cumulative Frequency	Cumulative Percent
4	3	75.00	3	75.00
5	1	25.00	4	100.00

Adding the NOCUM option to your TABLES statement suppresses the display of cumulative frequencies and cumulative percentages in one-way frequency tables and in list output. The syntax for the NOCUM option is shown below.

```
TABLES variable(s) / NOCUM;
```

Creating Two-Way Tables

So far, you have used the FREQ procedure to create one-way frequency tables. The table results show total frequency counts for the values within the data set. However, it is often helpful to **crosstabulate** frequencies with the values of other variables. For example, census data is typically crosstabulated with a variable that represents geographical regions.

The simplest crosstabulation is a **two-way** table. To create a two-way table, join two variables with an asterisk (*) in the TABLES statement of a PROC FREQ step.

General form, TABLES statement for crosstabulation:

     TABLES *variable-1*variable-2 <* ... variable-n>*;

where

- *variable-1* specifies table rows

- *variable-2* specifies table columns

- *variable-n* specifies a multi-way table.

When crosstabulations are specified, PROC FREQ produces tables with cells that contain
- cell frequency
- cell percentage of total frequency
- cell percentage of row frequency
- cell percentage of column frequency.

For example, the following program creates the two-way table shown on the following page.

```
proc format;
    value wtfmt low-139='< 140'
                140-180='140-180'
                181-high='> 180';
    value htfmt low-64='< 5''5"'
                65-70='5''5-10"'
                71-high='> 5''10"';
run;
proc freq data=clinic.diabetes;
    tables weight*height;
    format weight wtfmt. height htfmt.;
run;
```

Frequency Percent Row Pct Col Pct	Table of Weight by Height			
		Height		
Weight	**< 5'5"**	**5'5-10"**	**> 5'10"**	**Total**
< 140	2	0	0	2
	10.00	0.00	0.00	10.00
	100.00	0.00	0.00	
	28.57	0.00	0.00	
140-180	5	5	0	10
	25.00	25.00	0.00	50.00
	50.00	50.00	0.00	
	71.43	62.50	0.00	
> 180	0	3	5	8
	0.00	15.00	25.00	40.00
	0.00	37.50	62.50	
	0.00	37.50	100.00	
Total	7	8	5	20
	35.00	40.00	25.00	100.00

Note that the first variable, Weight, forms the table rows, and the second variable, Height, forms the columns; reversing the order of the variables in the TABLES statement would reverse their positions in the table. Note also that the statistics are listed in the legend box.

Creating *N*-Way Tables

For a frequency analysis of more than two variables, use PROC FREO ⁺ crosstabulation tables. A series of two-way tables is produced, wⁱᵗⁱ variables.

For example, suppose you want to add the variable Sex to ˥ Height in the data set **Clinic.Diabetes**. Add Sex to the TA variables with an asterisk (*).

```
tables sex*weight*height;
```

Determining the Table Layout

The order of the variables is important. In *n*-way tables, the last two variables of the TABLES statement become the two-way rows and columns. Variables that precede the last two variables in the TABLES statement stratify the crosstabulation tables.

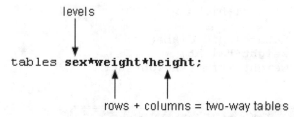

Notice the structure of the output that is produced by the program shown below. Two crosstabulation tables, one for each value of Sex, are produced.

```
proc format;
   value wtfmt low-139='< 140'
               140-180='140-180'
               181-high='> 180';
   value htfmt low-64='< 5''5"'
               65-70='5''5-10"'
               71-high='> 5''10"';
run;
proc freq data=clinic.diabetes;
   tables sex*weight*height;
   format weight wtfmt. height htfmt.;
run;
```

Frequency Percent Row Pct Col Pct	Table 1 of Weight by Height			
	Controlling for Sex=F			
	Height			
Weight	< 5'5"	5'5-10"	> 5'10"	Total
< 140	2 18.18 100.00 28.57	0 0.00 0.00 0.00	0 0.00 0.00 .	2 18.18
140-180	5 45.45 55.56 71.43	4 36.36 44.44 100.00	0 0.00 0.00 .	9 81.82
> 180	0 0.00 . 0.00	0 0.00 . 0.00	0 0.00 . .	0 0.00
Total	7 63.64	4 36.36	0 0.00	11 100.00

Frequency Percent Row Pct Col Pct	Table 2 of Weight by Height			
	Controlling for Sex=M			
	Height			
Weight	< 5'5"	5'5-10"	> 5'10"	Total
< 140	0 0.00 . .	0 0.00 . 0.00	0 0.00 . 0.00	0 0.00
140-180	0 0.00 0.00 .	1 11.11 100.00 25.00	0 0.00 0.00 0.00	1 11.11
> 180	0 0.00 0.00 .	3 33.33 37.50 75.00	5 55.56 62.50 100.00	8 88.89
Total	0 0.00	4 44.44	5 55.56	9 100.00

Changing the Table Format

Beginning in SAS 9, adding the **CROSSLIST** option to your TABLES statement displays crosstabulation tables in ODS column format. This option creates a table that has a table definition that you can customize by using the TEMPLATE procedure.

Notice the structure of the output that is produced by the program shown below.

```
proc format;
   value wtfmt low-139='< 140'
               140-180='140-180'
               181-high='> 180';
   value htfmt low-64='< 5''5"'
               65-70='5''5-10"'
               71-high='> 5''10"';
run;
proc freq data=clinic.diabetes;
   tables sex*weight*height/crosslist;
   format weight wtfmt. height htfmt.;
run;
```

Table of Weight by Height					
Controlling for Sex=F					
Weight	Height	Frequency	Percent	Row Percent	Column Percent
< 140	< 5'5"	2	18.18	100.00	28.57
	5'5-10"	0	0.00	0.00	0.00
	>5'10"	0	0.00	0.00	.
	Total	2	18.18	100.00	
140-180	< 5'5"	5	45.45	55.56	71.43
	5'5-10"	4	36.36	44.44	100.00
	>5'10"	0	0.00	0.00	.
	Total	9	81.82	100.00	
> 180	< 5'5"	0	0.00	.	0.00
	5'5-10"	0	0.00	.	0.00
	>5'10"	0	0.00	.	.
	Total	0	0.00	.	
Total	< 5'5"	7	63.64		100.00
	5'5-10"	4	36.36		100.00
	>5'10"	0	0.00		.
	Total	11	100.00		

Table of Weight by Height					
Controlling for Sex=M					
Weight	Height	Frequency	Percent	Row Percent	Column Percent
< 140	< 5'5"	0	0.00	.	.
	5'5-10"	0	0.00	.	0.00
	>5'10"	0	0.00	.	0.00
	Total	0	0.00	.	
140-180	< 5'5"	0	0.00	0.00	.
	5'5-10"	1	11.11	100.00	25.00
	>5'10"	0	0.00	0.00	0.00
	Total	1	11.11	100.00	
> 180	< 5'5"	0	0.00	0.00	
	5'5-10"	3	3.33	37.50	75.00
	>5'10"	5	55.56	62.50	100.00
	Total	8	88.89	100.00	
Total	< 5'5"	0	0.00		
	5'5-10"	4	44.44		100.00
	>5'10"	5	55.56		100.00
	Total	9	100.00		

Creating Tables in List Formats

When three or more variables are specified, the multiple levels of *n*-way tables can produce considerable output. Such bulky, often complex crosstabulations are often easier to read as a continuous list. Although this eliminates row and column frequencies and percents, the results are compact and clear.

To generate list output for crosstabulations, add a slash (*/*) and the **LIST** option to the TABLES statement in your PROC FREQ step.

```
TABLES variable-1*variable-2 <* ... variable-n> / LIST;
```

Example

Adding the LIST option to our **Clinic.Diabetes** program puts the program's frequencies in a simple, short table.

```
proc format;
    value wtfmt low-139='< 140'
                140-180='140-180'
                181-high='> 180';
    value htfmt low-64='< 5''5"'
                65-70='5''5-10"'
                71-high='> 5''10"';
run;
proc freq data=clinic.diabetes;
    tables sex*weight*height /list;
    format weight wtfmt. height htfmt.;
run;
```

Sex	Weight	Height	Frequency	Percent	Cumulative Frequency	Cumulative Percent
F	< 140	< 5'5"	2	10.00	2	10.00
F	140-180	< 5'5"	5	25.00	7	35.00
F	140-180	5'5-10"	4	20.00	11	55.00
M	140-180	5'5-10"	1	5.00	12	60.00
M	> 180	5'5-10"	3	15.00	15	75.00
M	> 180	> 5'10"	5	25.00	20	100.00

Suppressing Table Information

Another way to control the format of crosstabulation tables is to limit the output of the FREQ procedure to a **few specific statistics**. Remember that when crosstabulations are run, PROC FREQ produces tables with cells that contain

- cell frequency

- cell percentage of total frequency

- cell percentage of row frequency

- cell percentage of column frequency.

You can use options to suppress any of these statistics. To control the depth of crosstabulation results, add a slash (/) and any combination of the following options to the TABLES statement:

- **NOFREQ** suppresses cell frequencies.

- **NOPERCENT** suppresses cell percentages

- **NOROW** supresses row percentages.

- **NOCOL** suppresses column percentages.

Example

Suppose you want to use only the percentages of `Sex` and `Weight` combinations in the data set **Clinic.Diabetes**. To block frequency counts and row and column percentages, add the NOFREQ, NOROW, and NOCOL options to your program's TABLES statement.

```
proc format;
    value wtfmt low-139='< 140'
                140-180='140-180'
                181-high='> 180';
run;
proc freq data=clinic.diabetes;
    tables sex*weight /nofreq norow nocol;
    format weight wtfmt.;
run;
```

Percent	Table of Sex by Weight			
		Weight		
Sex	< 140	140-180	> 180	Total
F	10.00	45.00	0.00	55.00
M	0.00	5.00	40.00	45.00
Total	2 10.00	10 50.00	8 40.00	20 100.00

Notice that Percent is the only statistic that remains in the table's legend box.

Summary

Text Summary

Purpose of PROC MEANS

The MEANS procedure provides an easy way to compute descriptive statistics. Descriptive statistics such as the mean, minimum, and maximum provide useful information about numeric data.

Specifying Statistics

By default, PROC MEANS computes the *n*-count (the number of nonmissing values), the mean, the standard deviation, and the minimum and maximum values for variables. To specify statistics, list their keywords in the PROC MEANS statement.

Descriptive Statistics

Keyword	Description
CLM	Two-sided confidence limit for the mean
CSS	Corrected sum of squares
CV	Coefficient of variation
KURTOSIS / KURT	Kurtosis
LCLM	One-sided confidence limit below the mean
MAX	Maximum value
MEAN	Average
MIN	Minimum value
N	Number of observations with nonmissing values
NMISS	Number of observations with missing values
RANGE	Range
SKEWNESS / SKEW	Skewness
STDDEV / STD	Standard Deviation
STDERR / STDMEAN	Standard error of the mean
SUM	Sum
SUMWGT	Sum of the `Weight` variable values
UCLM	One-sided confidence limit above the mean
USS	Uncorrected sum of squares
VAR	Variance

Quantile Statistics

Keyword	Description
MEDIAN / P50	Median or 50th percentile
P1	1st percentile
P5	5th percentile
P10	10th percentile
Q1 / P25	Lower quartile or 25th percentile
Q3 / P75	Upper quartile or 75th percentile
P90	90th percentile
P95	95th percentile
P99	99th percentile
QRANGE	Difference between upper and lower quartiles: Q3-Q1

Hypothesis Testing

Keyword	Description
PROBT	Probability of a greater absolute value for the *t* value
T	Student's *t* for testing the hypothesis that the population mean is 0

Limiting Decimal Places

Because PROC MEANS uses the BEST. format by default, procedure output can contain unnecessary decimal places. To limit decimal places, use the **MAXDEC= option** and set it equal to the length that you prefer.

Specifying Variables in PROC MEANS

By default, PROC MEANS computes statistics for all numeric variables. To specify the variables to include in PROC MEANS output, list them in a VAR statement.

Group Processing Using the CLASS Statement

Include a **CLASS statement**, specifying variable names, in order to group PROC MEANS output by variable values. Statistics are not computed for the CLASS variables.

Group Processing Using the BY Statement

Include a **BY statement**, specifying variable names, in order to group PROC MEANS output by variable values. Your data must be sorted according to those variables. Statistics are not computed for the BY variables.

Creating a Summarized Data Set Using PROC MEANS

You can create an output SAS data set that contains summarized variables by using the **OUTPUT statement** in **PROC MEANS**. When you use the OUTPUT statement without specifying the *statistic-keyword=* option, the summary statistics N, MEAN, STD, MIN, and MAX are produced for all of the numeric variables or for all of the variables that are listed in a VAR statement.

Creating a Summarized Data Set Using PROC SUMMARY

You can also create a summarized output data set by using **PROC SUMMARY**. The PROC SUMMARY code for producing an output data set is exactly the same as the code for producing an output data set with PROC MEANS. The difference between the two procedures is that PROC MEANS produces a report by default, whereas PROC SUMMARY produces an output data set by default.

The FREQ Procedure

The **FREQ procedure** is a descriptive procedure as well as a statistical procedure that produces one-way and n-way frequency tables. It concisely describes your data by reporting the distribution of variable values.

Specifying Variables

By default, the FREQ procedure creates frequency tables for every variable in your data set. To specify the variables to analyze, include them in a **TABLES** statement.

Creating Two-Way Tables

When a TABLES statement contains two variables joined by an asterisk (*), PROC FREQ produces crosstabulation tables. The resulting table displays values for

- cell frequency
- cell percentage of total frequency
- cell percentage of row frequency
- cell percentage of column frequency.

Creating *N*-Way Tables

Crosstabulations can include more than two variables. When three or more variables are joined in a TABLES statement, the result is a series of two-way tables that are grouped by the values of the first two variables that are listed. You can use the CROSSLIST option to format your tables in ODS column format.

Creating Tables in List Format

To reduce the bulk of *n*-way table output, add a slash (/) and the **LIST** option to the end of the TABLES statement. PROC FREQ then prints compact, multicolumn lists instead of a series of tables.

Suppressing Table Information

You can suppress the display of specific statistics by adding a slash (/) and one or more options to the TABLES statement:

- **NOFREQ** suppresses cell frequencies.
- **NOPERCENT** suppresses cell percentages.
- **NOROW** suppresses row percentages.
- **NOCOL** suppresses column percentages.

Points to Remember

- In PROC MEANS, use a VAR statement to limit output to relevant variables. Exclude statistics for nominal variables such as ID or ProductCode.

- By default, PROC MEANS prints the full width of each numeric variable. Use the MAXDEC= option to limit decimal places and to improve legibility.

- Data must be sorted for BY-group processing. You might need to run PROC SORT before using PROC MEANS with a BY statement.

- PROC MEANS and PROC SUMMARY produce the same results; however, the default output is different. PROC MEANS produces a report, whereas PROC SUMMARY produces an output data set.

- If you do not include a TABLES statement, PROC FREQ produces statistics for every variable in the data set.

- Variables that have continuous numeric values can create a large amount of output. Use a TABLES statement to exclude such variables, or group their values by applying a FORMAT statement.

Practice

After you complete this chapter, practice what you learned by using the sample data and SAS programs for Chapter 9, **Producing Descriptive Statistics**, which are located on the CD-ROM. Make sure that you follow the directions for creating your sample data in the Before You Begin section.

Quiz

Select the best answer for each question. After completing the quiz, check your answers using the answer key in the appendix.

1. The default statistics produced by the MEANS procedure are **n-count**, **mean**, **minimum**, **maximum**, and

   a. median.
   b. range.
   c. standard deviation.
   d. standard error of the mean.

2. Which statement will limit a PROC MEANS analysis to the variables `Boarded`, `Transfer`, and `Deplane`?

   a. `by boarded transfer deplane;`
   b. `class boarded transfer deplane;`
   c. `output boarded transfer deplane;`
   d. `var boarded transfer deplane;`

3. The data set **Survey.Health** includes the following variables. Which is a poor candidate for PROC MEANS analysis?

   a. `IDnum`
   b. `Age`
   c. `Height`
   d. `Weight`

4. Which of the following statements is true regarding BY-group processing?

   a. BY variables must be either indexed or sorted.
   b. Summary statistics are computed for BY variables.
   c. BY-group processing is preferred when you are categorizing data that contains few variables.
   d. BY-group processing overwrites your data set with the newly grouped observations.

5. Which group processing statement produced the PROC MEANS output shown below?

Survive	Sex	N Obs	Variable	N	Mean	Std Dev	Minimum	Maximum
DIED	1	4	Arterial	4	92.5	10.5	83.0	103.0
			Heart	4	111.0	53.4	54.0	183.0
			Cardiac	4	176.8	75.2	95.0	260.0
			Urinary	4	98.0	186.1	0.0	377.0
	2	6	Arterial	6	94.2	27.3	72.0	145.0
			Heart	6	103.7	16.7	81.0	130.0
			Cardiac	6	318.3	102.6	156.0	424.0
			Urinary	6	100.3	155.7	0.0	405.0
SURV	1	5	Arterial	5	77.2	12.2	61.0	88.0
			Heart	5	109.0	32.0	77.0	149.0
			Cardiac	5	298.0	139.8	66.0	410.0
			Urinary	5	100.8	60.2	44.0	200.0
	2	5	Arterial	5	78.8	6.8	72.0	87.0
			Heart	5	100.0	13.4	84.0	111.0
			Cardiac	5	330.2	87.0	256.0	471.0
			Urinary	5	111.2	152.4	12.0	377.0

a. `class sex survive;`

b. `class survive sex;`

c. `by sex survive;`

d. `by survive sex;`

6. Which program can be used to create the following output?

Sex	N Obs	Variable	N	Mean	Std Dev	Minimum	Maximum
F	11	Age	11	48.9090909	13.3075508	16.0000000	63.0000000
		Height	11	63.9090909	2.1191765	61.0000000	68.0000000
		Weight	11	150.4545455	18.4464828	102.0000000	168.0000000
M	9	Age	9	44.0000000	12.3895117	15.0000000	54.0000000
		Height	9	70.6666667	2.6457513	66.0000000	75.0000000
		Weight	9	204.2222222	30.2893454	140.0000000	240.0000000

a.
```
proc means data=clinic.diabetes;
     var age height weight;
     class sex;
     output out=work.sum_gender
        mean=AvgAge AvgHeight AvgWeight;
   run;
```

b.
```
proc summary data=clinic.diabetes print;
     var age height weight;
     class sex;
     output out=work.sum_gender
        mean=AvgAge AvgHeight AvgWeight;
```

```
   run;
c. proc means data=clinic.diabetes noprint;
      var age height weight;
      class sex;
      output out=work.sum_gender
        mean=AvgAge AvgHeight AvgWeight;
   run;
```

d. Both *a* and *b.*

7. By default, PROC FREQ creates a table of frequencies and percentages for which data set variables?

   a. character variables

   b. numeric variables

   c. both character and numeric variables

   d. none: variables must always be specified

8. Frequency distributions work best with variables that contain

   a. continuous values.

   b. numeric values.

   c. categorical values.

   d. unique values.

9. Which PROC FREQ step produced this two-way table?

Frequency Percent Row Pct Col Pct	Table of Weight by Height			
		Height		
Weight	< 5'5"	5'5-10"	> 5'10"	Total
< 140	2 10.00 100.00 28.57	0 0.00 0.00 0.00	0 0.00 0.00 0.00	2 10.00
140-180	5 25.00 50.00 71.43	5 25.00 50.00 62.50	0 0.00 0.00 0.00	10 50.00
> 180	0 0.00 0.00 0.00	3 15.00 37.50 37.50	5 25.00 62.50 100.00	8 40.00
Total	7 35.00	8 40.00	5 25.00	20 100.00

```
a. proc freq data=clinic.diabetes;
      tables height weight;
      format height htfmt. weight wtfmt.;
   run;
b. proc freq data=clinic.diabetes;
      tables weight height;
      format weight wtfmt. height htfmt.;
   run;
c. proc freq data=clinic.diabetes;
      tables height*weight;
      format height htfmt. weight wtfmt.;
   run;
d. proc freq data=clinic.diabetes;
      tables weight*height;
      format weight wtfmt. height htfmt.;
   run;
```

10. Which PROC FREQ step produced this table?

Percent	Table of Sex by Weight			
		Weight		
Sex	< 140	140-180	> 180	Total
F	10.00	45.00	0.00	55.00
M	0.00	5.00	40.00	45.00
Total	2 10.00	10 50.00	8 40.00	20 100.00

```
a. proc freq data=clinic.diabetes;
      tables sex weight / list;
      format weight wtfmt.;
   run;
b. proc freq data=clinic.diabetes;
      tables sex*weight / nocol;
      format weight wtfmt.;
   run;
c. proc freq data=clinic.diabetes;
      tables sex weight / norow nocol;
      format weight wtfmt.;
   run;
d. proc freq data=clinic.diabetes;
      tables sex*weight / nofreq norow nocol;
      format weight wtfmt.;
   run;
```

Producing HTML Output

Overview

Introduction

In previous chapters, you've seen both traditional SAS listing output and HTML output. When you set options to create HTML output, SAS uses **Output Delivery System (ODS)** statements to generate the output.

Using ODS, you can create, customize, and manage HTML output in any operating environment by submitting programming statements. After you create HTML files, you can view them using Internet Explorer, Netscape Navigator, or any Web browser that fully supports HTML 3.2.

This chapter shows you how to create and view HTML output using ODS. You also learn how to apply styles to ODS output.

 By default, all code that you submit to SAS Enterprise Guide has ODS statements included to create HTML output. Before you submit your own ODS statements, you must turn off this default behavior. The practice programs on your companion CD include instructions for turning off the default behavior.

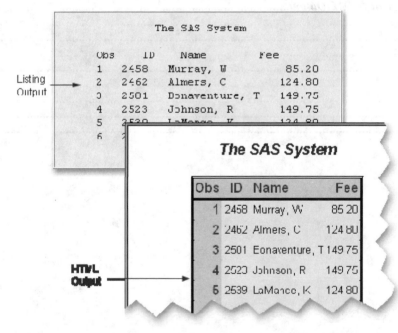

Objectives

In this chapter, you learn to

- open and close ODS destinations
- create a simple HTML file with the output of one or more procedures
- create HTML output with a linked table of contents in a frame
- use options to specify links and file paths
- view HTML output
- apply styles to HTML output.

The Output Delivery System

Before you learn to write ODS programming statements, it's helpful to understand a little about ODS.

Advantages of ODS

ODS gives you formatting options and makes procedure output much more flexible. With ODS, you can easily create output in a variety of formats, including

- **HTML output**

Obs	ID	Name	Fee
1	2458	Murray, W	85.20
2	2462	Almers, C	124.80
3	2501	Bonaventure, T	149.75
4	2523	Johnson, R	149.75
5	2539	LaMance, K	124.80
6	2544	Jones, M	124.80

- An **output data set** of procedure results

VarName	Quantile	Estimate
RestHR	100% Max	80
RestHR	99%	80
RestHR	95%	79
RestHR	90%	78
RestHR	75% Q3	76
RestHR	50% Median	72
RestHR	25% Q1	70
RestHR	10%	68

- Traditional **SAS listing output**

```
                    The SAS System

        Obs    ID   Name               Fee
        1     2458  Murray, W         85.20
        2     2462  Almers, C        124.80
        3     2501  Bonaventure, T   149.75
        4     2523  Johnson, R       149.75
        5     2539  LaMance, K       124.80
        6     2544  Jones, M         124.80
```

Also, ODS holds your output in its component parts (**data** and **table definition**) so that numerical data retains its full data precision.

Let's see how ODS creates output.

How ODS Works

When you submit your ODS statements and the SAS program that creates your output, ODS does the following:

1. ODS creates your output in the form of output objects.

    Each output object contains the results of a procedure or DATA step (the **data component**) and can also contain information about how to render the results (the **table definition**).

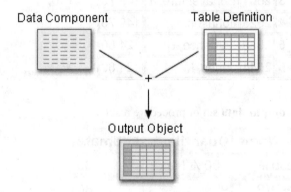

2. ODS sends the output object to the **ODS destination(s)** that you specify and creates formatted output as specified by the destination. For example, when the Listing and HTML destinations are open, ODS creates Listing and HTML output.

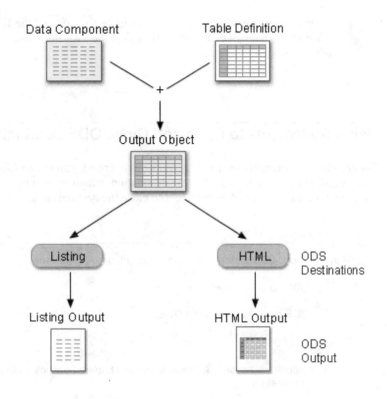

In the SAS windowing environment, ODS also creates a link to each output object in the **Results window** and identifies each output object by the appropriate icon.

Opening and Closing ODS Destinations

ODS Destinations

You use ODS statements to specify **destinations** for your output. Each destination creates a specific type of formatted output. The table that follows lists the ODS destinations that are supported.

This destination...	Produces...
HTML	output that is formatted in HyperText Markup Language (HTML)
Listing	output that is formatted like traditional SAS procedure (listing) output
Markup Language Family	output that is formatted using markup languages such as Extensible Markup Language (XML)
ODS Document	a hierarchy of output objects that enables you to render multiple ODS output without re-running procedures
Output	SAS data sets
Printer Family	output that is formatted for a high-resolution printer, such as PostScript (PS), Portable Document Format (PDF), or Printer Control Language (PCL) files
RTF	Rich Text Format output for use with Microsoft Word

In this chapter, we will discuss the **Listing** destination and the **HTML** destination. For information about all ODS destinations, see the SAS documentation for the Output Delivery System.

Using Statements to Open and Close ODS Destinations

For each type of formatted output that you want to create, you use an ODS statement to open the destination. The exception is the Listing destination, which is open by default. At the end of your program, you use another ODS statement to close the destination so that you can access your output.

General form, ODS statement to open and close destinations:

> **ODS** *open-destination*;

> **ODS** *close-destination* **CLOSE;**

where

- *open-destination* is a keyword and any required options for the type of output that you want to create, such as

  - **HTML FILE='**_html-file-pathname_**'**
  - **LISTING**.

- *close-destination* is a keyword for the type of output.

You can issue ODS statements in any order, depending on whether you need to open or close the ODS destination. Most ODS destinations are closed by default, and you open them at the beginning of your program and close them at the end. The exception is the Listing destination, which is open by default.

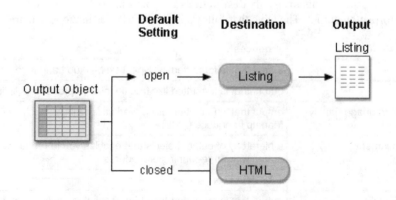

Example

The following program creates SAS listing output because the Listing destination is open by default. No other ODS destinations are open, so no other output formats are produced.

```
proc print data=sasuser.mydata;
run;
```

The following program produces HTML **and** listing output:

```
ods html body='c:\mydata.html';
proc print data=sasuser.mydata;
run;
ods html close;
```

 This example is meant to demonstrate how you open and close ODS destinations. You learn the specifics of creating HTML output later in this chapter.

Closing the Listing Destination

As you have learned, the Listing destination is open by default. Because open destinations use system resources, it's a good idea to close the Listing destination at the **beginning** of your program if you don't want to produce listing output. Here is an example:

```
ods listing close;
```

The Listing destination remains closed until you end your current SAS session or until you re-open the destination. It's a good programming practice to re-set ODS to listing output (the default setting) at the end of your programs. Here is an example:

```
ods listing;
```

Example

The following program produces only HTML output:

```
ods listing close;
ods html body='c:\mydata.html';
proc print data=sasuser.mydata;
run;
ods html close;
ods listing;
```

Closing Multiple ODS Destinations Concurrently

One of the features of ODS is that you can produce output in multiple formats concurrently by opening each ODS destination at the beginning of the program.

When you have more than one open ODS destination, you can use the keyword **_ALL_** in the ODS CLOSE statement to close all open destinations concurrently.

Example

The program below opens the HTML and PDF destinations before the PROC step and closes all ODS destinations at the end of the program:

```
ods html file='HTML-file-pathname';
ods pdf file='PDF-file-pathname';
proc print data=sasuser.admit;
run;
ods _all_ close;
ods listing;
```

Notice that the last ODS statement re-opens the Listing destination so that ODS returns to producing listing output for subsequent DATA or PROC steps in the current session.

Creating Simple HTML

To create HTML output, you open the HTML destination using the **ODS HTML statement**.

General form, ODS HTML statement:

    ODS HTML BODY=file-specification;
    ODS HTML CLOSE;

where *file-specification* identifies the file that contains the HTML output. The specification can be

- an HTML filename (include the complete pathname if you want to save the HTML file to a specific location)

- a fileref (file shortcut) that has been assigned to an HTML file

- a SAS catalog entry in the form *entry-name*.html.

FILE= can also be used to specify the file that contains the HTML output. FILE= is an alias for BODY=.

Example

The program below creates PROC PRINT output in an HTML file. The BODY= option specifies the file **F:\admit.html** in the Windows operating environment as the file that contains the PROC PRINT results.

```
ods listing close;
ods html body='f:\admit.html';
proc print data=clinic.admit label;
   var sex age height weight actlevel;
   label actlevel='Activity Level';
run;
ods html close;
ods listing;
```

Notice that ODS statements close the Listing destination and open the HTML destination. Then, after the RUN statement, you close the HTML destination and open the Listing destination.

The HTML file **admit.html** contains the results of all procedure steps **between** the ODS HTML statement and ODS HTML CLOSE statement.

Obs	Sex	Age	Height	Weight	Activity Level
1	M	27	72	168	HIGH
2	F	34	66	152	HIGH
3	F	31	61	123	LOW
4	F	43	63	137	MOD
5	M	51	71	158	LOW
6	M	29	76	193	HIGH
7	F	32	67	151	MOD
8	M	35	70	173	MOD
9	M	34	73	154	LOW
10	F	49	64	172	LOW
11	F	44	66	140	HIGH
12	F	28	62	118	LOW
13	M	30	69	147	MOD
14	F	40	69	163	HIGH
15	M	47	72	173	MOD
16	M	60	71	191	LOW
17	F	43	65	123	MOD
18	M	25	75	188	HIGH
19	F	22	63	139	LOW
20	F	41	67	141	HIGH
21	M	54	71	183	MOD

Viewing Your HTML Output

 If you're working in the SAS windowing environment, when you submit the program, the body file will automatically appear in the SAS internal browser or your preferred Web browser.

When you submit the program, two HTML results will appear in the Project window. One uses the HTML style that is active in SAS Enterprise Guide. The other uses the ODS statements from the code that you submitted and creates a temporary file labeled with the path and filename that you designated. It is similar in style to the actual HTML file that gets created in the location that you specify.

Creating HTML Output from Multiple Procedures

You can also use the ODS HTML statement to direct the results from multiple procedures to the same HTML file.

The program below generates HTML output for the PRINT and TABULATE procedures. The results for both procedures are saved to the file **C:\Records\data.html** (in the Windows operating system).

 In the SAS windowing environment, a link for each output object (one for each procedure) appears in the Results window.

```
ods listing close;
ods html body='c:\records\data.html';
proc print data=clinic.admit label;
    var id sex age height weight actlevel;
    label actlevel='Activity Level';
run;
proc tabulate data=clinic.stress2;
    var resthr maxhr rechr;
    table min mean, resthr maxhr rechr;
run;
ods html close;
ods listing;
```

The following is a representation of the HTML file containing the results from the program above. Notice that the results from each procedure are appended.

The SAS System

Obs	ID	Sex	Age	Height	Weight	Activity Level
1	2458	M	27	72	168	HIGH
2	2462	F	34	66	152	HIGH
3	2501	F	31	61	123	LOW
4	2523	F	43	63	137	MOD
5	2539	M	51	71	158	LOW
6	2544	M	29	76	193	HIGH
7	2552	F	32	67	151	MOD
8	2555	M	35	70	173	MOD
9	2563	M	34	73	154	LOW
10	2568	F	49	64	172	LOW
11	2571	F	44	66	140	HIGH
12	2572	F	28	62	118	LOW
13	2574	M	30	69	147	MOD
14	2575	F	40	69	163	HIGH
15	2578	M	47	72	173	MOD

Obs	ID	Sex	Age	Height	Weight	Activity Level
16	2579	M	60	71	191	LOW
17	2584	F	43	65	123	MOD
18	2586	M	25	75	188	HIGH
19	2588	F	22	63	139	LOW
20	2589	F	41	67	141	HIGH
21	2595	M	54	71	183	MOD

The SAS System

	RestHR	MaxHR	RecHR
Min	65.00	152.00	108.00
Mean	72.95	171.10	128.95

Creating HTML Output with a Table of Contents

So far in this chapter, you've used the BODY= option to create a simple HTML file containing your procedure output. Suppose you want to create an HTML file that has a table of contents with links to the output of each specific procedure. You can do this by specifying additional files in the ODS HTML statement.

General form, ODS HTML statement to create a linked table of contents:

    ODS HTML
        BODY=*body-file-specification*
        CONTENTS=*contents-file-specification*
        FRAME=*frame-file-specification*;
    ODS HTML CLOSE;

where

- *body-file-specification* is the name of an HTML file that contains the procedure output.

- *contents-file-specification* is the name of an HTML file that contains a table of contents with links to the procedure output.

- *frame-file-specification* is the name of an HTML file that integrates the table of contents and the body file. If you specify FRAME=, you must also specify CONTENTS=.

To direct the HTML output to a specific storage location, specify the complete pathname of the HTML file in the *file-specification*.

Example

In the program below,

- the BODY= option creates **data.html** in the **c:\records** directory. The body file contains the results of the two procedures.

- the CONTENTS= option creates **toc.html** in the **c:\records** directory. The table of contents file has links to each procedure output in the body file.

- the FRAME= option creates **frame.html** in the **c:\records** directory. The frame file integrates the table of contents and the body file.

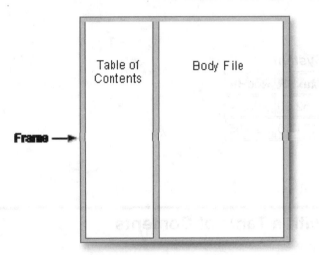

```
ods listing close;
ods html body='c:\records\data.html'
         contents='c:\records\toc.html'
         frame='c:\records\frame.html';
proc print data=clinic.admit label;
   var id sex age height weight actlevel;
   label actlevel='Activity Level';
run;
proc print data=clinic.stress2;
   var id resthr maxhr rechr;
run;
ods html close;
ods listing;
```

The frame file, **frame.html**, is shown below.

File C:\Records\frame.html

The SAS System

Obs	ID	Sex	Age	Height	Weight	Activity Level
1	2458	M	27	72	168	HIGH
2	2462	F	34	66	152	HIGH
3	2501	F	31	61	123	LOW
4	2523	F	43	63	137	MOD
5	2539	M	51	71	158	LOW
6	2544	M	29	76	193	HIGH
7	2552	F	32	67	151	MOD

FRAME=
frame.html

CONTENTS=
toc.html

BODY=
data.html

Viewing Frame Files

In the SAS windowing environment, the Results window does not display links to frame files. Only the body file will automatically appear in the internal browser or your preferred Web browser. To view the frame file that integrates the body file **and** the table of contents, select **File→ Open** from within the internal browser or your preferred Web browser. Then open the frame file that you specified using FRAME=. In the example above, this file is **frame.html**, which is stored in the **Records** directory in the Windows environment.

In SAS Enterprise Guide, use Windows Explorer to locate the frame file **frame.html** in the **Records** directory, and then double-click the file to open it in your browser. If you are using SAS Enterprise Guide 4.1, you can double-click the shortcut to **frame.html** in the Project Explorer window.

Using the Table of Contents

The table of contents created by the CONTENTS= option contains a numbered heading for each procedure that creates output. Below each heading is a link to the output for that procedure.

On some browsers, you can select a heading to contract or expand the table of contents.

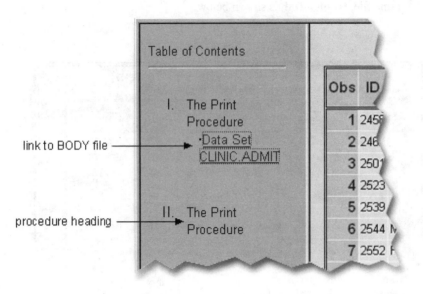

Using Options to Specify Links and Paths

When ODS generates HTML files for the body, contents, and frame, it also generates links between the files by using the HTML filenames that you specify in the ODS HTML statement. If you specify complete pathnames, then ODS uses those pathnames in the links it generates.

The ODS statement below creates a frame file that has links to **C:\Records\toc.html** and **C:\Records\data.html**, and a contents file that has links to **C:\Records\data.html**.

```
ods html body='c:\records\data.html'
         contents='c:\records\toc.html'
         frame='c:\records\frame.html';
```

A portion of the source code for the HTML file **frame.html** is shown below. Notice that the links have the complete pathnames specified in the file specifications for the contents and body files. Links in the contents file contain the same pathname.

```
<FRAME MARGINWIDTH="4" MARGINHEIGHT="0" SRC="c:\records\toc.html"
    NAME="contents" SCROLLING=auto>
<FRAME MARGINWIDTH="9" MARGINHEIGHT="0" SRC="c:\records\data.html"
    NAME="body" SCROLLING=auto>
```

These links work when you are viewing the HTML files locally, but if you want to place these files on a Web server so that other people can access them, then the links need to include either the complete URL for an absolute link or the HTML filename for a relative link.

The URL= Suboption

By specifying the **URL= suboption** in the BODY= or CONTENTS= file specification, you can provide a URL that ODS uses in all the links that it creates to the file. You can use the URL= suboption in any ODS file specification except FRAME= (because no ODS file references the frame file).

General form, URL= suboption in a file specification:

   (**URL=***'Uniform-Resource-Locator'*)

where *Uniform-Resource-Locator* is the name of an HTML file or the full URL of an HTML file. ODS uses this URL instead of the filename in all the links and references that it creates that point to the file.

 The URL= suboption is useful for building HTML files that can be moved from one location to another. If the links from the contents and page files are constructed with a simple URL (one name), they work as long as the contents, page, and body files are all in the same location.

Example: Relative URLs

In this ODS HTML statement, the URL= suboption specifies only the HTML filename. This is the most common style of linking between files because maintenance is easier and the files can be moved as long as they all remain in the same directory or storage location.

```
ods html body='c:\records\data.html' (url='data.html')
         contents='c:\records\toc.html' (url='toc.html')
         frame='c:\records\frame.html';
```

The source code for **frame.html** has only the HTML filename as specified in the URL= suboptions for the body and contents files.

```
<FRAME MARGINWIDTH="4" MARGINHEIGHT="0" SRC="toc.html"
    NAME="contents" SCROLLING=auto>
<FRAME MARGINWIDTH="9" MARGINHEIGHT="0" SRC="data.html"
    NAME="body" SCROLLING=auto>
```

Example: Absolute URLs

Alternatively, in this ODS HTML statement, the URL= suboptions specify complete URLs by using HyperText Transfer Protocol (HTTP). These files can be stored in the same or different locations.

```
ods html body='c:\records\data.html'
         (url='http://mysite.com/myreports/data.html')
         contents='c:\records\toc.html'
         (url='http://mysite.com/mycontents/toc.html')
         frame='c:\records\frame.html';
```

As you would expect, the source code for **frame.html** has the entire HTTP addresses that you specified in the URL= suboptions for the body and contents files.

```
<FRAME MARGINWIDTH="4" MARGINHEIGHT="0" SRC="http://mysite.com/myreports/toc.html"
    NAME="contents" SCROLLING=auto>
<FRAME MARGINWIDTH="9" MARGINHEIGHT="0" SRC="http://mysite.com/myreports/data.html"
    NAME="body" SCROLLING=auto>
```

 When you use the URL= suboption to specify a complete URL, you might need to move your files to that location before you can view them.

The PATH= Option

So far, you've learned to specify the complete pathname for HTML files in the BODY=, CONTENTS=, and FRAME= specifications when you want to save HTML files to specific locations. To streamline your ODS HTML statement, you can also use the **PATH= option** to specify the location where you want to store your HTML output, and you can use the **URL=NONE** to prevent ODS from using the pathname in any links it creates in your files.

General form, PATH= option:

    PATH=_file-specification_ <(**URL=**'_Uniform-Resource-Locator_' | **NONE**)>

where

- _file-location-specification_ identifies the location where you want HTML files to be saved. It can be one of the following:

    - the complete pathname to an aggregate storage location, such as a directory or partitioned data set

    - a fileref (file shortcut) that has been assigned to a storage location

    - a SAS catalog (_libname.catalog_).

- _Uniform-Resource-Locator_ provides a URL for links in the HTML files that ODS generates. If you specify the keyword **NONE**, no information from the PATH= option appears in the links or references.

    If you do not use the URL= suboption, then information from the PATH= option is added to links and references in the files that are created.

Example: PATH= Option with URL=NONE

In the program below, the PATH= option directs the files **data.html**, **toc.html**, and **frame.html** to the **C:\Records** directory in the Windows operating environment. The links from the frame file to the body and contents files contain only the HTML filenames **data.html** and **toc.html**.

```
ods listing close;
ods html path='c:\records' (url=none)
         body='data.html'
         contents='toc.html'
         frame='frame.html';
proc print data=clinic.admit;
run;
proc print data=clinic.stress2;
run;
ods html close;
ods listing;
```

This program generates the same files and links as the previous example in which you learned to use the URL= suboption with the BODY= and CONTENTS= file specifications. However, it's a bit simpler to specify the path only once in the PATH= option and to specify URL=NONE.

 If you plan to move your HTML files, you should specify **URL=NONE** with the PATH= option to prevent information from the PATH= option from creating URLs that are invalid or incorrect.

Example: PATH= Option without the URL= Suboption

In the program below, the PATH= option directs the files **data.html**, **toc.html**, and **frame.html** to the **C:\Records** directory in the Windows operating environment. The links from the frame file to the body and contents files contain the complete pathname, **c:\records\data.html** and **c:\records\toc.html**:

```
ods listing close;
ods html path='c:\records'
         body='data.html'
         contents='toc.html'
         frame='frame.html';
proc print data=clinic.admit;
run;
proc print data=clinic.stress2;
run;
ods html close;
ods listing;
```

Example: PATH= Option with a Specified URL

In the program below, the PATH= option directs the files **data.html**, **toc.html**, and **frame.html** to the **C:\Records** directory in the Windows operating environment. The links from the frame file to the body and contents files contain the specified URL, **http://mysite.com/myreports/data.html** and **http://mysite.com/myreports/toc.html**:

```
ods listing close;
ods html path='c:\records'(url='http://mysite.com/myreports/')
         body='data.html'
         contents='toc.html'
         frame='frame.html';
proc print data=clinic.admit;
run;
proc print data=clinic.stress2;
run;
ods html close;
ods listing;
```

Changing the Appearance of HTML Output

The STYLE= Option

You can change the appearance of your HTML output by using the **STYLE= option** in the ODS HTML statement.

General form, STYLE= option:

>   **STYLE=**_style-name_

where _style-name_ is the name of a valid SAS or user-defined style definition.

 Don't enclose _style-name_ in quotation marks.

Example

Predefined styles are shipped with SAS. In the program below, the STYLE= option applies the **Brick** style to the output for both PROC PRINT steps.

```
ods listing close;
ods html body='c:\records\data.html'(url='data.html')
         contents='c:\records\toc.html'(url='toc.html')
         frame='c:\records\frame.html'
         style=brick;
proc print data=clinic.admit label;
    var id sex age height weight actlevel;
    label actlevel='Activity Level';
run;
proc print data=clinic.stress2;
    var id resthr maxhr rechr;
run;
ods html close;
ods listing;
```

The following example shows PROC PRINT output with the Brick style applied.

Obs	Sex	Age	Date	Height	Weight	ActLevel
1	M	27	1	72	168	HIGH
2	F	34	3	66	152	HIGH
3	F	31	17	61	123	LOW
4	F	43	31	63	137	MOD
5	M	51	4	71	158	LOW
6	M	29	6	76	193	HIGH
7	F	32	9	67	151	MOD
8	M	35	13	70	173	MOD
9	M	34	22	73	154	LOW
10	F	49	27	64	172	LOW

 Your site might have its own customized style definitions.

Additional Features

Customizing HTML Output

You've seen that you can use the STYLE= option to apply predefined styles to your HTML output. However, you might want to further customize your results.

ODS provides ways for you to customize HTML output using **definitions** for tables, columns, headers, and so forth. These definitions describe how to render the HTML output or part of the HTML output. You can create style definitions using PROC TEMPLATE.

Summary

Text Summary

The OUTPUT Delivery System

The Output Delivery System (ODS) makes new report formatting options available in SAS. ODS separates your output into component parts so that the output can be sent to any ODS destination that you specify.

Opening and Closing ODS Destinations

Each **ODS destination** creates a different type of formatted output. By default, the Listing destination is open and SAS creates listing output. Because an open destination uses system resources, it's a good idea to close the Listing destination if you don't need to create listing output. By using ODS statements, you can create multiple output formats concurrently. When you have several ODS destinations open, you can close them all by using the **ODS _ALL_ CLOSE statement**.

Creating Simple HTML Output

You use the **ODS HTML statement** to open the HTML destination. Use the BODY= or FILE= options to create an HTML body file containing procedure results. You can also use the ODS HTML statement to direct the HTML output from multiple procedures to the same HTML file.

Creating HTML Output with a Table of Contents

In order to manage multiple pieces of procedure output, you can use the **CONTENTS=** and **FRAME= options** with the ODS HTML statement to create a table of contents that links to your HTML output. The **table of contents** contains a heading for each procedure that creates output.

Using Options to Specify Links and Paths

By specifying the **URL=option** in the file specification, you can provide a URL that ODS uses in all the links that it creates to the file. You can also use **the PATH= option** to specify the directory where you want to store your HTML output. When you use the PATH= option, you don't need to specify the complete pathname for the body, contents, or frame files.

Changing the Appearance of HTML Output

You can change the appearance of your output by using the **STYLE= option** in the ODS HTML statement. Several predefined styles are shipped with SAS.

Additional Features

ODS provides ways for you to customize HTML output using style definitions. Definitions are created by using PROC TEMPLATE and describe how to render the HTML output or part of the HTML output.

Points to Remember

- An open destination uses system resources. Therefore, it's a good idea to close the Listing destination before you create HTML output and re-open the Listing destination after you close the HTML destination.

- The ODS HTML CLOSE statement closes the HTML destination and is added **after** the RUN statement for the procedure.

- If you use the CONTENTS= and FRAME= options, open the frame file from within your Web browser to view the procedure output **and** the table of contents.

Practice

After you complete this chapter, practice what you learned by using the sample data and SAS programs for Chapter 10, **Producing HTML Output**, which are located on the CD-ROM. Follow the directions for creating your sample data in the Before You Begin section.

Quiz

Select the best answer for each question. After completing the quiz, check your answers using the answer key in the appendix.

1. Using ODS statements, how many types of output can you generate concurrently?

    a. 1 (only listing output)
    b. 2
    c. 3
    d. as many as you want

2. If ODS is set to its default settings, what types of output are created by the code below?

    ```
    ods html file='c:\myhtml.htm';
    ods pdf file='c:\mypdf.pdf';
    ```

    a. HTML and PDF
    b. PDF only
    c. HTML, PDF, and listing
    d. No output is created because ODS is closed by default.

3. What is the purpose of closing the Listing destination in the code shown below?

    ```
    ods listing close;
    ods html ... ;
    ```

    a. It conserves system resources.
    b. It simplifies your program.
    c. It makes your program compatible with other hardware platforms.
    d. It makes your program compatible with previous versions of SAS software.

4. When the code shown below is run, what will the file **D:\Output\body.html** contain?

    ```
    ods html body='d:\output\body.html';
    proc print data=work.alpha;
    run;
    proc print data=work.beta;
    run;
    ods html close;
    ```

    a. The PROC PRINT output for **Work.Alpha**.
    b. The PROC PRINT output for **Work.Beta**.
    c. The PROC PRINT output for both **Work.Alpha** and **Work.Beta**.
    d. Nothing. No output will be written to **D:\Output\body.html**.

5. When the code shown below is run, what file will be loaded by the links in **D:\Output\contents.html**?

```
ods html body='d:\output\body.html'
          contents='d:\output\contents.html'
          frame='d:\output\frame.html';
```

   a. **D:\Output\body.html**
   b. **D:\Output\contents.html**
   c. **D:\Output\frame.html**
   d. There are no links from the file **D:\Output\contents.html**.

6. The table of contents created by the CONTENTS= option contains a numbered heading for

   a. each procedure.
   b. each procedure that creates output.
   c. each procedure and DATA step.
   d. each HTML file created by your program.

7. When the code shown below is run, what will the file **D:\Output\frame.html** display?

```
ods html body='d:\output\body.html'
          contents='d:\output\contents.html'
          frame='d:\output\frame.html';
```

   a. The file **D:\Output\contents.html**.
   b. The file **D:\Output\frame.html**.
   c. The files **D:\Output\contents.html** and **D:\Output\body.html**.
   d. It displays no other files.

8. What is the purpose of the URL= suboptions shown below?

```
ods html body='d:\output\body.html' (url='body.html')
          contents='d:\output\contents.html' (url='contents.html')
          frame='d:\output\frame.html';
```

   a. To create absolute link addresses for loading the files from a server.
   b. To create relative link addresses for loading the files from a server.
   c. To allow HTML files to be loaded from a local drive.
   d. To send HTML output to two locations.

9. Which ODS HTML option was used in creating the following table?

Obs	ID	Name	Sex	Age	Height	Weight
1	2458	Murray, W	M	27	72	168
2	2462	Almers, C	F	34	66	152
3	2501	Bonaventure, T	F	31	61	123
4	2523	Johnson, R	F	43	63	137

a. `format=brown`

b. `format='brown'`

c. `style=brown`

d. `style='brown'`

10. What is the purpose of the PATH= option?

```
ods html path='d:\output' (url=none)
         body='body.html'
         contents='contents.html'
         frame='frame.html';
```

a. It creates absolute link addresses for loading HTML files from a server.

b. It creates relative link addresses for loading HTML files from a server.

c. It allows HTML files to be loaded from a local drive.

d. It specifies the location of HTML file output.

Chapter 11 Creating and Managing Variables

Overview

Introduction

You've learned how to create a SAS data set from raw data that is stored in an external file. You've also learned how to subset observations and how to assign values to variables.

This chapter shows you additional techniques for creating and managing variables. In this chapter, you learn how to create accumulator variables, assign variable values conditionally, select variables, and assign permanent labels and formats to variables.

Obs	ID	Name	RestHR	MaxHR	RecHR	Tolerance	TotalTime	Cumulative Total Seconds (+5,400)	TestLength
1	2458	Murray, W	72	185	128	D	758	6,158	Normal
2	2539	LaMance, K	75	168	141	D	706	6,864	Short
3	2572	Oberon, M	74	177	138	D	731	7,595	Short
4	2574	Peterson, V	80	164	137	D	849	8,444	Long
5	2584	Takahashi, Y	76	163	135	D	967	9,411	Long

Objectives

In this chapter, you learn to

- create variables that accumulate variable values
- initialize values of accumulator variables
- assign values to variables conditionally
- specify an alternative action when a condition is false
- specify lengths for variables
- delete unwanted observations
- select variables
- assign permanent labels and formats.

Creating and Modifying Variables

Accumulating Totals

It is often useful to create a variable that accumulates the values of another variable.

Suppose you want to create the data set **Clinic.Stress** and to add a new variable, SumSec, to accumulate the total number of elapsed seconds in treadmill stress tests.

SAS Data Set Clinic.Stress (Partial Listing)

ID	Name	RestHr	MaxHR	RecHR	TimeMin	TimeSec	Tolerance	TotalTime
2458	Murray, W	72	185	128	12	38	D	758
2462	Almers, C	68	171	133	10	5	I	605
2501	Bonaventure, T	78	177	139	11	13	I	673
2523	Johnson, R	69	162	114	9	42	S	582
2539	LaMance, K	75	168	141	11	46	D	706

To add the result of an expression to an accumulator variable, you can use a **Sum statement** in your DATA step.

General form, Sum statement:

> *variable+expression*;

where

- *variable* specifies the name of the accumulator variable. This variable must be numeric. The variable is automatically set to 0 before the first observation is read. The variable's value is retained from one DATA step execution to the next.

- *expression* is any valid SAS expression.

⚠ If the *expression* produces a missing value, the Sum statement treats it like a zero. (By contrast, in an assignment statement, a missing value is assigned if the *expression* produces a missing value.)

📑 The Sum statement is one of the few SAS statements that doesn't begin with a keyword.

The Sum statement adds the result of the expression that is on the right side of the plus sign (+) to the numeric variable that is on the left side of the plus sign. At the beginning of the DATA step, the value of the numeric variable is not set to missing as it usually is when reading raw data. Instead, the variable retains the new value in the program data vector for use in processing the next observation.

Example

To find the total number of elapsed seconds in treadmill stress tests, you need a variable (in this example, SumSec) whose value begins at *0* and increases by the amount of the total seconds in each observation. To calculate the total number of elapsed seconds in treadmill stress tests, you use the Sum statement shown below.

```
data clinic.stress;
   infile tests;
   input ID $ 1-4 Name $ 6-25 RestHR 27-29 MaxHR 31-33
         RecHR 35-37 TimeMin 39-40 TimeSec 42-43
         Tolerance $ 45;
   TotalTime=(timemin*60)+timesec;
   SumSec+totaltime;
run;
```

The value of the variable on the left side of the plus sign (here, SumSec) begins at *0* and increases by the value of TotalTime with each observation.

SumSec	=	TotalTime	+	Previous Total
0				
758	=	758	+	0
1363	=	605	+	758
2036	=	673	+	1363
2618	=	582	+	2036
3324	=	706	+	2618

Initializing Accumulator Variables

In a previous example, the accumulator variable SumSec was initialized to *0* by default before the first observation was read. But what if you want to initialize SumSec to a different number, such as the total seconds from previous treadmill stress tests?

You can use the **RETAIN statement** to assign an initial value other than the default value of *0* to a variable whose value is assigned by a Sum statement.

The RETAIN statement

- assigns an initial value to a retained variable
- prevents variables from being initialized each time the DATA step executes.

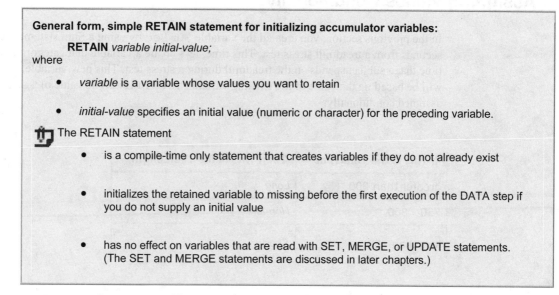

> **General form, simple RETAIN statement for initializing accumulator variables:**
>
> **RETAIN** *variable initial-value;*
> where
>
> - *variable* is a variable whose values you want to retain
>
> - *initial-value* specifies an initial value (numeric or character) for the preceding variable.
>
> The RETAIN statement
>
> - is a compile-time only statement that creates variables if they do not already exist
>
> - initializes the retained variable to missing before the first execution of the DATA step if you do not supply an initial value
>
> - has no effect on variables that are read with SET, MERGE, or UPDATE statements. (The SET and MERGE statements are discussed in later chapters.)

Example

Suppose you want to add 5400 seconds (the accumulated total seconds from a previous treadmill stress test) to the variable SumSec in the **Clinic.Stress** data set when you create the data set. To initialize SumSec with the value *5400*, you use the RETAIN statement shown below:

```
data clinic.stress;
   infile tests;
   input ID $ 1-4 Name $ 6-25 RestHR 27-29 MaxHR 31-33
         RecHR 35-37 TimeMin 39-40 TimeSec 42-43
         Tolerance $ 45;
   TotalTime=(timemin*60)+timesec;
   retain SumSec 5400;
   sumsec+totaltime;
run;
```

Now the value of SumSec begins at *5400* and increases by the value of TotalTime with each observation.

SumSec	=	TotalTime	+	Previous Total
5400				
6158	=	758	+	0
6763	=	605	+	6158
7436	=	673	+	6763
8018	=	582	+	7436
8724	=	706	+	8018

Assigning Values Conditionally

In the previous section, you created the variable SumSec by using a Sum statement to add total seconds from a treadmill stress test. This time, let's create a variable that categorizes the length of time that a subject spends on the treadmill during a stress test. This new variable, TestLength, will be based on the value of the existing variable TotalTime. The value of TestLength will be assigned conditionally.

If This Is the TotalTime	Then This Is the TestLength
greater than 800	*Long*
750 - 800	*Normal*
less than 750	*Short*

To perform an action conditionally, use an **IF-THEN** statement. The IF-THEN statement executes a SAS statement when the condition in the IF clause is true.

General form, IF-THEN statement:

    IF *expression* **THEN** *statement*;

where

- *expression* is any valid SAS expression

- *statement* is any executable SAS statement.

Example

To assign the value *Long* to the variable TestLength when the value of TotalTime is greater than 800, add the following IF-THEN statement to your DATA step:

```
data clinic.stress;
    infile tests;
    input ID $ 1-4 Name $ 6-25 RestHR 27-29 MaxHR 31-33
          RecHR 35-37 TimeMin 39-40 TimeSec 42-43
          Tolerance $ 45;
    TotalTime=(timemin*60)+timesec;
    retain SumSec 5400;
    sumsec+totaltime;
    if totaltime>800 then TestLength='Long';
run;
```

SAS executes the assignment statement only when the condition (`TotalTime>800`) is true. If the condition is false, then the value of `TestLength` will be missing.

Comparison and Logical Operators

When writing IF-THEN statements, you can use any of the following **comparison** operators:

Operator	Comparison Operation
= or **eq**	equal to
^= or **ne**	not equal to
> or **gt**	greater than
< or **lt**	less than
>= or **ge**	greater than or equal to
<= or **le**	less than or equal to
in	equal to one of a list

Examples

```
if test<85 and time<=20
   then Status='RETEST';
if region in ('NE','NW','SW')
   then Rate=fee-25;
if target gt 300 or sales ge 50000
   then Bonus=salary*.05;
```

You can also use these **logical** operators:

Operator	Logical Operation
&	and
|	or
^ or ~	not

Use the AND operator to execute the THEN statement if both expressions that are linked by AND are true.

```
if status='OK' and type=3
   then Count+1;
if (age^=agecheck | time^=3)
   & error=1 then Test=1;
```

Use the OR operator to execute the THEN statement if either expression that is linked by OR is true.

```
if (age^=agecheck | time^=3)
   & error=1 then Test=1;
if status='S' or cond='E'
      then Control='Stop';
```

Use the NOT operator with other operators to reverse the logic of a comparison.

```
if not(loghours<7500)
   then Schedule='Quarterly';
if region not in ('NE','SE')
   then Bonus=200;
```

Character values must be specified in the same case in which they appear in the data set and must be enclosed in quotation marks.

```
if status='OK' and type=3
   then Count+1;
if status='S' or cond='E'
   then Control='Stop';
if not(loghours<7500)
   then Schedule='Quarterly';
if region not in ('NE','SE')
   then Bonus=200;
```

Logical comparisons that are enclosed in parentheses are evaluated as true or false before they are compared to other expressions. In the example below, the OR comparison in parentheses is evaluated before the first expression and the AND operator are evaluated.

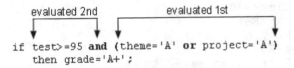

```
if test>=95 and (theme='A' or project='A')
   then grade='A+';
```

 In SAS, **any numeric value other than 0 or missing is true, and a value of 0 or missing is false**. Therefore, a numeric variable or expression can stand alone in a condition. If its value is a number other than 0 or missing, the condition is true; if its value is 0 or missing, the condition is false.

0 = False
. = False
1 = True

As a result, you need to **be careful when using the OR operator** with a series of comparisons. Remember that only one comparison in a series of OR comparisons must be true to make a condition true, and any nonzero, nonmissing constant is always evaluated as true. Therefore, the following subsetting IF statement is always true:

```
if x=1 or 2;
```

SAS first evaluates x=1, and the result can be either true or false. However, because the 2 is evaluated as nonzero and nonmissing (true), the entire expression is true. In the following statement, however, the condition is not necessarily true because either comparison can evaluate as true or false:

```
if x=1 or x=2;
```

Providing an Alternative Action

Now suppose you want to assign a value to `TestLength` that is based on the other possible values of `TotalTime`. One way to do this is to add IF-THEN statements to the other two conditions, as shown below.

```
if totaltime>800 then TestLength='Long';
if 750<=totaltime<=800 then TestLength='Normal';
if totaltime<750 then TestLength='Short';
```

However, when the DATA step executes, each IF statement is evaluated in order, even if the first condition is true. This wastes system resources and slows the processing of your program.

Instead of using a series of IF-THEN statements, you can use the **ELSE** statement to specify an alternative action to be performed when the condition in an IF-THEN statement is false. As shown below, you can write multiple ELSE statements to specify a series of mutually exclusive conditions.

```
if totaltime>800 then TestLength='Long';
else if 750<=totaltime<=800 then TestLength='Normal';
else if totaltime<750 then TestLength='Short';
```

The ELSE statement must immediately follow the IF-THEN statement in your program. An ELSE statement executes only if the previous IF-THEN/ELSE statement is false.

> **General form, ELSE statement:**
>
> > **ELSE** *statement*;
>
> where *statement* is any executable SAS statement, including another IF-THEN statement.

So to assign a value to `TestLength` when the condition in your IF-THEN statement is false, you can add the ELSE statement to your DATA step, as shown below:

```
data clinic.stress;
    infile tests;
    input ID $ 1-4 Name $ 6-25 RestHR 27-29 MaxHR 31-33
          RecHR 35-37 TimeMin 39-40 TimeSec 42-43
          Tolerance $ 45;
    TotalTime=(timemin*60)+timesec;
    retain SumSec 5400;
    sumsec+totaltime;
    if totaltime>800 then TestLength='Long';
    else if 750<=totaltime<=800 then TestLength='Normal';
    else if totaltime<750 then TestLength='Short';
run;
```

Using ELSE statements with IF-THEN statements can save resources:

- Using IF-THEN statements **without** the ELSE statement causes SAS to evaluate all IF-THEN statements.

- Using IF-THEN statements **with** the ELSE statement causes SAS to execute IF-THEN statements until it encounters the first true statement. Subsequent IF-THEN statements are not evaluated.

For greater efficiency, construct your IF-THEN/ELSE statements with conditions of decreasing probability.

Remember that you can use PUT statements to test your conditional logic.

```
data clinic.stress;
    infile tests;
    input ID $ 1-4 Name $ 6-25 RestHR 27-29 MaxHR 31-33
          RecHR 35-37 TimeMin 39-40 TimeSec 42-43
          Tolerance $ 45;
    TotalTime=(timemin*60)+timesec;
    retain SumSec 5400;
    sumsec+totaltime;
    if totaltime>800 then TestLength='Long';
    else if 750<=totaltime<=800 then TestLength='Normal';
    else put 'NOTE: Check this Length: ' totaltime=;
run;
```

Specifying Lengths for Variables

Previously, you added IF-THEN and ELSE statements to a DATA step in order to create the variable `TestLength`. Values for `TestLength` were assigned conditionally, based on the value for `TotalTime`.

```
data clinic.stress;
    infile tests;
    input ID $ 1-4 Name $ 6-25 RestHR 27-29 MaxHR 31-33
          RecHR 35-37 TimeMin 39-40 TimeSec 42-43
          Tolerance $ 45;
    TotalTime=(timemin*60)+timesec;
    retain SumSec 5400;
    sumsec+totaltime;
    if totaltime>800 then TestLength='Long';
    else if 750<=totaltime<=800 then TestLength='Normal';
    else if totaltime<750 then TestLength='Short';
run;
```

But look what happens when you submit this program.

During compilation, when creating a new character variable in an assignment statement, SAS allocates as many bytes of storage space as there are characters in the **first value** that it encounters for that variable. In this case, the first value for `TestLength` occurs in the IF-THEN statement, which specifies a four-character value (*Long*). So `TestLength` is assigned a length of 4, and any longer values (*Normal* and *Short*) are truncated.

Variable TestLength
(Partial Listing)

TestLength
Norm
Shor
Shor
Shor
Norm
Shor
Long
...

The example above assigns a character constant as the value of the new variable. The table that follows lists more examples of the default type and length that SAS assigns when the type and length of a variable are not explicitly set.

Expression	Example	Resulting Type of X	Resulting Length of X	Explanation
Character variable	`length a $ 4;` `x=a;`	Character variable	4	Length of source variable
Character literal (character constant)	`x='ABC';` `x='ABCDE';`	Character variable	3	Length of first literal (constant) encountered

Concatenation of variables	`length a $ 4`
	`b $ 6`
	`c $ 2;`
	`x=a||b||c;`
		Character variable	12	Sum of the lengths of all variables

Concatenation of variables and literals	`length a $ 4;`
	`x=a||'CAT';`
	`x=a||'CATNIP';`
		Character variable	7	Sum of the lengths of variables and literals (constants) encountered in first assignment statement

Numeric variable	`length a 4;` `x=a;`	Numeric variable	8	Default numeric length (8 bytes unless otherwise specified) Note: In general, it is not recommended that you change the default length of numeric variables, as this can affect numeric precision. See the SAS documentation for your operating environment for more information.

You can use a **LENGTH statement** to specify a length (the number of bytes) for `TestLength` before the first value is referenced elsewhere in the DATA step.

General form, LENGTH statement:

> **LENGTH** *variable(s)* <$> *length*;

where

- *variable(s)* names the variable(s) to be assigned a length

- $ is specified if the variable is a character variable

- *length* is an integer that specifies the length of the variable.

Examples

```
length Type $ 8;
length Address1 Address2 Address3 $ 200;
length FirstName $ 12 LastName $ 16;
```

Within your program, you include a LENGTH statement to assign a length to accommodate the longest value of the variable `TestLength`. The longest value is *Normal*, which has six characters. Because `TestLength` is a character variable, you must follow the variable name with a dollar sign ($).

```
data clinic.stress;
    infile tests;
    input ID $ 1-4 Name $ 6-25 RestHR 27-29 MaxHR 31-33
          RecHR 35-37 TimeMin 39-40 TimeSec 42-43
          Tolerance $ 45;
    TotalTime=(timemin*60)+timesec;
    retain SumSec 5400;
    sumsec+totaltime;
    length TestLength $ 6;
    if totaltime>800 then testlength='Long';
    else if 750<=totaltime<=800 then testlength='Normal';
    else if totaltime<750 then TestLength='Short';
run;
```

Make sure the LENGTH statement appears before any other reference to the variable in the DATA step. If the variable has been created by another statement, then a later use of the LENGTH statement will not change its size.

Now that you have added the LENGTH statement to your program, the values of `TestLength` are no longer truncated.

Variable TestLength
(Partial Listing)

TestLength
Normal
Short
Short
Short
Normal
Short
Long
...

Subsetting Data

Deleting Unwanted Observations

So far in this chapter, you've learned to use IF-THEN statements to execute assignment statements conditionally. But you can specify any executable SAS statement in an IF-THEN statement. For example, you can use an **IF-THEN statement** with a **DELETE statement** to determine which observations to omit from the data set that SAS is creating as it reads raw data.

- The IF-THEN statement executes a SAS statement when the condition in the IF clause is true.

- The DELETE statement stops processing the current observation.

General form, DELETE statement:

DELETE;

To conditionally execute a DELETE statement, you submit a statement in the following general form:

IF *expression* **THEN DELETE;**

If the *expression* is

- **true**, the DELETE statement executes, and control returns to the top of the DATA step (the observation is deleted).

- **false**, the DELETE statement does not execute, and processing continues with the next statement in the DATA step.

Example

The IF-THEN and DELETE statements below omit any observations whose values for `RestHR` are lower than 70.

```
data clinic.stress;
   infile tests;
   input ID $ 1-4 Name $ 6-25 RestHR 27-29 MaxHR 31-33
         RecHR 35-37 TimeMin 39-40 TimeSec 42-43
         Tolerance $ 45;
   if resthr<70 then delete;
   TotalTime=(timemin*60)+timesec;
   retain SumSec 5400;
   sumsec+totaltime;
   length TestLength $ 6;
   if totaltime>800 then testlength='Long';
   else if 750<=totaltime<=800 then testlength='Normal';
   else if totaltime<750 then TestLength='Short';
run;
```

Selecting Variables with the DROP= and KEEP= Data Set Options

Sometimes you might need to read and process fields that you don't want to keep in your data set. In this case, you can use the **DROP= and KEEP= data set options** to specify the variables that you want to drop or keep.

Use the KEEP= option instead of the DROP= option if more variables are dropped than kept. You specify data set options in parentheses after a SAS data set name.

General form, DROP= and KEEP= data set options:

> **(DROP=**variable(s)**)**
> **(KEEP=**variable(s)**)**

where

- the **DROP=** or **KEEP=** option, in parentheses, follows the name of the data set that contains the variables to be dropped or kept

- variable(s) identifies the variables to drop or keep.

Example

Suppose you are interested in keeping only the new variable `TotalTime` and not the original variables `TimeMin` and `TimeSec`. You can drop `TimeMin` and `TimeSec` when you create the **Stress** data set.

```
data clinic.stress(drop=timemin timesec);
    infile tests;
    input ID $ 1-4 Name $ 6-25 RestHR 27-29 MaxHR 31-33
          RecHR 35-37 TimeMin 39-40 TimeSec 42-43
          Tolerance $ 45;
    if tolerance='D';
    TotalTime=(timemin*60)+timesec;
    retain SumSec 5400;
    sumsec+totaltime;
    length TestLength $ 6;
    if totaltime>800 then testlength='Long';
    else if 750<=totaltime<=800 then testlength='Normal';
    else if totaltime<750 then TestLength='Short';
run;
```

SAS Data Set Clinic.Stress

ID	Name	RestHR	MaxHR	RecHR	Tolerance	TotalTime	SumSec	TestLength
2458	Murray, W	72	185	128	D	758	6158	Normal
2539	LaMance, K	75	168	141	D	706	6864	Short
2552	Reberson, P	69	158	139	D	941	7805	Long
2572	Oberon, M	74	177	138	D	731	8536	Short
2574	Peterson, V	80	164	137	D	849	9385	Long
2584	Takahashi, Y	76	163	135	D	967	10352	Long

Another way to exclude variables from your data set is to use the **DROP statement** or the **KEEP statement**. Like the DROP= and KEEP= data set options, these statements drop or keep variables. However, the DROP statement differs from the DROP= data set option in the following ways:

- You cannot use the DROP statement in SAS procedure steps.

- The DROP statement applies to all output data sets that are named in the DATA statement.

- To exclude variables from some data sets but not from others, place the appropriate DROP= data set option next to each data set name that is specified in the DATA statement.

The KEEP statement is similar to the DROP statement, except that the KEEP statement specifies a list of variables to write to output data sets. Use the KEEP statement instead of the DROP statement if the number of variables to keep is significantly smaller than the number to drop.

General form, DROP and KEEP statements:

> **DROP** *variable(s)*;
> **KEEP** *variable(s)*;

where *variable(s)* identifies the variables to drop or keep.

Example

The two programs below produce the same results. The first example uses the DROP= data set option; the second example uses the DROP statement.

```
data clinic.stress (drop=timemin timesec);
    infile tests;
    input ID $ 1-4 Name $ 6-25 RestHR 27-29 MaxHR 31-33
          RecHR 35-37 TimeMin 39-40 TimeSec 42-43
          Tolerance $ 45;
    if tolerance='D';
    TotalTime=(timemin*60)+timesec;
    retain SumSec 5400;
    sumsec+totaltime;
    length TestLength $ 6;
    if totaltime>800 then testlength='Long';
    else if 750<=totaltime<=800 then testlength='Normal';
    else if totaltime<750 then TestLength='Short';
run;

data clinic.stress;
    infile tests;
    input ID $ 1-4 Name $ 6-25 RestHR 27-29 MaxHR 31-33
          RecHR 35-37 TimeMin 39-40 TimeSec 42-43
          Tolerance $ 45;
    if tolerance='D';
    drop timemin timesec;
    TotalTime=(timemin*60)+timesec;
    retain SumSec 5400;
    sumsec+totaltime;
    length TestLength $ 6;
    if totaltime>800 then testlength='Long';
    else if 750<=totaltime<=800 then testlength='Normal';
    else if totaltime<750 then TestLength='Short';
run;
```

Assigning Permanent Labels and Formats

At this point, you've read and manipulated your raw data to obtain the observations, variables, and variable values that you want. Your final task in this chapter is to permanently assign **labels** and **formats** to variables.

In Chapter 4, **Creating List Reports**, you practiced temporarily assigning labels and formats within a PROC step. These temporary labels and formats are applicable only for the duration of the step. To permanently assign labels and formats, you use **LABEL and FORMAT statements in DATA steps**.

 Remember that labels and formats do not affect how data is stored in the data set, only how data appears in output.

Example

To specify the label **Cumulative Total Seconds (+5,400)** and the format COMMA6. for the variable SumSec, you can submit the following program:

```
data clinic.stress;
   infile tests;
   input ID $ 1-4 Name $ 6-25 RestHR 27-29 MaxHR 31-33
         RecHR 35-37 TimeMin 39-40 TimeSec 42-43
         Tolerance $ 45;
   if resthr<70 then delete;
   if tolerance='D';
   drop timemin timesec;
   TotalTime=(timemin*60)+timesec;
   retain SumSec 5400;
   sumsec+totaltime;
   length TestLength $ 6;

   if totaltime>800 then testlength='Long';
   else if 750<=totaltime<=800 then testlength='Normal';
   else if totaltime<750 then TestLength='Short';
   label sumsec='Cumulative Total Seconds (+5,400)';
   format sumsec comma6.;
run;
```

You're finished! When you print the new data set, SumSec is labeled and formatted as specified. (Don't forget to include the LABEL option in the PROC PRINT statement.)

```
proc print data=clinic.stress label;
run;
```

Obs	ID	Name	RestHR	MaxHR	RecHR	Tolerance	TotalTime	Cumulative Total Seconds (+5,400)	TestLength
1	2458	Murray, W	72	185	128	D	758	6,158	Normal
2	2539	LaMance, K	75	168	141	D	706	6,864	Short
3	2572	Oberon, M	74	177	138	D	731	7,595	Short
4	2574	Peterson, V	80	164	137	D	849	8,444	Long
5	2584	Takahashi, Y	76	163	135	D	967	9,411	Long

 Remember that many SAS procedures automatically use permanent labels and formats in output, without requiring additional statements or options.

 If you assign temporary labels or formats within a PROC step, they override any permanent labels or formats that were assigned during the DATA step.

Assigning Values Conditionally Using SELECT Groups

Earlier in this chapter, you learned to assign values conditionally by using IF-THEN/ELSE statements. You can also use **SELECT groups** in DATA steps to perform conditional processing. A SELECT group contains these statements:

Use This Statement	To Perform This Action
SELECT	begins a SELECT group.
WHEN	identifies SAS statements that are executed when a particular condition is true.
OTHERWISE (optional)	specifies a statement to be executed if no WHEN condition is met.
END	ends a SELECT group.

You can decide whether to use IF-THEN/ELSE statements or SELECT groups based on the following criteria.

When you have a **long series** of mutually exclusive conditions and the comparison is numeric, using a SELECT group is slightly more efficient than using a series of IF-THEN or IF-THEN/ELSE statements because CPU time is reduced. SELECT groups also make the program easier to read and debug.

For programs with **few conditions**, use IF-THEN/ELSE statements.

General form, SELECT group:

> **SELECT** <(*select-expression*)>;
>   **WHEN**-1 (*when-expression-1* <..., *when-expression-n*>) *statement*;
>   **WHEN**-*n* (*when-expression-1* <..., *when-expression-n*>) *statement*;
>   <**OTHERWISE** *statement*;>
> **END**;

where

- **SELECT** begins a SELECT group.

- the optional *select-expression* specifies any SAS expression that evaluates to a single value.

- **WHEN** identifies SAS statements that are executed when a particular condition is true.

- *when-expression* specifies any SAS expression, including a compound expression. You must specify at least one *when-expression*.

- *statement* is any executable SAS statement. You must specify the *statement* argument.

- the optional **OTHERWISE** statement specifies a statement to be executed if no WHEN condition is met.

- **END** ends a SELECT group.

Example

The following code is a simple example of a SELECT group. Notice that the variable a is specified in the SELECT statement, and various values to compare to a are specified in the WHEN statements. When the value of the variable a is

- *1*, x is multiplied by 10

- *3*, *4*, or *5*, x is multiplied by 100

- *2* or any other value, nothing happens.

```
select (a);
   when (1) x=x*10;
   when (3,4,5) x=x*100;
   otherwise;
end;
```

Example: SELECT Group in a DATA Step

Now let's look at a SELECT group in context. In the DATA step below, the SELECT group assigns values to the variable `Group` based on values of the variable `JobCode`. Most of the assignments are one-to-one correspondences, but ticket agents (the `JobCode` values *TA1*, *TA2*, and *TA3*) are grouped together, as are values in the *Other* category.

```
data emps(keep=salary group);
   set sasuser.payrollmaster;
   length Group $ 20;
   select(jobcode);
      when ("FA1") group="Flight Attendant I";
      when ("FA2") group="Flight Attendant II";
      when ("FA3") group="Flight Attendant III";
      when ("ME1") group="Mechanic I";
      when ("ME2") group="Mechanic II";
      when ("ME3") group="Mechanic III";
      when ("NA1") group="Navigator I";
      when ("NA2") group="Navigator II";
      when ("NA3") group="Navigator III";
      when ("PT1") group="Pilot I";
      when ("PT2") group="Pilot II";
      when ("PT3") group="Pilot III";
      when ("TA1","TA2","TA3") group="Ticket Agents";
      otherwise group="Other";
   end;
run;
```

Notice that in this case the SELECT statement does contain a *select-expression*. You are checking values of a single variable, so using **select(jobcode)** and only the `JobCode` value in each WHEN statement is more concise than eliminating the *select-expression* and repeating the variable in each *when-expression*, as in **when(jobcode="FA1")**.

 Notice that the LENGTH statement in the DATA step above specifies a length of 20 for `Group`. Remember that without the LENGTH statement, values for `Group` might be truncated, as the first value for `Group` (*Flight Attendant I*) is not the longest possible value.

 When you are comparing values in the *when-expression*, be sure to express the values exactly as they are coded in the data. For example, the *when-expression* below would be evaluated as false because the values for `JobCode` in **Sasuser.Payrollmaster** are stored in uppercase letters.

```
when ("fa1") group="Flight Attendant I";
```

In this case, given the SELECT group above, `Group` would be assigned the value *Other*.

Specifying SELECT Statements with Expressions

As you saw in the general form for SELECT groups, you can optionally specify a *select-expression* in the SELECT statement. The way SAS evaluates a *when-expression* depends on whether you specify a *select-expression*.

If you **do** specify a *select-expression* in the SELECT statement, SAS compares the value of the *select-expression* with the value of each *when-expression*. That is, SAS evaluates the *select-expression* and *when-expression,* compares the two for equality, and returns a value of true or false.

- If the comparison is **true**, SAS executes the *statement* in the WHEN statement.

- If the comparison is **false**, SAS proceeds either to the next *when-expression* in the current WHEN statement, or to the next WHEN statement if no more expressions are present. If no WHEN statements remain, execution proceeds to the OTHERWISE statement, if one is present.

If the result of all SELECT-WHEN comparisons is false and no OTHERWISE statement is present, SAS issues an **error message** and **stops executing** the DATA step.

In the following SELECT group, SAS determines the value of `toy` and compares it to values in each WHEN statement in turn. If a WHEN statement is true compared to the `toy` value, then SAS assigns the related price and continues processing the rest of the DATA step. If none of the comparisons is true, then SAS executes the OTHERWISE statement and writes a debugging message to the SAS log.

```
select (toy);
    when ("Bear") price=35.00;
    when ("Violin") price=139.00;
    when ("Top","Whistle","Duck") price=7.99;
    otherwise put "Check unknown toy: " toy=;
end;
```

Specifying SELECT Statements without Expressions

If you **don't** specify a *select-expression*, SAS evaluates each *when-expression* to produce a result of true or false.

- If the result is **true**, SAS executes the *statement* in the WHEN statement.

- If the result is **false**, SAS proceeds either to the next *when-expression* in the current WHEN statement, or to the next WHEN statement if no more expressions are present, or to the OTHERWISE statement if one is present. (That is, SAS performs the action that is indicated in the first true WHEN statement.)

If more than one WHEN statement has a true *when-expression*, **only the first** WHEN statement is used; once a *when-expression* is true, no other *when-expressions* are evaluated.

If the result of all *when-expressions* is false and no OTHERWISE statement is present, SAS issues an **error message**.

In the example below, the SELECT statement does not specify a *select-expression*. The WHEN statements are evaluated in order, and only one is used. For example, if the value of `toy` is *Bear* and the value of `month` is *FEB*, only the second WHEN statement is used, even though the condition in the third WHEN statement is also met. In this case, the variable `price` is assigned the value *25.00*.

```
select;
 when (toy="Bear" and month in ('OCT', 'NOV', 'DEC')) price=45.00;
 when (toy="Bear" and month in ('JAN', 'FEB')) price=25.00;
 when (toy="Bear") price=35.00;
 otherwise;
end;
```

Grouping Statements Using DO Groups

So far in this chapter, you've seen examples of conditional processing (IF-THEN/ELSE statements and SELECT groups) that execute only a single SAS statement when a condition is true. However, you can also execute a group of statements as a unit by using **DO groups**.

To construct a DO group, you use the DO and END statements along with other SAS statements.

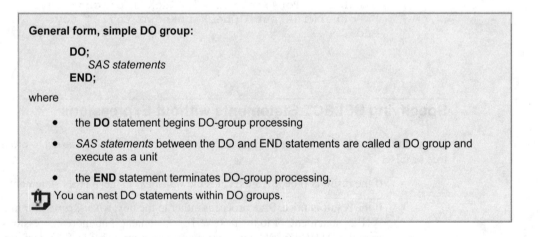

General form, simple DO group:

> **DO;**
> > *SAS statements*
> **END;**

where

- the **DO** statement begins DO-group processing
- *SAS statements* between the DO and END statements are called a DO group and execute as a unit
- the **END** statement terminates DO-group processing.

You can nest DO statements within DO groups.

You can use DO groups in IF-THEN/ELSE statements and SELECT groups to perform many statements as part of the conditional action.

Examples

In this simple DO group, the statements between DO and END are performed only when `TotalTime` is greater than 800. If `TotalTime` is less than or equal to 800, statements in the DO group do not execute, and the program continues with the assignment statement that follows the appropriate ELSE statement.

```
data clinic.stress;
    infile tests;
    input ID $ 1-4 Name $ 6-25 RestHR 27-29 MaxHR 31-33
          RecHR 35-37 TimeMin 39-40 TimeSec 42-43
          Tolerance $ 45;
    TotalTime=(timemin*60)+timesec;
    retain SumSec 5400;
    sumsec+totaltime;
    length TestLength $ 6 Message $ 20;
    if totaltime>800 then
        do;
            testlength='Long';
            message='Run blood panel';
        end;
    else if 750<=totaltime<=800 then testlength='Normal';
    else if totaltime<750 then TestLength='Short';
run;
```

In the SELECT group below, the statements between DO and END are performed only when the value of `Payclass` is *hourly*. Notice that an IF-THEN statement appears in the DO group; the PUT statement executes only when `Hours` is greater than 40. The second END statement in the program closes the SELECT group.

```
data payroll;
    set salaries;
    select(payclass);
    when ('monthly')  amt=salary;
    when ('hourly')
        do;
            amt=hrlywage*min(hrs,40);
            if hrs>40 then put 'CHECK TIMECARD';
        end;
    otherwise put 'PROBLEM OBSERVATION';
    end;
run;
```

Indenting and Nesting DO Groups

You can nest DO groups to any level, just like you nest IF-THEN/ELSE statements. (The memory capabilities of your system might limit the number of nested DO statements that you can use. For details, see the SAS documentation about how many levels of nested DO statements your system's memory can support.)

The following is an example of nested DO groups:

```
do;
    statements;
        do;
            statements;
                do;
                    statements;
                end;
        end;
end;
```

It is good practice to indent the statements in DO groups, as shown in the preceding statements, so that their position indicates the levels of nesting.

 There are three other forms of the DO statement:

- The **iterative DO statement** executes statements between DO and END statements repetitively based on the value of an index variable. The iterative DO statement can contain a WHILE or UNTIL clause.

- The **DO UNTIL statement** executes statements in a DO loop repetitively until a condition is true, checking the condition after each iteration of the DO loop.

- The **DO WHILE statement** executes statements in a DO loop repetitively while a condition is true, checking the condition before each iteration of the DO loop.

You can learn about these forms of the DO statement in Chapter 15, **Generating Data with DO Loops**.

Summary

Text Summary

Accumulating Totals

Use a **Sum statement** to add the result of an expression to an accumulator variable.

Initializing Accumulator Variables

You can use the **RETAIN statement** to assign an initial value to a variable whose value is assigned by a Sum statement.

Assigning Values Conditionally

To perform an action conditionally, use an **IF-THEN statement**. The IF-THEN statement executes a SAS statement when the condition in the IF clause is true. You can include comparison and logical operators; logical comparisons that are enclosed in parentheses are evaluated as true or false before other expressions are evaluated. Use the **ELSE statement** to specify an alternative action when the condition in an IF-THEN statement is false.

Specifying Lengths for Variables

When creating a new variable, SAS allocates as many bytes of storage space as there are characters in the first value that it encounters for that variable. This can result in truncated values. You can use the **LENGTH statement** to specify a length before the variable's first value is referenced in the DATA step.

Subsetting Data

To omit observations as you read raw data, include the **DELETE statement** in an IF-THEN statement. If you need to read and process variables that you don't want to keep in the data set, then use the **DROP=** and **KEEP= data set options** or the **DROP** and **KEEP statements**.

Assigning Permanent Labels and Formats

You can use **LABEL** and **FORMAT statements** in DATA steps to permanently assign labels and formats. These do not affect how data is stored in the data set, only how it appears in output.

Assigning Values Conditionally Using SELECT Groups

As an alternative to IF-THEN/ELSE statements, you can use **SELECT groups** in DATA steps to perform conditional processing. SELECT groups are more efficient than IF-THEN/ELSE statements when you have a long series of mutually exclusive conditions.

Grouping Statements Using DO Groups

You can execute a group of statements as a unit by **DO groups** in DATA steps. You can use DO groups in IF-THEN/ELSE statements and SELECT groups to perform many statements as part of the conditional action.

Points to Remember

- Like the assignment statement, the Sum statement does not contain a keyword.

- If the expression in a Sum statement produces a missing value, the Sum statement ignores it. (By contrast, assignment statements assign a missing value if the expression produces a missing value.)

- Using ELSE statements with IF-THEN statements can save resources. For greater efficiency, construct your IF-THEN/ELSE statements with conditions of decreasing probability.

- When you create a new variable, make sure the LENGTH statement appears before any other reference to the variable in the DATA step. If the variable has been created by another statement, a later use of the LENGTH statement will not change its size.

- Labels and formats do not affect how data is stored in the data set, only how it appears in output. You assign labels and formats temporarily in PROC steps and permanently in DATA steps.

Practice

After you complete this chapter, practice what you learned by using the sample data and SAS programs for Chapter 11, **Creating and Managing Variables**, which are located on the CD-ROM. Follow the directions for creating your sample data in the Before You Begin section.

Quiz

Select the best answer for each question. After completing the quiz, check your answers using the answer key in the appendix.

1. Which program creates the output shown below?

   Raw Data File Furnture

   ```
   1---+-----10---+-----20---+-----30---+
   310 oak    pedestal table  329.99
   311 maple pedestal table  369.99
   312 brass floor     lamp   79.99
   313 glass table     lamp   59.99
   314 oak    rocking  chair  153.99
   ```

StockNum	Finish	Style	Item	TotalPrice
310	oak	pedestal	table	329.99
311	maple	pedestal	table	699.98
312	brass	floor	lamp	779.97
313	glass	table	lamp	839.96

   a.
   ```
   data test2;
        infile furnture;
        input StockNum $ 1-3 Finish $ 5-9 Style $ 11-18
            Item $ 20-24 Price 26-31;
        if finish='oak' then delete;
        retain TotPrice 100;
        totalprice+price;
        drop price;
   run;
   proc print data=test2 noobs;
   run;
   ```

   b.
   ```
   data test2;
        infile furnture;
        input StockNum $ 1-3 Finish $ 5-9 Style $ 11-18
            Item $ 20-24 Price 26-31;
        if finish='oak' and price<200 then delete;
        TotalPrice+price;
   run;
   proc print data=test2 noobs;
   run;
   ```

c.
```
data test2(drop=price);
    infile furnture;
    input StockNum $ 1-3 Finish $ 5-9 Style $ 11-18
        Item $ 20-24 Price 26-31;
    if finish='oak' and price<200 then delete;
    TotalPrice+price;
run;
proc print data=test2 noobs;
run;
```

d.
```
data test2;
    infile furnture;
    input StockNum $ 1-3 Finish $ 5-9 Style $ 11-18
        Item $ 20-24 Price 26-31;
    if finish=oak and price<200 then delete price;
    TotalPrice+price;
run;
proc print data=test2 noobs;
run;
```

2. How is the variable `Amount` labeled and formatted in the PROC PRINT output?

```
data credit;
    infile creddata;
    input Account $ 1-5 Name $ 7-25 Type $ 27
        Transact $ 29-35 Amount 37-50;
    label amount='Amount of Loan';
    format amount dollar12.2;

run;
proc print data=credit label;
    label amount='Total Amount Loaned';
    format amount comma10.;
run;
```

a. label **Amount of Loan**, format **DOLLAR12.2**

b. label **Total Amount Loaned**, format **COMMA10.**

c. label **Amount**, default format

d. The PROC PRINT step does not execute because two labels and two formats are assigned to the same variable.

3. Consider the IF-THEN statement shown below. When the statement is executed, which expression is evaluated first?

```
if finlexam>=95
    and (research='A' or
        (project='A' and present='A'))
    then Grade='A+';
```

a. `finlexam>=95`

b. `research='A'`

c. `project='A' and present='A'`

d. `research='A' or`
   `(project='A' and present='A')`

4. Consider the small raw data file and program shown below. What is the value of `Count` after the fourth record is read?

```
1---+----10
  10
  20

  40
  50
```

```
data work.newnums;
     infile numbers;
     input Tens 2-3;
     Count+tens;
run;
```

a. missing

b. *0*

c. *30*

d. *70*

5. Now consider the revised program below. What is the value of `Count` after the **third** observation is read?

```
1---+----10
  10
  20

  40
  50
```

```
data work.newnums;
     infile numbers;
     input Tens 2-3;
     retain Count 100;
     count+tens;
run;
```

a. missing

b. *0*

c. *100*

d. *130*

6. For the observation shown below, what is the result of the IF-THEN statement?

Status	Type	Count	Action	Control
ok	3	12	E	Go

```
if status='OK' and type=3
   then Count+1;
if status='S' or action='E'
   then Control='Stop';
```

a. Count = *12*   Control = *Go*

b. Count = *13*   Control = *Stop*

c. Count = *12*   Control = *Stop*

d. Count = *13*   Control = *Go*

7. Which of the following can determine the length of a new variable?

a. the length of the variable's first value

b. the assignment statement

c. the LENGTH statement

d. all of the above

8. Which set of statements is the most efficient equivalent to the code shown below?

```
if code='1' then Type='Fixed';
if code='2' then Type='Variable';
if code^='1' and code^='2' then Type='Unknown';
```

a. ```
if code='1' then Type='Fixed';
   else if code='2' then Type='Variable';
   else Type='Unknown';
```

b. ```
if code='1' then Type='Fixed';
   if code='2' then Type='Variable';
   else Type='Unknown';
```

c. ```
if code='1' then type='Fixed';
   else code='2' and type='Variable';
   else type='Unknown';
```

d. ```
if code='1' and type='Fixed';
   then code='2' and type='Variable';
   else type='Unknown';
```

9. What is the length of the variable `Type`, as created in the DATA step below?

```
data finance.newloan;
   set finance.records;
   TotLoan+payment;
   if code='1' then Type='Fixed';
   else Type='Variable';
   length type $ 10;
run;
```

    a. 5

    b. 8

    c. 10

    d. It depends on the first value of Type.

10. Which program contains an error?

    a.
```
data clinic.stress(drop=timemin timesec);
    infile tests;
    input ID $ 1-4 Name $ 6-25 RestHR 27-29 MaxHR 31-33
          RecHR 35-37 TimeMin 39-40 TimeSec 42-43
          Tolerance $ 45;
    TotalTime=(timemin*60)+timesec;
    SumSec+totaltime;
run;
```

    b.
```
proc print data=clinic.stress;
    label totaltime='Total Duration of Test';
    format timemin 5.2;
    drop sumsec;
run;
```

    c.
```
proc print data=clinic.stress(keep=totaltime timemin);
    label totaltime='Total Duration of Test';
    format timemin 5.2;
run;
```

    d.
```
data clinic.stress;
    infile tests;
    input ID $ 1-4 Name $ 6-25 RestHR 27-29 MaxHR 31-33
          RecHR 35-37 TimeMin 39-40 TimeSec 42-43
          Tolerance $ 45;
    TotalTime=(timemin*60)+timesec;
    keep id totaltime tolerance;
run;
```

Chapter 12 Reading SAS Data Sets

Overview

Introduction

You've learned about creating a SAS data set from raw data. However, you might want to create a new data set from an existing SAS data set. To create the new data set, you can read a data set using the DATA step. As you read the data set, you can use all the programming features of the DATA step to manipulate your data.

SAS Data Set A

Num	VarA
1	A1
2	A2
3	A3

Read

SAS Data Set B

Num	VarA
1	A1
2	A2
3	A3

This chapter shows you how to use the DATA step to read an existing SAS data set. When you create your new data set, you can choose variables, select observations based on one or more conditions, and assign values conditionally. You can also assign variable attributes such as formats and labels.

 You can also **merge**, **concatenate**, or **interleave** two or more data sets. For details, see Chapter 13, **Combining SAS Data Sets**.

Objectives

In this chapter, you learn to

- create a new data set from an existing data set
- use BY groups to process observations
- read observations by observation number
- stop processing when necessary
- explicitly write observations to output

- detect the last observation in a data set
- identify differences in DATA step processing for raw data and DATA step processing for existing data sets.

Reading a Single Data Set

Suppose you want to create a small data set, **Lab23.Drug1H**, from the **Research.CLTrials** data set, which contains information about treadmill test time and relative tolerance levels.

To create the data set, you must first reference the library in which **CLTrials** is stored and then the library in which you want to store **Drug1H**. Then you write a DATA step to read your data and create a new data set.

General form, basic DATA step for reading a single data set:

    DATA *SAS-data-set*;
    SET *SAS-data-set*;
    RUN;

where

- *SAS-data-set* in the DATA statement is the name (*libref.filename*) of the SAS data set to be created
- *SAS-data-set* in the SET statement is the name (*libref.filename*) of the SAS data set to be read.

You write a DATA step to name the SAS data set to be created. Then, you specify the data set that will be read in the SET statement. The DATA statement below creates the permanent SAS data set **Drug1H**, which will be stored in a SAS data library to which the libref **Lab23** has been assigned. The SET statement below reads the permanent SAS data set **Research.CLTrials**.

```
libname lab23 'c:\drug\allergy\labtests';
libname research 'c:\drug\allergy';
data lab23.drug1h;
   set research.cltrials;
run;
```

The DATA step above reads all observations and variables from the existing data set into the new data set. When you submit this DATA step, the following messages appear in the log, confirming that the new data set was created:

SAS Log

```
 8  data lab23.drug1h;
 9     set research.cltrials;
10  run;

NOTE: The data set LAB23.DRUG1H has 21
      observations and 8 variables.
```

Manipulating Data

In the previous section of this chapter, the example program created a data set that was identical to the existing data set, **Research.CLTrials**. But you usually don't want an exact duplicate of the existing data set. When you read a data set, you can use any of the programming features of the DATA step to manipulate your data.

For example, you can use any of the statements and data set options that you learned in previous chapters.

To Do This	Use This Type of Statement
Subset data	`if resthr<70 then delete;` `if tolerance='D';`
Drop unwanted variables	`drop timemin timesec;`
Create or modify a variable	`TotalTime=(timemin*60)+timesec;`
Initialize a sum variable Sum accumulated values	`retain SumSec 5400;` `sumsec+totaltime;`
Specify a variable's length	`length TestLength $ 6;`

Execute statements conditionally	`if totaltime>800 then TestLength='Long';`
	`else if 750<=totaltime<=800`
	`    then TestLength='Normal';`
	`else if totaltime<750`
	`    then TestLength='Short';`

Label a variable Format a variable	`label sumsec='Cumulative Total Seconds';` `format sumsec comma6.;`

Example

The following DATA step reads the data set **Research.CLTrials**, selects observations and variables, and creates new variables.

```
data lab23.drug1h(drop=placebo uric);
   set research.cltrials(drop=triglyc);
   if sex='M' then delete;
   if placebo='YES';
   TestDate='22MAY1999'd;
   retain Days 30;
   days+1;
   length Retest $ 5;
   if cholesterol>190 then retest='YES';
   else if 150<=cholesterol<=190 then retest='CHECK';
   else if cholesterol<150 then retest='NO';
   label retest='Perform Cholesterol Test 2?';
   format enddate mmddyy10.;
run;
```

Where to Specify the DROP= and KEEP= Data Set Options

You've learned that you can specify the DROP= and KEEP= data set options anywhere you name a SAS data set. However, using DROP= and KEEP= when reading an existing data set requires that you decide where to specify these options. You can specify DROP= and KEEP= in either the **DATA statement** or the **SET statement**, depending on whether or not you want to process values of the variables in that DATA step:

- If you **don't** process certain variables and you don't want them to appear in the new data set, then specify them in the DROP= option in the SET statement.

  In the DATA step shown below, the DROP= option in the SET statement prevents the variables `Triglycerides` and `UricAcid` from being read. These variables won't appear in the **Lab23.Drug1H** data set.

  ```
  data lab23.drug1h(drop=placebo);
     set research.cltrials(drop=triglycerides uricacid);
     if placebo='YES';
  run;
  ```

- If you **do** need to process a variable in the original data set (in a subsetting IF statement, for example), you must specify the variable in the DROP= option in the DATA statement. Otherwise, the statement that is using the variable for processing causes an error.

  This DATA step uses the variable `Placebo` to select observations. To drop `Placebo` from the new data set, the DROP= option must appear in the DATA statement.

  ```
  data lab23.drug1h(drop=placebo);
     set research.cltrials(drop=triglycerides uricacid);
     if placebo='YES';
  run;
  ```

When used in the DATA statement, the DROP= option simply drops the variables from the new data set. However, the variables are still read from the original data set and are available within the DATA step.

- Remember, in either situation, you can use the KEEP= option instead of the DROP= option if more variables are dropped than kept.

Using BY-Group Processing

Finding the First and Last Observations in a Group

In Chapter 4, **Creating List Reports**, you learned to use a BY statement in PROC SORT to sort observations and in PROC PRINT to group observations for subtotals. You can also use the BY statement in the DATA step to group observations for processing.

```
data temp;
   set salary;
   by dept;
run;
```

When you use the BY statement with the SET statement,

- the data sets that are listed in the SET statement must be sorted by the values of the BY variable(s), or the data sets must have an appropriate index.

- the DATA step creates two temporary variables for each BY variable. One is named **FIRST.*variable***, where *variable* is the name of the BY variable, and the other is named **LAST.*variable***. Their values are either *1* or *0*. FIRST.*variable* and LAST.*variable* identify the first and last observation in each BY group.

This Variable	Equals
FIRST.*variable*	*1* for the **first** observation in a BY group *0* for any other observation in a BY group
LAST.*variable*	*1* for the **last** observation in a BY group *0* for any other observation in a BY group

Example

To work with FIRST.*variable* and LAST.*variable*, let's look at a different set of data. The **Company.USA** data set contains payroll information for individual employees. Suppose you want to compute the annual payroll by department. Assume 2,000 work hours per year for hourly employees.

Before computing the annual payroll, you need to group observations by values of the variable Dept.

SAS Data Set Company.USA
(Partial Listing)

Dept	WageCat	WageRate
ADM20	S	3392.50
ADM30	S	5093.75
CAM10	S	1813.30
CAM10	S	1572.50
CAM10	H	13.48
ADM30	S	2192.25

The following program computes the annual payroll by department. Notice that the variable name Dept has been appended to FIRST. and LAST.

```
proc sort data=company.usa out=work.temp;
   by dept;
run;
data company.budget(keep=dept payroll);
   set work.temp;
   by dept;
   if wagecat='S' then Yearly=wagerate*12;
   else if wagecat='H' then Yearly=wagerate*2000;
   if first.dept then Payroll=0;
   payroll+yearly;
   if last.dept;
run;
```

If you could look behind the scenes at the program data vector (PDV) as the **Company.Budget** data set is being created, you would see the following. Notice the values for FIRST.Dept and LAST.Dept.

Selected PDV Variables

_N_	Dept	Payroll	FIRST.Dept	LAST.Dept
1	ADM10	70929.0	1	0
1	ADM10	119479.2	0	0
1	ADM10	173245.2	0	0
1	ADM10	255516.0	0	0
1	ADM10	293472.0	0	1
1	ADM20	40710.0	1	0
1	ADM20	68010.0	0	0
1	ADM20	94980.0	0	0
1	ADM20	136020.0	0	0
1	ADM20	177330.0	0	1
1	ADM30	61125.0	1	1

When you print the new data set, you can now list and sum the annual payroll by department.

```
proc print data=company.budget noobs;
   sum payroll;
   format payroll dollar12.2;
run;
```

Dept	Payroll
ADM10	$293,472.00
ADM20	$177,330.00
ADM30	$173,388.00
CAM10	$130,709.60
CAM20	$156,731.20
	$931,630.80

Finding the First and Last Observations in Subgroups

When you specify multiple BY variables,

- FIRST.*variable* for each variable is set to *1* at the first occurrence of a new value for the variable

- a change in the value of a primary BY variable forces LAST.*variable* to equal *1* for the secondary BY variables.

Example

Suppose you now want to compute the annual payroll by job type for each manager. In your program, you specify two BY variables, Manager and JobType.

```
proc sort data=company.usa out=work.temp2;
   by manager jobtype;
data company.budget2(keep=manager jobtype payroll);
   set work.temp2;
   by manager jobtype;
   if wagecat='S' then Yearly=wagerate*12;
   else if wagecat='H' then Yearly=wagerate*2000;
   if first.jobtype then Payroll=0;
   payroll+yearly;
   if last.jobtype;
run;
```

If you could look at the PDV now, you would see the following. Notice that the values for FIRST.JobType and LAST.JobType change according to values of FIRST.Manager and LAST.Manager.

Selected PDV Variables

_N_	Manager	JobType	Payroll	FIRST. Manager	LAST. Manager	FIRST. JobType	LAST. JobType
1	Coxe	3	40710.0	1	0	1	1
2	Coxe	50	41040.0	0	0	1	0
3	Coxe	50	82350.0	0	0	0	1
4	Coxe	240	27300.0	0	0	1	0
5	Coxe	240	54270.0	0	1	0	1
6	Delgado	240	35520.0	1	0	1	0
7	Delgado	240	63120.0	0	0	0	1
8	Delgado	420	18870.0	0	0	1	0
9	Delgado	420	45830.0	0	0	0	1
10	Delgado	440	21759.6	0	1	1	1
11	Overby	1	82270.8	1	0	1	1
12	Overby	5	48550.2	0	0	1	1
13	Overby	10	53766.0	0	0	1	1
14	Overby	20	70929.0	0	0	1	0
15	Overby	20	108885.0	0	1	0	1

Now you can sum the annual payroll by job type for each manager. In the following output, the payroll for only two managers (*Coxe* and *Delgado*) is listed. Remember, neither the FIRST. *variable* nor the LAST. *variable* is stored in the new data set.

```
proc print data=company.budget2 noobs;;
   by manager;
   var jobtype;
   sum payroll;
   where manager in ('Coxe','Delgado');
   format payroll dollar12.2;
run;
```

Manager=Coxe

JobType	Payroll
3	$40,710.00
50	$123,390.00
240	$81,570.00
Manager	**$245,670.00**

Manager=Delgado

JobType	Payroll
240	$98,640.00
420	$64,700.00
440	$21,759.00
Manager	**$185,099.00**

Reading Observations Using Direct Access

The POINT= Option

So far in this chapter, you've read the observations in an input data set **sequentially**. That is, you have accessed observations in the order in which they appear in the physical file. However, you can also access observations **directly**, by going straight to an observation in a SAS data set without having to process each observation that precedes it.

To access observations directly by their observation number, you use the **POINT= option** in the SET statement.

General form, POINT= option:

      POINT=*variable*;

where *variable*

- specifies a temporary numeric variable that contains the **observation number** of the observation to be read

- must be given a value before the SET statement is executed.

Example

Let's suppose you want to read only the fifth observation from a data set. In the following DATA step, the value 5 is assigned to the variable ObsNum. The POINT= option reads the value of ObsNum to determine which observation to read from the data set **Company.USA**.

```
data work.getobs5;
   obsnum=5;
   set company.usa(keep=manager payroll) point=obsnum;
run;
```

Preventing Continuous Looping with the POINT= Option

As you learned in a previous chapter, the DATA step continues to read observations until it reaches the end-of-file marker in the input data. However, because the POINT= option reads only specified observations, SAS cannot read an end-of-file indicator as it would if the file were being read sequentially. So submitting the following program would cause **continuous looping**:

```
data work.getobs5(drop=obsnum);
   obsnum=5;
   set company.usa(keep=manager payroll) point=obsnum;
run;
```

Because there is no end-of-file condition when you use direct access to read data, you **must** take either or both of the following precautions:

- Use a **STOP statement** to prevent continuous looping. The STOP statement causes SAS to stop processing the current DATA step immediately and to resume processing statements after the end of the current DATA step.

- Use programming logic that checks for an **invalid value of the POINT= variable**. If SAS reads an invalid value for the POINT= variable, it sets the automatic variable _ERROR_ to *1*. You can use this information to check for conditions that cause continuous processing.

> **General form, STOP statement:**
>
> **STOP;**

So if you add a STOP statement, your program no longer loops continuously.

```
data work.getobs5(drop=obsnum);
   obsnum=5;
   set company.usa(keep=manager payroll) point=obsnum;
   stop;
run;
```

But your program doesn't write any observations to output, either. Remember from Chapter 6, **Understanding DATA Step Processing**, that the DATA step writes observations to output at the end of the DATA step. However, in this program, the STOP statement immediately stops processing before the end of the DATA step.

The following section shows you how to write the observation to output before processing stops.

Writing Observations Explicitly

To override the default way in which the DATA step writes observations to output, you can use an **OUTPUT statement** in the DATA step. Placing an explicit OUTPUT statement in a DATA step overrides the automatic output, so that observations are added to a data set only when the explicit OUTPUT statement is executed.

General form, OUTPUT statement:

> **OUTPUT** *<SAS-data-set(s)>*;

where *SAS-data-set(s)* names the data set(s) to which the observation is written. All data set names that are specified in the OUTPUT statement **must** also appear in the DATA statement.

Using an OUTPUT statement without a following data set name causes the current observation to be written to all data sets that are named in the DATA statement.

With an OUTPUT statement, your program now writes a single observation to output—observation 5.

```
data work.getobs5(drop=obsnum);
    obsnum=5;
    set company.usa(keep=manager payroll) point=obsnum;
    output;
    stop;
run;
proc print data=work.getobs5 noobs;
run;
```

Manager	Payroll
Delgado	45830

Suppose your DATA statement contains two data set names, and you include an OUTPUT statement that only references one of the data sets. The DATA step will create both data sets, but only the data set that is named in the OUTPUT statement will contain output. For example, the program below creates two temporary data sets, **Empty** and **Full**. The result of this DATA step is that the data set **Empty** is created but contains no observations, and the data set **Full** contains all of the observations from **Company.Usa**.

```
data empty full;
    set company.use;
    output full;
run;
```

More Complex Ways of Using Direct Access

To convey concepts clearly, the examples in this section have been as simple as possible. However, most uses of the POINT= option are more complex. For example, POINT= is commonly used in combining data sets, not simply in reading a single data set.

You can see more complex examples of using POINT= in Chapter 15, **Generating Data with DO Loops**.

Detecting the End of a Data Set

The END= Option

Instead of reading specific observations, you might want to determine when the last observation in an input data set has been read, so that you can perform specific processing. For example, you might want to write to output only an observation that contains totals for variables in all observations in the data set.

To create a temporary numeric variable whose value is used to detect the last observation, you can use the **END= option** in the SET statement.

> **General form, END= option:**
>
> **END=***variable*
>
> where *variable* creates and names a temporary variable that contains an end-of-file marker. The variable, which is initialized to *0*, is set to *1* when the SET statement reads the last observation of the data set.
>
> This variable is **not** added to the data set.
>
> Do not specify END= with POINT=. POINT= reads only a specific observation, so the last observation in the data set is not encountered.

Examples

Suppose you want to sum the number of seconds for treadmill stress tests. If you submit the following program, you produce a new data set that contains cumulative totals for each of the values of TotalTime.

```
data work.addtoend(drop=timemin timesec);
   set clinic.stress2(keep=timemin timesec);
   TotalMin+timemin;
   TotalSec+timesec;
   TotalTime=totalmin*60+timesec;
run;
proc print data=work.addtoend noobs;
run;
```

TotalMin	TotalSec	TotalTime
12	38	758
22	43	1325
33	56	1993
42	98	2562
53	144	3226
65	170	3926
80	211	4841
93	224	5593
103	246	6202
119	295	7189
134	297	8042
146	308	8771
160	317	9609
171	343	10286
185	370	11127
198	389	11899
214	396	12847
231	431	13895
246	472	14801
260	529	15657
272	539	16330

But what if you want only the **final** total (the last observation) in the new data set? The following program uses the END= variable `last` to select only the last observation of the data set. You specify END= in the SET statement and `last` wherever you need it in processing (here, in the subsetting IF statement).

```
data work.addtoend(drop=timemin timesec);
    set clinic.stress2(keep=timemin timesec) end=last;
    TotalMin+timemin;
    TotalSec+timesec;
    TotalTime=totalmin*60+timesec;
    if last;
run;
proc print data=work.addtoend noobs;
run;
```

Now the new data set has one observation:

TotalMin	TotalSec	TotalTime
272	539	16330

Understanding How Data Sets Are Read

In a previous chapter, you learned about the compilation and execution phases of the DATA step as they pertain to reading raw data. DATA step processing for reading existing SAS data sets is very similar. The main difference is that while reading an existing data set with the SET statement, SAS retains the values of the variables from one observation to the next.

Let's briefly look at the compilation and execution phases of DATA steps that use a SET statement. In this example, the DATA step reads the data set **Finance.Loans**, creates the variable `Interest`, and creates the new data set **Finance.DueJan**.

```
data finance.duejan;
   set finance.loans;
   Interest=amount*(rate/12);
run;
```

SAS Data Set Finance.Loans

Account	Amount	Rate	Months	Payment
101-1092	22000	0.100	60	467.43
101-1731	114000	0.095	360	958.57
101-1289	10000	0.105	36	325.02
101-3144	3500	0.105	12	308.52

Compilation Phase

The compilation phase includes the following steps:

1. The program data vector is created and contains the automatic variables _N_ and _ERROR_.

   Program Data Vector

_N_	_ERROR_
1	0

2. SAS also scans each statement in the DATA step, looking for syntax errors.

3. When the SET statement is compiled, a slot is added to the program data vector for each variable in the input data set. The input data set supplies the variable names, as well as attributes such as type and length.

   Program Data Vector

_N_	_ERROR_	Account	Amount	Rate	Months	Payment

4. Any variables that are created in the DATA step are also added to the program data vector. The attributes of each of these variables are determined by the expression in the statement.

Program Data Vector

_N_	_ERROR_	Account	Amount	Rate	Months	Payment	Interest

5. At the bottom of the DATA step, the compilation phase is complete, and the descriptor portion of the new SAS data set is created. There are no observations because the DATA step has not yet executed.

When the compilation phase is complete, the execution phase begins.

Execution Phase

The execution phase includes the following steps:

1. The DATA step executes once for each observation in the input data set. For example, this DATA step will execute four times because there are four observations in the input data set **Finance.Loans**.

2. At the beginning of the execution phase, the value of _N_ is *1*. Because there are no data errors, the value of _ERROR_ is *0*. The remaining variables are initialized to missing. Missing numeric values are represented by a period, and missing character values are represented by a blank.

```
data finance.duejan;
    set finance.loans;
    Interest=amount*(rate/12);
run;
```

SAS Data Set Finance.Loans

Account	Amount	Rate	Months	Payment
101-1092	22000	0.1000	60	467.43
101-1731	114000	0.0950	360	958.57
101-1289	10000	0.1050	36	325.02
101-3144	3500	0.1050	12	308.52

Program Data Vector

_N_	_ERROR_	Account	Amount	Rate	Months	Payment	Interest
1	0		.	.	.	.	.

Character Value — Numeric Values

SAS Data Set Finance.Duejan

Account	Amount	Rate	Months	Payment	Interest

3. The SET statement reads the first observation from the input data set and writes the values to the program data vector.

```
data finance.duejan;
   set finance.loans;
   Interest=amount*(rate/12);
run;
```

SAS Data Set Finance.Loans

Account	Amount	Rate	Months	Payment
101-1092	22000	0.1000	60	467.43
101-1731	114000	0.0950	360	958.57
101-1289	10000	0.1050	36	325.02
101-3144	3500	0.1050	12	308.52

Program Data Vector

N	ERROR	Account	Amount	Rate	Months	Payment	Interest
1	0	101-1092	22000	0.1000	60	467.43	.

SAS Data Set Finance.Duejan

Account	Amount	Rate	Months	Payment	Interest

4. Then, the assignment statement executes to compute the value for Interest.

```
data finance.duejan;
   set finance.loans;
   Interest=amount*(rate/12);
run;
```

SAS Data Set Finance.Loans

Account	Amount	Rate	Months	Payment
101-1092	22000	0.1000	60	467.43
101-1731	114000	0.0950	360	958.57
101-1289	10000	0.1050	36	325.02
101-3144	3500	0.1050	12	308.52

Program Data Vector

N	ERROR	Account	Amount	Rate	Months	Payment	Interest
1	0	101-1092	22000	0.1000	60	467.43	183.333

SAS Data Set Finance.Duejan

Account	Amount	Rate	Months	Payment	Interest

5. At the end of the first iteration of the DATA step, the values in the program data vector are written to the new data set as the first observation.

```
data finance.duejan;
   set finance.loans;
   Interest=amount*(rate/12);
run;
```

SAS Data Set Finance.Loans

Account	Amount	Rate	Months	Payment
101-1092	22000	0.1000	60	467.43
101-1731	114000	0.0950	360	958.57
101-1289	10000	0.1050	36	325.02
101-3144	3500	0.1050	12	308.52

Program Data Vector

_N_	_ERROR_	Account	Amount	Rate	Months	Payment	Interest
1	0	101-1092	22000	0.1000	60	467.43	183.333

SAS Data Set Finance.Duejan

Account	Amount	Rate	Months	Payment	Interest
101-1092	22000	0.1000	60	467.43	183.333

6. The value of _N_ is set to 2, and control returns to the top of the DATA step. Remember, the automatic variable _N_ keeps track of how many times the DATA step has begun to execute.

```
data finance.duejan;
   set finance.loans;
   Interest=amount*(rate/12);
run;
```

SAS Data Set Finance.Loans

Account	Amount	Rate	Months	Payment
101-1092	22000	0.1000	60	467.43
101-1731	114000	0.0950	360	958.57
101-1289	10000	0.1050	36	325.02
101-3144	3500	0.1050	12	308.52

Program Data Vector

_N_	_ERROR_	Account	Amount	Rate	Months	Payment	Interest
2	0	101-1092	22000	0.1000	60	467.43	183.333

SAS Data Set Finance.Duejan

Account	Amount	Rate	Months	Payment	Interest
101-1092	22000	0.1000	60	467.43	183.333

7. SAS retains the values of variables that were read from a SAS data set with the SET statement, or that were created by a Sum statement. All other variable values, such as the values of the variable `Interest`, are set to missing.

```
data finance.duejan;
    set finance.loans;
    Interest=amount*(rate/12);
run;
```

SAS Data Set Finance.Loans

Account	Amount	Rate	Months	Payment
101-1092	22000	0.1000	60	467.43
101-1731	114000	0.0950	360	958.57
101-1289	10000	0.1050	36	325.02
101-3144	3500	0.1050	12	308.52

Program Data Vector

N	ERROR	Account	Amount	Rate	Months	Payment	Interest
2	0	101-1092	22000	0.1000	60	467.43	•

Values Retained — Reset to Missing

SAS Data Set Finance.Duejan

Account	Amount	Rate	Months	Payment	Interest
101-1092	22000	0.1000	60	467.43	183.333

When SAS reads **raw data**, the situation is different. In that case, SAS sets the value of each variable in the DATA step to missing at the beginning of each iteration, with these exceptions:

- variables named in a RETAIN statement

- variables created in a Sum statement

- data elements in a _TEMPORARY_ array

- any variables created by using options in the FILE or INFILE statements

- automatic variables.

8. At the beginning of the second iteration, the value of _N_ is set to *2*, and the value of _ERROR_ is re-set to *0*. Remember, the automatic variable _N_ keeps track of how many times the DATA step has begun to execute.

```
data finance.duejan;
    set finance.loans;
    Interest=amount*(rate/12);
run;
```

SAS Data Set Finance.Loans

Account	Amount	Rate	Months	Payment
101-1092	22000	0.1000	60	467.43
101-1731	114000	0.0950	360	958.57
101-1289	10000	0.1050	36	325.02
101-3144	3500	0.1050	12	308.52

Program Data Vector

N	ERROR	Account	Amount	Rate	Months	Payment	Interest
2	0	101-1092	22000	0.1000	60	467.43	.

SAS Data Set Finance.Duejan

Account	Amount	Rate	Months	Payment	Interest
101-1092	22000	0.1000	60	467.43	183.333

9. As the SET statement executes, the values from the second observation are written to the program data vector.

```
data finance.duejan;
    set finance.loans;
    Interest=amount*(rate/12);
run;
```

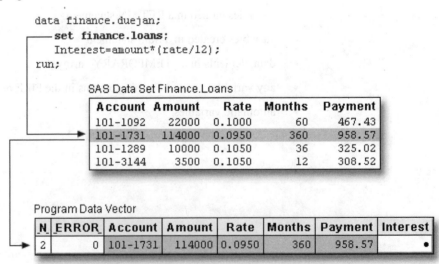

SAS Data Set Finance.Loans

Account	Amount	Rate	Months	Payment
101-1092	22000	0.1000	60	467.43
101-1731	114000	0.0950	360	958.57
101-1289	10000	0.1050	36	325.02
101-3144	3500	0.1050	12	308.52

Program Data Vector

N	ERROR	Account	Amount	Rate	Months	Payment	Interest
2	0	101-1731	114000	0.0950	360	958.57	.

SAS Data Set Finance.Duejan

Account	Amount	Rate	Months	Payment	Interest
101-1092	22000	0.1000	60	467.43	183.333

10. The assignment statement executes again to compute the value for `Interest` for the second observation.

```
data finance.duejan;
   set finance.loans;
   Interest=amount*(rate/12);
run;
```

SAS Data Set Finance.Loans

Account	Amount	Rate	Months	Payment
101-1092	22000	0.1000	60	467.43
101-1731	114000	0.0950	360	950.57
101-1289	10000	0.1050	36	325.02
101-3144	3500	0.1050	12	308.52

Program Data Vector

_N_	_ERROR_	Account	Amount	Rate	Months	Payment	Interest
2	0	101-1731	114000	0.0950	360	958.57	902.5

SAS Data Set Finance.Duejan

Account	Amount	Rate	Months	Payment	Interest
101-1092	22000	0.1000	60	467.43	183.333

11. At the bottom of the DATA step, the values in the program data vector are written to the data set as the second observation.

```
data finance.duejan;
   set finance.loans;
   Interest=amount*(rate/12);
run;
```

SAS Data Set Finance.Loans

Account	Amount	Rate	Months	Payment
101-1092	22000	0.1000	60	467.43
101-1731	114000	0.0950	360	958.57
101-1289	10000	0.1050	36	325.02
101-3144	3500	0.1050	12	308.52

Program Data Vector

_N_	_ERROR_	Account	Amount	Rate	Months	Payment	Interest
2	0	101-1731	114000	0.0950	360	958.57	902.5

SAS Data Set Finance.Duejan

Account	Amount	Rate	Months	Payment	Interest
101-1092	22000	0.1000	60	467.43	183.333
101-1731	114000	0.0950	360	958.57	902.5

12. The value of _N_ is set to 3, and control returns to the top of the DATA step. SAS retains the values of variables that were read from a SAS data set with the SET statement, or that were created by a Sum statement. All other variable values, such as the values of the variable Interest, are set to missing.

```
data finance.duejan;
    set finance.loans;
    Interest=amount*(rate/12);
run;
```

SAS Data Set Finance.Loans

Account	Amount	Rate	Months	Payment
101-1092	22000	0.1000	60	467.43
101-1731	114000	0.0950	360	958.57
101-1289	10000	0.1050	36	325.02
101-3144	3500	0.1050	12	308.52

Program Data Vector

_N_	_ERROR_	Account	Amount	Rate	Months	Payment	Interest
3	0	101-1731	114000	0.0950	360	958.57	.

|← Values Retained →| |← Reset to Missing →|

SAS Data Set Finance.Duejan

Account	Amount	Rate	Months	Payment	Interest
101-1092	22000	0.1000	60	467.43	183.333
101-1731	114000	0.0950	360	958.57	902.5

This process continues until all of the observations are read.

Additional Features

The DATA step provides many other programming features for manipulating data sets. For example, you can

- use IF-THEN/ELSE logic with DO groups and DO loops to control processing that is based on one or more conditions

- specify additional data set options

- process variables in arrays

- use SAS functions.

You can also combine SAS data sets in several ways, including match merging, interleaving, one-to-one merging, and updating. You will learn how to do these tasks in later chapters.

Summary

Text Summary

Setting Up

Before you can create a new data set, you must assign a libref to the SAS data library that will store the data set.

Reading a Single Data Set

After you have referenced the library in which your data set is stored, you can write a DATA step to name the SAS data set to be created. You then specify the data set to be read in the SET statement.

Selecting Variables

You can select the variables that you want to drop or keep by using the **DROP=** and **KEEP=** data set options in parentheses after a SAS data set name. For convenience, use DROP= if more variables are kept than dropped.

BY-Group Processing

Use the BY statement in the DATA step to group observations for processing. When you use the BY statement with the SET statement, the DATA step automatically creates two temporary variables, FIRST. and LAST. When you specify multiple BY variables, a change in the value of a primary BY variable forces LAST. *variable* to equal *1* for the secondary BY variables.

Reading Observations Using Direct Access

In addition to reading input data sequentially, you can access observations directly by using the POINT= option to go directly to a data set observation. There is no end-of-file condition when you use direct access, so include an explicit **OUTPUT statement** and then the **STOP statement** to prevent continuous looping.

Detecting the End of a Data Set

To determine when the last observation in an input data set has been read, use the END= option in the SET statement. The specified variable is initialized to *0*, then set to *1* when the SET statement reads the last observation of the data set.

Points to Remember

- When you perform BY-group processing, the data sets that are listed in the SET statement must either be sorted by the values of the BY variable(s), or they must have an appropriate index.
- When using direct access to read data, you **must** prevent continuous looping. Add a STOP statement to the DATA step, or use programming logic that checks for an invalid value of the POINT= variable.
- Do not specify the END= option with the POINT= option in a SET statement.

Practice

After you complete this chapter, practice what you learned by using the sample data and SAS programs for Chapter 12, **Reading SAS Data Sets**, which are located on the CD-ROM. Follow the directions for creating your sample data in the Before You Begin section.

Quiz

Select the best answer for each question. After completing the quiz, check your answers using the answer key in the appendix.

1. If you submit the following program, which variables appear in the new data set?

   ```
   data work.cardiac(drop=age group);
      set clinic.fitness(keep=age weight group);
      if group=2 and age>40;
   run;
   ```

   a. none
   b. Weight
   c. Age, Group
   d. Age, Weight, Group

2. Which of the following programs correctly reads the data set **Orders** and creates the data set **FastOrdr?**

   a. ```
      data catalog.fastordr(drop=ordrtime);
         set july.orders(keep=product units price);
         if ordrtime<4;
         Total=units*price;
      run;
      ```
   b. ```
      data catalog.orders(drop=ordrtime);
         set july.fastordr(keep=product units price);
         if ordrtime<4;
         Total=units*price;
      run;
      ```
   c. ```
      data catalog.fastordr(drop=ordrtime);
         set july.orders(keep=product units price
                         ordrtime);
         if ordrtime<4;
         Total=units*price;
      run;
      ```
   d. none of the above

3. Which of the following statements is **false** about BY-group processing?

   When you use the BY statement with the SET statement,

   a. the data sets that are listed in the SET statement must be indexed or sorted by the values of the BY variable(s).
   b. the DATA step automatically creates two variables, FIRST. and LAST., for each variable in the BY statement.
   c. FIRST. and LAST. identify the first and last observation in each BY group, in that order.
   d. FIRST. and LAST. are stored in the data set.
      ```

4. There are 500 observations in the data set **Company.USA**. What is the result of submitting the following program?

```
data work.getobs5(drop=obsnum);
   obsnum=5;
   set company.usa(keep=manager payroll) point=obsnum;
   stop;
run;
```

    a. an error

    b. an empty data set

    c. a continuous loop

    d. a data set that contains one observation

5. There is no end-of-file condition when you use direct access to read data, so how can your program prevent a continuous loop?

    a. Do not use a POINT= variable.

    b. Check for an invalid value of the POINT= variable.

    c. Do not use an END= variable.

    d. Include an OUTPUT statement.

6. Assuming that the data set **Company.USA** has five or more observations, what is the result of submitting the following program?

```
data work.getobs5(drop=obsnum);
   obsnum=5;
   set company.usa(keep=manager payroll) point=obsnum;
   output;
   stop;
run;
```

    a. an error

    b. an empty data set

    c. a continuous loop

    d. a data set that contains one observation

7. Which of the following statements is **true** regarding direct access of data sets?

    a. You cannot specify END= with POINT=.

    b. You cannot specify OUTPUT with POINT=.

    c. You cannot specify STOP with END=.

    d. You cannot specify FIRST. with LAST.

8. What is the result of submitting the following program?

```
data work.addtoend;
   set clinic.stress2 end=last;
   if last;
run;
```

    a. an error

    b. an empty data set

    c. a continuous loop

    d. a data set that contains one observation

9. At the start of DATA step processing, during the compilation phase, variables are created in the program data vector (PDV), and observations are set to

    a. blank

    b. missing

    c. 0

    d. there are no observations.

10. The DATA step executes

    a. continuously if you use the POINT= option and the STOP statement.

    b. once for each variable in the output data set.

    c. once for each observation in the input data set.

    d. until it encounters an OUTPUT statement.

Chapter 13 Combining SAS Data Sets

Overview

Introduction

In SAS programming, a common task is to combine observations from two or more data sets into a new data set. By using the DATA step, you can combine data sets in several ways, including the following:

Method of Combining	Illustration
One-to-one reading Creates observations that contain all of the variables from each contributing data set. Combines observations based on their relative position in each data set. Statement: SET	SAS Data Set C SAS Data Set D Num VarA Num VarB 1 A1 2 B1 3 A2 4 B2 5 A3 ── Read ── Combined SAS Data Set Num VarA VarB 2 A1 B1 4 A2 B2
Concatenating Appends the observations from one data set to another. Statement: SET	SAS Data Set A SAS Data Set C Num VarA Num VarB 1 A1 1 B1 2 A2 2 B2 3 A3 4 B3 ── Concatenate ── Combined SAS Data Set Num VarA VarB 1 A1 2 A2 3 A3 1 B1 2 B2 4 B3

Interleaving

Intersperses observations from two or more data sets, based on one or more common variables.

Statements: SET, BY

Match-merging

Matches observations from two or more data sets into a single observation in a new data set according to the values of a common variable.

Statements: MERGE, BY

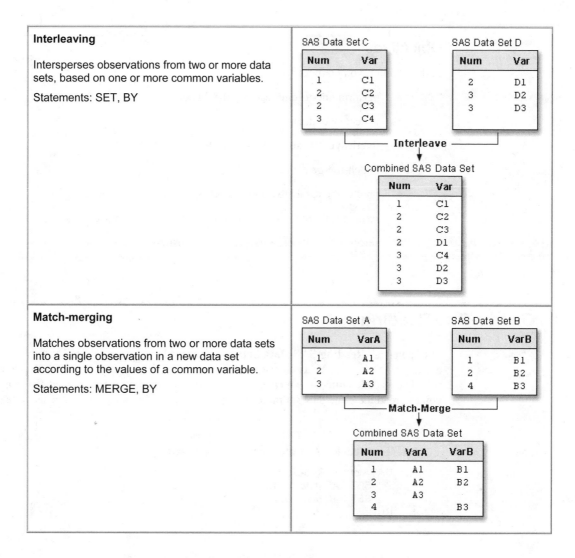

You can also use PROC SQL to join data sets according to common values. PROC SQL enables you to perform many other types of data set joins. See the **SQL Processing with SAS** e-learning course for additional training.

This chapter shows you how to combine SAS data sets by using one-to-one reading, concatenating, interleaving, and match-merging. When you use the DATA step to combine data sets, you have a high degree of control in creating and manipulating data sets.

Objectives

In this chapter, you learn to

- perform one-to-one reading of data sets

- concatenate data sets

- interleave data sets

- match-merge data sets

- predict the results by understanding match-merge processing

- re-name any like-named variables to avoid overwriting values

- select only matched observations, if desired.

One-to-One Reading

In Chapter 12, **Reading SAS Data Sets**, you learned how to use the SET statement to read an existing SAS data set. You can also use multiple SET statements in a DATA step to combine data sets. This is called **one-to-one reading**. In one-to-one reading, you can read different data sets, or you can read the same data set more than once, as if you were reading from separate data sets.

General form, basic DATA step for one-to-one reading:

> **DATA** *output-SAS-data-set*;
>   **SET** *SAS-data-set-1*;
>   **SET** *SAS-data-set-2*;
> **RUN;**

where

- *output-SAS-data-set* names the data set to be created

- *SAS-data-set-1* and *SAS-data-set-2* specify the data sets to be read.

📋 You can specify any number of data sets in the SET statement.

How One-to-One Reading Selects Data

When you perform one-to-one reading,

- the new data set contains **all the variables** from all the input data sets. If the data sets contain variables that have the same names, the values that are read in from the last data set overwrite the values that were read in from earlier data sets.

- the number of observations in the new data set is the **number of observations in the smallest original data set**. Observations are combined based on their relative position in each data set; that is, the first observation in one data set is joined with the first observation in the other, and so on. The DATA step stops after it has read the last observation from the smallest data set.

How One-to-One Reading Works

Let's look at a simple case of one-to-one reading.

```
data one2one;
   set c;
   set d;
run;
```

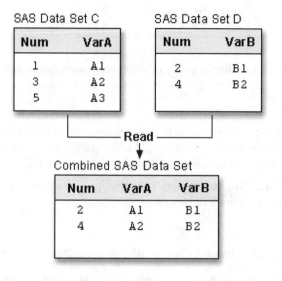

1. The first SET statement reads one observation from data set **C**.

Num	VarA	VarB
1	A1	

2. Then the second SET statement reads one observation from data set **D**. The value for Num in data set **D** overwrites the value for Num in data set **C**.

Num	VarA	VarB
2	A1	B1

3. Next, the first SET statement reads the second observation from data set **C**.

Num	VarA	VarB
2	A1	B1
3	A2	

4. Finally, the second SET statement reads the second observation from data set **D**, overwriting the value for Num in data set **C**. Because this is the last observation in the smallest data set, processing stops. The DATA step does not read the third observation in data set **C**.

Num	VarA	VarB
2	A1	B1
4	A2	B2

The following section shows how you might use one-to-one reading.

Example

Suppose you have basic patient data (ID, sex, and age) in the data set **Clinic.Patients** and want to combine it with other patient data (height and weight) for patients under age 60. The height and weight data is stored in the data set **Clinic.Measure**. Both data sets are sorted by the variable ID.

Notice that **Clinic.Patients** contains 7 observations in which the patient age is less than 60, and **Clinic.Measure** contains 6 observations.

SAS Data Set Clinic.Patients

Obs	ID	Sex	Age
1	1129	F	48
2	1387	F	57
3	2304	F	16
4	2486	F	63
5	4759	F	60
6	5438	F	42
7	6488	F	59
8	9012	F	39
9	9125	F	56

SAS Data Set Clinic.Measure

Obs	ID	Height	Weight
1	1129	61	137
2	1387	64	142
3	2304	61	102
4	5438	62	168
5	6488	64	154
6	9012	63	157

To subset observations from the first data set and combine them with observations from the second data set, you can submit the following program:

```
data clinic.one2one;
   set clinic.patients;
   if age<60;
   set clinic.measure;
run;
```

The resulting data set, **Clinic.One2one**, contains 6 observations (the number of observations read from the smallest data set, here **Clinic.Measure**). The last observation in **Clinic.Patients** is not read.

SAS Data Set Clinic.One2one

Obs	ID	Sex	Age	Height	Weight
1	1129	F	48	61	137
2	1387	F	57	64	142
3	2304	F	16	61	102
4	5438	F	42	62	168
5	6488	F	59	64	154
6	9012	F	39	63	157

Concatenating

Another way to combine SAS data sets with the SET statement is **concatenating**, which appends the observations from one data set to another data set. To concatenate SAS data sets, you specify a list of data set names in the SET statement.

General form, basic DATA step for concatenating:

> **DATA** *output-SAS-data-set*;
>   **SET** *SAS-data-set-1 SAS-data-set-2*;
> **RUN;**

where

- *output-SAS-data-set* names the data set to be created

- *SAS-data-set-1* and *SAS-data-set-2* specify the data sets to be read.

You can specify any number of data sets in the SET statement.

How Concatenating Selects Data

When a program concatenates data sets, all of the observations are read from the first data set that is listed in the SET statement. Then all of the observations are read from the second data set that is listed, and so on, until all of the listed data sets have been read. The new data set contains all of the variables and observations from all of the input data sets.

```
data concat;
   set a b;
run;
```

Notice that **A** and **C** contain a common variable named Num:

- Both instances of Num (or any common variable) must have the same **type** attribute, or SAS stops processing the DATA step and issues an error message stating that the variables are incompatible.

- However, if the **length** attribute is different, SAS takes the length from the **first data set** that contains the variable. In this case, the length of Num in **A** determines the length of Num in **Concat**.

- The same is true for the **label**, **format**, and **informat** attributes: If any of these attributes are different, SAS takes the attribute from the first data set that contains the variable with that attribute.

Example

The following DATA step creates **Clinic.Concat** by concatenating **Clinic.Therapy1999** and **Clinic.Therapy2000**.

```
data clinic.concat;
   set clinic.therapy1999 clinic.therapy2000;
run;
```

The listing of **Clinic.Concat** follows. The first 12 observations were read from **Clinic.Therapy1999**, and the last 12 observations were read from **Clinic.Therapy2000**.

SAS Data Set Clinic.Concat

Obs	Month	Year	AerClass	WalkJogRun	Swim
1	01	1999	26	78	14
2	02	1999	32	109	19
3	03	1999	15	106	22
4	04	1999	47	115	24
5	05	1999	95	121	31
6	06	1999	61	114	67
7	07	1999	67	102	72
8	08	1999	24	76	77
9	09	1999	78	77	54
10	10	1999	81	62	47
11	11	1999	84	31	52
12	12	1999	92	44	55
13	01	2000	37	91	83
14	02	2000	41	102	27
15	03	2000	52	98	19
16	04	2000	61	118	22
17	05	2000	49	88	29
18	06	2000	24	101	54
19	07	2000	45	91	69
20	08	2000	63	65	53
21	09	2000	60	49	68
22	10	2000	78	70	41
23	11	2000	82	44	58
24	12	2000	93	57	47

Interleaving

If you use a BY statement when you concatenate data sets, the result is **interleaving**. Interleaving intersperses observations from two or more data sets, based on one or more common variables.

To interleave SAS data sets, specify a list of data set names in the SET statement, and specify one or more BY variables in the BY statement.

> **General form, basic DATA step for interleaving:**
>
> >   **DATA** *output-SAS-data-set*;
> >   **SET** *SAS-data-set-1 SAS-data-set-2*;
> >   **BY** *variable(s)*;
> >   **RUN;**
>
> where
>
> - *output-SAS-data-set* names the data set to be created
>
> - *SAS-data-set-1* and *SAS-data-set-2* specify the data sets to be read
>
> - *variable(s)* specifies one or more variables that are used to interleave observations.
>
> You can specify any number of data sets in the SET statement. Each input data set **must** be sorted or indexed in ascending order based on the BY variable(s).

How Interleaving Selects Data

When SAS interleaves data sets, observations in each BY group in each data set in the SET statement are read sequentially, in the order in which the data sets and BY variables are listed, until all observations have been processed. The new data set includes all the variables from all the input data sets, and it contains the total number of observations from all input data sets.

```
data interlv;
   set c d;
   by num;
run;
```

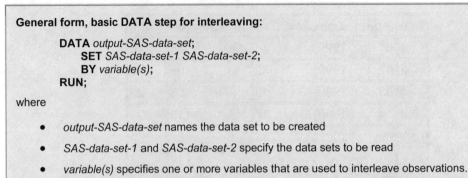

Example

The following DATA step creates **Clinic.Interlv** by interleaving **Clinic.Therapy1999** and **Clinic.Therapy2000**:

```
data clinic.interlv;
    set clinic.therapy1999 clinic.therapy2000;
    by month;
run;
```

Below is the listing of **Clinic.Interlv**. Notice that, unlike the previous example, observations are interleaved by month instead of being concatenated.

SAS Data Set Clinic.Interlv

Obs	Month	Year	AerClass	WalkJogRun	Swim
1	01	1999	26	78	14
2	01	2000	37	91	83
3	02	1999	32	109	19
4	02	2000	41	102	27
5	03	1999	15	106	22
6	03	2000	52	98	19
7	04	1999	47	115	24
8	04	2000	61	118	22
9	05	1999	95	121	31
10	05	2000	49	88	29
11	06	1999	61	114	67
12	06	2000	24	101	54
13	07	1999	67	102	72
14	07	2000	45	91	69
15	08	1999	24	76	77
16	08	2000	63	65	53
17	09	1999	78	77	54
18	09	2000	60	49	68
19	10	1999	81	62	47
20	10	2000	78	70	41
21	11	1999	84	31	52
22	11	2000	82	44	58
23	12	1999	92	44	55
24	12	2000	93	57	47

Simple Match-Merging

So far in this chapter, you've learned how to combine data sets based on the order of the observations in the input data sets. But sometimes you need to combine observations from two or more data sets into a single observation in a new data set according to the values of a common variable. This is called **match-merging**.

When you match-merge, you use a MERGE statement rather than a SET statement to combine data sets.

General form, basic DATA step for match-merging:

> **DATA** *output-SAS-data-set*;
>   **MERGE** *SAS-data-set-1 SAS-data-set-2*;
>   **BY** <DESCENDING> *variable(s)*;
> **RUN**;

where

- *output-SAS-data-set* names the data set to be created.

- *SAS-data-set-1* and *SAS-data-set-2* specify the data sets to be read.

- *variable(s)* in the **BY** statement specifies one or more variables whose values are used to match observations.

- DESCENDING indicates that the input data sets are sorted in descending order (largest to smallest numerically, or reverse alphabetical for character variables) by the variable that is specified. If you have more than one variable in the BY statement, DESCENDING applies only to the variable that immediately follows it.

Each input data set in the MERGE statement **must** be sorted in order of the values of the BY variable(s), or it must have an appropriate index. Each BY variable must have the same type in all data sets to be merged.

You cannot use the DESCENDING option with indexed data sets because indexes are always stored in ascending order.

How Match-Merging Selects Data

Generally speaking, during match-merging SAS sequentially checks each observation of each data set to see whether the BY values match, then writes the combined observation to the new data set.

```
data merged;
   merge a b;
   by num;
run;
```

SAS Data Set A

Num	VarA
1	A1
2	A2
3	A3

SAS Data Set B

Num	VarB
1	B1
2	B2
4	B3

————Match-Merge————

Combined SAS Data Set

Num	VarA	VarB
1	A1	B1
2	A2	B2
3	A3	
4		B3

Basic DATA step match-merging produces an output data set that contains values from **all observations in all input data sets**. (You can add statements and options to select only observations that match for two or more specific input data sets.)

If an input data set doesn't have any observations for a particular value of the same-named variable, then the observation in the output data set contains **missing values** for the variables that are unique to that input data set.

Table 1			+	Table 2			=	All		
Year	Var_X			Year	Var_Y			Year	Var_X	Var_Y
1991	X1			1991	Y1			1991	X1	Y1
1992	X2			1991	Y2			1991	X1	Y2
1993	X3			1993	Y3			1992	X2	
1994	X4			1994	Y4			1993	X3	Y3
1995	X5			1995	Y5			1994	X4	Y4
								1995	X5	Y5

 In match-merging, often one data set contains unique values for the same-named variable and other data sets contain multiple values for the same-named variable.

Example: Merging Data Sets That Are Sorted in Ascending Order

Suppose you have sorted the data sets **Clinic.Demog** and **Clinic.Visit** as follows:

```
proc sort data=clinic.demog;
   by id;
run;
proc print data=clinic.demog;
run;
```

Obs	ID	Age	Sex	Date
1	A001	21	m	05/22/75
2	A002	32	m	06/15/63
3	A003	24	f	08/17/72
4	A004	.		03/27/69
5	A005	44	f	02/24/52
6	A007	39	m	11/11/57

```
proc sort data=clinic.visit;
   by id;
run;
proc print data=clinic.visit;
run;
```

Obs	ID	Visit	SysBP	DiasBP	Weight	Date
1	A001	1	140	85	195	11/05/98
2	A001	2	138	90	198	10/13/98
3	A001	3	145	95	200	07/04/98
4	A002	1	121	75	168	04/14/98
5	A003	1	118	68	125	08/12/98
6	A003	2	112	65	123	08/21/98
7	A004	1	143	86	204	03/30/98
8	A005	1	132	76	174	02/27/98
9	A005	2	132	78	175	07/11/98
10	A005	3	134	78	176	04/16/98
11	A008	1	126	80	182	05/22/98

You can then submit this DATA step to create **Clinic.Merged** by merging **Clinic.Demog** and **Clinic.Visit** according to values of the variable ID:

```
data clinic.merged;
   merge clinic.demog clinic.visit;
   by id;
run;
proc print data=clinic.merged;
run;
```

Notice that all observations, including unmatched observations and observations that have missing data, are written to the output data set.

Obs	ID	Age	Sex	Date	Visit	SysBP	DiasBP	Weight
1	A001	21	m	11/05/98	1	140	85	195
2	A001	21	m	10/13/98	2	138	90	198
3	A001	21	m	07/04/98	3	145	95	200
4	A002	32	m	04/14/98	1	121	75	168
5	A003	24	f	08/12/98	1	118	68	125
6	A003	24	f	08/21/98	2	112	65	123
7	A004	.		03/30/98	1	143	86	204
8	A005	44	f	02/27/98	1	132	76	174
9	A005	44	f	07/11/98	2	132	78	175
10	A005	44	f	04/16/98	3	134	78	176
11	A007	39	m	11/11/57		.	.	.
12	A008	.		05/22/98	1	126	80	182

Example: Sorting and Merging Data Sets in Descending Order

The example above illustrates merging two data sets that are sorted in ascending order of the BY variable ID. To sort the data sets in **descending** order and then merge them, you can submit the following program:

```
proc sort data=clinic.demog;
   by descending id;
run;
proc sort data=clinic.visit;
   by descending id;
run;
data clinic.merged;
   merge clinic.demog clinic.visit;
   by descending id;
run;
proc print data=clinic.merged;
run;
```

Notice that you specify the DESCENDING option in the BY statements in both the PROC SORT steps and the DATA step. If you omit the DESCENDING option in the DATA step, you generate error messages about improperly sorted BY variables.

Now the data sets are merged in descending order of the BY variable ID.

Obs	ID	Age	Sex	Date	Visit	SysBP	DiasBP	Weight
1	A008	.		05/22/98	1	126	80	182
2	A007	39	m	11/11/57		.	.	.
3	A005	44	f	02/27/98	1	132	76	174
4	A005	44	f	07/11/98	2	132	78	175
5	A005	44	f	04/16/98	3	134	78	176
6	A004	.		03/30/98	1	143	86	204
7	A003	24	f	08/12/98	1	118	68	125
8	A003	24	f	08/21/98	2	112	65	123
9	A002	32	m	04/14/98	1	121	75	168
10	A001	21	m	11/05/98	1	140	85	195
11	A001	21	m	10/13/98	2	138	90	198
12	A001	21	m	07/04/98	3	145	95	200

Match-Merge Processing

Introduction

The match-merging examples in this chapter are straightforward. However, match-merging can be more complex, depending on your data and on the output data set that you want to create. To predict the results of match-merges correctly, you need to understand how the DATA step performs match-merges.

When you submit a DATA step, it is processed in two phases:

- the **compilation phase**, in which SAS checks the syntax of the SAS statements and compiles them (translates them into machine code). During this phase, SAS also sets up descriptor information for the output data set and creates the **program data vector** (PDV), an area of memory where SAS builds your data set, one observation at a time.

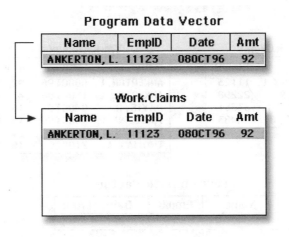

- the **execution phase**, in which the DATA step reads data and executes any subsequent programming statements. When the DATA step executes, data values are read into the appropriate variables in the program data vector. From here, the variables are written to the output data set as a single observation.

The following sections cover match-merge processing in greater detail. In those sections, you learn

- how the DATA step sets up the new output data set
- what happens when variables in different data sets have the same name
- how the DATA step matches observations in input data sets
- what happens when observations don't match
- how missing values are handled.

The Compilation Phase: Setting Up the New Data Set

To prepare to merge data sets, SAS

1. reads the descriptor portions of the data sets that are listed in the MERGE statement

2. reads the rest of the DATA step program

3. creates the program data vector (PDV) for the merged data set

4. assigns a tracking pointer to each data set that is listed in the MERGE statement.

If variables that have the same name appear in more than one data set, then the variable from the first data set that contains the variable (in the order listed in the MERGE statement) determines the length of the variable. (Recall that the value of the variable is the value in the last data set that contains it.)

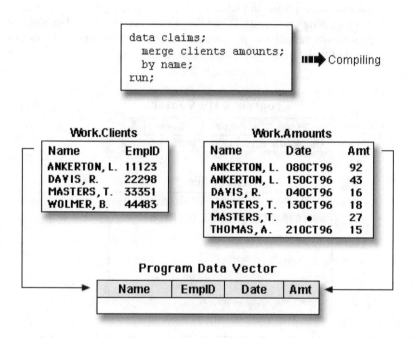

The illustration above shows match-merging during the compilation phase. After reading the descriptor portions of the data sets **Clients** and **Amounts**, SAS

1. creates a program data vector for the new **Claims** data set. The program data vector contains all variables from the two data sets. Note that although Name appears in both input data sets, it appears in the program data vector only once.

2. assigns tracking pointers to **Clients** and **Amounts**.

The Execution Phase: Match-Merging Observations

After compiling the DATA step, SAS sequentially match-merges observations by moving the pointers down each observation of each data set and checking to see **whether the BY values match**.

- If **Yes**, the observations are written to the PDV in the order in which the data sets appear in the MERGE statement. Values of any same-named variable are overwritten by values of the same-named variable in subsequent data sets. SAS writes the combined observation to the new data set and retains the values in the PDV until the BY value changes in all the data sets.

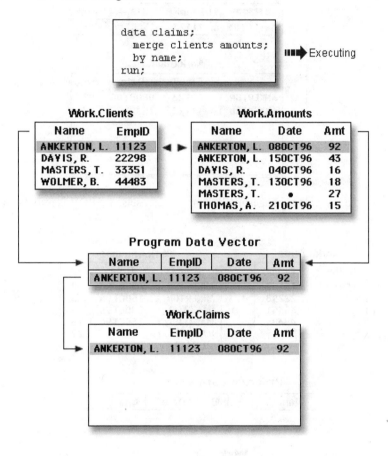

- If **No**, SAS determines which of the values comes first and writes the observation that contains this value to the PDV. Then the contents of the PDV are written to the new data set.

Work.Clients

Name	EmpID
ANKERTON, L.	11123
DAVIS, R.	22298
MASTERS, T.	33351
WOLMER, B.	44483

Work.Amounts

Name	Date	Amt
ANKERTON, L.	08OCT96	92
ANKERTON, L.	15OCT96	43
DAVIS, R.	04OCT96	16
MASTERS, T.	13OCT96	18
MASTERS, T.	•	27
THOMAS, A.	21OCT96	15

Program Data Vector

Name	EmpID	Date	Amt
ANKERTON, L.	11123	15OCT96	43

Work.Claims

Name	EmpID	Date	Amt
ANKERTON, L.	11123	08OCT96	92
ANKERTON, L.	11123	15OCT96	43

When the BY value changes in all the input data sets, the PDV is initialized to missing.

Work.Clients

Name	EmpID
ANKERTON, L.	11123
DAVIS, R.	22298
MASTERS, T.	33351
WOLMER, B.	44483

Work.Amounts

Name	Date	Amt
ANKERTON, L.	08OCT96	92
ANKERTON, L.	15OCT96	43
DAVIS, R.	04OCT96	16
MASTERS, T.	13OCT96	18
MASTERS, T.	•	27
THOMAS, A.	21OCT96	15

Program Data Vector

Name	EmpID	Date	Amt
		•	

Work.Claims

Name	EmpID	Date	Amt
ANKERTON, L.	11123	08OCT96	92
ANKERTON, L.	11123	15OCT96	43

The DATA step continues to process every observation in each data set until it has processed all observations in all data sets.

Handling Unmatched Observations and Missing Values

By default, **all observations** that are written to the PDV, including observations that have missing data and no matching BY values, are written to the output data set. (If you specify a subsetting IF statement to select observations, then only those that meet the IF condition are written.)

- If an observation contains **missing values for a variable**, then the observation in the output data set contains the missing values as well. Observations that have missing values for the BY variable appear at the top of the output data set.

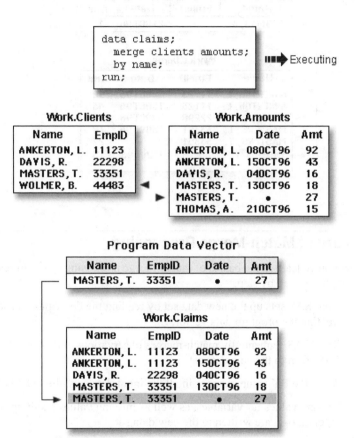

- If an input data set **doesn't have a matching BY value**, then the observation in the output data set contains missing values for the variables that are unique to that input data set.

Work.Clients	
Name	**EmpID**
ANKERTON, L.	11123
DAVIS, R.	22298
MASTERS, T.	33351
WOLMER, B.	44483

Work.Amounts		
Name	**Date**	**Amt**
ANKERTON, L.	08OCT96	92
ANKERTON, L.	15OCT96	43
DAVIS, R.	04OCT96	16
MASTERS, T.	13OCT96	18
MASTERS, T.	•	27
THOMAS, A.	21OCT96	15

Program Data Vector

Name	EmpID	Date	Amt
THOMAS, A.		21OCT96	15

Work.Claims

Name	EmpID	Date	Amt
ANKERTON, L.	11123	08OCT96	92
ANKERTON, L.	11123	15OCT96	43
DAVIS, R.	22298	04OCT96	16
MASTERS, T.	33351	13OCT96	18
MASTERS, T.	33351	•	27
THOMAS, A.		21OCT96	15

Summary of Match-Merge Processing

Now that you've learned the basics of match-merge processing, you can review the compilation and execution phases step by step.

1. First, SAS sets up the new data set by reading the descriptor portions of the data sets and creating the program data vector.

2. Next, SAS sequentially match-merges observations and writes the new observation to the PDV, then to the new data set.

3. When the BY value changes in all the input data sets, the PDV is initialized to missing.

4. Missing values for variables, as well as missing values resulting form unmatched observations, are written to the new data set.

Renaming Variables

Sometimes you might have same-named variables in more than one input data set. In this case, DATA step match-merging **overwrites values** of the like-named variable in the first data set in which it appears with values of the like-named variable in subsequent data sets.

For example, **Clinic.Demog** contains the variable Date (date of birth), and **Clinic.Visit** also contains Date (date of the clinic visit in 1998). The DATA step below overwrites the date of birth with the date of the clinic visit.

```
data clinic.merged;
   merge clinic.demog clinic.visit;
   by id;
run;
proc print data=clinic.merged;
run;
```

The following output shows the effects of overwriting the values of a variable in the **Clinic.Merged** data set. In most observations, the date is now the date of the clinic visit. In observation 11, the date is still the birth date because **Clinic.Visit** did not contain a matching ID value and did not contribute to the observation.

Obs	ID	Age	Sex	Date	Visit	SysBP	DiasBP	Weight
1	A001	21	m	11/05/98	1	140	85	195
2	A001	21	m	10/13/98	2	138	90	198
3	A001	21	m	07/04/98	3	145	95	200
4	A002	32	m	04/14/98	1	121	75	168
5	A003	24	f	08/12/98	1	118	68	125
6	A003	24	f	08/21/98	2	112	65	123
7	A004	.		03/30/98	1	143	86	204
8	A005	44	f	02/27/98	1	132	76	174
9	A005	44	f	07/11/98	2	132	78	175
10	A005	44	f	04/16/98	3	134	78	176
11	A007	39	m	11/11/57		.	.	.
12	A008	.		05/22/98	1	126	80	182

You now have a data set with values for Date that mean two different things: date of birth and date of clinic visit.

To prevent overwriting, you can rename variables by using the **RENAME= data set option** in the MERGE statement.

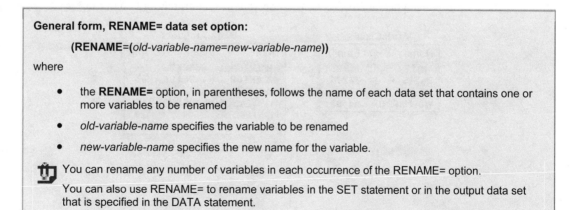

General form, RENAME= data set option:

(RENAME=(old-variable-name=new-variable-name**))**

where

- the **RENAME=** option, in parentheses, follows the name of each data set that contains one or more variables to be renamed
- *old-variable-name* specifies the variable to be renamed
- *new-variable-name* specifies the new name for the variable.

You can rename any number of variables in each occurrence of the RENAME= option.

You can also use RENAME= to rename variables in the SET statement or in the output data set that is specified in the DATA statement.

In the following example, the RENAME= option renames the variable `Date` in **Clinic.Demog** to `BirthDate`, and it renames the variable `Date` in **Clinic.Visit** to `VisitDate`.

```
data clinic.merged;
   merge clinic.demog(rename=(date=BirthDate))
         clinic.visit(rename=(date=VisitDate));
   by id;
run;
proc print data=clinic.merged;
run;
```

The following output shows the effect of the RENAME= option.

Obs	ID	Age	Sex	BirthDate	Visit	SysBP	DiasBP	Weight	VisitDate
1	A001	21	m	05/22/75	1	140	85	195	11/05/98
2	A001	21	m	05/22/75	2	138	90	198	10/13/98
3	A001	21	m	05/22/75	3	145	95	200	07/04/98
4	A002	32	m	06/15/63	1	121	75	168	04/14/98
5	A003	24	f	08/17/72	1	118	68	125	08/12/98
6	A003	24	f	08/17/72	2	112	65	123	08/21/98
7	A004	.		03/27/69	1	143	86	204	03/30/98
8	A005	44	f	02/24/52	1	132	76	174	02/27/98
9	A005	44	f	02/24/52	2	132	78	175	07/11/98
10	A005	44	f	02/24/52	3	134	78	176	04/16/98
11	A007	39	m	11/11/57		.	.	.	.
12	A008	.		.	1	126	80	182	05/22/98

Excluding Unmatched Observations

By default, DATA step match-merging combines all observations in all input data sets. However, you might want to select only observations that **match** for two or more specific input data sets.

Work.Clients

Name	EmpID
ANKERTON, L.	11123
DAVIS, R.	22298
MASTERS, T.	33351
WOLMER, B.	44483

Work.Amounts

Name	Date	Amt
ANKERTON, L.	08OCT96	92
ANKERTON, L.	15OCT96	43
DAVIS, R.	04OCT96	16
MASTERS, T.	13OCT96	18
MASTERS, T.	.	27
THOMAS, A.	21OCT96	15

To exclude unmatched observations from your output data set, you can use the **IN= data set option** and the **subsetting IF statement** in your DATA step. In this case, you use

- the IN= data set option to create and name a variable that indicates whether the data set contributed data to the current observation

- the subsetting IF statement to check the IN= values and to write to the merged data set only those observations that appear in the data sets for which IN= is specified.

Creating Temporary IN= Variables

Suppose you want to match-merge the data sets **Clinic.Demog** and **Clinic.Visit** and select only observations that appear in both data sets.

First, you use IN= to create two temporary variables, `indemog` and `invisit`. The IN= variable is a temporary variable that is available to program statements during the DATA step, but it is not included in the SAS data set that is being created.

General form, IN= data set option:

> **(IN=**variable**)**

where

- the **IN=** option, in parentheses, follows the data set name
- variable names the variable to be created.

Within the DATA step, the value of the variable is *1* if the data set contributed data to the current observation. Otherwise, its value is *0*.

The DATA step that contains the IN= options appears below. The first IN= creates the temporary variable `indemog`, which is set to *1* when an observation from **Clinic.Demog** contributes to the current observation; otherwise, it is set to *0*. Likewise, the value of `invisit` depends on whether **Clinic.Visit** contributes to an observation or not.

```
data clinic.merged;
   merge clinic.demog(in=indemog)
         clinic.visit(in=invisit
                      rename=(date=BirthDate));
   by id;
run;
```

 When you specify multiple data set options for a given data set, enclose them in a single set of parentheses.

Selecting Matching Observations

Next, to select only observations that appear in both **Clinic.Demog** and **Clinic.Visit**, you specify a subsetting IF statement in the DATA step.

In the DATA step below, the subsetting IF statement checks the values of indemog and invisit and continues processing only those observations that meet the condition of the expression. Here the condition is that both **Clinic.Demog** and **Clinic.Visit** contribute to the observation. If the condition is met, the new observation is written to **Clinic.Merged**. Otherwise, the observation is deleted.

```
data clinic.merged;
   merge clinic.demog(in=indemog
                      rename=(date=BirthDate))
         clinic.visit(in=invisit
                      rename=(date=VisitDate));
   by id;
   if indemog=1 and invisit=1;
run;
proc print data=clinic.merged;
run;
```

In previous examples, **Clinic.Merged** contained 12 observations. In the output below, notice that only 10 observations met the condition in the IF expression.

Obs	ID	Age	Sex	BirthDate	Visit	SysBP	DiasBP	Weight	VisitDate
1	A001	21	m	05/22/75	1	140	85	195	11/05/98
2	A001	21	m	05/22/75	2	138	90	198	10/13/98
3	A001	21	m	05/22/75	3	145	95	200	07/04/98
4	A002	32	m	06/15/63	1	121	75	168	04/14/98
5	A003	24	f	08/17/72	1	118	68	125	08/12/98
6	A003	24	f	08/17/72	2	112	65	123	08/21/98
7	A004	.		03/27/69	1	143	86	204	03/30/98
8	A005	44	f	02/24/52	1	132	76	174	02/27/98
9	A005	44	f	02/24/52	2	132	78	175	07/11/98
10	A005	44	f	02/24/52	3	134	78	176	04/16/98

 SAS evaluates the expression within an IF statement to produce a result that is either nonzero, zero, or missing. A nonzero or nonmissing result causes the expression to be true; a zero or missing result causes the expression to be false.

Thus, you can specify the subsetting IF statement from the previous example in either of the following ways. The first IF statement checks specifically for a value of *1*. The second IF statement checks for a value that is neither missing nor *0* (which for IN= variables is always *1*).

```
   if indemog=1 and invisit=1;
```

```
   if indemog and invisit;
```

Selecting Variables

As with reading raw data or reading SAS data sets, you can specify the variables that you want to drop or keep by using the **DROP= and KEEP= data set options**.

For example, the DATA step below reads all variables from **Clinic.Demog** and all variables except `Weight` from **Clinic.Visit**. It then excludes the variable ID from **Clinic.Merged** after the merge processing is complete.

```
data clinic.merged(drop=id);
   merge clinic.demog(in=indemog
                       rename=(date=BirthDate))
         clinic.visit(drop=weight in=invisit
                       rename=(date=VisitDate));
   by id;
   if indemog and invisit;
run;
proc print data=clinic.merged;
run;
```

Obs	Age	Sex	BirthDate	Visit	SysBP	DiasBP	VisitDate
1	21	m	05/22/75	1	140	85	11/05/98
2	21	m	05/22/75	2	138	90	10/13/98
3	21	m	05/22/75	3	145	95	07/04/98
4	32	m	06/15/63	1	121	75	04/14/98
5	24	f	08/17/72	1	118	68	08/12/98
6	24	f	08/17/72	2	112	65	08/21/98
7	.		03/27/69	1	143	86	03/30/98
8	44	f	02/24/52	1	132	76	02/27/98
9	44	f	02/24/52	2	132	78	07/11/98
10	44	f	02/24/52	3	134	78	04/16/98

Where to Specify the DROP= and KEEP= Options

As you've seen in previous chapters, you can specify the DROP= and KEEP= options wherever you specify a SAS data set. When match-merging, you can specify these options in either the **DATA statement** or the **MERGE statement**, depending on whether or not you want to process values of the variables in that DATA step:

- If you **don't** process certain variables and you don't want them to appear in the new data set, then specify them in the DROP= option in the **MERGE statement**.

```
   merge clinic.demog(in=indemog
                       rename=(date=BirthDate))
         clinic.visit(drop=weight in=invisit
                       rename=(date=VisitDate));
```

- If you **do** need to process a variable in the original data set (in a subsetting IF statement, for example), then you must specify the variable in the DROP= option in the **DATA statement**. Otherwise, the statement that uses the variable for processing causes an error.

  ```
  data clinic.merged(drop=id);
  ```

When used in the DATA statement, the DROP= option simply drops the variables from the new data set. However, they are still read from the original data set and are available for processing within the DATA step.

Additional Features

The DATA step provides a large number of other programming features for manipulating data when you combine data sets. For example, you can

- use IF-THEN/ELSE logic to control processing based on one or more conditions
- specify additional data set options
- perform calculations
- create new variables
- process variables in arrays
- use SAS functions
- use special variables such as FIRST. and LAST. to control processing.

You can also combine SAS data sets in other ways:

- You can perform **one-to-one merging**, which creates a data set that contains all of the variables and observations from each contributing data set. Observations are combined based on their relative position in each data set.

  One-to-one merging is the same as one-to-one reading, with two exceptions:

  o You use the MERGE statement instead of multiple SET statements.

  o The DATA step reads all observations from all data sets.

  ```
  data work.onemerge;
     merge clinic.demog clinic.visit;
  run;
  ```

- You can perform a **conditional merge,** using DO loops or other conditional statements:

  ```
  data work.combine;
     set sales.pounds;
     do while(not(begin le date le last));
        set sales.rate;
     end;
     Dollars=(sales*1000)*rate;
  run;
  ```

You can learn about DO loops in Chapter 15, **Generating Data with DO Loops**.

- You can read the **same data set** in more than one SET statement:

```
data work.combine(drop=totpay);
   if _n_=1 then do until(last);
      set sales.budget(keep=payroll) end=last;
      end;
   set sales.budget;
   Percent=payroll/totpay;
run;
```

Summary

Text Summary

One-to-One Reading

You can combine data sets with **one-to-one reading** by including multiple SET statements in a DATA step. When you perform one-to-one reading, the new data set contains all the variables from all the input data sets. If the data sets contain same-named variables, the values that are read in from the last data set replace those that were read in from earlier ones. The number of observations in the new data set is the number of observations in the smallest original data set.

Concatenating

To append the observations from one data set to another data set, you **concatenate** them by specifying the data set names in the SET statement. When SAS concatenates, data sets in the SET statement are read sequentially, in the order in which they are listed. The new data set contains all the variables and the total number of observations from all input data sets.

Interleaving

If you use a BY statement when you concatenate data sets, the result is **interleaving**. Interleaving intersperses observations from two or more data sets, based on one or more common variables. Each input data set must be sorted or indexed in ascending order based on the BY variable(s). Observations in each BY group in each data set in the SET statement are read sequentially, in the order in which the data sets and BY variables are listed, until all observations have been processed. The new data set contains all the variables and the total number of observations from all input data sets.

Simple Match-Merging

Sometimes you need to combine observations from two or more data sets into a single observation in a new data set according to the values of a same-named variable. This is **match-merging**, which uses a MERGE statement rather than a SET statement to combine data sets. Each input data set must be sorted or indexed in ascending order based on the BY variable(s). During match-merging, SAS sequentially checks each observation of each data set to see whether the BY values match, then writes the combined observation to the new data set.

Match-Merge Processing

To predict the results of match-merging correctly, you need to understand how the DATA step processes data in match-merges.

Compiling

To prepare to merge data sets, SAS

1. reads the descriptor portions of the data sets that are listed in the MERGE statement
2. reads the rest of the DATA step program
3. creates the program data vector (PDV), an area of memory where SAS builds your data set one observation at a time
4. assigns a tracking pointer to each data set that is listed in the MERGE statement.

If variables with the same name appear in more than one data set, then the variable from the first data set that contains the variable (in the order listed in the MERGE statement) determines the length of the variable.

Executing

After compiling the DATA step, SAS sequentially match-merges observations by moving the pointers down each observation of each data set and checking to see **whether the BY values match**.

- If **Yes**, the observations are written to the PDV in the order in which the data sets appear in the MERGE statement. Values of any same-named variable are overwritten by values of the same-named variable in subsequent data sets. SAS writes the combined observation to the new data set and retains the values in the PDV until the BY value changes in all the data sets.

- If **No**, SAS determines which of the values comes first and writes the observation that contains this value to the PDV. Then the observation is written to the new data set.

When the BY value changes in all the input data sets, the PDV is initialized to missing. The DATA step merge continues to process every observation in each data set until it has processed all observations in all data sets.

Handling Unmatched Observations and Missing Values

All observations that are written to the PDV, including observations that have missing data and no matching BY values, are written to the output data set.

- If an observation contains missing values for a variable, then the observation in the output data set contains the missing values as well. Observations that have missing values for the BY variable appear at the top of the output data set.

- If an input data set doesn't have a matching BY value, then the observation in the output data set contains missing values for the variables that are unique to that input data set.

Renaming Variables

Sometimes you might have same-named variables in more than one input data set. In this case, match-merging overwrites values of the same-named variable in the first data set with values of the same-named variable in subsequent data sets. To prevent overwriting, use the RENAME= data set option in the MERGE statement to rename variables.

Excluding Unmatched Observations

By default, match-merging combines all observations in all input data sets. However, you might want to select only observations that match for two or more input data sets. To exclude **unmatched observations**, use the IN= data set option and the subsetting IF statement in your DATA step. The IN= data set option creates a variable to indicate whether the data set contributed data to the current observation. The subsetting IF statement then checks the IN= values and writes to the merged data set only observations that appear in the data sets for which IN= is specified.

Selecting Variables

You can specify the variables you want to drop or keep by using the **DROP=** and **KEEP=** data set options. When match-merging, you can specify these options in either the DATA statement or the MERGE statement, depending on whether or not you want to process values of the variables in that DATA step. When used in the DATA statement, the DROP= option simply drops the variables from the new data set. However, they are still read from the original data set and are available within the DATA step.

Points to Remember

- You can rename any number of variables in each occurrence of the RENAME= option.

- In match-merging, the IN= data set option can apply to any data set in the MERGE statement. The RENAME=, DROP=, and KEEP= options can apply to any data set in the DATA or MERGE statements.

- Use the KEEP= option instead of the DROP= option if more variables are dropped than kept.

- When you specify multiple data set options for a particular data set, enclose them in a single set of parentheses.

Practice

After you complete this chapter, practice what you learned by using the sample data and SAS programs for Chapter 13, **Combining SAS Data Sets**, which are located on the CD-ROM. Follow the directions for creating your sample data in the Before You Begin section.

Quiz

Select the best answer for each question. After completing the quiz, check your answers using the answer key in the appendix.

1. Which program will combine **Brothers.One** and **Brothers.Two** to produce **Brothers.Three**?

Brothers.One	
VarX	**VarY**
1	Groucho
3	Harpo
5	Karl

+

Brothers.Two	
VarX	**VarZ**
2	Chico
4	Zeppo

=

Brothers.Three		
VarX	**VarY**	**VarZ**
2	Groucho	Chico
4	Harpo	Zeppo

   a. ```
       data brothers.three;
           set brothers.one;
           set brothers.two;
       run;
       ```
   b.  ```
       data brothers.three;
           set brothers.one brothers.two;
       run;
       ```
   c. ```
       data brothers.three;
           set brothers.one brothers.two;
           by varx;
       run;
       ```
   d.  ```
       data brothers.three;
           merge brothers.one brothers.two;
           by varx;
       run;
       ```

2. Which program will combine **Actors.Props1** and **Actors.Props2** to produce **Actors.Props3**?

Actors.Props1	
Actor	**Prop**
Curly	Anvil
Larry	Ladder
Moe	Poker

+

Actors.Props2	
Actor	**Prop**
Curly	Ladder
Moe	Pliers

=

Actors.Props3	
Actor	**Prop**
Curly	Anvil
Curly	Ladder
Larry	Ladder
Moe	Poker
Moe	Pliers

   a. ```
       data actors.props3;
           set actors.props1;
           set actors.props2;
       run;
       ```
       ```

b.
```
data actors.props3;
    set actors.props1 actors.props2;
run;
```

c.
```
data actors.props3;
    set actors.props1 actors.props2;
    by actor;
run;
```

d.
```
data actors.props3;
    merge actors.props1 actors.props2;
    by actor;
run;
```

3. If you submit the following program, which new data set is created?

Work.Dataone

Career	Supervis	Finance
72	26	9
63	76	7
96	31	7
96	98	6
84	94	6

Work.Datatwo

Variety	Feedback	Autonomy
10	11	70
85	22	93
83	63	73
82	75	97
36	77	97

```
data work.jobsatis;
    set work.dataone work.datatwo;
run;
```

a.

Career	Supervis	Finance	Variety	Feedback	Autonomy
72	26	9	.	.	.
63	76	7	.	.	.
96	31	7	.	.	.
96	98	6	.	.	.
84	94	6	.	.	.
.	.	.	10	11	70
.	.	.	85	22	93
.	.	.	83	63	73
.	.	.	82	75	97
.	.	.	36	77	97

b.

Career	Supervis	Finance	Variety	Feedback	Autonomy
72	26	9	10	11	70
63	76	7	85	22	93
96	31	7	83	63	73
96	98	6	82	75	97
84	94	6	36	77	97

c.

Career	Supervis	Finance
72	26	9
63	76	7
96	31	7
96	98	6
84	94	6
10	11	70
85	22	93
83	63	73
82	75	97
36	77	97

d. none of the above

4. If you concatenate the data sets below in the order shown, what is the value of `Sale` in observation 2 of the new data set?

Sales.Reps

ID	Name
1	Nay Rong
2	Kelly Windsor
3	Julio Meraz
4	Richard Krabill

Sales.Close

ID	Sale
1	$28,000
2	$30,000
2	$40,000
3	$15,000
3	$20,000
3	$25,000
4	$35,000

Sales.Bonus

ID	Bonus
1	$2,000
2	$4,000
3	$3,000
4	$2,500

a. missing

b. $30,000

c. $40,000

d. you cannot concatenate these data sets

5. What happens if you merge the following data sets by variable SSN?

1st	
SSN	**Age**
029-46-9261	39
074-53-9892	34
228-88-9649	32
442-21-8075	12
446-93-2122	36
776-84-5391	28
929-75-0218	27

2nd		
SSN	**Age**	**Date**
029-46-9261	37	02/15/95
074-53-9892	32	05/22/97
228-88-9649	30	03/04/96
442-21-8075	10	11/22/95
446-93-2122	34	07/08/96
776-84-5391	26	12/15/96
929-75-0218	25	04/30/97

a. The values of Age in the 1st data set overwrite the values of Age in the 2nd data set.

b. The values of Age in the 2nd data set overwrite the values of Age in the 1st data set.

c. The DATA step fails because the two data sets contain same-named variables that have different values.

d. The values of Age in the 2nd data set are set to missing.

6. Suppose you merge data sets **Health.Set1** and **Health.Set2** below:

Health.Set1		
ID	**Sex**	**Age**
1129	F	48
1274	F	50
1387	F	57
2304	F	16
2486	F	63
4425	F	48
4759	F	60
5438	F	42
6488	F	59
9012	F	39
9125	F	56

Health.Set2		
ID	**Height**	**Weight**
1129	61	137
1387	64	142
2304	61	102
5438	62	168
6488	64	154
9012	63	157
9125	64	159

Which output does the following program create?

```
data work.merged;
    merge health.set1(in=in1) health.set2(in=in2);
    by id;
    if in1 and in2;
run;
proc print data=work.merged;
run;
```

a.

Obs	ID	Sex	Age	Height	Weight
1	1129	F	48	61	137
2	1274	F	50	.	.
3	1387	F	57	64	142
4	2304	F	16	61	102
5	2486	F	63	.	.
6	4425	F	48	.	.
7	4759	F	60	.	.
8	5438	F	42	62	168
9	6488	F	59	64	154
10	9012	F	39	63	157
11	9125	F	56	64	159

b.

Obs	ID	Sex	Age	Height	Weight
1	1129	F	48	61	137
2	1387	F	50	64	142
3	2304	F	57	61	102
4	5438	F	16	62	168
5	6488	F	63	64	154
6	9012	F	48	63	157
7	9125	F	60	64	159
8	5438	F	42	.	.
9	6488	F	59	.	.
10	9012	F	39	.	.
11	9125	F	56	.	.

c.

Obs	ID	Sex	Age	Height	Weight
1	1129	F	48	61	137
2	1387	F	57	64	142
3	2304	F	16	61	102
4	5438	F	42	62	168
5	6488	F	59	64	154
6	9012	F	39	63	157
7	9125	F	56	64	159

d. none of the above

7. The data sets **Ensemble.Spring** and **Ensemble.Summer** both contain a variable named `Blue`. How do you prevent the values of the variable `Blue` from being overwritten when you merge the two data sets?

a.
```
data ensemble.merged;
    merge ensemble.spring(in=blue)
          ensemble.summer;
    by fabric;
run;
```

b.
```
data ensemble.merged;
    merge ensemble.spring(out=blue)
          ensemble.summer;
    by fabric;
run;
```

c.
```
data ensemble.merged;
    merge ensemble.spring(blue=navy)
          ensemble.summer;
    by fabric;
run;
```

d.
```
data ensemble.merged;
    merge ensemble.spring(rename=(blue=navy))
          ensemble.summer;
    by fabric;
run;
```

8. What happens if you submit the following program to merge **Blood.Donors1** and **Blood.Donors2**, shown below?

```
data work.merged;
    merge blood.donors1 blood.donors2;
    by id;
run;
```

Blood.Donors1

ID	Type	Units
2304	O	16
1129	A	48
1129	A	50
1129	A	57
2486	B	63

Blood.Donors2

ID	Code	Units
6488	65	27
1129	63	32
5438	62	39
2304	61	45
1387	64	67

a. The Merged data set contains some missing values because not all observations have matching observations in the other data set.

b. The Merged data set contains 8 observations.

c. The DATA step produces errors.

d. Values for Units in **Blood.Donors2** overwrite values for Units in **Blood.Donors1**.

9. If you merge **Company.Staff1** and **Company.Staff2** below by ID, how many observations does the new data set contain?

Company.Staff1

ID	Name	Dept	Project
000	Miguel	A12	Document
111	Fred	B45	Survey
222	Diana	B45	Document
888	Monique	A12	Document
999	Vien	D03	Survey

Company.Staff2

ID	Name	Hours
111	Fred	35
222	Diana	40
777	Steve	0
888	Monique	37

a. 4

b. 5

c. 6

d. 9

10. If you merge data sets **Sales.Reps**, **Sales.Close**, and **Sales.Bonus** by `ID`, what is the value of `Bonus` in the third observation in the new data set?

Sales.Reps	
ID	**Name**
1	Nay Rong
2	Kelly Windsor
3	Julio Meraz
4	Richard Krabill

Sales.Close	
ID	**Sale**
1	$28,000
2	$30,000
2	$40,000
3	$15,000
3	$20,000
3	$25,000
4	$35,000

Sales.Bonus	
ID	**Bonus**
1	$2,000
2	$4,000
3	$3,000
4	$2,500

a. $4,000

b. $3,000

c. missing

d. can't tell from the information given

Chapter 14 Transforming Data with SAS Functions

Overview

Introduction

When planning modifications to SAS data sets, be sure to examine the many **SAS functions** that are available. SAS functions are prewritten expressions that provide programming shortcuts for many calculations and manipulations of data.

This chapter teaches you how to use a variety of functions, such as those shown in the table below. You learn to convert data from one data type to another, to work with SAS date and time values, and to manipulate the values of character variables.

Function	Description	Form	Sample Value
YEAR	Extracts the year value from a SAS date value.	YEAR(*date*)	*2006*
QTR	Extracts the quarter value from a SAS date value.	QTR(*date*)	*1*
MONTH	Extracts the month value from a SAS date value.	MONTH(*date*)	*12*
DAY	Extracts the day value from a SAS date value.	DAY(*date*)	*5*

Objectives

In this chapter, you learn to

- convert character data to numeric data

- convert numeric data to character data

- create SAS date values

- extract the month, year, and interval from a SAS date value

- perform calculations with date and datetime values and time intervals

- extract, edit, and search the values of character variables

- replace or remove all occurrences of a particular word within a character string.

Understanding SAS Functions

SAS **functions** are built-in routines that enable you to complete many types of data manipulations quickly and easily. Generally speaking, functions provide programming shortcuts. There are many categories of SAS functions: **arithmetic functions**, **financial functions**, **character functions**, **probability functions**, and more.

Categories of SAS Functions	
Array	Mathematical
Bitwise Logical Operations	Probability
Character	Quantile
Character String Matching	Random Number
Currency Conversion	SAS File I/O
Date and Time	Special
Descriptive Statistics	State and Zip Code
Double Byte Character Set	Trigonometric
External Files	Truncation
Financial	Variable Control
Hyperbolic	Variable Information
Macro	Web Tools

Some functions provide results that can also be obtained by using a SAS procedure. For example, functions that provide descriptive statistics return values that can also be obtained through the MEANS procedure.

SAS Functions That Compute Descriptive Statistics

Function	Syntax	Calculates
SUM	sum(*argument, argument,...*)	sum of values
MEAN	mean(*argument, argument,...*)	average of nonmissing values
MIN	min(*argument, argument,...*)	minimum value
MAX	max(*argument, argument,...*)	maximum value
VAR	var(*argument, argument,...*)	variance of the values
STD	std(*argument, argument,...*)	standard deviation of the values

Despite the similarity of certain SAS functions and procedures, don't assume that they can be used interchangeably. For example, missing values might be handled differently for a similar function and procedure.

Uses of SAS Functions

Using SAS functions, you can

- calculate sample statistics
- create SAS date values
- convert U.S. Zip codes to state postal codes
- round values
- generate random numbers
- extract a portion of a character value
- convert data from one data type to another.

This chapter concentrates on functions that

- convert data
- manipulate SAS date values
- modify values of character variables.

However, be sure to explore the many other SAS functions, which are described in the SAS documentation.

Example of a SAS Function

SAS functions can be used in DATA step programming statements and in some statistical procedures. A SAS function can be specified anywhere that you would use a SAS expression, as long as the function is part of a SAS statement.

Let's look at a simple example of a SAS function. The assignment statement below uses the MEAN function to calculate the average of three exam scores that are stored in the variables Exam1, Exam2, and Exam3.

```
AvgScore=mean(exam1,exam2,exam3);
```

When you reference a SAS function, the function returns a value that is based on the function arguments. The MEAN function above contains three arguments: the variables Exam1, Exam2, and Exam3. The function calculates the mean of the three variables that are listed as arguments.

 Some functions require a specific number of arguments, whereas other functions can contain any number of arguments. Some functions require no arguments.

General Form of SAS Functions

Arguments, Variable Lists, Arrays

To use a SAS function, specify the function name followed by the function arguments, which are enclosed in parentheses.

General form, SAS function:

> ***function-name**(argument-1<,argument-n>)*;

where *arguments* can be

- variables mean(*x,y,z*)
- constants mean(*456,502,612,498*)
- expressions mean(*37*2,192/5,mean(22,34,56)*)

⚠️ Even if the function does not require arguments, the function name must still be followed by parentheses—for example, *function-name*().

When a function contains more than one argument, the arguments are usually separated by commas.

```
function-name(argument-1,argument-2,argument-n)
```

However, for some functions, variable lists and arrays can also be used as arguments, as long as the list or the array is preceded by the word OF.

Example

Here is an example of a function that contains multiple arguments. Notice that the arguments are separated by commas.

```
mean(x1,x2,x3)
```

The arguments for this function can also be written as a variable list.

```
mean(of x1-x3)
```

Or, the variables can be referenced by an **array**.

```
mean(of newarray {*})
```

When specifying function arguments with a variable list or an array, be sure to precede the list or the array with the word OF. If you omit the word OF, the function arguments might not be interpreted as you expect. For example, the function below calculates the average of X1 minus X3, not the average of the variables X1, X2, and X3.

```
mean(x1-x3)
```

Target Variables

Now that you are familiar with the purpose and general form of SAS functions, let's think about **target variables**. A target variable is the variable to which the result of a function is assigned. For example, in the statement below, the variable `AvgScore` is the target variable.

```
AvgScore=mean(exam1,exam2,exam3);
```

Unless the length of the target variable has been previously defined, a **default length** is assigned. The default length depends on the function; the default for character functions can be as long as 200.

Default lengths could cause variables to use more space than necessary in your data set. So, when using SAS functions, consider the appropriate length for any target variables. If necessary, add a LENGTH statement to specify a length for the target variable before the statement that creates the values of that variable.

Converting Data with Functions

Introduction to Converting Data

Suppose you are asked to complete a number of modifications to the data set **Hrd.Temp**. The first modification is to create a new variable that contains the salary of temporary employees. Examining the data set, you realize that one of the variables needed to calculate salaries is the character variable `PayRate`. To complete the calculation, you need to convert `PayRate` from character to numeric.

SAS Data Set Hrd.Temp

City	State	Zip	Phone	StartDate	EndDate	PayRate	Days	Hours
CARY	NC	27513	6224549	14567	14621	**10**	11	88
CARY	NC	27513	6223251	14524	14565	**8**	25	200
CHAPEL HILL	NC	27514	9974749	14570	14608	**40**	26	208

```
data hrd.newtemp;
   set hrd.temp;
      Salary=payrate*hours;
run;
```

In such cases, you should use the **INPUT** function before attempting the calculation. The INPUT function converts character data values to numeric values. The **PUT** function converts numeric data values to character values. Both functions are discussed in this section.

Potential Problems of Omitting INPUT or PUT

What happens if you omit the INPUT function or the PUT function when converting data?

SAS will detect the mismatched variables and will try an automatic character-to-numeric or numeric-to-character conversion. However, this process doesn't always work. Suppose each value of PayRate begins with a dollar sign ($). When SAS tries to automatically convert the values of PayRate to numeric values, the dollar sign blocks the process. The values cannot be converted to numeric values. Similar problems can occur with automatic numeric-to-character conversion.

Therefore, it is **always** best to include INPUT and PUT functions in your programs when conversions occur.

Automatic Character-to-Numeric Conversion

Let's begin with the automatic conversion of character values to numeric values.

By default, if you reference a **character variable in a numeric context** such as an arithmetic operation, SAS tries to convert the variable values to numeric. For example, in the DATA step below, the character variable PayRate appears in a numeric context. It is multiplied by the numeric variable Hours to create a new variable named Salary.

```
data hrd.newtemp;
    set hrd.temp;
    Salary=payrate*hours;
run;
```

When this step is executed, SAS automatically converts the character values of PayRate to numeric values so that the calculation can occur. This conversion is completed by creating a temporary numeric value for each character value of PayRate. This temporary value is used in the calculation. The character values of PayRate are **not** replaced by numeric values.

Whenever data is automatically converted, a message is written to the SAS log stating that the conversion has occurred.

SAS Log

```
4         data hrd.newtemp;
5         set hrd.temp;
6         Salary=payrate*hours;
7         run;

NOTE: Character values have been converted  to
      numeric values at the places given by:
      (Line):(Column).

              6:11

NOTE: The data set Hrd.Newtemp has 40 observations
      and 19 variables.
NOTE: The data statement used 0.78 seconds.
```

When Automatic Conversion Occurs

Automatic character-to-numeric conversion occurs when a character value is

- assigned to a previously defined numeric variable, such as the numeric variable `Rate`

  ```
  Rate=payrate;
  ```

- used in an arithmetic operation

  ```
  Salary=payrate*hours;
  ```

- compared to a numeric value, using a comparison operator

  ```
  if payrate>=rate;
  ```

- specified in a function that requires numeric arguments.

  ```
  NewRate=sum(payrate,raise);
  ```

The automatic conversion

- uses the *w.d* informat, where *w* is the width of the character value that is being converted

- produces a numeric missing value from any character value that does not conform to standard numeric notation (digits with an optional decimal point or leading sign).

Character Value	automatic conversion	Numeric Value
12.47	▸	12.47
-8.96	▸	-8.96
1.243E1	▸	12.43
1,742.64	▸	.

Restriction for WHERE Expressions

The WHERE statement **does not** perform automatic conversions in comparisons. The simple program below demonstrates what happens when a WHERE expression encounters the wrong data type. The variable `Number` contains a numeric value, and the variable `Character` contains a character value, but the two WHERE statements specify the wrong data type.

```
data work.convtest;
   Number=4;
   Character='4';
run;
proc print data=work.convtest;
   where character=4;
run;
proc print data=work.convtest;
   where number='4';
run;
```

This mismatch of character and numeric variables and values prevents the program from processing the WHERE statements. Automatic conversion is not performed. Instead, the program stops, and error messages are written to the SAS log.

SAS Log

```
1       data work.convtest;
2           Number=4;
3           Character='4';
4       run;
NOTE: The data set Work.ConvTest has 1 observations and 2 variables.

5       proc print data=work.convtest;
6           where character=4;
7       run;
ERROR: Where clause operator requires compatible variables.

NOTE: The SAS System stopped processing this step because of errors.

8       proc print data=work.convtest;
9           where number='4';
10      run;
ERROR: Where clause operator requires compatible variables.

NOTE: The SAS System stopped processing this step because of errors.
```

Explicit Character-to-Numeric Conversion

In order to avoid the problems we saw in the previous section, use the **INPUT** function to convert character data values to numeric values. To learn how to use this function, let's examine one of the data set modifications needed for **Hrd.Temp**. As mentioned earlier, you need to calculate employee salaries by multiplying the character variable `PayRate` by the numeric variable `Hours`.

SAS Data Set Hrd.Temp

City	State	Zip	Phone	StartDate	EndDate	PayRate	Days	Hours
CARY	NC	27513	6224549	14567	14621	10	11	88
CARY	NC	27513	6223251	14524	14565	8	25	200
CHAPEL HILL	NC	27514	9974749	14570	14608	40	26	208
RALEIGH	NC	27612	6970450	14516	14527	15	10	80

To calculate salaries, you write the following DATA step. It creates a new data set, **Hrd.Newtemp**, to contain the original data plus the new variable `Salary`.

```
data hrd.newtemp;
   set hrd.temp;
   Salary=payrate*hours;
run;
```

However, you know that submitting this DATA step would cause an automatic character-to-numeric conversion, because the character variable `PayRate` is used in a numeric context. You can explicitly convert the character values of `PayRate` to numeric values by using the INPUT function.

General form, INPUT function:

> **INPUT**(*source,informat*)

where

- *source* indicates the character variable, constant, or expression to be converted to a numeric value

- a numeric *informat* must also be specified, as in this example:
  `input(payrate,2.)`

When choosing the informat, be sure to select a numeric informat that can read the form of the values.

Character Value	Informat
2115233	7.
2,115,233	COMMA9.

Here's an example of the INPUT function:

```
Test=input(saletest,comma9.);
```

The function uses the numeric informat COMMA9. to read the values of the character variable `SaleTest`. Then the resulting numeric values are stored in the variable `Test`.

Now let's use the INPUT function to convert the character values of `PayRate` to numeric values. You begin the function by specifying `PayRate` as the source. Because `PayRate` has a length of 2, you choose the numeric informat 2. to read the values of the variable.

```
input(payrate,2.)
```

Finally, you add the function to the assignment statement in your DATA step.

```
data hrd.newtemp;
   set hrd.temp;
   Salary=input(payrate,2.)*hours;
run;
```

After the DATA step is executed, the new data set (which contains the variable `Salary`) is created.

SAS Data Set Hrd.Newtemp

City	State	Zip	Phone	StartDate	EndDate	PayRate	Days	Hours	BirthDate	Salary
CARY	NC	27513	6224549	14567	14621	10	11	88	7054	880
CARY	NC	27513	6223251	14524	14565	8	25	200	5757	1600

Notice that no conversion messages appear in the SAS log when you use the INPUT function.

SAS Log

```
13      data hrd.newtemp;
14      set hrd.temp;
15      Salary=input(payrate,2.)*hours;
16      run;

NOTE: The data set Hrd.Newtemp has 40 observations
      and 19 variables.
NOTE: The DATA statement used 0.55 seconds.
```

The form of the INPUT function is very similar to the form of the PUT function (which performs numeric-to-character conversions).

INPUT(*source,informat*)

PUT(*source,format*)

However, note that the INPUT function requires an informat, whereas the PUT function requires a format. To remember which function requires a format versus an informat, note that the **IN**PUT function requires the **in**format.

Automatic Numeric-to-Character Conversion

The automatic conversion of numeric data to character data is very similar to character-to-numeric conversion. Numeric data values are converted to character values whenever they are used in a **character context**.

For example, the numeric values of the variable Site are converted to character values if you

- assign the numeric value to a previously defined character variable, such as the character variable SiteCode: SiteCode=site;

- use the numeric value with an operator that requires a character value, such as the concatenation operator: SiteCode=site||dept;

- specify the numeric value in a function that requires character arguments, such as the SUBSTR function: Region=substr(site,1,4);

Specifically, SAS writes the numeric value with the BEST12. format, and the resulting character value is right-aligned. This conversion occurs before the value is assigned or used with any operator or function. Automatic numeric-to-character conversion can cause unexpected results. For example, suppose the original numeric value has fewer than 12 digits. The resulting character value will have leading blanks, which might cause problems when you perform an operation or function.

Numeric-to-character conversion also causes a message to be written to the SAS log indicating that the conversion has occurred.

SAS Log

```
9     data hrd.newtemp;
10  .    set hrd.temp;
11        SiteCode=site;
12    run;

NOTE: Numeric values have been converted to character
      values at the places given by: (Line):(Column).

      11:13

NOTE: The data set HRD.NEWTEMP has 40 observations
      and 19 variables.
NOTE: The data statement used 1.06 seconds.
```

As we saw with the INPUT function, it is best not to rely on automatic conversion. When you know that numeric data must be converted to character data, perform an explicit conversion by including a PUT function in your SAS program. We look at the INPUT and PUT functions in the next section.

Explicit Numeric-to-Character Conversion

You can use the **PUT** function to explicitly convert numeric data values to character data values.

Let's use this function to complete one of the modifications that is needed for the data set **Hrd.Temp**. Suppose you are asked to create a new character variable named `Assignment` that concatenates the values of the numeric variable `Site` and the character variable `Dept`. The new variable values must contain the value of `Site` followed by a slash (/) and then the value of `Dept`— for example, *26/DP*.

SAS Data Set Hrd.Temp

Overtime	Job	Contact	Dept	Site
4	Word processing	Word Processor	DP	26
.	Filing, administrative duties	Admin. Asst.	PURH	57
.	Organizational dev. specialist	Consultant	PERS	34
.	Bookkeeping, word processing	Bookkeeper Asst.	BK	57

You write an assignment statement that contains the concatenation operator (||) to indicate that `Site` should be concatenated with `Dept`, using a slash as a separator. Note that the slash is enclosed in quotation marks. All character constants must be enclosed in quotation marks.

```
data hrd.newtemp;
   set hrd.temp;
   Assignment=site||'/'||dept;
run;
```

You know that submitting this DATA step will cause SAS to automatically convert the numeric values of `Site` to character values, because `Site` is used in a character context. The variable `Site` appears with the concatenation operator, which requires character values. To explicitly convert the numeric values of `Site` to character values, you must add the **PUT function** to your assignment statement.

General form, PUT function:
PUT(*source,format*)

where

- *source* indicates the numeric variable, constant, or expression to be converted to a character value

- a *format* matching the data type of the source must also be specified, as in this example: `put(site,2.)`

- The PUT function always returns a character string.

- The PUT function returns the *source* written with a *format*.

- The *format* must agree with the *source* in type.

- Numeric formats right-align the result; character formats left-align the result.

- If you use the PUT function to create a variable that has not been previously identified, it creates a character variable whose length is equal to the format width.

Because you are listing a numeric variable as the source, you must specify a numeric format.

Now that you know the general form of the PUT function, you can rewrite the assignment statement in your DATA step to explicitly convert the numeric values of `Site` to character values.

To perform this conversion, write the PUT function, specifying `Site` as the source. Because `Site` has a length of 2, choose 2. as the numeric format. After you add this PUT function to the assignment statement, the DATA step creates the new data set that contains `Assignment`.

```
data hrd.newtemp;
   set hrd.temp;
   Assignment=put(site,2.)||'/'||dept;
run;
```

SAS Data Set Hrd.Newtemp

Overtime	Job	Contact	Dept	Site	BirthDate	Assignment
4	Word processing	Word Processor	DP	26	7054	**26/DP**
.	Filing, administrative duties	Admin. Asst.	PURH	57	5757	**57/PURH**

Notice that no conversion messages appear in the SAS log when you use the PUT function.

SAS Log

```
13     data hrd.newtemp;
14     set hrd.temp;
15     Assignment=put(site,2.)||'/'||dept;
16     run;

NOTE: The data set Hrd.Newtemp has 40 observations
      and 19 variables.
NOTE: The DATA statement used 0.71 seconds.
```

Matching the Data Type

Remember that the format specified in the PUT function must match the data type of the source.

    PUT(_source,format_**)**

So, to do an explicit numeric-to-character data conversion, you specify a numeric source and a numeric format. The form of the PUT function is very similar to the form of the INPUT function.

    PUT(_source,format_**)**

    INPUT(_source,informat_**)**

Note that the PUT function requires a format, whereas the INPUT function requires an informat. To remember which function requires a format versus an informat, note that the **IN**PUT function requires the **in**format.

Manipulating SAS Date Values with Functions

SAS Date and Time Values

SAS includes a variety of functions that enable you to work with SAS **date values**. SAS stores a date value as the number of days from January 1, 1960, to a given date. Here is an example:

Jan. 1, 1959	Jan. 1, 1960	Jan. 1, 1961
← -365	0	366 →

A SAS **time value** is stored as the number of seconds since midnight. Here is an example:

(12:00 am) midnight	12:15 pm	17:00 (or 5:00 pm)
0	44100	61200 →

Consequently, a SAS **datetime value** is stored as the number of seconds between midnight on January 1, 1960, and a given date and time.

July 4, 1776 11:30:23	Jan. 1, 1960 midnight	July 4, 1994 16:10:45
← ‑5790400177	0	1088957445 →

SAS stores date values as numbers so that you can easily sort the values or perform arithmetic computations. You can use SAS date values as you use any other numeric values.

```
data test(keep=name totday);
    set hrd.temp;
    TotDay=enddate-startdate;
run;
```

SAS Data Set Hrd.Temp

City	State	Zip	Phone	StartDate	EndDate	PayRate	Days	Hours
CARY	NC	27513	6224549	14567	14621	10	11	88
CARY	NC	27513	6223251	14524	14565	8	25	200

You can display SAS date values in a variety of forms by associating a SAS format with the values. The format affects **only** the display of the dates, not the date values in the data set. For example, the FORMAT statement below associates the DATE9. format with the variables `StartDate` and `EndDate`. A portion of the output created by this PROC PRINT step appears below.

```
proc print data=hrd.temp;
    format startdate enddate date9.;
run;
```

City	State	Zip	Phone	StartDate	EndDate	Pay Rate	Days	Hours
CARY	NC	27513	6224549	19NOV1999	12JAN2000	10	11	88
CARY	NC	27513	6223251	07OCT1999	17NOV1999	8	25	200
CHAPEL HILL	NC	27514	9974749	22NOV1999	30DEC1999	40	26	208
RALEIGH	NC	27612	6970450	29SEP1999	10OCT1999	15	10	80

SAS date values are valid for dates that are based on the Gregorian calendar from A.D. 1582 through A.D. 20,000.

January 1, 1582	December 31, 20,000
←	**SAS Date Values** →

Use caution when working with historical dates. The Gregorian calendar was used throughout most of Europe from 1582, but Great Britain and the American colonies did not adopt the calendar until 1752.

SAS Date Functions

SAS stores dates, times, and datetimes as numeric values. You can use several functions to create these values.

Function	Typical Use	Result
MDY	`date=mdy(mon,day,yr);`	SAS date
TODAY DATE	`now=today();` `now=date();`	today's date as a SAS date
TIME	`curtime=time();`	current time as a SAS time

You use other functions to extract months, quarters, days, and years from SAS date values.

Function	Typical Use	Result
DAY	`day=day(date);`	day of month (1-31)
QTR	`quarter=qtr(date);`	quarter (1-4)
WEEKDAY	`wkday=weekday(date);`	day of week (1-7)
MONTH	`month=month(date);`	month (1-12)
YEAR	`yr=year(date);`	year (4 digits)

INTCK	`x=intck('day',d1,d2);`
	`x=intck('week',d1,d2);`
	`x=intck('month',d1,d2);`
	`x=intck('qtr',d1,d2);`
	`x=intck('year',d1,d2);`
		days from D1 to D2
		weeks from D1 to D2
		months from D1 to D2
		quarters from D1 to D2
		years from D1 to D2

INTNX	`x=intnx('interval',start-from,increment);`	date, time, or datetime value
DATDIF YRDIF	`x=datdif('date1',date2, ACT/ACT);` `x=yrdif('date1',date2, ACT/ACT);`	days between date1 and date2 years between date1 and date2

In the following pages, you will see several SAS date functions, showing how they are used to both create and extract date values.

YEAR, QTR, MONTH, and DAY Functions

Every SAS date value can be queried for the values of its year, month, and day. You extract these values by using the functions **YEAR**, **QTR**, **MONTH**, and **DAY**. They all work the same way, so we'll discuss them as a group.

General form, YEAR, QTR, MONTH, and DAY functions:

> **YEAR**(*date*)
> **QTR**(*date*)
> **MONTH**(*date*)
> **DAY**(*date*)

where *date* is a SAS date value that is specified either as a variable or as a SAS date constant. For more information about SAS date constants, see the SAS documentation.

The YEAR function returns a four-digit numeric value that represents the year—for example, 2002. The QTR function returns a value of 1, 2, 3, or 4 from a SAS date value to indicate the quarter of the year in which a date value falls. The MONTH function returns a numeric value that ranges from 1 to 12, representing the month of the year. The value *1* represents January, *2* represents February, and so on. The DAY function returns a numeric value from 1 to 31, representing the day of the month. As you can see, these functions are very similar in purpose and form.

Function	Description	Form	Sample Value
YEAR	Extracts the year value from a SAS date value.	YEAR(*date*)	*2005*
QTR	Extracts the quarter value from a SAS date value.	QTR(*date*)	*1*
MONTH	Extracts the month value from a SAS date value.	MONTH(*date*)	*12*
DAY	Extracts the day value from a SAS date value.	DAY(*date*)	*5*

Finding the Year

Now let's use the YEAR function to complete a task.

Suppose you need to create a subset of the data set **Hrd.Temp** that contains information about all temporary employees who were hired during a specific year, such as 1998. **Hrd.Temp** contains the dates on which employees began work with the company and their ending dates, but there is no year variable.

SAS Data Set Hrd.Temp

City	State	Zip	Phone	StartDate	EndDate	PayRate	Days	Hours
CARY	NC	27513	6224549	14567	14621	10	11	88
CARY	NC	27513	6223251	14524	14565	8	25	200
CHAPEL HILL	NC	27514	9974749	14570	14608	40	26	208
RALEIGH	NC	27612	6970450	14516	14527	15	10	80

To determine the year in which employees were hired, you can apply the YEAR function to the variable that contains the employee start date, `StartDate`. You write the YEAR function as

```
year(startdate)
```

Then, to create the new data set, you include this function in a subsetting IF statement within a DATA step. This subsetting IF statement specifies that only observations in which the YEAR function extracts a value of *1998* are placed in the new data set.

```
data hrd.temp98;
   set hrd.temp;
   if year(startdate)=1998;
run;
```

Finally, you add a PROC PRINT step to the program so that you can view the new data set. Notice that the PROC PRINT step includes a FORMAT statement to display the variables StartDate and EndDate with the DATE9. format.

```
data hrd.temp98;
   set hrd.temp;
   if year(startdate)=1998;
proc print data=hrd.temp98;
   format startdate enddate date9.;
run;
```

Here is a portion of the PROC PRINT output that is created by your program. Notice that the new data set contains information about those employees who were hired in 1998.

City	State	Zip	Phone	StartDate	EndDate	Pay Rate	Days	Hours
CHAPEL HILL	NC	27514	9972070	02AUG1998	17AUG1998	12	12	96
DURHAM	NC	27713	3633020	06OCT1998	10OCT1998	10	5	40

Finding the Year and Month

Let's use the YEAR and MONTH functions to complete a simple task.

Suppose you need to create a subset of the data set **Hrd.Temp** that contains information about all temporary employees who were hired in November 1999. **Hrd.Temp** contains the beginning and ending dates for staff employment, but there are no month or year variables in the data set.

SAS Data Set Hrd.Temp

City	State	Zip	Phone	StartDate	EndDate	PayRate	Days	Hours
CARY	NC	27513	6224549	14567	14621	10	11	88
CARY	NC	27513	6223251	14524	14565	8	25	200
CHAPEL HILL	NC	27514	9974749	14570	14608	40	26	208
RALEIGH	NC	27612	6970450	14516	14527	15	10	80

To determine the year in which employees were hired, you can apply the YEAR function to the variable that contains the employee start date, `StartDate`. You write the YEAR function as

```
year(startdate)
```

Likewise, to determine the month in which employees were hired, you apply the MONTH function to `StartDate`.

```
month(startdate)
```

To create the new data set, you include these functions in a subsetting IF statement within a DATA step. The subsetting IF statement specifies that the new data set includes only observations in which the YEAR function extracts a value of *1999* and the MONTH function extracts a value of *11* (for November).

```
data hrd.nov99;
   set hrd.temp;
   if year(startdate)=1999 and month(startdate)=11;
run;
```

Finally, you add a PROC PRINT step to the program so that you can view the new data set. Notice that the PROC PRINT step includes a FORMAT statement to display the variables `StartDate` and `EndDate` with the DATE9. format.

```
data hrd.nov99;
   set hrd.temp;
   if year(startdate)=1999 and month(startdate)=11;
proc print data=hrd.nov99;
   format startdate enddate date9.;
run;
```

Here is a portion of the PROC PRINT output that is created by your program. Notice that the new data set contains information about only those employees who were hired in November 1999.

City	State	Zip	Phone	StartDate	EndDate	PayRate	Days	Hours
CARY	NC	27513	6224549	19NOV1999	12JAN2000	10	11	88
CHAPEL HILL	NC	27514	9974749	22NOV1999	30DEC1999	40	26	208
DURHAM	NC	27713	3633618	02NOV1999	13NOV1999	12	9	72
CARRBORO	NC	27510	9976732	16NOV1999	04JAN2000	15	7	64

WEEKDAY Function

The **WEEKDAY** function enables you to extract the day of the week from a SAS date value.

General form, WEEKDAY function:

> **WEEKDAY**(*date*)

where *date* is a SAS date value that is specified either as a variable or as a SAS date constant. For more information about SAS date constants, see the SAS documentation.

The WEEKDAY function returns a numeric value from 1 to 7. The values represent the days of the week.

Value	equals	Day of the Week
1	=	Sunday
2	=	Monday
3	=	Tuesday
4	=	Wednesday
5	=	Thursday
6	=	Friday
7	=	Saturday

For example, suppose the data set **Radio.Sch** contains a broadcast schedule. The variable `AirDate` contains SAS date values. To create a data set that contains only weekend broadcasts, you use the WEEKDAY function in a subsetting IF statement. You include only observations in which the value of `AirDate` corresponds to a Saturday or Sunday.

```
data radio.schwkend;
   set radio.sch;
   if weekday(airdate)=7 or weekday(airdate)=1;
run;
```

MDY Function

The **MDY** function creates a SAS date value from numeric values that represent the month, day, and year. For example, suppose the data set **Hrd.Temp** contains the employee start date in three numeric variables, `Month`, `Day`, and `Year`.

SAS Data Set Hrd.Temp

City	State	Zip	Phone	Month	Day	Year	PayRate	Days	Hours
CARY	NC	27513	6224549	1	12	2000	10	11	88
CARY	NC	27513	6223251	11	17	1999	8	25	200
CHAPEL HILL	NC	27514	9974749	12	30	1999	40	26	208
RALEIGH	NC	27612	6970450	10	10	1999	15	10	80

Having the start date in three variables makes it difficult to perform calculations that are based on the length of employment. You can convert these numeric values to useful SAS date values by applying the MDY function.

General form, MDY function:

    MDY(*month,day,year*)

where

- *month* can be a variable that represents the month, or a number from 1-12
- *day* can be a variable that represents the day, or a number from 1-31
- *year* can be a variable that represents the year, or a number that has 2 or 4 digits.

In the data set **Hrd.Temp**, the values for month, day, and year are stored in the numeric variables `Month`, `Day`, and `Year`. You write the following MDY function to create the SAS date values:

```
mdy(month,day,year)
```

Then place this function in an assignment statement to create a new variable to contain the SAS date values.

```
data hrd.newtemp(drop=month day year);
   set hrd.temp;
   Date=mdy(month,day,year);
run;
```

Here is the new data set that contains the variable `Date`.

SAS Data Set Hrd.Newtemp

City	State	Zip	Phone	PayRate	Days	Hours	Date
CARY	NC	27513	6224549	10	11	88	**14621**
CARY	NC	27513	6223251	8	25	200	**14565**
CHAPEL HILL	NC	27514	9974749	40	26	208	**14608**
RALEIGH	NC	27612	6970450	15	10	80	**14527**

Remember, to display SAS date values in a more readable form, you can associate a SAS format with the values. For example, the FORMAT statement below associates the DATE9. format with the variable `Date`. A portion of the output that is created by this PROC PRINT step appears below.

```
proc print data=hrd.newtemp;
   format date date9.;
run;
```

City	State	Zip	Phone	PayRate	Days	Hours	Date
CARY	NC	27513	6224549	10	11	88	12JAN2000
CARY	NC	27513	6223251	8	25	200	17NOV1999
CHAPEL HILL	NC	27514	9974749	40	26	208	30DEC1999
RALEIGH	NC	27612	6970450	15	10	80	10OCT1999

The MDY function can also add the same SAS date to every observation. This might be useful if you want to compare a fixed beginning date with differing end dates. Just use numbers instead of data set variables when providing values to the MDY function.

```
data hrd.newtemp;
   set hrd.temp;
   DateCons=mdy(6,17,2002);
proc print data=hrd.newtemp;
   format datecons date9.;
run;
```

City	State	Zip	Phone	PayRate	Days	Hours	DateCons
CARY	NC	27513	6224549	10	11	88	17JUN2002
CARY	NC	27513	6223251	8	25	200	17JUN2002
CHAPEL HILL	NC	27514	9974749	40	26	208	17JUN2002
RALEIGH	NC	27612	6970450	15	10	80	17JUN2002

 Be careful when entering and formatting year values. The MDY function accepts two-digit values for the year, but SAS interprets two-digit values according to the 100-year span that is set by the **YEARCUTOFF= system option**. The default value of YEARCUTOFF= is 1920. For details, see Chapter 19, **Reading Date and Time Values**.

Whenever possible, use four-digit year values in the MDY function:

- `MDY(5,10,20)` = May 10, 1920
- `MDY(5,10,2020)` = May 10, 2020

To display the years clearly, format SAS dates with the DATE9. format. This forces the year to appear with four digits, as shown above in the `Date` and `DateCons` variables of your **Hrd.Newtemp** output.

Let's look at another example of the MDY function. The data set **Dec.Review** contains a variable named `Day`. This variable contains the day of the month for each employee's performance appraisal. The appraisals were all completed in December 1998.

SAS Data Set Dec.Review

Site	Day	Rate	Name
Westin	12	A2	Mitchell, K
Stockton	4	A5	Worton, M
Center City	17	B1	Smith, A

The following DATA step uses the MDY function to create a new variable named `ReviewDate`. This variable contains the SAS date value for the date of each performance appraisal.

```
data dec.review98;
   set dec.review;
   ReviewDate=mdy(12,day,1998);
run;
```

SAS Data Set Dec.Review98

Site	Day	Rate	Name	ReviewDate
Westin	12	A2	Mitchell, K	14225
Stockton	4	A5	Worton, M	14217
Center City	17	B1	Smith, A	14230

 If you specify an invalid date in the MDY function, SAS assigns a missing value to the target variable.

```
data dec.review98;
   set dec.review;
   ReviewDate=mdy(15,day,1998);
run;
```

SAS Data Set Dec.Review98

Site	Day	Rate	Name	ReviewDate
Westin	12	A2	Mitchell, K	.
Stockton	4	A5	Worton, M	.
Center City	17	B1	Smith, A	.

DATE and TODAY Functions

The **DATE** and **TODAY** functions return the current date from the system clock as a SAS date value. The DATE and TODAY functions have the same form and can be used interchangeably.

General form, DATE and TODAY functions:

> **DATE()**
> **TODAY()**

These functions require no arguments, but they must still be followed by parentheses.

Let's add a new variable, which contains the current date, to the data set **Hrd.Temp**. To create this variable, write an assignment statement such as the following:

```
EditDate=date();
```

After this statement is added to a DATA step and the step is submitted, the data set that contains EditDate is created.

```
data hrd.newtemp;
   set hrd.temp;
   EditDate=date();
run;
```

 For this example, the SAS date values shown below were created by submitting this program on January 15, 2000.

SAS Data Set Hrd.Newtemp

EndDate	EditDate
14621	**14624**
14565	**14624**
14608	**14624**

Remember, to display these SAS date values in a different form, you can associate a SAS format with the values. For example, the FORMAT statement below associates the DATE9. format with the variable `EditDate`. A portion of the output that is created by this PROC PRINT step appears below.

```
proc print data=hrd.newtemp;
   format editdate date9.;
run;
```

EndDate	EditDate
14621	15JAN2000
14565	15JAN2000
14608	15JAN2000

The DATE and TODAY functions can also create a SAS date value from the current date.

```
ThisDate=date();   or   ThisDate=today();
```

INTCK Function

The **INTCK** function returns the number of time intervals that occur in a given time span. You can use it to count the passage of days, weeks, months, and so on.

General form, INTCK function:

    INTCK('*interval*',*from*,*to*)

where

- *'interval'* specifies a character constant or variable. The value must be one of the following:

DAY	DTMONTH
WEEKDAY	DTWEEK
WEEK	HOUR
TENDAY	MINUTE
SEMIMONTH	SECOND
MONTH	
QTR	
SEMIYEAR	
YEAR	

- *from* specifies a SAS date, time, or datetime value that identifies the beginning of the time span.
- *to* specifies a SAS date, time, or datetime value that identifies the end of the time span.

The type of interval (date, time, or datetime) must match the type of value in *from*.

The INTCK function counts intervals from fixed interval beginnings, not in multiples of an interval unit from the *from* value. Partial intervals are not counted. For example, WEEK intervals are counted by Sundays rather than seven-day multiples from the *from* argument. MONTH intervals are counted by day 1 of each month, and YEAR intervals are counted from 01JAN, not in 365-day multiples.

Consider the results in the following table. The values that are assigned to the variables `Weeks`, `Months`, and `Years` are based on consecutive days.

SAS Statement	Value
Weeks=intck('week','31dec2000'd,'01jan2001'd);	0
Months=intck('month','31dec2000'd,'01jan2001'd);	1
Years=intck('year','31dec2000'd,'01jan2001'd);	1

Because December 31, 2000, is a Sunday, no WEEK interval is crossed between that day and January 1, 2001. However, both MONTH and YEAR intervals are crossed.

The following statement creates the variable `Years` and assigns it a value of *2*. The INTCK function determines that 2 years have elapsed between June 15, 1999, and June 15, 2001.

```
Years=intck('year','15jun1999'd,'15jun2001'd);
```

 As shown here, the *from* and *to* dates are often specified as **date constants**. A date constant is a date in the form *ddMMMyyyy* in quotation marks followed by the character *d*.

Likewise, the following statement assigns the value *24* to the variable `Months`.

```
Months=intck('month','15jun1999'd,'15jun2001'd);
```

However, the following statement assigns *0* to the variable Years, even though 364 days have elapsed. In this case the YEAR boundary (01JAN) is not crossed.

```
Years=intck('year','01jan2002'd,'31dec2002'd);
```

Example: The INTCK Function

A common use of the INTCK function is to identify periodic events such as due dates and anniversaries.

The following program identifies mechanics whose 20th year of employment occurs in the current month. It uses the INTCK function to compare the value of the variable `Hired` to the date on which the program is run.

```
data work.anniv20;
   set flights.mechanics
       (keep=id lastname firstname hired);
   Years=intck('year',hired,today());
   if years=20 and month(hired)=month(today());
proc print data=work.anniv20;
   title '20-Year Anniversaries This Month';
run;
```

The following output is created when the program is run in December 1999.

20-Year Anniversaries This Month

Obs	ID	LastName	FirstName	Hired	Years
1	1403	BOWDEN	EARL	24DEC79	20
2	1121	HERNANDEZ	MICHAEL	10DEC79	20
3	1412	MURPHEY	JOHN	08DEC79	20

INTNX Function

The **INTNX** function is similar to the INTCK function. The INTNX function applies multiples of a given interval to a date, time, or datetime value and returns the resulting value. You can use the INTNX function to identify past or future days, weeks, months, and so on.

General form, INTNX function:

    INTNX(*'interval',start-from,increment<,'alignment'>***)**

where

- *'interval'* specifies a character constant or variable
- *start-from* specifies a starting SAS date, time, or datetime value
- *increment* specifies a negative or positive integer that represents time intervals toward the past or future
- *'alignment'* (optional) forces the alignment of the returned date to the beginning, middle, or end of the interval.

The type of interval (date, time, or datetime) must match the type of value in *start-from* and *increment*.

When you specify date intervals, the value of the character constant or variable that is used in *interval* must be one of the following:

DAY	DTMONTH
WEEKDAY	DTWEEK
WEEK	HOUR
TENDAY	MINUTE
SEMIMONTH	SECOND
MONTH	
QTR	
SEMIYEAR	
YEAR	

For example, the following statement creates the variable `TargetYear` and assigns it a SAS date value of *13515*, which corresponds to January 1, 1997.

```
TargetYear=intnx('year','05feb94'd,3);
```

Likewise, the following statement assigns the value for the date July 1, 2001, to the variable `TargetMonth`.

```
TargetMonth=intnx('semiyear','01jan2001'd,1);
```

As you know, SAS date values are based on the number of days since January 1, 1960. Yet the INTNX function can use intervals of weeks, months, years, and so on. What day should be returned when these larger intervals are used?

That's the purpose of the optional *alignment* argument: it lets you specify whether the date value should be at the beginning, middle, or end of the interval. When specifying date alignment in the INTNX function, use the following arguments or their corresponding aliases:

BEGINNING	B
MIDDLE	M
END	E
SAMEDAY	S

The best way to understand the alignment argument is to see its effect on identical statements. The following table shows the results of three INTNX statements that differ only in the value of *alignment*.

SAS Statement	Date Value
`MonthX=intnx('month','01jan95'd,5,'b');`	*12935* (June 1, 1995)
`MonthX=intnx('month','01jan95'd,5,'m');`	*12949* (June 15, 1995)
`MonthX=intnx('month','01jan95'd,5,'e');`	*12964* (June 30, 1995)

These statements count five months from January, but the returned value depends on whether *alignment* specifies the beginning, middle, or end day of the resulting month. If *alignment* is not specified, the beginning day is returned by default.

DATDIF and YRDIF Functions

The **DATDIF** and **YRDIF** functions calculate the difference in days and years between two SAS dates, respectively. Both functions accept start dates and end dates that are specified as SAS date values. Also, both functions use a *basis* argument that describes how SAS calculates the date difference.

General form, DATDIF and YRDIF functions:

    DATDIF(*start_date,end_date,basis*)
    YRDIF(*start_date,end_date,basis*)

where

- *start_date* specifies the starting date as a SAS date value

- *end_date* specifies the ending date as a SAS date value

- *basis* specifies a character constant or variable that describes how SAS calculates the date difference.

There are two character strings that are valid for basis in the DATDIF function and four character strings that are valid for basis in the YRDIF function. These character strings and their meanings are listed in the table below.

Character String	Meaning	Valid In DATDIF	Valid In YRDIF
`'30/360'`	specifies a 30 day month and a 360 day year	yes	yes
`'ACT/ACT'`	uses the actual number of days or years between dates	yes	yes
`'ACT/360'`	uses the actual number of days between dates in calculating the number of years (calculated by the number of days divided by 360)	no	yes
`'ACT/365'`	uses the actual number of days between dates in calculating the number of years (calculated by the number of days divided by 365)	no	yes

Modifying Character Values with Functions

Introduction to Modifying Character Values

This section teaches you how to use SAS functions to manipulate the values of character variables. After completing this section, you will be able to

- replace the contents of a character value

- trim trailing blanks from a character value

- search a character value and extract a portion of the value

- convert a character value to uppercase or lowercase.

To begin, let's look at some of the modifications that need to be made to the character variables in **Hrd.Temp**. These modifications include

- separating the values of one variable into multiple variables

SAS Data

Name	LastName	FirstName	MiddleName
CICHOCK, ELIZABETH MARIE →	CICHOCK	ELIZABETH	MARIE
BENINCASA, HANNAH LEE →	BENINCASA	HANNAH	LEE

- replacing a portion of a character variable's values

SAS Data

Phone	Phone
6224549 →	**433**4549
6223251 →	**433**3251

- searching for a specific string within a variable's values.

SAS Data

Job
filing, administrative duties
bookkeeping, word processing, accounting

The character functions listed below can help you complete these tasks.

Function	Purpose
SCAN	returns a specified word from a character value.
SUBSTR	extracts a substring or replaces character values.
TRIM	trims trailing blanks from character values.
CATX	concatenates character strings, removes leading and trailing blanks, and inserts separators.
INDEX	searches a character value for a specific string.
FIND	searches for a specific substring of characters within a character string that you specify.
UPCASE	converts all letters in a value to uppercase.
LOWCASE	converts all letters in a value to lowercase.
PROPCASE	converts all letters in a value to proper case.
TRANWRD	replaces or removes all occurrences of a pattern of characters within a character string.

SCAN Function

The **SCAN** function enables you to separate a character value into words and to return a specified word. Let's look at the following example to see how the SCAN function works.

The data set **Hrd.Temp** stores the names of temporary employees in the variable `Name`. The `Name` variable contains the employees' first, middle, and last names.

SAS Data Set Hrd.Temp

Agency	ID	Name
Administrative Support, Inc.	F274	CICHOCK, ELIZABETH MARIE
Administrative Support, Inc.	F101	BENINCASA, HANNAH LEE

However, suppose you want to separate the value of `Name` into three variables: one variable to store the first name, one to store the middle name, and one to store the last name. You can use the SCAN function to create these new variables.

SAS Data Set Hrd.Temp

Agency	ID	LastName	FirstName	MiddleName
Administrative Support, Inc.	F274	CICHOCK	ELIZABETH	MARIE
Administrative Support, Inc.	F101	BENINCASA	HANNAH	LEE

Specifying Delimiters

The SCAN function uses **delimiters**, which are characters that are specified as word separators, to separate a character string into words. For example, if you are working with the character string below and you specify the comma as a delimiter, the SCAN function separates the string into three words.

Then the function returns whichever word you specify. In this example, if you specify the third word, the SCAN function returns the word *HIGH*.

Here's another example. Once again, let's use the comma as a delimiter, and specify that the third word be returned.

209 RADCLIFFE ROAD, CENTER CITY, NY, 92716

In this example, the word returned by the SCAN function is *NY*.

Specifying Multiple Delimiters

When using the SCAN function, you can specify as many delimiters as needed to correctly separate the character expression. When you specify multiple delimiters, SAS uses all of the delimiters as word separators. For example, if you specify both the slash and the hyphen as delimiters, the SCAN function separates the following text string into three words:

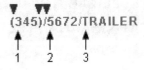

The SCAN function treats two or more contiguous delimiters, such as the parenthesis and slash below, as one delimiter. Also, leading delimiters have no effect.

```
(345)/5672/TRAILER
  1      2       3
```

Default Delimiters

If you do not specify delimiters when using the SCAN function, default delimiters are used. The default delimiters are

```
blank . < ( + | & ! $ * ) ; ^ - / , %
```

SYNTAX

Now that you are familiar with how the SCAN function works, let's examine the syntax of the function.

General form, SCAN function:

SCAN(*argument,n,delimiters*)

where

- *argument* specifies the character variable or expression to scan
- *n* specifies which word to read
- *delimiters* are special characters that must be enclosed in single quotation marks (' ').

Use the SCAN function to create your new name variables for **Hrd.Temp**. To begin, examine the values of the existing Name variable to determine which characters separate the names in the values. Notice that blanks and commas appear between the names and that the employee's last name appears first, then the first name, and then the middle name.

SAS Data Set Hrd.Temp

Agency	ID	Name
Administrative Support, Inc.	F274	**CICHOCK, ELIZABETH MARIE**
Administrative Support, Inc.	F101	**BENINCASA, HANNAH LEE**
OD Consulting, Inc.	F054	**SHERE, BRIAN THOMAS**
New Time Temps Agency	F077	**HODNOFF, RICHARD LEE**

To create the LastName variable to store the employee's last name, you write an assignment statement that contains the following SCAN function:

```
LastName=scan(name,1,' ,');
```

Note that a blank and a comma are specified as delimiters. You can also write the function without listing delimiters, because the blank and comma are default delimiters.

```
LastName=scan(name,1);
```

The complete DATA step that is needed to create LastName, FirstName, and MiddleName appears below. Notice that the original Name variable is dropped from the new data set.

```
data hrd.newtemp(drop=name);
   set hrd.temp;
   LastName=scan(name,1);
   FirstName=scan(name,2);
   MiddleName=scan(name,3);
run;
```

Specifying Variable Length

Note that the SCAN function assigns a length of 200 to each target variable. (Remember, a target variable is the variable that receives the result of the function.) So, if you submit the DATA step above, the LastName, FirstName, and MiddleName variables are each assigned a length of 200. This length is longer than necessary for these variables.

To save storage space, add a **LENGTH statement** to your DATA step, and specify an appropriate length for all three variables. Because SAS sets the length of a new character variable the first time it is encountered in the DATA step, be sure to place the LENGTH statement **before** the assignment statements that contain the SCAN function.

```
data hrd.newtemp(drop=name);
    set hrd.temp;
    length LastName FirstName MiddleName $ 10;
    lastname=scan(name,1);
    firstname=scan(name,2);
    middlename=scan(name,3);
run;
```

SUBSTR Function

The **SUBSTR** function can be used to

- extract a portion of a character value

- replace the contents of a character value.

Let's begin with the task of extracting a portion of a value. In the data set **Hrd.Newtemp**, the names of temporary employees are stored in three name variables: `LastName`, `FirstName`, and `MiddleName`.

SAS Data Set Hrd.Newtemp

Agency	ID	LastName	FirstName	MiddleName
Administrative Support, Inc.	F274	CICHOCK	ELIZABETH	MARIE
Administrative Support, Inc.	F101	BENINCASA	HANNAH	LEE
OD Consulting, Inc.	F054	SHERE	BRIAN	THOMAS
New Time Temps Agency	F077	HODNOFF	RICHARD	LEE

However, suppose you want to modify the data set to store only the middle initial instead of the full middle name. To do so, you must extract the first letter of the middle name values and assign these values to the new variable `MiddleInitial`.

SAS Data Set Work.Newtemp

Agency	ID	LastName	FirstName	MiddleInitial
Administrative Support, Inc.	F274	CICHOCK	ELIZABETH	M
Administrative Support, Inc.	F101	BENINCASA	HANNAH	L
OD Consulting, Inc.	F054	SHERE	BRIAN	T
New Time Temps Agency	F077	HODNOFF	RICHARD	L

The SUBSTR function enables you to extract any number of characters from a character string, starting at a specified position in the string.

General form, SUBSTR function:

   SUBSTR(*argument,position,<n>*)

where

- *argument* specifies the character variable or expression to scan.
- *position* is the character position to start from.
- *n* specifies the number of characters to extract. If *n* is omitted, all remaining characters are included in the substring.

Using the SUBSTR function, you can extract the first letter of the `MiddleName` value to create the new variable `MiddleInitial`.

SAS Data Set Hrd.Newtemp

Agency	ID	LastName	FirstName	MiddleName
Administrative Support, Inc.	F274	CICHOCK	ELIZABETH	**MARIE**
Administrative Support, Inc.	F101	BENINCASA	HANNAH	**LEE**
OD Consulting, Inc.	F054	SHERE	BRIAN	**THOMAS**
New Time Temps Agency	F077	HODNOFF	RICHARD	**LEE**

You write the SUBSTR function as:

```
substr(middlename,1,1)
```

This function specifies that a character string be extracted from the value of `MiddleName`. The string to be extracted begins in position 1 and contains one character. Then, you place this function in an assignment statement in your DATA step.

```
data work.newtemp(drop=middlename);
   set hrd.newtemp;
   MiddleInitial=substr(middlename,1,1);
run;
```

The new `MiddleInitial` variable is given the same length as `MiddleName`. The `MiddleName` variable is then dropped from the new data set.

SAS Data Set Work.Newtemp

Agency	ID	LastName	FirstName	MiddleInitial
Administrative Support, Inc.	F274	CICHOCK	ELIZABETH	**M**
Administrative Support, Inc.	F101	BENINCASA	HANNAH	**L**
OD Consulting, Inc.	F054	SHERE	BRIAN	**T**
New Time Temps Agency	F077	HODNOFF	RICHARD	**L**

You can use the SUBSTR function to extract a substring from any character value if you know the position of the value.

Positioning the SUBSTR Function

SAS uses the SUBSTR function to extract a substring or to modify a variable's values, depending on the position of the function in the assignment statement.

When the function is on the **right side** of an assignment statement, the function returns the requested string.

```
MiddleInitial=substr(middlename,1,1);
```

But if you place the SUBSTR function on the **left side** of an assignment statement, the function is used to modify variable values.

```
substr(region,1,3)='NNW';
```

When the SUBSTR function modifies variable values, the right side of the assignment statement must specify the **value** to place into the variable. For example, to replace the fourth and fifth characters of a variable named `Test` with the value *92*, you write the following assignment statement:

```
substr(test,4,2)='92';
```

Test		Test
S7381K2	→	S7392K2
S7381K7	→	S7392K7

Replacing Text

There is a second use for the SUBSTR function. This function can also be used to **replace the contents of a character variable**. For example, suppose the local phone exchange 622 was replaced by the exchange 433. You need to update the character variable `Phone` in **Hrd.Temp** to reflect this change.

SAS Data Set Hrd.Temp

City	State	Zip	Phone	StartDate	EndDate	PayRate	Days	Hours
CARY	NC	27513	**622**4549	14567	14621	10	11	88
CARY	NC	27513	**622**3251	14524	14565	8	25	200
CHAPEL HILL	NC	27514	9974749	14570	14608	40	26	208
RALEIGH	NC	27612	6970450	14516	14527	15	10	80

You can use the SUBSTR function to complete this modification. The syntax of the SUBSTR function, when used to replace a variable's values, is identical to the syntax for extracting a substring.

SUBSTR(*argument,position,n*)

However, in this case,

- the first argument specifies the character variable whose values are to be modified.

- the second argument specifies the position at which the replacement is to begin.

- the third argument specifies the number of characters to replace. If *n* is omitted, all remaining characters are replaced.

Now let's use the SUBSTR function to replace the 622 exchange in the variable Phone. You begin by writing this assignment statement:

```
data hrd.temp2;
   set hrd.temp;
   substr(phone,1,3)='433';
run;
```

This statement specifies that the new exchange 433 should be placed in the variable Phone, starting at character position 1 and replacing three characters.

SAS Data Set Hrd.Temp

City	State	Zip	Phone	StartDate	EndDate	PayRate	Days	Hours
CARY	NC	27513	**622**4549	14567	14621	10	11	88
CARY	NC	27513	**622**3251	14524	14565	8	25	200
CHAPEL HILL	NC	27514	9974749	14570	14608	40	26	208

But executing this DATA step places the value *433* into all values of Phone. You only need to replace the values of Phone that contain the 622 exchange. So, you add an assignment statement to the DATA step to extract the exchange from Phone. Notice that the SUBSTR function is used on the right side of the assignment statement.

```
data hrd.temp2(drop=exchange);
   set hrd.temp;
   Exchange=substr(phone,1,3);
   substr(phone,1,3)='433';
run;
```

Now the DATA step needs an **IF-THEN statement** to verify the value of the variable Exchange. If the exchange is 622, the assignment statement executes to replace the value of Phone.

```
data hrd.temp2(drop=exchange);
   set hrd.temp;
   Exchange=substr(phone,1,3);
   if exchange='622' then substr(phone,1,3)='433';
run;
```

After the DATA step is executed, the appropriate values of Phone contain the new exchange.

SAS Data Set Hrd.Temp2

City	State	Zip	Phone	StartDate	EndDate	PayRate	Days	Hours
CARY	NC	27513	**433**4549	14567	14621	10	11	88
CARY	NC	27513	**433**3251	14524	14565	8	25	200
CHAPEL HILL	NC	27514	9974749	14570	14608	40	26	208

Once again, remember the rules for using the SUBSTR function. If the SUBSTR function is on the right side of an assignment statement, the function extracts a substring.

```
MiddleInitial=substr(middlename,1,1);
```

If the SUBSTR function is on the left side of an assignment statement, the function replaces the contents of a character variable.

```
substr(region,1,3)='NNW';
```

SCAN Function Compared with SUBSTR Function

The SCAN function is similar to the SUBSTR function. Let's briefly compare the two. Both the SCAN and SUBSTR functions can extract a substring from a character value:

- **SCAN** extracts words within a value that is marked by delimiters.

- **SUBSTR** extracts a portion of a value by starting at a specified location.

The SUBSTR function is best used when you know the **exact position** of the substring that you want to extract from the character value. The substring does not need to be marked by delimiters. For example, the first two characters of the variable ID identify the class level of college students. The position of these characters does not vary within the values of ID.

SAS Data

Name	ID
Trentonson, Matthew Robert	**SO**45467
Truell, Marcia Elizabeth	**SR**32881

The SUBSTR function is the best choice to extract class level information from ID. By contrast, the SCAN function is best used when

- you know the order of the words in the character value

- the starting position of the words varies

- the words are marked by some delimiter.

TRIM Function

The **TRIM** function enables you to remove trailing blanks from character values. To learn about the TRIM function, let's modify the data set **Hrd.Temp**.

The data set **Hrd.Temp** contains four address variables: Address, City, State, and Zip.

SAS Data Set Hrd.Temp (Selected Variables)

Agency	ID	Name	Address	City	State	Zip	Phone	StartDate
Administrative Support, Inc.	F274	CICHOCK, ELIZABETH MARIE	**65 ELM DR**	**CARY**	**NC**	**27513**	6224549	14567
Administrative Support, Inc.	F101	BENINCASA, HANNAH LEE	**11 SUN DR**	**CARY**	**NC**	**27513**	6223251	14524

You need to create one address variable that contains the values of the three variables Address, City, and Zip. (Because all temporary employees are hired locally, the value of State does not need to be included in the new variable.)

SAS Data Set Hrd.NewTemp

Agency	ID	Name	NewAddress	Phone	StartDate	EndDate	PayRate	Days	Hours
Administrative Support, Inc.	F274	CICHOCK, ELIZABETH MARIE	**65 ELM DR, CARY, 27513**	6224549	14567	14621	10	11	88
Administrative Support, Inc.	F101	BENINCASA, HANNAH LEE	**11 SUN DR, CARY, 27513**	6223251	14524	14565	8	25	200

Writing a DATA step to create this new variable is easy. You include an assignment statement that contains the concatenation operator (||), as shown below.

```
data hrd.newtemp(drop=address city state zip);
   set hrd.temp;
   NewAddress=address||', '||city||', '||zip;
run;
```

The concatenation operator (||) enables you to concatenate character values. In this assignment statement, the character values of `Address`, `City`, and `Zip` are concatenated with two character constants that consist of a comma and a blank. The commas and blanks are needed to separate the street, city, and ZIP code values. The length of `NewAddress` is the sum of the length of each variable and constant that is used to create the new variable. Notice that this DATA step drops the original address variables from the new data set.

When the DATA step is executed, you notice that the values of `NewAddress` do not appear as expected. The values of the new variable contain embedded blanks.

SAS Data Set Hrd.NewTemp

NewAddress
65 ELM DRIVE   , CARY   , 27513
11 SUN DRIVE   , CARY   , 27513
712 HARDWICK STREET   , CHAPEL HILL   , 27514
5372 WHITEBUD ROAD   , RALEIGH   , 27612

These blanks appear in the values of `NewAddress` because the values of the original address variables contained trailing blanks. Whenever the value of a character variable does not match the length of the variable, SAS pads the value with trailing blanks.

Address length=32	City length=15	Zip length=5
65 ELM DRIVE ·	RALEIGH · · · · · · · ·	27612
11 SUN DRIVE ·	DURHAM · · · · · · · · ·	27612
712 HARTWICK STREET · · · · · · · · · · · · · ·	CHAPEL HILL · · · ·	27514

So, when the original address values are concatenated to create `NewAddress`, the trailing blanks in the original values are included in the values of the new variable. The variable `Zip` is the only one that does not contain trailing blanks.

NewAddress length=56
65 ELM DRIVE · · · · · · · · · · · · · · · · · · · , RALEIGH · · · · · · · · , 27612
11 SUN DRIVE · · · · · · · · · · · · · · · · · · · , DURHAM · · · · · · · · · , 27612
712 HARTWICK STREET · · · · · · · · · · · · · , CHAPEL HILL · · · · , 27514

The TRIM function enables you to remove trailing blanks from character values.

General form, TRIM function:

TRIM(*argument*)

where *argument* can be any character expression, such as

- a character variable: trim(address)

- another character function: trim(left(id)).

To remove the blanks from the variable `NewAddress`, include the TRIM function in your assignment statement. Trim the values of `Address` and `City`.

```
data hrd.newtemp(drop=address city state zip);
   set hrd.temp;
   NewAddress=trim(address)||', '||trim(city)||', '||zip;
run;
```

The revised DATA step creates the values that you expect for `NewAddress`.

SAS Data Set Hrd.Newtemp

NewAddress
65 ELM DRIVE, CARY, 27513
11 SUN DRIVE, CARY, 27513
712 HARDWICK STREET, CHAPEL HILL, 27514
5372 WHITEBUD ROAD, RALEIGH, 27612

Points to Remember

Keep in mind that the TRIM function does not affect how a variable is stored. Suppose you trim the values of a variable and then assign these values to a new variable. The trimmed values are padded with trailing blanks again if the values are shorter than the length of the new variable.

Here's an example. In the DATA step below, the trimmed value of `Address` is assigned to the new variable `Street`. When the trimmed value is assigned to `Street`, trailing blanks are added to the value to match the length of 20.

```
data temp;
   set hrd.temp;
   length Street $ 20;
   Street=trim(address);
run;
```

Address length=32	Street length=20
65 ELM DRIVE ·	65 ELM DRIVE · · · · · · ·
11 SUN DRIVE ·	11 SUN DRIVE · · · · · · ·
712 HARTWICK STREET · · · · · · · · · · · ·	712 HARTWICK STREET ·

CATX Function

The **CATX** function enables you to concatenate character strings, remove leading and trailing blanks, and insert separators. The CATX function returns a value to a variable, or returns a value to a temporary buffer. The results of the CATX function are usually equivalent to those that are produced by a combination of the concatenation operator and the TRIM and LEFT functions.

Remember that you learned to use the TRIM function along with the concatenation operator to create one address variable that contains the values of the three variables `Address`, `City`, and `Zip`, and to remove extra blanks from the new values. You used the DATA step shown below.

```
data hrd.newtemp(drop=address city state zip);
   set hrd.temp;
   NewAddress=trim(address)||', '||trim(city)||', '||zip;
run;
```

You can accomplish the same concatenation using only the CATX function.

General form, CATX function:

  CATX(*separator,string-1 <,...string-n>* **)**

where

- *separator* specifies the character string that is used as a separator between concatenated strings
- *string* specifies a SAS character string.

You want to create the new variable `NewAddress` by concatenating the values of the `Address`, `City`, and `Zip` variables from the data set **Hrd.Temp**. You want to strip excess blanks from the old variable values and separate the variable values with a comma. The DATA step below uses the CATX function to create `NewAddress`.

```
data hrd.newtemp(drop=address city state zip);
   set hrd.temp;
   NewAddress=catx(', ',address,city,zip);
run;
```

The revised DATA step creates the values that you expect for `NewAddress`.

SAS Data Set Hrd.Newtemp

NewAddress
65 ELM DRIVE, CARY, 27513
11 SUN DRIVE, CARY, 27513
712 HARDWICK STREET, CHAPEL HILL, 27514
5372 WHITEBUD ROAD, RALEIGH, 27612

INDEX Function

The **INDEX** function enables you to search a character value for a specified string. The INDEX function searches values from left to right, looking for the first occurrence of the string. It returns the position of the string's first character; if the string is not found, it returns a value of *0*.

Suppose you need to search the values of the variable `Job`, which lists job skills. You want to create a data set that contains the names of all temporary employees who have word processing experience.

SAS Data Set Hrd.Temp

Job	Contact	Dept	Site
word processing	WORD PROCESSOR	DP	26
filing, administrative duties	ADMIN. ASST.	PURH	57
organizational dev. specialist	CONSULTANT	PERS	34

The INDEX function can complete this search.

General form, INDEX function:

    INDEX(*source,excerpt*)

where

- *source* specifies the character variable or expression to search
- *excerpt* specifies a character string that is enclosed in quotation marks (' ').

To search for the occurrences of *word processing* in the values of the variable Job, you write the INDEX function as shown below. Note that the character string is enclosed in quotation marks.

```
index(job,'word processing')
```

Then, to create the new data set, include the INDEX function in a subsetting IF statement. Only those observations in which the function locates the string and returns a value greater than **0** are written to the data set.

```
data hrd.datapool;
   set hrd.temp;
   if index(job,'word processing') > 0;
run;
```

Here's your data set that shows the temporary employees who have word processing experience.

SAS Data Set Hrd.Datapool

Job	Contact	Dept	Site
word processing	WORD PROCESSOR	DP	26
bookkeeping, word processing	BOOKKEEPER AST	BK	57
word processing, sec. work	WORD PROCESSOR	DP	95
bookkeeping, word processing	BOOKKEEPER AST	BK	44
word processing	WORD PROCESSOR	DP	59
word processing, sec. work	WORD PROCESSOR	PUB	38
word processing	WORD PROCESSOR	DP	44
word processing	WORD PROCESSOR	DP	90

Note that the INDEX function is **case sensitive**, so the character string that you are searching for must be specified exactly as it is recorded in the data set. For example, the INDEX function shown below would not locate any employees who have word processing experience.

```
index(job,'WORD PROCESSING')
```

SAS Data Set Hrd.Temp

Job	Contact	Dept	Site
word processing	WORD PROCESSOR	DP	26
filing, administrative duties	ADMIN. ASST.	PURH	57
organizational dev. specialist	CONSULTANT	PERS	34
bookkeeping, word processing	BOOKKEEPER ASST.	BK	57

Finding a String Regardless of Case

To ensure that all occurrences of a character string are found, you can use the **UPCASE** or **LOWCASE** function with the INDEX function. The UPCASE and LOWCASE functions enable you to convert variable values to uppercase or lowercase letters. You can then specify the character string in the INDEX function accordingly.

```
index(upcase(job),'WORD PROCESSING')
index(lowcase(job),'word processing')
```

FIND Function

The **FIND** function enables you to search for a specific substring of characters within a character string that you specify. The FIND function searches a string for the first occurrence of the substring, and returns the position of that substring. If the substring is not found in the string, FIND returns a value of *0*.

The FIND function is similar to the INDEX function. Remember that you used the INDEX function to search the values of the variable `Job` in **Hrd.Temp** in order to create a data set that contains the names of all temporary employees who have word processing experience.

SAS Data Set Hrd.Temp

Job	Contact	Dept	Site
word processing	WORD PROCESSOR	DP	26
filing, administrative duties	ADMIN. ASST.	PURH	57
organizational dev. specialist	CONSULTANT	PERS	34

You can also use the FIND function to complete this search.

General form, FIND function:

FIND(*string,substring<,modifiers><,startpos>* **)**

where

- *string* specifies a character constant, variable, or expression that will be searched for substrings

- *substring* is a character constant, variable, or expression that specifies the substring of characters to seach for in *string*

- *modifiers* is a character constant, variable, or expression that specifies one or more modifiers

- *startpos* is an integer that specifies the position at which the search should start and the direction of the search.

If string or substring is a character literal, you must enclose it in quotation marks.

The *modifiers* argument enables you to specify one or more modifiers for the function, as listed below.

- The modifier **i** causes the FIND function to ignore character case during the search. If this modifier is not specified, FIND searches for character substrings with the same case as the characters in *substring*.

- The modifier **t** trims trailing blanks from *string* and *substring*.

 If the modifier is a constant, enclose it in quotation marks. Specify multiple constants in a single set of quotation marks.

If *startpos* is not specified, FIND starts the search at the beginning of the string and searches the string from left to right. If *startpos* is specified, the absolute value of *startpos* determines the position at which to start the search. The sign of *startpos* determines the direction of the search. If *startpos* is positive, FIND searches from *startpos* to the right; and if *startpos* is negative, FIND searches from *startpos* to the left.

Example

The values of the variable `Job` are all lowercase. Therefore, to search for the occurrence of *word processing* in the values of the variable `Job`, you write the FIND function as shown below. Note that the character substring is enclosed in quotation marks.

```
find(job,'word processing','t')
```

Then, to create the new data set, include the FIND function in a subsetting IF statement. Only those observations in which the function locates the string and returns a value greater than *0* are written to the data set.

```
data hrd.datapool;
   set hrd.temp;
   if find(job,'word processing','t') > 0;
run;
```

UPCASE Function

The **UPCASE** function converts all letters in a character expression to uppercase.

> **General form, UPCASE function:**
>
> **UPCASE**(*argument*)
>
> where *argument* can be any SAS expression, such as a character variable or constant.

Let's use the UPCASE function to convert the values of a character variable in **Hrd.Temp**. The values of the variable `Job` appear in lowercase letters.

SAS Data Set Hrd.Temp

Job	Contact	Dept	Site
word processing	WORD PROCESSOR	DP	26
filing, administrative duties	ADMIN. ASST.	PURH	57
organizational dev. specialist	CONSULTANT	PERS	34
bookkeeping, word processing	BOOKKEEPER ASST.	BK	57

To convert the values of Job to uppercase, you write the UPCASE function as follows:

```
upcase(job)
```

Then place the function in an assignment statement in a DATA step.

```
data hrd.newtemp;
   set hrd.temp;
   Job=upcase(job);
run;
```

Here's the new data set that contains the converted values of Job.

SAS Data Set Hrd.Newtemp

Job	Contact	Dept	Site
WORD PROCESSING	WORD PROCESSOR	DP	26
FILING, ADMINISTRATIVE DUTIES	ADMIN. ASST.	PURH	57
ORGANIZATIONAL DEV. SPECIALIST	CONSULTANT	PERS	34
BOOKKEEPING, WORD PROCESSING	BOOKKEEPER ASST.	BK	57

LOWCASE Function

The **LOWCASE** function converts all letters in a character expression to lowercase.

> **General form, LOWCASE function:**
>
> **LOWCASE**(*argument*)
>
> where *argument* can be any SAS expression, such as a character variable or constant.

Here's an example of the LOWCASE function. In this example, the function converts the values of a variable named Title to lowercase letters.

```
lowcase(title)
```

Another example of the LOWCASE function is shown below. The assignment statement in this DATA step uses the LOWCASE function to convert the values of the variable Contact to lowercase.

SAS Data Set Hrd.Temp

Job	Contact	Dept	Site
word processing	**WORD PROCESSOR**	DP	26
filing, administrative duties	**ADMIN. ASST.**	PURH	57
organizational dev. specialist	**CONSULTANT**	PERS	34

```
data hrd.newtemp;
   set hrd.temp;
   Contact=lowcase(contact);
run;
```

After this DATA step is executed, the new data set is created. Notice the converted values of the variable Contact.

SAS Data Set Hrd.Newtemp

Job	Contact	Dept	Site
word processing	**word processor**	DP	26
filing, administrative duties	**admin. asst.**	PURH	57
organizational dev. specialist	**consultant**	PERS	34

PROPCASE Function

The **PROPCASE** function converts all words in an argument to proper case (so that the first letter in each word is capitalized).

General form, PROPCASE function:

PROPCASE(*argument<,delimiter(s)>***)**

where

- *argument* can be any SAS expression, such as a character variable or constant

- *delimiter(s)* specifies one or more delimiters that are enclosed in quotation marks. The default delimiters are blank, forward slash, hyphen, open parenthesis, period, and tab.

If you specify *delimiter(s)*, then the default delimiters are no longer in effect.

The PROPCASE function copies a character argument and converts all uppercase letters to lowercase letters. It then converts to uppercase the first character of a word that is preceded by a delimiter. PROPCASE uses the default delimiters unless you use the *delimiter(s)* argument.

Here's an example of the PROPCASE function. In this example, the function converts the values of a variable named `Title` to proper case and uses the default delimiters.

```
lowcase(title)
```

Another example of the PROPCASE function is shown below. The assignment statement in this DATA step uses the PROPCASE function to convert the values of the variable `Contact` to proper case.

SAS Data Set Hrd.Temp

Job	Contact	Dept	Site
word processing	**WORD PROCESSOR**	DP	26
filing, administrative duties	**ADMIN. ASST.**	PURH	57
organizational dev. specialist	**CONSULTANT**	PERS	34

```
data hrd.newtemp;
   set hrd.temp;
   Contact=propcase(contact);
run;
```

After this DATA step is executed, the new data set is created. Notice the converted values of the variable `Contact`.

SAS Data Set Hrd.Newtemp

Job	Contact	Dept	Site
word processing	**Word Processor**	DP	26
filing, administrative duties	**Admin. Asst.**	PURH	57
organizational dev. specialist	**Consultant**	PERS	34

TRANWRD Function

The **TRANWRD** function replaces or removes all occurrences of a pattern of characters within a character string. The translated characters can be located anywhere in the string.

> **General form, TRANWRD function:**
>
> **TRANWRD**(*source,target,replacement*)
> where
> - *source* specifies the source string that you want to translate
> - *target* specifies the string that SAS searches for in *source*
> - *replacement* specifies the string that replaces *target*.
>
> 🔧 *target* and *replacement* can be specified as variables or as character strings. If you specify character strings, be sure to enclose the strings in quotation marks (' ' or " ").

You can use TRANWRD function to update variables in place. In this example, the function updates the values of Name by changing every occurrence of the string *Monroe* to *Manson*.

```
name=tranwrd(name,'Monroe','Manson')
```

Another example of the TRANWRD function is shown below. In this case, two assignment statements use the TRANWRD function to change all occurrences of *Miss* or *Mrs.* to *Ms.*

SAS Data Set Work.Before

Name
Mrs. Millicent Garrett Fawcett
Miss Charlotte Despard
Mrs. Emmeline Pankhurst
Miss Sylvia Pankhurst

```
data work.after;
   set work.before;
   name=tranwrd(name,'Miss','Ms.');
   name=tranwrd(name,'Mrs.','Ms.');
run;
```

After this DATA step is executed, the new data set is created. Notice the changed strings within the variable Name.

SAS Data Set Work.After

Name
Ms. Millicent Garrett Fawcett
Ms. Charlotte Despard
Ms. Emmeline Pankhurst
Ms. Sylvia Pankhurst

Modifying Numeric Values with Functions

Introduction

You've seen how SAS functions can be used to

- convert between character and numeric variable values

- manipulate SAS date values

- modify values of character variables.

SAS provides additional functions to create or modify numeric values. These include arithmetic, financial, and probability functions. There are far too many of these functions to explore them all in detail, but let's look at two examples.

INT Function

To return the integer portion of a numeric value, use the **INT function**. Any decimal portion of the INT function argument is discarded.

> **General form, INT function:**
>
>   **INT***(argument)*
>
> where *argument* is a numeric variable, constant, or expression.

The two data sets shown below give before-and-after views of values that are truncated by the INT function.

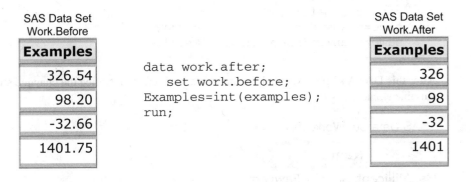

SAS Data Set
Work.Before

Examples
326.54
98.20
-32.66
1401.75

```
data work.after;
   set work.before;
Examples=int(examples);
run;
```

SAS Data Set
Work.After

Examples
326
98
-32
1401

ROUND Function

To round values to the nearest specified unit, use the **ROUND function**.

> **General form, ROUND function:**
>
>   **ROUND***(argument,round-off-unit)*
>
> where
>
> - *argument* is a numeric variable, constant, or expression.
> - *round-off-unit* is numeric and nonnegative.

If a round-off unit is not provided, a default value of 1 is used, and the argument is rounded to the nearest integer. The two data sets shown below give before-and-after views of values that are modified by the ROUND function.

SAS Data Set Work.Before
Examples
326.54
98.20
-32.66
1401.75

```
data work.after;
    set work.before;
Examples=round(examples,.2);
run;
```

SAS Data Set Work.After
Examples
326.6
98.2
-32.6
1401.80

To learn more about SAS functions that modify numeric values, see the SAS documentation.

Nesting SAS Functions

Throughout this lesson, you've seen examples of individual functions. For example, in this assignment statement the SCAN function selects the middle name (third word) from the variable Name:

```
MiddleName=scan(name,3);
```

Then this assignment statement uses the SUBSTR function to select the first letter from the variable MiddleName:

```
MiddleInitial=substr(MiddleName,1,1);
```

To write more efficient programs, however, you can **nest** functions as appropriate. For example, you can nest the SCAN function within the SUBSTR function in an assignment statement to compute the value for MiddleInitial:

```
MiddleInitial=substr(scan(name,3),1,1);
```

This example of nested numeric functions determines the number of years between June 15, 1999, and today:

```
Years=intck('year','15jun1999'd,today());
```

 You can nest any function as long as the function that is used as the argument meets the requirements for the argument.

Summary

Text Summary

Using SAS Functions

SAS functions can be used to convert data and to manipulate the values of character variables. Functions are written by specifying the function name, then its **arguments** in parentheses. Arguments can include variables, constants, or expressions. Although arguments are typically separated by commas, they can also be specified as variable lists or arrays.

Automatic Character-to-Numeric Conversion

When character variables are used in a numeric context, SAS tries to convert the character values to numeric values. Numeric context includes arithmetic operations, comparisons with numeric values, and assignment to previously defined numeric variables. The original character values are not changed. The conversion creates temporary numeric values and places a note in the SAS log.

Explicit Character-to-Numeric Conversion

The **INPUT function** provides direct, controlled conversion of character values to numeric values. When a character variable is specified in a numeric informat, the INPUT function generates numeric values without placing a note in the SAS log.

Automatic Numeric-to-Character Conversion

When numeric variables are used in a character context, SAS tries to convert the numeric values to character values. Character context includes concatenation operations, use in functions that require character arguments, and assignment to previously defined character variables. The original numeric values are not changed; the conversion creates temporary character values and places a note in the SAS log.

Explicit Numeric-to-Character Conversion

The **PUT function** provides direct, controlled conversion of numeric values to character values. The format specified in a PUT function must match the source, so use an appropriate numeric format to create the new character values. No note will appear in the SAS log.

SAS Date and Time Values

SAS **date values** are stored as the number of days from January 1, 1960; time values are stored as the number of seconds since midnight. These values can be displayed in a variety of forms by associating them with SAS formats.

YEAR, QTR, MONTH, and DAY Functions

To extract the year, quarter, month, or day value from a SAS date value, specify the YEAR, QTR, MONTH, or DAY function followed by the SAS date value in parentheses. The YEAR function returns a four-digit number; QTR returns a value of 1, 2, 3, or 4; MONTH returns a number from 1 to 12; and DAY returns 1 to 31.

WEEKDAY Function

To extract the day of the week from a SAS date value, specify the function WEEKDAY followed by the SAS date value in parentheses. The function returns a numeric value from 1 to 7, representing the day of the week.

MDY Function

To create a SAS date value for a month, day, and year, specify the MDY function followed by the date values. The result can be displayed in several ways by applying a SAS date format. SAS interprets two-digit values according to the 100-year span that is set by the YEARCUTOFF= system option. The default value of YEARCUTOFF= is 1920.

DATE and TODAY Functions

To convert the current date to a SAS date value, specify the DATE or TODAY function without arguments. The DATE and TODAY functions can be used interchangeably.

INTCK Function

To count the number of **time intervals** that occur in a time span, use the INTCK function and specify the interval constant or variable, the beginning date value, and the ending date value. The INTCK function counts intervals from fixed interval beginnings, not in multiples of an interval unit. Partial intervals are not counted.

INTNX Function

To apply multiples of an interval to a date value, use the INTNX function and specify the interval constant or variable, the start-from date value, and the increment. Include the alignment option to specify whether the date returned should be at the beginning, middle, or end of the interval.

DATDIF and YRDIF Functions

To calculate the difference between dates as a number of days or as a number of years, use the DATDIF or YRDIF function. These functions accept SAS date values and return a difference between the date values calculated according to the basis that you specify in the function.

SCAN Function

The SCAN function separates a character string to return a word based on its position. It defines words by counting delimiters, which are characters that are used as word separators. The name of the function is followed, in parentheses, by the name of the character variable, the number of delimiters to count, and the specified delimiters enclosed in quotation marks.

SUBSTR Function

The SUBSTR function can be used to extract or replace any portion of a character string. To extract values, place the function on the right side of an assignment statement and specify, in parentheses, the name of the character variable, the starting character position, and the number of characters to extract. To replace values, place the function on the left side of an assignment statement and specify, in parentheses, the name of the variable being modified, the starting character position, and the number of characters to replace.

SCAN Function versus SUBSTR Function

Both the SCAN and SUBSTR functions can extract a substring from a character value. SCAN relies on delimiters, whereas SUBSTR reads values from specified locations. Use SCAN when you know the delimiter and the order of words. Use SUBSTR when the positions of the characters don't vary.

TRIM Function

Because SAS pads the length of character values, unwanted spaces can sometimes appear after strings are concatenated. To remove trailing blanks from character values, specify the TRIM function with the name of a character variable. Remember that trimmed values will be padded with blanks again if they are shorter than the length of the new variable.

CATX Function

You can concatenate character strings, remove leading and trailing blanks, and insert separators in one step by using the CATX function. The results of the CATX function are usually equivalent to those that are produced by a combination of the concatenation operator and the TRIM and LEFT functions.

INDEX Function

To test character values for the presence of a string, use the INDEX function and specify, in parentheses, the name of the variable and the string enclosed in quotation marks. The INDEX function can be used with an IF statement when you are creating a data set. However, only those observations in which the function finds the string and returns a value greater than *0* are written to the new data set.

FIND Function

You can also use the FIND function to search for a specific substring of characters within a character string that you specify. The FIND function is similar to the INDEX function, but the FIND function enables you to ignore character case in your search and to trim trailing blanks. The FIND function can also begin the search at any position that you specify in the string.

UPCASE Function

The UPCASE function converts all letters in a character expression to uppercase. Include the function in an assignment statement, and specify the variable name in parentheses.

LOWCASE Function

Uppercase letters in character values can be converted to lowercase by using the LOWCASE function. Include the function in an assignment statement, and specify the variable name in parentheses.

PROPCASE Function

Character values can be converted to proper case by using the PROPCASE function. Include the function in an assignment statement, and specify the variable name in parentheses. Remember that you can specify delimiters or use the default delimiters.

TRANWRD Function

You can replace or remove patterns of characters in the values of character variables by using the TRANWRD function. Use the function in an assignment statement, and specify the source, target, and replacement strings or variables in parentheses.

INT Function

To return the integer portion of a numeric value, use the INT function. Any decimal portion of the INT function argument is discarded.

ROUND Function

To round values to the nearest specified unit, use the ROUND function. If a round-off unit is not provided, the argument is rounded to the nearest integer.

Nesting SAS Functions

To write more efficient programs, you can **nest functions** as appropriate. You can nest any functions as long as the function that is used as the argument meets the requirements for the argument.

Points to Remember

- Even if a function doesn't require arguments, the function name must still be followed by parentheses.

- When specifying a variable list or an array as a function argument, be sure to precede the list or the array with the word OF.

- To remember which function requires a format versus an informat, note that the **IN**PUT function requires the **in**format.

- If you specify an invalid date in the MDY function, a missing value is assigned to the target variable.

- The SCAN function treats contiguous delimiters as one delimiter; leading delimiters have no effect.

- When using the SCAN function, you can save storage space by adding a LENGTH statement to your DATA step to set an appropriate length for your new variable(s). Place the LENGTH statement before the assignment statements that contain the SCAN function.

- When the SUBSTR function is on the left side of an assignment statement, it replaces variable values. When SUBSTR is on the right side of an assignment statement, it extracts variable values. The syntax of the function is the same; only the placement of the function changes.

- The INDEX function is case sensitive. To ensure that all forms of a character string are found, use the UPCASE or LOWCASE function with the INDEX function.

Practice

After you complete this chapter, practice what you learned by using the sample data and SAS programs for Chapter 14, **Transforming Data with SAS Functions**, which are located on the CD-ROM. Follow the directions for creating your sample data in the Before You Begin section.

Quiz

Select the best answer for each question. After completing the quiz, check your answers using the answer key in the appendix.

1. Which function calculates the average of the variables `Var1`, `Var2`, `Var3`, and `Var4`?

    a. `mean(var1,var4)`

    b. `mean(var1-var4)`

    c. `mean(of var1,var4)`

    d. `mean(of var1-var4)`

2. Within the data set **Hrd.Temp**, `PayRate` is a character variable and `Hours` is a numeric variable. What happens when the following program is run?

    ```
    data work.temp;
        set hrd.temp;
        Salary=payrate*hours;
    run;
    ```

    a. SAS converts the values of `PayRate` to numeric values. No message is written to the log.

    b. SAS converts the values of `PayRate` to numeric values. A message is written to the log.

    c. SAS converts the values of `Hours` to character values. No message is written to the log.

    d. SAS converts the values of `Hours` to character values. A message is written to the log.

3. A typical value for the character variable `Target` is *123,456*. Which statement correctly converts the values of `Target` to numeric values when creating the variable `TargetNo`?

    a. `TargetNo=input(target,comma6.);`

    b. `TargetNo=input(target,comma7.);`

    c. `TargetNo=put(target,comma6.);`

    d. `TargetNo=put(target,comma7.);`

4. A typical value for the numeric variable `SiteNum` is *12.3*. Which statement correctly converts the values of `SiteNum` to character values when creating the variable `Location`?

    a. `Location=dept||'/'||input(sitenum,3.1);`

    b. `Location=dept||'/'||input(sitenum,4.1);`

    c. `Location=dept||'/'||put(sitenum,3.1);`

    d. `Location=dept||'/'||put(sitenum,4.1);`

5. Suppose the YEARCUTOFF= system option is set to 1920. Which MDY function creates the date value for January 3, 2020?

    a. `MDY(1,3,20)`

    b. `MDY(3,1,20)`

    c. `MDY(1,3,2020)`

    d. `MDY(3,1,2020)`

6. The variable `Address2` contains values such as *Piscataway, NJ*. How do you assign the two-letter state abbreviations to a new variable named `State`?

   a. `State=scan(address2,2);`

   b. `State=scan(address2,13,2);`

   c. `State=substr(address2,2);`

   d. `State=substr(address2,13,2);`

7. The variable `IDCode` contains values such as *123FA* and *321MB*. The fourth character identifies sex. How do you assign these character codes to a new variable named `Sex`?

   a. `Sex=scan(idcode,4);`

   b. `Sex=scan(idcode,4,1);`

   c. `Sex=substr(idcode,4);`

   d. `Sex=substr(idcode,4,1);`

8. Due to growth within the 919 area code, the telephone exchange 555 is being reassigned to the 920 area code. The data set **Clients.Piedmont** includes the variable `Phone`, which contains telephone numbers in the form *919-555-1234*. Which of the following programs will correctly change the values of `Phone`?

   a.
   ```
   data work.piedmont(drop=areacode exchange);
       set clients.piedmont;
       Areacode=substr(phone,1,3);
       Exchange=substr(phone,5,3);
       if areacode='919' and exchange='555'
           then scan(phone,1,3)='920';
   run;
   ```

   b.
   ```
   data work.piedmont(drop=areacode exchange);
       set clients.piedmont;
       Areacode=substr(phone,1,3);
       Exchange=substr(phone,5,3);
       if areacode='919' and exchange='555'
           then phone=scan('920',1,3);
   run;
   ```

   c.
   ```
   data work.piedmont(drop=areacode exchange);
       set clients.piedmont;
       Areacode=substr(phone,1,3);
       Exchange=substr(phone,5,3);
       if areacode='919' and exchange='555'
           then substr(phone,1,3)='920';
   run;
   ```

   d.
   ```
   data work.piedmont(drop=areacode exchange);
       set clients.piedmont;
       Areacode=substr(phone,1,3);
       Exchange=substr(phone,5,3);
       if areacode='919' and exchange='555'
           then phone=substr('920',1,3);
   run;
   ```

9. Suppose you need to create the variable `FullName` by concatenating the values of `FirstName`, which contains first names, and `LastName`, which contains last names. What's the best way to remove extra blanks between first names and last names?

    a.
    ```
    data work.maillist;
        set retail.maillist;
        length FullName $ 40;
        fullname=trim firstname||' '||lastname;
    run;
    ```

    b.
    ```
    data work.maillist;
        set retail.maillist;
        length FullName $ 40;
        fullname=trim(firstname)||' '||lastname;
    run;
    ```

    c.
    ```
    data work.maillist;
        set retail.maillist;
        length FullName $ 40;
        fullname=trim(firstname)||' '||trim(lastname);
    run;
    ```

    d.
    ```
    data work.maillist;
        set retail.maillist;
        length FullName $ 40;
        fullname=trim(firstname||' '||lastname);
    run;
    ```

10. Within the data set **Furnitur.Bookcase**, the variable `Finish` contains values such as *ash/cherry/teak/matte-black*. Which of the following creates a subset of the data in which the values of `Finish` contain the string *walnut*? Make the search for the string case-insensitive.

    a.
    ```
    data work.bookcase;
        set furnitur.bookcase;
        if index(finish,walnut) = 0;
    run;
    ```

    b.
    ```
    data work.bookcase;
        set furnitur.bookcase;
        if index(finish,'walnut') > 0;
    run;
    ```

    c.
    ```
    data work.bookcase;
        set furnitur.bookcase;
        if index(lowcase(finish),walnut) = 0;
    run;
    ```

    d.
    ```
    data work.bookcase;
        set furnitur.bookcase;
        if index(lowcase(finish),'walnut') > 0;
    run;
    ```

15 Generating Data with DO Loops

Overview

Introduction

You can execute SAS statements repeatedly by placing them in a **DO loop**. DO loops can execute any number of times in a single iteration of the DATA step. Using DO loops enables you to write concise DATA steps that are easier to change and debug.

For example, the DO loop in this program eliminates the need for 12 separate programming statements to calculate annual earnings:

```
data finance.earnings;
   set finance.master;
   Earned=0;
   do count=1 to 12;
      earned+(amount+earned)*(rate/12);
   end;
run;
```

You can also use DO loops to

- generate data

- conditionally execute statements

- read data.

This chapter shows you how to construct DO loops and how to include DO loops in your programs.

Objectives

In this chapter, you learn to

- construct a DO loop to perform repetitive calculations

- control the execution of a DO loop

- generate multiple observations in one iteration of the DATA step

- construct nested DO loops.

Constructing DO Loops

Introduction

DO loops process a group of statements repeatedly rather than once. This can greatly reduce the number of statements required for a repetitive calculation. For example, these 12 Sum statements compute a company's annual earnings from investments. Notice that all 12 statements are identical.

```
data finance.earnings;
   set finance.master;
   Earned=0;
   earned+(amount+earned)*(rate/12);
   earned+(amount+earned)*(rate/12);
```

```
        earned+(amount+earned)*(rate/12);
        earned+(amount+earned)*(rate/12);
        earned+(amount+earned)*(rate/12);
        earned+(amount+earned)*(rate/12);
        earned+(amount+earned)*(rate/12);
        earned+(amount+earned)*(rate/12);
        earned+(amount+earned)*(rate/12);
        earned+(amount+earned)*(rate/12);
        earned+(amount+earned)*(rate/12);
        earned+(amount+earned)*(rate/12);
    run;
```

Each Sum statement accumulates the calculated interest earned for an investment for one month. The variable `Earned` is created in the DATA step to store the earned interest. The investment is compounded monthly, meaning that the value of the earned interest is cumulative.

A DO loop enables you to achieve the same results with fewer statements. In this case, the Sum statement executes 12 times within the DO loop during each iteration of the DATA step.

```
data finance.earnings;
    set finance.master;
    Earned=0;
    do count=1 to 12;
        earned+(amount+earned)*(rate/12);
    end;
run;
```

General Form of DO Loops

To construct a DO loop, you use the DO and END statements along with other SAS statements.

General form, simple iterative DO loop:

> **DO** *index-variable=start* **TO** *stop* **BY** *increment*;
> *SAS statements*
> **END;**

where the *start*, *stop*, and *increment* values

- are set upon entry into the DO loop
- cannot be changed during the processing of the DO loop
- can be numbers, variables, or SAS expressions.

The **END** statement terminates the loop.

The value of the index variable can be changed within the loop.

When creating a DO loop with the iterative DO statement, you must specify an **index variable**. The index variable stores the value of the current iteration of the DO loop. You can use any valid SAS name.

```
DO index-variable=start TO stop BY increment;
    SAS statements
END;
```

Next, specify the conditions that execute the DO loop. A simple **specification** contains a **start value**, a **stop value**, and an **increment value** for the DO loop.

```
DO index-variable=start TO stop BY increment;
    SAS statements
END;
```

The start value specifies the initial value of the index variable.

```
DO index-variable=start TO stop BY increment;
    SAS statements
END;
```

The TO clause specifies the stop value. The stop value is the last index value that executes the DO loop.

```
DO index-variable=start TO stop BY increment;
    SAS statements
END;
```

The optional BY clause specifies an increment value for the index variable. Typically, you want the DO loop to increment by 1 for each iteration. If you do not specify a BY clause, the default increment value is *1*.

```
DO index-variable=start TO stop BY increment;
    SAS statements
END;
```

For example, the specification below increments the index variable by 1, resulting in `quiz` values of *1, 2, 3, 4,* and *5*:

```
do quiz=1 to 5;
```

By contrast, the following specification increments the index variable by 2, resulting in `rows` values of *2, 4, 6, 8, 10,* and *12*:

```
do rows=2 to 12 by 2;
```

DO Loop Execution

Using the form of the DO loop that was just presented, let's see how the DO loop executes in the DATA step. This example calculates how much interest was earned each month for a one-year investment.

```
data finance.earnings;
    Amount=1000;
    Rate=.075/12;
    do month=1 to 12;
        Earned+(amount+earned)*(rate);
    end;
run;
```

This DATA step does not read data from an external source. When submitted, it compiles and then executes only once to generate data. During compilation, the program data vector is created for the **Finance.Earnings** data set.

Program Data Vector

N	Amount	Rate	month	Earned
.	.	.	.	.

When the DATA step executes, the values of Amount and Rate are assigned.

Program Data Vector

N	Amount	Rate	month	Earned
1	1000	0.00625	•	•

Next, the DO loop executes. During each execution of the DO loop, the value of Earned is calculated and is added to its previous value; then the value of month is incremented. On the twelfth execution of the DO loop, the program data vector looks like this:

Program Data Vector

N	Amount	Rate	month	Earned
1	1000	0.00625	12	77.6326

After the twelfth execution of the DO loop, the value of month is incremented to 13. Because 13 exceeds the stop value of the iterative DO statement, the DO loop stops executing, and processing continues to the next DATA step statement. The end of the DATA step is reached, the values are written to the **Finance.Earnings** data set, and in this example, the DATA step ends. Only one observation is written to the data set.

SAS Data Set Finance.Earnings

Amount	Rate	month	Earned
1000	0.00625	13	77.6326

Notice that the index variable month is also stored in the data set. In most cases, the index variable is needed only for processing the DO loop and can be dropped from the data set.

Counting Iterations of DO Loops

In some cases, it is useful to create an index variable to count and store the number of iterations in the DO loop. Then you can drop the index variable from the data set.

```
data work.earn (drop=counter);
   Value=2000;
   do counter=1 to 20;
       Interest=value*.075;
       value+interest;
       Year+1;
   end;
run;
```

SAS Data Set Work.Earn

Value	Interest	Year
8495.70	592.723	20

The Sum statement Year+1 accumulates the number of iterations of the DO loop and stores the total in the new variable Year. The final value of Year is then stored in the data set, whereas the index variable counter is dropped. The data set has one observation.

Explicit OUTPUT Statements

To create an observation for each iteration of the DO loop, place an OUTPUT statement inside the loop. By default, every DATA step contains an implicit OUTPUT statement at the end of the step. But placing an explicit OUTPUT statement in a DATA step overrides automatic output, causing SAS to add an observation to the data set only when the explicit OUTPUT statement is executed.

The previous example created one observation because it used automatic output at the end of the DATA step. In the following example, the OUTPUT statement overrides automatic output, so the DATA step writes 20 observations.

SAS Data Set Work.Earn
(Partial Listing)

Value	Year	Interest
2150.00	1	150.000
2311.25	2	161.250
2484.59	3	173.344
2670.94	4	186.345
2871.26	5	200.320
3086.60	6	215.344
3318.10	7	231.495
3566.96	8	248.857
...	...	...
8495.70	20	592.723

```
data work.earn;
   Value=2000;
   do Year=1 to 20;
        Interest=value*.075;
        value+interest;
        output;
   end;
run;
```

Decrementing DO Loops

You can decrement a DO loop's index variable by specifying a negative value for the BY clause. For example, the specification in this iterative DO statement decreases the index variable by 1, resulting in values of *5, 4, 3, 2,* and *1.*

```
DO index-variable=5 to 1 by -1;
   SAS statements
END;
```

When you use a negative BY clause value, the start value must always be greater than the stop value in order to decrease the index variable during each iteration.

```
DO index-variable=5 to 1 by -1;
   SAS statements
END;
```

Specifying a Series of Items

You can also specify how many times a DO loop executes by listing items in a series.

General form, DO loop with a variable list:

> **DO** *index-variable=value1, value2, value3...;*
> *SAS statements*
> **END;**

where *values* can be character or numeric.

When the DO loop executes, it executes once for each item in the series. The index variable equals the value of the current item. You must use commas to separate items in the series.

To list items in a series, you must specify either

- all numeric values

```
DO index-variable=2,5,9,13,27;
   SAS statements
END;
```

- all character values, with each value enclosed in quotation marks

```
DO index-variable='MON','TUE','WED','THR','FRI';
   SAS statements
END;
```

- all variable names—the index variable takes on the values of the specified variables.

```
DO index-variable=win,place,show;
   SAS statements
END;
```

Variable names must represent either all numeric or all character values. Do **not** enclose variable names in quotation marks.

Nesting DO Loops

Iterative DO statements can be executed within a DO loop. Putting a DO loop within a DO loop is called **nesting**.

```
do i=1 to 20;
   SAS statements
   do j=1 to 10;
      SAS statements
   end;
   SAS statements
end;
```

The following DATA step computes the value of a one-year investment that earns 7.5% annual interest, compounded monthly.

```
data work.earn;
   Capital=2000;
   do month=1 to 12;
      Interest=capital*(.075/12);
      capital+interest;
   end;
run;
```

Let's assume the same amount of capital is to be added to the investment each year for 20 years. The new program must perform the calculation for each month during each of the 20 years. To do this, you can include the monthly calculations within another DO loop that executes 20 times.

```
data work.earn;
   do year=1 to 20;
      Capital+2000;
      do month=1 to 12;
         Interest=capital*(.075/12);
         capital+interest;
      end;
   end;
run;
```

During each iteration of the outside DO loop, an additional 2,000 is added to the capital, and the nested DO loop executes 12 times.

```
data work.earn;
   do year=1 to 20;
      Capital+2000;
      do month=1 to 12;
         Interest=capital*(.075/12);
         capital+interest;
      end;
   end;
run;
```

Remember, in order for nested DO loops to execute correctly, you must

- assign a unique index-variable name in each iterative DO statement.

```
data work.earn;
   do year=1 to 20;
      Capital+2000;
      do month=1 to 12;
         Interest=capital*(.075/12);
         capital+interest;
      end;
   end;
run;
```

- end each DO loop with an END statement.

```
data work.earn;
   do year=1 to 20;
      Capital+2000;
      do month=1 to 12;
         Interest=capital*(.075/12);
         capital+interest;
      end;
   end;
run;
```

 It is easier to manage nested DO loops if you indent the statements in each DO loop as shown above.

Iteratively Processing Data That Is Read from a Data Set

So far you have seen examples of DATA steps that use DO loops to generate one or more observations from one iteration of the DATA step. Now let's look at a DATA step that reads a data set to compute the value of a new variable.

The SAS data set **Finance.CDRates**, shown below, contains interest rates for certificates of deposit (CDs) that are available from several institutions.

SAS Data Set Finance.CDRates

Institution	Rate	Years
MBNA America	0.0817	5
Metropolitan Bank	0.0814	3
Standard Pacific	0.0806	4

Suppose you want to compare how much each CD will earn at maturity with an investment of $5,000. The DATA step below creates a new data set, **Work.Compare**, that contains the added variable, Investment.

```
data work.compare(drop=i);
    set finance.cdrates;
    Investment=5000;
    do i=1 to years;
        investment+rate*investment;
    end;
run;
```

SAS Data Set Work.Compare

Institution	Rate	Years	Investment

The index variable is used only to execute the DO loop, so it is dropped from the new data set. Notice that the data set variable Years is used as the stop value in the iterative DO statement. As a result, the DO loop executes the number of times that are specified by the current value of Years. During the first iteration of the DATA step, for example, the DO loop executes five times.

During each iteration of the DATA step,

- an observation is read from **Finance.CDRates**

- the value *5000* is assigned to the variable Investment

- the DO loop executes, based on the current value of Years

- the value of Investment is computed (each time that the DO loop executes), using the current value of Rate.

At the bottom of the DATA step, the first observation is written to the **Work.Compare** data set. Control returns to the top of the DATA step, and the next observation is read from **Finance.CDRates**. These steps are repeated for each observation in **Finance.CDRates**. The resulting data set contains the computed values of Investment for all observations that have been read from **Finance.CDRates**.

SAS Data Set Work.Compare

Institution	Rate	Years	Investment
MBNA America	0.0817	5	7404.64
Metropolitan Bank	0.0814	3	6323.09
Standard Pacific	0.0806	4	6817.57

Conditionally Executing DO Loops

The iterative DO statement requires that you specify the number of iterations for the DO loop. However, there are times when you want to execute a DO loop until a condition is reached or while a condition exists, but you don't know how many iterations are needed.

Suppose you want to calculate the number of years that are required for an investment to reach $50,000. In the DATA step below, using an iterative DO statement is inappropriate because you are trying to determine the number of iterations required for Capital to reach $50,000.

```
data work.invest;
   do year=1 to ? ;
       Capital+2000;
       capital+capital*.10;
   end;
run;
```

The DO WHILE and DO UNTIL statements enable you to execute DO loops based on whether a condition is true or false.

Using the DO UNTIL Statement

The DO UNTIL statement executes a DO loop **until** the expression is true.

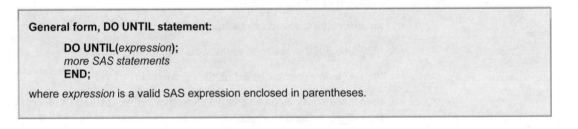

General form, DO UNTIL statement:

    DO UNTIL(*expression*);
    more SAS statements
    END;

where *expression* is a valid SAS expression enclosed in parentheses.

The expression is not evaluated until the bottom of the loop, so a DO UNTIL loop always executes at least once. When the expression is evaluated as true, the DO loop is not executed again.

Assume you want to know how many years it will take to earn $50,000 if you deposit $2,000 each year into an account that earns 10% interest. The DATA step that follows uses a DO UNTIL statement to perform the calculation until the value is reached. Each iteration of the DO loop represents one year of earning.

```
data work.invest;
   do until(Capital>=50000);
      capital+2000;
      capital+capital*.10;
      Year+1;
   end;
run;
```

During each iteration of the DO loop,

- *2000* is added to the value of `Capital` to reflect the annual deposit of $2,000

- the value of `Capital` with 10% interest is calculated

- the value of `Year` is incremented by 1.

Because there is no index variable in the DO UNTIL statement, the variable `Year` is created in a Sum statement to count the number of iterations of the DO loop. This program produces a data set that contains the single observation shown below. To accumulate more than $50,000 in capital requires 13 years (and 13 iterations of the DO loop).

SAS Data Set Work.Invest

Capital	Year
53949.97	13

Using the DO WHILE Statement

Like the DO UNTIL statement, the DO WHILE statement executes DO loops conditionally. You can use the DO WHILE statement to execute a DO loop **while** the expression is true.

General form, DO WHILE statement:

> **DO WHILE(***expression***);**
> *more SAS statements*
> **END;**

where *expression* is a valid SAS expression enclosed in parentheses.

An important difference between the DO UNTIL and DO WHILE statements is that the DO WHILE expression is evaluated at the top of the DO loop. If the expression is false the first time it is evaluated, then the DO loop never executes. For example, in the following program, if the value of `Capital` is less than 50,000, the DO loop does not execute.

```
data work.invest;
   do while(Capital>=50000);
      capital+2000;
      capital+capital*.10;
      Year+1;
   end;
run;
```

Using Conditional Clauses with the Iterative DO Statement

You have seen how the DO WHILE and DO UNTIL statements enable you to execute statements conditionally and how the iterative DO statement enables you to execute statements a set number of times, unconditionally.

```
DO WHILE(expression);
DO UNTIL(expression);
DO index-variable=start TO stop BY increment;
```

Now let's look at a form of the iterative DO statement that combines features of both conditional and unconditional execution of DO loops.

In this DATA step, the DO UNTIL statement determines how many years it takes (13) for an investment to reach $50,000.

```
data work.invest;
   do until(Capital>=50000);
      Year+1;
      capital+2000;
      capital+capital*.10;
   end;
run;
```

SAS Data Set Work.Invest

Capital	Year
53949.97	13

Suppose you also want to limit the number of years that you invest your capital to 10 years. You can add the UNTIL or WHILE expression to an iterative DO statement to further control the number of iterations. This iterative DO statement enables you to execute the DO loop until Capital is greater than or equal to *50000* or until the DO loop executes 10 times, whichever occurs first.

```
data work.invest(drop=i);
   do i=1 to 10 until(Capital>=50000);
      Year+1;
      capital+2000;
      capital+capital*.10;
   end;
run;
```

SAS Data Set Work.Invest

Capital	Year
35062.33	10

In this case, the DO loop stops executing after 10 iterations, and the value of Capital never reaches *50000*. If you increase the amount added to Capital each year to *4000*, the DO loop stops executing after the eighth iteration when the value of Capital exceeds *50000*.

```
data work.invest(drop=i);
   do i=1 to 10 until(Capital>=50000);
      Year+1;
      capital+4000;
      capital+capital*.10;
   end;
run;
```

SAS Data Set Work.Invest

Capital	Year
50317.91	8

The UNTIL and WHILE specifications in an iterative DO statement function similarly to the DO UNTIL and DO WHILE statements. Both statements require a valid SAS expression enclosed in parentheses.

UNTIL(*expression*);

DO *index-variable*=start TO *stop* BY *increment* **WHILE(*expression*);**

The UNTIL expression is evaluated at the **bottom** of the DO loop, so the DO loop always executes at least once. The WHILE expression is evaluated **before** the execution of the DO loop. So, if the condition is not true, the DO loop never executes.

Creating Samples

Because it performs iterative processing, a DO loop provides an easy way to draw sample observations from a data set. For example, suppose you would like to sample every tenth observation of the 5,000 observations in **Factory.Widgets**. Start with a simple DATA step:

```
data work.subset;
   set factory.widgets;
run;
```

You can create the sample data set by enclosing the SET statement in a DO loop. Use the start, stop, and increment values to select every tenth observation of the 5,000. Add the POINT= option to the SET statement, setting the POINT= option equal to the index variable that is used in the DO loop. (You learned about the POINT= option in Chapter 12, **Reading SAS Data Sets**.)

```
data work.subset;
   do sample=10 to 5000 by 10;
      set factory.widgets point=sample;
   end;
run;
```

Remember that, in order to prevent continuous DATA step looping, you need to add a STOP statement when using the POINT= option. Then, because the STOP statement prevents the output of observations at the end of the DATA step, you also need to add an OUTPUT statement. Place the statement inside the DO loop in order to output each observation that is selected. (If the OUTPUT statement were placed after the DO loop, only the last observation would be written.)

```
data work.subset;
   do sample=10 to 5000 by 10;
      set factory.widgets point=sample;
      output;
   end;
   stop;
run;
```

When the program runs, the DATA step reads the observations that are identified by the POINT= option in **Factory.Widgets**. The values of the POINT= option are provided by the DO loop, which starts at 10 and goes to 5,000 in increments of 10. The data set **Work.Subset** contains 500 observations.

Summary

Text Summary

Purpose of DO Loops

DO loops process groups of SAS statements repeatedly, reducing the number of statements that are required in repetitive calculations.

Syntax of Iterative DO Loops

To construct an iterative DO loop, specify an **index variable** and the conditions that will execute the loop. These conditions include a start value for the index variable, a stop value, and an increment value. Start, stop, and increment values can be any number, numeric variable, or SAS expression that results in a number.

DO Loop Execution

During each iteration of a DO loop, new values are created in the SAS program data vector. When the loop's index value exceeds the stop value, the DO loop stops, and processing continues with the following DATA step statement.

Counting DO Loop Iterations

A simple way to track DO loop iterations is to create a temporary counting variable, then drop this variable from the data set. Or, include an OUTPUT statement within the DO loop to write an observation for each iteration. This overrides the automatic generation of output at the end of the DATA step.

Decrementing DO Loops

You can decrement a DO loop by specifying a negative value for the BY clause. The start value must be greater than the stop value.

Specifying a Series of Items

You can specify how many times a DO loop executes by listing items in a series; the DO loop will execute once for each item, with the index variable equal to the value of each item. A series can consist of all numeric values, all character values (enclosed in quotation marks), or all variable names (without quotation marks).

Nesting DO Loops

DO loops can run within DO loops, as long as you assign a unique index variable to each loop and terminate each DO loop with its own END statement.

Iteratively Processing Data That Is Read from a Data Set

You can use a DO loop to read a data set and compute the value of a new variable. DO loop start and stop values, for example, can be read from a data set.

Conditionally Executing DO Loops

The **DO UNTIL** statement executes a DO loop until a condition is true. Because the expression is not evaluated until the bottom of the loop, a DO UNTIL loop will execute at least once. The **DO WHILE** statement is used to execute a DO loop while a condition is true. Because the DO WHILE statement is evaluated at the top of the DO loop, if the expression is false the first time it is evaluated, then the DO loop never executes.

Using Conditional Clauses within Iterative DO Statements

DO WHILE and DO UNTIL statements can be used within iterative DO loops to combine conditional and unconditional execution.

Creating Samples

DO loops provide an easy way to create samples from other data sets. Enclose the SET statement in a DO loop, using the start, stop, and increment values to select the observations. Add the POINT= option to the SET statement, setting it equal to the index variable of the DO loop. Then add a STOP statement to prevent DATA step looping, and add an OUTPUT statement to write DATA step output.

Points to Remember

- If you do not specify a BY clause, then the increment value for DO loops is 1.

- In most cases, the index variable is needed only for processing the DO loop and can be dropped from the data set.

- The index variable is always incremented by one value beyond the stop value unless you terminate the DO loop in some other manner.

- It's easier to manage nested DO loops if you indent the statements in each loop.

- In order for nested DO loops to execute correctly, you must

  o   assign a unique index-variable name in each iterative DO statement

  o   end each DO loop with an END statement.

Practice

After you complete this chapter, practice what you learned by using the sample data and SAS programs for Chapter 15, **Generating Data with DO Loops**, which are located on the CD-ROM. Follow the directions for creating your sample data in the Before You Begin section.

Quiz

Select the best answer for each question. After completing the quiz, check your answers using the answer key in the appendix.

1. Which statement is **false** regarding the use of DO loops?

   a. They can contain conditional clauses.

   b. They can generate multiple observations.

   c. They can be used to combine DATA and PROC steps.

   d. They can be used to read data.

2. During each execution of the following DO loop, the value of Earned is calculated and is added to its previous value. How many times does this DO loop execute?

   ```
   data finance.earnings;
      Amount=1000;
      Rate=.075/12;
      do month=1 to 12;
         Earned+(amount+earned)*rate;
      end;
   run;
   ```

   a. 0

   b. 1

   c. 12

   d. 13

3. On January 1 of each year, $5,000 is invested in an account. Complete the DATA step below to determine the value of the account after 15 years if a constant interest rate of 10% is expected.

   ```
   data work.invest;
      ...
         Capital+5000;
         capital+(capital*.10);
      end;
   run;
   ```

   a. do count=1 to 15;

   b. do count=1 to 15 by 10%;

   c. do count=1 to capital;

   d. do count=capital to (capital*.10);

4. In the data set **Work.Invest**, what would be the stored value for `Year`?

```
data work.invest;
   do year=1990 to 2004;
      Capital+5000;
      capital+(capital*.10);
   end;
run;
```

   a. missing

   b. *1990*

   c. *2004*

   d. *2005*

5. Which of the following statements is **false** regarding the program shown below?

```
data work.invest;
   do year=1990 to 2004;
      Capital+5000;
      capital+(capital*.10);
      output;
   end;
run;
```

   a. The OUTPUT statement writes current values to the data set immediately.

   b. The stored value for `Year` is *2005*.

   c. The OUTPUT statement overrides the automatic output at the end of the DATA step.

   d. The DO loop performs 15 iterations.

6. How many observations will the data set **Work.Earn** contain?

```
data work.earn;
   Value=2000;
   do year=1 to 20;
      Interest=value*.075;
      value+interest;
      output;
   end;
run;
```

   a. 0

   b. 1

   c. 19

   d. 20

7. Which of the following would you use to compare the result of investing $4,000 a year for five years in three different banks that compound interest monthly? Assume a fixed rate for the five-year period.

   a. DO WHILE statement
   b. nested DO loops
   c. DO UNTIL statement
   d. a DO group

8. Which statement is **false** regarding DO UNTIL statements?

   a. The condition is evaluated at the top of the loop, before the enclosed statements are executed.
   b. The enclosed statements are always executed at least once.
   c. SAS statements in the DO loop are executed until the specified condition is true.
   d. The DO loop must have a closing END statement.

9. Select the DO WHILE statement that would generate the same result as the program below.

```
data work.invest;
capital=100000;
   do until(Capital gt 500000);
      Year+1;
      capital+(capital*.10);
   end;
run;
```

   a. do while(Capital ge 500000);
   b. do while(Capital=500000);
   c. do while(Capital le 500000);
   d. do while(Capital<500000);

10. In the following program, complete the statement so that the program stops generating observations when Distance reaches 250 miles or when 10 gallons of fuel have been used.

```
data work.go250;
   set perm.cars;
   do gallons=1 to 10 ... ;
      Distance=gallons*mpg;
      output;
   end;
run;
```

   a. while(Distance<250)
   b. when(Distance>250)
   c. over(Distance le 250)
   d. until(Distance=250)

Chapter 16 Processing Variables with Arrays

Overview

Introduction

In DATA step programming, you often need to perform the same action on more than one variable. Although you can process variables individually, it is easier to handle them as a group. You can do this by using array processing.

For example, using an array and DO loop, the program below eliminates the need for 365 separate programming statements to convert the daily temperature from Fahrenheit to Celsius for the year.

```
data work.report (drop=i);
   set master.temps;
   array daytemp{365} day1-day365;
   do i=1 to 365;
      daytemp{i}=5*(daytemp{i}-32)/9;
   end;
run;
```

You can use arrays to simplify the code needed to

- perform repetitive calculations

- create many variables that have the same attributes

- read data

- rotate SAS data sets by changing variables to observations or observations to variables

- compare variables

- perform a table lookup.

This chapter teaches you how to define an array and how to reference elements of the array in the DATA step.

Objectives

In this chapter, you learn to

- group variables into one- and two-dimensional arrays

- perform an action on array elements

- create new variables with an ARRAY statement

- assign initial values to array elements

- create temporary array elements with an ARRAY statement.

Creating One-Dimensional Arrays

Understanding SAS Arrays

A SAS **array** is a temporary grouping of SAS variables under a single name. An array exists only for the duration of the DATA step.

One reason for using an array is to reduce the number of statements that are required for processing variables. For example, in the DATA step below, the values of seven data set variables are converted from Fahrenheit to Celsius temperatures.

```
data work.report;
   set master.temps;
   mon=5*(mon-32)/9;
   tue=5*(tue-32)/9;
   wed=5*(wed-32)/9;
   thr=5*(thr-32)/9;
   fri=5*(fri-32)/9;
   sat=5*(sat-32)/9;
   sun=5*(sun-32)/9;
run;
```

As you can see, the assignment statements perform the same calculation on each variable in this series of statements. Only the name of the variable changes in each statement.

By grouping the variables into a one-dimensional array, you can process the variables in a DO loop. You use fewer statements, and the DATA step program is more easily modified or corrected.

```
data work.report(drop=i);
   set master.temps;
   array wkday{7} mon tue wed thr fri sat sun;
   do i=1 to 7;
      wkday{i}=5*(wkday{i}-32)/9;
   end;
run;
```

You will learn other uses for arrays in this chapter.

General Form of an Array

To group previously defined data set variables into an array, use an ARRAY statement.

General form, ARRAY statement:

> **ARRAY** *array-name{dimension}* *<elements>*;

where

- *array-name* specifies the name of the array.
- *dimension* describes the number and arrangement of array elements. The default dimension is one.
- *elements* lists the variables to include in the array. Array elements must be either all numeric or all character. If no elements are listed, new variables will be created with default names.

 Do not give an array the same name as a variable in the same DATA step. Also, avoid using the name of a SAS function; the array will be correct, but you won't be able to use the function in the same DATA step, and a warning message will appear in the SAS log.

 You cannot use array names in LABEL, FORMAT, DROP, KEEP, or LENGTH statements. Arrays exist only for the duration of the DATA step. They do not become part of the output data set.

For example, in the data set **Finance.Sales91**, you might want to process the variables Qtr1, Qtr2, Qtr3, and Qtr4 in the same way.

Description of Finance.Sales91

Variable	Type	Length
SalesRep	char	8
Qtr1	num	8
Qtr2	num	8
Qtr3	num	8
Qtr4	num	8

Specifying the Array Name

To group the variables in the array, first give the array a **name**. In this example, make the array name sales.

```
array sales{4} qtr1 qtr2 qtr3 qtr4;
```

Specifying the Dimension

Following the array name, you must specify the **dimension** of the array. The dimension describes the number and arrangement of **elements** in the array. There are several ways to specify the dimension.

- In a one-dimensional array, you can simply specify the number of array elements. The array elements are the existing variables that you want to reference and process elsewhere in the DATA step.

```
array sales{4} qtr1 qtr2 qtr3 qtr4;
```

- The dimension of an array doesn't have to be the number of array elements. You can specify a range of values for the dimension when you define the array. For example, you can define the array sales as follows:

```
array sales{96:99} totals96 totals97 totals98 totals99;
```

- You can also indicate the dimension of a one-dimensional array by using an asterisk (*). This way, SAS determines the dimension of the array by counting the number of elements.

```
array sales{*} qtr1 qtr2 qtr3 qtr4;
```

- Enclose the dimension in either parentheses, braces, or brackets.

```
            ( )
array sales{4} qtr1 qtr2 qtr3 qtr4;
            [ ]
```

Specifying Array Elements

When specifying the elements of an array, you can list each **variable name** that you want to include in the array. When listing elements, separate each element with a space. As with all SAS statements, you end the ARRAY statement with a semicolon (;).

```
        array sales{4} qtr1 qtr2 qtr3 qtr4;
```

You can also specify array elements as a **variable list**. Here is an example of an ARRAY statement that groups the variables Qtr1 through Qtr4 into a one-dimensional array, using a variable list.

```
        array sales{4} qtr1-qtr4;
```

Let's look more closely at array elements that are specified as variable lists.

Variable Lists as Array Elements

You can specify variable lists in the forms shown below. Each type of variable list is explained in more detail following the table.

Variables	Form
a numbered range of variables	Var1-Var*n*
all numeric variables	_NUMERIC_
all character variables	_CHARACTER_
all variables	_ALL_

Specifying a Numbered Range of Variables

```
Qtr1 Qtr2 Qtr3 Qtr4 → Qtr1-Qtr4
```

When specifying a numbered range of variables,

- the variables must have the same name except for the last character or characters
- the last character of each variable must be numeric
- the variables must be numbered consecutively.

```
array sales{4} qtr1-qtr4;
```

In the preceding example, you would use `sales{4}` to reference `Qtr4`. However, the index of an array doesn't have to range from one to the number of array elements. You can specify a range of values for the index when you define the array. For example, you can define the array `sales` as follows:

```
array sales{96:99} totals96-totals99;
```

Specifying All Numeric Variables

```
Amount Rate Term → _NUMERIC_
```

NUMERIC specifies all numeric variables that have already been defined in the current DATA step.

```
array sales{*} _numeric_;
```

Specifying All Character Variables

```
FrstName LastName Address → _CHARACTER_
```

CHARACTER specifies all character variables that have already been defined in the current DATA step.

```
array sales{*} _character_;
```

Specifying All Variables

```
FrstName LastName Address Amount Rate Term → _ALL_
```

ALL specifies all variables of the same type (all character or all numeric) that have been defined in the current DATA step.

```
array sales{*} _all_;
```

Referencing Elements of an Array

Now let's look at some ways you can use arrays to process variables in the DATA step.

```
data work.report(drop=i);
   set master.temps;
   array wkday{7} mon tue wed thr fri sat sun;
   do i=1 to 7;
      if wkday{i}>95 then output;
   end;
run;
```

```
data work.weights(drop=i);
   set master.class;
   array wt{6} w1-w6;
   do i=1 to 6;
      wt{i}=wt{i}*2.2;
   end;
run;
```

```
data work.new(drop=i);
   set master.synyms;
   array term{9} also1-also9;
   do i=1 to 9;
      if term{i} ne ' ' then output;
   end;
run;
```

The ability to reference the elements of an array by an **index value** is what gives arrays their power. Typically, arrays are used with DO loops to process multiple variables and to perform repetitive calculations.

```
array quarter{4} jan apr jul oct;
do i=1 to 4;
   YearGoal=quarter{i}*1.2;
end;
```

When you define an array in a DATA step, an index value is assigned to each array element. The index values are assigned in the order of the array elements.

```
                   1    2    3    4
array quarter{4} jan apr jul oct;
do i=1 to 4;
   YearGoal=quarter{i}*1.2;
end;
```

You use an **array reference** to perform an action on an array element during execution. To reference an array element in the DATA step, specify the name of the array, followed by an index value enclosed in brackets.

> **General form, ARRAY reference:**
>
> *array-name{index value}*
>
> where *index value*
> - is enclosed in parentheses, braces, or brackets
> - specifies an integer, a numeric variable, or a SAS numeric expression
> - is within the lower and upper bounds of the dimension of the array.

When used in a DO loop, the index variable of the iterative DO statement can reference each element of the array.

```
array quarter {4} jan apr jul oct;
do i=1 to 4;
    YearGoal=qtr{i}*1.2;
end;
```

For example, the DO loop above increments the index variable i from the lower bound of the quarter array, *1*, to the upper bound, *4*. The following sequence illustrates this process:

```
               1
array quarter{4} jan apr jul oct;
do i=1 to 4;
    YearGoal=quarter{1}*1.2;
end;
```

```
                   2
    array quarter{4} jan apr jul oct;
    do i=1 to 4;
        YearGoal=quarter{2}*1.2;
    end;
```

```
                       3
        array quarter{4} jan apr jul oct;
        do i=1 to 4;
            YearGoal=quarter{3}*1.2;
        end;
```

```
                           4
            array quarter{4} jan apr jul oct;
            do i=1 to 4;
                YearGoal=quarter{4}*1.2;
            end;
```

During each iteration of the DO loop, quarter{i} refers to an element of the array quarter in the order listed.

Compilation and Execution

Let's look at another example of a DATA step that contains an array with a DO loop.

The Health Center of a company conducts a fitness class for its employees. Each week, participants are weighed so that they can monitor their progress. The weight data, currently stored in kilograms, needs to be converted to pounds.

SAS Data Set Hrd.Fitclass

Name	Weight1	Weight2	Weight3	Weight4	Weight5	Weight6
Alicia	69.6	68.9	68.8	67.4	66.0	66.2
Betsy	52.6	52.6	51.7	50.4	49.8	49.1
Brenda	68.6	67.6	67.0	66.4	65.8	65.2
Carl	67.6	66.6	66.0	65.4	64.8	64.2
Carmela	63.6	62.5	61.9	61.4	60.8	58.2
David	70.6	69.8	69.2	68.4	67.8	67.0

You can use a DO loop to update the variables `Weight1` through `Weight6` for each observation in the **Hrd.Fitclass** data set.

```
data hrd.convert;
   set hrd.fitclass;
   array wt{6} weight1-weight6;
   do i=1 to 6;
      wt{i}=wt{i}*2.2046;
   end;
run;
```

The `wt{i}` that appears on the right side of the equal sign (=) is an array reference, **not** a variable name, so it does not violate the rule against having the same variable and array name in a DATA step.

To understand how the DO loop processes the array elements, let's examine the compilation and execution phases of this DATA step.

During compilation, the program data vector is created for the **Hrd.Convert** data set.

Program Data Vector

N	Name	Weight1	Weight2	Weight3	Weight4	Weight5	Weight6	i

The DATA step is scanned for syntax errors. If there are any syntax errors in the ARRAY statement, they are detected at this time.

The index values of the array elements are assigned. Note that the array name and the array references are not included in the program data vector. The array name and array references exist only for the duration of the DATA step.

During the first iteration of the DATA step, the first observation in **Hrd.Fitclass** is read into the program data vector.

```
data hrd.convert;
    set hrd.fitclass;
    array wt{6} weight1-weight6;
    do i=1 to 6;
        wt{i}=wt{i}*2.2046;
    end;
run;
```

Program Data Vector

		wt{1}	wt{2}	wt{3}	wt{4}	wt{5}	wt{6}	
N	Name	Weight1	Weight2	Weight3	Weight4	Weight5	Weight6	i
1	Alicia	69.6	68.9	68.8	67.4	66.0	66.2	

Because the ARRAY statement is a compile-time only statement, it is ignored during execution. The DO loop is executed next.

During the first iteration of the DO loop, the index variable i is set to *1*. As a result, the array reference wt{*i*} becomes wt{*1*}. Because wt{*1*} refers to the first array element, Weight1, the value of Weight1 is converted from kilograms to pounds.

```
data hrd.convert;
    set hrd.fitclass;
    array wt{6} weight1-weight6;
    do i=1 to 6;
        wt{i}=wt{i}*2.2046;
    end;
run;
```

Program Data Vector

		wt{1}	wt{2}	wt{3}	wt{4}	wt{5}	wt{6}	
N	Name	Weight1	Weight2	Weight3	Weight4	Weight5	Weight6	i
1	Alicia	153.4	68.9	68.8	67.4	66.0	66.2	1

As the DATA step continues its DO loop iterations, the index variable i is changed from *1* to *2, 3, 4, 5,* and *6*, causing Weight2 through Weight6 to receive new values in the program data vector, as shown below.

```
data hrd.convert;
    set hrd.fitclass;
    array wt{6} weight1-weight6;
►   do i=1 to 6;
        wt{6}=wt{6}*2.2046;
    end;
run;
```

Program Data Vector

		wt(1)	wt(2)	wt(3)	wt(4)	wt(5)	wt(6)	
N_	Name	Weight1	Weight2	Weight3	Weight4	Weight5	Weight6	i
1	Alicia	153.4	151.9	151.7	148.6	145.5	145.9	6

Using the DIM Function in an Iterative DO Statement

You can also use the **DIM** function to return the number of elements in the array. When using DO loops to process arrays, you can use the DIM function in the TO clause of the iterative DO statement. For a one-dimensional array, specify the array name as the argument for the DIM function.

General form, DIM function:

DIM(*array-name*)

where *array-name* specifies the array.

In this example, `dim(wt)` returns a value of *6*.

```
data hrd.convert;
    set hrd.fitclass;
    array wt{*} weight1-weight6;
    do i=1 to dim(wt);
        wt{i}=wt{i}*2.2046;
    end;
run;
```

When you use the DIM function, you do not have to re-specify the stop value of an iterative DO statement if you change the dimension of the array.

```
data hrd.convert;                       data hrd.convert;
    set hrd.fitclass;                       set hrd.fitclass;
    array wt{*} weight1-weight6;            array wt{*} weight1-weight10;
    do i=1 to dim(wt);                      do i=1 to dim(wt);
        wt{i}=wt(i)*2.2046;                     wt{i}=wt{i}*2.2046;
    end;                                    end;
run;                                    run;
```

Expanding Your Use of Arrays

Creating Variables in an ARRAY Statement

So far you have learned several ways to reference existing variables in an ARRAY statement. You can also **create** variables in an ARRAY statement by omitting the array elements from the statement. Because you are not referencing existing variables, SAS automatically creates the variables for you and assigns default names to them.

> **General form, ARRAY statement to create new variables:**
>   **ARRAY** *array-name*{*dimension*};
> where
>
> - *array-name* specifies the name of the array.
> - *dimension* describes the number and arrangement of array elements. The default dimension is 1.

For example, suppose you need to calculate the weight gain or loss from week to week for each member of a fitness class, as shown below.

SAS Data Set Hrd.Convert

Name	Weight1	Weight2	Weight3	Weight4	Weight5	Weight6
Alicia	153.4	151.9	151.7	148.6	145.5	145.9
Betsy	116.0	116.0	114.0	111.1	109.8	108.2
Brenda	151.2	149.0	147.7	146.4	145.1	143.7
Carl	149.0	146.8	145.5	144.2	142.9	141.5
Carmela	140.2	137.8	136.5	135.4	134.0	128.3

You'd like to create variables that contain this weekly difference. To perform the calculation, you first group the variables Weight1 through Weight6 into an array.

```
data hrd.diff;
   set hrd.convert;
   array wt{6} weight1-weight6;
```

Next, you want to create the new variables to store the differences between the six recorded weights. You can use an additional ARRAY statement without elements to create the new variables.

```
data hrd.diff;
   set hrd.convert;
   array wt{6} weight1-weight6;
   array WgtDiff{5};
```

SAS Data Set Hrd.Convert

Name	Weight1	Weight2	Weight3	Weight4	Weight5	Weight6
Alicia	153.4	<-1->151.9	<-2->151.7	<-3->148.6	<-4->145.5	<-5->145.9
Betsy	116.0	116.0	114.0	111.1	109.8	108.2
Brenda	151.2	149.0	147.7	146.4	145.1	143.7
Carl	149.0	146.8	145.5	144.2	142.9	141.5
Carmela	140.2	137.8	136.5	135.4	134.0	128.3

Remember, when creating variables in an ARRAY statement, you do not need to specify array elements as long as you specify how many elements will be in the array.

```
array WgtDiff{5};
```

Creating Default Variable Names

SAS creates default variable names by concatenating the array name and the numbers 1, 2, 3, and so on, up to the array dimension.

```
              array WgtDiff{5};
```

```
       WgtDiff1  WgtDiff2  WgtDiff3  WgtDiff4  WgtDiff5
```

 If you prefer, you can specify individual variable names. To specify variable names, you list each name as an element of the array. The following ARRAY statement creates the numeric variables `Oct12`, `Oct19`, `Oct26`, `Nov02`, and `Nov09`.

```
  array WgtDiff{5} Oct12 Oct19 Oct26 Nov02 Nov09;
```

```
              array WgtDiff{5};
```

```
        Oct12   Oct19   Oct26   Nov02   Nov09
```

Creating Arrays of Character Variables

To create an array of character variables, add a dollar sign ($) after the array dimension.

```
array firstname{5} $;
```

By default, all character variables that are created in an ARRAY statement are assigned a length of 8. You can assign your own length by specifying the length after the dollar sign.

```
array firstname{5} $ 24;
```

The length that you specify is automatically assigned to all variables that are created by the ARRAY statement.

Using an ARRAY Statement with an Iterative DO Statement

During the compilation of the DATA step, the variables that this ARRAY statement creates are added to the program data vector and are stored in the resulting data set.

```
data hrd.diff;
   set hrd.convert;
   array wt{6} Weight1-Weight6;
   array WgtDiff{5};
```

Program Data Vector

N_	Name	Weight1	Weight2	Weight3	Weight4	Weight5	Weight6

WgtDiff1	WgtDiff2	WgtDiff3	WgtDiff4	WgtDiff5

When referencing the array elements, be careful not to confuse the **array references** `WgtDiff{1}` through `WgtDiff{5}` (note the braces) with the **variable names** `WgtDiff1` through `WgtDiff5`. The program data vector below shows the relationship between the array references and the corresponding variable names.

Program Data Vector

N_	Name	Weight1	Weight2	Weight3	Weight4	Weight5	Weight6

WgtDiff{1}	WgtDiff{2}	WgtDiff{3}	WgtDiff{4}	WgtDiff{5}
WgtDiff1	WgtDiff2	WgtDiff3	WgtDiff4	WgtDiff5

Now you can use a DO loop to calculate the differences between each of the recorded weights. Notice that each value of `WgtDiff{i}` is calculated by subtracting `wt{i}` from `wt(i+1)`. By manipulating the index variable, you can easily reference any array element.

```
data hrd.diff;
   set hrd.convert;
   array wt{6} weight1-weight6;
   array WgtDiff{5};
   do i=1 to 5;
      wgtdiff{i}=wt{i+1}-wt{i};
   end;
run;
```

A portion of the resulting data set is shown below.

SAS Data Set Hrd.Diff

Name	WgtDiff1	WgtDiff2	WgtDiff3	WgtDiff4	WgtDiff5
Alicia	-1.54322	-0.22046	-3.08644	-3.08644	0.44092
Betsy	0.00000	-1.98414	-2.86598	-1.32276	-1.54322
Brenda	-2.20460	-1.32276	-1.32276	-1.32276	-1.32276

Assigning Initial Values to Arrays

Sometimes it is useful to assign **initial values** to elements of an array when you define the array.

```
array goal{4} g1 g2 g3 g4 (initial values);
```

Here is an example:

```
array goal{4} g1 g2 g3 g4 (9000 9300 9600 9900);
```

To assign initial values in an ARRAY statement,

- place the values after the array elements

- specify one initial value for each corresponding array element

- separate each value with a comma or blank

- enclose the initial values in parentheses.

Enclose each character value in quotation marks.

```
array col{3} $ color1-color3 ('red','green','blue');
```

It's also possible to assign initial values to an array without specifying each array element. The following statement creates the variables Var1, Var2, Var3, and Var4, and assigns them initial values of *1*, *2*, *3*, and *4*:

```
array Var{4} (1 2 3 4);
```

For this example, assume that you have the task of comparing the actual sales figures in the **Finance.Qsales** data set to the sales goals for each sales representative at the beginning of the year. The sales goals are not recorded in **Finance.Qsales**.

Description of Finance.Qsales

Variable	Type	Length
SalesRep	char	8
Sales1	num	8
Sales2	num	8
Sales3	num	8
Sales4	num	8

The DATA step below reads the **Finance.Qsales** data set to create the **Finance.Report** data set. The ARRAY statement creates an array to process sales data for each quarter.

```
data finance.report;
   set finance.qsales;
   array sale{4} sales1-sales4;
```

To compare the actual sales to the sales goals, you must create the variables for the sales goals and assign values to them.

```
data finance.report;
   set finance.qsales;
   array sale{4} sales1-sales4;
   array Goal{4} (9000 9300 9600 9900);
```

A third ARRAY statement creates the variables Achieved1 through Achieved4 to store the comparison of actual sales versus sales goals.

```
data finance.report;
   set finance.qsales;
   array sale{4} sales1-sales4;
   array Goal{4} (9000 9300 9600 9900);
   array Achieved{4};
   do i=1 to 4;
      achieved{i}=100*sale{i}/goal{i};
   end;
run;
```

A DO loop executes four times to calculate the value of each element of the achieved array (expressed as a percentage).

```
data finance.report;
   set finance.qsales;
   array sale{4} sales1-sales4;
   array Goal{4} (9000 9300 9600 9900);
   array Achieved{4};
   do i=1 to 4;
      achieved{i}=100*sale{i}/goal{i};
   end;
run;
```

Before submitting this DATA step, you can drop the index variable from the new data set by adding a DROP= option to the DATA statement.

```
data finance.report(drop=i);
   set finance.qsales;
   array sale{4} sales1-sales4;
   array Goal{4} (9000 9300 9600 9900);
   array Achieved{4};
   do i=1 to 4;
      achieved{i}=100*sale{i}/goal{i};
   end;
run;
```

This is an example of a simple **table-lookup** program. The resulting data set contains the variables that were read from **Finance.Qsales**, plus the eight variables that were created with ARRAY statements.

SAS Data Set Finance.Report

SalesRep	Sales1	Sales2	Sales3	Sales4	Goal1	Goal2
Britt	8400	8800	9300	9800	9000	9300
Fruchten	9500	9300	9800	8900	9000	9300
Goodyear	9150	9200	9650	11000	9000	9300

Goal3	Goal4	Achieved1	Achieved2	Achieved3	Achieved4
9600	9900	93.333	94.624	96.875	98.990
9600	9900	105.556	100.000	102.083	89.899
9600	9900	101.667	98.925	100.521	111.111

 Variables to which initial values are assigned in an ARRAY statement are automatically retained.

The variables Goal1 through Goal4 should not be stored in the data set, because they are needed only to calculate the values of Achieved1 through Achieved4. The next example shows you how to create temporary array elements.

Creating Temporary Array Elements

To create temporary array elements for DATA step processing without creating new variables, specify **_TEMPORARY_** after the array name and dimension.

```
data finance.report;
   set finance.qsales;
   array sale{4} sales1-sales4;
   array goal{4} _temporary_ (9000 9300 9600 9900);
   array Achieved{4};
   do i=1 to 4;
      achieved{i}=100*sale{i}/goal{i};
   end;
run;
```

Temporary array elements do not appear in the resulting data set.

SAS Data Set Finance.Report

SalesRep	Sales1	Sales2	Sales3	Sales4
Britt	8400	8800	9300	9800
Fruchten	9500	9300	9800	8900
Goodyear	9150	9200	9650	11000

Achieved1	Achieved2	Achieved3	Achieved4
93.333	94.624	96.875	98.990
105.556	100.000	102.083	89.899
101.667	98.925	100.521	111.111

Temporary array elements are useful when the array is needed only to perform a calculation. You can improve performance time by using temporary array elements.

Understanding Multidimensional Arrays

So far you have learned how to group variables into one-dimensional arrays. You can also group variables into table-like structures called **multidimensional** arrays. This section teaches you how to define and use two-dimensional arrays, which are a common type of multidimensional array.

Suppose you want to write a DATA step to compare responses on a quiz to the correct answers. As long as there is only one correct answer per question, this is a simple one-to-one comparison.

```
Resp1  →  Answer1
Resp2  →  Answer2
Resp3  →  Answer3
Resp4  →  Answer4
```

However, if there is more than one correct answer per question, you must compare each response to each possible correct answer in order to determine whether there is a match.

```
Resp1  →  Answer1    Answer2    Answer3
Resp2  →  Answer4    Answer5    Answer6
Resp3  →  Answer7    Answer8    Answer9
Resp4  →  Answer10   Answer11   Answer12
```

You can process the above data more easily by grouping the Answer variables into a two-dimensional array. Think of a one-dimensional array as a single row of variables, as in this example:

```
Answer1 Answer2 Answer3 Answer4 ... Answer9 Answer10 Answer11 Answer12
```

And think of a two-dimensional array as **multiple rows of variables**, as in this example:

```
Answer1    Answer2    Answer3
Answer4    Answer5    Answer6
Answer7    Answer8    Answer9
Answer10   Answer11   Answer12
```

Defining a Multidimensional Array

To define a multidimensional array, you specify the number of elements in each dimension, separated by a comma. This ARRAY statement defines a two-dimensional array:

```
array new{3,4} x1-x12;
```

In a two-dimensional array, the two dimensions can be thought of as a table of rows and columns.

```
array new{r,c} x1-x12;
```

The first dimension in the ARRAY statement specifies the number of rows.

```
array new{3,4} x1-x12;
```

The second dimension specifies the number of columns.

```
array new{3,4} x1-x12;
```

You can reference any element of the array by specifying the two dimensions. In the example below, you can perform an action on the variable x7 by specifying the array reference new{2,3}. You can easily locate the array element in the table by finding the row (2), then the column (3).

```
array new{3,4} x1-x12;
new{2,3}=0;
```

When you define a two-dimensional array, the array elements are grouped in the order in which they are listed in the ARRAY statement. For example, the array elements x1 through x4 can be thought of as the first row of the table.

```
array new{3,4} x1 x2 x3 x4 x5 x6 x7 x8 x9 x10 x11 x12;
```

x1	x2	x3	x4
x5	x6	x7	x8
x9	x10	x11	x12

The elements x5 through x8 become the second row of the table, and so on.

```
array new{3,4} x1 x2 x3 x4 x5 x6 x7 x8 x9 x10 x11 x12;
```

x1	x2	x3	x4
x5	x6	x7	x8
x9	x10	x11	x12

Example: Referencing Elements of a Two-Dimensional Array

Multidimensional arrays are typically used with **nested DO loops**. The next example uses a one-dimensional array, a two-dimensional array, and a nested DO loop to restructure a set of variables.

Your company's sales figures are stored by month in the SAS data set **Finance.Monthly**. Your task is to generate a new data set of quarterly sales rather than monthly sales.

Description of Finance.Monthly

Variable	Type	Length
Year	num	8
Month1	num	8
Month2	num	8
Month3	num	8
Month4	num	8
Month5	num	8
Month6	num	8
Month7	num	8
Month8	num	8
Month9	num	8
Month10	num	8
Month11	num	8
Month12	num	8

Defining the array m{4,3} puts the variables Month1 through Month12 into four groups of three months (yearly quarters).

Table Representation of m Array

Month1	Month2	Month3
Month4	Month5	Month6
Month7	Month8	Month9
Month10	Month11	Month12

```
data finance.quarters;
   set finance.monthly;
   array m{4,3} month1-month12;
```

Defining the array Qtr{4} creates the numeric variables Qtr1, Qtr2, Qtr3, Qtr4, which will be used to sum the sales for each quarter.

```
data finance.quarters;
   set finance.monthly;
   array m{4,3} month1-month12;
   array Qtr{4};
```

A nested DO loop is used to reference the values of the variables Month1 through Month12 and to calculate the values of Qtr1 through Qtr4. Because the variables i and j are used only for loop processing, the DROP= option is used to exclude them from the **Finance.Quarters** data set.

```
data finance.quarters(drop=i j);
   set finance.monthly;
   array m{4,3} month1-month12;
   array Qtr{4};
   do i=1 to 4;
     qtr{i}=0;
       do j=1 to 3;
          qtr{i}+m{i,j};
       end;
   end;
run;
```

Each element in the Qtr array represents the sum of one row in the m array. The number of elements in the Qtr array should match the first dimension of the m array (that is, the number of rows in the m array). The first DO loop executes once for each of the four elements of the Qtr array.

The assignment statement, qtr{i}=0, sets the value of qtr{i} to zero after each iteration of the first DO loop. Without the assignment statement, the values of Qtr1, Qtr2, Qtr3, and Qtr4 would accumulate across iterations of the DATA step due to the qtr{i}+m{i,j} Sum statement within the DO loop.

```
data finance.quarters(drop=i j);
   set finance.monthly;
   array m{4,3} month1-month12;
   array Qtr{4};
   do i=1 to 4;
     qtr{i}=0;
       do j=1 to 3;
          qtr{i}+m{i,j};
       end;
   end;
run;
```

The second DO loop executes the same number of times as the second dimension of the m array (that is, the number of columns in each row of the m array).

```
data finance.quarters(drop=i j);
   set finance.monthly;
   array m{4,3} month1-month12;
   array Qtr{4};
   do i=1 to 4;
     qtr{i}=0;
       do j=1 to 3;
          qtr{i}+m{i,j};
       end;
   end;
run;
```

To see how the nested DO loop processes these arrays, let's examine the execution of this DATA step.

When this DATA step is compiled, the program data vector is created. The PDV contains the variables Year, Month1 through Month12, and the new variables Qtr1 through Qtr4. (Only the beginning and ending portions of the program data vector are represented here.)

```
data finance.quarters(drop=i j);
   set finance.monthly;
   array m{4,3} month1-month12;
   array Qtr{4};
   do i=1 to 4;
     qtr{i}=0;
       do j=1 to 3;
          qtr{i}+m{i,j};
       end;
   end;
run;
```

Program Data Vector

N_	Year	Month1	Month2	Month3	Qtr1	Qtr2	Qtr3	Qtr4	i	j
.	.	.	.	.	.	.	.	.	.	.

During the first execution of the DATA step, the values of the first observation of **Finance.Monthly** are read into the program data vector. When the first DO loop executes the first time, the index variable i is set to *1*.

```
data finance.quarters(drop=i j);
   set finance.monthly;
   array m{4,3} month1-month12;
   array Qtr{4};
 > do i=1 to 4;                i=1
     qtr{i}=0;
      do j=1 to 3;
         qtr{i}+m{i,j};
      end;
   end;
run;
```

Program Data Vector

N	Year	Month1	Month2	Month3		Qtr1	Qtr2	Qtr3	Qtr4	i	j
1	1989	23000	21500	24600		•	•	•	•	1	•

During the first iteration of the nested DO loop, the value of Month1, which is referenced by m{i,j}, is added to Qtr1.

```
data finance.quarters(drop=i j);
   set finance.monthly;
   array m{4,3} month1-month12;
   array Qtr{4};
   do i=1 to 4;                i=1
     qtr{i}=0;
    > do j=1 to 3;            j=1
         qtr{1}+m{1,1};
      end;
   end;
run;
```

Program Data Vector

N	Year	Month1	Month2	Month3		Qtr1	Qtr2	Qtr3	Qtr4	i	j
1	1989	23000	21500	24600		23000	•	•	•	1	1

During the second iteration of the nested DO loop, the value of Month2, which is referenced by m{i,j}, is added to Qtr1.

```
data finance.quarters(drop=i j);
   set finance.monthly;
   array m{4,3} month1-month12;
   array Qtr{4};
   do i=1 to 4;                i=1
     qtr{i}=0;
    > do j=1 to 3;            j=2
         qtr{1}+m{1,2};
      end;
   end;
run;
```

Program Data Vector

N	Year	Month1	Month2	Month3	Qtr1	Qtr2	Qtr3	Qtr4	i	j
1	1989	23000	21500	24600	44500	•	•	•	1	2

The nested DO loop continues to execute until the index variable j **exceeds** the stop value, *3*. When the nested DO loop completes execution, the total sales for the first quarter, Qtr1, have been computed.

```
data finance.quarters(drop=i j);
   set finance.monthly;
   array m{4,3} month1-month12;
   array Qtr{4};
   do i=1 to 4;              i=1
     qtr{i}=0;
   > do j=1 to 3;            j=3
         qtr{1}+m{1,3};
      end;
   end;
run;
```

Program Data Vector

N	Year	Month1	Month2	Month3	Qtr1	Qtr2	Qtr3	Qtr4	i	j
1	1989	23000	21500	24600	69100	•	•	•	1	4

The outer DO loop increments i to *2*, and the process continues for the array element Qtr2 and the m array elements Month4 through Month6.

```
data finance.quarters(drop=i j);
   set finance.monthly;
   array m{4,3} month1-month12;
   array Qtr{4};
 > do i=1 to 4;              i=2
     qtr{i}=0;
       do j=1 to 3;          j=1
          qtr{i}+m{i,j};
       end;
   end;
run;
```

Program Data Vector

N	Month2	Month3	Month4	Qtr1	Qtr2	Qtr3	Qtr4	i	j
1	21500	24600	23300	69100	23300	•	•	2	1

After the outer DO loop completes execution, the end of the DATA step is reached, and the variable values for the first observation are written to the data set **Finance.Quarters**.

```
data finance.quarters(drop=i j);
   set finance.monthly;
   array m{4,3} month1-month12;
   array Qtr{4};
 > do i=1 to 4;                    i=5 (loop ends)
     qtr{i}=0;
      do j=1 to 3;
         qtr{i}+m{i,j};
      end;
   end;
run;
```

Program Data Vector

N	Month2	Month3	Month4	Qtr1	Qtr2	Qtr3	Qtr4	i	j
1	21500	24600	23300	69100	23300	69200	71800	5	4

What you have seen so far represents the first iteration of the DATA step. All observations in the data set **Finance.Monthly** are processed in the same manner. Below is a portion of the resulting data set, which contains the sales figures grouped by quarters.

SAS Data Set Finance.Quarters
(Partial Listing)

Year	Qtr1	Qtr2	Qtr3	Qtr4
1989	69100	64400	69200	71800
1990	73100	72000	83200	82800
1991	73400	81800	85200	87800

Additional Features

You've seen a number of uses for arrays, including creating variables, performing repetitive calculations, and performing table lookups. You can also use arrays for rotating (transposing) a SAS data set.

When you rotate a SAS data set, you change variables to observations or observations to variables. For example, suppose you want to rotate the **Finance.Funddrive** data set to create four output observations from each input observation.

SAS Data Set Finance.Funddrive

LastName	Qtr1	Qtr2	Qtr3	Qtr4
ADAMS	18	18	20	20
ALEXANDE	15	18	15	10
APPLE	25	25	25	25
ARTHUR	10	25	20	30
AVERY	15	15	15	15
BAREFOOT	20	20	20	20
BAUCOM	25	20	20	30
BLAIR	10	10	5	10
BLALOCK	5	10	10	15
BOSTIC	20	25	30	25
BRADLEY	12	16	14	18
BRADY	20	20	20	20
BROWN	18	18	18	18
BRYANT	16	18	20	18
BURNETTE	10	10	10	10
CHEUNG	30	30	30	30
LEHMAN	20	20	20	20
VALADEZ	14	18	40	25

The following program rotates the data set and lists the first 16 observations in the new data set.

```
data work.rotate(drop=qtr1-qtr4);
   set finance.funddrive;
   array contrib{4} qtr1-qtr4;
   do Qtr=1 to 4;
      Amount=contrib{qtr};
      output;
   end;
run;
proc print data=rotate(obs=16) noobs;
run;
```

LastName	Qtr	Amount
ADAMS	1	18
ADAMS	2	18
ADAMS	3	20
ADAMS	4	20
ALEXANDER	1	15
ALEXANDER	2	18
ALEXANDER	3	15
ALEXANDER	4	10
APPLE	1	25
APPLE	2	25
APPLE	3	25
APPLE	4	25
ARTHUR	1	10
ARTHUR	2	25
ARTHUR	3	20
ARTHUR	4	30

Summary

Text Summary

Purpose of SAS Arrays

An array is a temporary grouping of variables under a single name. This can reduce the number of statements that are needed to process variables and can simplify the maintenance of DATA step programs.

Defining an Array

To group previously defined data set variables into an array, use an **ARRAY statement** that specifies the array's name, its dimension enclosed in braces, brackets, or parentheses, and the elements to include. For example: `array sales{4} qtr1 qtr2 qtr3 qtr4;`

Variable Lists as Array Elements

You can use a **variable list** to specify array elements. Depending on the form of the variable list, it can specify all numeric or all character variables, or a numbered range of variables.

Referencing Elements of an Array

When you define an array in a DATA step, an index value is assigned to each element. During execution, you can use an **array reference** to perform actions on specific array elements. When used in a DO loop, for example, the index variable of the iterative DO statement can reference each element of the array.

The DIM Function

When using DO loops to process arrays, you can also use the **DIM function** in the TO clause of the iterative DO statement. When you use the DIM function, you do not have to re-specify the stop value of a DO statement if you change the dimension of the array.

Creating Variables with the ARRAY Statement

If you don't specify array elements in an ARRAY statement, SAS automatically creates the variables for you by concatenating the array name and the numbers 1, 2, 3... up to the array dimension. To create an array of character variables, add a dollar sign ($) after the array dimension. By default, all character variables that are created with an ARRAY statement are assigned a length of 8. However, you can specify a different length after the dollar sign.

Assigning Initial Values to Arrays

To assign **initial values** in an ARRAY statement, place the values in parentheses after the array elements, specifying one initial value for each array element and separating each value with a comma or blank. To assign initial values to character variables, enclose each value in quotation marks and separate the values with commas.

Creating Temporary Array Elements

You can create temporary array elements for DATA step processing without creating additional variables. Just specify **_TEMPORARY_** after the array name and dimension. This is useful when the array is needed only to perform a calculation.

Multidimensional Arrays

To define a multidimensional array, specify the number of elements in each dimension, separated by a comma. For example, array new{3,4} x1-x12; defines a two-dimensional array, with the first dimension specifying the number of rows (3) and the second dimension specifying the number of columns (4).

Referencing Elements of a Two-Dimensional Array

Multidimensional arrays are typically used with nested DO loops. If a DO loop processes a two-dimensional array, you can reference any element within the array by specifying the two dimensions.

Rotating Data Sets

You can use arrays to rotate a data set. Rotating a data set changes variables to observations or observations to variables.

Points to Remember

- A SAS array exists only for the duration of the DATA step.

- Do not give an array the same name as a variable in the same DATA step. Also, avoid using the name of a SAS function as an array name—the array will be correct, but you won't be able to use the function in the same DATA step, and a warning will be written to the SAS log.

- You can indicate the dimension of a one-dimensional array with an asterisk (*) as long as you specify the elements of the array.

- When referencing array elements, be careful not to confuse variable names with the array references. `WgtDiff1` through `WgtDiff5` is not the same as `WgtDiff{1}` through `WgtDiff{5}`.

Practice

After you complete this chapter, practice what you learned by using the sample data and SAS programs for Chapter 16, **Processing Variables with Arrays**, which are located on the CD-ROM. Follow the directions for creating your sample data in the Before You Begin section.

Quiz

Select the best answer for each question. After completing the quiz, check your answers using the answer key in the appendix.

1. Which statement is **false** regarding an ARRAY statement?

   a. It is an executable statement.

   b. It can be used to create variables.

   c. It must contain either all numeric or all character elements.

   d. It must be used to define an array before the array name can be referenced.

2. What belongs within the braces of this ARRAY statement?
   ```
   array contrib{?} qtr1-qtr4;
   ```

   a. quarter

   b. quarter*

   c. 1-4

   d. 4

3. For the program below, select an iterative DO statement to process all elements in the contrib array.
   ```
   data work.contrib;
      array contrib{4} qtr1-qtr4;
         ...
            contrib{i}=contrib{i}*1.25;
      end;
   run;
   ```

   a. do i=4;

   b. do i=1 to 4;

   c. do until i=4;

   d. do while i le 4;

4. What is the value of the index variable that references Jul in the statements below?
   ```
   array quarter{4} Jan Apr Jul Oct;
   do i=1 to 4;
      yeargoal=quarter{i}*1.2;
   end;
   ```

   a. 1

   b. 2

   c. 3

   d. 4

5. Which DO statement would **not** process all the elements in the `factors` array shown below?

   ```
   array factors{*} age height weight bloodpr;
   ```

   a. `do i=1 to dim(factors);`
   b. `do i=1 to dim(*);`
   c. `do i=1,2,3,4;`
   d. `do i=1 to 4;`

6. Which statement below is **false** regarding the use of arrays to create variables?

   a. The variables are added to the program data vector during the compilation of the DATA step.
   b. You do not need to specify the array elements in the ARRAY statement.
   c. By default, all character variables are assigned a length of eight.
   d. Only character variables can be created.

7. For the first observation, what is the value of `diff{i}` at the end of the **second** iteration of the DO loop?

Weight1	Weight2	Weight3
192	200	215
137	130	125
220	210	213

   ```
   array wt{*} weight1-weight10;
   array diff{9};
   do i=1 to 9;
      diff{i}=wt{i+1}-wt{i};
   end;
   ```

   a. 15
   b. 10
   c. 8
   d. -7

8. Finish the ARRAY statement below to create temporary array elements that have initial values of *9000, 9300, 9600,* and *9900.*

   ```
   array goal{4} ... ;
   ```

   a. `_temporary_ (9000 9300 9600 9900)`
   b. `temporary (9000 9300 9600 9900)`
   c. `_temporary_ 9000 9300 9600 9900`
   d. `(temporary) 9000 9300 9600 9900`

9. Based on the ARRAY statement below, select the array reference for the array element q50.

   ```
   array ques{3,25} q1-q75;
   ```

   a. ques{q50}
   b. ques{1,50}
   c. ques{2,25}
   d. ques{3,0}

10. Select the ARRAY statement that defines the array in the following program.

    ```
    data rainwear.coat;
       input category high1-high3 / low1-low3;
       ...
       do i=1 to 2;
          do j=1 to 3;
             compare{i,j}=round(compare{i,j}*1.12);
          end;
       end;
    run;
    ```

    a. array compare{1,6} high1-high3 low1-low3;
    b. array compare{2,3} high1-high3 low1-low3;
    c. array compare{3,2} high1-high3 low1-low3;
    d. array compare{3,3} high1-high3 low1-low3;

Chapter **17** Reading Raw Data in Fixed Fields

Overview

Introduction

Raw data can be organized in several ways.

This external file contains data that is arranged in **columns** or fixed fields. You can specify a beginning and ending column for each field. However, this file contains nonstandard data, because one of the variable's values includes a special character, the dollar sign ($).

```
1---+----10---+----20---+----
BIRD FEEDER    LG088   3 $29.95
GLASS MUGS     SB082   6 $25.00
GLASS TRAY     BQ049  12 $39.95
PADDED HANGRS  MN256  15 $9.95
JEWELRY BOX    AJ498  23 $45.00
RED APRON      AQ072   9 $6.50
CRYSTAL VASE   AQ672  27 $29.95
PICNIC BASKET  LS930  21 $15.00
```

This external file contains no special characters, but its data is free format, meaning that it is not arranged in columns. Notice that the values for a particular field do not begin and end in the same columns.

```
1---+----10---+----20---+--
BARNES NORTHWEST 36098.45
FARLSON SOUTHWEST 24394.09
LAWRENCE NORTHEAST 19504.26
NELSON SOUTHEAST 16930.84
STEWART MIDWEST 23845.13
TAYLOR MIDWEST 12354.42
TREADWAY SOUTHWEST 41092.84
WALSTON SOUTHEAST 28938.71
```

How your data is organized and what type of data you have determine which input style you should use to read the data. SAS provides three primary input styles—column input, formatted input, and list input. This chapter teaches you how to use **column input** and **formatted input** to read standard and nonstandard data that is arranged in fixed fields.

Objectives

In this chapter, you learn to

- distinguish between standard and nonstandard numeric data
- read standard fixed-field data
- read nonstandard fixed-field data.

Review of Column Input

Introduction

In Chapter 5, **Creating SAS Data Sets from Raw Data**, you learned how to use column input to read raw data that is stored in an external file.

You can use column input to read the values for Item, IDnum, InStock, and BackOrd from the raw data file that is referenced by the fileref **Invent**.

```
input Item $ 1-13 IDnum $ 15-19 InStock 21-22
      BackOrd 24-25;
```

Raw Data File Invent

```
1---+----10---+----20---+--
BIRD FEEDER    LG088   3 20
GLASS MUGS     SB082   6 12
GLASS TRAY     BQ049  12  6
PADDED HANGRS  MN256  15 20
JEWELRY BOX    AJ498  23  0
RED APRON      AQ072   9 12
CRYSTAL VASE   AQ672  27  0
PICNIC BASKET  LS930  21  0
```

Notice that the INPUT statement lists the variables with their corresponding column locations in order from left to right. However, one of the features of column input is the ability to read fields in any order.

For example, you could have read the values for InStock and BackOrd before the values for Item and IDnum.

```
input InStock 21-22 BackOrd 24-25 Item $ 1-13
      IDnum $ 15-19;
```

When you print a report that is based on this data set, by default, the variables will be listed in the order in which they were created.

InStock	BackOrd	Item	IDnum
3	20	BIRD FEEDER	LG088
6	12	GLASS MUGS	SB082
12	6	GLASS TRAY	BQ049
15	20	PADDED HANGRS	MN256
23	0	JEWELRY BOX	AJ498
9	12	RED APRON	AQ072
27	0	CRYSTAL VASE	AQ672
21	0	PICNIC BASKET	LS930

Column Input Features

Column input has several features that make it useful for reading raw data.

- It can be used to read character variable values that contain embedded blanks.

      input Name $ **1-25**;

```
1---+----10---+----20---+-
JOSEPH PAUL THACKERY JR.
```

- No placeholder is required for missing data. A blank field is read as missing and does not cause other fields to be read incorrectly.

      input Item $ 1-13 IDnum $ 15-19
            InStock 21-22 BackOrd 24-25;

```
1---+----10---+----20---+-
BIRD FEEDER   LG088   3 20
6 GLASS MUGS  SB082     12
GLASS TRAY    BQ049  12  6
```

- Fields or parts of fields can be re-read.

      input Item $ 1-13 IDnum $ 15-19 **Supplier $ 15-16**
            InStock 21-22 BackOrd 24-25;

```
1---+----10---+----20---+--
PADDED HANGRS MN256 15 20
JEWELRY BOX   AJ498 23  0
RED APRON     AQ072  9 12
```

- Fields do not have to be separated by blanks or other delimiters.

      input Item $ **1-13** IDnum $ **14-18** InStock **19-20**
            BackOrd **21-22**;

```
1---+----10---+----20---+--
PADDED HANGRSMN2561520
JEWELRY BOX   AJ49823 0
RED APRON     AQ072 912
```

Identifying Standard and Nonstandard Numeric Data

Standard Numeric Data

Standard numeric data values can contain only

- numbers
- decimal points
- numbers in scientific, or E, notation (23E4)
- minus signs and plus signs.

Some examples of standard numeric data are *15, -15, 15.4, +.05, 1.54E3*, and *-1.54E-3*.

Nonstandard Numeric Data

Nonstandard numeric data includes

- values that contain special characters, such as percent signs (%), dollar signs ($), and commas (,)
- date and time values
- data in fraction, integer binary, real binary, and hexadecimal forms.

The external file that is referenced by the fileref **Empdata** contains the personnel information for the technical writing department of a small computer manufacturer. The fields contain values for each employee's last name, first name, job title, and annual salary.

Raw Data File Empdata

```
1---+----10---+----20---+---
EVANS    DONNY 112 29,996.63
HELMS    LISA  105 18,567.23
HIGGINS  JOHN  111 25,309.00
LARSON   AMY   113 32,696.78
MOORE    MARY  112 28,945.89
POWELL   JASON 103 35,099.50
RILEY    JUDY  111 25,309.00
RYAN     NEAL  112 28,180.00
WILSON   HENRY 113 31,875.46
WOODS    CHIP  105 17,098.71
```

Notice that the values for `Salary` contain commas. So, the values for `Salary` are considered to be nonstandard numeric values.

Choosing an Input Style

Nonstandard data values require an input style that has more flexibility than column input.

You can use **formatted input**, which combines the features of column input with the ability to read both standard and nonstandard data.

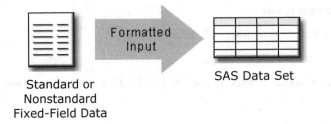

Whenever you encounter raw data that is organized into fixed fields, you can use

- column input to read standard data only
- formatted input to read both standard and nonstandard data.

Using Formatted Input

General Form of the INPUT Statement Using Formatted Input

Formatted input is a very powerful method for reading both standard and nonstandard data in fixed fields.

> **General form, INPUT statement using formatted input:**
>
> **INPUT** <*pointer-control*> *variable informat.*;
>
> where
>
> - *pointer-control* positions the input pointer on a specified column
> - *variable* is the name of the variable that is being created
> - *informat* is the special instruction that specifies how SAS reads raw data.

In this chapter, you will learn to work with two **column pointer controls**.

- The *@n* moves the input pointer to a specific column number.
- The *+n* moves the input pointer forward to a column number that is relative to the current position.

Let's first take a look at the *@n* column pointer control.

Using the @*n* Column Pointer Control

The @*n* is an absolute pointer control that moves the input pointer to a specific column number. The @ moves the pointer to column *n*, which is the first column of the field that is being read.

General form, INPUT statement using formatted input and the @*n* pointer control:

INPUT @*n* variable informat.;

- *variable* is the name of the variable that is being created
- *informat* is the special instruction that specifies how SAS reads raw data.

Let's use the @*n* pointer control to locate variable values in the external file **Empdata**. As you can see, the values for LastName begin in column 1. We could start with the @1 pointer control.

```
input @1 LastName $7.
```

However, the default column pointer location is column 1, so you do not need to use a column pointer control to read the first field.

```
input LastName $7.
```

```
↓---+----10---+----20---+---
EVANS    DONNY 112 29,996.63
HELMS    LISA  105 18,567.23
HIGGINS  JOHN  111 25,309.00
LARSON   AMY   113 32,696.78
MOORE    MARY  112 28,945.89
POWELL   JASON 103 35,099.50
RILEY    JUDY  111 25,309.00
```

Next, the values for FirstName begin in column 9. To point to column 9, use an @ sign and the column number in the INPUT statement:

```
input LastName $7. @9 FirstName $5.
```

```
1---+---↓10---+----20---+---
EVANS    DONNY 112 29,996.63
HELMS    LISA  105 18,567.23
HIGGINS  JOHN  111 25,309.00
LARSON   AMY   113 32,696.78
MOORE    MARY  112 28,945.89
POWELL   JASON 103 35,099.50
RILEY    JUDY  111 25,309.00
```

The $7. and $5. informats are explained later in this chapter.

Reading Columns in Any Order

Column pointer controls are very useful. For example, you can use the *@n* to move a pointer forward or backward when reading a record.

In this INPUT statement, the value for FirstName is read first, starting in column 9.

```
input @9 FirstName $5.
```

```
1---+---↓10---+----20---+---
EVANS    DONNY 112 29,996.63
HELMS    LISA  105 18,567.23
HIGGINS  JOHN  111 25,309.00
```

Now let's read the values for LastName, which begin in the first column. Here you must use the *@n* pointer control to move the pointer back to column 1.

```
input @9 FirstName $5. @1 LastName $7.
```

```
↓---+----10---+----20---+---
EVANS    DONNY 112 29,996.63
HELMS    LISA  105 18,567.23
HIGGINS  JOHN  111 25,309.00
```

The rest of the INPUT statement specifies the column locations of the raw data value for JobTitle and Salary.

```
input @9 FirstName $5. @1 LastName $7. @15 JobTitle 3.
      @19 Salary comma9.;
```

```
1---+----10---↓---↓20---+---
EVANS    DONNY 112 29,996.63
HELMS    LISA  105 18,567.23
HIGGINS  JOHN  111 25,309.00
```

 The $5., $7., 3., and comma9. informats are explained later in this chapter.

The +*n* Pointer Control

The +*n* pointer control moves the input pointer forward to a column number that is relative to the current position. The + moves the pointer forward *n* columns.

General form, INPUT statement using formatted input and the +*n* pointer control:

INPUT +*n* *variable informat.***;**

- *variable* is the name of the variable that is being created
- *informat* is the special instruction that specifies how SAS reads raw data.

In order to count correctly, it is important to understand where the column pointer control is located after each data value is read. Let's look at an example.

Suppose you want to read the data from **Empdata** in the following order: LastName, FirstName, Salary, JobTitle. Like the @*n* pointer control, the default column location for the +*n* pointer control is column 1. Because the values for LastName begin in column 1, a column pointer control is not needed.

```
input LastName $7.
```

```
↓---+----10---+----20---+---
EVANS    DONNY 112 29,996.63
HELMS    LISA  105 18,567.23
HIGGINS  JOHN  111 25,309.00
```

With formatted input, the column pointer control moves to the first column following the field that was just read. In this example, after LastName is read, the pointer moves to column 8.

```
1---+--↓-10---+----20---+---
EVANS    DONNY 112 29,996.63
HELMS    LISA  105 18,567.23
HIGGINS  JOHN  111 25,309.00
```

To start reading FirstName, which begins in column 9, you move the column pointer control ahead 1 column with +1.

```
input LastName $7. +1 FirstName $5.
```

```
1---+---↓10---+----20---+---
EVANS    DONNY 112 29,996.63
HELMS    LISA  105 18,567.23
HIGGINS  JOHN  111 25,309.00
```

After reading `FirstName`, the column pointer moves to column 14. Now you want to skip over the values for `JobTitle` and read the values for `Salary`, which begin in column 19. Move the column pointer ahead 5 columns from column 14.

```
input LastName $7. +1 FirstName $5. +5 Salary comma9.
```

```
             1 2 3 4 5
1---+----10---↓---↓20---+---
EVANS   DONNY 112 29,996.63
HELMS   LISA  105 18,567.23
HIGGINS JOHN  111 25,309.00
```

The last field to be read contains the values for `JobTitle`. You can use the `@n` column pointer control to return to column 15.

```
input LastName $7. +1 FirstName $5. +5 Salary comma9.
      @15 JobTitle 3.;
```

```
1---+----10---↓----20---+---
EVANS   DONNY 112 29,996.63
HELMS   LISA  105 18,567.23
HIGGINS JOHN  111 25,309.00
```

The $7., $5., comma9., and 3. informats are explained later in this chapter.

You can use the notation +(-n) to move the +n pointer control backward.

For more information about the +(-n) notation, see the SAS documentation.

Using Informats

Remember that the general form of the INPUT statement for formatted input is

> **INPUT** *<pointer-control> variable informat.*;

An informat is an instruction that tells SAS how to read raw data. SAS provides many informats for reading standard and nonstandard data values. Here is a small sample.

PERCENT*w.d*	DATE*w.*	NENGO*w.*
$BINARY*w.*	DATETIME*w.*	PD*w.d*
$VARYING*w.*	HEX*w.*	PERCENT*w.*
$*w.*	JULIAN*w.*	TIME*w.*
COMMA*w.d*	MMDDYY*w.*	*w.d*

Note that

- each informat contains a *w* value to indicate the width of the raw data field

- each informat also contains a period, which is a required delimiter

- for some informats, the optional *d* value specifies the number of implied decimal places

- informats for reading character data always begin with a dollar sign ($).

ⓘ   For a complete list of informats, see the SAS documentation.

Reading Character Values

The $*w.* informat enables you to read character data. The *w* represents the field width of the data value (the total number of columns that contain the raw data field).

In the example below, the $ indicates that `FirstName` is a character variable, the 5 indicates a field width of five columns, and a period ends the informat.

```
input @9 FirstName $5.;
```

```
         12345
1---+---↓10---+----20---+---
EVANS    DONNY 112 29,996.63
HELMS    LISA  105 18,567.23
HIGGINS  JOHN  111 25,309.00
LARSON   AMY   113 32,696.78
MOORE    MARY  112 28,945.89
POWELL   JASON 103 35,099.50
RILEY    JUDY  111 25,309.00
RYAN     NEAL  112 28,180.00
WILSON   HENRY 113 31,875.46
WOODS    CHIP  105 17,098.71
```

Reading Standard Numeric Data

The informat for reading standard numeric data is the *w.d* informat.

The *w* specifies the field width of the raw data value, the period serves as a delimiter, and the *d* optionally specifies the number of implied decimal places for the value. The *w.d* informat ignores any specified *d* value if the data already contains a decimal point.

For example, the raw data value that is shown below contains 6 digits (4 are decimals) and 1 decimal point. Therefore, the *w.* informat requires a field width of only 7 to correctly read the raw data value.

Raw Data Value	w. Informat	Variable Value
34.0008 →	7. →	34.0008

In the example that is shown below, the values for `JobTitle` in columns 15-17 contain only numbers. Remember that standard numeric data values can contain only numbers, decimal points, scientific notation, and plus and minus signs.

A *d* value is not necessary to read the values for `JobTitle`. Simply move the column pointer control forward 7 spaces to column 15, name the variable, and specify a field width of 3.

```
input @9 FirstName $5. @1 LastName $7. +7 JobTitle 3.;
```

```
                 123
1---+----10---↓----20---+---
EVANS    DONNY 112 29,996.63
HELMS    LISA  105 18,567.23
HIGGINS  JOHN  111 25,309.00
LARSON   AMY   113 32,696.78
MOORE    MARY  112 28,945.89
POWELL   JASON 103 35,099.50
RILEY    JUDY  111 25,309.00
```

 Remember to specify the **period** in the informat name. For example, if you omit the period in the following INPUT statement, SAS assigns a length of *3* to `JobTitle` instead of reading `JobTitle` with the 3. informat.

```
input @9 FirstName $5. @1 LastName $7. +7 JobTitle 3;
```

Reading Nonstandard Numeric Data

The COMMA*w.d* informat is used to read numeric values and to remove embedded

- blanks
- commas
- dashes
- dollar signs
- percent signs
- right parentheses
- left parentheses, which are converted to minus signs.

The COMMA*w.d* informat has three parts:

1.	the informat name	**COMMA**
2.	a value that specifies the width of the field to be read (including dollar signs, decimal places, or other special characters), followed by a period	*w.*
3.	an optional value that specifies the number of implied decimal places for a value (not necessary if the value already contains decimal places).	*d*

In the example below, the values for `Salary` contain commas, which means that they are nonstandard numeric values.

The values for `Salary` begin in column 19, so use the @*n* or +*n* pointer control to point to column 19, and then name the variable.

```
data perm.empinfo;
   infile empdata;
   input @9 FirstName $5. @1 LastName $7. +7 JobTitle 3.
         @19 Salary
```

```
1---+----10---+---↓20---+---
EVANS    DONNY 112 29,996.63
HELMS    LISA  105 18,567.23
HIGGINS  JOHN  111 25,309.00
LARSON   AMY   113 32,696.78
MOORE    MARY  112 28,945.89
POWELL   JASON 103 35,099.50
RILEY    JUDY  111 25,309.00
```

Now add the COMMA*w.d* informat and specify the field width. The values end in column 27, so the field width is 9 columns. Add a RUN statement to complete the DATA step.

```
data perm.empinfo;
   infile empdata;
   input @9 FirstName $5. @1 LastName $7. +7 JobTitle 3.
      @19 Salary comma9.;
run;
```

```
                        123456789
1---+----10---+---↓20---+-↓-
EVANS    DONNY 112 29,996.63
HELMS    LISA  105 18,567.23
HIGGINS  JOHN  111 25,309.00
LARSON   AMY   113 32,696.78
MOORE    MARY  112 28,945.89
POWELL   JASON 103 35,099.50
RILEY    JUDY  111 25,309.00
```

If you use PROC PRINT to display the data set, the commas are removed from the values for `Salary` in the resulting output.

```
data perm.empinfo;
   infile empdata;
   input @9 FirstName $5. @1 LastName $7. +7 JobTitle 3.
      @19 Salary comma9.;
run;
proc print data=perm.empinfo;
run;
```

Obs	FirstName	LastName	JobTitle	Salary
1	DONNY	EVANS	112	29996.63
2	ALISA	HELMS	105	18567.23
3	JOHN	HIGGINS	111	25309.00
4	AMY	LARSON	113	32696.78
5	MARY	MOORE	112	28945.89
6	JASON	POWELL	103	35099.50
7	JUDY	RILEY	111	25309.00

Thus, the COMMA*w.d* informat does more than simply read the raw data values. It removes special characters such as commas from numeric data and stores only numeric values in a SAS data set.

DATA Step Processing of Informats

Let's place our INPUT statement in a DATA step and submit it for processing. Remember that after the DATA step is submitted, it is compiled and then executed.

```
data perm.empinfo;
    infile empdata;
    input @9 FirstName $5. @1 LastName $7. +7 JobTitle 3.
          @19 Salary comma9.;
run;
```

During the compile phase, the character variables in the program data vector are defined with the exact length that is specified by the informat. But notice that the lengths that are defined for JobTitle and Salary in the program data vector are different from the lengths that are specified by their informats.

```
                  123   123456789
1---+----10---↓-↓-↓20---+-↓-
EVANS    DONNY  112  29,996.63
HELMS    LISA   105  18,567.23
HIGGINS  JOHN   111  25,309.00
```

Program Data Vector

N	ERROR	FirstName	LastName	JobTitle	Salary
		$5.	$7.	8.	8.
				112	29996.63

Remember, by default, SAS stores numeric values (no matter how many digits the value contains) as floating-point numbers in 8 bytes of storage. The length of a stored numeric variable is not affected by an informat's width nor by other column specifications in an INPUT statement.

However, it is still necessary to specify the actual width of a raw data field in an INPUT statement. Otherwise, if you specify a default field width of 8 for all numeric values, you'll get inappropriate variable values when the program executes.

In the following example, the values for JobTitle would contain embedded blanks, thus creating invalid numeric values.

```
data perm.empinfo;
    infile empdata;
    input @9 FirstName $5. @1 LastName $7.
          +7 JobTitle 8. @19 Salary comma8.;
run;
```

```
                    12345678
                       12345678
  1---+----10---↓---↓20↓--+↓--
  EVANS   DONNY  112 29,996.63
  HELMS   LISA   105 18,567.23
  HIGGINS JOHN   111 25,309.00
```

Program Data Vector

N	ERROR	FirstName	LastName	JobTitle	Salary
		$5.	$7.	8.	8.
				•	29996.63

> Remember that the *w* value of the informat represents the width of the field in the raw data file. The values for JobTitle only have a width of 3 in the raw data file. However, because they are numeric values, SAS stores them with a default length of 8.

Record Formats

The record format of an external file might affect how data is read with column input and formatted input. A record format specifies how records are organized in a file.

In some operating environments, external files can have different types of record formats. Two common record formats are fixed-length records and variable-length records.

Fixed-Length Records

External files that have a fixed-length record format have an end-of-record marker after a predetermined number of columns. A typical record length is 80 columns.

```
123456789..................................80
< field1 >< field2 >< field3 >..unused space    record 1
123456789..................................80
< field1 >< field2 >< field3 >< field4 >....    record 2
123456789..................................80
< field1 >< field2 >.... unused space ......    record 3
```

Variable-Length Records

Files that have a variable-length record format have an end-of-record marker after the last field in each record.

As you can see, the length of each record varies.

```
123456789..................*
< field1 >< field2 >< field3 >   record 1
123456789.........................*
< field1 >< field2 >< field3 >< field4 >   record 2
123456789..........*
< field1 >< field2 >   record 3
```

Reading Variable-Length Records

When you are working with variable-length records that contain fixed-field data, you might have values that are shorter than others or that are missing. This can cause problems when you try to read the raw data into your SAS data set.

For example, notice that the following INPUT statement specifies a field width of 8 columns for `Receipts`. In the third record, the input pointer encounters an end-of-record marker before the 8th column.

```
input Dept $ 1-11 @13 Receipts comma8.;
```

 The asterisk symbolizes the end-of-record marker and is not part of the data.

```
          12345678
1---+----10---+---↓20--
BED/BATH    1,354.93*
HOUSEWARES  2,464.05*
GARDEN        923.34*
GRILL         598.34*
SHOES       1,345.82*
SPORTS*
TOYS        6,536.53*
```

The input pointer moves down to the next record in an attempt to find a value for `Receipts`. However, *GRILL* is a character value, and `Receipts` is a numeric variable. Thus, an **invalid data** error occurs, and `Receipts` is set to missing.

```
↓---+----10---+----20--
BED/BATH    1,354.93*
HOUSEWARES  2,464.05*
GARDEN        923.34*
GRILL         598.34*
SHOES       1,345.82*
SPORTS*
TOYS        6,536.53*
```

The PAD Option

When you use column input or formatted input to read fixed-field data in variable-length records, you can avoid problems by using the PAD option in the INFILE statement. The PAD option pads each record with blanks so that all data lines have the same length.

```
infile receipts pad;
```

```
1---+----10---+----20--
BED/BATH    1,354.93
HOUSEWARES  2,464.05
GARDEN        923.34
GRILL         598.34
SHOES       1,345.82
SPORTS
TOYS        6,536.53
```

The examples in this chapter have not required the PAD option. However, when you use column input or formatted input to read fixed-field data in variable-length records, remember to determine whether or not you need to use the PAD option. For more information about the PAD option, see the SAS documentation for your operating environment.

 The PAD option is useful only when missing data occurs at the end of a record and when SAS encounters an end-of-record marker before the last field is completely read.

The default value of the maximum record length is determined by your operating environment. If you get unexpected results when reading many variables, you might need to change the maximum record length by specifying the **LRECL=option** in the INFILE statement. For more information about the LRECL= option, see the SAS documentation for your operating environment.

Summary

Text Summary

Review of Column Input

When data is arranged in columns or fixed fields, you can use **column input** to read them. With column input, the beginning and ending column are specified for each field. Character variables are identified by a dollar ($) sign.

Column input has several features:

- Fields can be read in any order.

- It can be used to read character variables that contain embedded blanks.

- No placeholder is required for missing data. A blank field is read as missing and does not cause other fields to be read incorrectly.

- Fields or parts of fields can be re-read.

- Fields do not have to be separated by blanks or other delimiters.

- It can be used to read standard character and numeric data.

Identifying Nonstandard Numeric Data

Standard numeric data values are values that contain only numbers, scientific notation, decimal points, and plus and minus signs. When numeric data contains characters such as commas or dollar signs, the data is considered to be nonstandard.

Nonstandard numeric data includes

- values that contain special characters, such as percent signs, dollar signs, and commas

- date and time values

- data in fraction, integer binary, real binary, and hexadecimal forms.

Choosing an Input Style

SAS provides two input styles for reading data in fixed fields—**column input** and **formatted input**. You can use

- column input to read standard data only

- formatted input to read both standard and nonstandard data.

Using Formatted Input

Formatted input uses column pointer controls to position the input pointer on a specified column. A column pointer control is optional when the first variable is in the first column.

The **@n** is an absolute pointer control that moves the input pointer to a specific column number. You can read columns in any order with the @n column pointer control.

The **+n** is a relative pointer control that moves the input pointer forward to a column number that is relative to the current position. The +n pointer control cannot move backward. However, you can use the notation +(-n) to move the pointer control backward.

Using Informats

An informat tells SAS how to read raw data. There are informats for reading standard and nonstandard character values and for reading standard and nonstandard numeric data values.

Informats always contain a *w* value to indicate the width of the raw data field. A period (.) ends the informat or separates the *w* value from the optional *d* value, which specifies the number of implied decimal places.

Record Formats

A record format specifies how records are organized in a file. Some operating environments have different types of record formats; the two most common are **fixed-length records** and **variable-length records**.

When you read variable-length records that contain fixed-field data into a SAS data set, there might be values that are shorter than others or that are missing. The **PAD option** pads each record with blanks so that all data lines have the same length.

Points to Remember

- When you use column input or formatted input, the input pointer stops on the column following the last column that was read.

- When you use informats, you do not need to specify a *d* value if the data values already contain decimal places.

- Column input can be used to read standard character or standard numeric data only.

- Formatted input can be used to read both standard and nonstandard data.

- When reading variable-length records that contain fixed-field data, you can avoid problems by using the PAD option in the INFILE statement.

Practice

After you complete this chapter, practice what you learned by using the sample data and SAS programs for Chapter 17, **Reading Raw Data in Fixed Fields**, which are located on the CD-ROM. Follow the directions for creating your sample data in the Before You Begin section.

Quiz

Select the best answer for each question. After completing the quiz, check your answers using the answer key in the appendix.

1. Which SAS statement correctly uses column input to read the values in the raw data file below in this order: Address (4th field), SquareFeet (second field), Style (first field), Bedrooms (third field)?

    ```
    1---+----10---+----20---+----30
    2STORY 1810 4 SHEPPARD AVENUE
    CONDO  1200 2 RAND STREET
    RANCH  1550 3 MARKET STREET
    ```

    a. input Address 15-29 SquareFeet 8-11 Style 1-6
            Bedrooms 13;

    b. input $ 15-29 Address 8-11 SquareFeet $ 1-6 Style
            13 Bedrooms;

    c. input Address $ 15-29 SquareFeet 8-11 Style $ 1-6
            Bedrooms 13;

    d. input Address 15-29 $ SquareFeet 8-11 Style 1-6
            $ Bedrooms 13;

2. Which is **not** an advantage of column input?

    a. It can be used to read character variables that contain embedded blanks.
    b. No placeholder is required for missing data.
    c. Standard as well as nonstandard data values can be read.
    d. Fields do not have to be separated by blanks or other delimiters.

3. Which is an example of standard numeric data?

    a. -34.245
    b. $24,234.25
    c. 1/2
    d. 50%

4. Formatted input can be used to read

    a. standard free-format data
    b. standard data in fixed fields
    c. nonstandard data in fixed fields
    d. both standard and nonstandard data in fixed fields

5. Which informat should you use to read the values in column 1-5?

```
1---+----10---+----20---+----30
DG345 CD PLAYER    $174.99
HJ756 VCR          $298.99
AS658 CAMCORDER $1,195.99
```

   a. w.

   b. $w.

   c. w.d

   d. COMMAw.d

6. The COMMAw.d informat can be used to read which of the following values?

   a. 12,805

   b. $177.95

   c. 18 %

   d. all of the above

7. Which INPUT statement correctly reads the values for ModelNumber (first field) after the values for Item (second field)? Both Item and ModelNumber are character variables.

```
1---+----10---+----20---+----30
DG345 CD PLAYER    $174.99
HJ756 VCR          $298.99
AS658 CAMCORDER $1,195.99
```

   a. input +7 Item $9. @1 ModelNumber $5.;

   b. input +6 Item $9. @1 ModelNumber $5.;

   c. input @7 Item $9. +1 ModelNumber $5.;

   d. input @7 Item $9 @1 ModelNumber 5.;

8. Which INPUT statement correctly reads the numeric values for Cost (third field)?

```
1---+----10---+----20---+----30
DG345 CD PLAYER    $174.99
HJ756 VCR          $298.99
AS658 CAMCORDER $1,195.99
```

   a. input @17 Cost 7.2;

   b. input @17 Cost 9.2.;

   c. input @17 Cost comma7.;

   d. input @17 Cost comma9.;

9. Which SAS statement correctly uses formatted input to read the values in this order: Item (first field), UnitCost (second field), Quantity (third field)?

   ```
   1---+----10---+----20---+
   ENVELOPE  $13.25 500
   DISKETTES $29.50  10
   BANDS     $2.50  600
   RIBBON    $94.20  12
   ```

   a. input @1 Item $9. +1 UnitCost comma6.
            @18 Quantity 3.;

   b. input Item $9. @11 UnitCost comma6.
            @18 Quantity 3.;

   c. input Item $9. +1 UnitCost comma6.
            @18 Quantity 3.;

   d. all of the above

10. Which raw data file requires the PAD option in the INFILE statement in order to correctly read the data using either column input or formatted input?

    a.
    ```
    1---+----10---+----20---+
    JONES     M 48 128.6
    LAVERNE   M 58 158
    JAFFE     F 33 115.5
    WILSON    M 28 130
    ```

    b.
    ```
    1---+----10---+----20---+
    JONES     M 48 128.6
    LAVERNE   M 58 158.0
    JAFFE     F 33 115.5
    WILSON    M 28 130.0
    ```

    c.
    ```
    1---+----10---+----20---+
    JONES     M 48 128.6
    LAVERNE   M 58    158
    JAFFE     F 33 115.5
    WILSON    M 28    130
    ```

    d.
    ```
    1---+----10---+----20---+
       JONES    M 48 128.6
    LAVERNE     M 58 158.0
       JAFFE    F 33 115.5
    WILSON      M 28 130.0
    ```

Chapter 18 Reading Free-Format Data

Overview

Introduction

As you learned in Chapter 17, **Reading Raw Data in Fixed Fields**, raw data can be organized in several ways.

This external file contains data that is arranged in **columns**, or fixed fields. You can specify a beginning and ending column for each field.

```
1---+----10---+----20---+----30--
BIRD FEEDER    LG088    3  20
GLASS MUGS     SB082    6  12
GLASS TRAY     BQ049   12   6
PADDED HANGRS  MN256   15  20
JEWELRY BOX    AJ498   23   0
RED APRON      AQ072    9  12
CRYSTAL VASE   AQ672   27   0
PICNIC BASKET  LS930   21   0
```

By contrast, the following external file contains data that is **free format**, meaning data that is not arranged in columns. Notice that the values for a particular field do not begin and end in the same columns.

```
1---+----10---+----20---+----30--
ABRAMS L.MARKETING $18,209.03
BARCLAY M.MARKETING $18,435.71
COURTNEY W.MARKETING $20,006.16
FARLEY J.PUBLICATIONS $21,305.89
HEINS W.PUBLICATIONS $20,539.23
```

In the previous chapter, you learned that how your data is organized determines which input style you should use to read the data. SAS provides three primary input styles: column, formatted, and list input. Previously, you learned how to use column input and formatted input. This chapter teaches you how to use list input to read free-format data that is not arranged in fixed fields.

Objectives

In this chapter, you learn to use the INPUT statement with list input to read

- free-format data (data that is not organized in fixed fields)
- free-format data that is separated by nonblank delimiters, such as commas
- free-format data that contains missing values
- character values that exceed eight characters
- nonstandard free-format data
- character values that contain embedded blanks.

In addition, you learn how to mix column, formatted, and list input styles in a single INPUT statement.

Reading Free-Format Data

You have already worked with raw data that is in fixed fields. In doing so, you used column input to read standard data values in fixed fields. You have also used formatted input to read both standard and nonstandard data in fixed fields.

Suppose you have raw data that is **free format**; that is, it is not arranged in fixed fields. The fields are often separated by blanks or by some other delimiter, such as the pound sign (#) shown below. In this case, column input and formatted input that you might have used before to read standard and nonstandard data in fixed fields will not enable you to read all of the values in the raw data file.

```
1---+----10---+----20---+----30
ABRAMS#L.#MARKETING#$8,209
BARCLAY#M.#MARKETING#$8,435
COURTNEY#W.#MARKETING#$9,006
FARLEY#J.#PUBLICATIONS#$8,305
HEINS#W.#PUBLICATIONS#$9,539
```

Using List Input

List input is a powerful tool for reading both standard and nonstandard free-format data.

> **General form, INPUT statement using list input:**
>> **INPUT** *variable* <$>;
>
> where
>
> * *variable* specifies the variable whose value the INPUT statement is to read
> * $ specifies that the variable is a character variable.

Suppose you have an external data file like the one that follows. The file, which is referenced by the fileref **Credit**, contains the results of a survey on the use of credit cards by males and females in the 18-39 age range.

Raw Data File Credit

```
1---+----10---+----20
MALE 27 1 8 0 0
FEMALE 29 3 14 5 10
FEMALE 34 2 10 3 3
MALE 35 2 12 4 8
FEMALE 36 4 16 3 7
MALE 21 1 5 0 0
MALE 25 2 9 2 1
FEMALE 21 1 4 2 6
MALE 38 3 11 4 3
FEMALE 30 3 5 1 0
```

You need to read the data values for

- gender
- age
- number of bank credit cards
- bank card use per month
- number of department store credit cards
- department store card use per month.

List input might be the easiest input style to use because, as shown in the INPUT statement below, you simply list the variable names in the same order as the corresponding raw data fields. Remember to distinguish character variables from numeric variables.

```
input Gender $ Age Bankcard FreqBank Deptcard
      FreqDept;
```

Because list input, by default, does not specify column locations,

- all fields must be separated by at least **one** blank or other delimiter
- fields must be read **in order** from left to right
- you cannot skip or re-read fields.

Processing List Input

It's important to remember that list input causes SAS to scan the input lines for values rather than reading from specific columns. When the INPUT statement is submitted for processing, the input pointer is positioned at column 1 of the raw data file, as shown below.

```
data perm.survey;
   infile credit;
   input Gender $ Age Bankcard FreqBank Deptcard
         FreqDept;
run;
```

```
↓---+----10---+----20
MALE 27 1 8 0 0
FEMALE 29 3 14 5 10
FEMALE 34 2 10 3 3
```

SAS reads the first field until it encounters a blank space. The blank space indicates the end of the field, and the data value is assigned to the program data vector for the first variable in the INPUT statement.

```
1---↓----10---+----20
MALE 27 1 8 0 0
FEMALE 29 3 14 5 10
FEMALE 34 2 10 3 3
```

Next, SAS scans the record until the next nonblank space is found, and the second value is read until another blank is encountered. Then the value is assigned to its corresponding variable in the program data vector.

```
1---+--↓-10---+----20
MALE 27 1 8 0 0
FEMALE 29 3 14 5 10
FEMALE 34 2 10 3 3
```

This process of scanning ahead to the next nonblank column, reading the data value until a blank is encountered, and assigning the value to a variable in the program data vector continues until all the fields have been read and values have been assigned to variables in the program data vector.

Program Data Vector

N	Gender	Age	Bankcard	FreqBank	Deptcard	FreqDept
1	MALE	27	1	8	0	0

When the DATA step has finished executing, you can display the data set with the PRINT procedure. The code below produces the output that follows.

```
proc print data=perm.survey;
run;
```

(Partial Output)

Obs	Gender	Age	Bankcard	FreqBank	Deptcard	FreqDept
1	MALE	27	1	8	0	0
2	FEMALE	29	3	14	5	10
3	FEMALE	34	2	10	3	3
4	MALE	35	2	12	4	8
5	FEMALE	36	4	16	3	7
6	MALE	21	1	5	0	0
7	MALE	25	2	9	2	1

Working with Delimiters

Most free-format data fields are clearly separated by blanks and are easy to imagine as variables and observations. But fields can also be separated by other delimiters, such as commas, as shown below.

Raw Data File Credit

```
1---+----10---+----20
MALE,27,1,8,0,0
FEMALE,29,3,14,5,10
FEMALE,34,2,10,3,3
MALE,35,2,12,4,8
FEMALE,36,4,16,3 7
MALE,21,1,5,0,0
MALE,25,2,9,2,1
FEMALE,21,1,4,2 6
MALE,38,3,11,4,3
FEMALE,30,3,5,1,0
```

When characters other than blanks are used to separate the data values, you can tell SAS which field delimiter to use. Use the **DLM= option in the INFILE statement** to specify a delimiter other than a blank (the default).

General form, DLM= option:

> **DLM=***delimiter(s)*

where *delimiter(s)* specifies a delimiter for list input in either of the following forms:

- *'list-of-delimiting-characters'* specifies one or more characters (up to 200) to read as delimiters. The list of characters must be enclosed in quotation marks.

- *character-variable* specifies a character variable whose value becomes the delimiter.

Example

The following program creates the output shown below.

```
data perm.survey;
   infile credit dlm=',';
   input Gender $ Age Bankcard FreqBank
         Deptcard FreqDept;
run;
proc print data=perm.survey;
run;
```

Obs	Gender	Age	Bankcard	FreqBank	Deptcard	FreqDept
1	MALE	27	1	8	0	0
2	FEMALE	29	3	14	5	10
3	FEMALE	34	2	10	3	3
4	MALE	35	2	12	4	8
5	FEMALE	36	4	16	3	7
6	MALE	21	1	5	0	0
7	MALE	25	2	9	2	1
8	FEMALE	21	1	4	2	6
9	MALE	38	3	11	4	3
10	FEMALE	30	3	5	1	0

The field delimiter must **not** be a character that occurs in a data value. For example, this raw data file contains values for `LastName` and `Salary`. Notice that the values for `Salary` contain commas.

```
1---+----10---+----20
BROWN 24,456.09
JOHNSON 25,467.17
McABE 21,766.36
```

If the field delimiter is also a comma, the fields are identified incorrectly, as shown below.

```
1---+----10---+----20
BROWN,24,456.09
JOHNSON,25,467.17
McABE,21,766.36
```

SAS Data Set

Obs	LastName	Salary
1	BROWN	24
2	JOHNSON	25
3	McABE	21

 Later in this chapter, you'll learn how to work with data values that contain delimiters.

Reading a Range of Variables

When the variable values in the raw data file are sequential and are separated by a blank (or by another delimiter), you can specify a range of variables in the INPUT statement. This is especially useful if your data contains similar variables, such as the answers to a questionnaire.

For example, the following INPUT statement creates five new numeric variables and assigns them the names Ques1, Ques2, Ques3, and so on. You can also specify a range in the VAR statement in the PROC PRINT step to list a range of specific variables.

Raw Data File Survey

```
1---+----10---+----20
1000 23 94 56 85 99
1001 26 55 49 87 85
1002 33 99 54 82 94
1003 71 33 22 44 92
1004 88 49 29 57 83
```

```
data survey.phone;
   infile survey;
   input IDnum $ Ques1-Ques5;
run;
proc print data=survey.phone;
   var ques1-ques3;
run;
```

Obs	Ques1	Ques2	Ques3
1	23	94	56
2	26	55	49
3	33	99	54
4	71	33	22
5	88	49	29

If you are specifying a range of character variables, both the variable list and the $ sign must be enclosed in parentheses.

```
data survey.stores;
   infile stordata;
   input Age (Store1-Store3) ($);
run;
proc print data=survey.stores;
run;
```

 You can also specify a range of variables using formatted input. If you specify a range of variables using formatted input, both the variable list and the format must be enclosed in parentheses, regardless of the variable's type.

```
data test.scores;
   infile group3;
   input Age (Score1-Score4) (6.);
run;
```

Limitations of List Input

In its default form, list input places several limitations on the types of data that can be read:

- Although the width of a field can be greater than eight columns, both character and numeric variables have a default length of 8. Character values that are longer than eight characters will be truncated.

- Data must be in standard numeric or character format.

- Character values cannot contain embedded delimiters.

- Missing numeric and character values must be represented by a period or some other character.

 There are ways to work around these limitations using modified list input, which will be discussed later in this chapter.

Reading Missing Values

Reading Missing Values at the End of a Record

Suppose the third person represented in the raw data file below did not answer the questions about how many department store credit cards she has and how often she uses them.

```
1---+----10---+----20
MALE 27 1 8 0 0
FEMALE   3 14 5 10
FEMALE 34 2 10 ▮ ▮
MALE 35 2 12 4 8
FEMALE 36 4 16 3 7
MALE 21 1 5 0 0
MALE 25 2 9 2 1
FEMALE 21 1 4 2 6
MALE 38 3 11 4 3
FEMALE 30 3 5 1 0
```

Because the missing values occur at the **end** of the record, you can use the MISSOVER option in the INFILE statement to read the missing values at the end of the record. The MISSOVER option prevents SAS from going to another record if, when using list input, it does not find values in the current line for all the INPUT statement variables. At the **end** of the current record, values that are expected but not found are set to missing.

For the raw data file shown above, the MISSOVER option prevents the fields in the fourth record from being read as values for `Deptcard` and `FreqDept` in the third observation. Note that `Deptcard` and `FreqDept` are set to missing.

```
data perm.survey;
    infile credit missover;
    input Gender $ Age Bankcard FreqBank
          Deptcard FreqDept;
run;
proc print data=perm.survey;
run;
```

Obs	Gender	Age	Bankcard	FreqBank	Deptcard	FreqDept
1	MALE	27	1	8	0	0
2	FEMALE	29	3	14	5	10
3	FEMALE	34	2	10	.	.
4	MALE	35	2	12	4	8
5	FEMALE	36	4	16	3	7
6	MALE	21	1	5	0	0

> The MISSOVER option works only for missing values that occur at the **end** of the record.

Reading Missing Values at the Beginning or Middle of a Record

Remember that the MISSOVER option works only for missing values that occur at the end of the record. A different method is required when you are using list input to read raw data that contains missing values at the beginning or middle of a record. Let's look at what happens when a missing value occurs at the beginning or middle of a record.

Suppose the value for Age is missing in the first record.

Raw Data File Credit2

```
1---+----10---+----20
MALE,,1,8,0,0
FEMALE,29,3,14,5,10
FEMALE,34,2,10,3,3
MALE,35,2,12,4,8
FEMALE,36,4,16,3,7
```

When the program below executes, each field in the raw data file is read one by one. The INPUT statement tells SAS to read six data values from each record. However, the first record contains only five values.

```
data perm.survey;
    infile credit dlm=',';
    input Gender $ Age Bankcard FreqBank
          Deptcard FreqDept;
run;
proc print data=perm.survey;
run;
```

The two commas in the first record are interpreted as one delimiter. The incorrect value (*1*) is read for Age. The program continues to read subsequent incorrect values for Bankcard (*8*), FreqBank (*0*), and Deptcard (*0*). The program then attempts to read the character filed *FEMALE*, at the beginning of the second record, as the value for the numeric variable FreqDept. This causes the value of FreqDept in the first observation to be interpreted as missing. The input pointer then moves down to the third record to begin reading values for the second observation. Therefore, the first observation in the data set contains incorrect values and values from the second in the raw data file are not included.

Obs	Gender	Age	Bankcard	FreqBank	Deptcard	FreqDept
1	MALE	1	8	0	0	.
2	FEMALE	34	2	10	3	3
3	MALE	35	2	12	4	8
4	FEMALE	36	4	16	3	7

The DSD Option

You can use the DSD option in the INFILE statement to correctly read the raw data. The DSD option changes how SAS treats delimiters when list input is used. Specifically, the DSD option

- sets the default delimiter to a comma
- treats two consecutive delimiters as a missing value
- removes quotation marks from values.

When the following program reads the raw data file, the DSD option sets the default delimiter to a comma and treats the two consecutive delimiters as a missing value. Therefore, the data is read correctly.

```
data perm.survey;
   infile credit dsd;
   input Gender $ Age Bankcard FreqBank
         Deptcard FreqDept;
run;
proc print data=perm.survey;
run;
```

Raw Data File Credit2

```
1---+----10---+----20
MALE,,1,8,0,0
FEMALE,29,3,14,5,10
FEMALE,34,2,10,3,3
MALE,35,2,12,4,8
FEMALE,36,4,16,3,7
```

Obs	Gender	Age	Bankcard	FreqBank	Deptcard	FreqDept
1	MALE	.	1	8	0	0
2	FEMALE	29	3	14	5	10
3	FEMALE	34	2	10	3	3
4	MALE	35	2	12	4	8
5	FEMALE	36	4	16	3	7

The DLM= Option

If the data uses multiple delimiters or a single delimiter other than a comma, then simply specify the delimiter value(s) with the DLM= option. In the following example, an asterisk (*) is used as a delimiter. However, the data is still read correctly because of the DSD option.

```
data perm.survey;
    infile credit dsd dlm='*';
    input Gender $ Age Bankcard FreqBank
        Deptcard FreqDept;
run;
proc print data=perm.survey;
run;
```

Raw Data File Credit3

```
1---+----10---+----20
MALE**1*8*0*0
FEMALE*29*3*14*5*10
FEMALE*34*2*10*3*3
MALE*35*2*12*4*8
FEMALE*36*4*16*3*7
```

Obs	Gender	Age	Bankcard	FreqBank	Deptcard	FreqDept
1	MALE	.	1	8	0	0
2	FEMALE	29	3	14	5	10
3	FEMALE	34	2	10	3	3
4	MALE	35	2	12	4	8
5	FEMALE	36	4	16	3	7

The DSD option can also be used to read raw data when there is a missing value at the beginning of a record, as long as a delimiter precedes the first value in the record.

```
data perm.survey;
    infile credit dsd;
    input Gender $ Age Bankcard FreqBank
        Deptcard FreqDept;
run;
proc print data=perm.survey;
run;
```

Raw Data File Credit4

```
1---+----10---+----20
,27,1,8,0,0
FEMALE,29,3,14,5,10
FEMALE,34,2,10,3,3
MALE,35,2,12,4,8
FEMALE,36,4,16,3,7
```

Obs	Gender	Age	Bankcard	FreqBank	Deptcard	FreqDept
1		27	1	8	0	0
2	FEMALE	29	3	14	5	10
3	FEMALE	34	2	10	3	3
4	MALE	35	2	12	4	8
5	FEMALE	36	4	16	3	7

You can also use the DSD and DLM= options to read fields that are delimited by blanks.

```
data perm.survey;
    infile credit dsd dlm=' ';
    input Gender $ Age Bankcard FreqBank
          Deptcard FreqDept;
run;
```

Later in this chapter, you'll learn how to use the DSD option to remove quotation marks from values in raw data.

Specifying the Length of Character Values

Remember that when you use list input to read raw data, **character** values are assigned a default length of 8. Let's look at what happens when list input is used to read character variables whose values are longer than 8.

The raw data file that is referenced by the fileref **Citydata** contains 1970 and 1980 population figures for several large U.S. cities. Notice that some city names are rather long.

```
1---+----10---+----20---+----
ANCHORAGE 48081 174431
ATLANTA 495039 425022
BOSTON 641071 562994
CHARLOTTE 241420 314447
CHICAGO 3369357 3005072
DALLAS 844401 904078
DENVER 514678 492365
DETROIT 1514063 1203339
MIAMI 334859 346865
PHILADELPHIA 1949996 1688210
SACRAMENTO 257105 275741
```

The longer character values are truncated when they are written to the program data vector.

Program Data Vector

N	Rank	City	Pop70	Pop80
1	1	ANCHORAG	48081	174431

PROC PRINT output shows the truncated values for `City`.

```
data perm.growth;
    infile citydata;
    input City $ Pop70 Pop80;
run;
proc print data=perm.growth;
run;
```

Obs	City	Pop70	Pop80
1	ANCHORAG	48081	174431
2	ATLANTA	495039	425022
3	BOSTON	641071	562994
4	CHARLOTT	241420	314447
5	CHICAGO	3369357	3005072
6	DALLAS	844401	904078
7	DENVER	514678	492365
8	DETROIT	1514063	1203339
9	MIAMI	334859	346865
10	PHILADEL	1949996	1688210
11	SACRAMEN	257105	275741

The LENGTH Statement

Remember, variable attributes are defined when the variable is **first** encountered in the DATA step. In the program below, the LENGTH statement precedes the INPUT statement and defines both the length and type of the variable `City`. A length of 12 has been assigned to accommodate *PHILADELPHIA*, which is the longest value for `City`.

```
data perm.growth;
   infile citydata;
   length City $ 12;
   input city $ Pop70 Pop80;
run;
proc print data=perm.growth;
run;
```

```
1---+----10---+----20---+----
ANCHORAGE 48081 174431
ATLANTA 495039 425022
BOSTON 641071 562994
CHARLOTTE 241420 314447
CHICAGO 3369357 3005072
DALLAS 844401 904078
DENVER 514678 492365
DETROIT 1514063 1203339
MIAMI 334859 346865
PHILADELPHIA 1949996 1688210
SACRAMENTO 257105 275741
```

Using this method, you do not need to specify `City`'s type in the INPUT statement. However, leaving the $ in the INPUT statement will not produce an error. Your output should now display the complete values for `City`.

Obs	City	Pop70	Pop80
1	ANCHORAGE	48081	174431
2	ATLANTA	495039	425022
3	BOSTON	641071	562994
4	CHARLOTTE	241420	314447
5	CHICAGO	3369357	3005072
6	DALLAS	844401	904078
7	DENVER	514678	492365
8	DETROIT	1514063	1203339
9	MIAMI	334859	346865
10	PHILADELPHIA	1949996	1688210
11	SACRAMENTO	257105	275741

Because variable attributes are defined when the variable is first encountered in the DATA step, a variable that is defined in a LENGTH statement (if it precedes an INPUT statement) will appear first in the data set, regardless of the order of the variables in the INPUT statement.

Modifying List Input

You can make list input more versatile by using **modified** list input. There are two modifiers that can be used with list input.

- The ampersand (**&**) modifier is used to read character values that contain embedded blanks.

- The colon (:) modifier is used to read nonstandard data values and character values that are longer than eight characters, but which contain no embedded blanks.

You can use modified list input to read the file shown below. This file contains the names of the 10 largest U.S. cities ranked in order based on their 1986 estimated population figures.

Notice that some of the values for city names contain embedded blanks. Also, note that the values representing the population of each city are nonstandard numeric values (they contain commas).

Raw Data File Topten

```
1---+----10---+----20---+--
 1 NEW YORK  7,262,700
 2 LOS ANGELES  3,259,340
 3 CHICAGO  3,009,530
 4 HOUSTON  1,728,910
 5 PHILADELPHIA  1,642,900
 6 DETROIT  1,086,220
 7 SAN DIEGO  1,015,190
 8 DALLAS  1,003,520
 9 SAN ANTONIO  914,350
10 PHOENIX  894,070
```

In the following sections you will learn how to use the ampersand (&) modifier to read the values for city (City). Then you will learn how the colon (:) modifier can be used to read the nonstandard numeric values that represent population (Pop86).

Reading Values That Contain Embedded Blanks

The ampersand (&) modifier enables you to read character values that contain single embedded blanks. The & indicates that a character value that is being read with list input might contain one or more single embedded blanks. The value is read until **two or more consecutive blanks** are encountered. The & modifier precedes a specified informat if one is used.

```
input Rank City &;
```

In the raw data file shown below, each value of City is followed by two consecutive blanks. There are two ways that you can use list input to read the values of City.

Using the Ampersand (&) Modifier with a LENGTH Statement

As shown below, you can use a LENGTH statement to define the length of City, and then add an & modifier to the INPUT statement to indicate that the values contain embedded blanks.

```
data perm.cityrank;
   infile topten;
   length City $ 12;
   input Rank city &;
```

Raw Data File Topten

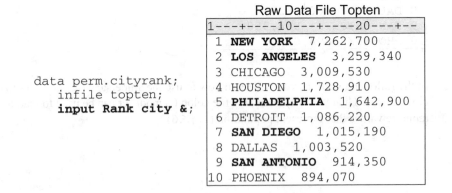

```
1---+----10---+----20---+--
 1 NEW YORK  7,262,700
 2 LOS ANGELES  3,259,340
 3 CHICAGO  3,009,530
 4 HOUSTON  1,728,910
 5 PHILADELPHIA  1,642,900
 6 DETROIT  1,086,220
 7 SAN DIEGO  1,015,190
 8 DALLAS  1,003,520
 9 SAN ANTONIO  914,350
10 PHOENIX  894,070
```

Using the Ampersand (&) Modifier with an Informat

You can also read the values for City with the & modifier followed by the $w. informat, which reads standard character values, as shown below. When you do this, the w value in the informat determines the variable's length and should be large enough to accommodate the longest value.

```
data perm.cityrank;
   infile topten;
   input Rank city &;
```

Raw Data File Topten

```
1---+----10---+----20---+--
 1 NEW YORK  7,262,700
 2 LOS ANGELES  3,259,340
 3 CHICAGO  3,009,530
 4 HOUSTON  1,728,910
 5 PHILADELPHIA  1,642,900
 6 DETROIT  1,086,220
 7 SAN DIEGO  1,015,190
 8 DALLAS  1,003,520
 9 SAN ANTONIO  914,350
10 PHOENIX  894,070
```

 Remember that you must use **two consecutive blanks** as delimiters when you use the & modifier. You cannot use any other delimiter to indicate the end of each field.

Reading Nonstandard Values

The colon (:) modifier enables you to read nonstandard data values and character values that are longer than eight characters, but which contain no embedded blanks. The colon (:) indicates that values are read until a blank (or other delimiter) is encountered, and then an informat is applied. If an informat for reading character values is specified, the *w* value specifies the variable's length, overriding the default length.

Notice the values representing the 1986 population of each city in the raw data file below. Because they contain commas, these values are **nonstandard** numeric values.

Raw Data File Topten

```
1---+----10---+----20---+--
 1 NEW YORK  7,262,700
 2 LOS ANGELES  3,259,340
 3 CHICAGO  3,009,530
 4 HOUSTON  1,728,910
 5 PHILADELPHIA  1,642,900
 6 DETROIT  1,086,220
 7 SAN DIEGO  1,015,190
 8 DALLAS  1,003,520
 9 SAN ANTONIO  914,350
10 PHOENIX  894,070
```

In order to read these values, you can modify list input with the colon (:) modifier, followed by the COMMA*w.d* informat, as shown in the program below. Notice that the COMMA*w.d* informat does **not** specify a *w* value.

```
data perm.cityrank;
    infile topten;
    input Rank City & $12.
        Pop86 : comma.;
```

Remember that list input reads each value until the next blank is detected. The default length of numeric variables is 8, so you don't need to specify a *w* value to indicate the length of a numeric variable.

This is different from using a numeric informat with **formatted** input. In that case, you must specify a *w* value in order to indicate the number of columns to be read.

Processing the DATA Step

At compile time, the informat $12. in the example below sets the length of `City` to 12 and stores this information in the descriptor portion of the data set. During the execution phase, however, the *w* value of 12 does **not** determine the number of columns that are read. This is different from the function of informats in the formatted input style.

```
data perm.cityrank;
    infile topten;
    input Rank City & $12.
          Pop86 : comma.;
run;
```

```
1---+----10---+----20---+--
1 NEW YORK  7,262,700
2 LOS ANGELES  3,259,340
3 CHICAGO  3,009,530
4 HOUSTON  1,728,910
5 PHILADELPHIA  1,642,900
```

The & modifier indicates that the values for `City` should be read until two consecutive blanks are encountered. Therefore, the value *NEW YORK* is read from column 4 to column 11, a total of only 8 columns. When blanks are encountered in both columns 12 and 13, the value *NEW YORK* is written to the program data vector.

```
data perm.cityrank;
    infile topten;
    input Rank City & $12.
          Pop86 : comma.;
run;
```

```
 12345678
1---+----10↓--+----20---+--
1 NEW YORK  7,262,700
2 LOS ANGELES  3,259,340
3 CHICAGO  3,009,530
4 HOUSTON  1,728,910
5 PHILADELPHIA  1,642,900
```

Program Data Vector

N_	Rank	City	Pop86
1	1	New York	.

The input pointer moves forward to the next **nonblank** column, which is column 14 in the first record. Now the values for `Pop86` are read from column 14 **until the next blank** is encountered. The COMMA*w.d* informat removes the commas, and the value is written to the program data vector.

```
data perm.cityrank;
   infile topten;
   input Rank City & $12.
         Pop86 : comma.;
run;
```

```
1---+----10---+----20-↓-+--
1 NEW YORK  7,262,700
2 LOS ANGELES  3,259,340
3 CHICAGO  3,009,530
4 HOUSTON  1,728,910
5 PHILADELPHIA  1,642,900
```

Program Data Vector

N	Rank	City	Pop86
1	1	New York	7262700

Notice that the **character** values for City and the **nonstandard** values for Pop86 are stored correctly in the data set.

SAS Data Set Perm.Cityrank

Rank	City	Pop86
1	NEW YORK	7262700
2	LOS ANGELES	3259340
3	CHICAGO	3009530
4	HOUSTON	1728910
5	PHILADELPHIA	1642900
6	DETROIT	1086220
7	SAN DIEGO	1015190
8	DALLAS	1003520
9	SAN ANTONIO	914350
10	PHOENIX	894070

Comparing Formatted Input and Modified List Input

As you have seen, informats work differently in modified list input than they do in formatted input. With formatted input, the informat determines both the length of character variables and the number of columns that are read. The same number of columns are read from each record.

```
input @3 City $12.;
```

```
   123456789-12
1---+----10---+----20---+--
1 NEW YORK    7,262,700
2 LOS ANGELES 3,259,340
3 CHICAGO     3,009,530
4 HOUSTON     1,728,910
5 PHILADELPHIA 1,642,900
```

```
   123456789--12
1---+----10---+----20---+--
1 NEW YORK    7,262,700
2 LOS ANGELES 3,259,340
3 CHICAGO     3,009,530
4 HOUSTON     1,728,910
5 PHILADELPHIA 1,642,900
```

The informat in modified list input determines only the **length** of the variable, **not** the number of columns that are read. Here, the raw data values are read until two consecutive blanks are encountered.

```
input City & $12.;
```

```
   12345678
1---+----10---+----20---+--
1 NEW YORK   7,262,700
2 LOS ANGELES  3,259,340
3 CHICAGO  3,009,530
4 HOUSTON  1,728,910
5 PHILADELPHIA   1,642,900
```

```
   123456789--12
1---+----10---+----20---+--
1 NEW YORK   7,262,700
2 LOS ANGELES  3,259,340
3 CHICAGO  3,009,530
4 HOUSTON  1,728,910
5 PHILADELPHIA  1,642,900
```

Creating Free-Format Data

In Chapter 5, **Creating SAS Data Sets from Raw Data**, you learned how the PUT statement can be used with column output to write observations from a SAS data set to a raw data file. The PUT statement can also be used with **list output** to create free-format raw data files.

List output is similar to list input. With list output, you simply list the names of the variables whose values you want to write. The PUT statement writes a variable, leaves a blank, then writes the next value.

General form, PUT statement using list output:

    PUT *variable* **<:** *format***>;**

where

- *variable* specifies the variable whose value you want to write
- a colon (:) precedes a format
- *format.* specifies a format to use for writing the data values.

The following program creates the raw data file **Findat**, using the SAS data set **Perm.Finance**. The DATE*w.* format is used to write the value of Date in the form *DDMMYYYY*.

```
data _null_;
   set perm.finance;
   file 'c:\data\findat';
   put ssn name salary date : date9.;
run;
```

SAS Data Set Finance

SSN	Name	Salary	Date
074-53-9892	Vincent	35000	05/22/97
776-84-5391	Phillipon	29750	12/15/96
929-75-0218	Gunter	27500	04/30/97
446-93-2122	Harbinger	33900	07/08/96
228-88-9649	Benito	28000	03/04/96
029-46-9261	Rudelich	35000	02/15/95
442-21-8075	Sirignano	5000	11/22/95

Raw Data File Findat

```
1---+----10---+----20---+----30---+----40
074-53-9892 Vincent 35000 22MAY1997
776-84-5391 Phillipon 29750 15DEC1996
929-75-0218 Gunter 27500 30APR1997
446-93-2122 Harbinger 33900 08JUL1996
228-88-9649 Benito 2800 04MAR1996
029-46-9261 Rudelich 3500 15FEB1995
442-21-2122 Sirigano 5000 22NOV1995
```

Specifying a Delimiter

You can use the DLM= option with a FILE statement to create a character-delimited raw data file.

```
data _null_;
   set perm.finance;
   file 'c:\data\findat2' dlm=',';
   put ssn name salary date : date9.;
run;
```

SAS Data Set Finance

SSN	Name	Salary	Date
074-53-9892	Vincent	35000	05/22/97
776-84-5391	Phillipon	29750	12/15/96
929-75-0218	Gunter	27500	04/30/97
446-93-2122	Harbinger	33900	07/08/96
228-88-9649	Benito	28000	03/04/96
029-46-9261	Rudelich	35000	02/15/95
442-21-8075	Sirignano	5000	11/22/95

Raw Data File Findat2

```
1---+----10---+----20---+----30---+----40
074-53-9892,Vincent,35000,22MAY1997
776-84-5391,Phillipon,29750,15DEC1996
929-75-0218,Gunter,27500,30APR1997
446-93-2122,Harbinger,33900,08JUL1996
228-88-9649,Benito,28000,04MAR1996
029-46-9261,Rudelich,35000,15FEB1995
442-21-8075,Sirignano,5000,22NOV1995
```

 For creating a simple raw data file, an alternative to the DATA step is the EXPORT procedure.

General form, PROC EXPORT:

> **PROC EXPORT** DATA=*SAS-data-set*;
>   **OUTFILE**=*filename* <**DELIMITER**=*'delimiter'*>;
> **RUN**;

where

- *SAS-data-set* names the input SAS data set
- *filename* specifies the complete path and file name of the output
- *delimiter* specifies the delimiter to separate columns of data in the output file.

 For more information about the EXPORT procedure, see the SAS documentation.

Using the DSD Option

What happens if you need to create a comma-delimited file that requires the use of a format that writes out values using commas?

If you used the following program, the resulting raw data file would contain five fields rather than four.

```
data _null_;
   set perm.finance;
   file 'c:\data\findat2' dlm=',';
   put ssn name salary : comma6. date date9.;
run;
```

SAS Data Set Finance

SSN	Name	Salary	Date
074-53-9892	Vincent	35000	05/22/97
776-84-5391	Phillipon	29750	12/15/96
929-75-0218	Gunter	27500	04/30/97
446-93-2122	Harbinger	33900	07/08/96
228-88-9649	Benito	28000	03/04/96
029-46-9261	Rudelich	35000	02/15/95
442-21-8075	Sirignano	5000	11/22/95

Raw Data File Findat2

```
1---+----10---+----20---+----30---+----40
074-53-9892,Vincent,35,000,22MAY1997
776-84-5391,Phillipon,29,750,15DEC1996
929-75-0218,Gunter,27,500,30APR1997
446-93-2122,Harbinger,33,900,08JUL1996
228-88-9649,Benito,28,000,04MAR1996
029-46-9261,Rudelich,35,000,15FEB1995
442-21-8075,Sirignano,5,000,22NOV1995
```

You can use the DSD option in the FILE statement to specify that data values containing commas should be enclosed in quotation marks. Remember that the DSD option uses a comma as a delimiter, so a DLM= option isn't necessary here.

```
data _null_;
   set perm.finance;
   file 'c:\data\findat2' dsd;
   put ssn name salary : comma. date : date9.;
run;
```

Raw Data File Findat2

```
1---+----10---+----20---+----30---+----40
074-53-9892,Vincent,"35,000",22MAY1997
776-84-5391,Phillipon,"29,750",15DEC1996
929-75-0218,Gunter,"27,500",30APR1997
446-93-2122,Harbinger,"33,900",08JUL1996
228-88-9649,Benito,"28,000",04MAR1996
029-46-9261,Rudelich,"35,000",15FEB1995
442-21-8075,Sirignano,"5,000",22NOV1995
```

Reading Values That Contain Delimiters within a Quoted String

You can also use the DSD option in an INFILE statement to read values that contain delimiters within a quoted string. As shown in the following PROC PRINT output, the INPUT statement treats the commas within the values for Salary as valid characters and removes the quotation marks from the character strings before the value is stored.

```
data work.finance2;
   infile findat2 dsd;
   length SSN $ 11 Name $ 9;
   input ssn name Salary : comma. Date date9.;
run;

proc print data=work.finance2;
   format date date9.;
run;
```

Raw Data File Findat2

```
1---+----10---+----20---+----30---+----40
074-53-9892,Vincent,"35,000",22MAY1997
776-84-5391,Phillipon,"29,750",15DEC1996
929-75-0218,Gunter,"27,500",30APR1997
446-93-2122,Harbinger,"33,900",08JUL1996
228-88-9649,Benito,"28,000",04MAR1996
029-46-9261,Rudelich,"35,000",15FEB1995
442-21-8075,Sirignano,"5,000",22NOV1995
```

Obs	SSN	Name	Salary	Date
1	074-53-9892	Vincent	35000	22MAY1997
2	776-84-5391	Phillipon	29750	15DEC1996
3	929-75-0218	Gunter	27500	30APR1997
4	446-93-2122	Harbinger	33900	08JUL1996
5	228-88-9649	Benito	28000	04MAR1996
6	029-46-9261	Rudelich	35000	15FEB1995
7	442-21-8075	Sirignano	5000	22NOV1995

Mixing Input Styles

Evaluating your raw data and choosing the most appropriate input style is a very important task. You have already worked with three input styles for reading raw data.

Input Style	Reads
Column	standard data values in fixed fields
Formatted	nonstandard data values in fixed fields
List	data values that are not arranged in fixed fields, but are separated by blanks or other delimiters

With some file layouts, you might need to mix input styles in the same INPUT statement in order to read the data correctly.

Look at the raw data file below and think about how to combine input styles to read these values.

```
1---+----10---+----20---+----30---+----40-
209-20-3721 07JAN78 41,983 SALES 2896
223-96-8933 03MAY86 27,356 EDUCATION 2344
232-18-3485 17AUG81 33,167 MARKETING 2674
251-25-9392 08SEP84 34,033 RESEARCH 2956
```

- Column input is an appropriate choice for the first field because the values can be read as standard character values and are located in fixed columns.

- The next two fields are also located in fixed columns, but the values require an informat. So, formatted input is a good choice here.

- Values in the fourth field begin in column 28 but do not end in the same column. List input is appropriate here, but notice that some values are longer than eight characters. You need to use the : format modifier with an informat to read these values.

- The last field does not always begin or end in the same column, so list input is the best input style for those values.

Field Description	Starting Column	Field Width	Data Type	Input Style
Social Security #	1	11	character	column
Date of Hire	13	7	date	formatted
Annual Salary	21	6	numeric	formatted
Department	28	5 to 9	character	list
Phone Extension	??	4	numeric	list

The INPUT statement to read the data should look like this:

```
data perm.mixed;
   infile rawdata;
   input SSN $ 1-11 @13 HireDate date7.
         @21 Salary comma6. Department : $9. Phone;
run;
proc print data=perm.mixed;
run;
```

When you submit the PRINT procedure, the output displays values for each variable.

Obs	SSN	HireDate	Salary	Department	Phone
1	209-20-3721	6581	41983	SALES	2896
2	223-96-8933	9619	27356	EDUCATION	2344
3	232-18-3485	7899	33167	MARKETING	2674
4	251-25-9392	9017	34033	RESEARCH	2956

Additional Features

Writing Character Strings and Variable Values

You can use a PUT statement to write both character strings and variable values to a raw data file. To write out a character string, simply add a character string, enclosed in quotation marks, to the PUT statement. It's a good idea to include a blank space as the last character in the string to avoid spacing problems.

```
filename totaldat 'c:\records\junsales';
data _null_;
   set work.totals;
   file totaldat;
   put 'Sales for salesrep ' salesrep
       'totaled ' sales : dollar9.;
run;
```

SAS Data Set Work.Totals

Obs	SalesRep	Sales
1	Friedman	$14,893
2	Keane	$14,324
3	Schuster	$13,914
4	Davidson	$13,674

Raw Data File Totaldat

```
1---+----10---+----20---+----30---+----40---+
Sales for salesrep Friedman totaled $14,893
Sales for salesrep Keane totaled $14,324
Sales for salesrep Schuster totaled $13,914
Sales for salesrep Davidson totaled $13,674
```

 For more information about using the PUT statement to write character strings, see the SAS documentation for your operating environment.

Summary

Text Summary

Free-Format Data

External files can contain raw data that is **free format**; that is, the data is not arranged in fixed fields. The fields can be separated by blanks or by some other delimiter, such as commas.

Using List Input

Free-format data can easily be read with **list input** because you do not need to specify column locations of the data. You simply list the variable names in the same order as the corresponding raw data fields. You must distinguish character variables from numeric variables by using the dollar ($) sign.

When characters other than blanks are used to separate the data values, you can specify the field delimiter by using the **DLM= option** in the INFILE statement.

You can also specify a range of variables in the INPUT statement when the variable values in the raw data file are sequential and are separated by blanks (or by some other delimiter). This is especially useful if your data contains similar variables, such as the answers to a questionnaire.

In its simplest form, list input places several limitations on the types of data that can be read.

Reading Missing Values

If your data contains missing values at the end of a record, you can use the INFILE statement with the MISSOVER option to prevent SAS from going to the next record to find the missing values.

If your data contains missing values at the beginning or in the middle of a record, you might be able to use the **DSD option** in the INFILE statement to correctly read the raw data. The DSD option sets the default delimiter to a comma and treats two consecutive delimiters as a missing value.

If the data uses multiple delimiters or a single delimiter other than a comma, you can use both the DSD option and the DLM= option in the INFILE statement.

The DSD option can also be used to read raw data when there is a missing value at the beginning of a record, as long as a delimiter precedes the first value in the record.

Specifying the Length of Character Values

You can specify the length of character variables by using the **LENGTH statement**. The LENGTH statement enables you to use list input to read names that are longer than eight characters without truncating them.

Because variable attributes are defined when the variable is first encountered in the DATA step, the LENGTH statement precedes the INPUT statement and defines both the length and the type of the variable.

When you use the LENGTH statement, you do not need to specify the variable type again in the INPUT statement.

Modifying List Input

Modified list input can be used to read values that contain embedded blanks and nonstandard values. Modified list input uses two format modifiers:

- the **ampersand (&) modifier** enables you to read character values that contain single embedded blanks

- the **colon (:) modifier** enables you to read nonstandard data values and character values that are longer than eight characters, but which contain no embedded blanks.

Remember that informats work differently in modified list input than they do in formatted input.

Creating Free-Format Data

You can create a raw data file using **list output**. With list output, you simply list the names of the variables whose values you want to write. The PUT statement writes a variable, leaves a blank, then writes the next value.

You can use the DLM= option with a FILE statement to create a delimited raw data file. You can use the DSD option in a FILE statement to specify that data values containing commas should be enclosed in quotation marks. You can also use the DSD option to read values that contain delimiters within a quoted string.

Mixing Input Styles

With some file layouts, you might need to mix input styles in the same INPUT statement in order to read the data correctly.

Points to Remember

- When you use list input,

    o fields must be separated by at least one blank or other delimiter.

    o fields must be read in order, from left to right. You cannot skip or re-read fields.

    o use a LENGTH statement to avoid truncating character values that are longer than eight characters.

- In formatted input, the informat determines both the length of character variables and the number of columns that are read. The same number of columns are read from each record.

- The informat in modified list input determines only the length of the variable value, not the number of columns that are read.

Practice

After you complete this chapter, practice what you learned by using the sample data and SAS programs for Chapter 18, **Reading Free-Format Data**, which are located on the CD-ROM. Follow the directions for creating your sample data in the Before You Begin section.

Quiz

Select the best answer for each question. After completing the quiz, check your answers using the answer key in the appendix.

1. The raw data file referenced by the fileref **Students** contains data that is

   Raw Data File Students

   ```
   1---+----10---+----20---+
   FRED JOHNSON 18 USC 1
   ASHLEY FERRIS 20 NCSU 3
   BETH ROSEMONT 21 UNC 4
   ```

   a. arranged in fixed fields
   b. free format
   c. mixed format
   d. arranged in columns

2. Which input style should be used to read the values in the raw data file that is referenced by the fileref **Students**?

   Raw Data File Students

   ```
   1---+----10---+----20---+
   FRED JOHNSON 18 USC 1
   ASHLEY FERRIS 20 NCSU 3
   BETH ROSEMONT 21 UNC 4
   ```

   a. column
   b. formatted
   c. list
   d. mixed

3. Which SAS program was used to create the raw data file **Teamdat** from the SAS data set **Work.Scores**?

   SAS Data Set Work.Scores

Obs	Name	HighScore	Team
1	Joe	87	Blue Beetles, Durham
2	Dani	79	Raleigh Racers, Raleigh
3	Lisa	85	Sand Sharks, Cary
4	Matthew	76	Blue Beetles, Durham

Raw Data File Teamdat

```
1---+----10---+----20---+----30---+
Joe,87,"Blue Beetles, Durham"
Dani,79,"Raleigh Racers, Raleigh"
Lisa,85,"Sand Sharks, Cary"
Matthew,76,"Blue Beetles, Durham"
```

a. ```
   data _null_;
       set work.scores;
       file 'c:\data\teamdat' dlm=',';
       put name highscore team;
   run;
   ```

b. ```
   data _null_;
       set work.scores;
       file 'c:\data\teamdat' dlm=' ';
       put name highscore team;
   run;
   ```

c. ```
   data _null_;
       set work.scores;
       file 'c:\data\teamdat' dsd;
       put name highscore team;
   run;
   ```

d. ```
   data _null_;
       set work.scores;
       file 'c:\data\teamdat';
       put name highscore team;
   run;
   ```

4. Which SAS statement reads the raw data values in order and assigns them to the variables shown below?

Variables: FirstName (character), LastName (character), Age (numeric), School (character), Class (numeric)

Raw Data File Students

```
1---+----10---+----20---+
FRED JOHNSON 18 USC 1
ASHLEY FERRIS 20 NCSU 3
BETH ROSEMONT 21 UNC 4
```

a. ```
   input FirstName $ LastName $ Age School $ Class;
   ```

b. ```
   input FirstName LastName Age School Class;
   ```

c. ```
   input FirstName $ 1-4 LastName $ 6-12 Age 14-15
         School $ 17-19 Class 21;
   ```

d. ```
   input FirstName 1-4 LastName 6-12 Age 14-15
         School 17-19 Class 21;
   ```

5. Which SAS statement should be used to read the raw data file that is referenced by the fileref **Salesrep**?

Raw Data File Salesrep

```
1---+----10---+----20---+----30
ELAINE:FRIEDMAN:WILMINGTON:2102
JIM:LLOYD:20:RALEIGH:38392
JENNIFER:WU:21:GREENSBORO:1436
```

    a. `infile salesrep;`

    b. `infile salesrep ':';`

    c. `infile salesrep dlm;`

    d. `infile salesrep dlm=':';`

6. Which of the following raw data files can be read by using the MISSOVER option in the INFILE statement? Missing values are indicated with colored blocks.

    a.
```
1---+----10---+----20---+----
ORANGE SUNNYDALE 20 10
PINEAPPLE ALOHA 7 10
GRAPE FARMFRESH 3 ▉
APPLE FARMFRESH 16 5
GRAPEFRUIT SUNNYDALE 12 8
```

    b.
```
1---+----10---+----20---+----
ORANGE SUNNYDALE 20 10
PINEAPPLE ALOHA 7 10
GRAPE FARMFRESH ▉ 17
APPLE FARMFRESH 16 5
GRAPEFRUIT SUNNYDALE 12 8
```

    c.
```
1---+----10---+----20---+----
ORANGE SUNNYDALE 20 10
PINEAPPLE ALOHA 7 10
GRAPE ▉▉▉▉▉ 3 17
APPLE FARMFRESH 16 5
GRAPEFRUIT SUNNYDALE 12 8
```

    d.
```
1---+----10---+----20---+----
ORANGE SUNNYDALE 20 10
PINEAPPLE ALOHA 7 10
▉▉▉ FARMFRESH 3
APPLE FARMFRESH 16 5
GRAPEFRUIT SUNNYDALE 12 8
```

7. Which SAS program correctly reads the data in the raw data file that is referenced by the fileref **Volunteer**?

    Raw Data File Volunteer

    ```
    1---+----10---+----20---+----30
    ARLENE BIGGERSTAFF 19 UNC 2
    JOSEPH CONSTANTINO 21 CLEM 2
    MARTIN FIELDS 18 UNCG 1
    ```

    a. ```
       data perm.contest;
           infile volunteer;
           input FirstName $ LastName $ Age School $ Class;
       run;
       ```

    b. ```
       data perm.contest;
           infile volunteer;
           length LastName $ 11;
           input FirstName $ lastname $ Age School $ Class;
       run;
       ```

    c. ```
       data perm.contest;
           infile volunteer;
           input FirstName $ lastname $ Age School $ Class;
           length LastName $ 11;
       run;
       ```

    d. ```
       data perm.contest;
           infile volunteer;
           input FirstName $ LastName $ 11. Age School $ Class;
       run;
       ```

8. Which type of input should be used to read the values in the raw data file that is referenced by the fileref **University**?

    Raw Data File University

    ```
    1---+----10---+----20---+----30
    UNC ASHEVILLE  2,712
    UNC CHAPEL HILL  24,189
    UNC CHARLOTTE  15,031
    UNC GREENSBORO  12,323
    ```

    a. column
    b. formatted
    c. list
    d. modified list

9. Which SAS statement correctly reads the values for `Flavor` and `Quantity`? Make sure the length of each variable can accommodate the values that are shown.

Raw Data File Cookies

```
1---+----10---+----20---+----30
CHOCOLATE CHIP  10,453
OATMEAL  12,187
PEANUT BUTTER  11,546
SUGAR  12,331
```

a. `input Flavor & $9. Quantity : comma.;`

b. `input Flavor & $14. Quantity : comma.;`

c. `input Flavor : $14. Quantity & comma.;`

d. `input Flavor $14. Quantity : comma.;`

10. Which SAS statement correctly reads the raw data values in order and assigns them to these corresponding variables: `Year` (numeric), `School` (character), `Enrolled` (numeric)?

Raw Data File Founding

```
1---+----10---+----20---+----30---+----40
1868 U OF CALIFORNIA BERKELEY  31,612
1906 U OF CALIFORNIA DAVIS  21,838
1965 U OF CALIFORNIA IRVINE  15,874
1919 U OF CALIFORNIA LOS ANGELES  35,730
```

a. `input Year School & $27.`
    `Enrolled : comma.;`

b. `input Year 1-4 School & $27.`
    `Enrolled : comma.;`

c. `input @1 Year 4. +1 School & $27.`
    `Enrolled : comma.;`

d. all of the above

19 Reading Date and Time Values

Overview

Introduction

SAS provides many informats for reading raw data values in various forms. In Chapter 17, **Reading Raw Data in Fixed Fields**, you learned how to use informats to read standard and nonstandard data. In this chapter, you learn how to use a special category of SAS informats called **date** and **time informats**. These informats enable you to read a variety of common date and time expressions. After you read date and time values, you can also perform calculations with them.

```
options yearcutoff=1920;
data perm.aprbills;
    infile aprdata;
    input LastName $8. @10 DateIn mmddyy8. +1 DateOut
        mmddyy8. +1 RoomRate 6. @35 EquipCost 6.;
    Days=dateout-datein+1;
    RoomCharge=days*roomrate;
    Total=roomcharge+equipcost;
run;
```

Program Data Vector

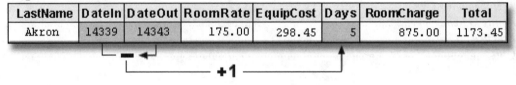

LastName	DateIn	DateOut	RoomRate	EquipCost	Days	RoomCharge	Total
Akron	14339	14343	175.00	298.45	5	875.00	1173.45

Objectives

In this chapter, you learn how

- SAS stores date and time values
- to use SAS informats to read common date and time expressions
- to handle two-digit date values
- to calculate time intervals by subtracting two dates
- to multiply a time interval by a rate
- to display various date and time values.

How SAS Stores Date Values

Before you read date or time values into a SAS data set or use those values in calculations, you should understand how SAS stores date and time values.

When you use a SAS informat to read a date, SAS converts it to a numeric **date value**. A SAS date value is the number of days from January 1, 1960, to the given date.

Jan. 1, 1959	Jan. 1, 1960	Jan. 1, 1961
← ‾365	0	366 →

Here are some examples of how the appropriate SAS informat can convert different expressions for the date January 2, 2000, to a single SAS date value:

Date Expression	SAS Date Informat	SAS Date Value
02Jan00	DATE*w*.	14611
01-02-2000	MMDDYY*w*.	14611
02/01/00	DDMMYY*w*.	14611
2000/01/02	YYMMDD*w*.	14611

Storing dates and times as numeric values enables you to use dates and times in calculations in much the same way as you would use any other number.

How SAS Stores Time Values

SAS stores **time values** similar to the way it stores date values. A SAS time value is stored as the number of seconds since midnight.

(12:00 am) midnight	12:15 pm	17:00 (or 5:00 pm)
0	44100	61200 →

A SAS **datetime** is a special value that combines both date and time information. A SAS datetime value is stored as the number of seconds between midnight on January 1, 1960, and a given date and time.

July 4, 1776 11:30:23	Jan. 1, 1960 midnight	April 22, 1989 16:10:45
← ‾5790400177	0	92488384 →

More about SAS Date and Time Values

As you use SAS date and time values, remember that

- SAS date values are based on the Gregorian calendar, and they are valid for dates from A.D. 1582 through A.D. 20,000. Use caution when working with historical dates. Most of Europe started to use the Gregorian calendar in 1582. Great Britain and the American colonies adopted it in 1752. Check the adoption date for other parts of the world before making important calculations.

- SAS makes adjustments for leap years but ignores leap seconds.

- SAS does not make adjustments for daylight saving time.

Reading Date and Time Informats

You use SAS date and time **informats** to read date and time expressions and convert them to SAS date and time values. Like other SAS informats, date and time informats are composed of

- an informat name
- a field width
- a period delimiter.

SAS informat names indicate the form of date expression that can be read using that particular informat. Here are some examples of common date and time informats:

- DATE*w*.
- DATETIME*w*.
- MMDDYY*w*.
- TIME*w*.

As you know, there are several ways to write a particular date. For example, all the following expressions represent the date October 15, 1999. Each of these common date expressions can be read using the appropriate SAS date informat.

Date Expression	SAS Date Informat
10/15/99	MMDDYY*w.*
15Oct99	DATE*w.*
10-15-99	MMDDYY*w.*
99/10/15	YYMMDD*w.*

Specifying Informats

Using the INPUT statement with an informat after a variable name is the simplest way to read date and time values into a variable.

General form, INPUT statement with an informat:

    INPUT *<pointer-control> variable informat.*;

where

- *pointer-control* gives the absolute or relative position of the pointer.
- *variable* is the name of the variable that is being read.
- *informat.* is any valid SAS informat. Note that the informat includes a final period.

For example, the following INPUT statement uses two informats:

```
input @15 Style $3. @21 Price 5.2;
```

The $*w.* character informat ($3.) reads values, starting at column 15 of the raw data, into the variable `Style`. The *w.d* numeric informat (5.2) reads values, starting at column 21, into the variable `Price`.

Now let's look at some specific informats that you can use.

MMDDYY*w.* Informat

You can tell by its name that the informat MMDDYY*w.* reads date values in the form 10/15/99.

General form, values that are read with the MMDDYY*w.* informat:

    mmddyy or *mmddyyyy*

where

- *mm* is an integer between 01 and 12, representing the month
- *dd* is an integer between 01 and 31, representing the day
- *yy* or *yyyy* is an integer that represents the year.

In the MMDDYY*w*. informat, the month, day, and year fields can be separated by blanks or delimiters such as hyphens (-) or slashes (/). If you use delimiters, you must place them between all fields in the values. Remember to specify a field width that includes not only the month, day, and year values, but any delimiters as well. Here are some date expressions that you can read using the MMDDYY*w*. informat:

Date Expression	SAS Date Informat
101599	MMDDYY6.
10/15/99	MMDDYY8.
10 15 99	MMDDYY8.
10-15-1999	MMDDYY10.

DATE*w*. Informat

The DATE*w*. informat reads date values in the form 30May2000.

> **General form, values that are read with the DATE*w*. informat:**
>
>   *ddmmmyy* or *ddmmmyyyy*
>
> where
>
> - *dd* is an integer from 01 to 31, representing the day
> - *mmm* is the first three letters of the month's name
> - *yy* or *yyyy* is an integer that represents the year.

You can place blanks or other special characters between the day, month, and year, as long as you increase the width of the informat to include these delimiters. Here are some date expressions that you can read using the DATE*w*. informat:

Date Expression	SAS Date Informat
30May00	DATE7.
30May2000	DATE9.
30-May-2000	DATE11.

TIME*w*. Informat

The TIME*w*. informat reads values in the form *hh:mm:ss.ss*.

General form, values that are read with the TIME*w*. informat:

    hh:mm:ss.ss

where

- *hh* is an integer from 00 to 23, representing the hour
- *mm* is an integer from 00 to 59, representing the minute
- *ss.ss* is an optional field that represents seconds and hundredths of seconds.

If you do not enter a value for *ss.ss*, a value of zero is assumed. Here are some examples of time expressions that you can read using the TIME*w*. informat:

Time Expression	SAS Time Informat
17:00:01.34	TIME11.
17:00	TIME5.
2:34	TIME5.

 Notice the last example. The field is only 4 columns wide, but a *w* value of 5 is specified. Five is the minimum acceptable field width for the TIME*w*. informat. If you specify a *w* value less than 5, you'll receive the following error message in the SAS log:

SAS Log

```
ERROR 29 - 85: Width specified for informat
               TIME is invalid.
```

DATETIME*w.* Informat

The DATETIME*w.* informat reads expressions that are composed of two parts, a date value and a time value, in the form: *ddmmmyy hh:mm:ss.ss*.

General form, values that are read with the DATETIME*w.* informat:

　　ddmmmyy hh:mm:ss.ss

where

- *ddmmmyy* is the date value, the same form as for the DATE*w.* informat
- the time value must be in the form *hh:mm:ss.ss*
- *hh* is an integer from 00 to 23, representing the hour
- *mm* is an integer from 00 to 59, representing the minute
- *ss.ss* is an optional field that represents seconds and hundredths of seconds
- the date value and time value are separated by a blank or other delimiter.

If you do not enter a value for *ss.ss*, a value of zero is assumed.

Here are some examples of the DATETIME*w.* informat. Note that in the time value, you must use delimiters to separate the values for hour, minutes, and seconds.

Date and Time Expression	SAS Datetime Informat
30May2000:10:03:17.2	DATETIME20.
30May00 10:03:17.2	DATETIME18.
30May2000/10:03	DATETIME15.

YEARCUTOFF= SAS System Option

Recall from Chapter 2, **Referencing Files and Setting Options,** that the value of the YEARCUTOFF= system option affects only **two-digit year values**. A date value that contains a four-digit year value will be interpreted correctly even if it does not fall within the 100-year span set by the YEARCUTOFF= system option.

Date Expression	SAS Date Informat	Interpreted As
06Oct59	date7.	06Oct1959
17Mar1783	date9.	17Mar1783

However, if you specify an inappropriate field width, you will receive incorrect results. Notice that the date expression in the table below contains a four-digit year value. The informat specifies a *w* value that is too small to read the entire value, so the last two digits of the year are truncated.

Date Expression	SAS Date Informat	Interpreted As
17Mar1783	date7.	17Mar1917

Another problem arises if you use the wrong informat to read a date or time expression. The SAS log displays an invalid data message, and the variable's values are set to missing.

```
1---+----10
03/23/98
```

SAS Log

```
3   input birthday date8.;
4   run;
NOTE: Invalid data for BIRTHDAY in line 3 1-8.
RULE: ----+----1----+----3----+----4----+----5
3      03/23/98
BIRTHDAY=. _ERROR_=1 _N_=1
```

When you work with date and time values,

- check the default value of the YEARCUTOFF= system option, and change it if necessary. The default YEARCUTOFF= value is 1920. Recall that you can use the OPTIONS procedure to display the current setting of system options.

- specify the proper informat for reading a date value.

- specify the correct field width so that the entire date value is read.

 Later in this chapter, you'll learn how to work with data values that contain delimiters.

Using Dates and Times in Calculations

Introduction

In this chapter so far, you've learned how date and time informats read common date and time expressions in specific forms. Now you will see how converting date and time expressions to numeric SAS date values can be useful, particularly for determining time intervals or performing calculations.

Suppose you work in the billing department of a small community hospital. It's your job to create a SAS data set from the raw data file that is referenced by the fileref **Aprdata**. A portion of the raw data file below shows data values that represent each patient's

- last name
- date checked in
- date checked out
- daily room rate
- equipment cost.

Raw Data File Aprdata

```
1---+----10---+----20---+----30---+----40
Akron     04/05/99 04/09/99 175.00 298.45
Brown     04/12/99 05/01/99 125.00 326.78
Carnes    04/27/99 04/29/99 125.00 174.24
Denison   04/11/99 04/12/99 175.00  87.41
Fields    04/15/99 04/22/99 175.00 378.96
Jamison   04/16/99 04/23/99 125.00 346.28
```

The data set that you create must also include variable values that represent how many days each person stayed in the hospital, the total room charges, and the total of all expenses that each patient incurred. When building the SAS program, you must first name the data set, identify the raw data file **Aprdata**, and use formatted input to read the data.

Example

 The following example is shown with the YEARCUTOFF= system option. When you work with two-digit year data, remember to check the default value of the YEARCUTOFF= option, and change it if necessary.

```
options yearcutoff=1920;
data perm.aprbills;
   infile aprdata;
   input LastName $8.
```

Notice that the values in the second and third fields are in the form *mmddyy*. To complete the INPUT statement, add instructions to read the values for `RoomRate` (third field) and `EquipCost` (fourth field), and add a semicolon.

```
options yearcutoff=1920;
data perm.aprbills;
   infile aprdata;
   input LastName $8. @10 DateIn mmddyy8. +1 DateOut
         mmddyy8. +1 RoomRate 6. @35 EquipCost 6.;
```

Now that the INPUT statement is complete, calculate how many days each patient was hospitalized. Because `DateIn` and `DateOut` are numeric variables, you can simply subtract to find the difference. But because the dates should be inclusive (patients are charged for both the first and last days), you must add 1 to the difference. Call this new variable `Days`.

```
options yearcutoff=1920;
data perm.aprbills;
   infile aprdata;
   input LastName $8. @10 DateIn mmddyy8. +1 DateOut
         mmddyy8. +1 RoomRate 6. @35 EquipCost 6.;
Days=dateout-datein+1;
```

You can calculate a total room charge by multiplying the variable values for `Days` and `RoomRate`.

```
options yearcutoff=1920;
data perm.aprbills;
   infile aprdata;
   input LastName $8. @10 DateIn mmddyy8. +1 DateOut
       mmddyy8. +1 RoomRate 6. @35 EquipCost 6.;
   Days=dateout-datein+1;
   RoomCharge=days*roomrate;
```

Calculating the total cost for each patient is easy. Create a variable named `Total` whose value is the sum of `RoomCharge` and `EquipCost`. Then add a PROC PRINT step and a RUN statement to view the new data.

```
options yearcutoff=1920;
data perm.aprbills;
   infile aprdata;
   input LastName $8. @10 DateIn mmddyy8. +1 DateOut
       mmddyy8. +1 RoomRate 6. @35 EquipCost 6.;
   Days=dateout-datein+1;
   RoomCharge=days*roomrate;
   Total=roomcharge+equipcost;
run;
proc print data=perm.aprbills;
run;
```

Obs	LastName	DateIn	DateOut	RoomRate	EquipCost	Days	RoomCharge	Total
1	Akron	14339	14343	175	298.45	5	875	1173.45
2	Brown	14346	14365	125	326.78	20	2500	2826.78
3	Carnes	14361	14363	125	174.24	3	375	549.24
4	Denison	14345	14346	175	87.41	2	350	437.41
5	Fields	14349	14356	175	378.96	8	1400	1778.96
6	Jamison	14350	14357	125	346.28	8	1000	1346.28

If the values for `DateIn` and `DateOut` look odd to you, remember that these are SAS date values. Applying a format such as MMDDYY8. displays them as they appeared in **Aprdata**. You'll work with some other date and time formats later in this chapter.

Follow the execution of the program that you've written. When the DATA step executes, the values for `DateIn` and `DateOut` are converted to SAS date values.

```
options yearcutoff=1920;
data perm.aprbills;
   infile aprdata;
   input LastName $8. @10 DateIn mmddyy8. +1 DateOut
      mmddyy8. +1 RoomRate 6. @35 EquipCost 6.;
   Days=dateout-datein+1;
   RoomCharge=days*roomrate;
   Total=roomcharge+equipcost;
run;
```

Raw Data File Aprdata

```
1---+----10---+----20---+----30---+----40
Akron     04/05/99 04/09/99 175.00 298.45
Brown     04/12/99 05/01/99 125.00 326.78
Carnes    04/27/99 04/29/99 125.00 174.24
Denison   04/11/99 04/12/99 175.00  87.41
Fields    04/15/99 04/22/99 175.00 378.96
Jamison   04/16/99 04/23/99 125.00 346.28
```

Program Data Vector

LastName	DateIn	DateOut	RoomRate	EquipCost	Days	RoomCharge	Total
Akron	14339	14343	.	.	.	.	.

After the rest of the INPUT statement executes, the value for `Days` is created by subtracting the SAS date value for `DateIn` from the value for `DateOut` and then adding 1.

```
options yearcutoff=1920;
data perm.aprbills;
   infile aprdata;
   input LastName $8. @10 DateIn mmddyy8. +1 DateOut
      mmddyy8. +1 RoomRate 6. @35 EquipCost 6.;
   Days=dateout-datein+1;
   RoomCharge=days*roomrate;
   Total=roomcharge+equipcost;
run;
```

Program Data Vector

LastName	DateIn	DateOut	RoomRate	EquipCost	Days	RoomCharge	Total
Akron	14339	14343	175.00	298.45	5	.	.

The value for RoomCharge is calculated next. RoomCharge is the product of Days and RoomRate.

```
options yearcutoff=1920;
data perm.aprbills;
   infile aprdata;
   input LastName $8. @10 DateIn mmddyy8. +1 DateOut
      mmddyy8. +1 RoomRate 6. @35 EquipCost 6.;
   Days=dateout-datein+1;
   RoomCharge=days*roomrate;
   Total=roomcharge+equipcost;
run;
```

Raw Data File Aprdata

```
1---+----10---+----20---+----30---+----40
Akron     04/05/99 04/09/99 175.00 298.45
Brown     04/12/99 05/01/99 125.00 326.78
Carnes    04/27/99 04/29/99 125.00 174.24
Denison   04/11/99 04/12/99 175.00  87.41
Fields    04/15/99 04/22/99 175.00 378.96
Jamison   04/16/99 04/23/99 125.00 346.28
```

Program Data Vector

LastName	DateIn	DateOut	RoomRate	EquipCost	Days	RoomCharge	Total
Akron	14339	14343	175.00	298.45	5	875.00	1173.45

The value for `Total` is the final calculation. `Total` is the sum of `EquipCost` and `RoomCharge`.

```
options yearcutoff=1920;
data perm.aprbills;
    infile aprdata;
    input LastName $8. @10 DateIn mmddyy8. +1 DateOut
        mmddyy8. +1 RoomRate 6. @35 EquipCost 6.;
    Days=dateout-datein+1;
    RoomCharge=days*roomrate;
    Total=roomcharge+equipcost;
run;
```

Raw Data File Aprdata

```
1---+----10---+----20---+----30---+----40
Akron      04/05/99 04/09/99 175.00 298.45
Brown      04/12/99 05/01/99 125.00 326.78
Carnes     04/27/99 04/29/99 125.00 174.24
Denison    04/11/99 04/12/99 175.00  87.41
Fields     04/15/99 04/22/99 175.00 378.96
Jamison    04/16/99 04/23/99 125.00 346.28
```

Program Data Vector

LastName	DateIn	DateOut	RoomRate	EquipCost	Days	RoomCharge	Total
Akron	14339	14343	175.00	298.45	5	875.00	•

Using Date and Time Formats

Remember that when **Perm.Aprbills** is printed, the values for `DateIn` and `DateOut` appear as SAS date values.

```
options yearcutoff=1920;
data perm.aprbills;
    infile aprdata;
    input LastName $8. @10 DateIn mmddyy8. +1 DateOut
        mmddyy8. +1 RoomRate 6. @35 EquipCost 6.;
    Days=dateout-datein+1;
    RoomCharge=days*roomrate;
    Total=roomcharge+equipcost;
run;
proc print data=perm.aprbills;
run;
```

Raw Data File Aprdata

```
1---+----10---+----20---+----30---+----40
Akron      04/05/99 04/09/99 175.00 298.45
Brown      04/12/99 05/01/99 125.00 326.78
Carnes     04/27/99 04/29/99 125.00 174.24
Denison    04/11/99 04/12/99 175.00  87.41
Fields     04/15/99 04/22/99 175.00 378.96
Jamison    04/16/99 04/23/99 125.00 346.28
```

Obs	LastName	DateIn	DateOut	RoomRate	EquipCost	Days	RoomCharge	Total
1	Akron	14339	14343	175	298.45	5	875	1173.45
2	Brown	14346	14365	125	326.78	20	2500	2826.78
3	Carnes	14361	14363	125	174.24	3	375	549.24
4	Denison	14345	14346	175	87.41	2	350	437.41
5	Fields	14349	14356	175	378.96	8	1400	1778.96
6	Jamison	14350	14357	125	346.28	8	1000	1346.28

SAS provides many specialized date and time formats that enable you to specify how date and time values are displayed and stored. Let's take a closer look at two date formats: **WEEKDATE*w*.** and **WORDDATE*w*.**

The WEEKDATE*w*. Format

You can use the WEEKDATE*w*. format to write these values out in a format that displays the day of the week, month, day, and year.

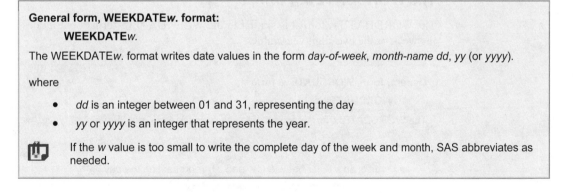

General form, WEEKDATE*w*. format:

> **WEEKDATE*w*.**

The WEEKDATE*w*. format writes date values in the form *day-of-week, month-name dd, yy* (or *yyyy*).

where

- *dd* is an integer between 01 and 31, representing the day
- *yy* or *yyyy* is an integer that represents the year.

If the *w* value is too small to write the complete day of the week and month, SAS abbreviates as needed.

```
proc print data=perm.aprbills;
   format datein dateout weekdate17.;
run;
```

Obs	LastName	DateIn	DateOut	RoomRate	EquipCost	Days	RoomCharge	Total
1	Akron	Mon, Apr 5, 1999	Fri, Apr 9, 1999	175	298.45	5	875	1173.45
2	Brown	Mon, Apr 12, 1999	Sat, May 1, 1999	125	326.78	20	2500	2826.78
3	Carnes	Tue, Apr 27, 1999	Thu, Apr 29, 1999	125	174.24	3	375	549.24
4	Denison	Sun, Apr 11, 1999	Mon, Apr 12, 1999	175	87.41	2	350	437.41
5	Fields	Thu, Apr 15, 1999	Thu, Apr 22, 1999	175	378.96	8	1400	1778.96
6	Jamison	Fri, Apr 16, 1999	Fri, Apr 23, 1999	125	346.28	8	1000	1346.28

You can vary the results by changing the *w* value in the format.

FORMAT Statement	Result
`format datein weekdate3.;`	Mon
`format datein weekdate6.;`	Monday
`format datein weekdate17.;`	Monday, Apr 5, 99
`format datein weekdate21.;`	Monday, April 5, 1999

The WORDDATE*w.* Format

The WORDDATE*w.* format is similar to the WEEKDATE*w.* format, but it does not display the day of the week or the two-digit year values.

General form, WORDDATE*w.* format:

> **WORDDATE*w.***

The WORDDATE*w.* format writes date values in the form *month-name dd, yyyy*.

where

- *dd* is an integer between 01 and 31, representing the day
- *yyyy* is an integer that represents the year.

If the *w* value is too small to write the complete month, SAS abbreviates as needed.

```
proc print data=perm.aprbills;
   format datein dateout worddate12.;
run;
```

Obs	LastName	DateIn	DateOut	RoomRate	EquipCost	Days	RoomCharge	Total
1	Akron	Apr 5, 1999	Apr 9, 1999	175	298.45	5	875	1173.45
2	Brown	Apr 12, 1999	May 1, 1999	125	326.78	20	2500	2826.78
3	Carnes	Apr 27,1999	Apr 29, 1999	125	174.24	3	375	549.24
4	Denison	Apr 11, 1999	Apr 12, 1999	175	87.41	2	350	437.41
5	Fields	Apr 15, 1999	Apr 22, 1999	175	378.96	8	1400	1778.96
6	Jamison	Apr 16, 1999	Apr 23, 1999	125	346.28	8	1000	1346.28

You can vary the results by changing the *w* value in the format.

FORMAT Statement	Result
`format datein worddate3.;`	Apr
`format datein worddate5.;`	April
`format datein worddate14.;`	April 15, 1999

Remember that you can permanently assign a format to variable values by including a FORMAT statement in the DATA step.

```
options yearcutoff=1920;
data work.aprbills;
   infile aprdata;
   input LastName $8. @10 DateIn mmddyy8. +1 DateOut
      mmddyy8. +1 RoomRate 6. @35 EquipCost 6.;
   Days=dateout-datein+1;
   RoomCharge=days*roomrate;
   Total=roomcharge+equipcost;
   format datein dateout worddate12.;
run;
proc print data=work.aprbills;
run;
```

Summary

Text Summary

How SAS Stores Date and Time Values

SAS stores date values as numeric **SAS date values**, which are the number of days from January 1, 1960. **SAS time values** are the number of seconds since midnight.

Reading Dates and Times with Informats

Use SAS informats to read date and time expressions and convert them to SAS date and time values.

- **MMDDYY***w.* reads dates such as 053090, 05/30/90, or 05 30 1990.

- **DATE***w.* reads dates such as 30May1990, 30May90, or 30-May-1990.

- **TIME***w.* reads times such as 17:00, 17:00:01.34, or 2:34.

- **DATETIME***w.* reads dates and times such as 30May1990:10:03:17.2, 30May90 10:03:17.2, or 30May1990/10:03.

Two-digit year values require special consideration. When a two-digit year value is read, SAS defaults to a year within a 100-year span that is determined by the **YEARCUTOFF=** system option. The default value of YEARCUTOFF= is 1920. You can check or reset the value of this option in your SAS session to use a different 100-year span for date informats.

Using Dates and Times in Calculations

Date and time values can be used in calculations like other numeric values. In addition to tracking time intervals, SAS date and time values can be used with SAS functions and with complex calculations.

Using Date and Time Formats

SAS provides many specialized date and time formats that enable you to specify how date and time values are displayed and stored. You can use the **WEEKDATE***w.* format to write date values in the form *day-of-week, month-name dd, yy* (or *yyyy*). You can use the **WORDDATE***w.* format to write date values in the form *month-name dd, yyyy*.

Points to Remember

- SAS makes adjustments for leap years, but not for leap seconds or daylight saving time.

- The minimum acceptable field width for the TIME*w.* informat is 5. If you specify a *w* value less than 5, you'll receive an error message in the SAS log.

- The default value of the YEARCUTOFF= option is 1920. When you work with two-digit year data, remember to check the default value of the YEARCUTOFF= option, and change it if necessary.

- The value of the YEARCUTOFF= system option does not affect four-digit year values. Four-digit values are always read correctly.

- Be sure to specify the proper informat for reading a date value, and specify the correct field width so that the entire value is read.

- If SAS date values appear in your program output, use a date format to display them in legible form.

Practice

After you complete this chapter, practice what you learned by using the sample data and SAS programs for Chapter 19, **Reading Date and Time Values**, which are located on the CD-ROM. Follow the directions for creating your sample data in the Before You Begin section.

Quiz

Select the best answer for each question. After completing the quiz, check your answers using the answer key in the appendix.

1. SAS date values are the number of days since which date?

   a. January 1, 1900
   b. January 1, 1950
   c. January 1, 1960
   d. January 1, 1970

2. A great advantage of storing dates and times as SAS numeric date and time values is that

   a. they can easily be edited.
   b. they can easily be read and understood.
   c. they can be used in text strings like other character values.
   d. they can be used in calculations like other numeric values.

3. SAS does not automatically make adjustments for daylight saving time, but it **does** make adjustments for

   a. leap seconds
   b. leap years
   c. Julian dates
   d. time zones

4. An input data file has date expressions in the form 10222001. Which SAS informat should you use to read these dates?

   a. DATE6.
   b. DATE8.
   c. MMDDYY6.
   d. MMDDYY8.

5. The minimum width of the TIME*w*. informat is

   a. 4
   b. 5
   c. 6
   d. 7

6. Shown below are date and time expressions and corresponding SAS datetime informats. Which date and time expresssion **cannot** be read by the informat that is shown beside it?

    a. 30May2000:10:03:17.2 DATETIME20.
    b. 30May00 10:03:17.2 DATETIME18.
    c. 30May2000/10:03 DATETIME15.
    d. 30May2000/1003 DATETIME14.

7. What is the default value of the YEARCUTOFF= system option?

    a. 1920
    b. 1910
    c. 1900
    d. 1930

8. Suppose your input data file contains the date expression *13APR2009*. The YEARCUTOFF= system option is set to 1910. SAS will read the date as

    a. 13APR1909
    b. 13APR1920
    c. 13APR2009
    d. 13APR2020

9. Suppose the YEARCUTOFF= system option is set to 1920. An input file contains the date expression *12/08/1925*, which is being read with the MMDDYY8. informat. Which date will appear in your data?

    a. 08DEC1920
    b. 08DEC1925
    c. 08DEC2019
    d. 08DEC2025

10. Suppose your program creates two variables from an input file. Both variables are stored as SAS date values: FirstDay records the start of a billing cycle, and LastDay records the end of that cycle. The code for calculating the total number of days in the cycle would be

    a. TotDays=lastday-firstday;
    b. TotDays=lastday-firstday+1;
    c. TotDays=lastday/firstday;
    d. You cannot use date values in calculations.

Chapter 20 Creating a Single Observation from Multiple Records

Overview

Introduction

Information for one observation can be spread out over several records. You can write multiple INPUT statements to read each record that comprises a single observation, as in this example:

```
input Lname $ 1-8 Fname $ 10-15;
input Department $ 1-12 JobCode $ 15-19;
input Salary comma10.;
```

```
1---+----10---+----
ABRAMS    THOMAS
MARKETING        SR01
$25,209.03
BARCLAY   ROBERT
EDUCATION        IN01
$24,435.71
COURTNEY MARK
PUBLICATIONS  TW01
$24,006.16
```

Or, you can write one INPUT statement that contains a line pointer control to specify the record(s) from which values are to be read, as in this example:

```
input #1 Lname $ 1-8 Fname $ 10-15
      #2 Department $ 1-12 JobCode $ 15-19
      #3 Salary comma10.;
```

```
1---+----10---+----
ABRAMS    THOMAS
MARKETING        SR01
$25,209.03
BARCLAY   ROBERT
EDUCATION        IN01
$24,435.71
COURTNEY MARK
PUBLICATIONS  TW01
$24,006.16
```

Objectives

In this chapter, you learn to

- read multiple records sequentially and create a single observation
- read multiple records non-sequentially and create a single observation.

Use Line Pointer Controls

You know that as SAS reads raw data values, it keeps track of its position with an input pointer. You have used column pointer controls and column specifications to determine the column placement of the input pointer.

Column Specifications	`input Name $ 1-12 Age 15-16 Gender $ 18;`
Column Pointer Controls	`input Name $12. @15 Age 2. @18 Gender $1.;`

But you can also position the input pointer on a specific record by using a **line pointer control** in the INPUT statement.

```
input #2 Name $ 1-12 Age 15-16 Gender $ 18;
```

Raw Data File Admit

```
1---+----10---+----
S. Thompson    37 M
L. Rochester   31 F
M. Sabatello   43 M
```

There are two types of line pointer controls.

- The **forward slash (/)** specifies a line location that is relative to the current one.

- The **#n** specifies the absolute number of the line to which you want to move the pointer.

First we'll look at the forward slash (/). Later in this chapter, you'll learn how to use the #*n*, and you will see how these two controls can be combined.

Reading Multiple Records Sequentially

The Forward Slash (/) Line Pointer Control

You use the forward slash (/) line pointer control to read multiple records sequentially. The / advances the input pointer to the next record. The / line pointer control only moves the input pointer forward and must be specified **after** the instructions for reading the values in the current record.

The single INPUT statement below reads the values for `Lname` and `Fname` in the first record, followed by the values for `Department` and `JobCode` in the second record. Then the value for `Salary` is read in the third record.

```
input Lname $ 1-8 Fname $ 10-15 /
      Department $ 1-12 JobCode $ 15-19 /
      Salary comma10.;
```

```
1---+----10---+----
ABRAMS    THOMAS
MARKETING        SR01
$25,209.03
BARCLAY   ROBERT
EDUCATION        IN01
$24,435.71
COURTNEY  MARK
PUBLICATIONS  TW01
$24,006.16
```

Take a closer look at using the forward slash (/) line pointer control in the following example.

The raw data file **Memdata** contains the mailing list of a professional organization. Your task is to combine the information for each member into one data set observation. We'll begin by reading each member's name, followed by the street address, and finally the city, state, and zip code.

- As you write the instructions to read the values for Fname and Lname, notice that not all of the values for Lname begin in the same column. So, you should use standard list input to read these values.

```
data perm.members;
   infile memdata;
   input Fname $ Lname $
```

```
1---+----10---+----20
LEE ATHNOS
1215 RAINTREE CIRCLE
PHOENIX  AZ 85044
HEIDIE BAKER
1751 DIEHL ROAD
VIENNA   VA 22124
MYRON BARKER
131 DONERAIL DRIVE
ATLANTA  GA 30363
JOYCE BENEFIT
85 MAPLE AVENUE
MENLO PARK CA  94025
```

- Now you want to read the values for Address from the second record. The / line pointer control advances the input pointer to the next record. At this point the INPUT statement is incomplete, so you should not place a semicolon after the line pointer control.

```
data perm.members;
    infile memdata;
    input Fname $ Lname $ /
```

```
1---+----10---+----20
LEE ATHNOS
1215 RAINTREE CIRCLE
PHOENIX   AZ 85044
HEIDIE BAKER
1751 DIEHL ROAD
VIENNA   VA 22124
MYRON BARKER
131 DONERAIL DRIVE
ATLANTA   GA 30363
JOYCE BENEFIT
85 MAPLE AVENUE
MENLO PARK   CA 94025
```

- You can use column input to read the values in the next record as one variable named `Address`. Then add a line pointer control to move the input pointer to the next record.

```
data perm.members;
    infile memdata;
    input Fname $ Lname $ /
          Address $ 1-20 /
```

```
1---+----10---+----20
LEE ATHNOS
1215 RAINTREE CIRCLE
PHOENIX   AZ 85044
HEIDIE BAKER
1751 DIEHL ROAD
VIENNA   VA 22124
MYRON BARKER
131 DONERAIL DRIVE
ATLANTA   GA 30363
JOYCE BENEFIT
85 MAPLE AVENUE
MENLO PARK   CA 94025
```

- As you write the statements to read the values for `City`, notice that one of the values is longer than eight characters and contains embedded blanks. Also note that each value is followed by two consecutive blanks. To read these values, you should use modified list input with the ampersand (&) modifier.

  The values for `State` and the values for `Zip` do not begin in the same column. Therefore, you should use list input to read these values.

```
data perm.members;
    infile memdata;
    input Fname $ Lname $ /
          Address $ 1-20 /
          City & $10. State $ Zip $;
run;
```

```
1---+----10---+----20
LEE ATHNOS
1215 RAINTREE CIRCLE
PHOENIX   AZ 85044
HEIDIE BAKER
1751 DIEHL ROAD
VIENNA   VA 22124
MYRON BARKER
131 DONERAIL DRIVE
ATLANTA   GA 30363
JOYCE BENEFIT
85 MAPLE AVENUE
MENLO PARK   CA 94025
```

Sequential Processing of Multiple Records in the DATA Step

Now that you've learned the basics of using the / line pointer control, let's take a closer look at the sequential processing of multiple records in the DATA step.

During compilation, the program data vector is created for the **Perm.Members** data set. When the DATA step executes, the values in the first record are read, and the / line pointer control moves the input pointer to the second record.

```
data perm.members;
    infile memdata;
    input Fname $ Lname $ /
          Address $ 1-20 /
          City & $10. State $ Zip $;
run;
```

```
>----+----10---+----20
LEE ATHNOS
1215 RAINTREE CIRCLE
PHOENIX   AZ 85044
HEIDIE BAKER
1751 DIEHL ROAD
VIENNA   VA 22124
```

Program Data Vector

N	Fname	Lname	Address	City	State	Zip
1	LEE	ATHNOS				

The values for Address are read, and the second / line pointer control advances the input pointer to the third record.

```
data perm.members;
   infile memdata;
   input Fname $ Lname $ /
         Address $ 1-20 /
         City & $10. State $ Zip $;
run;
```

```
>----+----10---+----20
LEE ATHNOS
1215 RAINTREE CIRCLE
PHOENIX   AZ 85044
HEIDIE BAKER
1751 DIEHL ROAD
VIENNA   VA 22124
```

Program Data Vector

N	Fname	Lname	Address	City	State	Zip
1	LEE	ATHNOS	1215 RAINTREE CIRCLE			

The values for City, State, and Zip are read, and the INPUT statement is completely executed.

```
data perm.members;
   infile memdata;
   input Fname $ Lname $ /
         Address $ 1-20 /
         City & $10. State $ Zip $;
run;
```

```
>----+----10---+----20
LEE ATHNOS
1215 RAINTREE CIRCLE
PHOENIX   AZ 85044
HEIDIE BAKER
1751 DIEHL ROAD
VIENNA   VA 22124
```

Program Data Vector

N	Fname	Lname	Address	City	State	Zip
1	LEE	ATHNOS	1215 RAINTREE CIRCLE	PHOENIX	AZ	85044

The values in the program data vector are written to the data set as the first observation.

Program Data Vector

N	Fname	Lname	Address	City	State	Zip
1	LEE	ATHNOS	1215 RAINTREE CIRCLE	PHOENIX	AZ	85044

SAS Data Set Perm.Members

Fname	Lname	Address	City	State	Zip
LEE	ATHNOS	1215 RAINTREE CIRCLE	PHOENIX	AZ	85044

Control returns to the top of the DATA step, and the variable values are reinitialized to missing.

```
data perm.members;
    infile memdata;
    input Fname $ Lname $ /
          Address $ 1-20 /
          City & $10. State $ Zip $;
run;
```

```
>----+----10---+----20
LEE ATHNOS
1215 RAINTREE CIRCLE
PHOENIX   AZ 85044
HEIDIE BAKER
1751 DIEHL ROAD
VIENNA   VA 22124
```

Program Data Vector

N	Fname	Lname	Address	City	State	Zip
2						

During the second iteration, values for Fname and Lname are read beginning in column one of the fourth record.

```
data perm.members;
   infile memdata;
   input Fname $ Lname $ /
         Address $ 1-20 /
         City & $10. State $ Zip $;
run;
```

```
>----+----10---+----20

LEE ATHNOS
1215 RAINTREE CIRCLE
PHOENIX  AZ 85044
HEIDIE BAKER
1751 DIEHL ROAD
VIENNA  VA 22124
```

Program Data Vector

N	Fname	Lname	Address	City	State	Zip
2	HEIDIE	BAKER				

The values for Address are read and the / line pointer control advances the input pointer to the fifth record.

```
data perm.members;
   infile memdata;
   input Fname $ Lname $ /
         Address $ 1-20 /
         City & $10. State $ Zip $;
run;
```

```
>----+----10---+----20

LEE ATHNOS
1215 RAINTREE CIRCLE
PHOENIX  AZ 85044
HEIDIE BAKER
1751 DIEHL ROAD
VIENNA  VA 22124
```

Program Data Vector

N	Fname	Lname	Address	City	State	Zip
2	HEIDIE	BAKER	1751 DIEHL ROAD			

The values for City, State, and Zip are read, and the INPUT statement is completely executed.

```
data perm.members;
    infile memdata;
    input Fname $ Lname $ /
          Address $ 1-20 /
          City & $10. State $ Zip $;
run;
```

```
>----+----10---+----20

LEE ATHNOS
1215 RAINTREE CIRCLE
PHOENIX   AZ 85044
HEIDIE BAKER
1751 DIEHL ROAD
VIENNA   VA 22124
```

Program Data Vector

N	Fname	Lname	Address	City	State	Zip
2	HEIDIE	BAKER	1751 DIEHL ROAD	VIENNA	VA	22124

The values for City, State, and Zip are read, and the INPUT
statement is completely executed.

The values in the program data vector are written to the data set as the second observation.

Program Data Vector

N	Fname	Lname	Address	City	State	Zip
2	HEIDIE	BAKER	1751 DIEHL ROAD	VIENNA	VA	22124

SAS Data Set Perm.Members

Fname	Lname	Address	City	State	Zip
LEE	ATHNOS	1215 RAINTREE CIRCLE	PHOENIX	AZ	85044

The values in the program data vector are written to the data set
as the second observation.

After the data set is complete, PROC PRINT output for **Perm.Members** shows that a single observation contains the complete information for each member.

```
proc print data=perm.members;
run;
```

Obs	Fname	Lname	Address	City	State	Zip
1	LEE	ATHNOS	1215 RAINTREE CIRCLE	PHOENIX	AZ	85044
2	HEIDIE	BAKER	1751 DIEHL ROAD	VIENNA	VA	22124
3	MYRON	BARKER	131 DONERAIL DRIVE	ATLANTA	GA	30363
4	JOYCE	BENEFIT	85 MAPLE AVENUE	MENLO PARK	CA	94025

Number of Records Per Observation

Note that the raw data file must contain the **same number of records** for each observation that is being created.

For example, suppose there are only two records for the second member. However, the INPUT statement is set up to read three records.

```
data perm.members;
   infile memdata;
   input Fname $ Lname $ /
   Address $ 1-20 /
   City & $10. State $ Zip $;
```

```
1---+----10---+----20
LEE ATHNOS
1215 RAINTREE CIRCLE
PHOENIX   AZ 85044
HEIDIE BAKER
1751 DIEHL ROAD
VIENNA   VA 22124
MYRON BARKER
131 DONERAIL DRIVE
ATLANTA   GA 30363
JOYCE BENEFIT
85 MAPLE AVENUE
MENLO PARK   CA 94025
```

The second member's name and address are read and assigned to corresponding variables. Then the input pointer advances to the next record, as directed by the INPUT statement, and the third member's name is read as a value for City.

The DATA step is still looking for a value for State and Zip, so the input pointer advances to the next record and reads the values for the member's address.

The PROC PRINT output for this data set illustrates the problem.

Obs	Fname	Lname	Address	City	State	Zip
1	LEE	ATHNOS	1215 RAINTREE CIRCLE	PHOENIX	AZ	85044
2	HEIDIE	BAKER	1751 DIEHL ROAD	MYRON BARK	131	DONERAIL
3	ATLANTA	GA	JOYCE BENEFIT	85 MAPLE A	MENLO	PARK

So, before you write the INPUT statement, ensure that the raw data file contains the same number of records for each observation.

```
1---+----10---+----20
1 LEE ATHNOS
2 1215 RAINTREE CIRCLE
3 PHOENIX   AZ 85044
1 HEIDIE BAKER
2 1751 DIEHL ROAD
3 VIENNA   VA 22124
1 MYRON BARKER
2 131 DONERAIL DRIVE
3 ATLANTA   GA 30363
1 JOYCE BENEFIT
2 85 MAPLE AVENUE
3 MENLO PARK   CA 94025
```

 For more information about working with raw data files that contain missing records, see the SAS documentation.

Reading Multiple Records Non-Sequentially

The #*n* Line Pointer Control

You already know how to read multiple records sequentially by using the / line pointer control. Now let's look at reading multiple records non-sequentially by using the #*n* line pointer control.

The #*n* specifies the absolute number of the line to which you want to move the input pointer. The #*n* pointer control can read records in any order; therefore, it must be specified **before** the instructions for reading values in a specific record.

The INPUT statement below first reads the values for Department and JobCode in the second record, then the values for Lname and Fname in the first record. Finally, it reads the value for Salary in the third record.

```
input #2 Department $ 1-12 JobCode $ 15-19
      #1 Lname $ Fname $
      #3 Salary comma10.;
```

```
1---+----10---+----
ABRAMS THOMAS
MARKETING       SR01
$25,209.03
BARCLAY ROBERT
EDUCATION       IN01
$24,435.71
COURTNEY MARK
PUBLICATIONS    TW01
$24,006.16
```

Example: Using the #*n* Line Pointer Control

Take a closer look at using the #*n* line pointer control in the following example.

The raw data file **Patdata** contains information about the patients of a small group of general surgeons.

The first three records contain a patient's name, address, city, state, and zip code. The fourth record contains the patient's ID number followed by the name of the primary physician.

```
1---+----10---+----20---
1 ALEX BEDWAN
2 609 WILTON MEADOW DRIVE
3 GARNER NC 27529
4 XM034 FLOYD
  ALISON BEYER
  8521 HOLLY SPRINGS ROAD
  APEX NC 27502
  XF124 LAWSON
```

Suppose you want to read each patient's information in the following order:

1. ID number (`ID`)

2. first name (`Fname`)

3. last name (`Lname`)

4. address (`Address`)

5. city (`City`)

6. state (`State`)

7. zip (`Zip`)

8. doctor (`Doctor`)

- To read the values for ID in the fourth record, specify **#4** before naming the variable and defining its attributes.

```
data perm.patients;
   infile patdata;
   input #4 ID $5.
```

```
1---+----10---+----20---
ALEX BEDWAN
609 WILTON MEADOW DRIVE
GARNER NC 27529
XM034 FLOYD
```

- To read the values for Fname and Lname in the first record, specify **#1** before naming the variables and defining their attributes.

```
data perm.patients;
   infile patdata;
   input #4 ID $5.
         #1 Fname $ Lname $
```

```
1---+----10---+----20---
ALEX BEDWAN
609 WILTON MEADOW DRIVE
GARNER NC 27529
XM034 FLOYD
```

- Use the *#n* line pointer control to move the input pointer to the second record and read the value for Address.

```
data perm.patients;
   infile patdata;
   input #4 ID $5.
         #1 Fname $ Lname $
         #2 Address $23.
```

```
1---+----10---+----20---
ALEX BEDWAN
609 WILTON MEADOW DRIVE
GARNER NC 27529
XM034 FLOYD
```

- Now move the input pointer to the third record and read the values for City, State, and Zip, in that order.

In this raw data file, the values for City contain eight or fewer characters and do not contain embedded blanks. So, you can use standard list input to read these values.

```
data perm.patients;
   infile patdata;
   input #4 ID $5.
         #1 Fname $ Lname $
         #2 Address $23.
         #3 City $ State $ Zip $
```

```
1---+----10---+----20---
ALEX BEDWAN
609 WILTON MEADOW DRIVE
GARNER NC 27529
XM034 FLOYD
```

- Now you need to move the input pointer down to the fourth record to read the values for `Doctor`, which begin in column 7. Don't forget to add a semicolon at the end of the INPUT statement. A RUN statement completes the program.

```
data perm.patients;
        infile patdata;
        input #4 ID $5.
              #1 Fname $ Lname $
              #2 Address $23.
              #3 City $ State $ Zip $
              #4 @7 Doctor $6.;
    run;
```

```
1---+----10---+----20---
ALEX BEDWAN
609 WILTON MEADOW DRIVE
GARNER NC 27529
XM034 FLOYD
```

Execution of the DATA Step

The *#n* pointer controls in the program below cause four records to be read for each execution of the DATA step.

```
data perm.patients;
    infile patdata;
    input #4 ID $5.
          #1 Fname $ Lname $
          #2 Address $23.
          #3 City $ State $ Zip $
          #4 @7 Doctor $6.;
run;
```

The first time the DATA step executes, the first four records are read, and an observation is written to the data set.

```
1---+----10---+----20---
ALEX BEDWAN
609 WILTON MEADOW DRIVE
GARNER NC 27529
XM034 FLOYD
ALISON BEYER
8521 HOLLY SPRINGS ROAD
APEX NC 27502
XF124 LAWSON
```

During the second iteration, the next four records are read, and the second observation is written to the data set, and so on.

```
1---+----10---+----20---
ALEX BEDWAN
609 WILTON MEADOW DRIVE
GARNER NC 27529
XM034 FLOYD
ALISON BEYER
8521 HOLLY SPRINGS ROAD
APEX NC 27502
XF124 LAWSON
```

The PROC PRINT output of the data set shows how information that was spread over several records has been condensed into one observation.

```
proc print data=perm.patients noobs;
run;
```

ID	Fname	Lname	Address	City	State	Zip	Doctor
XM034	ALEX	BEDWAN	609 WILTON MEADOW DRIVE	GARNER	NC	27529	FLOYD
XF124	ALISON	BEYER	8521 HOLLY SPRINGS ROAD	APEX	NC	27502	LAWSON
XF232	LISA	BONNER	109 BRAMPTON AVENUE	CARY	NC	27511	LAWSON
XM065	GEORGE	CHESSON	3801 WOODSIDE COURT	GARNER	NC	27529	FLOYD

Combining Line Pointer Controls

The forward slash (/) line pointer control and the #*n* line pointer control can be used together in a SAS program to read multiple records both sequentially and non-sequentially.

For example, you could use both the / line pointer control and the #*n* line pointer control to read the variables in the raw data file **Patdata** in the following order:

1. ID
2. Fname
3. Lname
4. Address
5. City
6. State
7. Zip
8. Doctor

```
data perm.patients;
   infile patdata;
   input #4 ID $5.
        #1 Fname $ Lname $ /
           Address $23. /
           City $ State $ Zip $ /
           @7 Doctor $6.;
   run;
```

```
1---+----10---+----20---
ALEX BEDWAN
609 WILTON MEADOW DRIVE
GARNER NC 27529
XM034 FLOYD
ALISON BEYER
8521 HOLLY SPRINGS ROAD
APEX NC 27502
XF124 LAWSON
```

- To read the values for ID in the fourth record, specify **#4** before naming the variable and defining its attributes.

- Specify **#1** to move the input pointer back to the first record, where the values for Fname and Lname are read.

- Because the next record to be read is sequential, you can use the / line pointer control after the variable Lname to move the input pointer to the second record, where the value for Address is read.

- The / line pointer control in the next line directs the input pointer to the third record, where the values for City, State, and Zip are read.

- The final / line pointer control moves the input pointer back to the fourth record, where the value for Doctor is read.

Alternatively, you can use only the *#n* line pointer control (as shown earlier in this chapter and below) to read the variables in the order shown above.

```
data perm.patients;
   infile patdata;
   input #4 ID $5.
        #1 Fname $ Lname $
        #2 Address $23.
        #3 City $ State $ Zip $
        #4 @7 Doctor $6.;
   run;
```

```
1---+----10---+----20---
ALEX BEDWAN
609 WILTON MEADOW DRIVE
GARNER NC 27529
XM034 FLOYD
ALISON BEYER
8521 HOLLY SPRINGS ROAD
APEX NC 27502
XF124 LAWSON
```

Summary

Text Summary

Multiple Records Per Observation

Information for one observation can be spread out over several records. You can write one INPUT statement that contains line pointer controls to specify the records from which values are read.

Reading Multiple Records Sequentially

The forward slash (/) line pointer control is used to read multiple records sequentially. Each time a / pointer is encountered, the input pointer advances to the next line.

Reading Multiple Records Non-Sequentially

The #n line pointer control is used to read multiple records non-sequentially. The #n specifies the absolute number of the line to which you want to move the pointer.

Combining Line Pointer Controls

The / line pointer control and the #n line pointer control can be combined within a SAS program to read multiple records both sequentially and non-sequentially.

Points to Remember

- When a file contains multiple records per observation, the file must contain the same number of records for each observation that is being created.

- Because the / pointer control can only move forward, the pointer control is specified **after** the values in the current record are read.

- The #*n* pointer control can read records in any order and must be specified **before** the variable names are defined.

- A semicolon should be placed at the end of the **complete** INPUT statement.

Practice

After you complete this chapter, practice what you learned by using the sample data and SAS programs for Chapter 20, **Creating a Single Observation from Multiple Records**, which are located on the CD-ROM. Follow the directions for creating your sample data in the Before You Begin section.

Quiz

Select the best answer for each question. After completing the quiz, check your answers using the answer key in the appendix.

1. You can position the input pointer on a specific record by using

   a. column pointer controls.
   b. column specifications.
   c. line pointer controls.
   d. line hold specifiers.

2. Which pointer control is used to read multiple records sequentially?

   a. @n
   b. +n
   c. /
   d. all of the above

3. Which pointer control can be used to read records non-sequentially?

   a. @n
   b. #n
   c. +n
   d. /

4. Which SAS statement correctly reads the values for Fname, Lname, Address, City, State, and Zip in order?

   ```
   1---+----10---+----20---
   LAWRENCE CALDWELL
   1010 LAKE STREET
   ANAHEIM CA 94122
   RACHEL CHEVONT
   3719 OLIVE VIEW ROAD
   HARTFORD CT 06183
   ```

a. input Fname $ Lname $ /
          Address $20. /
          City $ State $ Zip $;

b. input Fname $ Lname $ /;
          Address $20. /;
          City $ State $ Zip $;

c. input / Fname $ Lname $
          / Address $20.
          City $ State $ Zip $;

d. input / Fname $ Lname $;
          / Address $20.;
          City $ State $ Zip $;

5. Which INPUT statement correctly reads the values for ID in the fourth record, then returns to the first record to read the values for Fname and Lname?

```
1---+----10---+----20---
GEORGE CHESSON
3801 WOODSIDE COURT
GARNER NC 27529
XM065 FLOYD
JAMES COLDWELL
123-A TARBERT
APEX NC 27529
XMO65 LAWSON
```

a. input #4 ID $5.
          #1 Fname $ Lname $;

b. input #4 ID $ 1-5
          #1 Fname $ Lname $;

c. input #4 ID $
          #1 Fname $ Lname $;

d. all of the above

6. How many records will be read for each iteration of the DATA step?

```
1---+----10---+----20---
SKIRT BLACK
COTTON
036499 $44.98
SKIRT NAVY
LINEN
036899 $51.50
DRESS RED
SILK
037299 $76.98
```

```
data spring.sportswr;
    infile newitems;
    input #1 Item $ Color $
          #3 @8 Price comma6.
          #2 Fabric $
          #3 SKU $ 1-6;
run;
```

 a. one

 b. two

 c. three

 d. four

7. Which INPUT statement correctly reads the values for `City`, `State`, and `Zip`?

```
1---+----10---+----20---
DINA  FIELDS
904  MAPLE  CIRCLE
DURHAM  NC  27713
ELIZABETH  GARRISON
1293  OAK  AVENUE
CHAPEL  HILL  NC  27614
DAVID  HARRINGTON
2426  ELMWOOD  LANE
RALEIGH  NC  27803
```

 a. `input #3 City $ State $ Zip $;`

 b. `input #3 City & $11. State $ Zip $;`

 c. `input #3 City $11. +2 State $2. + 2 Zip $5.;`

 d. all of the above

8. Which program does **not** read the values in the first record as a variable named `Item` and the values in the second record as two variables named `Inventory` and `Type`?

```
1---+----10---+----20---
COLORED PENCILS
12 BOXES
WATERCOLOR PAINT
8 PALETTES
DRAWING PAPER
15 PADS
```

a. ```
data perm.supplies;
    infile instock pad;
    input Item & $16. /
        Inventory 2. Type $8.;
run;
```

*b.* ```
data perm.supplies;
    infile instock pad;
    input Item & $16.
            / Inventory 2. Type $8.;
run;
```

c. ```
data perm.supplies;
    infile instock pad;
    input #1 Item & $16.
        Inventory 2. Type $8.;
run;
```

*d.* ```
data perm.supplies;
    infile instock pad;
    input Item & $16.
        #2 Inventory 2. Type $8.;
run;
```

9. Which INPUT statement reads the values for Lname, Fname, Department, and Salary (in that order)?

```
1---+----10---+----20---
ABRAMS THOMAS
SALES $25,209.03
BARCLAY ROBERT
MARKETING $29,180.36
COURTNEY MARK
PUBLICATIONS $24,006.16
```

a. ```
input #1 Lname $ Fname $ /
        Department $12. Salary comma10.;
```

*b.* ```
input #1 Lname $ Fname $ /
        Department : $12. Salary : comma.;
```

c. ```
input #1 Lname $ Fname $
        #2 Department : $12. Salary : comma.;
```

*d.* both *b* and *c*
```

10. Which raw data file poses potential problems when you are reading multiple records for each observation?

a.
```
1---+----10---+----20---
LAWRENCE CALDWELL
1010 LAKE STREET
ANAHEIM CA 94122
RACHEL CHEVONT
3719 OLIVE VIEW ROAD
HARTFORD CT 06183
```

b.
```
1---+----10---+----20---
SHIRT LT BLUE SOLID
SKU 128699
$38.99
SHIRT DK BLUE STRIPE
SKU 128799
$41.99
```

c.
```
1---+----10---+----20---
MARCUS JONES
SR01 $26,134.00
MARY ROBERTSON
COURTNEY NEILS
TWO1 $28,342.00
```

d.
```
1---+----10---+----20---
CROCUS MIX
10 CASES
DAFFODIL
12 CASES
HYACINTH BLUE
8 BAGS
```

Chapter **21** Creating Multiple Observations from a Single Record

Overview

Introduction

Sometimes raw data files contain data for several observations in one record. Data is stored in this manner to reduce the size of the entire data file.

Each record can contain

- **repeating blocks** of data that represent separate observations

```
1---+----10---+----20---+----30--
01APR90 68 02APR90 67 03APR90 70
04APR90 74 05APR90 72 06APR90 73
07APR90 71 08APR90 75 09APR90 76
```

- an ID field followed by an **equal number** of repeating fields that represent separate observations

```
1---+----10---+----20---+----30--
001 WALKING AEROBICS CYCLING
002 SWIMMING CYCLING SKIING
003 TENNIS SWIMMING AEROBICS
```

- an ID field followed by a **varying number** of repeating fields that represent separate observations.

```
1---+----10---+----20---+----30--
001 WALKING
002 SWIMMING CYCLING SKIING
003 TENNIS SWIMMING
```

This chapter shows you several ways of creating multiple observations from a single record.

Objectives

In this chapter, you learn to

- create multiple observations from a single record that contains repeating blocks of data
- create multiple observations from a single record that contains one ID field followed by the **same** number of repeating fields
- create multiple observations from a single record that contains one ID field followed by a **varying** number of repeating fields.

Additionally, you learn to

- hold the current record across iterations of the DATA step
- hold the current record for the next INPUT statement
- execute SAS statements based on a variable's value
- explicitly write an observation to a data set
- execute SAS statements while a condition is true.

Reading Repeating Blocks of Data

Each record in the file **Tempdata** contains three blocks of data. Each block contains a date followed by the day's high temperature in a small city that is located in the southern United States.

Raw Data File Tempdata

```
1---+----10---+----20---+----30--
01APR90 68 02APR90 67 03APR90 70
04APR90 74 05APR90 72 06APR90 73
07APR90 71 08APR90 75 09APR90 76
10APR90 78 11APR90 70 12APR90 69
13APR90 71 14APR90 72 15APR90 74
16APR90 73 17APR90 71 18APR90 75
19APR90 75 20APR90 73 21APR90 75
22APR90 77 23APR90 78 24APR90 80
25APR90 78 26APR90 77 27APR90 79
28APR90 81 29APR90 81 30APR90 84
```

You could write a DATA step that reads each record and creates three different `Date` and `Temp` variables.

SAS Data Set

Date1	Temp1	Date2	Temp2	Date3	Temp3
11048	68	11049	67	11050	70

But if you create a separate observation for each block of data in a record, you can later use several statistical procedures to analyze the data for each day.

SAS Data Set

Date	HighTemp
11048	68
11049	67
11050	70

Holding the Current Record with a Line-Hold Specifier

As you begin to write the INPUT statement, you need to hold the current record until each block of data has been read and written to the data set as an observation. This is easily accomplished by using a line-hold specifier in the INPUT statement.

SAS provides two line-hold specifiers.

- The trailing at sign (@) holds the input record for the execution of the next INPUT statement.

- The double trailing at sign (@@) holds the input record for the execution of the next INPUT statement, even across iterations of the DATA step.

The term **trailing** indicates that the @ or @@ must be the **last** item that is specified in the INPUT statement. Here is an example:

```
input Name $20. @;   or   input Name $20. @@;
```

This chapter teaches you how the trailing @@ can be used to hold a record across multiple iterations of the DATA step.

Using the Double Trailing At Sign (@) to Hold the Current Record

Typically, each time a DATA step executes, the INPUT statement reads a new record. But when you use the trailing @@, the INPUT statement holds the current record and reads the next value.

input Score;

```
1---+----10---+-
102 92 78 103
84 23 36 75
```

Program Data Vector

N	Score
2	84

input Score;

```
1---+----10---+-
102 92 78 103
84 23 36 75
```

Program Data Vector

N	Score
2	92

The double trailing at sign (@@)

- works like the trailing @ except it also holds the data line in the input buffer **across multiple executions** of the DATA step

- typically is used to read multiple SAS observations from a single data line

- should not be used with the @ pointer control, with column input, nor with the MISSOVER option.

A record that is being held by the double trailing at sign (@@) is not released until one of the following events occurs:

- the input pointer moves past the end of the record. Then the input pointer moves down to the next record.

```
1---+----10--↓+-
102 92 78 103
84 23 36 75
```

- an INPUT statement that has no line-hold specifier executes.

```
      input ID $ @@;
      .
      .
      .
input Department 5.;
```

This example requires only one INPUT statement to read the values for Date and HighTemp, but the INPUT statement must execute three times for each record.

The INPUT statement reads a block of values for Date and HighTemp, and then holds the current record by using the trailing @@. The values in the program data vector are written to the data set as an observation, and control returns to the top of the DATA step.

```
data perm.april90;
   infile tempdata;
   input Date : date. HighTemp @@;
```

Raw Data File Tempdata

```
1---+----1↓---+----20---+----30--
01APR90 68 02APR90 67 03APR90 70
04APR90 74 05APR90 72 06APR90 73
07APR90 71 08APR90 75 09APR90 76
```

In the next iteration, the INPUT statement reads the next block of values for `Date` and `HighTemp` from the same record.

Raw Data File Tempdata

```
1---+----10---+----2↓---+----30--
01APR90 68 02APR90 67 03APR90 70
04APR90 74 05APR90 72 06APR90 73
07APR90 71 08APR90 75 09APR90 76
```

Completing the DATA Step

You can add a FORMAT statement to the DATA step to display the date or time values with a format that you specify in the data set. In the FORMAT statement below, the DATE*w.* format is used to display the values for `Date` in the form **ddmmmyyyy**.

```
data perm.april90;
   infile tempdata;
   input Date : date. HighTemp @@;
   format date date9.;
run;
```

Raw Data File Tempdata

```
1---+----10---+----20---+----30--
01APR90 68 02APR90 67 03APR90 70
04APR90 74 05APR90 72 06APR90 73
07APR90 71 08APR90 75 09APR90 76
```

DATA Step Processing of Repeating Blocks of Data

Here is the complete DATA step.

```
data perm.april90;
   infile tempdata;
   input Date : date. HighTemp @@;
   format date date9.;
run;
```

Example

As the execution phase begins, the input pointer rests on column 1 of record 1.

Raw Data File Tempdata

```
>↓---+----10---+----20---+----30--

01APR90 68 02APR90 67 03APR90 70
04APR90 74 05APR90 72 06APR90 73
07APR90 71 08APR90 75 09APR90 76
10APR90 78 11APR90 70 12APR90 69
13APR90 71 14APR90 72 15APR90 74
```

Program Data Vector

N	Date	HighTemp
1	.	.

During the first iteration of the DATA step, the first block of values for `Date` and `HighTemp` are read and stored in the program data vector.

Raw Data File Tempdata

```
>----+----1↓---+----20---+----30--

01APR90 68 02APR90 67 03APR90 70
04APR90 74 05APR90 72 06APR90 73
07APR90 71 08APR90 75 09APR90 76
10APR90 78 11APR90 70 12APR90 69
13APR90 71 14APR90 72 15APR90 74
```

Program Data Vector

N	Date	HighTemp
1	11048	68

The first observation is written to the data set, control returns to the top of the DATA step, and values are reset to missing.

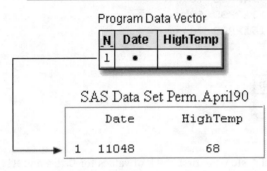

Raw Data File Tempdata

```
>----+----1↓---+----20---+----30--

01APR90 68 02APR90 67 03APR90 70
04APR90 74 05APR90 72 06APR90 73
07APR90 71 08APR90 75 09APR90 76
10APR90 78 11APR90 70 12APR90 69
13APR90 71 14APR90 72 15APR90 74
```

Program Data Vector

N	Date	HighTemp
1	.	.

SAS Data Set Perm.April90

	Date	HighTemp
1	11048	68

During the second iteration, the @@ prevents the input pointer from moving down to column 1 of the next record.

Raw Data File Tempdata

```
>----+----1↓---+----20---+----30--

01APR90 68 02APR90 67 03APR90 70
04APR90 74 05APR90 72 06APR90 73
07APR90 71 08APR90 75 09APR90 76
10APR90 78 11APR90 70 12APR90 69
13APR90 71 14APR90 72 15APR90 74
```

Program Data Vector

N	Date	HighTemp
2	.	.

SAS Data Set Perm.April90

	Date	HighTemp
1	11048	68

The INPUT statement reads the second block of values for `Date` and `HighTemp` in the first record.

Raw Data File Tempdata

```
>----+----10---+----20↓--+----30--

  01APR90  68  02APR90  67  03APR90  70
  04APR90  74  05APR90  72  06APR90  73
  07APR90  71  08APR90  75  09APR90  76
  10APR90  78  11APR90  70  12APR90  69
  13APR90  71  14APR90  72  15APR90  74
```

Program Data Vector

N	Date	HighTemp
2	11049	67

SAS Data Set Perm.April90

	Date	HighTemp
1	11048	68

The second observation is written to the data set, and control returns to the top of the DATA step.

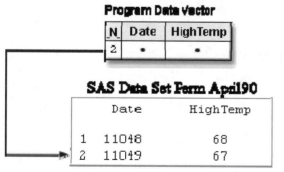

Raw Data File Tempdata

```
>----+----10---+----20↓--+----30--

  01APR90  68  02APR90  67  03APR90  70
  04APR90  74  05APR90  72  06APR90  73
  07APR90  71  08APR90  75  09APR90  76
  10APR90  78  11APR90  70  12APR90  69
  13APR90  71  14APR90  72  15APR90  74
```

Program Data Vector

N	Date	HighTemp
2	.	.

SAS Data Set Perm April90

	Date	HighTemp
1	11048	68
2	11049	67

During the third iteration, the last block of values is read and written to the data set as the third observation. Control returns to the top of the DATA step, and values are reset to missing.

Raw Data File Tempdata

```
>----+----10---+----20---+----30-↓
 01APR90  68  02APR90  67  03APR90  70
 04APR90  74  05APR90  72  06APR90  73
 07APR90  71  08APR90  75  09APR90  76
 10APR90  78  11APR90  70  12APR90  69
 13APR90  71  14APR90  72  15APR90  74
```

Program Data Vector

N	Date	HighTemp
3	.	.

SAS Data Set Perm.April90

	Date	HighTemp
1	11048	68
2	11049	67
3	11050	70

During the fourth iteration, the first block of values in the second record is read and written as the fourth observation. Control returns to the top of the DATA step, and values are reset to missing.

Raw Data File Tempdata

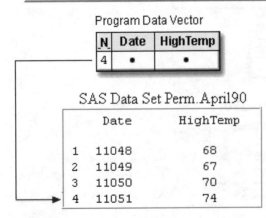

```
>----+----1↓---+----20---+----30--
 01APR90  68  02APR90  67  03APR90  70
 04APR90  74  05APR90  72  06APR90  73
 07APR90  71  08APR90  75  09APR90  76
 10APR90  78  11APR90  70  12APR90  69
 13APR90  71  14APR90  72  15APR90  74
```

Program Data Vector

N	Date	HighTemp
4	.	.

SAS Data Set Perm.April90

	Date	HighTemp
1	11048	68
2	11049	67
3	11050	70
4	11051	74

The execution phase continues until the last block of data is read.

Raw Data File Tempdata

```
>----+----10---+----20---+----30-↓
 01APR90 68 02APR90 67 03APR90 70
 04APR90 74 05APR90 72 06APR90 73
 07APR90 71 08APR90 75 09APR90 76
 10APR90 78 11APR90 70 12APR90 69
 13APR90 71 14APR90 72 15APR90 74
```

SAS Data Set Perm.April90

```
        Date        HighTemp

    1   11048          68
        .
        .
        .
   13   11060          71
   14   11061          72
   15   11062          74
```

You can display the data set with the PRINT procedure.

```
proc print data=perm.april90;
run;
```

Obs	Date	HighTemp
1	01APR1990	68
2	02APR1990	67
3	03APR1990	70
4	04APR1990	74
5	05APR1990	72
6	06APR1990	73
7	07APR1990	71
8	08APR1990	75
9	09APR1990	76
10	10APR1990	78
11	11APR1990	70
12	12APR1990	69
13	13APR1990	71
14	14APR1990	71
15	15APR1990	74

Reading the Same Number of Repeating Fields

So far you have created multiple observations from a single record by executing the DATA step once for each block of data in a record.

Now look at another file that is organized differently.

Each record in the file **Data97** contains a sales representative's ID number, followed by four repeating fields that represent his or her quarterly sales totals for 1997.

You want to pair each sales representative's ID number with one quarterly sales total to produce a single observation. That way, four observations can be derived from one record.

Raw Data File Data97

```
1---+----10---+----20---+----30---+----40
0734 1,323.34 2,472.85 3,276.65 5,345.52
0943 1,908.34 2,560.38 3,472.09 5,290.86
1009 2,934.12 3,308.41 4,176.18 7,581.81
1043 1,295.38 5,980.28 8,876.84 6,345.94
1190 2,189.84 5,023.57 2,794.67 4,243.35
1382 3,456.34 2,065.83 3,139.08 6,503.49
1734 2,345.83 3,423.32 1,034.43 1,942.28
```

ID	Quarter	Sales
0734	1	1323.34
0734	2	2472.85
0734	3	3276.65
0734	4	5345.52
0943	1	1908.34
0943	2	2560.38
0943	3	3472.09
0943	4	5290.86

To accomplish this, you must execute the DATA step once for each record, repetitively reading and writing values in one iteration.

This means that a DATA step must

- read the value for ID and hold the current record

- create a new variable named Quarter to identify the fiscal quarter for each sales figure

- read a new value for Sales and write the values to the data set as an observation

- continue reading a new value for Sales and writing values to the data set three more times.

Using the Single Trailing At Sign (@) to Hold the Current Record

First, you need to read the value for ID and hold the record so that subsequent values for Sales can be read.

```
data perm.sales97;
    infile data97;
    input ID $
```

Raw Data File Data97

```
1---↓----10---+----20---+----30---+----40
0734 1,323.34 2,472.85 3,276.65 5,345.52
0943 1,908.34 2,560.38 3,472.09 5,290.86
1009 2,934.12 3,308.41 4,176.18 7,581.81
```

You are already familiar with the double trailing @@, which holds the current record across multiple iterations of the DATA step.

However, in this case, you want to hold the record with the trailing @ line-hold specifier so that a second INPUT statement can read the values for Sales within the same iteration of the DATA step. Like the double trailing @@, the single trailing @

- enables the next INPUT statement to read from the same record

- releases the current record when a subsequent INPUT statement executes without a line-hold specifier.

It's easy to distinguish between the trailing @@ and the trailing @ by remembering that

- the double trailing at sign (@@) holds a record across multiple iterations of the DATA step until the end of the record is reached.

- the single trailing at sign (@) releases a record when control returns to the top of the DATA step.

In this example, the first INPUT statement reads the value for ID and uses the trailing @ to hold the current record for the next INPUT statement in the DATA step.

```
data perm.sales97;
    infile data97;
    input ID $ @;
    input Sales : comma. @;
    output;
```

Raw Data File Data97

```
1---↓----10---+----20---+----30---+----40
0734 1,323.34 2,472.85 3,276.65 5,345.52
0943 1,908.34 2,560.38 3,472.09 5,290.86
1009 2,934.12 3,308.41 4,176.18 7,581.81
```

The second INPUT statement reads a value for Sales and holds the record. The COMMA*w.d* informat in the INPUT statement reads the numeric value for Sales and removes the embedded commas. An OUTPUT statement writes the observation to the SAS data set, and the DATA step continues processing.

 Notice that the COMMA*w.d* informat does **not** specify a *w* value. Remember that list input reads values until the next blank is detected. The default length of numeric variables is 8 bytes, so you don't need to specify a *w* value to determine the length of a numeric variable.

When all of the repeating fields have been read and sent to output, control returns to the top of the DATA step, and the record is released.

Raw Data File Data97

```
1---+----10--↓+----20---+----30---+----40
0734 1,323.34 2,472.85 3,276.65 5,345.52
0943 1,908.34 2,560.38 3,472.09 5,290.86
1009 2,934.12 3,308.41 4,176.18 7,581.81
```

```
data perm.sales97;
   infile data97;
   input ID $ @;
   input Sales : comma. @;
   output;
   input Sales : comma. @;
   output;
   input Sales : comma. @;
   output;
   input Sales : comma. @;
   output;
run;
```

More Efficient Programming

Each record contains four different values for the variable Sales, so the INPUT statement must execute four times. Rather than writing four INPUT statements, you can execute one INPUT statement repeatedly in an iterative DO loop.

Each time the loop executes, you need to write the values for ID, Quarter, and Sales as an observation to the data set. This is easily accomplished by using the OUTPUT statement.

```
data perm.sales97;
   infile data97;
   input ID $ @;
   do Quarter=1 to 4;
      input Sales : comma. @;
      output;
   end;
run;
```

By default, every DATA step contains an implicit OUTPUT statement at the end of the step. Placing an explicit OUTPUT statement in a DATA step overrides the automatic output, and SAS adds an observation to a data set only when the explicit OUTPUT statement is executed.

Processing a DATA Step That Contains an Iterative DO Loop

Now that the program is complete, let's see how SAS processes a DATA step that contains an iterative DO loop.

```
data perm.sales97;
    infile data97;
    input ID $ @;
    do Quarter=1 to 4;
        input Sales : comma. @;
        output;
    end;
run;
```

During the first iteration, the value for ID is read and Quarter is initialized to 1, so the loop begins to execute.

Raw Data File Data97

```
>----↓----10---+----20---+----30---+----40-
 0734 1,323.34 2,472.85 3,276.65 5,345.52
 0943 1,908.34 2,560.38 3,472.09 5,290.86
 1009 2,934.12 3,308.41 4,176.18 7,581.81
```

Program Data Vector

N	ID	Quarter	Sales
1	0734	1	•

The INPUT statement reads the first repeating field and assigns the value to Sales in the program data vector. The @ holds the current record.

Raw Data File Data97

```
>----+----10--↓+----20---+----30---+----40-
 0734 1,323.34 2,472.85 3,276.65 5,345.52
 0943 1,908.34 2,560.38 3,472.09 5,290.86
 1009 2,934.12 3,308.41 4,176.18 7,581.81
```

Program Data Vector

N	ID	Quarter	Sales
1	0734	1	1323.34

The OUTPUT statement writes the values in the program data vector to the data set as the first observation.

Raw Data File Data97

```
>----+----10--↓+----20---+----30---+----40-
0734 1,323.34 2,472.85 3,276.65 5,345.52
0943 1,908.34 2,560.38 3,472.09 5,290.86
1009 2,934.12 3,308.41 4,176.18 7,581.81
```

Program Data Vector

N	ID	Quarter	Sales
1	0734	1	1323.34

SAS Data Set Perm.Sales97

	ID	Quarter	Sales
1	0734	1	1323.34

The END statement indicates the bottom of the loop, but control returns to the DO statement, not to the top of the DATA step. Now the value of Quarter is incremented to 2.

Raw Data File Data97

```
>----+----10---↓----20---+----30---+----40-
0734 1,323.34 2,472.85 3,276.65 5,345.52
0943 1,908.34 2,560.38 3,472.09 5,290.86
1009 2,934.12 3,308.41 4,176.18 7,581.81
```

Program Data Vector

N	ID	Quarter	Sales
1	0734	2	1323.34

SAS Data Set Perm.Sales97

	ID	Quarter	Sales
1	0734	1	1323.34

The INPUT statement executes again, reading the second repeating field and storing the value for Sales in the program data vector.

Raw Data File Data97

```
>----+----10---+----20-↓-+----30---+----40-
 0734 1,323.34 2,472.85 3,276.65 5,345.52
 0943 1,908.34 2,560.38 3,472.09 5,290.86
 1009 2,934.12 3,308.41 4,176.18 7,581.81
```

Program Data Vector

N	ID	Quarter	Sales
1	0734	2	2472.85

SAS Data Set Perm.Sales97

	ID	Quarter	Sales
1	0734	1	1323.34

The OUTPUT statement writes the values in the program data vector as the second observation.

Raw Data File Data97

```
>----+----10---+----20-↓-+----30---+----40-
 0734 1,323.34 2,472.85 3,276.65 5,345.52
 0943 1,908.34 2,560.38 3,472.09 5,290.86
 1009 2,934.12 3,308.41 4,176.18 7,581.81
```

Program Data Vector

N	ID	Quarter	Sales
1	0734	2	2472.85

SAS Data Set Perm.Sales97

	ID	Quarter	Sales
1	0734	1	1323.34
2	0734	2	2472.85

The loop continues executing while the value for Quarter is 3, then 4. In the process, the third and fourth observations are created.

Raw Data File Data97

```
>----+----10---+----20---+----30---+----4↓-
0734 1,323.34 2,472.85 3,276.65 5,345.52
0943 1,908.34 2,560.38 3,472.09 5,290.86
1009 2,934.12 3,308.41 4,176.18 7,581.81
```

Program Data Vector

N	ID	Quarter	Sales
1	0734	4	5345.52

SAS Data Set Perm.Sales97

	ID	Quarter	Sales
1	0734	1	1323.34
2	0734	2	2472.85
3	0731	3	3276.65
4	0734	4	5345.52

After the fourth observation is created, `Quarter` is incremented to 5 at the bottom of the DO loop and control returns to the top of the loop. The loop does not execute again because the value of `Quarter` is now greater than 4.

The RUN statement executes. Control returns to the top of the DATA step, and the input pointer moves to column 1 of the next record. The variable values in the program data vector are reset to missing. Notice that SAS is reading the second record from the original file but has created four observations in the new SAS data set.

Raw Data File Data97

```
>↓---+----10---+----20---+----30---+----40-
0734 1,323.34 2,472.85 3,276.65 5,345.52
0943 1,908.34 2,560.38 3,472.09 5,290.86
1009 2,934.12 3,308.41 4,176.18 7,581.81
```

Program Data Vector

N	ID	Quarter	Sales
2	.	.	.

SAS Data Set Perm.Sales97

	ID	Quarter	Sales
1	0734	1	1323.34
2	0734	2	2472.85
3	0734	3	3276.65
4	0734	4	5345.52

When the execution phase is complete, you can display the data set with the PRINT procedure.

```
proc print data=perm.sales97;
run;
```

Obs	ID	Quarter	Sales
1	0734	1	1323.34
2	0734	2	2472.85
3	0734	3	3276.65
4	0734	4	5345.52
5	0943	1	1908.34
6	0943	2	2560.38
7	0943	3	3472.09
8	0943	4	5290.86
9	1009	1	2934.12
10	1009	2	3308.41
11	1009	3	4176.18
12	1009	4	7581.81

Reading a Varying Number of Repeating Fields

So far each record in the file **Data97** has contained the same number of repeating fields.

Raw Data File Data97

```
1---+----10---+----20---+----30---+----40
0734 1,323.34 2,472.85 3,276.65 5,345.52
0943 1,908.34 2,560.38 3,472.09 5,290.86
1009 2,934.12 3,308.41 4,176.18 7,581.81
1043 1,295.38 5,980.28 8,876.84 6,345.94
1190 2,189.84 5,023.57 2,794.67 4,243.35
1382 3,456.34 2,065.83 3,139.08 6,503.49
1734 2,345.83 3,423.32 1,034.43 1,942.28
```

But suppose some of the employees quit after the first quarter. Records that contain information for those employees might not contain sales totals for the second, third, or fourth quarter. These records contain a varying number of repeating fields.

Raw Data File Data97

```
1---+----10---+----20---+----30---+----40
1824 1,323.34 2,472.85
1943 1,908.34
2046 1,423.52 1,673.46 3,276.65
2063 2,345.34 2,452.45 3,523.52 2,983.01
```

The DATA step that you just wrote won't work with a varying number of repeating fields because now the value of `Quarter` is not constant for every record.

```
data perm.sales97;
    infile data97;
    input ID $ @;
    do Quarter=1 to 4;
        input Sales : comma. @;
        output;
    end;
run;
```

Using the MISSOVER Option

You can adapt the DATA step to accommodate a varying number of values for `Sales`.

Like the previous example with the same number of repeating fields, your DATA step must read the same record more than once. However, you need to prevent the input pointer from moving to the next record when there are missing values for `Sales`.

You can use the MISSOVER option in an INFILE statement to prevent SAS from reading the next record when missing values are encountered at the end of a record. Essentially, records that have a varying number of repeating fields are records that contain missing values, so you need to specify the MISSOVER option here as well.

Because there is at least one value for the repeating field, `Sales`, in each record, the first INPUT statement reads **both** the value for `ID` and the first value for `Sales` in the first record. The trailing @ holds the record so that any subsequent repeating fields can be read.

```
data perm.sales97;
    infile data97 missover;

    input ID $ Sales : comma. @;
```

Raw Data File Data97

```
1---+----10--↓+----20---+----30---+----40
1824 1,323.34 2,472.85
1943 1,908.34
2046 1,423.52 1,673.46 3,276.65
2063 2,345.34 2,452.45 3,523.52 2,983.01
```

 SAS provides several options to control reading past the end of a line. You've seen the MISSOVER option for setting remaining INPUT statement variables to missing values if the pointer reaches the end of a record. You can also use other options such as the **TRUNCOVER option**, which reads column or formatted input when the last variable that is read by the INPUT statement contains varying-length data. The TRUNCOVER option assigns the contents of the input buffer to a variable when the field is shorter than expected.

Other related options include FLOWOVER (the default), STOPOVER, and SCANOVER. For more information about TRUNCOVER and related options, see the SAS documentation.

Executing SAS Statements While a Condition Is True

Now consider how many times to read each record. Earlier, you created an index variable named `Quarter` whose value ranged from *1* to *4* because there were four repeating fields.

Now you want to read the record only while a value for Sales exists. Use a DO WHILE statement instead of the iterative DO statement, enclosing the expression in parentheses. In the example below, the DO WHILE statement executes while the value of Sales is not equal to a missing value (which is represented by a period).

```
data perm.sales97;
    infile data97 missover;
    input ID $ Sales : comma. @;
    do while (sales ne .);
```

Creating a Counter Variable

Because the DO WHILE statement does not create an index variable, you can create your own "counter" variable. You can then use a Sum statement to increment the value of the counter variable each time the DO WHILE loop executes.

In the example below, the assignment statement that precedes the loop creates the counter variable Quarter and assigns it an initial value of zero. Each time the DO WHILE loop executes, the Sum statement increments the value of Quarter by one.

```
data perm.sales97;
    infile data97 missover;
    input ID $ Sales : comma. @;
    Quarter=0;
    do while (sales ne .);
        quarter+1;
```

Completing the DO WHILE Loop

Now look at the other statements that should be executed in the DO WHILE loop. First, you need an OUTPUT statement to write the current observation to the data set. Then, another INPUT statement reads the next value for Sales and holds the record. You complete the DO WHILE loop with an END statement.

```
data perm.sales97;
    infile data97 missover;
    input ID $ Sales : comma. @;
    Quarter=0;
    do while (sales ne .);
        quarter+1;
        output;
        input sales : comma. @;
    end;
run;
```

Processing a DATA Step That Has a Varying Number of Repeating Fields

Here is the new version of the DATA step.

```
data perm.sales97;
    infile data97 missover;
    input ID $ Sales : comma. @;
    Quarter=0;
    do while (sales ne .);
        quarter+1;
        output;
        input sales : comma. @;
    end;
run;
```

During the first iteration of the DATA step, values for ID and Sales are read. Quarter is initialized to zero.

Raw Data File Data97

```
>----+----10--↓+----20---+----30---+----40-
1824 1,323.34 2,472.85
1943 1,908.34
2046 1,423.52 1,673.46 3,276.65
2063 2,345.34 2,452.45 3,523.52 2,983.01
```

Program Data Vector

N	ID	Sales	Quarter
1	1824	1323.34	0

The DO WHILE statement checks to see if Sales has a value at the top of the loop. Because it does have a value, the other statements in the DO loop execute.

Raw Data File Data97

```
>----+----10--↓+----20---+----30---+----40-
1824 1,323.34 2,472.85
1943 1,908.34
2046 1,423.52 1,673.46 3,276.65
2063 2,345.34 2,452.45 3,523.52 2,983.01
```

Program Data Vector

N	ID	Sales	Quarter
1	1824	1323.34	1

SAS Data Set Perm.Sales97

	ID	Sales	Quarter
1	1824	1323.34	1

The INPUT statement reads the next value for Sales, the end of the loop is reached, and control returns to the DO WHILE statement.

Raw Data File Data97

```
>----+----10---+----20-↓-+----30---+----40-
 1824 1,323.34 2,472.85
 1943 1,908.34
 2046 1,423.52 1,673.46 3,276.65
 2063 2,345.34 2,452.45 3,523.52 2,983.01
```

Program Data Vector

N	ID	Sales	Quarter
1	1824	2472.85	1

SAS Data Set Perm.Sales97

	ID	Sales	Quarter
1	1824	1323.34	1

The condition is checked at the top of the loop and Sales still has a value, so the loop executes again.

Raw Data File Data97

```
>----+----10---+----20-↓-+----30---+----40-
 1824 1,323.34 2,472.85
 1943 1,908.34
 2046 1,423.52 1,673.46 3,276.65
 2063 2,345.34 2,452.45 3,523.52 2,983.01
```

Program Data Vector

N	ID	Sales	Quarter
1	1824	2472.85	1

SAS Data Set Perm.Sales97

	ID	Sales	Quarter
1	1824	1323.34	1

Quarter is incremented to 2, and the values in the program data vector are written as the second observation.

Raw Data File Data97

```
>----+----10---+----20-↓-+----30---+----40-
 1824 1,323.34 2,472.85
 1943 1,908.34
 2046 1,423.52 1,673.46 3,276.65
 2063 2,345.34 2,452.45 3,523.52 2,983.01
```

Program Data Vector

N	ID	Sales	Quarter
1	1824	2472.85	2

SAS Data Set Perm.Sales97

	ID	Sales	Quarter
1	1824	1323.34	1
2	1824	2472.85	2

The MISSOVER option prevents the input pointer from moving to the next record in search of another value for Sales. At this point, Sales has no value.

Raw Data File Data97

```
>----+----10---+----20-↓-+----30---+----40-
 1824 1,323.34 2,472.85
 1943 1,908.34
 2046 1,423.52 1,673.46 3,276.65
 2063 2,345.34 2,452.45 3,523.52 2,983.01
```

Program Data Vector

N	ID	Sales	Quarter
1	1824	•	2

SAS Data Set Perm.Sales97

	ID	Sales	Quarter
1	1824	1323.34	1
2	1824	2472.85	2

Because the condition is now false, the statements in the loop are not executed.

Raw Data File Data97

```
>----+----10---+----20-↓-+----30---+----40-
1824 1,323.34 2,472.85
1943 1,908.34
2046 1,423.52 1,673.46 3,276.65
2063 2,345.34 2,452.45 3,523.52 2,983.01
```

Program Data Vector

N	ID	Sales	Quarter
1	1824	•	2

SAS Data Set Perm.Sales97

	ID	Sales	Quarter
1	1824	1323.34	1
2	1824	2472.85	2

Instead, control returns to the top of the DATA step, the values in the program data vector are reset to missing, and the input pointer moves to column 1 of the next record. The DATA step continues executing until all the values for Sales are read.

Raw Data File Data97

```
>↓---+----10---+----20---+----30---+----40-
1824 1,323.34 2,472.85
1943 1,908.34
2046 1,423.52 1,673.46 3,276.65
2063 2,345.34 2,452.45 3,523.52 2,983.01
```

Program Data Vector

N	ID	Sales	Quarter
2	•	•	•

SAS Data Set Perm.Sales97

	ID	Sales	Quarter
1	1824	1323.34	1
2	1824	2472.85	2

PROC PRINT output for the data set shows a varying number of observations for each employee.

```
proc print data=perm.sales97;
run;
```

Obs	ID	Sales	Quarter
1	1824	1323.34	1
2	1824	2472.85	2
3	1943	2199.23	1
4	2046	3598.48	1
5	2046	4697.98	2
6	2046	4598.45	3
7	2063	4963.87	1
8	2063	3434.42	2
9	2063	2241.64	3
10	2063	2759.11	4

Summary

Text Summary

File Formats

One raw data record can contain enough information to produce several observations. Data is stored in this manner in order to reduce the size of the entire file. The data can be organized into

- repeating blocks of data
- an ID field followed by the same number of repeating fields
- an ID field followed by a varying number of repeating fields.

Reading Repeating Blocks of Data

To create multiple observations from a record that contains repeating blocks of data, the DATA step needs to hold the current record until each block of data has been read and written to the data set as an observation. The DATA step should include statements that

- read the first block of values and hold the current record with the **double trailing at sign (@@)** line-hold specifier
- optionally add a FORMAT statement to display date or time values with a specified format
- write the first block of values as an observation
- execute the DATA step until all repeating blocks have been read.

Reading the Same Number of Repeating Fields

To create multiple observations from a record that contains an ID field and the same number of repeating fields, you must execute the DATA step once for each record, repetitively reading and writing values in one iteration. The DATA step should include statements that

- read the ID field and hold the current record with the **single trailing at sign (@)** line-hold specifier
- execute SAS statements using an **iterative DO loop**. The iterative DO loop repetitively processes statements that

  o read the next value of the repeating field and hold the record with the @ line-hold specifier

  o explicitly write an observation to the data set by using an OUTPUT statement.
- complete the iterative DO loop with an END statement.

Reading a Varying Number of Repeating Fields

To create multiple observations from a record that contains an ID field and a varying number of repeating fields, you must execute the DATA step once for each record, repetitively reading and writing values in one iteration while the value of the repeating field exists. The DATA step should include statements that

- prevent SAS from reading the next record if missing values were encountered in the current record by using the **MISSOVER option**
- read the ID field and the first repeating field, and then hold the record with the single trailing at sign (@) line-hold specifier
- optionally create a counter variable
- execute SAS statements while a condition is true, using a DO WHILE loop. A DO WHILE loop repetitively processes statements that

  o optionally increment the value of the counter variable by using a Sum statement

  o explicitly add an observation to the data set by using an OUTPUT statement

  o read the next value of the repeating field and hold the record with the single trailing at sign (@) line-hold specifier.
- complete the DO WHILE loop with an END statement.

Points to Remember

- The double trailing at sign (@@) holds a record across multiple iterations of the DATA step until the end of the record is reached.
- The single trailing at sign (@) releases a record when control returns to the top of the DATA step.
- Use an END statement to complete DO loops and DO WHILE loops.

Practice

After you complete this chapter, practice what you learned by using the sample data and SAS programs for Chapter 21, **Creating Multiple Observations from a Single Record**, which are located on the CD-ROM. Follow the directions for creating your sample data in the Before You Begin section.

Quiz

Select the best answer for each question. After completing the quiz, check your answers using the answer key in the appendix.

1. Which is true for the double trailing at sign (@@)?

    a. It enables the next INPUT statement to read from the current record across multiple iterations of the DATA step.
    b. It must be the last item that is specified in the INPUT statement.
    c. It is released when the input pointer moves past the end of the record.
    d. All of the above.

2. A record that is being held by a single trailing at sign (@) is automatically released when

    a. the input pointer moves past the end of the record.
    b. the next iteration of the DATA step begins.
    c. another INPUT statement that has a single trailing at sign (@) executes.
    d. another value is read from the observation.

3. Which SAS program correctly creates a separate observation for each block of data?

    ```
    1---+----10---+----20---+----30---+----40---+
    1001 apple 1002 banana 1003 cherry
    1004 guava 1005 kiwi 1006 papaya
    1007 pineapple 1008 raspberry 1009 strawberry
    ```

    a.
    ```
    data perm.produce;
        infile fruit;
        input Item $4. Variety : $10.;
    run;
    ```
    b.
    ```
    data perm.produce;
        infile fruit;
        input Item $4. Variety : $10. @;
    run;
    ```
    c.
    ```
    data perm.produce;
        infile fruit;
        input Item $ Variety : $10. @@;
    run;
    ```
    d.
    ```
    data perm.produce;
        infile fruit @@;
        input Item $4. Variety : $10.;
    run;
    ```

4. Which SAS program segment reads the values for ID and holds the record for each value of `Quantity`, so that three observations are created for each record?

```
1---+----10---+----20---+----30
2101 21,208 19,047 22,890
2102 18,775 20,214 22,654
2103 19,763 22,927 21,862
```

a.
```
data work.sales;
    infile unitsold;
    input ID $;
    do week=1 to 3;
        input Quantity : comma.;
        output;
    end;
run;
```

b.
```
data work.sales;
    infile unitsold;
    input ID $ @@;
    do week=1 to 3;
        input Quantity : comma.;
        output;
    end;
run;
```

c.
```
data work.sales;
    infile unitsold;
    input ID $ @;
    do week=1 to 3;
        input Quantity : comma.;
        output;
    end;
run;
```

d.
```
data work.sales;
    infile unitsold;
    input ID $ @;
    do week=1 to 3;
        input Quantity : comma. @;
        output;
    end;
run;
```

5. Which SAS statement repetitively executes several statements when the value of an index variable named `Count` ranges from 1 to 50, incremented by 5?

a. `do count=1 to 50 by 5;`

b. `do while count=1 to 50 by 5;`

c. `do count=1 to 50 + 5;`

d. `do while (count=1 to 50 + 5);`

6. Which option below, when used in a DATA step, writes an observation to the data set after each value for `Activity` has been read?

   a.
   ```
   do choice=1 to 3;
       input Activity : $10. @;
       output;
   end;
   run;
   ```

   b.
   ```
   do choice=1 to 3;
       input Activity : $10. @;
   end;
   output;
   run;
   ```

   c.
   ```
   do choice=1 to 3;
       input Activity : $10. @;
   end;
   run;
   ```

   d. *a* and *b*

7. Which SAS statement repetitively executes several statements while the value of `Cholesterol` is greater than 200?

   a. `do cholesterol > 200;`
   b. `do cholesterol gt 200;`
   c. `do while (cholesterol > 200);`
   d. `do while cholesterol > 200;`

8. Which choice below is an example of a Sum statement?

   a. `totalpay=1;`
   b. `totalpay+1;`
   c. `totalpay*1;`
   d. `totalpay by 1;`

9. Which program creates the SAS data set **Perm.Topstore** from the raw data file shown below?

   ```
   1---+----10---+----20---+----30---+
   1001 77,163.19 76,804.75 74,384.27
   1002 76,612.93 81,456.34 82,063.97
   1003 82,185.16 79,742.33
   ```

SAS Data Set Perm.Topstore

Store	Sales	Month
1001	77163.19	1
1001	76804.75	2
1001	74384.27	3
1002	76612.93	1
1002	81456.34	2
1002	82063.97	3
1003	82185.16	1
1003	79742.33	2

a.
```
data perm.topstores;
    infile sales98 missover;
    input Store Sales : comma. @;
    do while (sales ne .);
       month + 1;
        output;
        input sales : comma. @;
    end;
run;
```

b.
```
data perm.topstores;
    infile sales98 missover;
    input Store Sales : comma. @;
    do while (sales ne .);
       Month=0;
       month + 1;
       output;
       input sales : comma. @;
    end;
run;
```

c.
```
data perm.topstores;
    infile sales98 missover;
    input Store Sales : comma. Month @;
    do while (sales ne .);
       month + 1;
        input sales : comma. @;
    end;
    output;
run;
```

d.
```
data perm.topstores;
    infile sales98 missover;
    input Store Sales : comma. @;
    Month=0;
    do while (sales ne .);
        month + 1;
        output;
        input sales : comma. @;
    end;
run;
```

10. How many observations are produced by the DATA step that reads this external file?

```
1---+----10---+----20---+----30---+----40
01 CHOCOLATE VANILLA RASPBERRY
02 VANILLA PEACH
03 CHOCOLATE
04 RASPBERRY PEACH CHOCOLATE
05 STRAWBERRY VANILLA CHOCOLATE
```

```
data perm.choices;
    infile icecream missover;
    input Day $ Flavor : $10. @;
    do while (flavor ne ' ');
        output;
        input flavor : $10. @;
    end;

run;
```

a. 3

b. 5

c. 12

d. 15

Overview

Introduction

Raw data files can be hierarchical in structure, consisting of a header record and one or more detail records. Typically, each record contains a field that identifies the record type.

Here, the *P* indicates a **header record** that contains a patient's ID number. The *C* indicates a **detail record** that contains the date of the patient's appointment and the charges that the patient has incurred.

Raw Data File

```
1---+----10---+----20
P    1095
C    01-08-89   $45.0
C    01-17-89   $37.5
P    1096
C    01-09-89   $156.5
P    1097
C    01-02-89   $109.0
P    1099
C    01-03-89   $45.0
C    01-05-89   $45.0
P    1201
C    01-05-89   $37.0
C    01-10-89   $45.0
```

You can build a SAS data set from a hierarchical file by creating one observation **per detail record** and storing each header record as part of the observation.

SAS Data Set

Obs	ID	Date	Amount
1	1095	01/08/89	$45.00
2	1095	01/17/89	$37.50
3	1096	01/09/89	$156.50
4	1097	01/02/89	$109.00
5	1099	01/03/89	$45.00
6	1099	01/05/89	$45.00
7	1201	01/05/89	$37.00
8	1201	01/10/89	$45.00

You can also build a SAS data set from a hierarchical file by creating one observation **per header record** and combining the information from detail records into **summary variables.**

SAS Data Set

Obs	ID	Total
1	1095	$82.50
2	1096	$156.50
3	1097	$109.00
4	1099	$90.00
5	1201	$82.00

In this chapter, you learn how to read from a hierarchical file and create a SAS data set that contains either one observation for each detail record or one observation for each header record.

Objectives

In this chapter, you learn to

- retain the value of a variable

- conditionally execute a SAS statement

- determine when the last observation is being processed

- conditionally execute multiple SAS statements.

You can also review how to

- use a line-hold specifier to hold the current record

- explicitly write an observation to a data set.

Creating One Observation Per Detail Record

In order to create one observation per detail record, it is necessary to distinguish between header and detail records. Having a field that identifies the type of the record makes this task easier.

In the raw data file **Census** that follows, *H* indicates a **header record** that contains a street address, and *P* indicates a **detail record** that contains information about a person who lives at that address.

Raw Data File

```
1---+----10---+----
H 321 S. MAIN ST
P MARY E      21 F
P WILLIAM M 23 M
P SUSAN K      3 F
H 324 S. MAIN ST
P THOMAS H  79 M
P WALTER S  46 M
P ALICE A    42 F
P MARYANN A 20 F
P JOHN S     16 M
H 325A S. MAIN ST
```

Let's see how you can create a data set that contains one observation for **each** person who lives at a specific address.

SAS Data Set

Obs	Address	Name	Age	Gender
1	321 S. MAIN ST	MARY E	21	F
2	321 S. MAIN ST	WILLIAM M	23	M
3	321 S. MAIN ST	SUSAN K	3	F
4	324 S. MAIN ST	THOMAS H	79	M
5	324 S. MAIN ST	WALTER S	46	M
6	324 S. MAIN ST	ALICE A	42	F
7	324 S. MAIN ST	MARYANN A	20	F
8	324 S. MAIN ST	JOHN S	16	M
9	325A S. MAIN ST	JAMES L	34	M
10	325A S. MAIN S	T LIZA A	31	F
11	325B S. MAIN S	T MARGO K	27	F

Retaining the Values of Variables

As you write the DATA step to read this file, remember that you want to **keep the header record** as a part of each observation until the next header record is encountered. To do this, you need to use a RETAIN statement to retain the values for Address across iterations of the DATA step.

```
data perm.people;
   infile census;
   retain Address;
```

```
1---+----10---+----
H 321 S. MAIN ST
P MARY E      21 F
P WILLIAM M 23 M
P SUSAN K     3 F
```

> ⚠ When a RETAIN statement specifies variables, new variables are created. Therefore, you must give any variables that you use in a RETAIN statement the same name as you want them to have in the data set.

Next, you need to read the first field in each record, which identifies the record's type. You also need to use the single trailing @ line-hold specifier (which you learned about in Chapter 21, **Creating Multiple Observations from a Single Record**) to hold the current record so that the other values in the record can be read.

```
data perm.people;
   infile census;
   retain Address;
   input type $1. @;
```

```
↓---+----10---+----
H 321 S. MAIN ST
P MARY E      21 F
P WILLIAM M 23 M
P SUSAN K     3 F
```

Conditionally Executing SAS Statements

You can use the value of type to identify each record. If type is *H*, execute an INPUT statement to read the values for Address. However, if type is *P*, then execute an INPUT statement to read the values for Name, Age, and Gender.

You can tell SAS to perform a given task based on a specific condition by using an IF-THEN statement.

```
data perm.people;
   infile census;
   retain Address;
   input type $1. @;
   if type='H' then
      input @3 address $15.;
```

```
↓---+----10---+----
H 321 S. MAIN ST
P MARY E      21 F
P WILLIAM M 23 M
P SUSAN K     3 F
```

Expressions in conditional statements usually involve some kind of comparison. In the previous example, `type` is being compared to a value that is found in the raw data. When the condition is met, the expression is evaluated as true, and the statement that follows the keyword THEN is executed.

The expression defines a condition so that when the value of `type` is *H*, the INPUT statement reads the values for `Address`. However, when the value of `type` is not *H*, the expression is evaluated as false, and the INPUT statement is not executed. Notice that the value is enclosed in quotation marks because it is a character value.

 When you are comparing values, be sure to express the values exactly as they are coded in the data. For example, the expression below would be evaluated as false because the values in the data are stored in uppercase letters.

`if type='h' then ... ;`

Reading a Detail Record

Now think about what needs to happen when a **detail** record is read. Remember, you want to write an observation to the data set only when the value of `type` is *P*.

```
↓---+-----10---+----
H 321 S. MAIN ST
P MARY E     21 F
P WILLIAM M 23 M
P SUSAN K    3 F
```

You can use a subsetting IF statement to check for the condition that `type` is *P*. The remaining DATA step statements execute only when the condition is true. If `type` is not *P*, then the values for `Name`, `Age`, and `Gender` are not read, the values in the program data vector are not written to the data set as an observation, and control returns to the top of the DATA step.

The values for `Address` are retained only as a part of the observation. Remember, you do not want to create an observation for each header record.

```
data perm.people;
    infile census;
    retain Address;
    input type $1. @;
    if type='H' then input @3 address $15.;
    if type='P';
    input @3 Name $10. @13 Age 3. @16 Gender $1.;
run;
```

Dropping Variables

Because `type` is useful only for identifying a record's type, drop the variable from the data set. The DROP= option in the DATA statement shown here prevents the values of `type` from being written to the data set.

```
data perm.people (drop=type);
    infile census;
    retain Address;
    input type $1. @;
    if type='H' then input @3 address $15.;
    if type='P';
    input @3 Name $10. @13 Age 3. @16 Gender $1.;
run;
```

Processing a DATA Step That Creates One Observation Per Detail Record

Let's take a look at how this DATA step is processed.

```
data perm.people (drop=type);
    infile census;
    retain Address;
    input type $1. @;
    if type='H' then input @3 address $15.;
    if type='P';
input @3 Name $10. @13 Age 3. @16 Gender $1.;
    run;
```

At compile time, the variable `type` is flagged so that its values are not written to the data set. `Address` is flagged so that its value is retained across iterations of the DATA step.

```
>----+----10---+----
H 321 S. MAIN ST
P MARY E      21 F
P WILLIAM M 23 M
P SUSAN K     3 F
H 324 S. MAIN ST
```

	Retain	Drop			
N	Address	type	Name	Age	Gender
.				.	

As the DATA step begins to execute, the INPUT statement reads the value for `type` and holds the first record.

```
>----+----10---+----
H 321 S. MAIN ST
P MARY E      21 F
P WILLIAM M 23 M
P SUSAN K      3 F
H 324 S. MAIN ST
```

N	Address	type	Name	Age	Gender
		H		•	
1					

The condition `type='H'` is checked and found to be true, so the INPUT statement reads the value for `Address` in the first record.

```
>----+----10---+----
H 321 S. MAIN ST
P MARY E      21 F
P WILLIAM M 23 M
P SUSAN K      3 F
H 324 S. MAIN ST
```

N	Address	type	Name	Age	Gender
1	321 S. MAIN ST	H		•	

Next, the subsetting IF statement checks for the condition `type='P'`. Because the condition is not true, the remaining statements are not executed and control returns to the top of the DATA step.

```
>----+----10---+----
H 321 S. MAIN ST
P MARY E      21 F
P WILLIAM M 23 M
P SUSAN K      3 F
H 324 S. MAIN ST
```

N	Address	type	Name	Age	Gender
1	321 S. MAIN ST	H		•	

As the second iteration begins, the input pointer moves to the next record and a new value for `type` is read. The condition that is expressed in the IF-THEN statement is not true, so the statement following the THEN keyword is not executed.

```
>----+----10---+----

H 321 S. MAIN ST
P MARY E      21 F
P WILLIAM M 23 M
P SUSAN K      3 F
H 324 S. MAIN ST
```

		Retain	Drop		
N	Address	type	Name	Age	Gender
2	321 S. MAIN ST	P		•	

Now the subsetting IF statement checks for the condition `type='P'`. In this iteration, the condition is true, so the remaining INPUT statement is executed.

```
>----+----10---+----

H 321 S. MAIN ST
P MARY E      21 F
P WILLIAM M 23 M
P SUSAN K      3 F
H 324 S. MAIN ST
```

		Retain	Drop		
N	Address	type	Name	Age	Gender
2	321 S. MAIN ST	P		•	

The INPUT statement reads the values for `Name`, `Age`, and `Gender`.

```
>----+----10---+----

H 321 S. MAIN ST
P MARY E      21 F
P WILLIAM M 23 M
P SUSAN K      3 F
H 324 S. MAIN ST
```

		Retain	Drop		
N	Address	type	Name	Age	Gender
2	321 S. MAIN ST	P	MARY E	21	F

Then the values in the program data vector are written as the first observation, and control returns to the top of the DATA step. Notice that the values for `type` are not included.

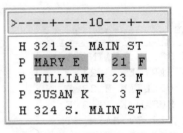

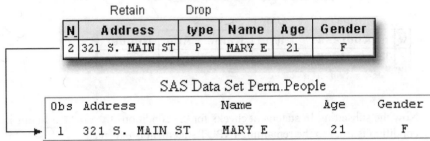

As the execution phase continues, observations are produced from the third and fourth records. However, notice that the fifth record is a header record. During the fifth iteration, the condition `type='H'` is true, so the new value for `Address` is read in to the program data vector.

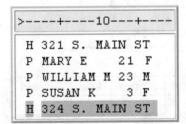

Printing Your Results

When the execution phase is complete, you can display the data set by using the PRINT procedure.

```
proc print data=perm.people;
run;
```

Obs	Address	Name	Age	Gender
1	321 S. MAIN ST	MARY E	21	F
2	321 S. MAIN ST	WILLIAM M	23	M
3	321 S. MAIN ST	SUSAN K	3	F
4	324 S. MAIN ST	THOMAS H	79	M
5	324 S. MAIN ST	WALTER S	46	M
6	324 S. MAIN ST	ALICE A	42	F
7	324 S. MAIN ST	MARYANN A	20	F
8	324 S. MAIN ST	JOHN S	16	M
9	325A S. MAIN ST	JAMES L	34	M
10	325A S. MAIN ST	LIZA A	31	F

Creating One Observation Per Header Record

In the previous example, you learned how to create one observation per detail record. But suppose you only want to know how many people reside at each address. You can create a data set that reads each detail record, counts the number of people, and stores this value in a summary variable.

In the example below, this summary variable, `Total`, is combined with the header record to form an observation in the data set. As you can see, creating one observation per header record condenses a large amount of information into a concise data set.

Raw Data File

```
1---+----10---+----20
H 321 S. MAIN ST
P MARY E      21 F
P WILLIAM M 23 M
P SUSAN K     3 F
H 324 S. MAIN ST
P THOMAS H  79 M
P WALTER S  46 M
P ALICE A   42 F
P MARYANN A 20
P JOHN S     16 M
H 325A S. MAIN ST
P JAMES L 34 M
P LIZA A 31 F
H 325B S. MAIN ST
P MARGO K 27 F
P WILLIAM R 27 M
P ROBERT W 1 M
```

SAS Data Set

Address	Total
321 S. MAIN ST	3
324 S. MAIN ST	5
325A S. MAIN ST	2
325B S. MAIN ST	3

As you write the DATA step to read this file, you need to think about performing several tasks. First, the value of `Address` must be retained as detail records are read and summarized.

```
data perm.people;
   infile census;
   retain Address;
```

```
1---+----10---+----
H 321 S. MAIN ST
P MARY E      21 F
P WILLIAM M 23 M
P SUSAN K     3 F
```

Next, the value of `type` must be read in order to determine whether the current record is a header record or a detail record. Add a single trailing at sign (@) to hold the record so that another INPUT statement can read the remaining values.

```
data perm.people;
   infile census;
   retain Address;
   input type $1. @;
```

```
↓---+----10---+----
H 321 S. MAIN ST
P MARY E      21 F
P WILLIAM M 23 M
P SUSAN K     3 F
```

When the value of `type` indicates a header record, you need to execute several statements. When the value of `type` indicates a detail record, you need to define an alternative set of actions. Let's look at executing different sets of statements for each value of `type`.

DO Group Actions for Header Records

To execute **multiple** SAS statements based on the value of a variable, you can use a simple **DO group** with an IF-THEN statement. When the condition `type='H'` is true, you need to execute several statements.

```
data perm.residnts;
   infile census;
   retain Address;
   input type $1. @;
   if type='H' then do;
```

- First, you need to determine whether this is the first header record in the external file. You do not want the first header record to be written as an observation until the related detail records have been read and summarized.

  _N_ is an automatic variable whose value is the number of times the DATA step has begun to execute. The expression `_n_ > 1` defines a condition where the DATA step has executed more than once. Use this expression in conjunction with the previous IF-THEN statement to check for these two conditions:

  o   The current record is a header record.

  o   The DATA step has executed more than once.

  ```
  data perm.residnts;
     infile census;
     retain Address;
     input type $1. @;
     if type='H' then do;
        if _n_ > 1
  ```

- When the conditions `type='H'` and `_n_ > 1` are true, an OUTPUT statement is executed. Thus, each header record except for the first one causes an observation to be written to the data set.

  ```
  data perm.residnts;
     infile census;
     retain Address;
     input type $1. @;
     if type='H' then do;
        if _n_ > 1 then output;
  ```

- An assignment statement creates the summary variable `Total` and sets its value to *0*.

  ```
  data perm.residnts;
     infile census;
     retain Address;
     input type $1. @;
     if type='H' then do;
        if _n_ > 1 then output;
        Total=0;
  ```

- An INPUT statement reads the values for `Address`.

```
data perm.residnts;
   infile census;
   retain Address;
   input type $1. @;
   if type='H' then do;
      if _n_ > 1 then output;
      Total=0;
      input address $ 3-17;
```

- An END statement closes the DO group.

```
data perm.residnts;
   infile census;
   retain Address;
   input type $1. @;
   if type='H' then do;
      if _n_ > 1 then output;
      Total=0;
      input address $ 3-17;
   end;
```

Reading Detail Records

When the value of `type` is not *H*, you need to define an alternative action. You can do this by adding an ELSE statement to the IF-THEN statement.

Remember that the IF-THEN statement executes a SAS statement when the condition that is specified in the IF clause is true. By adding an ELSE statement after the IF-THEN statement, you define an alternative action to be performed when the THEN clause is not executed.

```
data perm.residnts;
   infile census;
   retain Address;
   input type $1. @;
   if type='H' then do;
      if _n_ > 1 then output;
      Total=0;
      input address $ 3-17;
   end;
   else
```

The only other type of record is a detail record, represented by a *P*. You want to count each person who is represented by a detail record and store the accumulated value in the summary variable `Total`. You do not need to read the values for `Name`, `Age`, and `Gender`.

```
1---+----10---+----20
H 321 S. MAIN ST
P MARY E      21 F
P WILLIAM M 23 M
P SUSAN K     3 F
H 324 S. MAIN ST
P THOMAS H   79 M
P WALTER S   46 M
P ALICE A    42 F
P MARYANN A 20 F
P JOHN S     16 M
```

```
data perm.residnts;
   infile census;
   retain Address;
   input type $1. @;
   if type='H' then do;
      if _n_ > 1 then output;
      Total=0;
      input address $ 3-17;
   end;
   else if type='P' then
```

You have already initialized the value of Total to *0* each time a header record is read. Now, as each detail record is read, you can increment the value of Total by using a Sum statement. In this example you're counting the number of detail records for each header record, so you increment the value of Total by 1 when the value of type is *P*.

```
data perm.residnts;
   infile census;
   retain Address;
   input type $1. @;
   if type='H' then do;
      if _n_ > 1 then output;
      Total=0;
      input address $ 3-17;
   end;
   else if type='P' then total+1;
```

 Remember that a Sum statement enables you to add any valid SAS expression to an accumulator variable. Depending on your data, you might need to add the value of another variable to the accumulator variable.

```
      else if type='B' then total+cost;
```

 Remember also that the value that is generated by a Sum statement is automatically retained throughout the DATA step. That is why it is important to set the value of Total to *0* each time a header record is read.

Determining the End of the External File

Your program writes an observation to the data set only when another header record is read and the DATA step has executed more than once. But after the last detail record is read, there are no more header records to cause the last observation to be written to the data set.

```
data perm.residnts;
   infile census;
   retain Address;
   input type $1. @;
   if type='H' then do;
      if _n_ > 1 then
         output;
      Total=0;
      input address $ 3-17;
   end;
   else if type='P'
      then total+1;
```

```
1---+----10---+----20
H 321 S. MAIN ST
P MARY E      21 F
P WILLIAM M 23 M
P SUSAN K     3 F
H 324 S. MAIN ST
P THOMAS H  79 M
P WALTER S  46 M
P ALICE A   42 F
P MARYANN A 20 F
P JOHN S    16 M
H 325A S. MAIN ST
P JAMES L 34 M
P LIZA A 31 F
H 325B S. MAIN ST
P MARGO K 27 F
P WILLIAM R 27 M
P ROBERT W 1 M
```

You need to determine when the last record in the file is read so that you can then execute another explicit OUTPUT statement. You can determine when the current record is the last record in an external file by specifying the END= option in the INFILE statement. (You learned how to use the END= option with a SET statement in Chapter 12, **Reading SAS Data Sets**.)

> **General form, INFILE statement with the END= option:**
>
> **INFILE** *file-specification* **END=***variable*;
>
> where *variable* is a temporary numeric variable whose value is *0* until the last line is read and *1* after the last line is read.
>
> Like automatic variables, the END= variable is not written to the data set.

In the following example, the END= variable is defined in the INFILE statement as last. When last has a value other than *0*, the OUTPUT statement writes the last observation to the data set.

```
data perm.residnts;
    infile census end=last;
    retain Address;
    input type $1. @;
    if type='H' then do;
        if _n_ > 1 then output;
        Total=0;
        input address $ 3-17;
    end;
    else if type='P' then total+1;
    if last then output;
```

A DROP= option in the DATA statement drops the variable type from the data set, and a RUN statement completes the DATA step.

```
data perm.residnts (drop=type);
    infile census end=last;
    retain Address;
    input type $1. @;
    if type='H' then do;
        if _n_ > 1 then output;
        Total=0;
        input address $ 3-17;
    end;
    else if type='P' then total+1;
    if last then output;
run;
```

Processing a DATA Step That Creates One Observation Per Header Record

Let's look at how this DATA step is processed.

```
data perm.people (drop=type);
    infile census end=last;
    retain Address;
    input type $1. A;
    if type='H' then do;
        if _n_ > 1 then output;
        Total=0;
        input Address $3-17;
    end;
    else if type='P' then total+1;
    if last then output;
run;
```

During the compile phase, the variable type is flagged so that it can be dropped later. The value for `Address` is retained.

```
data perm.people (drop=type);
   infile census end=last;
   retain Address;
   input type $1. @;
   if type='H'then do;
      if _n_ > 1 then output;
      Total=0;
      input Address $3-17;
   end;
   else if type='P' then total+1;
   if last then output;
run;
```

```
>----+----10---+----

H 321 S. MAIN ST
P MARY E     21  F
P WILLIAM M 23  M
P SUSAN K     3  F
H 324 S. MAIN ST
```

		Retain	Drop	
N	**last**	**Address**	**type**	**Total**
•	•			•

As the execution phase begins, `_n_` is *1* and `last` is *0*.

```
data perm.people (drop=type);
   infile census end=last;
   retain Address;
   input type $1. @;
   if type='H'then do;
      if _n_ > 1 then output;
      Total=0;
      input Address $3-17;
   end;
   else if type='P' then total+1;
   if last then output;
run;
```

```
>↓---+----10---+----

H 321 S. MAIN ST
P MARY E     21  F
P WILLIAM M 23  M
P SUSAN K     3  F
H 324 S. MAIN ST
```

		Retain	Drop	
N	**last**	**Address**	**type**	**Total**
1	0			•

Now the value for `type` is read, the condition `type='H'` is true, so the statements in the DO group execute.

```
data perm.people (drop=type);
   infile census end=last;
   retain Address;
   input type $1. @;
   if type='H'then do;
      if _n_ > 1 then output;
      Total=0;
      input Address $3-17;
   end;
   else if type='P' then total+1;
   if last then output;
run;
```

```
>-↓--+----10---+----
H 321 S. MAIN ST
P MARY E     21 F
P WILLIAM M 23 M
P SUSAN K     3 F
H 324 S. MAIN ST
```

		Retain	Drop	
N	last	Address	type	Total
1	0		H	•

The condition `_n_` > 1 is not true, so the OUTPUT statement is not executed. However, `Total` is assigned the value of *0* and the value for `Address` is read.

```
data perm.people (drop=type);
   infile census end=last;
   retain Address;
   input type $1. @;
   if type='H'then do;
      if _n_ > 1 then output;
      Total=0;
      input Address $3-17;
   end;
   else if type='P' then total+1;
   if last then output;
run;
```

```
>----+----10---+--↓-
H 321 S. MAIN ST
P MARY E     21 F
P WILLIAM M 23 M
P SUSAN K     3 F
H 324 S. MAIN ST
```

		Retain	Drop	
N	last	Address	type	Total
1	0	321 S. MAIN ST	H	0

The END statement closes the DO group. The alternative condition that is expressed in the ELSE statement is not checked because the first condition, `type='H'`, was true.

```
data perm.people (drop=type);
   infile census end=last;
   retain Address;
   input type $1. @;
   if type='H'then do;
      if _n_ > 1 then output;
      Total=0;
      input Address $3-17;
   end;
   else if type='P' then total+1;
   if last then output;
run;
```

```
>----+----10---+----

H 321 S. MAIN ST
P MARY E      21 F
P WILLIAM M 23 M
P SUSAN K      3 F
H 324 S. MAIN ST
```

| | | Retain | Drop | |
N	last	Address	type	Total
1	0	321 S. MAIN ST	H	0

The value of `last` is still *0*, so the OUTPUT statement is not executed. The RUN statement passes control back to the top of the DATA step.

```
data perm.people (drop=type);
   infile census end=last;
   retain Address;
   input type $1. @;
   if type='H'then do;
      if _n_ > 1 then output;
      Total=0;
      input Address $3-17;
   end;
   else if type='P' then total+1;
   if last then output;
run;
```

```
>↓---+----10---+----

H 321 S. MAIN ST
P MARY E      21 F
P WILLIAM M 23 M
P SUSAN K      3 F
H 324 S. MAIN ST
```

| | | Retain | Drop | |
N	last	Address	type	Total
1	0	321 S. MAIN ST	H	0

During the second iteration, the value of `type` is *'P'* and `Total` is incremented by 1. Again, the value of `last` is *0*, so control returns to the top of the DATA step.

```
data perm.people (drop=type);
   infile census end=last;
   retain Address;
   input type $1. @;
   if type='H'then do;
      if _n_ > 1 then output;
      Total=0;
      input Address $3-17;
   end;
   else if type='P' then total+1;
   if last then output;
run;
```

```
>-↓--+----10---+----

H 321 S. MAIN ST
P MARY E     21 F
P WILLIAM M 23 M
P SUSAN K    3 F
H 324 S. MAIN ST
```

		Retain	Drop	
N	last	Address	type	Total
2	0	321 S. MAIN ST	P	1

During the fifth iteration, the value of type is '*H*' and _n_ is greater than *1*, so the values for Address and Total are written to the data set as the first observation.

```
data perm.people (drop=type);
   infile census end=last;
   retain Address;
   input type $1. @;
   if type='H'then do;
      if _n_ > 1 then output;
      Total=0;
      input Address $3-17;
   end;
   else if type='P' then total+1;
   if last then output;
run;
```

```
>-↓--+----10---+----

H 321 S. MAIN ST
P MARY E     21 F
P WILLIAM M 23 M
P SUSAN K    3 F
H 324 S. MAIN ST
```

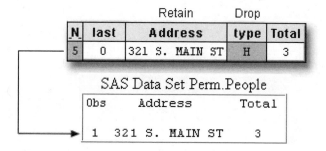

		Retain	Drop	
N	last	Address	type	Total
5	0	321 S. MAIN ST	H	3

SAS Data Set Perm.People

Obs	Address	Total
1	321 S. MAIN ST	3

As the last record in the file is read, the variable last is set to *1*. Now that the condition for last is true, the values in the program data vector are written to the data set as the final observation.

```
data perm.people (drop=type);
   infile census end=last;
   retain Address;
   input type $1. @;
   if type='H'then do;
      if _n_ > 1 then output;
      Total=0;
      input Address $3-17;
   end;
   else if type='P' then total+1;
   if last then output;
run;
```

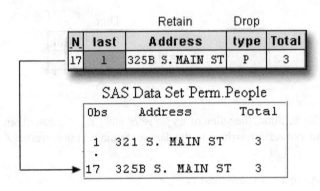

```
>-↓--+----10---+----

P LIZA A      31 F
H 325B S. MAIN ST
P MARGO K     27 F
P WILLIAM R 27 F
P ROBERT W    1 M
```

		Retain	Drop	
N	**last**	**Address**	**type**	**Total**
17	1	325B S.MAIN ST	P	3

SAS Data Set Perm.People

```
Obs     Address        Total

 1   321 S. MAIN ST      3
 .
17   325B S. MAIN ST     3
```

Summary

Text Summary

Hierarchical Raw Data Files

Raw data files can be hierarchical in structure, consisting of a header record and one or more detail records. You can build a SAS data set from a hierarchical file by creating one observation

- per detail record and storing each header record as part of the observation

- per header record and combining the information from detail records into summary variables.

Creating One Observation Per Detail Record

In order to create one observation per detail record, it is necessary to distinguish between header and detail records. Having a field that identifies the type of the record makes this task easier.

As you write the DATA step, use a **RETAIN statement** to keep the header record as a part of each observation until the next header record is encountered.

Next, you need to read the field in each record that identifies the record's type. Remember to use the **@ line-hold specifier** to hold the current value of each record type so that the other values in the record can be read.

Use an **IF-THEN statement** to check for the condition that the record is a header record. If the record is a header record, then you need to execute an INPUT statement to read the variable values for that record.

You can use a **subsetting IF statement** to check for the condition that the record is a detail record. If the record is a detail record, then use another INPUT statement to read the variable values in that record.

You can use the **DROP= option** to prevent the variable that identifies each record's type from being included in the data set.

Creating One Observation Per Header Record

Creating one observation per header record condenses a large amount of information into a concise data set. As you write the DATA step, you need to think about performing several tasks.

As with creating one observation per detail record, use a RETAIN statement to keep the header record as a part of each observation until the next header record is encountered. Then read the field in each record that identifies the record's type. Remember to use the @ line-hold specifier to hold the current record so that the other values in the record can be read.

When the record is a header record, **multiple** statements need to be executed. You can do this by adding a **simple DO group** to an IF-THEN statement. Within the DO group, you need to

1. determine whether this is the **first** header record in the external file by using the automatic variable _N_

2. use an OUTPUT statement to write each header record except for the first one to the data set

3. use an assignment statement to create a summary variable, and set its value to *0*

4. add an INPUT statement to read the variable values in the header record

5. close the loop with an END statement.

When the record is a detail record, you need to define an alternative set of actions. You can do this by adding an **ELSE statement** to an IF-THEN statement. As each detail record is read, you can increment the value of the summary variable by using a Sum statement.

After the last detail record is read, there are no more header records to cause the last observation to be written to the data set. You can determine when the current record is the last record in an external file by specifying the **END= option** in the INFILE statement.

Again, you can use the **DROP= option** to prevent the variable that identifies each record's type from being included in the data set.

Points to Remember

- As with automatic variables, the END= variable is not written to the data set.

- Values are automatically retained when using a Sum statement. Therefore, it might be necessary to set the value of the counter variable back to 0 when a new header is encountered.

Practice

After you complete this chapter, practice what you learned by using the sample data and SAS programs for Chapter 22, **Reading Hierarchical Files**, which are located on the CD-ROM. Follow the directions for creating your sample data in the Before You Begin section.

Quiz

Select the best answer for each question. After completing the quiz, check your answers using the answer key in the appendix.

1. When you write a DATA step to create one observation per detail record you need to

    a. distinguish between header and detail records.

    b. keep the header record as part of each observation until the next header record is encountered.

    c. hold the current value of each record type so that the other values in the record can be read.

    d. all of the above

2. Which SAS statement reads the value for code (in the first field), and then holds the value until an INPUT statement reads the remaining value in each observation in the same iteration of the DATA step?

    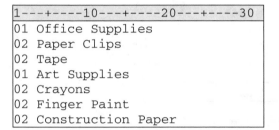

    ```
    1---+----10---+----20---+----30
    01 Office Supplies
    02 Paper Clips
    02 Tape
    01 Art Supplies
    02 Crayons
    02 Finger Paint
    02 Construction Paper
    ```

    a. `input code $2. @;`

    b. `input code $2. @@;`

    c. `retain code;`

    d. none of the above

3. Which SAS statement checks for the condition that Record equals *C* and executes a single statement to read the values for Amount?

    a. `if record=c then input @3 Amount comma7.;`

    b. `if record='C' then input @3 Amount comma7.;`

    c. `if record='C' then do input @3 Amount comma7.;`

    d. `if record=C then do input @3 Amount comma7.;`

4. After the value for code is read in the sixth iteration, which illustration of the program data vector is correct?

```
1---+----10---+----20---+----30
H Lettuce
P Green Leaf   Quality Growers
P Iceberg      Pleasant Farm
P Romaine      Quality Growers
H Squash
P Yellow       Tasty Acres
P Zucchini     Pleasant Farm
```

```
data perm.produce (drop=code);
    infile orders;
    retain Vegetable;
    input code $1. @;
    if code='H' then input @3 vegetable $6.;
    if code='P';
    input @3 Variety : $10. @15 Supplier : $15.;
run;
proc print data=perm.produce;
run;
```

a.

N	Vegetable	code	Variety	Supplier
6		P		

b.

N	Vegetable	code	Variety	Supplier
6	Squash	P		

c.

N	Vegetable	code	Variety	Supplier
6	Squash	H		

d.

N	Vegetable	code	Variety	Supplier
6	Squash	H	Yellow	

5. What happens when the fourth iteration of the DATA step is complete?

```
1---+----10---+----20---+----30
F Apples
V Gala                $2.50
V Golden Delicious $1.99
V Rome                $2.35
F Oranges
V Navel               $2.79
V Temple              $2.99
```

```
data perm.orders (drop=type);
    infile produce;
    retain Fruit;
    input type $1. @;
    if type='F' then input @3 fruit $7.;
    if type='V';
    input @3 Variety : $16. @20 Price comma5.;
run;
```

    a. All of the values in the program data vector are written to the data set as the third observation.

    b. All of the values in the program data vector are written to the data set as the fourth observation.

    c. The values for `Fruit`, `Variety`, and `Price` are written to the data set as the third observation.

    d. The values for `Fruit`, `Variety`, and `Price` are written to the data set as the fourth observation.

6. Which SAS statement indicates that several other statements should be executed when `Record` has a value of *A*?

```
1---+----10---+----20---+----30
A 124153-01
C $153.02
D $20.00
D $20.00
```

    a. `if record='A' then do;`

    b. `if record=A then do;`

    c. `if record='A' then;`

    d. `if record=A then;`

7. Which is true for the following statements (*X* indicates a header record)?

```
if code='X' then do;
   if _n_ > 1 then output;
   Total=0;
   input Name $ 3-20;
end;
```

   a. _N_ equals the number of times the DATA step has begun to execute.

   b. When code='X' and _n_ > 1 are true, an OUTPUT statement is executed.

   c. Each header record causes an observation to be written to the data set.

   d. *a* and *b*

8. What happens when the condition type= 'P' is false?

```
if type='P' then input @3 ID $5. @9 Address $20.;
else if type='V' then input @3 Charge 6.;
```

   a. The values for ID and Address are read.

   b. The values for Charge are read.

   c. Type is assigned the value of *V*.

   d. The ELSE statement is executed.

9. What happens when last has a value other than zero?

```
data perm.househld (drop=code);
   infile citydata end=last;
   retain Address;
   input type $1. @;
   if code='A' then do;
      if _n_ > 1 then output;
      Total=0;
      input address $ 3-17;
   end;
   else if code='N' then total+1;
   if last then output;
run;
```

   a. Last has a value of *1*.

   b. The OUTPUT statement writes the last observation to the data set.

   c. The current value of last is written to the DATA set.

   d. *a* and *b*

10. Based on the values in the program data vector, what happens next?

N	last	Department	Extension	type	Total	Amount
5	0	Accounting	x3808	D	16.50	.

```
1---+----10---+----20---+----30
D Accounting   x3808
S Paper Clips  $2.50
S Paper        $4.95
S Binders      $9.05
D Personnel    x3810
S Markers      $8.98
S Pencils      $3.35
```

```
data work.supplies (drop=type amount);
    infile orders end=last;
    retain Department Extension;
    input type $1. @;
    if type='D' then do;
        if _n_ > 1 then output;
        Total=0;
        input @3 department $10. @16 extension $5.;
    end;
    else if type='S' then do;
        input @16 Amount comma5.;
        total+amount;
        if last then output;
    end;
run;
```

a. All the values in the program data vector are written to the data set as the first observation.

b. The values for `Department`, `Total`, and `Extension` are written to the data set as the first observation.

c. The values for `Department`, `Total`, and `Extension` are written to the data set as the fourth observation.

d. The value of `last` changes to *1*.

Quiz Answer Keys

Chapter 1: Basic Concepts Answer Key

1. How many observations and variables does the data set below contain?

Name	Sex	Age
Picker	M	32
Fletcher		28
Romano	F	.
Choi	M	42

   a. 3 observations, 4 variables
   b. 3 observations, 3 variables
   c. 4 observations, 3 variables
   d. can't tell because some values are missing

Correct answer: c

Rows in the data set are called **observations**, and columns are called **variables**. Missing values don't affect the structure of the data set.

2. How many program steps are executed when the program below is processed?

```
data user.tables;
    infile jobs;
    input date name $ job $;
run;
proc sort data=user.tables;
    by name;
run;
proc print data=user.tables;
run;
```

   a. three
   b. four
   c. five
   d. six

Correct answer: a

When it encounters a DATA, PROC, or RUN statement, SAS stops reading statements and executes the previous step in the program. The program above contains one DATA step and two PROC steps, for a total of three program steps.

3. What type of variable is the variable AcctNum in the data set below?

AcctNum	Balance
3456_1	M
2451_2	
Romano	F
Choi	M

a. numeric
b. character
c. can be either character or numeric
d. can't tell from the data shown

Correct answer: b

It must be a **character variable**, because the values contain letters and underscores, which are not valid characters for numeric values.

4. What type of variable is the variable Wear in the data set below?

Brand	Wear
Acme	43
Ajax	34
Atlas	.

a. numeric
b. character
c. can be either character or numeric
d. can't tell from the data shown

Correct answer: a

It must be a **numeric variable**, because the missing value is indicated by a period rather than by a blank.

5. Which of the following variable names is valid?

a. 4BirthDate
b. $Cost
c. _Items_
d. Tax-Rate

Correct answer: c

Variable names follow the same rules as SAS data set names. They can be 1 to 32 characters long, must begin with a letter (A–Z, either uppercase or lowercase) or an underscore, and can continue with any combination of numbers, letters, or underscores.

6.   Which of the following files is a permanent SAS file?

    a.   **Sashelp.PrdSale**
    b.   **Sasuser.MySales**
    c.   **Profits.Quarter1**
    d.   all of the above

Correct answer: d

To store a file permanently in a SAS data library, you assign it a libref other than the default **Work**. For example, by assigning the libref **Profits** to a SAS data library, you specify that files within the library are to be stored until you delete them. Therefore, SAS files in the **Sashelp** and **Sasuser** libraries are permanent files.

7.   In a DATA step, how can you reference a temporary SAS data set named **Forecast**?

    a.   **Forecast**
    b.   **Work.Forecast**
    c.   **Sales.Forecast** (after assigning the libref **Sales**)
    d.   only a and b above

Correct answer: d

To reference a temporary SAS file in a DATA step or PROC step, you can specify the one-level name of the file (for example, **Forecast**) or the two-level name using the libref **Work** (for example, **Work.Forecast**).

8.   What is the default length for the numeric variable `Balance`?

Name	Balance
Adams	105.73
Geller	107.89
Martinez	97.45
Noble	182.50

    a.   5
    b.   6
    c.   7
    d.   8

Correct answer: d

The numeric variable `Balance` has a default length of 8. Numeric values (no matter how many digits they contain) are stored in 8 bytes of storage unless you specify a different length.

9. How many statements does the following SAS program contain?

```
proc print data=new.prodsale
                  label double;
   var state day price1 price2; where state='NC';
   label state='Name of State';
run;
```

a. three
b. four
c. five
d. six

Correct answer: c

The five statements are

- PROC PRINT statement (two lines long)

- VAR statement

- WHERE statement (on the same line as the VAR statement)

- LABEL statement

- RUN statement (on the same line as the LABEL statement).

10. What is a SAS data library?

a. a collection of SAS files, such as SAS data sets and catalogs
b. in some operating environments, a physical collection of SAS files
c. in some operating environments, a logically related collection of SAS files
d. all of the above

Correct answer: d

Every SAS file is stored in a **SAS data library**, which is a collection of SAS files, such as SAS data sets and catalogs. In some operating environments, a SAS data library is a physical collection of files. In others, the files are only logically related. In the Windows and UNIX environments, a SAS data library is typically a group of SAS files in the same folder or directory.

Chapter 2: Referencing Files and Setting Options Answer Key

1. If you submit the following program, how does the output look?

    ```
    options pagesize=55 nonumber;
    proc tabulate data=clinic.admit;
       class actlevel;
       var age height weight;
       table actlevel,(age height weight)*mean;
    run;
    options linesize=80;
      proc means data=clinic.heart min max maxdec=1;
      var arterial heart cardiac urinary;
      class survive sex;
    run;
    ```

    a. The PROC MEANS output has a print line width of 80 characters, but the PROC TABULATE output has no print line width.

    b. The PROC TABULATE output has no page numbers, but the PROC MEANS output has page numbers.

    c. Each page of output from both PROC steps is 55 lines long and has no page numbers, and the PROC MEANS output has a print line width of 80 characters.

    d. The date does not appear on output from either PROC step.

    Correct: answer: c

    When you specify a system option, it remains in effect until you change the option or end your SAS session, so both PROC steps generate output that is printed 55 lines per page with no page numbers. If you don't specify a system option, SAS uses the default value for that system option.

2. In order for the date values 05May1955 and 04Mar2046 to be read correctly, what value must the YEARCUTOFF= option have?

    a. a value between 1947 and 1954, inclusive

    b. 1955 or higher

    c. 1946 or higher

    d. any value

    Correct answer: d

    As long as you specify an informat with the correct field width for reading the entire date value, the YEARCUTOFF= option doesn't affect date values that have four-digit years.

3. When you specify an engine for a library, you are always specifying

   a. the file format for files that are stored in the library.
   b. the version of SAS that you are using.
   c. access to other software vendors' files.
   d. instructions for creating temporary SAS files.

   Correct answer: a

   A SAS engine is a set of internal instructions that SAS uses for writing to and reading from files in a SAS library. Each engine specifies the file format for files that are stored in the library, which in turn enables SAS to access files with a particular format. Some engines access SAS files, and other engines support access to other vendors' files.

4. Which statement prints a summary of all the files stored in the library named **Area51**?

   a. `proc contents data=area51._all_ nods;`
   b. `proc contents data=area51 _all_ nods;`
   c. `proc contents data=area51 _all_ noobs;`
   d. `proc contents data=area51 _all_.nods;`

   Correct answer: a

   To print a summary of library contents with the CONTENTS procedure, use a period to append the _ALL_ option to the libref. Adding the NODS option suppresses detailed information about the files.

5. The following PROC PRINT output was created immediately after PROC TABULATE output. Which SAS system options were specified when the report was created?

```
                                                       1
                        10:03 Friday, March 17, 2000


                                   Act
       Obs  ID   Height  Weight  Level     Fee

        1   2458   72      168    HIGH     85.20
        2   2462   66      152    HIGH    124.80
        3   2501   61      123    LOW     149.75
        4   2523   63      137    MOD     149.75
        5   2539   71      158    LOW     124.80
        6   2544   76      193    HIGH    124.80
        7   2552   67      151    MOD     149.75
        8   2555   70      173    MOD     149.75
        9   2563   73      154    LOW     124.80
```

    a.   OBS=, DATE, and NONUMBER

    b.   PAGENO=1, and DATE

    c.   NUMBER and DATE only

    d.   none of the above

Correct answer: b

Clearly, the DATE and PAGENO= options are specified. Because the page number on the output is 1, even though PROC TABULATE output was just produced. If you don't specify PAGENO=, all output in the Output window is numbered sequentially throughout your SAS session.

6.   Which of the following programs correctly references a SAS data set named **SalesAnalysis** that is stored in a permanent SAS library?

    a.
```
data saleslibrary.salesanalysis;
    set mydata.quarter1sales;
    if sales>100000;
run;
```

    b.
```
data mysales.totals;
    set sales_99.salesanalysis;
    if totalsales>50000;
run;
```

    c.
```
proc print data=salesanalysis.quarter1;
    var sales salesrep month;
run;
```

    d.
```
proc freq data=1999data.salesanalysis;
    tables quarter*sales;
run;
```

Correct answer: b

Librefs must be 1 to 8 characters long, must begin with a letter or underscore, and can contain only letters, numbers, or underscores. After you assign a libref, you specify it as the first element in the two-level name for a SAS file.

7. Which time span is used to interpret two-digit year values if the YEARCUTOFF= option is set to 1950?

   a. 1950-2049
   b. 1950-2050
   c. 1949-2050
   d. 1950-2000

   Correct answer: a

   The YEARCUTOFF= option specifies which 100-year span is used to interpret two-digit year values. The default value of YEARCUTOFF= is 1920. However, you can override the default and change the value of YEARCUTOFF= to the first year of another 100-year span. If you specify YEARCUTOFF=1950, then the 100-year span will be from 1950 to 2049.

8. Asssuming you are using SAS code and not special SAS windows, which one of the following statements is false?

   a. LIBNAME statements can be stored with a SAS program to reference the SAS library automatically when you submit the program.
   b. When you delete a libref, SAS no longer has access to the files in the library. However, the contents of the library still exist on your operating system.
   c. Librefs can last from one SAS session to another.
   d. You can access files that were created with other vendors' software by submitting a LIBNAME statement.

   Correct answer: c

   The LIBNAME statement is global, which means that librefs remain in effect until you modify them, cancel them, or end your SAS session. Therefore, the LIBNAME statement assigns the libref for the current SAS session only. You must assign a libref before accessing SAS files that are stored in a permanent SAS data library.

9. What does the following statement do?

   ```
   libname osiris spss 'c:\myfiles\sasdata\data';
   ```

   a. defines a library called Spss using the OSIRIS engine
   b. defines a library called Osiris using the SPSS engine
   c. defines two libraries called Osiris and Spss using the default engine
   d. defines the default library using the OSIRIS and SPSS engines

   Correct answer: b

   In the LIBNAME statement, you specify the library name before the engine name. Both are followed by the path.

10. What does the following OPTIONS statement do?

```
options pagesize=15 nodate;
```

 a. suppresses the date and limits the page size of the log
 b. suppresses the date and limits the vertical page size for text output
 c. suppresses the date and limits the vertical page size for text and HTML output
 d. suppresses the date and limits the horizontal page size for text output

Correct answer: b

These options affect the format of listing output only. NODATE suppresses the date and PAGESIZE= determines the number of rows to print on the page.

Chapter 3: Editing and Debugging SAS Programs Answer Key

1. As you write and edit SAS programs it's a good idea to

    a. begin DATA and PROC steps in column one.
    b. indent statements within a step.
    c. begin RUN statements in column one.
    d. all of the above

    Correct answer: d

    Although you can write SAS statements in almost any format, a consistent layout enhances readability and enables you to understand the program's purpose. It's a good idea to begin DATA and PROC steps in column one, to indent statements within a step, to begin RUN statements in column one, and to include a RUN statement after every DATA step or PROC step.

2. What usually happens when an error is detected?

    a. SAS continues processing the step.
    b. SAS continues to process the step, and the log displays messages about the error.
    c. SAS stops processing the step in which the error occurred, and the log displays messages about the error.
    d. SAS stops processing the step in which the error occurred, and the program output displays messages about the error.

    Correct answer: c

    Syntax errors generally cause SAS to stop processing the step in which the error occurred. When a program that contains an error is submitted, messages regarding the problem also appear in the SAS log. When a syntax error is detected, the SAS log displays the word ERROR, identifies the possible location of the error, and gives an explanation of the error.

3. A syntax error occurs when

    a. some data values are not appropriate for the SAS statements that are specified in a program.
    b. the form of the elements in a SAS statement is correct, but the elements are not valid for that usage.
    c. program statements do not conform to the rules of the SAS language.
    d. none of the above

    Correct answer: c

    Syntax errors are common types of errors. Some SAS system options, features of the Editor window, and the DATA step debugger can help you identify syntax errors. Other types of errors include data errors, semantic errors, and execution-time errors.

4. How can you tell whether you have specified an invalid option in a SAS program?

   a.   A log message indicates an error in a statement that seems to be valid.

   b.   A log message indicates that an option is not valid or not recognized.

   c.   The message "PROC running" or "DATA step running" appears at the top of the active window.

   d.   You can't tell until you view the output from the program.

Correct answer: b

When you submit a SAS statement that contains an invalid option, a log message notifies you that the option is not valid or not recognized. You should recall the program, remove or replace the invalid option, check your statement syntax as needed, and resubmit the corrected program.

5. Which of the following programs contains a syntax error?

   a.
```
proc sort data=sasuser.mysales;
   by region;
run;
```
   b.
```
dat sasuser.mysales;
   set mydata.sales99;
run;
```
   c.
```
proc print data=sasuser.mysales label;
   label region='Sales Region';
run;
```
   d.   none of the above

Correct answer: b

The DATA step contains a misspelled keyword (**dat** instead of **data**). However, this is such a common (and easily interpretable) error that SAS produces only a warning message, not an error.

6. What does the following log indicate about your program?

```
proc print data=sasuser.cargo99
  var origin dest cargorev;
   22
   76
ERROR 22-322: Syntax error, expecting one of the
following:
             ;, (, DATA, DOUBLE, HEADING, LABEL,
             N, NOOBS, OBS, ROUND, ROWS, SPLIT,
STYLE,
             UNIFORM, WIDTH.
ERROR 76-322: Syntax error, statement will be
ignored.
11        run;
```

a. SAS identifies a syntax error at the position of the VAR statement.

b. SAS is reading VAR as an option in the PROC PRINT statement.

c. SAS has stopped processing the program because of errors.

d. all of the above

Correct answer: d

Because there is a missing semicolon at the end of the PROC PRINT statement, SAS interprets VAR as an option in PROC PRINT and finds a syntax error at that location. SAS stops processing programs when it encounters a syntax error.

1. Which PROC PRINT step below creates the following output?

Date	On	Changed	Flight
04MAR99	232	18	219
05MAR99	160	4	219
06MAR99	163	14	219
07MAR99	241	9	219
08MAR99	183	11	219
09MAR99	211	18	219
10MAR99	167	7	219

a.
```
proc print data=flights.laguardia noobs;
   var on changed flight;
   where on>=160;
run;
```

b.
```
proc print data=flights.laguardia;
   var date on changed flight;
   where changed>3;
run;
```

c.
```
proc print data=flights.laguardia label;
   id date;
   var boarded transferred flight;
   label boarded='On' transferred='Changed';
   where flight='219';
run;
```

d.
```
proc print flights.laguardia noobs;
   id date;
   var date on changed flight;
   where flight='219';
run;
```

Correct answer: c

The **DATA= option** specifies the data set that you are listing, and the **ID statement** replaces the Obs column with the specified variable. The **VAR statement** specifies variables and controls the order in which they appear, and the **WHERE statement** selects rows based on a condition. The **LABEL option** in the PROC PRINT statement causes the labels that are specified in the LABEL statement to be displayed.

2. Which of the following PROC PRINT steps is correct if labels are not stored with the data set?

   a.
```
proc print data=allsales.totals label;
   label region8='Region 8 Yearly Totals';
run;
```
   b.
```
proc print data=allsales.totals;
   label region8='Region 8 Yearly Totals';
run;
```
   c.
```
proc print data allsales.totals label noobs;
run;
```
   d.
```
proc print allsales.totals label;
run;
```

Correct answer: a

You use the **DATA=** option to specify the data set to be printed. The **LABEL** option specifies that variable labels appear in output instead of variable names.

3. Which of the following statements selects from a data set only those observations for which the value of the variable `Style` is *RANCH*, *SPLIT*, or *TWOSTORY*?

   a. `where style='RANCH' or 'SPLIT' or 'TWOSTORY';`

   b. `where style in 'RANCH' or 'SPLIT' or 'TWOSTORY';`

   c. `where style in (RANCH, SPLIT, TWOSTORY);`

   d. `where style in ('RANCH','SPLIT','TWOSTORY');`

Correct answer: d

In the WHERE statement, the **IN operator** enables you to select observations based on several values. You specify values in parentheses and separate them by spaces or commas. Character values must be enclosed in quotation marks and must be in the same case as in the data set.

4. If you want to sort your data and create a temporary data set named **Calc** to store the sorted data, which of the following steps should you submit?

   a. ```
proc sort data=work.calc out=finance.dividend;
run;
```

   *b.* ```
proc sort dividend out=calc;
    by account;
run;
```

   c. ```
proc sort data=finance.dividend out=work.calc;
    by account;
run;
```

   *d.* ```
proc sort from finance.dividend to calc;
    by account;
run;
```

   Correct answer: c

   In a **PROC SORT** step, you specify the DATA= option to specify the data set to sort. The OUT= option specifies an output data set. The required BY statement specifies the variable(s) to use in sorting the data.

5. Which options are used to create the following PROC PRINT output?

   ```
                                    13:27 Monday, March 22, 1999

        Patient     Arterial    Heart    Cardiac    Urinary

          203          88         95        66         110

           54          83        183        95           0

          664          72        111       332          12

          210          74         97       369           0

          101          80        130       291           0
   ```

   a. the DATE system option and the LABEL option in PROC PRINT
   b. the DATE and NONUMBER system options and the DOUBLE and NOOBS options in PROC PRINT
   c. the DATE and NONUMBER system options and the DOUBLE option in PROC PRINT
   d. the DATE and NONUMBER system options and the NOOBS option in PROC PRINT

Correct answer: b

The DATE and NONUMBER system options cause the output to appear with the date but without page numbers. In the PROC PRINT step, the **DOUBLE** option specifies double spacing, and the **NOOBS** option removes the default Obs column.

6.   Which of the following statements can you use in a PROC PRINT step to create this output?

Month	Instructors	AerClass	WalkJogRun	Swim
01	1	37	91	83
02	2	41	102	27
03	1	52	98	19
04	1	61	118	22
05	3	49	88	29
	8	240	497	180

a. var month instructors;
    sum instructors aerclass walkjogrun swim;

b. var month;
    sum instructors aerclass walkjogrun swim;

c. var month instructors aerclass;
    sum instructors aerclass walkjogrun swim;

d. all of the above

Correct answer: d

You do not need to name the variables in a VAR statement if you specify them in the SUM statement, but you can. If you choose not to name the variables in the VAR statement as well, then the **SUM statement** determines the order of the variables in the output.

7.   What happens if you submit the following program?

```
proc sort data=clinic.diabetes;
run;
proc print data=clinic.diabetes;
  var age height weight pulse;
  where sex='F';
run;
```

a. The PROC PRINT step runs successfully, printing observations in their sorted order.

b. The PROC SORT step permanently sorts the input data set.

c. The PROC SORT step generates errors and stops processing, but the PROC PRINT step runs successfully, printing observations in their original (unsorted) order.

d. The PROC SORT step runs successfully, but the PROC PRINT step generates errors and stops processing.

Correct answer: c

The **BY statement** is required in PROC SORT. Without it, the PROC SORT step fails. However, the PROC PRINT step prints the original data set as requested.

8. If you submit the following program, which output does it create?

```
proc sort data=finance.loans out=work.loans;
   by months amount;
run;
proc print data=work.loans noobs;
   var months;
   sum amount payment;
   where months<360;
run;
```

a.

Months	Amount	Payment
12	$3,500	$308.52
24	$8,700	$403.47
36	$10,000	$325.02
48	$5,000	$128.02
	$27,200	$1,165.03

b.

Months	Amount	Payment
12	$3,500	$308.52
24	$8,700	$403.47
36	$10,000	$325.02
48	$5,000	$128.02
	27,200	1,165.03

c.

Months	Amount	Payment
12	$3,500	$308.52
48	$5,000	$128.02
24	$8,700	$403.47
36	$10,000	$325.02
	$27,200	$1,165.03

d.

Months	Amount	Payment
12	$3,500	$308.52
24	$8,700	$403.47
36	$10,000	$325.02
48	$5,000	$128.02
		$1,165.03

Correct answer: a

Column totals appear at the end of the report in the same format as the values of the variables, so b is incorrect. **Work.Loans** is sorted by Month and Amount, so c is incorrect. The program sums both **Amount** and **Payment**, so d is incorrect.

9. Choose the statement below that selects rows which

   - the amount is less than or equal to $5000

   - the account is 101-1092 or the rate equals 0.095.

   a. ```
where amount <= 5000 and
    account='101-1092' or rate = 0.095;
```
   b. ```
where (amount le 5000 and account='101-1092')
    or rate = 0.095;
```
   c. ```
where amount <= 5000 and
    (account='101-1092' or rate eq 0.095);
```
   d. ```
where amount <= 5000 or account='101-1092'
    and rate = 0.095;
```

Correct answer: c

To ensure that the compound expression is evaluated correctly, you can use parentheses to group

```
account='101-1092' or rate eq 0.095
```

```
OBS Account    Amount   Rate   MonthsPayment

1    101-1092   $22,000 10.00%60     $467.43
2    101-1731   $114,0009.50% 360    $958.57
3    101-1289   $10,000 10.50%36     $325.02
4    101-3144   $3,500  10.50%12     $308.52
5    103-1135   $8,700  10.50%24     $403.47
6    103-1994   $18,500 10.00%60     $393.07
7    103-2335   $5,000  10.50%48     $128.02
8    103-3864   $87,500 9.50% 360    $735.75
9    103-3891   $30,000 9.75% 360    $257.75
```

For example, from the data set above, a and b above select observations 2 and 8 (those that have a rate of 0.095); c selects no observations; and d selects observations 4 and 7 (those that have an amount less than or equal to 5000).

10. What does PROC PRINT display by default?

   a. PROC PRINT does not create a default report; you must specify the rows and columns to be displayed.

   b. PROC PRINT displays all observations and variables in the data set. If you want an additional column for observation numbers, you can request it.

   c. PROC PRINT displays columns in the following order: a column for observation numbers, all character variables, and all numeric variables.

   d. PROC PRINT displays all observations and variables in the data set, a column for observation numbers on the far left, and variables in the order in which they occur in the data set.

Correct answer: d

You can remove the column for observation numbers. You can also specify the variables you want, and you can select observations according to conditions.

Chapter 5: Creating SAS Data Sets from Raw Data Answer Key

1. Which SAS statement associates the fileref **Crime** with the raw data file **C:\States\Data\Crime**?

   a. `filename crime 'c:\states\data\crime';`
   b. `filename crime c:\states\data\crime;`
   c. `fileref crime 'c:\states\data\crime';`
   d. `filename 'c:\states\data\crime' crime;`

   Correct answer: a

   Before you can read your raw data, you must reference the raw data file by creating a fileref. You assign a fileref by using a FILENAME statement in the same way that you assign a libref by using a LIBNAME statement.

2. Filerefs remain in effect until

   a. you change them.
   b. you cancel them.
   c. you end your SAS session.
   d. all of the above

   Correct answer: d

   Like LIBNAME statements, FILENAME statements are global; they remain in effect until you change them, cancel them, or end your SAS session.

3. Which statement identifies the name of a raw data file to be read with the fileref **Products** and specifies that the DATA step read only records 1-15?

   a. `infile products obs 15;`
   b. `infile products obs=15;`
   c. `input products obs=15;`
   d. `input products 1-15;`

   Correct answer: b

   You use an INFILE statement to specify the raw data file to be read. You can specify a fileref or an actual filename (in quotation marks). The OBS= option in the INFILE statement enables you to process only records 1 through *n*.

4.   Which of the following programs correctly writes the observations from the data set below to a raw data file?

SAS Data Set Work.Patients

ID	Sex	Age	Height	Weight	Pulse
2304	F	16	61	102	100
1128	M	43	71	218	76
4425	F	48	66	162	80
1387	F	57	64	142	70
9012	F	39	63	157	68
6312	M	52	72	240	77
5438	F	42	62	168	83
3788	M	38	73	234	71
9125	F	56	64	159	70
3438	M	15	66	140	67

a.
```
data _null_;
   set work.patients;
   infile 'c:\clinic\patients\referrals.dat';
   input id 1-4 sex 6 age 8-9 height 11-12
       weight 14-16 pulse 18-20;
run;
```

b.
```
data referrals.dat;
   set work.patients;
   input id 1-4 sex 6 age 8-9 height 11-12
       weight 14-16 pulse 18-20;
run;
```

c.
```
data _null_;
   set work.patients;
   file c:\clinic\patients\referrals.dat;
   put id 1-4 sex 6 age 8-9 height 11-12
       weight 14-16 pulse 18-20;
    run;
```

d.
```
data _null_;
   set work.patients;
   file 'c:\clinic\patients\referrals.dat';
   put id 1-4 sex 6 age 8-9 height 11-12
       weight 14-16 pulse 18-20;
run;
```

Correct answer: d

The keyword _NULL_ in the DATA statement enables you to use the power of the DATA step without actually creating a SAS data set. You use the FILE and PUT statements to write out the observations from a SAS data set to a raw data file. The FILE statement specifies the raw data file and the PUT statement describes the lines to write to the raw data file. The filename and location that are specified in the FILE statement must be enclosed in quotation marks.

5. Which raw data file can be read using column input?

a.
```
1---+----10---+----20---+
Henderson CA 26 ADM
Josephs SC 33 SALES
Williams MN 40 HRD
Rogan NY RECRTN
```

b.
```
1---+----10---+----20---+----30
2803 Deborah Campos  173.97
2912 Bill    Marin   205.14
3015 Helen   Stinson 194.08
3122 Nicole  Terry   187.65
```

c.
```
1---+----10---+----20---+
Avery John        $601.23
Davison Sherrill $723.15
Holbrook Grace   $489.76
Jansen Mike      $638.42
```

d. all of the above

Correct answer: b

Column input is appropriate only in some situations. When you use column input, your data must be standard character or numeric values, and they must be in fixed fields. That is, values for a particular variable must be in the same location in all records.

6. Which program creates the output shown below?

```
1---+----10---+----20---+----30
3427 Chen     Steve Raleigh
1436 Davis    Lee   Atlanta
2812 King     Vicky Memphis
1653 Sanchez  Jack  Atlanta
```

Obs	ID	LastName	FirstName	City
1	3427	Chen	Steve	Raleigh
2	1436	Davis	Lee	Atlanta
3	2812	King	Vicky	Memphis
4	1653	Sanchez	Jack	Atlanta

```
a.   data work.salesrep;
         infile empdata;
         input ID $ 1-4 LastName $ 6-12
               FirstName $ 14-18 City $ 20-29;
     run;
     proc print data=work.salesrep;
     run;

b.   data work.salesrep;
         infile empdata;
         input ID $ 1-4 Name $ 6-12
               FirstName $ 14-18 City $ 20-29;
     run;
     proc print data=work.salesrep;
     run;

c.   data work.salesrep;
         infile empdata;
         input ID $ 1-4 name1 $ 6-12
               name2 $ 14-18 City $ 20-29;
     run;
     proc print data=work.salesrep;
     run;
```

d.   all of the above

Correct answer: a

The INPUT statement creates a variable using the name that you assign to each field. Therefore, when you write an INPUT statement, you need to specify the variable names exactly as you want them to appear in the SAS data set.

7.   Which statement correctly reads the fields in the following order: StockNumber, Price, Item, Finish, Style?

Field Name	Start Column	End Column	Data Type
StockNumber	1	3	character
Finish	5	9	character
Style	11	18	character
Item	20	24	character
Price	27	32	numeric

```
1---+----10---+----20---+----30---+
310 oak   pedestal table  329.99
311 maple pedestal table  369.99
312 brass floor    lamp    79.99
313 glass table     lamp    59.99
313 oak   rocking  chair  153.99
```

a. input StockNumber $ 1-3 Finish $ 5-9 Style $ 11-18
        Item $ 20-24 Price 27-32;

b. input StockNumber $ 1-3 Price 27-32
        Item $ 20-24 Finish $ 5-9 Style $ 11-18;

c. input $ StockNumber 1-3 Price 27-32
        $ Item 20-24 $ Finish 5-9 $ Style 11-18;

d. input StockNumber $ 1-3 Price $ 27-32
        Item $ 20-24 Finish $ 5-9 Style $ 11-18;

Correct answer: b

You can use column input to read fields in any order. You must specify the variable name to be created, identify character values with a $, and name the correct starting column and ending column for each field.

8. Which statement correctly re-defines the values of the variable Income as 100 percent higher?

   a. income=income*1.00;
   b. income=income+(income*2.00);
   c. income=income*2;
   d. income=*2;

Correct answer: c

To re-define the values of the variable Income in an Assignment statement, you specify the variable name on the left side of the equal sign and an appropriate expression including the variable name on the right side of the equal sign.

9. Which program correctly reads instream data?

a.
```
data finance.newloan;
    input datalines;
    if country='JAPAN';
    MonthAvg=amount/12;
1998 US      CARS    194324.12
1998 US      TRUCKS  142290.30
1998 CANADA  CARS     10483.44
1998 CANADA  TRUCKS   93543.64
1998 MEXICO  CARS     22500.57
1998 MEXICO  TRUCKS   10098.88
1998 JAPAN   CARS     15066.43
1998 JAPAN   TRUCKS   40700.34
;
```

b.
```
data finance.newloan;
    input Year 1-4 Country $ 6-11
        Vehicle $ 13-18 Amount 20-28;
    if country='JAPAN';
    MonthAvg=amount/12;
    datalines;
run;
```

c.
```
data finance.newloan;
    input Year 1-4 Country 6-11
        Vehicle 13-18 Amount 20-28;
    if country='JAPAN';
    MonthAvg=amount/12;
    datalines;
1998 US      CARS    194324.12
1998 US      TRUCKS  142290.30
1998 CANADA  CARS     10483.44
1998 CANADA  TRUCKS   93543.64
1998 MEXICO  CARS     22500.57
1998 MEXICO  TRUCKS   10098.88
1998 JAPAN   CARS     15066.43
1998 JAPAN   TRUCKS   40700.34
;
```

d.
```
data finance.newloan;
    input Year 1-4 Country $ 6-11
        Vehicle $ 13-18 Amount 20-28;
    if country='JAPAN';
    MonthAvg=amount/12;
    datalines;
1998 US      CARS    194324.12
1998 US      TRUCKS  142290.30
1998 CANADA  CARS     10483.44
1998 CANADA  TRUCKS   93543.64
1998 MEXICO  CARS     22500.57
1998 MEXICO  TRUCKS   10098.88
1998 JAPAN   CARS     15066.43
1998 JAPAN   TRUCKS   40700.34
;
```

Correct answer: d

To read instream data, you specify a DATALINES statement and data lines, followed by a null statement (single semicolon) to indicate the end of the input data. Program *a* contains no DATALINES statement, and the INPUT statement doesn't specify the fields to read. Program *b* contains no data lines, and the INPUT statement in program *c* doesn't specify the necessary dollar signs for the character variables `Country` and `Vehicle`.

10. Which SAS statement subsets the raw data shown below so that only the observations in which Sex (in the second field) has a value of *F* are processed?

```
1----+----10---+----20---+--
Alfred  M 14 69.0 112.5
Becka   F 13 65.3 98.0
Gail    F 14 64.3 90.0
Jeffrey M 13 62.5 84.0
John    M 12 59.0 99.5
Karen   F 12 56.3 77.0
Mary    F 15 66.5 112.0
Philip  M 16 72.0 150.0
Sandy   F 11 51.3 50.5
Tammy   F 14 62.8 102.5
William M 15 66.5 112.0
```

    a. if sex=f;

    b. if sex=F;

    c. if sex='F';

    d. *a* or *b*

Correct answer: c

To subset data, you can use a subsetting IF statement in any DATA step to process only those observations that meet a specified condition. Because `Sex` is a character variable, the value *F* must be enclosed in quotation marks and must be in the same case as in the data set.

1. Which of the following is **not** created during the compilation phase?

   a. the data set descriptor
   b. the first observation
   c. the program data vector
   d. the _N_ and _ERROR_ automatic variables

Correct answer: b

At the beginning of the compilation phase, the program data vector is created. The program data vector includes the two automatic variables _N_ and _ERROR_. The descriptor portion of the new SAS data set is created at the end of the compilation phase. The descriptor portion includes the name of the data set, the number of observations and variables, and the names and attributes of the variables. Observations are not written until the execution phase.

2. During the compilation phase, SAS scans each statement in the DATA step, looking for syntax errors. Which of the following is **not** considered a syntax error?

   a. incorrect values and formats
   b. invalid options or variable names
   c. missing or invalid punctuation
   d. missing or misspelled keywords

Correct answer: a

Syntax checking can detect many common errors, but it cannot verify the values of variables or the correctness of formats.

3. Unless otherwise directed, the DATA step executes

   a. once for each compilation phase.
   b. once for each DATA step statement.
   c. once for each record in the input file.
   d. once for each variable in the input file.

Correct answer: c

The DATA step executes once for each record in the input file, unless otherwise directed.

4. At the beginning of the execution phase, the value of _N_ is *1*, the value of _ERROR_ is *0*, and the values of the remaining variables are set to

    a. *0*
    b. *1*
    c. undefined
    d. missing

    Correct answer: d

    The remaining variables are initialized to missing. Missing numeric values are represented by periods, and missing character values are represented by blanks.

5. Suppose you run a program that causes three DATA step errors. What is the value of the automatic variable _ERROR_ when the observation that contains the third error is processed?

    a. *0*
    b. *1*
    c. *2*
    d. *3*

    Correct answer: b

    The default value of _ERROR_ is *0*, which means there is no error. When an error occurs, whether it is one error or multiple errors, the value is set to *1*.

6. Which of the following actions occurs at the end of the DATA step?

    a. The automatic variables _N_ and _ERROR_ are incremented by one.
    b. The DATA step stops execution.
    c. The descriptor portion of the data set is written.
    d. The values of variables created in programming statements are re-set to missing in the program data vector.

    Correct answer: d

    By default, at the end of the DATA step, the values in the program data vector are written to the data set as an observation, the value of the automatic variable _N_ is incremented by one, control returns to the top of the DATA step, and the values of variables created in programming statements are set to missing. The automatic variable _ERROR_ retains its value.

7. Look carefully at the DATA step shown below. Based on the INPUT statement, in what order will the variables be stored in the new data set?

```
data perm.update;
   infile invent;
   input IDnum $ 15-19 Item $ 1-13 Instock 21-22
         BackOrd 24-25;
   Total=instock+backord;
run;
```

    a.   IDnum Item InStock BackOrd Total

    b.   Item IDnum InStock BackOrd Total

    c.   Total IDnum Item InStock BackOrd

    d.   Total Item IDnum InStock BackOrd

Correct answer: a

The order in which variables are defined in the DATA step determines the order in which the variables are stored in the data set.

8. If SAS cannot interpret syntax errors, then

    a.   data set variables will contain missing values.

    b.   the DATA step does not compile.

    c.   the DATA step still compiles, but it does not execute.

    d.   the DATA step still compiles and executes.

Correct answer: c

When SAS can't interpret syntax errors, the DATA step compiles, but it does not execute.

9. What is wrong with this program?

    ```
    data perm.update;
        infile invent
        input Item $ 1-13 IDnum $ 15-19 Instock 21-22
             BackOrd 24-25;
        total=instock+backord;
    run;
    ```

    a. missing semicolon on second line
    b. missing semicolon on third line
    c. incorrect order of variables
    d. incorrect variable type

    Correct answer: a

    A semicolon is missing from the second line. It will cause an error because the INPUT statement will be interpreted as invalid INFILE statement options.

10. Look carefully at this section of a SAS session log. Based on the note, what was the most likely problem with the DATA step?

    ```
    NOTE: Invalid data for IDnum in line 7 15-19.
    RULE: ----+----1----+----2----+----3----+----4
    7         Bird Feeder LG088 3 20
    Item=Bird Feeder IDnum=. InStock=3 BackOrd=20
    Total=23 _ERROR_=1 _N_=1
    ```

    a. A keyword was misspelled in the DATA step.
    b. A semicolon was missing from the INFILE statement.
    c. A variable was misspelled in the INPUT statement.
    d. A dollar sign was missing in the INPUT statement.

    Correct answer: d

    The third line of the log displays the values for IDnum, which are clearly character values. The fourth line displays the values in the program data vector and shows that the values for IDnum are missing, even though the other values are correctly assigned. Thus, it appears that numeric values were expected for IDnum. A dollar sign, to indicate character values, must be missing from the INPUT statement.

Chapter 7: Creating and Applying User-Defined Formats Answer Key

1. If you don't specify the LIBRARY= option, your formats are stored in **Work.Formats**, and they exist

    a.   only for the current procedure.
    b.   only for the current DATA step.
    c.   only for the current SAS session.
    d.   permanently.

    Correct answer: c

    If you do not specify the LIBRARY= option, formats are stored in a default format catalog named **Work.Formats**. As the libref **Work** implies, any format that is stored in **Work.Formats** is a temporary format that exists only for the current SAS session.

2. Which of the following statements will store your formats in a permanent catalog?

    a.
    ```
    libname library 'c:\sas\formats\lib';
    proc format lib=library
       ...;
    ```
    b.
    ```
    libname library 'c:\sas\formats\lib';
    format lib=library
       ...;
    ```
    c.
    ```
    library='c:\sas\formats\lib';
    proc format library
       ...;
    ```
    d.
    ```
    library='c:\sas\formats\lib';
    proc library
       ...;
    ```

    Correct answer: a

    To store formats in a permanent catalog, you first write a LIBNAME statement to associate the libref with the SAS data library in which the catalog will be stored. Then add the LIB= (or LIBRARY=) option to the PROC FORMAT statement, specifying the name of the catalog.

3. When creating a format with the VALUE statement, the new format's name

    - cannot end with a number
    - cannot end with a period
    - cannot be the name of a SAS format, and

    a. cannot be the name of a data set variable.

    b. must be at least two characters long.

    c. must be at least eight characters long.

    d. must begin with a dollar sign ($) if used with a character variable.

Correct answer: d

The name of a format that is created with a VALUE statement must begin with a dollar sign ($) if it applies to a character variable.

4. Which of the following FORMAT procedures is written correctly?

    a.
    ```
    proc format lib=library
        value colorfmt;
            1='Red'
            2='Green'
            3='Blue'
    run;
    ```
    b.
    ```
    proc format lib=library;
        value colorfmt
            1='Red'
            2='Green'
            3='Blue';
    run;
    ```
    c.
    ```
    proc format lib=library;
        value colorfmt;
            1='Red'
            2='Green'
            3='Blue'
    run;
    ```
    d.
    ```
    proc format lib=library;
        value colorfmt
            1='Red';
            2='Green';
            3='Blue';
    run;
    ```

Correct answer: b

A semicolon is needed after the PROC FORMAT statement. The VALUE statement begins with the keyword VALUE and ends with a semicolon after all the labels have been defined.

5. Which of these is **false**? Ranges in the VALUE statement can specify

    a. a single value, such as *24* or *'S'*.
    b. a range of numeric values, such as *0–1500*.
    c. a range of character values, such as *'A–'M'*.
    d. a list of numeric and character values separated by commas, such as *90,'B',180,'D',270*.

    Correct answer: d

    You can list values separated by commas, but the list must contain either all numeric values or all character values. Data set variables are either numeric or character.

6. How many characters can be used in a label?

    a. 40
    b. 96
    c. 200
    d. 256

    Correct answer: d

    When specifying a label, enclose it in quotation marks and limit the label to 256 characters.

7. Which keyword can be used to label missing values as well as any values that are not specified in a range?

    a. LOW
    b. MISS
    c. MISSING
    d. OTHER

    Correct answer: d

    MISS and MISSING are invalid keywords, and LOW does not include missing values. The keyword OTHER can be used in the VALUE statement to label missing values as well as any values that are not specifically included in a range.

8. You can place the FORMAT statement in either a DATA step or a PROC step. What happens when you place the FORMAT statement in a DATA step?

    a. You temporarily associate the formats with variables.

    b. You permanently associate the formats with variables.

    c. You replace the original data with the format labels.

    d. You make the formats available to other data sets

Correct answer: b

By placing the FORMAT statement in a DATA step, you permanently associate the defined formats with variables.

9. The format JOBFMT was created in a FORMAT procedure. Which FORMAT statement will apply it to the variable `JobTitle` in the program output?

    a.   `format jobtitle jobfmt;`

    b.   `format jobtitle jobfmt.;`

    c.   `format jobtitle=jobfmt;`

    d.   `format jobtitle='jobfmt';`

Correct answer: b

To associate a user-defined format with a variable, place a period at the end of the format name when it is used in the FORMAT statement.

10. Which keyword, when added to the PROC FORMAT statement, will display all the formats in your catalog?

    a. CATALOG

    b. LISTFMT

    c. FMTCAT

    d. FMTLIB

Correct answer: d

Adding the keyword FMTLIB to the PROC FORMAT statement displays a list of all the formats in your catalog, along with descriptions of their values.

1. If `Style` has four unique values and you submit the following program, which output do you get? (Assume that all the other variables are numeric.)

```
proc report data=sasuser.houses nowd;
   column style sqfeet bedrooms price;
   define style / group;
run;
```

a.

Style	SqFeet	Bedrooms	Price
CONDO	6755	11	$397,250
RANCH	5005	9	$274,300
SPLIT	4110	8	$233,950
TWOSTORY	5835	12	$335,300

b.

Style	SqFeet	Bedrooms	Price
CONDO	1400	2	$80,050
	1390	3	$79,350
	2105	4	$127,150
	1860	2	$110,700
RANCH	1250	2	$64,000
	1500	3	$86,650
	1535	3	$89,100
	720	1	$34,550
SPLIT	1190	1	$65,850
	1615	4	$94,450
	1305	3	$73,650
TWOSTORY	1810	4	$107,250
	1040	2	$55,850
	1240	2	$69,250
	1745	4	$102,950

c.

Style	SqFeet	Bedrooms	Price
15	21705	40	$1,240,800

d.

Style	SqFeet	Bedrooms	Price
RANCH	1250	2	$64,000
SPLIT	1190	1	$65,850
CONDO	1400	2	$80,050
TWOSTORY	1810	4	$107,250
RANCH	1500	3	$86,650
SPLIT	1615	4	$94,450
SPLIT	1305	3	$73,650
CONDO	1390	3	$79,350
TWOSTORY	1040	2	$55,850
CONDO	2105	4	$127,150
RANCH	1535	3	$89,100
TWOSTORY	1240	2	$69,250
RANCH	720	1	$34,550
TWOSTORY	1745	4	$102,950
CONDO	1860	2	$110,700

Correct answer: a

This program creates a summary report, which consolidates into one row all observations from the data set that have a unique combination of values for the variable `Style`.

2. When you define an order variable,

   a. the detail rows are ordered according to their formatted values.
   b. you can't create summary reports.
   c. PROC REPORT displays only the first occurrence of each order variable value in a set of rows that have the same value for all order variables.
   d. all of the above

Correct answer: d

Order variables do order rows according to the formatted values of the order variable, and PROC REPORT suppresses repetitive printing of order values. However, you can't use order variables in a summary report.

3. Which attributes or options are reflected in this PROC REPORT output?

Style	SqFeet	Price
RANCH	720	$34,550
TWOSTORY	1040	$55,850
SPLIT	1190	$65,850
TWOSTORY	1240	$69,250
RANCH	1250	$64,000
SPLIT	1305	$73,650
CONDO	1390	$79,350
CONDO	1400	$80,050
RANCH	1500	$86,650
RANCH	1535	$89,100
SPLIT	1615	$94,450
TWOSTORY	1745	$102,950
TWOSTORY	1810	$107,250
CONDO	1860	$110,700
CONDO	2105	$127,150

- *a.* SKIPLINE and FORMAT=
- *b.* CENTER, HEADLINE, HEADSKIP, and either WIDTH=, SPACING=, or FORMAT=
- *c.* SPACING= only
- *d.* CENTER, FORMAT=, and HEADLINE

Correct answer: b

The **HEADLINE** option underlines the headings, and the **HEADSKIP** option skips a line between the headings and the rows in the report. Also, `Style` is centered, and the column for `Price` is wider than the default.

4. To create a summary report that shows the average number of bedrooms and the maximum number of baths for each style of house, which DEFINE statements do you use in your PROC REPORT step?

- *a.*
  ```
  define style / center 'Style of/House';
  define bedrooms / mean 'Average/Bedrooms';
  define baths / max 'Maximum/Baths';
  ```
- *b.*
  ```
  define style / group;
  define bedrooms / mean 'Average/Bedrooms';
  define baths / max 'Maximum/Baths';
  ```
- *c.*
  ```
  define style / order;
  define bedrooms / mean 'Average/Bedrooms';
  define baths / max 'Maximum/Baths';
  ```
- *d.*
  ```
  define style / group;
  define bedrooms / 'Average/Bedrooms';
  define baths / 'Maximum/Baths'
  ```

Correct answer: b

To create a summary report, you must define a group variable. To produce the statistics that you want, you must specify the MEAN and MAX statistics for `Bedrooms` and `Baths`.

5. Which program does **not** contain an error?

```
a. proc report data=sasuser.houses nowd;
      column style bedrooms baths;
      define style / order;
      define bedbathratio / computed format=4.2;
      compute bedbathratio;
         bedbathratio=baths.sum/bedrooms.sum;
      endcomp;
   run;
```

```
b. proc report data=sasuser.houses nowd;
      column style bedrooms baths BedBathRatio;
      define style / order;
      define bedbathratio / order format=4.2;
      compute bedbathratio;
         bedbathratio=baths.sum/bedrooms.sum;
      endcomp;
   run;
```

```
c. proc report data=sasuser.houses nowd;
      column style bedrooms baths BedBathRatio;
      define style / order;
      define bedbathratio / computed format=4.2;
      compute bedbathratio;
         bedbathratio=baths.sum/bedrooms.sum;
      endcomp;
   run;
```

```
d. proc report data=sasuser.houses nowd;
      column style bedrooms baths BedBathRatio;
      define style / order;
      define bedbathratio / computed format=4.2;
      compute bedbathratio;
         bedbathratio=baths/bedrooms;
      endcomp;
   run;
```

Correct answer: c

Program c correctly specifies a **computed variable** in the COLUMN statement, defines the variable in a DEFINE statement, and computes values using the form *variable-name.statistic* in a compute block.

6. What output does this PROC REPORT step produce?

```
proc report data=sasuser.houses nowd;
   column style sqfeet bedrooms price;
run;
```

   a. a list report ordered by values of the first variable in the COLUMN statement

   b. a summary report ordered by values of the first variable in the COLUMN statement

   c. a list report that displays a row for each observation in the input data set and which calculates the SUM statistic for numeric variables

   d. a list report that calculates the N (frequency) statistic for character variables

Correct answer: c

By default, PROC REPORT displays character variables as display variables. A report that contains one or more display variables has a detail row for each observation in the data set. By default, PROC REPORT displays numeric variables as analysis variables, which are used to calculate the default statistic SUM.

7. Which of the following programs produces this output?

Style				
CONDO	RANCH	SPLIT	TWOSTORY	Average Price
4	4	3	4	$82,720

   a.
```
proc report data=sasuser.houses nowd;
   column style condo range split
          twostory price;

   define price / mean 'Average Price';
run;
```

   b.
```
proc report data=sasuser.houses nowd;
   column style price;
   define style / group;
   define price / mean 'Average Price';
run;
```

   c.
```
proc report data=sasuser.houses nowd;
   column style price;
   define style / across;
   define price / mean 'Average Price';
run;
```

   d.
```
proc report data=sasuser.houses nowd;
   column style price;
   define style / across 'CONDO' 'RANCH'
          'SPLIT' 'TWOSTORY';
   define price / mean 'Average Price';
run;
```

Correct answer: c

In this output, the table cells contain a frequency count for each unique value of an **across** variable, `Style`. You don't have to specify across variable values in your PROC REPORT step.

8. If you submit this program, where does your PROC REPORT output appear?

```
proc report data=sasuser.houses nowd;
   column style sqfeet bedrooms price;
   define style / group;
run;
```

   a. in the PROC REPORT window
   b. as HTML and/or SAS listing output
   c. both of the above
   d. neither of the above

Correct answer: b

In nonwindowing mode, your PROC REPORT output appears as HTML and/or as SAS listing output, depending on your option settings.

9. How can you create output with headings that break as shown below?

```
Style of     Average    Maximum
  House      Bedrooms      Baths
  CONDO        2.75         2.5
  RANCH        2.25           3
  SPLIT     2.666666          3
TWOSTORY         3            3
```

   a. You must specify the SPLIT= option in the PROC REPORT statement and use the split character in column headings in DEFINE statements.
   b. You must use the default split character in column headings in DEFINE statements.
   c. You must specify either the WIDTH= or the SPACING= attribute in DEFINE statements.
   d. These headings split this way by default.

Correct answer: d

By default, columns for character variables are the same as the variable's length, and columns for numeric variables have a width of 9. So these headings split this way by default.

10. Suppose you want to create a report using both character and numeric variables. If you don't use any DEFINE statements in your PROC REPORT step,

    a. your PROC REPORT step will not execute successfully.

    b. you can produce only list reports.

    c. you can order rows by specifying options in the PROC REPORT statement.

    d. you can produce only summary reports.

Correct answer: b

Unless you use **DEFINE statements** to define order variables or group variables, you can't order rows or produce summary reports. However, DEFINE statements are not required in all PROC REPORT steps.

Chapter 9: Producing Descriptive Statistics Answer Key

1. The default statistics produced by the MEANS procedure are **n-count**, **mean**, **minimum**, **maximum**, and

   a. median.
   b. range.
   c. standard deviation.
   d. standard error of the mean.

   Correct answer: c

   By default, the MEANS procedure produces the n-cout, mean, minimum, and standard deviation.

2. Which statement will limit a PROC MEANS analysis to the variables `Boarded`, `Transfer`, and `Deplane`?

   a. `by boarded transfer deplane;`
   b. `class boarded transfer deplane;`
   c. `output boarded transfer deplane;`
   d. `var boarded transfer deplane;`

   Correct answer: d

   To specify the variables that PROC MEANS analyzes, add a VAR statement and list the variable names.

3. The data set **Survey.Health** includes the following variables. Which is a poor candidate for PROC MEANS analysis?

   a. `IDnum`
   b. `Age`
   c. `Height`
   d. `Weight`

   Correct answer: a

   Unlike `Age`, `Height`, or `Weight`, the values of IDnum are unlikely to yield any useful statistics.

4. Which of the following statements is true regarding BY-group processing?

   a. BY variables must be either indexed or sorted.

   b. Summary statistics are computed for BY variables.

   c. BY-group processing is preferred when you are categorizing data that contains few variables.

   d. BY-group processing overwrites your data set with the newly grouped observations.

Correct answer: a

Unlike CLASS processing, BY-group processing requires that your data already be indexed or sorted in the order of the BY variables. You might need to run the SORT procedure before using PROC MEANS with a BY group.

5. Which group processing statement produced the PROC MEANS output shown below?

Survive	Sex	N Obs	Variable	N	Mean	Std Dev	Minimum	Maximum
DIED	1	4	Arterial	4	92.5	10.5	83.0	103.0
			Heart	4	111.0	53.4	54.0	183.0
			Cardiac	4	176.8	75.2	95.0	260.0
			Urinary	4	98.0	186.1	0.0	377.0
	2	6	Arterial	6	94.2	27.3	72.0	145.0
			Heart	6	103.7	16.7	81.0	130.0
			Cardiac	6	318.3	102.6	156.0	424.0
			Urinary	6	100.3	155.7	0.0	405.0
SURV	1	5	Arterial	5	77.2	12.2	61.0	88.0
			Heart	5	109.0	32.0	77.0	149.0
			Cardiac	5	298.0	139.8	66.0	410.0
			Urinary	5	100.8	60.2	44.0	200.0
	2	5	Arterial	5	78.8	6.8	72.0	87.0
			Heart	5	100.0	13.4	84.0	111.0
			Cardiac	5	330.2	87.0	256.0	471.0
			Urinary	5	111.2	152.4	12.0	377.0

   a. `class sex survive;`

   b. `class survive sex;`

   c. `by sex survive;`

   d. `by survive sex;`

Correct answer: b

A CLASS statement produces a single large table, whereas BY-group processing creates a series of small tables. The order of the variables in the CLASS statement determines their order in the output table.

6. Which program can be used to create the following output?

Sex	N Obs	Variable	N	Mean	Std Dev	Minimum	Maximum
F	11	Age	11	48.9090909	13.3075508	16.0000000	63.0000000
		Height	11	63.9090909	2.1191765	61.0000000	68.0000000
		Weight	11	150.4545455	18.4464828	102.0000000	168.0000000
M	9	Age	9	44.0000000	12.3895117	15.0000000	54.0000000
		Height	9	70.6666667	2.6457513	66.0000000	75.0000000
		Weight	9	204.2222222	30.2893454	140.0000000	240.0000000

a.
```
proc means data=clinic.diabetes;
    var age height weight;
    class sex;
    output out=work.sum_gender
       mean=AvgAge AvgHeight AvgWeight;
run;
```
b.
```
proc summary data=clinic.diabetes print;
    var age height weight;
    class sex;
    output out=work.sum_gender
       mean=AvgAge AvgHeight AvgWeight;
run;
```
c.
```
proc means data=clinic.diabetes noprint;
    var age height weight;
    class sex;
    output out=work.sum_gender
       mean=AvgAge AvgHeight AvgWeight;
run;
```
d. Both *a* and *b*.

Correct answer: d

You can use either PROC MEANS or PROC SUMMARY to create the table. Adding a PRINT option to the PROC SUMMARY statement produces the same reports as if you used PROC MEANS.

7. By default, PROC FREQ creates a table of frequencies and percentages for which data set variables?

    a. character variables

    b. numeric variables

    c. both character and numeric variables

    d. none: variables must always be specified

Correct answer: c

By default, the PROC FREQ creates a table for all variables in a data set.

8. Frequency distributions work best with variables that contain

    a. continuous values.

    b. numeric values.

    c. categorical values.

    d. unique values.

Correct answer: c

Both continuous values and many unique values can result in lengthy and meaningless tables. Frequency distributors work best with categorical values.

9. Which PROC FREQ step produced this two-way table?

Frequency Percent Row Pct Col Pct	Table of Weight by Height			
		Height		
Weight	< 5'5"	5'5-10"	> 5'10"	Total
< 140	2 10.00 100.00 28.57	0 0.00 0.00 0.00	0 0.00 0.00 0.00	2 10.00
140-180	5 25.00 50.00 71.43	5 25.00 50.00 62.50	0 0.00 0.00 0.00	10 50.00
> 180	0 0.00 0.00 0.00	3 15.00 37.50 37.50	5 25.00 62.50 100.00	8 40.00
Total	7 35.00	8 40.00	5 25.00	20 100.00

a.
```
proc freq data=clinic.diabetes;
    tables height weight;
    format height htfmt. weight wtfmt.;
run;
```
b.
```
proc freq data=clinic.diabetes;
    tables weight height;
    format weight wtfmt. height htfmt.;
run;
```
c.
```
proc freq data=clinic.diabetes;
    tables height*weight;
    format height htfmt. weight wtfmt.;
run;
```
d.
```
proc freq data=clinic.diabetes;
    tables weight*height;
    format weight wtfmt. height htfmt.;
run;
```

Correct answer: d

An asterisk is used to join the variables in a two-way TABLES statement. The first variable forms the table rows, and the second variable forms the table columns.

10. Which PROC FREQ step produced this table?

Percent	Table of Sex by Weight			
		Weight		
Sex	**< 140**	**140-180**	**> 180**	**Total**
F	10.00	45.00	0.00	55.00
M	0.00	5.00	40.00	45.00
Total	2 10.00	10 50.00	8 40.00	20 100.00

a.
```
proc freq data=clinic.diabetes;
     tables sex weight / list;
     format weight wtfmt.;
run;
```
b.
```
proc freq data=clinic.diabetes;
     tables sex*weight / nocol;
     format weight wtfmt.;
run;
```
c.
```
proc freq data=clinic.diabetes;
     tables sex weight / norow nocol;
     format weight wtfmt.;
run;
```
d.
```
proc freq data=clinic.diabetes;
     tables sex*weight / nofreq norow nocol;
     format weight wtfmt.;
run;
```

Correct answer: d

An asterisk is used to join the variables in crosstabulation tables. The only results that are shown in this table are cell percentages. The NOFREQ option suppresses cell frequencies, the NOROW option suppresses row percentages, and the NOCOL option suppresses column percentages.

Chapter 10: Producing HTML Output Answer Key

1. Using ODS statements, how many types of output can you generate concurrently?

    a. 1 (only listing output)
    b. 2
    c. 3
    d. as many as you want

    Correct answer: d

    You can generate any number of output types as long as you open the ODS destination for each type of output that you want to create.

2. If ODS is set to its default settings, what types of output are created by the code below?

    ```
    ods html file='c:\myhtml.htm';
    ods pdf file='c:\mypdf.pdf';
    ```

    a. HTML and PDF
    b. PDF only
    c. HTML, PDF, and listing
    d. No output is created because ODS is closed by default.

    Correct answer: c

    Listing output is created by default, so these statements create HTML, PDF, and listing output.

3. What is the purpose of closing the Listing destination in the code shown below?

    ```
    ods listing close;
    ods html ... ;
    ```

    a. It conserves system resources.
    b. It simplifies your program.
    c. It makes your program compatible with other hardware platforms.
    d. It makes your program compatible with previous versions of SAS software.

    Correct answer: a

    By default, SAS programs produce listing output. If you want only HTML output, it's a good idea to close the Listing destination before creating HTML output, because an open destination uses system resources.

4. When the code shown below is run, what will the file **D:\Output\body.html** contain?

```
ods html body='d:\output\body.html';
proc print data=work.alpha;
run;
proc print data=work.beta;
run;
ods html close;
```

   a. The PROC PRINT output for **Work.Alpha**.

   b. The PROC PRINT output for **Work.Beta**.

   c. The PROC PRINT output for both **Work.Alpha** and **Work.Beta**.

   d. Nothing. No output will be written to **D:\Output\body.html**.

Correct answer: c

When multiple procedures are run while HTML output is open, procedure output is appended to the same body file.

5. When the code shown below is run, what file will be loaded by the links in **D:\Output\contents.html**?

```
ods html body='d:\output\body.html'
         contents='d:\output\contents.html'
         frame='d:\output\frame.html';
```

   a. **D:\Output\body.html**

   b. **D:\Output\contents.html**

   c. **D:\Output\frame.html**

   d. There are no links from the file **D:\Output\contents.html**.

Correct answer: a

The CONTENTS= option creates a table of contents containing links to the body file, **D:\Output\body.html**.

6. The table of contents created by the CONTENTS= option contains a numbered heading for

   a. each procedure.

   b. each procedure that creates output.

   c. each procedure and DATA step.

   d. each HTML file created by your program.

Correct answer: b

The table of contents contains a numbered heading for each procedure that creates output.

7. When the code shown below is run, what will the file **D:\Output\frame.html** display?

```
ods html body='d:\output\body.html'
         contents='d:\output\contents.html'
         frame='d:\output\frame.html';
```

 a. The file **D:\Output\contents.html**.
 b. The file **D:\Output\frame.html**.
 c. The files **D:\Output\contents.html** and **D:\Output\body.html**.
 d. It displays no other files.

Correct answer: c

The FRAME= option creates an HTML file that integrates the table of contents and the body file.

8. What is the purpose of the URL= suboptions shown below?

```
ods html body='d:\output\body.html' (url='body.html')
         contents='d:\output\contents.html' (url='contents.html')
         frame='d:\output\frame.html';
```

 a. To create absolute link addresses for loading the files from a server.
 b. To create relative link addresses for loading the files from a server.
 c. To allow HTML files to be loaded from a local drive.
 d. To send HTML output to two locations.

Correct answer: b

Specifying the URL= suboption in the file specification provides a URL that ODS uses in the links it creates. Specifying a simple (one name) URL creates a relative link address to the file.

9. Which ODS HTML option was used in creating the following table?

Obs	ID	Name	Sex	Age	Height	Weight
1	2458	Murray, W	M	27	72	168
2	2462	Almers, C	F	34	66	152
3	2501	Bonaventure, T	F	31	61	123
4	2523	Johnson, R	F	43	63	137

 a. `format=brown`
 b. `format='brown'`
 c. `style=brown`
 d. `style='brown'`

Correct answer: c

You can change the appearance of HTML output by using the STYLE= option in the ODS HTML statement. The style name doesn't need quotation marks.

10. What is the purpose of the PATH= option?

```
ods html path='d:\output' (url=none)
         body='body.html'
         contents='contents.html'
         frame='frame.html';
```

 a. It creates absolute link addresses for loading HTML files from a server.
 b. It creates relative link addresses for loading HTML files from a server.
 c. It allows HTML files to be loaded from a local drive.
 d. It specifies the location of HTML file output.

Correct answer: d

You use the PATH= option to specify the location for HTML output. When you use the PATH= option, you don't need to specify the full pathname for the body, contents, or frame files.

1. Which program creates the output shown below?

Raw Data File Furnture

```
1---+----10---+----20---+----30---+
310 oak    pedestal table  329.99
311 maple pedestal table  369.99
312 brass floor    lamp   79.99
313 glass table    lamp   59.99
314 oak    rocking  chair  153.99
```

StockNum	Finish	Style	Item	TotalPrice
310	oak	pedestal	table	329.99
311	maple	pedestal	table	699.98
312	brass	floor	lamp	779.97
313	glass	table	lamp	839.96

a.
```
data test2;
     infile furnture;
     input StockNum $ 1-3 Finish $ 5-9 Style $ 11-18
          Item $ 20-24 Price 26-31;
     if finish='oak' then delete;
     retain TotPrice 100;
     totalprice+price;
     drop price;
run;
proc print data=test2 noobs;
run;
```

b.
```
data test2;
     infile furnture;
     input StockNum $ 1-3 Finish $ 5-9 Style $ 11-18
          Item $ 20-24 Price 26-31;
     if finish='oak' and price<200 then delete;
     TotalPrice+price;
run;
proc print data=test2 noobs;
run;
```

c.
```
data test2(drop=price);
     infile furnture;
     input StockNum $ 1-3 Finish $ 5-9 Style $ 11-18
          Item $ 20-24 Price 26-31;
     if finish='oak' and price<200 then delete;
     TotalPrice+price;
run;
proc print data=test2 noobs;
run;
```

```
d. data test2;
      infile furnture;
      input StockNum $ 1-3 Finish $ 5-9 Style $ 11-18
            Item $ 20-24 Price 26-31;
      if finish=oak and price<200 then delete price;
      TotalPrice+price;
   run;
   proc print data=test2 noobs;
   run;
```

Correct answer: c

Program *c* correctly deletes the observation in which the value of Finish is *oak* and the value of Price is less than 200. It also creates TotalPrice by summing the variable Price down observations, then drops Price by using the DROP= data set option in the DATA statement.

2. How is the variable Amount labeled and formatted in the PROC PRINT output?

```
data credit;
   infile creddata;
   input Account $ 1-5 Name $ 7-25 Type $ 27
         Transact $ 29-35 Amount 37-50;
   label amount='Amount of Loan';
   format amount dollar12.2;

run;
proc print data=credit label;
   label amount='Total Amount Loaned';
   format amount comma10.;
run;
```

a. label **Amount of Loan**, format **DOLLAR12.2**
b. label **Total Amount Loaned**, format **COMMA10.**
c. label **Amount**, default format
d. The PROC PRINT step does not execute because two labels and two formats are assigned to the same variable.

Correct answer: b

The PROC PRINT output displays the label **Total Amount Loaned** for the variable Amount and formats this variable using the COMMA10. format. Temporary labels or formats that are assigned in a PROC step override permanent labels or formats that are assigned in a DATA step.

3. Consider the IF-THEN statement shown below. When the statement is executed, which expression is evaluated first?

```
if finlexam>=95
    and (research='A' or
        (project='A' and present='A'))
    then Grade='A+';
```

  a. `finlexam>=95`

  b. `research='A'`

  c. `project='A' and present='A'`

  d. `research='A' or`
     `(project='A' and present='A')`

Correct answer: c

Logical comparisons that are enclosed in parentheses are evaluated as true or false before they are compared to other expressions. In the example above, the AND comparison within the nested parentheses is evaluated before being compared to the OR comparison.

4. Consider the small raw data file and program shown below. What is the value of `Count` after the fourth record is read?

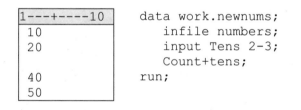

```
1---+----10          data work.newnums;
   10                    infile numbers;
   20                    input Tens 2-3;
                         Count+tens;
   40                run;
   50
```

  a. missing

  b. 0

  c. 30

  d. 70

Correct answer: d

The Sum statement adds the result of the expression that is on the right side of the plus sign to the numeric variable that is on the left side. The new value is then retained for subsequent observations. The Sum statement treats the missing value as a 0, so the value of `Count` in the fourth observation would be *10+20+0+40*, or *70*.

5. Now consider the revised program below. What is the value of Count after the **third** observation is read?

```
1---+----10        data work.newnums;
  10                  infile numbers;
  20                  input Tens 2-3;
                      retain Count 100;
  40                  count+tens;
  50               run;
```

   a.   missing
   b.   0
   c.   100
   d.   130

Correct answer: d

The RETAIN statement assigns an initial value of *100* to the variable Count, so the value of Count in the third observation would be *100+10+20+0*, or *130*.

6. For the observation shown below, what is the result of the IF-THEN statement?

Status	Type	Count	Action	Control
ok	3	12	E	Go

```
if status='OK' and type=3
   then Count+1;
if status='S' or action='E'
   then Control='Stop';
```

   a.   Count = *12*   Control = *Go*
   b.   Count = *13*   Control = *Stop*
   c.   Count = *12*   Control = *Stop*
   d.   Count = *13*   Control = *Go*

Correct answer: c

You must enclose character values in quotation marks, and you must specify them in the same case in which they appear in the data set. The value *ok* is not identical to *OK*, so the value of Count is not changed by the IF-THEN statement.

7. Which of the following can determine the length of a new variable?

    a. the length of the variable's first value

    b. the assignment statement

    c. the LENGTH statement

    d. all of the above

Correct answer: d

The length of a variable is determined by its first reference in the DATA step. When creating a new character variable, SAS allocates as many bytes of storage space as there are characters in the first value that it encounters for that variable. The first reference to a new variable can also be made with a LENGTH statement or an assignment statement. The length of the variable's first value does not matter once the variable has been referenced in your program.

8. Which set of statements is the most efficient equivalent to the code shown below?

```
if code='1' then Type='Fixed';
if code='2' then Type='Variable';
if code^='1' and code^='2' then Type='Unknown';
```

   a.
```
if code='1' then Type='Fixed';
   else if code='2' then Type='Variable';
   else Type='Unknown';
```
   b.
```
if code='1' then Type='Fixed';
   if code='2' then Type='Variable';
   else Type='Unknown';
```
   c.
```
if code='1' then type='Fixed';
   else code='2' and type='Variable';
   else type='Unknown';
```
   d.
```
if code='1' and type='Fixed';
   then code='2' and type='Variable';
   else type='Unknown';
```

Correct answer: a

Answer *a* is the most efficient. You can write multiple ELSE statements to specify a series of mutually exclusive conditions. The ELSE statement must immediately follow the IF-THEN statement in your program. An ELSE statement executes only if the previous IF-THEN/ELSE statement is false.

9. What is the length of the variable `Type`, as created in the DATA step below?

```
data finance.newloan;
   set finance.records;
   TotLoan+payment;
   if code='1' then Type='Fixed';
   else Type='Variable';
   length type $ 10;
run;
```

a. 5

b. 8

c. 10

d. It depends on the first value of `Type`.

Correct answer: a

The length of a new variable is determined by the first reference in the DATA step, not by data values. In this case, the length of `Type` is determined by the value *Fixed*. The LENGTH statement is in the wrong place; it must be read **before** any other reference to the variable in the DATA step. The LENGTH statement cannot change the length of an existing variable.

10. Which program contains an error?

a.
```
data clinic.stress(drop=timemin timesec);
    infile tests;
    input ID $ 1-4 Name $ 6-25 RestHR 27-29 MaxHR 31-33
        RecHR 35-37 TimeMin 39-40 TimeSec 42-43
        Tolerance $ 45;
    TotalTime=(timemin*60)+timesec;
    SumSec+totaltime;
run;
```

b.
```
proc print data=clinic.stress;
    label totaltime='Total Duration of Test';
    format timemin 5.2;
    drop sumsec;
run;
```

c.
```
proc print data=clinic.stress(keep=totaltime timemin);
    label totaltime='Total Duration of Test';
    format timemin 5.2;
run;
```

d.
```
data clinic.stress;
    infile tests;
    input ID $ 1-4 Name $ 6-25 RestHR 27-29 MaxHR 31-33
        RecHR 35-37 TimeMin 39-40 TimeSec 42-43
        Tolerance $ 45;
    TotalTime=(timemin*60)+timesec;
    keep id totaltime tolerance;
run;
```

Correct answer: b

To select variables, you can use a DROP or KEEP statement in any DATA step. You can also use the DROP= or KEEP= data set options following a data set name in any DATA or PROC step. However, you cannot use DROP or KEEP statements in PROC steps.

Chapter 12: Reading SAS Data Sets Answer Key

1. If you submit the following program, which variables appear in the new data set?

```
data work.cardiac(drop=age group);
   set clinic.fitness(keep=age weight group);
   if group=2 and age>40;
run;
```

   a. none

   b. Weight

   c. Age, Group

   d. Age, Weight, Group

Correct answer: b

The variables Age, Weight, and Group are specified using the KEEP= option in the SET statement. After processing, Age and Group are dropped in the DATA statement.

2. Which of the following programs correctly reads the data set **Orders** and creates the data set **FastOrdr?**

   a.
```
data catalog.fastordr(drop=ordrtime);
   set july.orders(keep=product units price);
   if ordrtime<4;
   Total=units*price;
run;
```
   b.
```
data catalog.orders(drop=ordrtime);
   set july.fastordr(keep=product units price);
   if ordrtime<4;
   Total=units*price;
run;
```
   c.
```
data catalog.fastordr(drop=ordrtime);
   set july.orders(keep=product units price
                   ordrtime);
   if ordrtime<4;
   Total=units*price;
run;
```
   d. none of the above

Correct answer: c

You specify the data set to be created in the DATA statement. The DROP= data set option prevents variables from being written to the data set. Because you use the variable OrdrTime when processing your data, you cannot drop OrdrTime in the SET statement. If you use the KEEP= option in the SET statement, then you must list OrdrTime as one of the variables to be kept.

3. Which of the following statements is **false** about BY-group processing?

    When you use the BY statement with the SET statement,

    a. the data sets that are listed in the SET statement must be indexed or sorted by the values of the BY variable(s).
    b. the DATA step automatically creates two variables, `FIRST.` and `LAST.`, for each variable in the BY statement.
    c. `FIRST.` and `LAST.` identify the first and last observation in each BY group, in that order.
    d. `FIRST.` and `LAST.` are stored in the data set.

    Correct answer: d

    When you use the BY statement with the SET statement, the DATA step creates the temporary variables `FIRST.` and `LAST.` They are not stored in the data set.

4. There are 500 observations in the data set **Company.USA**. What is the result of submitting the following program?

    ```
    data work.getobs5(drop=obsnum);
        obsnum=5;
        set company.usa(keep=manager payroll) point=obsnum;
        stop;
    run;
    ```

    a. an error
    b. an empty data set
    c. a continuous loop
    d. a data set that contains one observation

    Correct answer: b

    The DATA step writes observations to output at the end of the DATA step. However, in this program, the STOP statement stops processing before the end of the DATA step. An explicit OUTPUT statement is needed in order to produce observations.

5. There is no end-of-file condition when you use direct access to read data, so how can your program prevent a continuous loop?

    a. Do not use a POINT= variable.
    b. Check for an invalid value of the POINT= variable.
    c. Do not use an END= variable.
    d. Include an OUTPUT statement.

Correct answer: b

To avoid a continuous loop when using direct access, either include a STOP statement or use programming logic that checks for an invalid value of the POINT= variable. If SAS reads an invalid value of the POINT= variable, it sets the automatic variable _ERROR_ to *1*. You can use this information to check for conditions that cause continuous processing.

6. Assuming that the data set **Company.USA** has five or more observations, what is the result of submitting the following program?

```
data work.getobs5(drop=obsnum);
    obsnum=5;
    set company.usa(keep=manager payroll) point=obsnum;
    output;
    stop;
run;
```

   a. an error
   b. an empty data set
   c. a continuous loop
   d. a data set that contains one observation

Correct answer: d

By combining the POINT= option with the OUTPUT and STOP statements, your program can write a single observation to output.

7. Which of the following statements is **true** regarding direct access of data sets?

   a. You cannot specify END= with POINT=.
   b. You cannot specify OUTPUT with POINT=.
   c. You cannot specify STOP with END=.
   d. You cannot specify FIRST. with LAST.

Correct answer: a

The END= option and POINT= option are incompatible in the same SET statement. Use one or the other in your program.

8. What is the result of submitting the following program?

```
data work.addtoend;
    set clinic.stress2 end=last;
    if last;
run;
```

a. an error

b. an empty data set

c. a continuous loop

d. a data set that contains one observation

Correct answer: d

This program uses the END= option to name a temporary variable that contains an end-of-file marker. That variable, LAST, is set to *1* when the SET statement reads the last observation of the data set.

9. At the start of DATA step processing, during the compilation phase, variables are created in the program data vector (PDV), and observations are set to

a. blank

b. missing

c. *0*

d. there are no observations.

Correct answer: d

At the bottom of the DATA step, the compilation phase is complete, and the descriptor portion of the new SAS data set is created. There are no observations because the DATA step has not yet executed.

10. The DATA step executes

a. continuously if you use the POINT= option and the STOP statement.

b. once for each variable in the output data set.

c. once for each observation in the input data set.

d. until it encounters an OUTPUT statement.

Correct answer: c

The DATA step executes once for each observation in the input data set. You use the POINT= option with the STOP statement to prevent continuous looping.

Chapter 13: Combining SAS Data Sets Answer Key

1. Which program will combine **Brothers.One** and **Brothers.Two** to produce **Brothers.Three**?

Brothers.One			Brothers.Two			Brothers.Three		
VarX	**VarY**		**VarX**	**VarZ**		**VarX**	**VarY**	**VarZ**
1	Groucho		2	Chico		2	Groucho	Chico
3	Harpo		4	Zeppo		4	Harpo	Zeppo
5	Karl							

a.
```
data brothers.three;
    set brothers.one;
    set brothers.two;
run;
```
b.
```
data brothers.three;
    set brothers.one brothers.two;
run;
```
c.
```
data brothers.three;
    set brothers.one brothers.two;
    by varx;
run;
```
d.
```
data brothers.three;
    merge brothers.one brothers.two;
    by varx;
run;
```

Correct answer: a

This is a case of one-to-one reading, which requires multiple SET statements. Notice that where same-named variables occur, the values that are read in from the second data set replace those that are read in from the first one. Also, the number of observations in the new data set is the number of observations in the smallest original data set.

2. Which program will combine **Actors.Props1** and **Actors.Props2** to produce **Actors.Props3**?

Actors.Props1			Actors.Props2			Actors.Props3	
Actor	**Prop**		**Actor**	**Prop**		**Actor**	**Prop**
Curly	Anvil		Curly	Ladder		Curly	Anvil
Larry	Ladder		Moe	Pliers		Curly	Ladder
Moe	Poker					Larry	Ladder
						Moe	Poker
						Moe	Pliers

a.
```
data actors.props3;
    set actors.props1;
    set actors.props2;
run;
```

b.
```
data actors.props3;
    set actors.props1 actors.props2;
run;
```

c.
```
data actors.props3;
    set actors.props1 actors.props2;
    by actor;
run;
```

d.
```
data actors.props3;
    merge actors.props1 actors.props2;
    by actor;
run;
```

Correct answer: c

This is a case of interleaving, which requires a list of data set names in the SET statement and one or more BY variables in the BY statement. Notice that observations in each BY group are read sequentially, in the order in which the data sets and BY variables are listed. The new data set contains all the variables from all the input data sets, as well as the total number of records from all input data sets.

3. If you submit the following program, which new data set is created?

Work.Dataone

Career	Supervis	Finance
72	26	9
63	76	7
96	31	7
96	98	6
84	94	6

Work.Datatwo

Variety	Feedback	Autonomy
10	11	70
85	22	93
83	63	73
82	75	97
36	77	97

```
data work.jobsatis;
    set work.dataone work.datatwo;
run;
```

a.

Career	Supervis	Finance	Variety	Feedback	Autonomy
72	26	9	.	.	.
63	76	7	.	.	.
96	31	7	.	.	.
96	98	6	.	.	.
84	94	6	.	.	.
.	.	.	10	11	70
.	.	.	85	22	93
.	.	.	83	63	73
.	.	.	82	75	97
.	.	.	36	77	97

b.

Career	Supervis	Finance	Variety	Feedback	Autonomy
72	26	9	10	11	70
63	76	7	85	22	93
96	31	7	83	63	73
96	98	6	82	75	97
84	94	6	36	77	97

c.

Career	Supervis	Finance
72	26	9
63	76	7
96	31	7
96	98	6
84	94	6
10	11	70
85	22	93
83	63	73
82	75	97
36	77	97

d. none of the above

Correct answer: a

Concatenating appends the observations from one data set to another data set. The new data set contains the total number of records from all input data sets, so *b* is incorrect. All the variables from all the input data sets appear in the new data set, so *c* is incorrect.

4. If you concatenate the data sets below in the order shown, what is the value of Sale in observation 2 of the new data set?

Sales.Reps

ID	Name
1	Nay Rong
2	Kelly Windsor
3	Julio Meraz
4	Richard Krabill

Sales.Close

ID	Sale
1	$28,000
2	$30,000
2	$40,000
3	$15,000
3	$20,000
3	$25,000
4	$35,000

Sales.Bonus

ID	Bonus
1	$2,000
2	$4,000
3	$3,000
4	$2,500

a. missing
b. $30,000
c. $40,000
d. you cannot concatenate these data sets

Correct answer: a

The concatenated data sets are read sequentially, in the order in which they are listed in the SET statement. The second observation in **Sales.Reps** does not contain a value for Sale, so a missing value appears for this variable. (Note that if you merge the data sets, the value of Sale for the second observation is *$30,000*.)

5. What happens if you merge the following data sets by variable SSN?

1st

SSN	Age
029-46-9261	39
074-53-9892	34
228-88-9649	32
442-21-8075	12
446-93-2122	36
776-84-5391	28
929-75-0218	27

2nd

SSN	Age	Date
029-46-9261	37	02/15/95
074-53-9892	32	05/22/97
228-88-9649	30	03/04/96
442-21-8075	10	11/22/95
446-93-2122	34	07/08/96
776-84-5391	26	12/15/96
929-75-0218	25	04/30/97

a. The values of Age in the 1st data set overwrite the values of Age in the 2nd data set.

b. The values of Age in the 2nd data set overwrite the values of Age in the 1st data set.

c. The DATA step fails because the two data sets contain same-named variables that have different values.

d. The values of Age in the 2nd data set are set to missing.

Correct answer: b

If you have variables with the same name in more than one input data set, then values of the same-named variable in the first data set in which it appears are overwritten by values of the same-named variable in subsequent data sets.

6. Suppose you merge data sets **Health.Set1** and **Health.Set2** below:

Health.Set1

ID	Sex	Age
1129	F	48
1274	F	50
1387	F	57
2304	F	16
2486	F	63
4425	F	48
4759	F	60
5438	F	42
6488	F	59
9012	F	39
9125	F	56

Health.Set2

ID	Height	Weight
1129	61	137
1387	64	142
2304	61	102
5438	62	168
6488	64	154
9012	63	157
9125	64	159

Which output does the following program create?

```
data work.merged;
   merge health.set1(in=in1) health.set2(in=in2);
   by id;
   if in1 and in2;
run;
proc print data=work.merged;
run;
```

a.

Obs	ID	Sex	Age	Height	Weight
1	1129	F	48	61	137
2	1274	F	50	.	.
3	1387	F	57	64	142
4	2304	F	16	61	102
5	2486	F	63	.	.
6	4425	F	48	.	.
7	4759	F	60	.	.
8	5438	F	42	62	168
9	6488	F	59	64	154
10	9012	F	39	63	157
11	9125	F	56	64	159

b.

Obs	ID	Sex	Age	Height	Weight
1	1129	F	48	61	137
2	1387	F	50	64	142
3	2304	F	57	61	102
4	5438	F	16	62	168
5	6488	F	63	64	154
6	9012	F	48	63	157
7	9125	F	60	64	159
8	5438	F	42	.	.
9	6488	F	59	.	.
10	9012	F	39	.	.
11	9125	F	56	.	.

c.

Obs	ID	Sex	Age	Height	Weight
1	1129	F	48	61	137
2	1387	F	57	64	142
3	2304	F	16	61	102
4	5438	F	42	62	168
5	6488	F	59	64	154
6	9012	F	39	63	157
7	9125	F	56	64	159

d. none of the above

Correct answer: c

The DATA step uses the IN= data set option and the subsetting IF statement to exclude unmatched observations from the output data set. So *a* and *b*, which contain unmatched observations, are incorrect.

7. The data sets **Ensemble.Spring** and **Ensemble.Summer** both contain a variable named Blue. How do you prevent the values of the variable Blue from being overwritten when you merge the two data sets?

   a.
   ```
   data ensemble.merged;
       merge ensemble.spring(in=blue)
             ensemble.summer;
       by fabric;
   run;
   ```

   b.
   ```
   data ensemble.merged;
       merge ensemble.spring(out=blue)
             ensemble.summer;
       by fabric;
   run;
   ```

   c.
   ```
   data ensemble.merged;
       merge ensemble.spring(blue=navy)
             ensemble.summer;
       by fabric;
   run;
   ```

   d.
   ```
   data ensemble.merged;
       merge ensemble.spring(rename=(blue=navy))
             ensemble.summer;
       by fabric;
   run;
   ```

Correct answer: d

Match-merging overwrites same-named variables in the first data set with same-named variables in subsequent data sets. To prevent overwriting, rename variables by using the RENAME= data set option in the MERGE statement.

8. What happens if you submit the following program to merge **Blood.Donors1** and **Blood.Donors2**, shown below?

```
data work.merged;
   merge blood.donors1 blood.donors2;
   by id;
run;
```

Blood.Donors1		
ID	**Type**	**Units**
2304	O	16
1129	A	48
1129	A	50
1129	A	57
2486	B	63

Blood.Donors2		
ID	**Code**	**Units**
6488	65	27
1129	63	32
5438	62	39
2304	61	45
1387	64	67

a. The Merged data set contains some missing values because not all observations have matching observations in the other data set.

b. The Merged data set contains 8 observations.

c. The DATA step produces errors.

d. Values for Units in **Blood.Donors2** overwrite values for Units in **Blood.Donors1**.

Correct answer: c

The two input data sets are not sorted by values of the BY variable, so the DATA step produces errors and stops processing.

9. If you merge **Company.Staff1** and **Company.Staff2** below by ID, how many observations does the new data set contain?

Company.Staff1			
ID	**Name**	**Dept**	**Project**
000	Miguel	A12	Document
111	Fred	B45	Survey
222	Diana	B45	Document
888	Monique	A12	Document
999	Vien	D03	Survey

Company.Staff2		
ID	**Name**	**Hours**
111	Fred	35
222	Diana	40
777	Steve	0
888	Monique	37

a. 4

b. 5

c. 6

d. 9

Correct answer: c

In this example, the new data set contains one observation for each unique value of ID. The merged data set is shown below.

ID	Name	Dept	Project	Hours
000	Miguel	A12	Document	.
111	Fred	B45	Survey	35
222	Diana	B45	Document	40
777	Steve			0
888	Monique	A12	Document	37
999	Vien	D03	Survey	.

10. If you merge data sets **Sales.Reps**, **Sales.Close**, and **Sales.Bonus** by ID, what is the value of Bonus in the third observation in the new data set?

Sales.Reps

ID	Name
1	Nay Rong
2	Kelly Windsor
3	Julio Meraz
4	Richard Krabill

Sales.Close

ID	Sale
1	$28,000
2	$30,000
2	$40,000
3	$15,000
3	$20,000
3	$25,000
4	$35,000

Sales.Bonus

ID	Bonus
1	$2,000
2	$4,000
3	$3,000
4	$2,500

a. *$4,000*

b. *$3,000*

c. missing

d. can't tell from the information given

Correct answer: a

In the new data set, the third observation is the second observation for ID number *2* (*Kelly Windsor*). The value for Bonus is retained from the previous observation because the BY variable value didn't change. The new data set is shown below.

ID	Name	Sale	Bonus
1	Nay Rong	$28,000	$2,000
2	Kelly Windsor	$30,000	$4,000
2	Kelly Windsor	$40,000	$4,000
3	Julio Meraz	$15,000	$3,000
3	Julio Meraz	$20,000	$3,000
3	Julio Meraz	$25,000	$3,000
4	Richard Krabill	$35,000	$2,500

Chapter 14: Transforming Data with SAS Functions Answer Key

1. Which function calculates the average of the variables `Var1`, `Var2`, `Var3`, and `Var4`?

   a. `mean(var1,var4)`

   b. `mean(var1-var4)`

   c. `mean(of var1,var4)`

   d. `mean(of var1-var4)`

   Correct answer: d

   Use a variable list to specify a range of variables as the function argument. When specifying a variable list, be sure to precede the list with the word OF. If you omit the word OF, the function argument might not be interpreted as expected.

2. Within the data set **Hrd.Temp**, `PayRate` is a character variable and `Hours` is a numeric variable. What happens when the following program is run?

   ```
   data work.temp;
      set hrd.temp;
      Salary=payrate*hours;
   run;
   ```

   a. SAS converts the values of `PayRate` to numeric values. No message is written to the log.

   b. SAS converts the values of `PayRate` to numeric values. A message is written to the log.

   c. SAS converts the values of `Hours` to character values. No message is written to the log.

   d. SAS converts the values of `Hours` to character values. A message is written to the log.

   Correct answer: b

   When this DATA step is executed, SAS automatically converts the character values of `PayRate` to numeric values so that the calculation can occur. Whenever data is automatically converted, a message is written to the SAS log stating that the conversion has occurred.

3. A typical value for the character variable `Target` is *123,456*. Which statement correctly converts the values of `Target` to numeric values when creating the variable `TargetNo`?

   a. `TargetNo=input(target,comma6.);`

   b. `TargetNo=input(target,comma7.);`

   c. `TargetNo=put(target,comma6.);`

   d. `TargetNo=put(target,comma7.);`

Correct answer: b

You explicitly convert character values to numeric values by using the INPUT function. Be sure to select an informat that can read the form of the values.

4. A typical value for the numeric variable `SiteNum` is *12.3*. Which statement correctly converts the values of `SiteNum` to character values when creating the variable `Location`?

   a. `Location=dept||'/'||input(sitenum,3.1);`
   b. `Location=dept||'/'||input(sitenum,4.1);`
   c. `Location=dept||'/'||put(sitenum,3.1);`
   d. `Location=dept||'/'||put(sitenum,4.1);`

Correct answer: d

You explicitly convert numeric values to character values by using the PUT function. Be sure to select a format that can read the form of the values.

5. Suppose the YEARCUTOFF= system option is set to 1920. Which MDY function creates the date value for January 3, 2020?

   a. `MDY(1,3,20)`
   b. `MDY(3,1,20)`
   c. `MDY(1,3,2020)`
   d. `MDY(3,1,2020)`

Correct answer: c

Because the YEARCUTOFF= system option is set to 1920, SAS sees the two-digit year value *20* as *1920*. Four-digit year values are always read correctly

6. The variable `Address2` contains values such as *Piscataway, NJ*. How do you assign the two-letter state abbreviations to a new variable named `State`?

   a. `State=scan(address2,2);`
   b. `State=scan(address2,13,2);`
   c. `State=substr(address2,2);`
   d. `State=substr(address2,13,2);`

Correct answer: a

The SCAN function is used to extract words from a character value when you know the order of the words, when their position varies, and when the words are marked by some delimiter. In this case, you don't need to specify delimiters, because the blank and the comma are default delimiters.

7. The variable `IDCode` contains values such as *123FA* and *321MB*. The fourth character identifies sex. How do you assign these character codes to a new variable named `Sex`?

    a. `Sex=scan(idcode,4);`

    b. `Sex=scan(idcode,4,1);`

    c. `Sex=substr(idcode,4);`

    d. `Sex=substr(idcode,4,1);`

Correct answer: d

The SUBSTR function is best used when you know the exact position of the substring to extract from the character value. You specify the position to start from and the number of characters to extract.

8. Due to growth within the 919 area code, the telephone exchange 555 is being reassigned to the 920 area code. The data set **Clients.Piedmont** includes the variable `Phone`, which contains telephone numbers in the form *919-555-1234*. Which of the following programs will correctly change the values of `Phone`?

    a.
    ```
    data work.piedmont(drop=areacode exchange);
        set clients.piedmont;
        Areacode=substr(phone,1,3);
        Exchange=substr(phone,5,3);
        if areacode='919' and exchange='555'
            then scan(phone,1,3)='920';
    run;
    ```

    b.
    ```
    data work.piedmont(drop=areacode exchange);
        set clients.piedmont;
        Areacode=substr(phone,1,3);
        Exchange=substr(phone,5,3);
        if areacode='919' and exchange='555'
            then phone=scan('920',1,3);
    run;
    ```

```
c. data work.piedmont(drop=areacode exchange);
      set clients.piedmont;
      Areacode=substr(phone,1,3);
      Exchange=substr(phone,5,3);
      if areacode='919' and exchange='555'
         then substr(phone,1,3)='920';
   run;
d. data work.piedmont(drop=areacode exchange);
      set clients.piedmont;
      Areacode=substr(phone,1,3);
      Exchange=substr(phone,5,3);
      if areacode='919' and exchange='555'
         then phone=substr('920',1,3);
   run;
```

Correct answer: c

The SUBSTR function replaces variable values if it is placed on the left side of an assignment statement. When placed on the right side (as in **Question 7**), the function extracts a substring.

9. Suppose you need to create the variable `FullName` by concatenating the values of `FirstName`, which contains first names, and `LastName`, which contains last names. What's the best way to remove extra blanks between first names and last names?

```
a. data work.maillist;
      set retail.maillist;
      length FullName $ 40;
      fullname=trim firstname||' '||lastname;
   run;
b. data work.maillist;
      set retail.maillist;
      length FullName $ 40;
      fullname=trim(firstname)||' '||lastname;
   run;
c. data work.maillist;
      set retail.maillist;
      length FullName $ 40;
      fullname=trim(firstname)||' '||trim(lastname);
   run;
d. data work.maillist;
      set retail.maillist;
      length FullName $ 40;
      fullname=trim(firstname||' '||lastname);
   run;
```

Correct answer: b

The TRIM function removes trailing blanks from character values. In this case, extra blanks must be removed from the values of `FirstName`. Although answer *c* also works, the extra TRIM function for the variable `LastName` is unnecessary. Because of the LENGTH statement, all values of `FullName` are padded to 40 characters.

10. Within the data set **Furnitur.Bookcase**, the variable `Finish` contains values such as *ash/cherry/teak/matte-black*. Which of the following creates a subset of the data in which the values of `Finish` contain the string *walnut*? Make the search for the string case-insensitive.

   a.
```
data work.bookcase;
    set furnitur.bookcase;
    if index(finish,walnut) = 0;
run;
```

   b.
```
data work.bookcase;
    set furnitur.bookcase;
    if index(finish,'walnut') > 0;
run;
```

   c.
```
data work.bookcase;
    set furnitur.bookcase;
    if index(lowcase(finish),walnut) = 0;
run;
```

   d.
```
data work.bookcase;
    set furnitur.bookcase;
    if index(lowcase(finish),'walnut') > 0;
run;
```

Correct answer: d

Use the INDEX function in a subsetting IF statement, enclosing the character string in quotation marks. Only those observations in which the function locates the string and returns a value greater than *0* are written to the data set.

Chapter 15: Generating Data with DO Loops Answer Key

1. Which statement is **false** regarding the use of DO loops?

   a. They can contain conditional clauses.

   b. They can generate multiple observations.

   c. They can be used to combine DATA and PROC steps.

   d. They can be used to read data.

   Correct answer: c

   DO loops are DATA step statements and cannot be used in conjunction with PROC steps.

2. During each execution of the following DO loop, the value of `Earned` is calculated and is added to its previous value. How many times does this DO loop execute?

   ```
   data finance.earnings;
      Amount=1000;
      Rate=.075/12;
      do month=1 to 12;
         Earned+(amount+earned)*rate;
      end;
   run;
   ```

   a. 0

   b. 1

   c. 12

   d. 13

   Correct answer: c

   The number of iterations is determined by the DO statement's stop value, which in this case is 12.

3. On January 1 of each year, $5,000 is invested in an account. Complete the DATA step below to determine the value of the account after 15 years if a constant interest rate of 10% is expected.

   ```
   data work.invest;
      ...
         Capital+5000;
         capital+(capital*.10);
      end;
   run;
   ```

   a. `do count=1 to 15;`

   b. `do count=1 to 15 by 10%;`

   c. `do count=1 to capital;`

   d. `do count=capital to (capital*.10);`

Correct answer: a

Use a DO loop to perform repetitive calculations starting at 1 and looping 15 times.

4. In the data set **Work.Invest**, what would be the stored value for `Year`?

```
data work.invest;
   do year=1990 to 2004;
      Capital+5000;
      capital+(capital*.10);
   end;
 run;
```

   a. missing

   b. *1990*

   c. *2004*

   d. *2005*

Correct answer: d

At the end of the fifteenth iteration of the DO loop, the value for `Year` is incremented to *2005*. Because this value exceeds the stop value, the DO loop ends. At the bottom of the DATA step, the current values are written to the data set.

5. Which of the following statements is **false** regarding the program shown below?

```
data work.invest;
   do year=1990 to 2004;
      Capital+5000;
      capital+(capital*.10);
      output;
   end;
 run;
```

   a. The OUTPUT statement writes current values to the data set immediately.

   b. The stored value for Year is *2005*.

   c. The OUTPUT statement overrides the automatic output at the end of the DATA step.

   d. The DO loop performs 15 iterations.

Correct answer: b

The OUTPUT statement overrides the automatic output at the end of the DATA step. On the last iteration of the DO loop, the value of `Year`, *2004*, is written to the data set.

6. How many observations will the data set **Work.Earn** contain?

```
data work.earn;
   Value=2000;
   do year=1 to 20;
      Interest=value*.075;
      value+interest;
      output;
   end;
run;
```

 a. 0

 b. 1

 c. 19

 d. 20

Correct answer: d

The number of observations is based on the number of times the OUTPUT statement executes. The new data set has 20 observations, one for each iteration of the DO loop.

7. Which of the following would you use to compare the result of investing $4,000 a year for five years in three different banks that compound interest monthly? Assume a fixed rate for the five-year period.

 a. DO WHILE statement

 b. nested DO loops

 c. DO UNTIL statement

 d. a DO group

Correct answer: b

Place the monthly calculation in a DO loop within a DO loop that iterates once for each year. The DO WHILE and DO UNTIL statements are not used here because the number of required iterations is fixed. A non-iterative DO group would not be useful.

8. Which statement is **false** regarding DO UNTIL statements?

 a. The condition is evaluated at the top of the loop, before the enclosed statements are executed.

 b. The enclosed statements are always executed at least once.

 c. SAS statements in the DO loop are executed until the specified condition is true.

 d. The DO loop must have a closing END statement.

Correct answer: a

The DO UNTIL condition is evaluated at the bottom of the loop, so the enclosed statements are always executed at least once.

9. Select the DO WHILE statement that would generate the same result as the program below.

```
data work.invest
capital=100000
   do until(Capital gt 500000);
      Year+1;
      capital+(capital*.10);
   end;
run;
```

a. do while(Capital ge 500000);

b. do while(Capital=500000);

c. do while(Capital le 500000);

d. do while(Capital>500000);

Correct answer: c

Because the DO WHILE loop is evaluated at the top of the loop, you specify the condition that must exist in order to execute the enclosed statements.

10. In the following program, complete the statement so that the program stops generating observations when Distance reaches 250 miles or when 10 gallons of fuel have been used.

```
data work.go250;
   set perm.cars;
   do gallons=1 to 10 ... ;
      Distance=gallons*mpg;
      output;
   end;
run;
```

a. while(Distance<250)

b. when(Distance>250)

c. over(Distance le 250)

d. until(Distance=250)

Correct answer: a

The WHILE expression causes the DO loop to stop executing when the value of *Distance* becomes equal to or greater than 250.

Chapter 16: Processing Variables with Arrays Answer Key

1. Which statement is **false** regarding an ARRAY statement?

    a. It is an executable statement.
    b. It can be used to create variables.
    c. It must contain either all numeric or all character elements.
    d. It must be used to define an array before the array name can be referenced.

Correct answer: a

An ARRAY statement is not an executable statement; it merely defines an array.

2. What belongs within the braces of this ARRAY statement?
    ```
    array contrib{?} qtr1-qtr4;
    ```

    a. quarter
    b. quarter*
    c. 1-4
    d. 4

Correct answer: d

The value in braces indicates the number of elements in the array. In this case, there are four elements.

3. For the program below, select an iterative DO statement to process all elements in the `contrib` array.
    ```
    data work.contrib;
       array contrib{4} qtr1-qtr4;
          . . .
            contrib{i}=contrib{i}*1.25;
       end;
    run;
    ```

    a. do i=4;
    b. do i=1 to 4;
    c. do until i=4;
    d. do while i le 4;

Correct answer: b

In the DO statement, you specify the index variable that represents the values of the array elements. Then specify the start and stop positions of the array elements.

4. What is the value of the index variable that references `Jul` in the statements below?

```
array quarter{4} Jan Apr Jul Oct;
do i=1 to 4;
    yeargoal=quarter{i}*1.2;
end;
```

    a. 1

    b. 2

    c. 3

    d. 4

Correct answer: c

The index value represents the position of the array element. In this case, the third element is `Jul`.

5. Which DO statement would **not** process all the elements in the `factors` array shown below?

```
array factors{*} age height weight bloodpr;
```

    a. `do i=1 to dim(factors);`

    b. `do i=1 to dim(*);`

    c. `do i=1,2,3,4;`

    d. `do i=1 to 4;`

Correct answer: b

To process all the elements in an array, you can either specify the array dimension or use the DIM function with the array name as the argument.

6. Which statement below is **false** regarding the use of arrays to create variables?

    a. The variables are added to the program data vector during the compilation of the DATA step.

    b. You do not need to specify the array elements in the ARRAY statement.

    c. By default, all character variables are assigned a length of eight.

    d. Only character variables can be created.

Correct answer: d

Either numeric or character variables can be created by an ARRAY statement.

7. For the first observation, what is the value of diff{i} at the end of the **second** iteration of the DO loop?

Weight1	Weight2	Weight3
192	200	215
137	130	125
220	210	213

```
array wt{*} weight1-weight10;
array diff{9};
do i=1 to 9;
   diff{i}=wt{i+1}-wt{i};
end;
```

   a. 15
   b. 10
   c. 8
   d. -7

Correct answer: a

At the end of the second iteration, diff{i} resolves as follows:

```
diff{2}=wt{2+1}-wt{2};
diff{2}=215-200
```

8. Finish the ARRAY statement below to create temporary array elements that have initial values of *9000, 9300, 9600,* and *9900*.

```
   array goal{4} ... ;
```

   a. _temporary_ (9000 9300 9600 9900)
   b. temporary (9000 9300 9600 9900)
   c. _temporary_ 9000 9300 9600 9900
   d. (temporary) 9000 9300 9600 9900

Correct answer: a

To create temporary array elements, specify _TEMPORARY_ after the array name and dimension. Specify an initial value for each element, separated by either blanks or commas, and enclose the values in parentheses.

9. Based on the ARRAY statement below, select the array reference for the array element q50.

   ```
   array ques{3,25} q1-q75;
   ```

   a. ques{q50}
   b. ques{1,50}
   c. ques{2,25}
   d. ques{3,0}

   Correct answer: c

   This two-dimensional array would consist of three rows of 25 elements. The first row would contain q1 through q25, the second row would start with q26 and end with q50, and the third row would start with q51 and end with q75.

10. Select the ARRAY statement that defines the array in the following program.

    ```
    data rainwear.coat;
       input category high1-high3 / low1-low3;
       ...
       do i=1 to 2;
          do j=1 to 3;
             compare{i,j}=round(compare{i,j}*1.12);
          end;
       end;
    run;
    ```

    a. array compare{1,6} high1-high3 low1-low3;
    b. array compare{2,3} high1-high3 low1-low3;
    c. array compare{3,2} high1-high3 low1-low3;
    d. array compare{3,3} high1-high3 low1-low3;

    Correct answer: b

    The nested DO loops indicate that the array is named compare and is a two-dimensional array that has two rows and three columns.

1. Which SAS statement correctly uses column input to read the values in the raw data file below in this order: Address (4th field), SquareFeet (second field), Style (first field), Bedrooms (third field)?

```
1---+----10---+----20---+----30
2STORY 1810 4 SHEPPARD AVENUE
CONDO  1200 2 RAND STREET
RANCH  1550 3 MARKET STREET
```

  a. input Address 15-29 SquareFeet 8-11 Style 1-6
        Bedrooms 13;

  b. input $ 15-29 Address 8-11 SquareFeet $ 1-6 Style
        13 Bedrooms;

  c. input Address $ 15-29 SquareFeet 8-11 Style $ 1-6
        Bedrooms 13;

  d. input Address 15-29 $ SquareFeet 8-11 Style 1-6
        $ Bedrooms 13;

Correct answer: c

Column input specifies the variable's name, followed by a dollar ($) sign if the values are character values, and the beginning and ending column locations of the raw data values.

2. Which is **not** an advantage of column input?

  a. It can be used to read character variables that contain embedded blanks.
  b. No placeholder is required for missing data.
  c. Standard as well as nonstandard data values can be read.
  d. Fields do not have to be separated by blanks or other delimiters.

Correct answer: c

Column input is useful for reading standard values only.

3. Which is an example of standard numeric data?

  a. -34.245
  b. $24,234.25
  c. 1/2
  d. 50%

Correct answer: a

A standard numeric value can contain numbers, scientific notation, decimal points, and plus and minus signs. Nonstandard numeric data includes values that contain fractions or special characters such as commas, dollar signs, and percent signs.

4. Formatted input can be used to read

   a. standard free-format data
   b. standard data in fixed fields
   c. nonstandard data in fixed fields
   d. both standard and nonstandard data in fixed fields

Correct answer: d

Formatted input can be used to read both standard and nonstandard data in fixed fields.

5. Which informat should you use to read the values in column 1-5?

```
1---+----10---+----20---+----30
DG345 CD PLAYER    $174.99
HJ756 VCR          $298.99
AS658 CAMCORDER $1,195.99
```

   a. *w.*
   b. *$w.*
   c. *w.d*
   d. COMMA*w.d*

Correct answer: b

The *$w.* informat enables you to read character data. The *w* represents the field width of the data value or the total number of columns that contain the raw data field.

6. The COMMA*w.d* informat can be used to read which of the following values?

   a. *12,805*
   b. *$177.95*
   c. *18 %*
   d. all of the above

Correct answer: d

The COMMA*w.d* informat strips out special characters such as commas, dollar signs, and percent signs from numeric data, and stores only numeric values in a SAS data set.

7. Which INPUT statement correctly reads the values for `ModelNumber` (first field) after the values for `Item` (second field)? Both `Item` and `ModelNumber` are character variables.

```
1---+----10---+----20---+----30
DG345 CD PLAYER    $174.99
HJ756 VCR          $298.99
AS658 CAMCORDER $1,195.99
```

   a. input +7 Item $9. @1 ModelNumber $5.;

   b. input +6 Item $9. @1 ModelNumber $5.;

   c. input @7 Item $9. +1 ModelNumber $5.;

   d. input @7 Item $9 @1 ModelNumber 5.;

Correct answer: b

The +6 pointer control moves the input pointer to the beginning column of `Item`, and the values are read. Then the @1 pointer control returns to column 1, where the values for `ModelNumber` are located.

8. Which INPUT statement correctly reads the numeric values for `Cost` (third field)?

```
1---+----10---+----20---+----30
DG345 CD PLAYER    $174.99
HJ756 VCR          $298.99
AS658 CAMCORDER $1,195.99
```

   a. input @17 Cost 7.2;

   b. input @17 Cost 9.2.;

   c. input @17 Cost comma7.;

   d. input @17 Cost comma9.;

Correct answer: d

The values for `Cost` contain dollar signs and commas, so you must use the COMMA*w.d* informat. Counting the numbers, dollar sign, comma, and decimal point, the field width is 9 columns. Because the data value contains decimal places, a *d* value is not needed.

9. Which SAS statement correctly uses formatted input to read the values in this order: Item (first field), UnitCost (second field), Quantity (third field)?

```
1---+----10---+----20---+
ENVELOPE  $13.25 500
DISKETTES $29.50  10
BANDS      $2.50 600
RIBBON    $94.20  12
```

a. input @1 Item $9. +1 UnitCost comma6.
        @18 Quantity 3.;

b. input Item $9. @11 UnitCost comma6.
        @18 Quantity 3.;

c. input Item $9. +1 UnitCost comma6.
        @18 Quantity 3.;

d. all of the above

Correct answer: d

The default location of the column pointer control is column 1, so a column pointer control is optional for reading the first field. You can use the @*n* or +*n* pointer controls to specify the beginning column of the other fields. You can use the $*w*. informat to read the values for Item, the COMMA*w.d* informat for UnitCost, and the *w.d* informat for Quantity.

10. Which raw data file requires the PAD option in the INFILE statement in order to correctly read the data using either column input or formatted input?

a.
```
1---+----10---+----20---+
JONES     M 48 128.6
LAVERNE   M 58 158
JAFFE     F 33 115.5
WILSON    M 28 130
```

b.
```
1---+----10---+----20---+
JONES     M 48 128.6
LAVERNE   M 58 158.0
JAFFE     F 33 115.5
WILSON    M 28 130.0
```

c.
```
1---+----10---+----20---+
JONES     M 48 128.6
LAVERNE   M 58    158
JAFFE     F 33 115.5
WILSON    M 28    130
```

d.

```
1---+----10---+----20---+
   JONES    M 48 128.6
LAVERNE    M 58 158.0
   JAFFE    F 33 115.5
 WILSON    M 28 130.0
```

Correct answer: a

Use the PAD option in the INFILE statement to read variable-length records that contain fixed-field data. The PAD option pads each record with blanks so that all data lines have the same length.

Chapter 18: Reading Free-Format Data Answer Key

1. The raw data file referenced by the fileref **Students** contains data that is

    Raw Data File Students

    ```
    1---+----10---+----20---+
    FRED JOHNSON 18 USC 1
    ASHLEY FERRIS 20 NCSU 3
    BETH ROSEMONT 21 UNC 4
    ```

    a. arranged in fixed fields
    b. free format
    c. mixed format
    d. arranged in columns

    Correct answer: b

    The raw data file contains data that is free format, meaning that the data is not arranged in columns or fixed fields.

2. Which input style should be used to read the values in the raw data file that is referenced by the fileref **Students**?

    Raw Data File Students

    ```
    1---+----10---+----20---+
    FRED JOHNSON 18 USC 1
    ASHLEY FERRIS 20 NCSU 3
    BETH ROSEMONT 21 UNC 4
    ```

    a. column
    b. formatted
    c. list
    d. mixed

    Correct answer: c

    List input should be used to read data that is free format because you do not need to specify the column locations of the data.

3. Which SAS program was used to create the raw data file **Teamdat** from the SAS data set **Work.Scores**?

SAS Data Set Work.Scores

Obs	Name	HighScore	Team
1	Joe	87	Blue Beetles, Durham
2	Dani	79	Raleigh Racers, Raleigh
3	Lisa	85	Sand Sharks, Cary
4	Matthew	76	Blue Beetles, Durham

Raw Data File Teamdat

```
1---+----10---+----20---+----30---+
Joe,87,"Blue Beetles, Durham"
Dani,79,"Raleigh Racers, Raleigh"
Lisa,85,"Sand Sharks, Cary"
Matthew,76,"Blue Beetles, Durham"
```

a.
```
data _null_;
    set work.scores;
    file 'c:\data\teamdat' dlm=',';
    put name highscore team;
run;
```

b.
```
data _null_;
    set work.scores;
    file 'c:\data\teamdat' dlm=' ';
    put name highscore team;
run;
```

c.
```
data _null_;
    set work.scores;
    file 'c:\data\teamdat' dsd;
    put name highscore team;
run;
```

d.
```
data _null_;
    set work.scores;
    file 'c:\data\teamdat';
    put name highscore team;
run;
```

Correct answer: c

You can use the DSD option in the FILE statement to specify that data values containing commas should be enclosed in quotation marks. The DSD option uses a comma as the delimiter by default.

4. Which SAS statement reads the raw data values in order and assigns them to the variables shown below?

   Variables: `FirstName` (character), `LastName` (character), `Age` (numeric), `School` (character), `Class` (numeric)

   Raw Data File Students

   ```
   1---+----10---+----20---+
   FRED JOHNSON 18 USC 1
   ASHLEY FERRIS 20 NCSU 3
   BETH ROSEMONT 21 UNC 4
   ```

   a. `input FirstName $ LastName $ Age School $ Class;`

   b. `input FirstName LastName Age School Class;`

   c. `input FirstName $ 1-4 LastName $ 6-12 Age 14-15`
      `School $ 17-19 Class 21;`

   d. `input FirstName 1-4 LastName 6-12 Age 14-15`
      `School 17-19 Class 21;`

   Correct answer: a

   Because the data is free format, list input is used to read the values. With list input, you simply name each variable and identify its type.

5. Which SAS statement should be used to read the raw data file that is referenced by the fileref **Salesrep**?

   Raw Data File Salesrep

   ```
   1---+----10---+----20---+----30
   ELAINE:FRIEDMAN:WILMINGTON:2102
   JIM:LLOYD:20:RALEIGH:38392
   JENNIFER:WU:21:GREENSBORO:1436
   ```

   a. `infile salesrep;`
   b. `infile salesrep ':';`
   c. `infile salesrep dlm;`
   d. `infile salesrep dlm=':';`

   Correct answer: d

   The INFILE statement identifies the location of the external data file. The DLM= option specifies the colon (:) as the delimiter that separates each field.

6. Which of the following raw data files can be read by using the MISSOVER option in the INFILE statement? Missing values are indicated with colored blocks.

a.
```
1---+----10---+----20---+----
ORANGE SUNNYDALE 20 10
PINEAPPLE ALOHA 7 10
GRAPE FARMFRESH 3  ▓
APPLE FARMFRESH 16 5
GRAPEFRUIT SUNNYDALE 12 8
```

b.
```
1---+----10---+----20---+----
ORANGE SUNNYDALE 20 10
PINEAPPLE ALOHA 7 10
GRAPE FARMFRESH ▓  17
APPLE FARMFRESH 16 5
GRAPEFRUIT SUNNYDALE 12 8
```

c.
```
1---+----10---+----20---+----
ORANGE SUNNYDALE 20 10
PINEAPPLE ALOHA 7 10
GRAPE ▓▓▓▓▓▓ 3 17
APPLE FARMFRESH 16 5
GRAPEFRUIT SUNNYDALE 12 8
```

d.
```
1---+----10---+----20---+----
ORANGE SUNNYDALE 20 10
PINEAPPLE ALOHA 7 10
▓▓▓▓ FARMFRESH 3
APPLE FARMFRESH 16 5
GRAPEFRUIT SUNNYDALE 12 8
```

Correct answer: a

You can use the MISSOVER option in the INFILE statement to read the missing values at the end of a record. The MISSOVER option prevents SAS from moving to the next record if values are missing in the current record.

7. Which SAS program correctly reads the data in the raw data file that is referenced by the fileref **Volunteer**?

Raw Data File Volunteer

```
1---+----10---+----20---+----30
ARLENE BIGGERSTAFF 19 UNC 2
JOSEPH CONSTANTINO 21 CLEM 2
MARTIN FIELDS 18 UNCG 1
```

a. ```
data perm.contest;
    infile volunteer;
    input FirstName $ LastName $ Age School $ Class;
run;
```

b. ```
data perm.contest;
    infile volunteer;
    length LastName $ 11;
    input FirstName $ lastname $ Age School $ Class;
run;
```

c. ```
data perm.contest;
    infile volunteer;
    input FirstName $ lastname $ Age School $ Class;
    length LastName $ 11;
run;
```

d. ```
data perm.contest;
    infile volunteer;
    input FirstName $ LastName $ 11. Age School $ Class;
run;
```

Correct answer: b

The LENGTH statement extends the length of the character variable `LastName` so that it is large enough to accommodate the data. Variable attributes such as length are defined the first time a variable is named in a DATA step. The LENGTH statement should precede the INPUT statement so that the correct length is defined.

8. Which type of input should be used to read the values in the raw data file that is referenced by the fileref **University**?

Raw Data File University

```
1---+----10---+----20---+----30
UNC ASHEVILLE  2,712
UNC CHAPEL HILL  24,189
UNC CHARLOTTE  15,031
UNC GREENSBORO  2,323
```

   a. column
   b. formatted
   c. list
   d. modified list

Correct answer: d

Notice that the values for School contain embedded blanks, and the values for Enrolled are nonstandard numeric values. Modified list input can be used to read the values that contain embedded blanks and nonstandard values.

9. Which SAS statement correctly reads the values for Flavor and Quantity? Make sure the length of each variable can accommodate the values that are shown.

Raw Data File Cookies

```
1---+----10---+----20---+----30
CHOCOLATE CHIP  10,453
OATMEAL  12,187
PEANUT BUTTER  11,546
SUGAR  12,331
```

   a. input Flavor & $9. Quantity : comma.;
   b. input Flavor & $14. Quantity : comma.;
   c. input Flavor : $14. Quantity & comma.;
   d. input Flavor $14. Quantity : comma.;

Correct answer: b

The INPUT statement uses list input with format modifiers and informats to read the values for each variable. The ampersand (&) modifier enables you to read character values that contain single embedded blanks. The colon (:) modifier enables you to read nonstandard data values and character values that are longer than eight characters, and that contain no embedded blanks.

10. Which SAS statement correctly reads the raw data values in order and assigns them to these corresponding variables: `Year` (numeric), `School` (character), `Enrolled` (numeric)?

Raw Data File Founding

```
1---+----10---+----20---+----30---+----40
1868 U OF CALIFORNIA BERKELEY  31,612
1906 U OF CALIFORNIA DAVIS  21,838
1965 U OF CALIFORNIA IRVINE  15,874
1919 U OF CALIFORNIA LOS ANGELES  35,730
```

a. `input Year School & $27.`
`        Enrolled : comma.;`

b. `input Year 1-4 School & $27.`
`        Enrolled : comma.;`

c. `input @1 Year 4. +1 School & $27.`
`        Enrolled : comma.;`

d. all of the above

Correct answer: d

The values for `Year` can be read with column, formatted, or list input. However, the values for `School` and `Enrolled` are free-format data that contain embedded blanks or nonstandard values. Therefore, these last two variables must be read with modified list input.

Chapter 19: Reading Date and Time Values Answer Key

1. SAS date values are the number of days since which date?

   a. January 1, 1900
   b. January 1, 1950
   c. January 1, 1960
   d. January 1, 1970

   Correct answer: c

   A SAS date value is the number of days from January 1, 1960, to the given date.

2. A great advantage of storing dates and times as SAS numeric date and time values is that

   a. they can easily be edited.
   b. they can easily be read and understood.
   c. they can be used in text strings like other character values.
   d. they can be used in calculations like other numeric values.

   Correct answer: d

   In addition to tracking time intervals, SAS date and time values can be used in calculations like other numeric values. This lets you calculate values that involve dates much more easily than in other programming languages.

3. SAS does not automatically make adjustments for daylight saving time, but it **does** make adjustments for:

   a. leap seconds
   b. leap years
   c. Julian dates
   d. time zones

   Correct answer: b

   SAS automatically makes adjustments for leap years.

4. An input data file has date expressions in the form 10222001. Which SAS informat should you use to read these dates?

    a. DATE6.
    b. DATE8.
    c. MMDDYY6.
    d. MMDDYY8.

Correct answer: d

The SAS informat MMDDYY*w*. reads dates such as 10222001, 10/22/01, or 10-22-01. In this case, the field width is eight.

5. The minimum width of the TIME*w*. informat is

    a. 4
    b. 5
    c. 6
    d. 7

Correct answer: b

The minimum acceptable field width for the TIME*w*. informat is five. If you specify a *w* value less than five, you will receive an error message in the SAS log.

6. Shown below are date and time expressions and corresponding SAS datetime informats. Which date and time expresssion **cannot** be read by the informat that is shown beside it?

    a. 30May2000:10:03:17.2 DATETIME20.
    b. 30May00 10:03:17.2 DATETIME18.
    c. 30May2000/10:03 DATETIME15.
    d. 30May2000/1003 DATETIME14.

Correct answer: d

In the time value of a date and time expression, you must use delimiters to separate the values for hour, minutes, and seconds.

7. What is the default value of the YEARCUTOFF= system option?

   a. 1920

   b. 1910

   c. 1900

   d. 1930

   Correct answer: a

   The default value of YEARCUTOFF= is 1920. This enables you to read two-digit years from 00-19 as the years 2000 through 2019.

8. Suppose your input data file contains the date expression *13APR2009*. The YEARCUTOFF= system option is set to 1910. SAS will read the date as

   a. 13APR1909

   b. 13APR1920

   c. 13APR2009

   d. 13APR2020

   Correct answer: c

   The value of the YEARCUTOFF= system option does not affect four-digit year values. Four-digit values are always read correctly.

9. Suppose the YEARCUTOFF= system option is set to 1920. An input file contains the date expression *12/08/1925*, which is being read with the MMDDYY8. informat. Which date will appear in your data?

   a. 08DEC1920

   b. 08DEC1925

   c. 08DEC2019

   d. 08DEC2025

   Correct answer: c

   The *w* value of the informat MMDDYY8. is too small to read the entire value, so the last two digits of the year are truncated. The last two digits thus become 19 instead of 25. Because the YEARCUTOFF= system option is set to 1920, SAS interprets this year as 2019. To avoid such errors, be sure to specify an informat that is wide enough for your date expressions.

10. Suppose your program creates two variables from an input file. Both variables are stored as SAS date values: FirstDay records the start of a billing cycle, and LastDay records the end of that cycle. The code for calculating the total number of days in the cycle would be

   a. `TotDays=lastday-firstday;`

   b. `TotDays=lastday-firstday+1;`

   c. `TotDays=lastday/firstday;`

   d. You cannot use date values in calculations.

Correct answer: b

To find the number of days spanned by two dates, subtract the first day from the last day and add one. Because SAS date values are numeric values, they can easily be used in calculations.

Chapter 20: Creating a Single Observation from Multiple Records
Answer Key

1. You can position the input pointer on a specific record by using

   a. column pointer controls.
   b. column specifications.
   c. line pointer controls.
   d. line hold specifiers.

   Correct answer: c

   Information for one observation can be spread out over several records. You can write one INPUT statement that contains line pointer controls to specify the records from which values are read.

2. Which pointer control is used to read multiple records sequentially?

   a. @*n*
   b. +*n*
   c. /
   d. all of the above

   Correct answer: c

   The forward slash (/) line pointer control is used to read multiple records sequentially. Each time a / pointer is encountered, the input pointer advances to the next line. @*n* and +*n* are column pointer controls.

3. Which pointer control can be used to read records non-sequentially?

   a. @*n*
   b. #*n*
   c. +*n*
   d. /

   Correct answer: b

   The #*n* line pointer control is used to read records non-sequentially. The #*n* specifies the absolute number of the line to which you want to move the pointer.

4. Which SAS statement correctly reads the values for Fname, Lname, Address, City, State, and Zip in order?

```
1---+----10---+----20---
LAWRENCE CALDWELL
1010 LAKE STREET
ANAHEIM CA 94122
RACHEL CHEVONT
3719 OLIVE VIEW ROAD
HARTFORD CT 06183
```

a. input Fname $ Lname $ /
         Address $20. /
         City $ State $ Zip $;

b. input Fname $ Lname $ /;
         Address $20. /;
         City $ State $ Zip $;

c. input / Fname $ Lname $
         / Address $20.
         City $ State $ Zip $;

d. input / Fname $ Lname $;
         / Address $20.;
         City $ State $ Zip $;

Correct answer: a

The INPUT statement uses the / line pointer control to move the input pointer forward from the first record to the second record, and from the second record to the third record. The / line pointer control only moves the input pointer forward and must be specified after the instructions for reading the values in the current record. You should place a semicolon only at the end of a complete INPUT statement.

5. Which INPUT statement correctly reads the values for ID in the fourth record, then returns to the first record to read the values for Fname and Lname?

```
1---+----10---+----20---
GEORGE CHESSON
3801 WOODSIDE COURT
GARNER NC 27529
XM065 FLOYD
JAMES COLDWELL
123-A TARBERT
APEX NC 27529
XMO65 LAWSON
```

a. ```
input #4 ID $5.
      #1 Fname $ Lname $;
```

b. ```
input #4 ID $ 1-5
      #1 Fname $ Lname $;
```

c. ```
input #4 ID $
      #1 Fname $ Lname $;
```

d. all of the above

**Correct answer: d**

The first #*n* line pointer control enables you to read the values for ID from the fourth record. The second #*n* line pointer control moves back to the first record and reads the values for Fname and Lname. You can use formatted input, column input, or list input to read the values for ID.

6. How many records will be read for each iteration of the DATA step?

```
1---+----10---+----20---
SKIRT BLACK
COTTON
036499 $44.98
SKIRT NAVY
LINEN
036899 $51.50
DRESS RED
SILK
037299 $76.98
```

```
data spring.sportswr;
   infile newitems;
   input #1 Item $ Color $
         #3 @8 Price comma6.
         #2 Fabric $
         #3 SKU $ 1-6;
run;
```

a. one

b. two

c. three

d. four

Correct answer: c

The first time the DATA step executes, the first three records are read, and an observation is written to the data set. During the second iteration, the next three records are read, and the second observation is written to the data set. During the third iteration, the last three records are read, and the final observation is written to the data set.
```

7. Which INPUT statement correctly reads the values for `City`, `State`, and `Zip`?

    ```
    1---+----10---+----20---
    DINA FIELDS
    904 MAPLE CIRCLE
    DURHAM NC 27713
    ELIZABETH GARRISON
    1293 OAK AVENUE
    CHAPEL HILL NC 27614
    DAVID HARRINGTON
    2426 ELMWOOD LANE
    RALEIGH NC 27803
    ```

    a. `input #3 City $ State $ Zip $;`
    b. `input #3 City & $11. State $ Zip $;`
    c. `input #3 City $11. +2 State $2. + 2 Zip $5.;`
    d. all of the above

    Correct answer: b

    A combination of modified and simple list input can be used to read the values for `City`, `State`, and `Zip`. You need to use modified list input to read the values for `City`, because one of the values is longer than eight characters and contains an embedded blank. You cannot use formatted input, because the values do not begin and end in the same column in each record.

8. Which program does **not** read the values in the first record as a variable named `Item` and the values in the second record as two variables named `Inventory` and `Type`?

    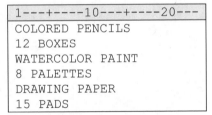

    ```
    1---+----10---+----20---
    COLORED PENCILS
    12 BOXES
    WATERCOLOR PAINT
    8 PALETTES
    DRAWING PAPER
    15 PADS
    ```

a.
```
data perm.supplies;
    infile instock pad;
    input Item & $16. /
          Inventory 2. Type $8.;
run;
```
b.
```
data perm.supplies;
    infile instock pad;
    input Item & $16.
              / Inventory 2. Type $8.;
run;
```
c.
```
data perm.supplies;
    infile instock pad;
    input #1 Item & $16.
          Inventory 2. Type $8.;
run;
```
d.
```
data perm.supplies;
    infile instock pad;
    input Item & $16.
          #2 Inventory 2. Type $8.;
run;
```

Correct answer: c

The values for `Item` in the first record are read, then the following / or #*n* line pointer control advances the input pointer to the second record to read the values for `Inventory` and `Type`.

9. Which INPUT statement reads the values for `Lname`, `Fname`, `Department`, and `Salary` (in that order)?

```
1---+-----10---+-----20---
ABRAMS THOMAS
SALES $25,209.03
BARCLAY ROBERT
MARKETING $29,180.36
COURTNEY MARK
PUBLICATIONS $24,006.16
```

a.
```
input #1 Lname $ Fname $ /
      Department $12. Salary comma10.;
```
b.
```
input #1 Lname $ Fname $ /
      Department : $12. Salary : comma.;
```
c.
```
input #1 Lname $ Fname $
      #2 Department : $12. Salary : comma.;
```
d. both *b* and *c*

Correct answer: d

You can use either the / or #*n* line pointer control to advance the input pointer to the second line, in order to read the values for `Department` and `Salary`. The colon (:) modifier is used to read the character values that are longer than eight characters (`Department`) and the nonstandard data values (`Salary`).

10. Which raw data file poses potential problems when you are reading multiple records for each observation?

a.
```
1---+----10---+----20---
LAWRENCE CALDWELL
1010 LAKE STREET
ANAHEIM CA 94122
RACHEL CHEVONT
3719 OLIVE VIEW ROAD
HARTFORD CT 06183
```

b.
```
1---+----10---+----20---
SHIRT LT BLUE SOLID
SKU 128699
$38.99
SHIRT DK BLUE STRIPE
SKU 128799
$41.99
```

c.
```
1---+----10---+----20---
MARCUS JONES
SR01 $26,134.00
MARY ROBERTSON
COURTNEY NEILS
TWO1 $28,342.00
```

d.
```
1---+----10---+----20---
CROCUS MIX
10 CASES
DAFFODIL
12 CASES
HYACINTH BLUE
8 BAGS
```

Correct answer: c

The third raw data file does not contain the same number of records for each observation, so the output from this data set will show invalid data for the ID and salary information in the fourth line.

1. Which is true for the double trailing at sign (@@)?

    a. It enables the next INPUT statement to read from the current record across multiple iterations of the DATA step.
    b. It must be the last item that is specified in the INPUT statement.
    c. It is released when the input pointer moves past the end of the record.
    d. All of the above.

    Correct answer: d

    The double trailing at sign (@@) enables the next INPUT statement to read from the current record across multiple iterations of the DATA step. It must be the last item that is specified in the INPUT statement. A record that is being held by the double trailing at sign (@@) is not released until the input pointer moves past the end of the record, or until an INPUT statement that has no line-hold specifier executes.

2. A record that is being held by a single trailing at sign (@) is automatically released when

    a. the input pointer moves past the end of the record.
    b. the next iteration of the DATA step begins.
    c. another INPUT statement that has a single trailing at sign (@) executes.
    d. another value is read from the observation.

    Correct answer: b

    Unlike the double trailing at sign (@@), the single trailing at sign (@) is automatically released when control returns to the top of the DATA step for the next iteration. The trailing @ does not toggle on and off. If another INPUT statement that has a trailing @ executes, the holding effect is still on.

3. Which SAS program correctly creates a separate observation for each block of data?

```
1---+----10---+----20---+----30---+----40---+
1001 apple 1002 banana 1003 cherry
1004 guava 1005 kiwi 1006 papaya
1007 pineapple 1008 raspberry 1009 strawberry
```

a.
```
data perm.produce;
    infile fruit;
    input Item $4. Variety : $10.;
run;
```

b.
```
data perm.produce;
    infile fruit;
    input Item $4. Variety : $10. @;
run;
```

c.
```
data perm.produce;
    infile fruit;
    input Item $ Variety : $10. @@;
run;
```

d.
```
data perm.produce;
    infile fruit @@;
    input Item $. Variety : $10.;
run;
```

Correct answer: c

Each record in this file contains three repeating blocks of data values for `Item` and `Variety`. The INPUT statement reads a block of values for `Item` and `Variety`, and then holds the current record by using the double trailing at sign (@@). The values in the program data vector are written to the data set as the first observation. In the next iteration, the INPUT statement reads the next block of values for `Item` and `Variety` from the same record.

4. Which SAS program segment reads the values for ID and holds the record for each value of `Quantity`, so that three observations are created for each record?

```
1---+----10---+----20---+----30
2101 21,208 19,047 22,890
2102 18,775 20,214 22,654
2103 19,763 22,927 21,862
```

a.
```
data work.sales;
    infile unitsold;
    input ID $;
    do week=1 to 3;
        input Quantity : comma.;
        output;
    end;
run;
```

b.
```
data work.sales;
    infile unitsold;
    input ID $ @@;
    do week=1 to 3;
        input Quantity : comma.;
        output;
    end;
run;
```

c.
```
data work.sales;
    infile unitsold;
    input ID $ @;
    do week=1 to 3;
        input Quantity : comma.;
        output;
    end;
run;
```

d.
```
data work.sales;
    infile unitsold;
    input ID $ @;
    do week=1 to 3;
        input Quantity : comma. @;
        output;
    end;
run;
```

Correct answer: d

This raw data file contains an ID fieldthat is followed by repeating fields. The first INPUT statement reads the values for ID and uses the @ line-hold specifier to hold the current record for the next INPUT statement in the DATA step. The second INPUT statement reads the values for Quantity. When all of the repeating fields have been read, control returns to the top of the DATA step, and the record is released.

5. Which SAS statement repetitively executes several statements when the value of an index variable named Count ranges from 1 to 50, incremented by 5?

    a. `do count=1 to 50 by 5;`
    b. `do while count=1 to 50 by 5;`
    c. `do count=1 to 50 + 5;`
    d. `do while (count=1 to 50 + 5);`

Correct answer: a

The iterative DO statement begins the execution of a loop based on the value of an index variable. Here, the loop executes when the value of Count ranges from 1 to 50, incremented by 5.

6. Which option below, when used in a DATA step, writes an observation to the data set after each value for `Activity` has been read?

    a.
    ```
    do choice=1 to 3;
        input Activity : $10. @;
        output;
    end;
    run;
    ```
    b.
    ```
    do choice=1 to 3;
        input Activity : $10. @;
    end;
    output;
    run;
    ```
    c.
    ```
    do choice=1 to 3;
        input Activity : $10. @;
    end;
    run;
    ```
    d. *a* and *b*

    Correct answer: a

    The OUTPUT statement must be included in the loop so that each time a value for `Activity` is read, an observation is immediately written to the data set.

7. Which SAS statement repetitively executes several statements while the value of `Cholesterol` is greater than 200?

    a. `do cholesterol > 200;`
    b. `do cholesterol gt 200;`
    c. `do while (cholesterol > 200);`
    d. `do while cholesterol > 200;`

    Correct answer: c

    The DO WHILE statement checks for the condition that `Cholesterol` is greater than *200*. The expression must be enclosed in parentheses. The expression is evaluated at the top of the loop, before any statements are executed. If the condition is true, the DO WHILE loop executes. If the expression is false the first time it is evaluated, then the loop never executes.

8. Which choice below is an example of a Sum statement?

    a. `totalpay=1;`

    b. `totalpay+1;`

    c. `totalpay*1;`

    d. `totalpay by 1;`

Correct answer: b

The Sum statement adds the result of an expression to a counter variable. So the + sign is an essential part of the Sum statement. Here, the value of `TotalPay` is incremented by 1.

9. Which program creates the SAS data set **Perm.Topstore** from the raw data file shown below?

```
1---+----10---+----20---+----30---+
1001 77,163.19 76,804.75 74,384.27
1002 76,612.93 81,456.34 82,063.97
1003 82,185.16 79,742.33
```

SAS Data Set Perm.Topstore

Store	Sales	Month
1001	77163.19	1
1001	76804.75	2
1001	74384.27	3
1002	76612.93	1
1002	81456.34	2
1002	82063.97	3
1003	82185.16	1
1003	79742.33	2

a.
```
data perm.topstores;
    infile sales98 missover;
    input Store Sales : comma. @;
    do while (sales ne .);
       month + 1;
       output;
       input sales : comma. @;
    end;
run;
```

b.
```
data perm.topstores;
    infile sales98 missover;
    input Store Sales : comma. @;
    do while (sales ne .);
       Month=0;
       month + 1;
       output;
       input sales : comma. @;
    end;
run;
```

c.
```
data perm.topstores;
    infile sales98 missover;
    input Store Sales : comma. Month @;
    do while (sales ne .);
       month + 1;
       input sales : comma. @;
    end;
    output;
run;
```

d.
```
data perm.topstores;
    infile sales98 missover;
    input Store Sales : comma. @;
    Month=0;
    do while (sales ne .);
       month + 1;
       output;
       input sales : comma. @;
    end;
run;
```

Correct answer: d

The assignment statement that **precedes** the DO WHILE loop creates the counter variable Month and assigns an initial value of zero to it. Each time the DO WHILE loop executes, the Sum statement increments the value of Month by 1.

10. How many observations are produced by the DATA step that reads this external file?

```
1---+----10---+----20---+----30---+----40
01 CHOCOLATE VANILLA RASPBERRY
02 VANILLA PEACH
03 CHOCOLATE
04 RASPBERRY PEACH CHOCOLATE
05 STRAWBERRY VANILLA CHOCOLATE
```

```
data perm.choices;
   infile icecream missover;
   input Day $ Flavor : $10. @;
   do while (flavor ne ' ');
      output;
      input flavor : $10. @;
   end;

run;
```

a. 3

b. 5

c. 12

d. 15

Correct answer: c

This DATA step produces one observation for each repeating field. The MISSOVER option in the INFILE statement prevents SAS from reading the next record when missing values occur at the end of a record. Every observation contains one value for Flavor, paired with the corresponding value for ID. Because there are 12 values for Flavor, there are 12 observations in the data set.

1. When you write a DATA step to create one observation per detail record you need to

    a. distinguish between header and detail records.

    b. keep the header record as part of each observation until the next header record is encountered.

    c. hold the current value of each record type so that the other values in the record can be read.

    d. all of the above

Correct answer: d

In order to create one observation per detail record, it is necessary to distinguish between header and detail records. Use a RETAIN statement to keep the header record as part of each observation until the next header record is encountered. You also need to use the @ line-hold specifier to hold the current value of each record type so that the other values in the record can be read.

2. Which SAS statement reads the value for code (in the first field), and then holds the value until an INPUT statement reads the remaining value in each observation in the same iteration of the DATA step?

```
1---+----10---+----20---+----30
01 Office Supplies
02 Paper Clips
02 Tape
01 Art Supplies
02 Crayons
02 Finger Paint
02 Construction Paper
```

    a. input code $2. @;

    b. input code $2. @@;

    c. retain code;

    d. none of the above

Correct answer: a

An INPUT statement is used to read the value for code. The single @ sign at the end of the INPUT statement holds the current record for a later INPUT statement in the same iteration of the DATA step.

3. Which SAS statement checks for the condition that Record equals *C* and executes a single statement to read the values for Amount?

   a. `if record=c then input @3 Amount comma7.;`

   b. `if record='C' then input @3 Amount comma7.;`

   c. `if record='C' then do input @3 Amount comma7.;`

   d. `if record=C then do input @3 Amount comma7.;`

Correct answer: b

The IF-THEN statement defines the condition that Record equals *C* and executes an INPUT statement to read the values for Amount when the condition is true. *C* must be enclosed in quotation marks and must be specified exactly as shown because it is a character value.

4. After the value for code is read in the sixth iteration, which illustration of the program data vector is correct?

```
1---+----10---+----20---+----30
H Lettuce
P Green Leaf   Quality Growers
P Iceberg      Pleasant Farm
P Romaine      Quality Growers
H Squash
P Yellow       Tasty Acres
P Zucchini     Pleasant Farm
```

```
data perm.produce (drop=code);
    infile orders;
    retain Vegetable;
    input code $1. @;
    if code='H' then input @3 vegetable $6.;
    if code='P';
    input @3 Variety : $10. @15 Supplier : $15.;
run;
proc print data=perm.produce;
run;
```

a.

N	Vegetable	code	Variety	Supplier
6		P		

b.

N	Vegetable	code	Variety	Supplier
6	Squash	P		

c.

N	Vegetable	code	Variety	Supplier
6	Squash	H		

d.

N	Vegetable	code	Variety	Supplier
6	Squash	H	Yellow	

Correct answer: b

The value of Vegetable is retained across iterations of the DATA step. As the sixth iteration begins, the INPUT statement reads the value for code and holds the record, so that the values for Variety and Supplier can be read with an additional INPUT statement.

5. What happens when the fourth iteration of the DATA step is complete?

```
1---+----10---+----20---+----30
F Apples
V Gala              $2.50
V Golden Delicious $1.99
V Rome              $2.35
F Oranges
V Navel             $2.79
V Temple            $2.99
```

```
data perm.orders (drop=type);
    infile produce;
    retain Fruit;
    input type $1. @;
    if type='F' then input @3 fruit $7.;
    if type='V';
    input @3 Variety : $16. @20 Price comma5.;
run;
```

a. All of the values in the program data vector are written to the data set as the third observation.

b. All of the values in the program data vector are written to the data set as the fourth observation.

c. The values for Fruit, Variety, and Price are written to the data set as the third observation.

d. The values for Fruit, Variety, and Price are written to the data set as the fourth observation.

Correct answer: c

This program creates one observation for each detail record. The RETAIN statement retains the value for Fruit as part of each observation until the values for Variety and Price can be read. The DROP= option in the DATA statement prevents the values for type from being written to the data set.

6. Which SAS statement indicates that several other statements should be executed when `Record` has a value of *A*?

```
1---+----10---+----20---+----30
A 124153-01
C $153.02
D $20.00
D $20.00
```

   a. `if record='A' then do;`

   b. `if record=A then do;`

   c. `if record='A' then;`

   d. `if record=A then;`

Correct answer: a

The IF-THEN statement defines the condition that `Record` equals *A* and specifies a simple DO group. The keyword DO indicates that several executable statements follow until the DO group is closed by an END statement. The value *A* must be enclosed in quotation marks and specified exactly as shown because it is a character value.

7. Which is true for the following statements (*X* indicates a header record)?

```
if code='X' then do;
   if _n_ > 1 then output;
   Total=0;
   input Name $ 3-20;
end;
```

   a. `_N_` equals the number of times the DATA step has begun to execute.

   b. When `code='X'` and `_n_ > 1` are true, an OUTPUT statement is executed.

   c. Each header record causes an observation to be written to the data set.

   d. *a* and *b*

Correct answer: d

`_N_` is an automatic variable whose value is the number of times the DATA step has begun to execute. The expression `_n_ > 1` defines a condition where the DATA step has executed more than once. When the conditions `code='X'` and `_n_ > 1` are true, an OUTPUT statement is executed, and `Total` is initialized to zero. Thus, each header record except for the first one causes an observation to be written to the data set.

8. What happens when the condition `type='P'` is false?

```
if type='P' then input @3 ID $5. @9 Address $20.;
else if type='V' then input @3 Charge 6.;
```

a. The values for `ID` and `Address` are read.

b. The values for `Charge` are read.

c. `Type` is assigned the value of *V*.

d. The ELSE statement is executed.

Correct answer: d

The condition is false, so the values for `ID` and `Address` are **not** read. Instead, the ELSE statement is executed and defines another condition which might or might not be true.

9. What happens when `last` has a value other than zero?

```
data perm.househld (drop=code);
    infile citydata end=last;
    retain Address;
    input type $1. @;
    if code='A' then do;
        if _n_ > 1 then output;
        Total=0;
        input address $ 3-17;
    end;
    else if code='N' then total+1;
    if last then output;
run;
```

a. `Last` has a value of *1*.

b. The OUTPUT statement writes the last observation to the data set.

c. The current value of `last` is written to the DATA set.

d. *a* and *b*

Correct answer: d

You can determine when the current record is the last record in an external file by specifying the END= option in the INFILE statement. `Last` is a temporary numeric variable whose value is zero until the last line is read. `Last` has a value of *1* after the last line is read. Like automatic variables, the END= variable is not written to the data set.

10. Based on the values in the program data vector, what happens next?

N	last	Department	Extension	type	Total	Amount
5	0	Accounting	x3808	D	16.50	•

```
1---+----10---+----20---+----30
D Accounting   x3808
S Paper Clips  $2.50
S Paper        $4.95
S Binders      $9.05
D Personnel    x3810
S Markers      $8.98
S Pencils      $3.35
```

```
data work.supplies (drop=type amount);
    infile orders end=last;
    retain Department Extension;
    input type $1. @;
    if type='D' then do;
        if _n_ > 1 then output;
        Total=0;
        input @3 department $10. @16 extension $5.;
    end;
    else if type='S' then do;
        input @16 Amount comma5.;
        total+amount;
        if last then output;
    end;
run;
```

a. All the values in the program data vector are written to the data set as the first observation.

b. The values for Department, Total, and Extension are written to the data set as the first observation.

c. The values for Department, Total, and Extension are written to the data set as the fourth observation.

d. The value of last changes to *1*.

Correct answer: b

This program creates one observation for each header record and combines information from each detail record into the summary variable, Total. When the value of type is *D* and the value of _N_ is greater than *1*, the OUTPUT statement executes, and the values for Department, Total, and Extension are written to the data set as the first observation. The variables _N_, last, type, and Amount are not written to the data set.

Glossary

aggregate storage location

a location on an operating system that can contain a group of distinct files. Different host operating systems call an aggregate grouping of files different names, such as a directory, a maclib, or a partitioned data set. The standard form for referencing an aggregate storage location from within SAS is *fileref* (*name*), where *fileref* is the entire aggregate and (*name*) is a specific file or member of that aggregate. See also fileref (file reference).

analysis variable

a numeric variable that is used to calculate statistics or to display values. Usually an analysis variable contains quantitative or continuous values, but this is not required.

argument

(1) the data values within parentheses on which a SAS function or CALL routine performs the indicated operation. (2) in syntax descriptions, any keyword in a SAS statement other than the statement name. (3) in macro processing, a character string that is used by a macro function.

arithmetic operator

any of the symbols (+, -, /, *, and **) that are used to perform addition, subtraction, division, multiplication, and exponentiation in SAS expressions.

array

(1) in the SAS programming language, a group of variables that are of the same data type and which are available for processing under a single name. (2) a method of defining an area of memory as a unit of information, such as _TEMPORARY_ arrays.

array name

a name that is selected to identify a group of variables or temporary data elements. It must be a valid SAS name that is not the name of a variable in the same DATA step or SCL (SAS Component Language) program. See also array.

array reference

a reference to an element to be processed in an array. See also array.

automatic variable

a variable that is created automatically by the DATA step, some DATA step statements, some SAS procedures, and the SAS macro facility.

Base SAS software

software that includes a programming language that manages your data, procedures for data analysis and reporting, procedures for managing SAS files, a macro facility, Help menus, and a windowing environment for text editing and file management.

buffer

a portion of computer memory that is used for special holding purposes or processes. For example, a buffer might simply store information before sending that information to main memory for processing, or it might hold data after the data is read or before the data is written.

BY group

a group of observations or rows that have the same value for a variable that is specified in a BY statement. If more than one variable is specified in a BY statement, then the BY group is a group of observations that have a unique combination of values for those variables.

BY value

the value of a BY variable.

BY variable

a variable that is named in a BY statement and whose values define groups of observations to process.

BY-group processing

the process of using the BY statement to process observations that are ordered, grouped, or indexed according to the values of one or more variables. Many SAS procedures and the DATA step support BY-group processing. For example, you can use BY-group processing with the PRINT procedure to print separate reports for different groups of observations in a single SAS data set.

catalog

See SAS catalog.

character format

a set of instructions that tell SAS to use a specific pattern for writing character data values.

character function

a type of function that enables you to manipulate, compare, evaluate, or analyze character strings.

character informat

a set of instructions that tell SAS to use a specific pattern for reading character data values into character variables.

character value

a value that can contain alphabetic characters, the numeric characters 0 through 9, and other special characters.

character variable

a variable whose values can consist of alphabetic characters and special characters as well as numeric characters.

class variable

a variable that is used to group, or classify, data. Class variables can be either character or numeric values. Class variables can have continuous values, but they typically have a few discrete values that define the classifications of the variable.

code editing window

a generic term for any window into which users can type or paste program code, or in which they can make changes to existing programs.

column input

in the DATA step, a style of input in which column numbers are included in the INPUT statement to tell SAS which columns contain the values for each variable. This style of input is useful when the values for each variable are in the same location in all records.

comment

text that provides additional information in a SAS program. SAS ignores comments during processing but writes them to the SAS log. Comments have two forms. A comment can appear as a statement that begins with an asterisk and ends with a semicolon: * *message* ; A comment can also appear as text that begins with a forward slash and an asterisk and ends with an asterisk and a forward slash: /* *message* */

comparison operator

a symbolic or mnemonic instruction that tests for a particular relationship between two values. If the comparison is true, the result of executing the instruction is the value 1; if the comparison is false, the result is the value 0.

compilation

the process of checking syntax and translating a portion of a program into a form that the computer can execute.

compound expression

an expression that contains more than one operator.

concatenate

(1) for character values, to combine two or more character values, one after the other, into a single character value. (2) for external files, to access two or more files as if they were one by specifying the filenames one after another in the same SAS statement. (3) for SAS data sets, to combine two or more SAS data sets, one after the other, into a single data set.

condition

(1) in a SAS program, one or more numeric or character expressions that result in a value upon which some decision depends. (2) in the SQL procedure, the part of the WHERE clause that contains the search criteria. In the condition, you specify which rows are to be retrieved.

constant

in SAS software, a number or a character string that indicates a fixed value. Character constants must be enclosed in quotation marks.

data error

a type of execution error that occurs when a SAS program analyzes data that contains invalid values. For example, a data error occurs if you specify numeric variables in the INPUT statement for character data. SAS reports these errors in the SAS log but continues to execute the program. See also programming error, syntax error.

data set option

a SAS language element that specifies actions that apply to only one particular SAS data set. For example, data set options enable you to rename variables, to select only the first or last *n* observations for processing, to drop variables from processing or from the output data set, and to specify a password for a SAS data set.

DATA step

a group of statements in a SAS program that begins with a DATA statement and which ends with either a RUN statement, another DATA statement, a PROC statement, the end of the job, or the semicolon that immediate follows lines of data. The DATA step enables you to read raw data or other SAS data sets and to use programming logic to create a SAS data set to write a report, or to write to an external file.

data value

(1) a unit of character or numeric information in a SAS data set. A data value represents one variable in an observation. (2) in the rectangular structure of a SAS data set, the intersection of a row and a column.

date and time format

the instructions that tell SAS how to write numeric values as dates, times, and datetimes.

date and time informat

the instructions that tell SAS how to read numeric values that are represented as dates, times, and datetimes.

date value

See SAS date value.

delimiter

a character that serves as a boundary that separates the elements of a character string, a program statement, a data line, or a list of arguments.

descriptor information

information about the contents and attributes of a SAS data set. For example, the descriptor information includes the data types and lengths of the variables, as well as which engine was used to create the data. SAS creates and maintains descriptor information within every SAS data set.

directory

a named subdivision on a disk or diskette, used in organizing files. A directory also contains information about the file, such as size and date of last change.

DO group

a sequence of statements that starts with a simple DO statement and that ends with a corresponding END statement. See also DO loop.

DO loop

a sequence of statements that starts with an iterative DO, DO WHILE, or DO UNTIL statement and that ends with a corresponding END statement. The statements are executed (usually repeatedly) according to directions that are specified in the DO statement. See also DO group.

double trailing at sign (@@)

a special symbol that is used to hold a line in the input buffer during multiple iterations of a DATA step.

duration

a value that represents the difference, in elapsed time or days, between any two time or date values.

engine

a component of SAS software that reads from or writes to a file. Each engine enables SAS to access files that are in a particular file format.

execution

(1) in the DATA step, the process in which SAS carries out statements for each observation or record in the file. (2) in contexts other than the DATA step, such as SAS macros, procedures, and global statements, the process in which SAS performs the actions that are indicated.

expression

See SAS expression.

external file

a file that is created and maintained by a host operating system or by another vendor's software application. SAS can read data from and route output to external files. External files can contain raw data, SAS programming statements, procedure output, or output that was created by the PUT statement. A SAS data set is not an external file. See also fileref (file reference).

field

in an external file, the smallest logical unit of data.

file reference

See fileref (file reference).

fileref (file reference)

a name that is temporarily assigned to an external file or to an aggregate storage location such as a directory or a folder. The fileref identifies the file or the storage location to SAS. See also libref (library reference).

FIRST.*variable*

a temporary variable that SAS creates to identify the first observation of each BY group. The variable is not added to the SAS data set. See also LAST.*variable*.

floating-point representation

a compact form of storing real numbers on a computer, similar to scientific notation. Different operating systems use different techniques for floating-point representation.

format

a pattern or set of instructions that SAS uses to determine how the values of a variable (or column) should be written or displayed. SAS provides a set of standard formats and also enables you to define your own formats.

format modifier

a special symbol that is used in the INPUT and PUT statements and which enables you to control how SAS reads input data and writes output data.

formatted input

a style of input that uses special instructions called informats in the INPUT statement to determine how values that are entered in data fields should be interpreted. See also informat.

function

a component of the SAS programming language that can accept arguments, perform a computation or other operation, and return a value. For example, the ABS function returns the absolute value of a numeric argument. Functions can return either numeric or character results. A wide variety of functions are included with SAS software.

global option

See SAS system option.

heading

in SAS output, the text that is located near the beginning of each page of output. This includes text produced by a HEADER= option in a FILE statement, titles written with a TITLE statement, and default information such as date and page numbers.

informat

a pattern or set of instructions that SAS uses to determine how data values in an input file should be interpreted. SAS provides a set of standard informats and also enables you to define your own informats.

input buffer

the temporary area of memory into which each record of data is read when the INPUT statement executes. Note that the input buffer is a logical concept that is independent of physical implementation.

integer

a number that does not contain a decimal point.

interleaving

a process in which SAS combines two or more sorted SAS data sets into one sorted SAS data set based on the values of the BY variables.

item

in the REPORT procedure, a data set variable, a statistic, or a computed variable. An item can occupy one or more columns in a report. Under some circumstances, multiple items can share a column.

label, variable

up to 256 characters of descriptive text that can be printed in the output by certain procedures instead of, or in addition to, the variable name.

LAST.*variable*

a temporary variable that SAS creates to identify the last observation of each BY group. This variable is not added to the SAS data set. See also FIRST.*variable*.

length variable

a numeric variable that is used with the $VARYING. informat or format to specify the actual length of a character variable whose values do not all have the same length.

length, variable

the number of bytes used to store each of a variable's values in a SAS data set.

library reference

See libref (library reference).

libref (library reference)

a name that is temporarily associated with a SAS library. The complete name of a SAS file consists of two words, separated by a period. The libref, which is the first word, indicates the library. The second word is the name of the specific SAS file. For example, in VLIB.NEWBDAY, the libref VLIB tells SAS which library contains the file NEWBDAY. You assign a libref with a LIBNAME statement or with an operating system command.

line-hold specifier

a special symbol used in INPUT and PUT statements that enables you to hold a record in the input or output buffer for further processing. Line-hold specifiers include the trailing at sign (@) and the double trailing at sign (@@).

list input

a style of input that supplies variable names, not column locations, in the INPUT statement to scan input records for data values that are separated by at least one blank or by some other delimiter.

listing output

SAS procedure output that is in a monospace font. All text in listing output has the same font size, and no special font styles are applied to it.

logical data model

a framework into which engines fit information for processing by SAS. This data model is a logical representation of data or files, not a physical structure.

logical operator

an operator that is used in expressions to link sequences of comparisons. The logical operators are AND, OR, and NOT.

match-merging

a process in which SAS joins observations from two or more SAS data sets according to the values of the BY variables. See also one-to-one merging.

member

a SAS file in a SAS library.

member name

a name that is assigned to a SAS file in a SAS library.

menu bar

the primary list of items at the top of a window, which represent the actions or classes of actions that can be executed. Selecting an item executes an action, opens a pull-down menu, or opens a dialog box that requests additional information.

merging

the process of combining observations from two or more SAS data sets into a single observation in a new SAS data set. See also match-merging, one-to-one merging.

missing value

(1) in SAS, a term that describes the contents of a variable that contains no data for a particular row or observation. By default, SAS prints or displays a missing numeric value as a single period, and it prints or displays a missing character value as a blank space. (2) in the SQL procedure, the equivalent of an SQL NULL value.

modified list input

a style of input that uses instructions called informats and format modifiers in the INPUT statement. Modified list input scans input records for data values that are separated by at least one blank (or by some other delimiter), or in some cases, by multiple blanks.

nonstandard data

data that appear in alternate or nonstandard forms, such as numbers that contain commas.

numeric format

a set of instructions that tell SAS to use a specific pattern for writing the values of numeric variables.

numeric informat

a set of instructions that tell SAS to use a specific pattern for reading numeric data values.

numeric value

a value that usually contains only numbers, which can include numbers in E-notation and hexadecimal notation. A numeric value can sometimes contain a decimal point, a plus sign, or a minus sign. Numeric values are stored in numeric variables.

numeric variable

a variable that contains only numeric values and related symbols, such as decimal points, plus signs, and minus signs. By default, SAS stores all numeric variables in floating-point representation.

observation

a row in a SAS data set. All of the data values in an observation are associated with a single entity such as a customer or a state. Each observation contains one data value for each variable.

one-level name

a one-part name for a SAS file in which the libref (library reference) is omitted and only the filename is specified. When you specify a one-level name, the default temporary library, Work, is assumed.

one-to-one matching

the process of combining observations from two or more data sets into one observation using two or more SET statements to read observations independently from each data set. See also match-merging.

one-to-one merging

the process of using the MERGE statement (without a BY statement) to combine observations from two or more data sets based on the observations' positions in the data sets. See also match-merging.

operand

any of the variables and constants in a SAS expression that contains operators, variables, and constants.

operator

in a SAS expression, any of several symbols that request a comparison, a logical operation, or an arithmetic calculation.

page size

(1) the size of a page of printed output. (2) the number of bytes of data that SAS moves between external storage and memory in one input/output operation. Page size is analogous to buffer size for SAS data sets.

PDV (program data vector)

See program data vector (PDV).

permanent SAS data library

a SAS library that is not deleted when a SAS session ends, and which is therefore available to subsequent SAS sessions. Unless the USER libref is defined, you use a two-level name to access a file in a permanent library. The first-level name is the libref, and the second-level name is the member name. See also libref (library reference), member.

permanent SAS file

a file in a SAS data library that is not deleted when the SAS session or job terminates.

physical filename

the name that the operating system uses to identify a file.

pointer

in the DATA step, a programming tool that SAS uses to keep track of its position in the input or output buffer.

pointer control

the process of instructing SAS to move the pointer before reading or writing data.

PROC step

a group of SAS statements that call and execute a SAS procedure. A PROC step usually takes a SAS data set as input.

procedure

See SAS procedure.

procedure output file

an external file that contains the result of the analysis that a SAS procedure performs or the report that the procedure produces. Most SAS procedures write output to the procedure output file by default. Reports that are produced by SAS DATA steps, using PUT statements and a FILE statement with the PRINT destination, also go to this file. See also external file, DATA step.

program data vector (PDV)

the temporary area of computer memory in which SAS builds a SAS data set, one observation at a time. The program data vector is a logical concept and does not necessarily correspond to a single contiguous area of memory.

programming error

a flaw in the logic of a SAS program that can cause the program to fail or to perform differently than the programmer intended. See also data error, syntax error.

pull-down menu

the list of menu items or choices that appears when you choose an item from a menu bar or from another menu.

raw data

(1) data that has not been read into a SAS data set. (2) in statistical analysis, data (including data in SAS data sets) that has not had a particular operation, such as standardization, performed on it.

SAS catalog

a SAS file that stores many different kinds of information in smaller units called catalog entries. A single SAS catalog can contain several different types of catalog entries.

SAS data file

a type of SAS data set that contains data values as well as descriptor information that is associated with the data. The descriptor information includes information such as the data types and lengths of the variables, as well as the name of the engine that was used to create the data. SAS data files are of member type DATA. A PROC SQL table is a SAS data file.

SAS data library

a collection of one or more SAS files that are recognized by SAS and which are referenced and stored as a unit. Each file is a member of the library.

SAS data set

a file whose contents are in one of the native SAS file formats. There are two types of SAS data sets: SAS data files and SAS data views. SAS data files contain data values in addition to descriptor information that is associated with the data. SAS data views contain only the descriptor information plus other information that is required for retrieving data values from other SAS data sets or from files whose contents are in other software vendors' file formats.

SAS data set option

an option that appears in parentheses after a SAS data set name. Data set options specify actions that apply only to the processing of that SAS data set.

SAS data view

a type of SAS data set that retrieves data values from other files. A SAS data view contains only descriptor information such as the data types and lengths of the variables (columns), plus other information that is required for retrieving data values from other SAS data sets or from files that are stored in other software vendors' file formats. SAS data views can be created by the ACCESS and SQL procedures, as well as by the SAS DATA step.

SAS date constant

a string in the form '*ddMMMyy*'d or '*ddMMMyyyy*'d that represents a date in a SAS statement. The string is enclosed in quotation marks and is followed by the character d (for example, '6JUL01'd, '06JUL01'd, '6 JUL2001'd, or '06JUL2001'd).

SAS date value

an integer that represents a date in SAS software. The integer represents the number of days between January 1, 1960, and another specified date. For example, the SAS date value 366 represents the calendar date January 1, 1961.

SAS datetime constant

a string in the form '*ddMMMyy*:*hh*:*mm*:*ss*'dt or '*ddMMMyyyy*:*hh*:*mm*:*ss*'dt that represents a date and time in SAS. The string is enclosed in quotation marks and is followed by the characters dt (for example, '06JUL2001:09:53:22'dt).

SAS datetime value

an integer that represents a date and a time in SAS software. The integer represents the number of seconds between midnight, January 1, 1960, and another specified date and time. For example, the SAS datetime value for 9:30 a.m., June 5, 2000, is 1275816600.

SAS Enterprise Guide

a software application with a point-and-click interface that gives users access to the functionality of many components of SAS software. Interactive dialog boxes guide users through data analysis tasks and reporting tasks, and users can easily export the results of those tasks to other Windows applications or servers. SAS Enterprise Guide provides access not only to SAS data files, but also to data that is in a wide variety of other software vendors' formats and in other operating system formats.

SAS expression

a sequence of operands and operators that form a set of instructions that SAS processes and which resolve to a single value. SAS expressions are used in SAS program statements to create variables, to assign values, to calculate new values, to transform variables, and to perform conditional processing. SAS expressions can resolve to numeric values, character values, or Boolean values.

SAS file

a specially structured file that is created, organized, and, optionally, maintained by SAS. A SAS file can be a SAS data set, a catalog, a stored program, an access descriptor, a utility file, a multidimensional database file, a financial database file, a data mining database file, or an item store file.

SAS function

See function.

SAS keyword

a literal that is a primary part of the SAS language. Keywords are statement names, function names, command names, macro statement names, and macro function names.

SAS log

a file that contains a record of the SAS statements that you enter as well as messages about the execution of your program.

SAS name

a name that is assigned to items such as SAS variables and SAS data sets. The first character must be a letter or an underscore. Subsequent characters can be letters, numbers, or underscores. Blanks and special characters (except the underscore) are not allowed. The maximum length of a SAS name depends on the language element that it is assigned to. Many SAS names, such as names of DATA step variables and array names, can be 32 characters long. Others, such as librefs and filerefs, have a maximum length of 8 characters.

SAS operator

See operator.

SAS procedure

a program that produces reports, manages files, or analyzes data and which is accessed with a PROC statement. Many procedures are included in SAS software.

SAS program

a sequence of related SAS statements.

SAS session

the activity between invoking and exiting a specific SAS software product.

SAS statement

a string of SAS keywords, SAS names, and special characters and operators that instructs SAS to perform an operation or that gives information to SAS. Each SAS statement ends with a semicolon.

SAS system option

an option that affects the processing of an entire SAS program or interactive SAS session from the time the option is specified until it is changed. Examples of items that are controlled by SAS system options include the appearance of SAS output, the handling of some files that are used by SAS, the use of system variables, the processing of observations in SAS data sets, features of SAS initialization, and the way SAS interacts with your host operating environment.

SAS time constant

a string in the form '*hh*:*mm*:*ss*'t that represents a time in a SAS statement. The string is enclosed in quotation marks and is followed by the character t (for example, '09:53:22't).

SAS time value

an integer that represents a time in SAS. The integer represents the number of seconds between midnight of the current day and another specified time value. (For example, the SAS time value for 9:30 a.m. is 34200.)

SAS windowing environment

an interactive windowing interface to SAS software. In this environment you can issue commands by typing them on the command line, by pressing function keys, or by selecting items from menus or menu bars. Within one session, you can perform many different tasks, including preparing and submitting programs, viewing and printing results, and debugging and resubmitting programs.

Sashelp library

a SAS data library supplied by SAS software that stores the text for Help windows, default function-key definitions and window definitions, and menus.

Sasuser library

a default, permanent SAS data library that is created at the beginning of your first SAS session. The Sasuser library contains a Profile catalog that stores the customized features or settings that you specify for SAS. You can also store other SAS files in this library.

statement option

a word that you specify in a particular SAS statement and which affects only the processing that that statement performs.

syntax checking

the process by which SAS checks each SAS statement for proper usage, correct spelling, proper SAS naming conventions, and so on.

syntax error

an error in the spelling or grammar of a SAS statement. SAS finds syntax errors as it compiles each SAS step before execution. See also data error, programming error.

system option

See SAS system option.

target variable

the variable to which the result of a function or expression is assigned.

taskbar

the bar at the bottom of the Windows desktop that displays active applications. The taskbar enables you to easily switch between applications and to restore, move, size, minimize, maximize, and close applications.

temporary SAS data library

a library that exists only for the current SAS session or job. The most common temporary library is the Work library. See also Work library.

temporary SAS file

a SAS file in a SAS data library (usually the Work library) that is deleted at the end of the SAS session or job.

text output

another term for listing output.

title

a heading that is printed at the top of each page of SAS output or of the SAS log.

toggle

an option, parameter, or other mechanism that enables you to turn on or turn off a processing feature.

trailing at sign (@)

a special symbol that is used to hold a line of input or output so that SAS can read from it or write to it in a subsequent INPUT or PUT statement.

type, variable

See variable type.

user-defined format

See format.

variable

a column in a SAS data set or in a SAS data view. The data values for each variable describe a single characteristic for all observations. Each SAS variable can have the following attributes: name, data type (character or numeric), length, format, informat, and label.

variable attributes

the name, label, format, informat, data type, and length that are associated with a particular variable.

variable list

a list of variables. You can use abbreviated variable lists in many SAS statements instead of listing all the variable names.

variable type

the classification of a variable as either numeric or character. Type is an attribute of SAS variables.

view

See SAS data view.

windowing environment

See SAS windowing environment.

Work library

a temporary SAS data library that is automatically defined by SAS at the beginning of each SAS session or SAS job. Unless you have specified a User library, any newly created SAS file that has a one-level name will be placed in the Work library by default and will be deleted at the end of the current SAS session or job.

Index

Symbols

: (colon)
   See colon
, (comma)
   See comma
. (period)
   See period
; (semicolon)
   See semicolon
+ (addition) 136
& (ampersand)
   See ampersand
   See AND logical operator
' (apostrophe) 195
* (asterisk)
   See asterisk
^ (caret) 424
|| (concatenation operator) 405–406, 431–432
$ (dollar sign)
   See dollar sign
@@ (double trailing at sign) 612–614, 621, 652
= (equal sign)
   See equal sign
! (exclamation point) 424
> (gt)
   See gt
% (percent sign)
   See percent sign
| (pipe)
   See pipe
+ (plus sign)
   See plus sign
(pound sign) 527
" (quotation marks)
   See quotation marks
@ (trailing at sign)
   See trailing at sign
_ (underscore) 17, 22
{ } (braces) 473, 476, 482
[ ] (brackets) 473, 475–476
/ (division) 136
- (hyphen) 424, 513, 568
- (minus sign)
   See minus sign
( ) parentheses
   See parentheses
/ (slash)
   See slash
- (subtraction) 136
>= (ge) comparison operator 89, 137, 301
<= (le) comparison operator 89, 137, 301
< (lt) comparison operator 89, 137, 301
^= (ne) comparison operator 89, 137, 301
~ (not) logical operator 301
^ (not) logical operator 301
< (less than) symbol 194, 424

A

absolute links 284
absolute URLs 285–286
accumulator variables 297–299, 655
ACROSS usage option, DEFINE statement
    (REPORT) 214, 223, 231
across variables 227, 230–231
ADABAS database 38
addition (+) 136
aggregate storage location 123–124
alignment argument, INTNX function 420–421
ALL automatic variable 182
ALL keyword, ODS CLOSE statement
    277–278
ALL variable list 473–474
ampersand (&)
   as delimiter 424, 542
   as list input modifier 541–542, 544, 589
ANALYSIS usage option, DEFINE statement
    (REPORT) 214, 223
analysis variables 223, 227–231
AND (&) logical operator 89, 137, 301–302
apostrophe (') 195
arguments
   alignment 420–421
   character context and 405
   character-to-numeric conversion 402
   functions and 398–399, 417, 443, 479
   OF keyword and 399
arithmetic functions 397
arithmetic operators 136, 402
array references 475–478, 482, 487–493
ARRAY statement
   array elements and 488
   assigning initial values 483–485
   creating variables in 480–483
   DATA step compilation phase and 477–479
   general form 472–473
arrays
   assigning initial values to 483–485
   compilation and execution 477–479
   creating variables in ARRAY statement
     480–483
   DIM function and 479
   dimensions of 472–473, 481, 489
   DO loops and 470–471, 475–479, 482–484
   elements of 472–473
   function arguments and 399
   multidimensional 486–493